THE MAKING OF THE COMMON LAW

THE MAKING OF THE
COMMON LAW

PAUL BRAND

THE HAMBLEDON PRESS

LONDON AND RIO GRANDE

Published by The Hambledon Press, 1992

102 Gloucester Avenue, London NW1 8HX (U.K.)

P.O. Box 162, Rio Grande, Ohio 45674 (U.S.A.)

ISBN 1 85285 070 1

A description of this book is available from the
British Library and from the Library of Congress

Printed on acid-free paper in
Great Britain and bound by
Cambridge University Press

Contents

Acknowledgements   vii

Introduction   ix

1   The Origins of the English Legal Profession   1

2   The Early History of the Legal Profession of the Lordship of Ireland, 1250-1350   21

3   Courtroom and Schoolroom: The Education of Lawyers in England Prior to 1400   57

4   'Multis Vigiliis Excogitatam et Inventam': Henry II and the Creation of the English Common Law   77

5   Edward I and the Judges: The 'State Trials' of 1289-93   103

6   Chief Justice and Felon: The Career of Thomas Weyland   113

7   Edward I and the Transformation of the English Judiciary   135

8   Medieval Legal Bureaucracy: The Clerks of the Courts in the Reign of Edward I   169

9   The Origins of English Land Law: Milsom and After   203

10   Formedon in the Remainder before *De Donis*   227

11   The Control of Mortmain Alienation in England, 1200-1300   233

12   King, Church and Property: The Enforcement of Restrictions on Alienations into Mortmain in the Lordship of Ireland in the Later Middle Ages   245

13   The Licensing of Mortmain Alienations in the Medieval Lordship of Ireland   267

14   Legal Change in the Later Thirteenth Century: Statutory and Judicial Remodelling of the Action of Replevin   287

15 Lordship and Distraint in Thirteenth-Century England 301

16 The Drafting of Legislation in Mid Thirteenth-Century England 325

17 *Hengham Magna*: A Thirteenth-Century English Common Law Treatise and its Composition 369

18 'Quo Waranto' Law in the Reign of Edward I: A Hitherto Undiscovered Opinion of Chief Justice Hengham 393

19 Ireland and the Literature of the Early Common Law 445

20 Ralph de Hengham and the Irish Common Law 465

Index 473

Acknowledgements

The articles and essays collected here first appeared in the following places and are reprinted by kind permission of the original publishers.

1 *Law and History Review*, 5 (1987), pp. 31-50 (Copyright: Cornell University).

2 *Brehons, Serjeants and Attorneys: Studies in the History of the Irish Legal Profession*, ed. Daire Hogan and W.N. Osborough (Irish Academic Press in association with the Irish Legal History Society, Blackrock, Co. Dublin, 1990), pp. 15-50.

3 *Historical Research*, 60 (1987), pp. 147-65.

4 *Haskins Society Journal*, 2 (1990), pp. 197-222.

5 *Thirteenth Century England*, i, ed. P.R. Coss and S.D. Lloyd (Woodbridge, 1986), pp. 31-40.

6 *The Political Context of Law*, ed. Richard Eales and David Sullivan (London, 1987), pp. 26-47.

7 This essay appears here for the first time.

8 This essay appears here for the first time.

9 This essay appears here for the first time.

10 *Irish Jurist*, new series, x (1975), pp. 318-23.

11 *Legal Records and the Historian*, ed. J.H. Baker (Royal Historical Society, London, 1978), pp. 29-40.

12 *Peritia*, 3 (1984), pp. 481-502 (Copyright: the Medieval Academy of Ireland).

13 *Irish Jurist*, new series, xxi (1986), pp. 125-44.

14 *American Journal of Legal History*, xxxi (1987), pp. 43-55 (Copyright: Temple University).

15 *Thirteenth Century England*, iii, ed. P.R. Coss and S.D. Lloyd (Woodbridge, 1991), pp. 1-24.

16 *Parliamentary History*, 9 (1990), pp. 243-85 (Copyright: the Parliamentary History Yearbook Trust).

17 *Irish Jurist*, new series, xi (1976), pp. 147-69.

18 *Irish Jurist*, new series, xiv (1979), pp. 124-72.

19 *Irish Jurist*, new series, xvi (1981), pp. 95-113.

20 *Irish Jurist*, new series, xix (1984), pp. 107-14.

Introduction

Legal history is too important a subject to be left to the legal historians.
Law plays and has played an important part in the life of most human
societies, articulating and enforcing rules that attempt to govern and
control important areas of human social behaviour. Legal history is the
endeavour to understand and recreate the law of past societies and to
explain how it changed over time. This involves reconstructing the legal
ideas and concepts of particular societies and discovering the legal rules
which were applied within them. It also requires the reconstitution of the
wider legal systems within which legal ideas and rules developed and
through which they were applied. The full understanding of a legal
system requires the investigation and analysis of the courts which
administered and developed the law to discover what jurisdiction they
exercised, what procedures they followed and who influenced or
determined their decisions. It is also necessary to know what business
was actually transacted through the courts and by whom and more
generally to assess what impact their decisions had on the surrounding
society. Legal history also requires investigation of the wider 'legal
culture' of the society through the surviving 'artifacts' which that culture
produced, its legal literature. Thus legal history is more than just a
history of legal ideas. It is also the history of institutions, social history,
even literary history.

The essays in this volume are all concerned with the history of one
particular legal system, the Common Law. Most are specifically about
the history of the English Common Law, but some are about aspects of
the history of the Common Law in Ireland. English law was taken to
Ireland by twelfth century settlers and what was recognisably a close
relative of the English Common Law, with close links of various kinds to
its English counterpart, became well established within the area of
English settlement during the thirteenth century. The legal systems both
of the Republic of Ireland and of Northern Ireland are lineal
descendants of that thirteenth-century Irish Common Law. Thus the
Common Law has almost as long a history in Ireland as it does in
England. No one who is interested in the development of the Common
Law as a legal system can afford to neglect its Irish dimension.

The first English common law treatise, *Glanvill*, was completed
shortly before the end of the reign of king Henry II. No such treatise
could have been written at the beginning of Henry's reign, less than forty
years earlier, for the Common Law itself did not then exist. Two of the
essays in this collection are concerned with the major changes associated
with Henry II's reign which brought the Common Law into being.
'"Multis Vigiliis Excogitatam et Inventam": Henry II and the Creation
of the English Common Law' (4) concentrates on the institutional
changes which created national royal courts in England and began the
process of integrating other existing courts into a single national legal
system. It argues that the new royal courts were much more radically
different from existing courts than most historians have supposed and
that their creation was the result of deliberate royal policy and was
intended to bring litigation into the king's courts. It also argues that it
was only these changes which made possible the emergence of a
genuinely national Common Law in England. 'The Origins of English
Land Law: Milsom and After' (9) concentrates on the beginnings of
English land law, one of the most important areas of the nascent English
Common Law. This has been the focus of an important body of recent
scholarly work, much of it hard for the non-specialist and some of it
difficult even for the specialist to grasp. This essay was originally written
in response to an invitation to 'explain Milsom' to a session of the
Colloquium on Medieval Welsh Law at Gregynog in April 1988. In it I
have attempted to provide a clear introduction to the work of Professor
Milsom for the non-specialist: to explain Milsom's picture of the 'feudal
world' of lords and tenant which existed prior to Henry II's reign; of the
changes which took place during the reign, of the intentions which lay
behind them and of their unintended but crucial long-term effects. It is,
however, a critical introduction to Professor Milsom's work in which I
attempt to explain some of my reasons for scepticism as to whether
Milsom's picture both of the 'feudal world' and of the Henrician changes
is really the right one.

The thirteenth century is the focus of most of the remaining essays.
This is a period of major significance in the history of the Common Law.
It is the century when the English legal profession and its Irish
counterpart first made their appearance and when the English and Irish
royal courts first came under the control of a small group of paid, full-
time, career professional royal judges. The thirteenth century also saw
the compilation of the greatest English legal treatise of the Middle Ages
(*Bracton*) and of a large and varied literature of other legal treatises. In
the second half of the century men first began to compile the unofficial
law reports of individual cases, which are forerunners of the later Year
Books and which allow us for the first time to hear individual lawyers
and judges talking in court and to penetrate the intellectual world of the
early common lawyers in a way that the courts' own official records, the

plea rolls, rarely permit. Legislation first began being enacted in England on a regular basis during the same half century and for the first time a distinction was made between 'statute law' and the 'common law' in its narrower sense. It was also in the thirteenth century that the momentous decision was taken that the English Common Law was to be the law of the lordship of Ireland and various practical steps taken to ensure that English law was communicated to Ireland and followed there.

The emergence of the English legal profession is the subject of 'The Origins of the English Legal Profession' (1). This essay re-examines and dismisses evidence that has been adduced for thinking that professional lawyers already existed in Anglo-Norman England and traces the gradual emergence of professional lawyers and then of an English legal profession during the course of the thirteenth century, themes I discuss at greater length in my book, *The Origins of the English Legal Profession*. An important element in the emergence of a distinct legal profession was the provision of professional education for future professional lawyers. Much recent work on legal education has argued or assumed that there was no real legal education in England for common lawyers before the fifteenth century. 'Courtroom and Schoolroom: The Education of Lawyers in England prior to 1400' (3) looks at the later thirteenth- and early fourteenth-century evidence which demonstrates that well before 1300 there existed arrangements for the provision of legal education and that by 1300 this existed at both an elementary and a more advanced level.

'Edward I and the Transformation of the English Judiciary' (7) argues that the general effect of a series of important changes in the English legal system during the second half of the thirteenth century was to place the royal courts much more firmly in the hands of a full-time, career professional judiciary. This development coincided with the emergence of the English legal profession but is quite distinct from it as the members of the new legal profession did not gain their monopoly of higher legal appointments for another half century. However, the coincidence of the two changes certainly had a marked effect on the character of royal courts and perhaps even on the nature of proceedings conducted in them. It greatly strengthened an existing tendency towards making the courts places where only the insiders could really feel at home and into institutions which professionals controlled.

One of the signs of the greater professionalisation of the judiciary was the enunciation and enforcement of a distinct code of professional judicial ethics. The high (as well as the low) point in the story of the enforcement of professional judicial ethics is the dismissal of most of the higher judiciary in 1289-90 and the trial and conviction of most of them for judicial misconduct in the so-called 'State Trials' of 1289-93. 'Edward I and the Transformation of the English Judiciary' (7) deals with certain aspects of this crisis; others are dealt with in 'Edward I and the Judges: the "State Trials" of 1289-93' (5). One of the most prominent of the judges to be dismissed in 1289-90 was Thomas Weyland, the chief justice of the Bench. In 'Chief Justice and Felon: The Career of Thomas Weyland' (6) I demonstrate that his dismissal and exile were not, as previously believed, punishments for judicial misconduct but the result of his involvement in a murder committed by his servants. Other evidence also discussed in the essay does, however, suggest that Weyland may well have been involved in misconduct of this kind. The essay also makes a start on the substantial task of compiling a satisfactory collective biography of the Edwardian judiciary using the many unprinted sources which previous judicial biographers have neglected, in particular the largely unpublished reports. Only when this work is completed will we have a full picture of the background and previous experience of these judges and be in a position to assess the contribution they made to the development of the Common Law.

The judges were clearly the most important single group in the functioning of the thirteenth-century English judicial system. Professional lawyers also clearly had an important part to play in it. It is only towards the end of the thirteenth century as new sources of information become available that we begin to see just how large a group the clerks working in the courts were and what an important role they too played in their operation. They are the subject of 'Medieval Legal Bureaucracy: The Clerks of the King's Courts in the reign of Edward I' (8), which is the first general survey of what is discoverable about this important group of legal bureaucrats during this period. This essay looks at their numbers, the functions they performed, the sources of their income, their ethical standards in theory and in practice and the significance of this group as a source for the recruitment of royal justices.

Professional lawyers, judges and court clerks were the main producers but also among the main consumers of the 'artifacts' of legal culture, the various legal treatises and miscellaneous legal works which circulated in manuscript in thirteenth century England. A number of these are discussed in 'Courtroom and Schoolroom: The Education of Lawyers in England prior to 1400' (3), where it is suggested that many may have been by-products of the process of legal education. 'Hengham Magna: A Thirteenth-Century Common Law Treatise and its Composition' (17) looks at one such treatise which was not derived from any kind of educational process but which, to judge from the large number of surviving manuscripts, was clearly found useful and probably played an important role in legal education in the broader sense, explaining the rudiments of legal process in land pleas and what went on in court to a wider and perhaps predominantly non-professional audience. The essay re-examines the question of the authorship of this treatise. It has been attributed since the thirteenth century to the well-known royal justice, Ralph de Hengham. The essay explains why this attribution is likely to be wrong and provides good reasons for reattributing it to a much less well-known court clerk, John Blundel. Hengham is, however, the probable author of the major part of another work printed in 'Quo Waranto Law in the Reign of Edward I: A Hitherto Undiscovered Opinion of Chief Justice Hengham' (18). This work derives from a set of questions on points of *quo waranto* law submitted to Hengham, then chief justice of King's Bench, by the justices of the 1285 Northamptonshire eyre and Hengham's answers to those questions. The essay also attempts to place both questions and answers in the wider context of the development of *quo waranto* law during this period, the period of the Edwardian *quo waranto* proceedings, when franchise-holders were made to justify their exercise of various franchisal rights and to answer for various lands and other properties allegedly usurped from the Crown.

Regular legislative modification of the Common Law began shortly after the middle of the thirteenth century with the enactment of the Provisions of Westminster in 1259. We know little about the drafting of most of the legislation of this period for it is rare for legislative drafts or other preparatory material to survive that sheds any real light on this process. Perhaps because the Provisions of Westminster were one of the main products of a period of major political upheaval, several texts relating to various stages of the drafting process of these Provisions do survive. 'The Drafting of Legislation in Mid Thirteenth-Century England' (16) uses these exceptionally plentiful and informative sources to elucidate the process by which the final text of the Provisions eventually emerged. It is unlikely that this drafting process was typical. It cannot, however, have been wholly different from what happened at other times, so these documents provide us with a privileged insight into the process of legislative drafting. A second essay, 'The Control of Mortmain Alienations in England, 1200-1300' (11), looks at the social, legal and legislative background to the enactment of one of the major pieces of Edwardian legislation, the Statute of Mortmain of 1279, which purported to impose a permanent ban on all future grants of property to the Church. It also examines how and why a system of royal licensing of mortmain alienations soon came to supersede the complete prohibition mandated by the statute.

By the later thirteenth century distraint (the seizure of animals or other property) without prior judicial authorisation had become a common way of enforcing obligations and duties of various kinds. Such distraints could be challenged in the courts by the action of replevin which made the distrainor appear and justify the distraint he had made. 'Legal Change in the Later Thirteenth Century: Statutory and Judicial Remodelling of the Action of Replevin' (14) looks at the changes made by c.2 of the statute of Westminster II (1285) and their effects on the working of the action and argues that these suggest that it is necessary to read between the lines of statutes when they talk of the reasons for making changes in the law. The essay also points to non-statutory changes in the working of the action and in the law of distraint during the reign of Edward I. These suggest the continuing importance of non-legislative legal change even in an era of major legislative innovation in the Common Law.

The single most important use of distraint by the later thirteenth century was by lords attempting to compel the performance of services by their tenants. Changes in the law relating to this kind of distraint and in the use of the action of replevin to challenge it over a longer period (from the later twelfth century onwards) are discussed in 'Lordship and Distraint in Thirteenth-Century England' (15). It argues that distraint without prior judicial authorisation to compel the performance of services is a practice that goes back to the Anglo-Norman period and is not, as Professor Milsom has recently suggested, a thirteenth-century development. Distraint has been seen by some legal historians as a powerful weapon in the hands of thirteenth-century lords which allowed them to extort additional services from their tenants. They have argued that it was only in the later thirteenth and early fourteenth centuries and through a series of statutory changes and judicial extensions of those statutes that this weapon was gradually brought under control. This essay argues that, on the contrary, the legal rules relating to distraint may have made it quite difficult for lords to compel their free tenants to perform even those services that they did owe by means of distraint in the first half of the thirteenth century; they certainly did not make it easy for lords to usurp additional services in this way. It also argues that the statutory changes in fact made it easier for lords in the second half of the century to use distraint and turned it into the normal method of enforcing services, but that this did not present lords with a new opportunity for usurping services since the tenant already had a handy weapon for challenging unjustified distraints in the action of replevin.

Non-statutory change in an era of plentiful legislation is also the underlying theme of the brief essay on 'Formedon in the Remainder before "De Donis"' (10). In a classic essay Professor Milsom established the existence of actions of formedon in the descender and in the reverter and the scope and limitations of these actions in protecting the interests of the heir and of the reversioner under entails prior to the enactment in 1285 of c.1 of the statute Westminster II ('de Donis'). He was not, however, able to establish the existence of any comparable remedy to provide any kind of protection for those given interests in remainder under pre-1285 entails. This essay established for the first time from direct plea roll evidence the existence of such a remedy. Initially the remainderman was allowed to use the apparently inappropriate actions of formedon in the reverter and formedon in the descender to assert his claim. It was only in 1279 that a distinct writ and action of formedon in the remainder were provided for his use. Thus the history of the remainderman's remedy prior to 1285 is important evidence for how litigants, with the cooperation of the courts and perhaps also of chancery, could extend the ambit of common law remedies without any statutory authority and without, initially at least, the invention of new writs.

Aspects of the history of the Common Law in Ireland are discussed in the remaining essays. 'Ireland and the Literature of the Early Common Law' (19) re-examines the mechanisms through which the Common Law came to be transmitted to Ireland in the later twelfth century and first half of the thirteenth century. The essay argues for the redating of the so-called 'Irish' register of writs from 1227 to the immediate aftermath of King John's visit to the lordship in 1210 and suggests that its immediate context is the decision, taken during John's visit and recorded in a charter now lost, that Ireland should follow the English Common Law. It also argues that the various certifications on matters of English legal custom sent to Ireland between 1223 and 1238 are to be seen not as evidence of ignorance in the lordship of basic principles of English law but in the context of changes in that law and as attempts to ensure uniformity between the law of the two countries. The linkages which existed between the English and Irish legal systems during the second half of the thirteenth century are discussed in 'Ralph de Hengham and the Irish Common Law' (20). This focuses in particular on evidence provided by a hitherto unknown 'consultation' of Hengham on a question about procedure in advowson cases for the informal consultation of senior English royal judges by their Irish counterparts.

'King, Church and Property: The Enforcement of Restrictions on Alienations into Mortmain in the Lordship of Ireland in the Later Middle Ages' (12) also concerns one of the mechanisms for the extension of English law to Ireland in the later thirteenth century. The essay examines the tangled story of how the English statute of Mortmain came ultimately to be extended to the lordship of Ireland and the extension to Ireland of a number of related legislative provisions. It also uses surviving English and Irish evidence to demonstrate the various different ways in which the statute was enforced within the lordship of Ireland in the later Middle Ages. 'The Licensing of Mortmain Alienations in the Medieval Lordship of Ireland' (13) is a complementary essay which looks at the other side of the working of the mortmain legislation in Ireland: the operation of the mortmain licensing system within the lordship during the later Middle Ages and the gradual process through which control of licensing passed from England to the rulers of the lordship in Dublin.

A final essay, 'The Early History of the Legal Profession of the Lordship of Ireland' (2), complements my own work on the beginnings of the legal profession in England. This essay examines the evidence for the existence of professional lawyers and a legal profession in the lordship of Ireland during the century between 1250 and 1350 and shows that there was indeed an Irish legal profession by *c.* 1300, which in many respects resembled its much larger English counterpart and was clearly modelled on it but also in some interesting respects departed from the English model.

Although I am a legal historian I have always believed that legal history should be a matter of interest not just to the narrow circle of my fellow specialists but also to a much wider world of non-specialist lawyers and historians. Knowledge and understanding of the past history of the legal ideas which developed within his own legal system and of how that legal system developed should be part of the mental equipment of any educated lawyer. The historian who is interested in the development of English or Irish society over the past eight centuries needs to know a great deal about legal development in our two neighbouring islands. Legal historians have not always shown themselves aware of the need to communicate with their wider audience, indeed have often written as though their fellow-specialists were the only conceivable readers of their work. There is some excuse for this. Legal ideas are often complex, legal procedures and legal institutions complicated. Non-specialists have often been deterred by the smallest of technicalities. In these essays I have tried to keep a lay audience in mind and to make my work accessible to that wider audience but without sacrificing the technical detail that is the necessary underpinning to any serious work in legal history. Legal history written only for legal historians is a story which has lost its most important audience.

Paul Brand
London
September 1992

1

The Origins of the English Legal Profession

I

Shortly after Henry II had succeeded to the English throne, Richard of Anstey commenced litigation against his cousin, Mabel de Francheville.[1] His uncle, William de Sackville, had held a sizeable mesne barony, consisting of at least seven Essex manors and the overlordship of ten knights' fees in Essex and three neighbouring counties. Richard's aim was to secure this property for himself. Mabel claimed that (as William's daughter and heiress) she was rightfully in possession. Richard asserted that she was illegitimate, the issue of a marriage that had been annulled by the Church; and that as Williams's nephew, the eldest son of William's sister, the lands should pass to him, as William's heir. The litigation began in 1158 in the king's court; but once the question of Mabel's status had been raised it was transferred to the Church courts. Her legitimacy was discussed in turn in the court of the archbishop of Canterbury, before papal judges delegate, and finally before the papal court of audience in Rome. The eventual decision was that Mabel was illegitimate. The case then returned to the king's court, and, some five years after the proceedings had begun, the king's court awarded William de Sackville's lands to Richard of Anstey.

Richard compiled a detailed memorandum giving full particulars of the money he had spent during the course of the litigation, a total of £ 350. The memorandum records the payments made to three canon lawyers who had given Richard professional legal assistance in the English ecclesiastical courts (master Peter of Meleti, master Stephen of Binham, master Ambrose). It also records a total of twelve and a half marks as having been spent by Richard in gifts of money and of horses to the 'pleaders' (*placitatores*) who had regularly come to court with him on the days appointed for the hearing of his case. These 'pleaders' were not, however,

Earlier versions of this paper were read to the members of the two medieval seminars in London and to the Medieval Society in Oxford and I would like to thank those who commented on the paper on those occasions. The paper also owes much to the help and encouragement of Dr. Paul Hyams and to the stimulus provided by Dr. Robert Palmer.

1. P.M. Barnes, 'The Anstey Case', in P.M. Barnes and C.F. Slade, eds., *A Medieval Miscellany for D.M. Stenton*, Pipe Roll Society, new ser., xxxvi (London, 1960) 1–23. Additional material on the case, including an identification of the lands which were at stake in it, will be found in P.A. Brand, 'New Light on the Anstey Case', *Essex Archaelogy and History* xv (1983) 68–83.

in any true sense the counterparts of the professionals which Richard of Anstey had employed in the ecclesiastical courts. The memorandum makes it plain that they were simply neighbours (*vicini*) who accompanied Richard to court to show solidarity with him, not men employed by Richard for any special skills or knowledge they possessed. Towards the end of the litigation, it is true, Richard sent for Ranulf de Glanvill, the future royal justice and justiciar. It is tempting to see this as the summoning of expert legal assistance. The memorandum suggests, however, that Richard only wanted Ranulf there to swell the numbers of his supporters present at the court and to make them look more impressive. Richard's memorandum speaks of him going to the court on that day with 'as many friends and helpers as I could get . . . '. If Ranulf de Glanvill did turn up (and there is no clear evidence that he did) he seems not to have been paid for doing so, for no payment to him is recorded in the memorandum. Richard of Anstey was after a valuable prize, and was willing to spend considerable sums in order to secure it. For his litigation in the church courts he employed professional lawyers and paid them accordingly. If there had been professional lawyers to be employed in the English law courts at this time he would surely have employed them as well. As yet then, in the 1150s, the evidence of the Anstey case suggests that there were no professional lawyers active in the lay courts in England.

Other evidence from the period between the Norman Conquest and the early years of the reign of Henry II confirms this view. The chronicle of Abingdon abbey mentions a number of lawyers (*causidici*) of English origin who helped in the defence and recovery of the abbey's rights during the reign of William the Conqueror.[2] Early professional lawyers, we might conclude—but we would be wrong, because the chronicler goes on to say who they were. One was a priest in charge of one of the abbey's churches, the others monks belonging to the abbey. They may have been legal experts, but they are most unlikely to have been professional lawyers even in the minimal sense of men recognized as having a specific professional expertise in legal matters who were willing to put that expertise at the disposal of clients and who were remunerated for so doing. In any case, the chronicler makes it clear that their main value to the abbey lay in their ability to recall the pre-conquest past and not in any more specifically legal skills.

When Robert of Chilton was summoned to the court of the abbey of Battle in 1102 to render his account of the period he had been in charge of the abbey's manor of Wye, like Richard of Anstey he came to the court with 'pleaders' (*placitatores*).[3] Again, it is tempting to suppose that we are dealing here with professional lawyers: but it seems clear that we are not. The chronicler names four of them and, as Eleanor Searle's identifications make plain, three out of the four were simply prominent members of the

2. J. Stevenson, ed., *Chronicon Monasterii de Abingdon*, 2 vols., Rolls Series (London, 1858) ii:2 [hereinafter: *Chronicon Monasterii de Abingdon*].

3. E. Searle, ed., *The Chronicle of Battle Abbey*, (Oxford, 1980) 109–10.

local gentry. They were there to give support, not professional advice, as the Battle abbey chronicle itself makes plain—for it goes on at once to mention the many other barons (*aliique barones quamplurimi*) who accompanied Robert. The same chronicle also has an account of the land litigation brought by the abbot of Battle against Gilbert de Balliol half a century later.[4] This litigation started in the court of the count of Eu but was eventually determined in the King's court. For the presentation of his case in the King's court the abbot relied on one of his monks and a local knight, Peter de Criol, and not on some hired professional lawyer, though his eventual success owed much to the efforts of his brother, Richard de Luci, the king's justiciar.

This was, indeed, a world in which powerful friends and not expert advisers were of most use to litigants. We know that religious houses, in particular, took good care to ensure that they would have such 'friends' when they needed them. The *Descriptio Militum* of the abbey of Peterborough, which belongs to the first decade of the twelfth century, mentions a half carucate holding at Riseholme in Lincolnshire which Picot son of Colswain held of the abbey. This land, the survey says, had been given to his father Colswain in return for the service of 'being at the abbot's law-suits, and supporting the abbot in his defence of the abbey's property and the abbey's tenants both in the county court and elsewhere'.[5] Colswain and Picot were great men, lords of the Lincolnshire barony of Brattleby, 'friends' well worth having.[6] In 1111 the abbey of St. Augustine's Canterbury granted land to Hamo *dapifer* in return for Hamo's 'advice and assistance' to the abbey in the county court of Kent and in the king's court against all barons other than those to whom Hamo was already bound by homage.[7] Hamo was again a powerful man—a royal steward and also at the time the sheriff of Kent, and clearly a 'friend' to cultivate. Around this same time, the abbot of Abingdon made an agreement with Nigel d'Oylly, the lord of the Oxfordshire barony of Hook Norton and also a royal constable, that in return for the land he held of the abbey, he would be on the abbot's side (*ipsius abbatis parti . . . adierit*) in any litigation the abbot had in the king's court, provided only that the opponent of the abbot was someone other than the king.[8] Agreements of this sort have been seen as arrangements

---

4. Ibid. at 211–19.

5. E. King, 'The Peterborough *Descriptio Militum* (Henry I)', *English Historical Review* lxxxiv (1969) 100.

6. J.F.W. Hill, *Medieval Lincoln* (Cambridge, 1948) 48–49.

7. G.J. Turner and H.E. Salter, eds., *The Black Book of St. Augustine's Canterbury*, 2 vols. (London, 1924) ii: 462–63; C. Johnson and H.A. Cronne, eds., *Regesta Regum Anglo-Normannorum*, 4 vols. (Oxford, 1913–69) ii: xi-xii.

8. *Chronicon Monasterii de Abingdon*, supra note 2 at ii: 132–33; I.J. Sanders, *English Baronies* (Oxford, 2nd ed. 1963) 54.

intended to secure expert, professional legal advice[9]; but this was a society where it was the 'friendship' of powerful men, and not legal expertise, that potential litigants needed; and such agreements were clearly intended to secure such 'friendships'.

In form, such agreements are not always easy to distinguish from agreements of a somewhat different kind also to be found in twelfth century sources, under which much less prominent and important individuals are granted land in perpetuity in return for the service of representing the grantor and his tenants and defending their interests at a particular court or courts.[10] Such grantees, too, have been seen as early professional lawyers and the grants as providing evidence for the existence of a legal profession in twelfth century England.[11] There is, however, no evidence that the grantees did possess any specialized legal skills, and the permanent nature of such agreements suggests that it was not professional skill that the grantor required from his grantee, since it was impossible to be certain that the grantee's heirs would inherit any special skill of this sort that he might have had. It seems much more likely that all that the grantor expected from the grantee and his heirs was regular attendance at the court(s) concerned in the place of the grantor; and that at a time when there were no professional lawyers it did not matter that the watching brief for the grantor and his men was held by just another unskilled tenant.

On other type of agreement has, on occasion, led the historian astray, into seeing a professional lawyer where there is none to be found. Between 1166 and 1176 a mill was granted by the abbot of Cirencester to Robert son of William of Blewbury in return for various services. One of these was that of 'assisting the abbot in the pleas of his church at Cirencester or wherever he was called upon to do so'. The editor of the cartulary comments that 'the services . . . are of a most unusual character, and seem to suggest that Robert was some kind of lawyer who would plead for the abbot wherever required . . . '.[12] The key to the understanding of this clause is, however, provided by a subsequent charter in the same cartulary, recording a grant to the same tenant of another mill by the abbot's successor. This time the charter stipulates that Robert is to 'assist the abbot in the pleas of his church

9. R. C. Palmer, 'The Origins of the Legal Profession in England', *The Irish Jurist*, new ser. xi (1976) 135 [hereinafter: Palmer, 'Origins of the Legal Profession'].

10. W. D. Macray, ed., *Chronicon Abbatiae Ramesiensis* Rolls Series (London, 1886) 260–61; C.J. Holdsworth, ed., *Rufford Charters* Thoroton Soc. Record Series, xxx (1974) ii: 289–90; W. Hunt, ed., *Two Chartularies of the Priory of St. Peter at Bath*, Somerset Record Soc., vii (1893) Lincoln's Inn Manuscript 11; C.G.O. Bridgeman, 'The Burton Abbey Twelfth Century Surveys', *William Salt Archaelogical Society: Collections for a History of Staffordshire*, (1916) 231.

11. Palmer, 'Origins of the Legal Profession', supra note 9 at 135.

12. C. Ross and M. Devine, eds., *The Cartulary of Cirencester Abbey* 3 vols., (Oxford, 1964–77) ii: 472 ('*et assistet abbati in placitis ecclesie sive apud Cyrencestriam sive alibi quocumque vocabitur . . .* ').

in his court, like the other free men of Hagbourne and Easton'.[13] This makes it plain that all that each of the abbots had wanted from their tenant was the common feudal service of acting as a suitor at his court, as one of the non-professional judges who made and gave judgments in seignorial and local courts. The only unusual feature of these charters is that the grantors specifically mention suit of court: most twelfth century enfeoffment do not, though the grantees seem normally to have performed it.

II

By 1300 a legal profession had come into being in England. There existed by that date a sizeable group of men who were recognised as having specific, professional skills in the representation of litigants and who spent much of their time and derived much of their income from putting those skills at the disposal of litigants.[14] They also, by 1300, constituted a profession in another sense, for by that date they were also subject to special rules governing their professional conduct[15]. As we have seen, there was no legal profession in England in the mid-twelfth century. When, how and why did a legal profession come into existence between those two dates?

A.

Lady Stenton's work on the surviving plea rolls of the king's courts of the reigns of kings Richard and John uncovered some fifteen men whose names, she thought, occurred on those rolls with sufficient frequency—in the role of attorney, essoiner or surety—to suggest the possibility that they were professional lawyers.[16] About two of these men (Reginald de Argentan and Fulk Bainard) she herself had doubts. A further two of her fifteen (Stephen Boncretien and William of Buckingham) seem to have been clerks serving in the courts; a third (Robert of Rockingham) was an Exchequer clerk; and a fourth (Richard Duket) was a man in the service of the justiciar, Geoffrey FitzPeter. Such men may have done 'professional' legal work for clients but were hardly professional lawyers. Another of her putative professional lawyers, Ralph Hareng, is shown by the references to have been the steward of Thomas de St. Valery as well as a royal justice, but not to have offered his services to any other clients. John de Planez, yet another member of the group, is shown by the sources to have been a professional lawyer in and after 1228, but they do not show that he was acting as such in John's reign.

13. Ibid. at ii: 473 ('*preterea assistet abbati in placitis ecclesie in curia sua sicut alii liberi homines de Hackeburne et Eston*').

14. I will discuss elsewhere in my forthcoming book on the origins and early history of the English legal profession the main features and characteristics of the Edwardian profession.

15. See discussion at 12-14 infra.

16. D. M. Stenton, ed., *Pleas before the King or his Justices, 1198–1212, vol III* Selden Society, lxxxiii (London, 1966) xxxvi-xl, ccxcv-cccxix.

This reduces the number of probable professional lawyers to just seven.[17] About one of these seven, at least, there can be little doubt, for in his case the evidence of the plea rolls receives independent confirmation from another source. John Bucuinte came of a London merchant family, perhaps of Italian origin; and a certain inherited verbal facility may be indicated by the family surname, which probably means 'oily mouth'. He is known to have acted as the serjeant of the abbot of Crowland in litigation with the prior of Spalding in 1200; and the case of 1201, in which he is recorded to have alleged that the champion of one of the parties had been hired was probably one where he was acting for the other party in the same capacity. In 1220 he was amerced by the justices of the Bench for 'sitting at [a] judgment, when he was serjeant in the case' (*eo quod ipse sedit ad judicium et fuit narrator loquele*). This may simply have been a breach of etiquette— an indication of disrespect to the justices who were giving judgment in the case. An alternative interpretation of the passage, however, is to see in it something rather more serious: Bucuinte sitting in at, and participating in, the making of a judgment in a case where he had previously acted as a serjeant[18]. Most of the references, however, are to him acting or being appointed as an attorney: an indication that, at this early stage in the development of the profession, the professional was still free to act in both capacities—though not necessarily in the same case.[19]

It is during the long reign of Henry III (1216–72) that we first begin to catch glimpses of what looks like a real group of professional lawyers—and of a group who were already specializing in the work of only one branch of the profession. Matthew Paris, the St. Alban's chronicler, in his account of the trial of Hubert de Burgh before the king's council in 1239, speaks of the king having for this trial the assistance of all of the *serjeants* of the Bench ('*cum omnibus prolocutoribus banci, quos 'narratores' vulgariter appellamus*') but Hubert having to make do with the services of his own steward, master Laurence of St. Alban's.[20] By 1239, then, there was a

---

17. Ibid. at ccxcv-cccxix.

18. There was a need for specific regulations against this practice in the London city courts in 1244. H. M. Chew and M. Weinbaum, eds., *The London Eyre of 1244* (London Record Society) vi (1970) 96 (no. 236). For possible evidence of John Bucuinte hearing litigation in the Bench earlier in 1220, see *Curia Regis Rolls* 16 vols. to date (London, 1922-) viii: 322 n.6.

19. *Pleas before the King or his Justices* supra note 16 at xxxviii-xl, cccvii-cccxi. W.O. Hassall, ed., *Cartulary of St. Mary, Clerkenwell*, Camden Society, 3rd series (1949), lxxxi, nos. 170, 180, 181; H.T. Riley, ed., *Munimenta Gildhalle Londoniensis, vol. I*, Rolls Series (1859) 109; G.A. Williams, *Medieval London: from Commune to Capital*, (London, 2nd ed. 1970) 20. Another of these men, Matthew of Bigstrup, appears to have been acting as a serjeant by 1228, see note 21 infra, but all the earlier references are to him acting as an attorney or as a county knight.

20. H. Luard, ed., *Matthaei Parisiensis Chronica Majora*, 7 vols., Rolls Series (1872–84) iii: 618–20. For evidence that Lawrence was Hubert's steward see ibid at 233. The proceedings as transcribed by Matthew Paris from the plea roll record are edited ibid. at vi: 63–74. This portion of the *Chronica Majora* may not be exactly contemporary

group of presumably professional lawyers able to specialize in the functions of the serjeant and in practice in the Bench, though also perhaps available for employment elsewhere. Unfortunately Matthew Paris gives us no real idea of the size of the group or guidance as to the identity of its members.[21]

We encounter the group again in Michaelmas term 1267 when one of its members, Robert de Coleville, assaulted Robert of Fulham, one of the justices of the Jews, in Westminster hall. Robert de Coleville was eventually induced to make an appearance before the Treasurer and the barons of the Exchequer and the justices of the Bench with tunic unbelted and head uncovered, in the guise of a humble suppliant, and to make a full and total submission to the victim of his assault, putting life and limb, land and property, at his disposal; then, honour being satisfied, the two men were reconciled with a kiss of peace. The mediators who brought about the submission and subsequent reconciliation were Robert de Coleville's *socii*, his fellow-serjeants, acting as a group.[22] Again, disappointingly, we are told of the existence of a recognizable group of Bench serjeants, but not how large that group was or who its other members were.[23]

---

with the events described but had been written up by 1251. R. Vaughan, *Matthew Paris* (Cambridge, 1958) 60. Matthew Paris also refers to the serjeants as *banci narratores* in a section of his *Gesta Abbatum*. John Mansel, one of Henry III's most trusted advisers, is said to have taken steps to ensure that none of them acted for the abbot of St. Alban's in litigation with Mansel's brother-in-law, Geoffrey of Childwick. As a result the abbot was forced to rely on the services of the abbey's cellarer instead. H. T. Riley, ed, *Gesta Abbatum Monasterii Sancti Albani*, 3 vols., Rolls Series (1867–69) i:316.

21. The names of a number of serjeants or possible serjeants of the first half of the reign of Henry III can be gleaned from the plea rolls. These include: (i) Robert of Sudbury, C.R.R. ix; 41 (amerced in 1220 *pro falsiloquio et mendacio*); (ii) Stephen of the Strand, C.R.R. ix: 59 (amerced in 1220 *pro stultioquio suo* (Stephen also appears frequently on the rolls as an attorney and as a pledge between 1219 and 1233)). (iii) Ralph of Bardfield, C.R.R. x: 203 (amerced in 1221 *pro stultiloquio* and specifically described as having spoken for the tenant in the case); (iv) Matthew of Bigstrup, C.R.R. xiii: no. 1107 (amerced in 1228 because the defendant's attorney had disavowed what he had said ('*deadvocat . . . dictum Mathei de Bikestrop*') (Matthew is one of the men whom Lady Stenton suggested might have been professional lawyers, see discussion supra at 35–36 and notes 16, 19); (v) John de Planaz, C.R.R. xiii: no. 1194 (amerced in 1228 because the demandant in the case had disavowed his count ('*deadvocat . . . narracionem Johannis de Planaz advocati sui*'—; (vi) Alan of Waxham, C.R.R. xv: no. 1026 (amerced in 1234 in king's bench because the person for whom he had spoken disavowed what he had said ('*quia . . . deadvocavit id quod pro eo narravit*'); (vii) Richard de Hottot, KB 26/132 m. 6. (client amerced in 1244 for avowing a count made by Richard which did not correspond with his writ).

22. The episode is recorded on both memoranda rolls; E 368/42 m. 3d (Lord Treasurer's Remembrancer) and E 159/42 m. 3d (King's Remembrancer), but it is only on the L.T.R. memoranda roll that interlineations in the entry tell us of Robert de Coleville's status as a serjeant of the Bench ('*narrator de banco*') and that the reconciliation was accomplished through the mediation of his colleagues ('*ad instanciam sociorum suorum narratorum*'). The entry is printed from the L.T.R. memoranda roll in T. Madox, *The History and Antiquities of the Exchequer* (London, 1711) 161 note k.

23. Some names of serjeants, or possible serjeants, of the Bench of the second half of the

Other evidence suggests that by the 1260s it had become the normal practice for litigants to have serjeants to plead for them and not to plead in person or have their attorney plead for them. The author of *Hengham Magna*, written during this period, assumes that when two litigants appear in the Bench for land litigation, they will both have serjeants to speak for them—even where all the defendant intends to do is the simple business of requesting a view of the land concerned.[24] The compiler of *Brevia Placitata*, a collection of specimen counts and defences for litigation in the Bench, also written at about the same time, does not say that these counts and defences are normally delivered by serjeants: but does go on at a number of points to give arguments following up a particular count and defence. These have every appearance of having been drawn from real cases. On almost every occasion that this occurs, the author specifically attributes one or both sides of the argument to the litigant's serjeants.[25]

It was, however, still possible in the 1260s for a litigant to have his attorney plead on his behalf. Hugh de Bladis, the attorney of the defendant in an action of right heard in the Bench in 1261, is recorded on the plea roll as having lost the land for his client because he had put himself on the grand assize—that is, used the form of words appropriate to the submission of the plaintiff's claim and his denial of it to the verdict of a grand assize of twelve knights—without having first made the necessary formal denial of the plaintiff's right. The case illustrates nicely the reason why attorneys did not normally double as serjeants for their clients: the attorney could not disavow

---

reign of Henry III can be gleaned from the plea rolls and from other sources. These include: (i) Abel de St. Martin, KB 26/150 m. 22 (1253, king's bench) (amerced and remanded to custody for speaking for the defendant, the bishop of Rochester, to whom he was probably related, but not being avowed ('*narravit pro episcopo et non fuit advocatus*')). Maitland's interpretation of this passage was that Abel was amerced for pleading when 'he was not a member of the legal profession . . . ', but this seems to be wrong. Cf. F. Pollock & F. Maitland, *The History of English Law*, 2 vols. (Cambridge, 1968) (i) 216 n. 3. Abel may not however, have been a professional serjeant. (ii) Nicholas of Lynn, *Calendar of Patent Rolls, 1247–58* 605 (1257) (described as '*narrator*', and probably (from other evidence) a Bench serjeant). (iii) Richard (de Ulmis) of Havering, *Calendar of Patent Rolls, 1247–58*, 617 (1258) (also described as '*narrator*', and probably from other evidence, a Bench serjeant). (iv) John Giffard, W.H. Dunham, ed., *Casus Placitorum*, Selden Society, lxix (London, 1950) 79–80. (v) John of Pakenham, KB 26/166 m. 2d; KB 26/195, m. 19 (1268), KB 26/196 m. 15 (1270) (sues for king in litigation in the Bench). (vi) William of Thorney *Calendar of Patent Rolls, 1266–72* 318 (1269) (described as king's serjeant, and other evidence suggests that he was a king's serjeant in the sense of a lawyer acting for the king). (vii) Richard of Boyland, Dunham, ed. *Casus Placitorum* supra at 79. (viii) John of Houghton, *Calendar of Patent Rolls, 1266–72* 551 (1271) (described as king's serjeant, and other evidence suggests that he was a lawyer).

24. *Radulphi de Hengham Summae*, p. 34. On the date and authorship of the treatise see
   P.A. Brand, '*Hengham Magna*: a Thirteenth Century English Common Law Treatise and its Composition', below, pp. 369-91.

25. G.J. Turner and T.F.T. Plucknett, ed., *Brevia Placitata* Selden Society, lxvi (London, 1951) 20, 25–26, 55–56, 59, 60, 64–65, 81–83, 100, 100–102, 103–106, 129, 130–131, 143, 165, etc. On the date of the treatise, see ibid at xviii-xxiv.

himself, and so any mistake that he made was final and could be fatal to his client.[26] The Bench plea-rolls of 1262 also provide us with one example of a litigant apparently having to plead on his own behalf. The case is one brought by Richard of Cornwall, the king's brother, against Hugh Gernegan for various lands that Richard claimed should have escheated to him after Hugh's outlawry for felony. Hugh is recorded as objecting to the form of Richard's writ—as asking, with a sigh (*suspirando*) for judgment of the writ—but as having been told by the king's council as well as by the justices of the court to answer over (because the writ was good). He is then recorded as seeking a view of the land, in tears (*lacrimando*). The sigh and the tears are surely not those of the serjeant and probably not those of an attorney [27]: they are most likely to have been those of the litigant himself.[28] Both entries are, however, quite exceptional, and neither can be easily paralleled, if parallelled at all, from Bench records of the next four decades.[29]

Of professional attorneys practising in the Bench during the reign of Henry III we hear very little. As yet, we find no proceedings brought against them for misconduct; no law-suits between them and their clients; and no attempts to regulate either their numbers or their conduct. All that we do have is the bare record, term by term, of the appointment of attorneys; and it is only from an analysis of these appointments that we can show that there were almost certainly already some professional attorneys practising in the Bench by 1260. As yet, however, their number was still very small— probably fewer than ten -and they only account for a very small proportion of the total number of appointments recorded on the plea rolls.[30] There were

26. Pillerton v. Fitz Roger, KB 26/171 m. 35d. The land concerned was only a small holding (one message, an acre and a half of woodland, four acres of arable and two and a half acres of medadow) and the defendant may have been attempting to avoid the expense of employing a serjeant.

27. But note that one of the two attorneys whom Hugh had appointed in Michaelmas term 1261 for this plea was his own son John, KB 26/171 m. 81, and that he appointed another attorney in the plea in Easter term 1262, KB 26/166 m. 40 (his opponent here becomes '*rex anemalie*' not '*alemanie*').

28. KB 26/166 m. 35. For earlier and later stages of the same case, KB 26/171 m. 9d; KB 26/172 m. 22; KB 26/173 m. 16d; KB 26/200A m. 26 and for its background, see 2 *Calendar of Patent Rolls, 1232–47* 11, 164.

29. But see the splendid story of the Peterborough chronicler about the earl of Gloucester's litigation against the abbot of Peterborough in the 1285 Northamtonshire eyre in which the earl was seeking the manor of 'Biggin'. On the day the case was to be heard the earl took the abbot by the hand ('*per manum accepit*') and sat with him, but this was just a trick to stop him getting a serjeant ('*et fraudulenter hoc fecit ut abbas non haberet serianciam pro negociis suis expendiendis nec ut aliquis pro causa isius abbatis se apponere seu defendere quoquomodo auderet*'). The abbot had then to use the services of his sacristan to speak for him, though only after the abbot had asked permission for this from the justices. Fortunately the sacristan was able to find a defect in the earl's writ and so got it quashed. British Library, Additional MS 39758, fol. 99r.

30. There is no whole year around 1260 with a good run of surviving attorney appointment membranes. For the purposes of analysis I have used the attorney membranes of the

professional lawyers practising also in other royal courts by the end of Henry III's reign: but of them very little is known.[31]

Outside the royal courts, it is only in London that there seems to be any clear evidence for the existence of the professional lawyer prior to the reign of Edward I. As early as 1244, it was found necessary to prohibit serjeants (*advocatus aut placitator*) from taking any part in the making or giving of judgments in the city courts in cases where they themselves had acted for one of the litigants.[32] Such serjeants may not have been professional lawyers, however. Subsequent legislation, of 1259, was clearly aimed at the professional serjeant. This made it illegal for any serjeant (*causidicus*) practising in the city courts to agree to act for a litigant in return for a share of the tenement or land which was at stake in the litigation. On conviction, the serjeant was not just to lose the share thereby acquired but also to be 'suspended from his office' (*et suspendatur ab officio suo . . .*), a punishment only appropriate to a professional serjeant. A further clause of the same legislation, as it is reported by the London chronicler, Arnulf fitz Thedmar, provided that it was not in future to be necessary (*non sit necesse*) for litigants to have a serjeant in any plea in the city other than pleas of the crown (criminal cases), land pleas, and pleas of replevin. In all other kinds of litigation, the litigants were just to explain their cases themselves and the courts, having thereby discovered the truth, were to give a just and an

---

rolls for Michaelmas term 1258 (KB 26/160 mm. 60–63), Hilary term 1259 (KB 26/162 mm. 43, 44, 46), Hilary term 1260 (KB 26/164 m. 35 only: the other membranes are lost), and Easter term 1260 (KB 26/165 mm. 36–39). The probable professional attorneys of the Bench found on these rolls are (with totals of appointments in brackets): Richer of Colchester (nine and also one appointment in King's Bench as an attorney in Michaelmas term 1259); John of Easton (fifteen); John of Harpley (thirteen); Reginald of St. Alban's (twelve); William of Skutterskelfe (nine, and twice appointed an attorney in the Exchequer in Hilary and Easter terms 1260), John of Wandsworth (seventeen), John son of William (sixteen), and Robert of Wolmerston (ten).

31. The Richard of Glen and Richard Gruys *narratores* amerced because they were disavowed by John le Paumer and his mother Isabel in the Warwickshire special eyre of 1260, see JUST 1/953 m. 2d, were perhaps professionals: Richard of Glen also appears in the Exchequer of Pleas as an attorney for the abbot of Leicester in 1259–60. E 13/1B mm. 2, 4d. Note also that the Peterborough chronicler, writing about the 1262 Lincolnshire eyre, mentions the great expenses and 'liberalities' ('*sumptus amplos et magnas liberalitates*') of the abbot of Peterborough both to the justices and to the serjeants ('*narratoribus*') as well as to other men of the county: British Library, Additional MS 39758, fol. 90r. The earliest identified Eyre Year-Book reports come from the following Lincolnshire eyre of 1272. One is Cambridge Univ. Library, MS. Dd VII. 14, fols. 370b–371a (report of a case on JUST 1/483 m. 30). The only serjeants named in this report are (Gilbert of) Thornton and 'Pageman' (William de Pakeman or more probably John of Pakenham). The other is the report printed by Dunham in *Casus Placitorum*, supra note 23 at 65–67 (report of JUST 1/483 m. 40d). In this report no serjeants are named.

32. *The London Eyre of 1244*, supra note 18 at 96 no. 236. A similar provision also applied to aldermen of the city who had 'stood with', or acted as counsel to, litigants.

equitable judgement.[33] Fitz Thedmar seems here to have conflated the legislation and its intended results. What the legislation probably said was that in all types of litigation other than those specified the formalities of pleading hitherto observed were no longer to be mandatory, the intention being to render the use of serjeants in such cases superfluous. The serjeants of London, however, clearly survived the blow, and continued to find employment in the city courts: in 1264 we find another ordinance prohibiting serjeants from acting as essoiners in the city courts.[34]

Once we reach the reign of Edward I, it begins to make sense to talk about the existence of a legal profession in England. From the 1270s onwards, surviving reports of pleading in cases in the Bench demonstrate the existence of a group of professional serjeants in the Bench and tell us something of their work in that court: they also tell us who these serjeants were.[35] From the late 1270s onwards other reports provide similar information about the serjeants who practised in the general eyre: and already there seems to be a substantial overlap between them and the serjeants practising in the Bench.[36] We now begin to find the king retaining serjeants to act on his behalf in the eyre and in the Bench.[37] Outside the royal courts altogether there are traces

33. T. Stapleton, ed., *Liber de Antiquis Legibus: Cronica Maiorum et Vicecomitum Londoniarum* Camden Society, original series, xxxiv (1846) 42–43.

34. Ibid. at 70. Note that an account roll of the abbot of Ramsey for 1241–42 includes a payment of thirteen shillings and four pence to two serjeants (*narratores*) at Norwich, British Library, Additional Roll 34332, m. 4. It is not, however, clear whether they were being paid for services in the city court or some other court.

35. The serjeants active in the Bench during the 1270s include: Adam de Arderne, Hamon de la Barre, John of Bocking, Robert of Bradfield, John Gifford, John of Houghton, Adam of Kinsham, John of Quy, John of Ramsey, William of Stowe, Gilbert of Thornton and Alan of Walkingham. The serjeants active in the Bench during the 1280s include: William of Barford (Bereford), Robert of Bradfield, Alexander of Coventry, Richard of Gosfield, Roger of Higham, John de Lisle, William of Kelloe, Hugh of Lowther, Gilbert of Thornton and Nicholas of Warwick. I will be discussing the evidence on which these lists are based in my forthcoming book on the early history of the English legal profession.

36. Most of the surviving reports come from the 'Northern' eyre circuit. The serjeants active on this circuit include: Robert of Bradfield, Richard of Arnesby, Thomas of Fishburn, Richard of Gosfield, William of Kelloe, John de Lisle, John of Ramsey, Roger of Scotter, William of Selby, Gilbert of Thornton. There are a few reports of cases from the 'Southern' eyre circuit, see Dunham, ed., *Casus Placitorum* supra note 23 at 111–12, 114, 130–31, and various manuscripts, but not enough to reach general conclusions about the serjeants active on the circuit. For further details see my forthcoming book on the early history of the English legal profession.

37. G. O. Sayles, ed., *Select Cases in the Court of King's Bench, vol. V* Selden Society, lxxvi (London, 1957) xl–xliv. Sayles dates the beginning of the regular retaining of serjeants by the king to 1278. This may well be true, though it should be noted that Alan of Walkingham, one of the king's serjeants, was paid in 1281 in respect of his services to the king during the previous *six* years. C 62/57 m. 10. It should also be noted that in 1278 there is a reference to the king's serjeants ('*narratores regis*') as though to a well-established institution. *Rotuli Parliamentorum* i: 7. For men described in 1269 and

of professional serjeants in city courts other than London's, and also in fair courts and in county courts.[38]

We cease now to be wholly reliant on analysis of the appointment of attorneys for evidence of the existence of professional attorneys practising in the Bench. From the late 1280s onwards, the court begins to entertain allegations of misconduct made against them by clients [39]; in 1291 we find for the first time a reference to a man 'claiming to be a common attorney of the court' (*qui se gerit pro communi attornato curio'*)[40]; and in 1292 we find an unsuccessful attempt to limit the number of professional attorneys practising in the Bench, and to restrict admission to their ranks, which, by envisaging a reduction to 140, clearly assumes that there are well over that number of professional attorneys currently practising in the Bench.[41] We also now begin to encounter references to professional attorneys practising in other royal courts[42] and in the city courts in London.[43] More significantly, professional lawyers were now also coming to be seen as men having, or needing, specific, professional skills. Those persons who wanted to become serjeants in the Bench had first, it seems, to have been 'apprentices'— persons learning the skills of the serjeant. One of the reasons given for the making of the ordinance of 1280 which restricted regular practice as a serjeant in the city courts of London to those who had been specially admitted to the office, was that there had been some men hitherto who had held themselves out to be serjeants when they did not know and had not learned the appropriate skills (*qi lour mestier ne savoient ne ne eurent apris*), and that this had led their clients to lose their cases.[44] The professional attorney, too, was recognized as having a special skill appropriate to his functions. In 1294 one of the professional attorneys practising in the Bench, Alan Prat, sued out further mesne process against

---

1271 as king's serjeants who are known from other evidence, to have been lawyers see note 23 supra.

38. For full references see my forthcoming book on the early history of the English legal profession.

39. The earliest instance seems to be in 1287, though it is not completely certain that the attorney here is professional. CP 40/67 m. 47d.

40. CP 40/89 m. 26d.

41. *Rotuli Parliamentorum*, supra note 37 at i: 84 (no. 22). For a full discussion of this episode see my forthcoming book on the early history of the English legal profession.

42. In the eyre: Burne v. Watergate, JUST 1/915 m. 39 (1279 Sussex eyre); Motekan v. Ingoldmells et al., CP 40/102 m. 160 (1282 Lincolnshire eyre); In the court of King's Bench: Brettevil vs. Abbot of Tichfield KB 27/94 m. 42d; *Calendar of City of London Letter-Book B*, p. 216; *Calendar of City of London Letter-Book C*, pp. 26, 115–16.

43. *Munimenta Gildhalle Londoniensis*, ii, part i: 280–82.

44. Ibid. More ambiguous is evidence from the 1278 Hertfordshire eyre. A plaintiff lost his case because of a faulty count by his serjeant. His amercement was pardoned because he was poor and because his serjeant had defrauded him (' . . . *et quia narrator ejus defraudavit eum* . . . '). But no action seems to have been taken against the serjeant. *Chepman v. Seriaunt*, JUST 1/323 m. 16d.

the jurors in a case after he had received word from his client that the other party to the plea had died. The jurors concerned complained to the court and got the attorney suspended. The enrollment recording the suspension goes on to give the reason for it. As a professional attorney, Alan 'ought not to have been ignorant of how pleas were to be prosecuted for his clients in accordance with the law and custom of the realm' ('*nec ignorare debuit qualiter pro dominis suis secundum legem et consuetudinem regni placita sunt prosequenda . . .* ').[45] A litigant suing in person or a non-professional attorney might be excused such an error: the professional attorney could not expect to be, for this was the area of his special knowledge and skills.[46]

It is also early in the reign of Edward I that we find the first general legislation to be concerned with professional misconduct by members of the legal profession: chapter twenty-nine of the statute of Westminster I, enacted in 1275.[47] This provided that any serjeant (*seriaunt countour*) convicted of deception or collusion or being a party to such—whether the intention was intended to deceive a litigant or the king's justices—was to go to prison for a year and a day, and be disbarred from further practice as serjeant. Anyone else ('*autre*') convicted of the same offences was simply to suffer the term of imprisonment. This sounds sufficiently general to apply to the non-professional legal representative or even to the litigant himself, as well as to the other type of professional lawyer, the professional attorney: but in practice it seems almost invariably to have been applied only in the case of offences committed by the latter. From the 1290s onward, the latter were also, commonly, though not invariably, debarred from practice as well upon conviction, even though this was not something that the legislation itself warranted.[48] This suggests that by the 1290s the professional attorney had

---

45. Gernun v. Gernun, CP 40/103 m. 70d.

46. In another case of 1292 a different professional attorney of the Bench, Simon of Stowe, was in trouble for failing to sue the writs required for his client at the proper time. Here it was held that he could not excuse his failure by ignorance, since he had long been a general attorney and knew sufficiently well what he ought to have done (*nec . . . per ignoranciam se potest in hoc casu excusare, eo quod generalis attornatus dudum extitit et sufficienter eruditus ad premissa exequenda si volebat*') and that the failure was therefore to be ascribed to deliberate deception. He was therefore sentenced to a year and a day in the Fleet prison. CP 40/95 m. 79d.

47. *Statutes of the Realm* i: 34.

48. For cases where attorneys were sentenced to a year and a day in the Fleet prison and also disbarred from practising, see CP 40/90 m. 146d (1291–Peter of Luffenham); CP 40/90 m. 57d (1291-Robert of 'Greshope'); CP 40/108 m. 145d (1295-Thomas de la Bere); CP 40/125 m. 236d (1298-Roger de Plat). For cases where only the term of imprisonment is mentioned, see CP 40/91 m. 210 (1291-Gerin le Lyndraper); CP 40/91 m. 191d (1291-John of Upton); CP 40/95 m. 79d (1292-Simon of Stowe). For an apprentice of the court sentenced to a year and a day in the Fleet and also disbarred from representing litigants ('*et inhibitum est ei ne se immisceat seu intromittat de aliquibus negociis in curia domini regis decetero prosequendo seu defendendo . . .* ') for deception of the court in a case in which he himself was a party, see CP 40/139 m. 106 (1301-Thomas Torel).

come to be seen as part of the same profession as the professional serjeant and that it had come to seem anomalous that they had not been made subject to the same penalty for the same offence of professional misconduct. But it also suggests that in 1275 the professional attorney was not as yet fully accepted as a member of the legal professsion, and that this acceptance took place between 1275 and 1290. It must also be significant that this same legislation of 1275 only applied to the activities of professional lawyers in the king's courts. This suggests that if there were professional lawyers practising outside the king's courts (and outside London) they were not as yet sufficiently numerous to be regarded as a normal feature of those courts. A subsequent chapter of the same statute (chapter 33) did deal with the perversion of legal process in the county court;[49] but its concern was not with the professional serjeant or attorney, but with 'barrators', members of the local gentry and others who supported litigants in litigation in the county court, and with the stewards of great men and others who gave judgements in the county court without being specially requested to do so by all the suitors. It was misconduct by them, rather than by professional lawyers, that was the obvious cause of concern for the legislator in the county court of 1275. This suggests that the spreading of the professional lawyer into the county court was a development which took place during the reign of Edward I and not before.

The evidence seems to suggest, then, that the first group of professional lawyers to emerge in England were the serjeants of the Bench, and that they already existed as a recognizable group by 1240; but that by 1260 at latest there was also a second recognizable group of professional lawyers in the shape of the professional serjeants practising in the courts of the city of London. By the 1270s professional serjeants were also clearly in evidence at sessions of the general eyre, but they seem largely, if not entirely, to have been drawn from the pool of serjeants who practised in the Bench. When, in the 1290s, we begin to get reports of pleading in the court of King's Bench, the same appears to be true there as well. During the course of the reign of Edward I, professional serjeants seem to have become established in some local courts—particularly city and county courts—as well.

There were also, it seems, a small group of professional attorneys practising in the Bench by 1260, but the real expansion in their numbers came only during the course of the reign of Edward I. There were over one hundred and forty by 1292, and at least two hundred and ten by 1300.[50] By this latter date there were also at least twenty-five professional attorneys in the court of King's Bench and around fourteen professional attorneys in the Exchequer (though many Bench attorneys also represented clients there as well). There is, however, much less evidence of professional attorneys being active in local courts except in London.

---

49. *Statutes of the Realm* i:35.

50. For full details see my forthcoming book on the early history of the English legal profession.

The emergence of what is recognizable as a legal profession is a slightly different matter. The raw material, clearly, is these sizeable groups of professional lawyers: but what was also needed were moves to 'professionalize' their members. The imposition of separate and higher standards of conduct for professional serjeants came first in the London city courts, and did not come to the professional serjeants practising in the king's courts until 1275; for the professional attorneys practising in the king's courts, or at least in the Bench, it did not come until the early 1290s. Control of admission into the ranks of professional serjeants was accomplished in the city of London by 1280; and a similar control may well by then have been accomplished for serjeants practising in the Bench; but moves made in 1292 to control admission into the ranks of professional attorneys practising in the Bench seem to have been ineffective. Quality control of professional lawyers through their suspension had come to the Bench for serjeants by 1275; for attorneys only after 1292.

B.

The main institutional prerequisite for the development of a legal profession was that it should be permissible for individuals to represent others in legal proceedings, without there having to be any wider preexisting or continuing relationship between them. The author of the *Leges Henrici Primi*, an unofficial legal treatise written during the second decade of the twelfth century, and one of our few sources on English legal custom in that period, clearly envisages the possibility that a litigant may not be present in person at litigation and may be represented by a third party. That representative, however, is not—and probably *cannot* be -someone specially appointed to represent the litigant in that case alone. He is—and probably *has* to be—that litigant's steward (*dapifer*) or other servant (*minister*), someone appointed by him to take charge of all his business affairs, managing his lands, presiding over his courts and so one.[51] It was, it seems, only during the reign of Henry II, and perhaps as the result of legislation now lost, that it became possible for a litigant to appoint whomever he wished to act for him as his representative in a single piece of litigation.[52] It is possible that this innovation was made for the benefit of litigants, and particularly of litigants in the king's courts. No longer would it be essential for litigants either to attend court in person or to send their stewards or bailiffs (whose services would be needed by their lord almost continuously on his own estates). Someone of much less importance could now be sent as the litigant's representative, particularly for these stages of the litigation where only the authorisation of a further stage of mesne process was

---

51. L.J. Downer, ed., *Leges Henrici Primi* (Oxford, 1972) 151 (42,2), 195 (61, 2), 197 (61, 10).

52. The institution is described in book XI of G.D.G. Hall, ed., *Glanvill* (London, 1965) 132–36, a treatise written at the very end of the reign of Henry II, but may have come into existence some time before this. The author describes such a representative as a *responsalis*, but in all except name he is the same as the attorney of the later common law.

required. It seems more probable, however, that the change was intended to solve a practical problem for the courts, caused by the major increase during the reign of Henry II in the amount of litigation coming before the royal courts, and the large increase in the number of litigants with business there: that of keeping proper track of whether or not someone claiming to be the representative of a litigant really did possess the authority to act for him. Certainly, in practice it was not a matter of the royal courts just allowing the appointment of attorneys. They *insisted* that anyone who was to represent a litigant should be appointed as his attorney, and specifically for that piece of litigation, whether or not he was the litigant's steward or bailiff.[53] The older type of more permanent representative, however, did not completely disappear, even in the king's courts. Throughout the thirteenth century we find references to the stewards and bailiffs of the lords of the greater franchises claiming cases for the hearing of their lords' courts—and it does not appear that they were specially appointed to do this on each occasion that they did so. The older type of more permanent representative seems also to have survived in the local courts. The legislation of 1234, which allowed the appointment of 'attorneys' in county, hundred and seignorial courts with power to claim for hearing in their principal's court any cases falling within the jurisdiction of that court, and also to act for them in any litigation brought by or against them that was initiated by plaint (rather than writ), probably preserved an existing institution and did not introduce a new one.[54] It may be significant that the legislation speaks of 'attorneys' rather than 'stewards' or 'bailiffs'. It might be the lord's steward who acted as his attorney—but it no longer had to be. It was the new type of representative, the representative appointed to act for his principal in one piece of litigation only, who is of greatest importance for the development of the legal profession. It was the emergence of this new type of representative during the reign of Henry II which ultimately made possible the development of the professional attorney—a representative whose only link with his client was that constituted by the contract made between them.

The serjeant was a representative of a somewhat different kind—one who only spoke on the litigant's behalf at the stage of formal pleading; one who was not formally appointed to speak for or represent the litigant; and one whose words could be disavowed by the litigant or the litigant's attorney, if need be. There seems to be a forerunner of the serjeant in the *Leges Henrici Primi* as well in the shape of the person giving 'advice' (*consilium*) in a plea, subject to a right of a correction. Such a person will be—and perhaps *has* to be—drawn from the litigant's friends and relations (*amicis et parentibus suis*), though his functions appear to be more limited than those of the later serjeant. The making of the count and the making of the formal defence both appear to have been matters for the litigants themselves. It was only when the defendant had asked permission to 'imparl', to seek advice, after making

53. Ibid. at 133 (XI,1).

54. *Close Rolls, 1231–34* 551.

the formal defence that the 'advisers' or proto-serjeants on both sides were able to join in.[55] The requirement, if such it was, that the serjeant speaking on behalf of a litigant be drawn from among his 'friends' and relations might just conceivably have been an enforceable on in the context of a local court, at least in the negative sense that it would be possible to prevent men who specialized in pleading for payment from practising in a particular court. It is much less clear that this would have been an enforceable rule in the case of pleading in the king's courts, once those courts began to attract a substantial amount of business. It is also much less clear that those courts would have had any interest in enforcing the rule. The extension of the permissible functions of the serjeant—in particular, allowing him to make the count on behalf of the plaintiff—though this cannot, at present, be dated precisely[56]—may perhaps be connected with the adoption of the writ as the standard form for the initiation of civil proceedings in the king's court, and the higher premium that this put on the need for accurate and standard counts that corresponded with the writs used in the case.

These institutional changes made it possible for the English legal profession to emerge. The professional serjeant, as we have seen, appeared first in the Bench and in the city of London. There had been no particular need for specialists, professional serjeants, in the older, local law courts of twelfth century England—feudal, county and hundred courts. Knowledge of the rules governing pleading and of the legal customs applied in those courts must have been widespread among those who regularly attended such courts in the role of suitors, but who might also less regularly appear in the courts as litigants or as the friends and advisers of litigants. The Bench, however, from its very beginnings in the reign of Henry II—initially as a part of the Exchequer—was a different kind of court. Its judgments were made not by suitors but by full-time, paid royal officials, and few of its litigants (or their friends) attended the court with sufficient regularity for them to acquire a reliable knowledge of the way in which the court's procedure worked, or the rules of law which it applied. Treatises like *Glanvill* and *Bracton* may have been intended, at least in part, to answer the demand of litigants for such knowledge, but inevitably, given the pace of legal development, they were soon out of date. Indeed, as Professor Thorne has shown, part of the confusion in the text of *Bracton* is directly caused by attempts to update

---

55. *Leges Henrici Primi* supra note 51 at 156–58 (46, 4–6; 48, 1-lc), 162 (49,3). It should, however, be noted that Maitland thought that the treatise showed 'counsel' able to speak for the litigants at all stages in proceedings: Pollock & Maitland, *History of English Law* supra note 23 at i: 211–12.

56. The earliest clear reference to a serjeant making a *count* for a plaintiff—and then being disavowed—seems to be in 1222 C.R.R. xiii: no. 1194. It may also be significant that when Glanvill gives a specimen count for the demandant in the action of right for land, it is in the first person (*'peto. . .'*). *Glanvill*, supra note 52 at 22–23 (II,3). When Bracton gives a similar count it is in the third person, as though spoken *for* the demandant (*'Hoc ostendit vobis A . . . '*). S.E. Thorne, ed., Bracton, *De Legibus et Consuetudinibus Angliae* Cambridge, Mass., 1968) iv: 169. Later evidence indicates that third person counts became the standard form.

the text to bring it into line with subsequent changes in the law.[57] There was, therefore, a demand from litigants with business in the court for assistance and representation by persons in regular attendance at the court, who possessed reliable and up-to-date information on the law and practice of the court. The serjeants met this demand.

The early emergence of the professional serjeant in the Bench must also have been assisted by the fact that the typical litigant in the court during the first half of the thirteenth century was among the wealthier of the litigants with business in the king's court. For most types of business it cost more to initiate litigation in the Bench (and probably also to prosecute it there) than to wait to initiate it at the next session of the eyre in the appropriate county.[58] Later in the century, other factors probably came into play to consolidate the hold of the professional serjeant on pleading in the Bench. Some attorneys were not even able to speak, or were not fluent in the language spoken in the court,[59] and the same was probably true of at least some of the litigants themselves. They needed a serjeant able to speak the language of the court. The professional serjeants were moreover a small group, in regular day to day contact with the justices of the court. The litigant—particularly the poorer and less powerful litigant engaged in litigation with a richer and more powerful opponent—may have seen himself as acquiring the services of a valuable intermediary in the serjeant, someone able to secure a full and fair hearing for his client's case in a way that the litigant himself would not have been able to do.

The early emergence of professional serjeants in the city courts in London is probably explicable in much the same kind of terms. Few of the inhabitants of London can have been in regular attendance at the city courts, and the court of the mayor and sheriff, in particular, soon came to bear a much closer resemblance to the royal courts than to the local courts in its constitution and ways of doing business.[60] Moreover, many of the litigants there were wealthy men, well able to pay for professional representation.

The predominance of Bench serjeants in pleading in the Eyre is presumably to be explained by the intermittent nature of the general eyre, which inhibited the growth of a separate group of serjeants specializing solely in work in the eyre. Further, in the earliest years of the professional serjeant in the Bench sessions were suspended while a major eyre visitation was in progress. Had there been groups of professional serjeants practising in the county court prior to the later years of the reign of Edward I, it might have been those serjeants who represented litigants in the eyre in the counties in which they practised, but their emergence was too late to prevent the Bench serjeants establishing a predominance in the eyre. The hegemony

---

57. Ibid. at III: xv-xxix.

58. E. de Haas and G.D.G. Hall, eds. *Early Registers of Writs*, Selden Society, lxxxvii (London, 1970) xxvii-xxix.

59. CP 40/110, m. 239.

60. Williams, *Medieval London*, supra note 19 at 83–84.

of the Bench serjeants in the court of King's Bench is more problematic. The court had been in continuous existence from the mid-1230s onwards, and practice in it was not easily combined with practice in the Bench, since King's Bench was most of the time an itinerant court, and the Bench normally stationary at Westminster. The comparatively late establishment of the court on a permanent basis may possibly provide the answer. By then it may have been the serjeants of the Bench who were accepted as the legal experts; and as they were willing to work in the Eyre, they may have proved willing to work in King's Bench as well, as and when clients required this. The eventual emergence of serjeants in the county court as well during the reign of Edward I is probably to be related to wider changes in the nature and constitution of those courts which transformed them into much more 'professional' and expert courts.

The later emergence of the professional attorney is probably a reflexion of the fact that the attorney's function was one which required a much smaller amount of expertise and knowledge. Certainly, there were from the earliest years of the Bench good reasons for litigants to appoint attorneys to represent them there: the journey from many, perhaps most, litigants' homes to the Bench was normally long and slow, and might often turn out to be dangerous. The litigant would normally need to stay at Westminster for several days when he arrived in order to sue out the next stage of process against his opponent or secure judgment against him on his default; and these journeys and stays would normally need to be repeated several times over two or three years before the litigation was at an end. But, if no special expertise was required, there was at this time probably no great advantage in employing a professional attorney who was unknown to the litigant (and perhaps therefore not to be relied upon) rather than using the services of a reliable friend or relative. The breakthrough to professionalization seems to have occurred as a direct consequence of an as yet unexplained phenomenon: the major increase in the business of the Bench during the second half of the thirteenth century.[61] What seems to have happened is that there came to be enough business from each area of the country to allow professional attorneys to make a living by representing persons from their area of the country (and a few others), charging enough to cover their traveling expenses, but being able to charge less than the non-professional attorney would need to be reimbursed by his one principal to cover his expenses. At this stage it became financially advantageous to appoint a professional and not an amateur attorney. Only when there had come to be a number of professional attorneys, so it seems, did those attorneys come also to be perceived as having the further advantage over the non-professional—possession of a special, detailed knowledge of the procedures of the court,

61. A rather crude indication of the scale of this increase is provided by counting the number of membranes required to record one year's business in the Bench. In 1200 forty-nine membranes sufficed; this had more than doubled by 1250 (108 membranes) and almost doubled again by 1260 (207); between 1260 and 1280 it more than doubled again (439) and by 1300 more than doubled once more (1056).

and how those could best be manipulated or used to the advantage of their clients. Volume of business, and its increase during the second half of the thirteenth century, may well also account for the emergence of the professional attorney in the court of King's Bench as well by 1300,[62] though again some sort of attorney must normally have been appointed by most litigants from an early date.

Professional lawyers—professional serjeants and professional attorneys—came first: a recognizable legal profession came subsequently. As far as can be seen, the movement in the direction of the transformation of professional lawyers into a legal profession was, at this early stage, as much, if not more, the product of external pressures as of any conscious wish or attempt by professional lawyers to turn themselves into a profession. The setting of special standards of professional conduct was achieved by statute and the maintenance of professional standards seems, as yet, to have been a matter entirely for the courts—and not for other members of the profession. The abortive attempt to limit the numbers of, and to control admission into, the ranks of professional attorneys in the Bench in 1292 seems to have had its origins in the concern of king and council with the low standards of existing attorneys, and not been the product of any attempt by those attorneys or some of their number to create an exclusive monopoly for themselves. The monopoly apparently enjoyed by Bench serjeants by the reign of Edward I may well have had a similar origin. So, too, the monopoly of regular practice in the city courts enjoyed by the London serjeants created by the ordinance of 1280 seems to have been the product of external pressure to raise standards, rather than any campaign by those serjeants to secure such a monopoly. As yet, then, in 1300 the legal profession was still the prisoner, and in some senses also itself the product, of outside forces beyond its own control: not yet the autonomous and powerful body it was later to become.

---

62. Using the same rather crude indication, in 1260 fifty-six membranes sufficed, by 1280 the roll had more than doubled (to 127) and by 1301 more than doubled again (to 273).

2

The Early History of the Legal Profession of the Lordship of Ireland, 1250-1350

I

In 1295 A COMPLAINANT alleged misconduct on the part of William de Morton, a clerk of the Dublin Bench.[1] William was responsible for making enrolments on the Bench plea-roll, the official record of litigation in the court. The complainant had brought litigation there to recover certain lands. His opponent had asked for an adjournment to give various other interested persons an opportunity to join in the litigation. The opponent had made an error in giving the names of those whom he wanted to be summoned, potentially a fatal mistake in litigation of this kind. The enrolment had, however, silently corrected his mistake and given the names in their correct form, thereby depriving the complainant of his chance to profit from his opponent's error. As enrolling clerk, William was responsible. William had no difficulty in clearing himself. He had, he said, simply enrolled the names as he had found them written on the dorse of the appropriate writ; and that endorsement had been the work of a different and more senior clerk, Nicholas of Berkeley, keeper of rolls and writs in the Bench. Nicholas accepted responsibility for the endorsement and did not deny that the endorsement itself had been altered. But, he said, he had not acted fraudulently or in return for a bribe. He had made the alteration by the direction of the justices of the court. To establish this and to clear himself of any misconduct he asked to be 'tried' by the verdict of those best in a position to know the truth of the matter: the serjeants (*narratores*) and attorneys who had then been present in the Bench.

1. *Cal. justic. rolls, Ire., 1295–1303*, pp. 5–6. For reasons that are unclear the complainant's name is not given in this entry and he is represented simply by the initial B.

It has long been known that 'serjeants' and 'attorneys' were the two main groups of professional lawyers active in the Westminster Bench at the end of the thirteenth century.[2] The main function of the serjeants was to speak in court on behalf of their clients when litigation came on for a hearing and in 1300 they were the much smaller (and the more select) of the two groups, numbering no more than about thirty individuals. The primary function of the professional attorneys active in the court was simply to put in an appearance at the court on behalf of their clients on each day appointed for a hearing; but by 1300 they had also become responsible for ensuring that the court took the necessary steps to ensure the appearance of their client's opponent and perhaps for engaging and briefing serjeants on behalf of those clients. In 1300 there were over two hundred professional attorneys practising in the Westminster Bench. This case suggests that by 1300 two similar groups of professional lawyers were also to be found in the Dublin counterpart of the Westminster Bench; and other evidence indicates that by the same date professional lawyers were also to be found in various other courts in the English lordship of Ireland (as they were also to be found in various other courts in England). In this essay I want to examine the evidence for the existence and functioning of these two types of professional lawyer not just in the Dublin Bench but also in the other law courts of the English lordship of Ireland during the half century or so preceding this case (which will take us back to the earliest evidence for the existence of professional lawyers in the lordship) and also during the half century or so after it (to *c.*1350).

II

The Westminster Bench seems to have been the centre of the English legal profession and to have contained the largest number of professional lawyers. The same was possibly also true of its Dublin counterpart, though deficiencies in the surviving evidence make it impossible to be certain about this. The Dublin Bench is, however, certainly the best documented of the courts of the lordship of Ireland and thus it is with its lawyers that we will start.

2. A detailed discussion of the English legal profession, its functions and organisation at the end of the thirteenth century will be found in my forthcoming book, *The origins of the English legal profession*. Wherever in the following discussion reference is made to the English legal profession the material is drawn from this much fuller study and so no supporting references will be given.

It is unfortunately the case that we possess virtually no direct evidence as to the functions performed by the serjeants of the Dublin Bench. However, it seems reasonable to suppose that these were much the same functions as those performed by their Westminster counterparts since litigation seems to have been conducted along the same general lines in both courts; and thus we can probably get a reasonably accurate picture of the functions of the Dublin serjeants from the unofficial Norman French reports of litigation heard in the Westminster Bench which survive from *c.*1270 onwards and are generally known as the Year Book reports. These show that hearings in the Bench normally commenced with a serjeant acting for the plaintiff making a formal count, expounding the plaintiff's claim or complaint, and with a serjeant acting for the defendant making a formal defence, a blank denial of everything contained in the plaintiff's count, before going on to make a more specific defence. They also indicate that it was at this point in the proceedings that the real skills of the serjeants on both sides came into play. The plaintiff's serjeant might respond that the defence advanced was not a valid one in law or answer by alleging other, additional facts which showed that the plaintiff's claim was nonetheless a good one. The defendant's serjeant would then have to answer the argument or reply to the allegation or might (since the pleading was normally only tentative and exploratory) abandon his first line of defence altogether and advance another one instead. Eventually, though generally only after a prolonged series of arguments between the serjeants for the two litigants, in which the justices of the court would also take an active part, the parties would reach an 'issue'. This was either an issue of law, a point of law which was to be decided by the justices after further consideration, or (more commonly) an issue of fact. The latter would be decided on the basis of a verdict by a jury as to whether or not certain facts alleged in the course of pleading by one of the serjeants and material to his client's claim or defence were true. A decision on either type of issue would then lead to judgment being given in favour of one of the parties. The skill of the serjeant lay in his ability to argue convincingly and in knowing when to continue or abandon a particular line of defence or of attack.

The Year Book reports make it clear that it was common practice in the Westminster Bench for litigants to have at least two serjeants to act and speak on their behalf. There is some evidence to suggest that this may also have been common practice in the Dublin Bench. From the Record Commission calendars of Bench plea-rolls formerly in the Public Record Office in Dublin but now destroyed it is known that between 1299 and 1317 those rolls sometimes recorded in detail the assignment by successful litigants of part or all of the damages which they had recovered.[3] When such assignments were made the clerks of the Bench commonly got a share, as did other officials associated with the court such as its marshal and usher. The most likely explanation is that the assignment was made in lieu of fees owed by the successful litigant. Serjeants also often commonly got a share of such damages: sometimes specifically as serjeants, more often simply by name. On occasion only one serjeant is assigned a share, but more commonly we find two, three, four or even five serjeants sharing a lump sum or being given individual shares.[4] The assignment of damages to the serjeants must normally have been a reward for their services. In these cases at least, therefore, there must be a strong presumption that the litigant had employed the services of a group of serjeants rather than just one; and there seems no reason to doubt that this was common practice in other cases as well.

The serjeant spoke on behalf of his client without any kind of prior formal authorisation from his client. At Westminster we know that it was possible for the litigant or the litigant's representative to disown what a serjeant had said after he had said it (the technical term for this was 'disavowing' him), although the normal expectation was that a serjeant would not be disowned in this way. Disavowal is also something specifically mentioned in the custumal of the city of Dublin which apparently belongs to this period, though only in connection with litigation in the city court.[5] This suggests that disavowal must also have been a possibility in the Dublin Bench although it is not specifically mentioned in any of the surviving evidence relating to the court from this period.

There must normally always have been some kind of prior contact between serjeant and litigant before the serjeant stood up

---

3. The first such assignment is recorded in the calendar of a plea-roll for Easter term 1299: PROI RC 7/6, p. 11; the latest in the calendar of a plea-roll for Hilary term 1317: RC 8/11, p. 175.

4. For an example of the assignment of damages to a single serjeant see PROI RC 8/2, p. 174; of individual assignments to two serjeants: RC 7/10, p. 103; of joint assignment to two serjeants: RC 8/2, p. 155; of individual assignments to three serjeants: RC 7/9, p. 299; of joint assignment to three serjeants: RC 7/9, pp. 275–6; of joint assignment to four serjeants: RC 8/5, p. 76; of individual assignments to five serjeants: RC 7/10, pp. 112–13; of joint assignment to five serjeants: RC 7/13/3, p. 76.

5. *Hist. & mun. doc. Ire.*, p. 257.

in court. The serjeant needed to have been properly instructed as to the main facts concerning the litigation in question and perhaps also about the strengths and weaknesses of his client's case. But even before that could take place the client needed to have secured the serjeant's agreement to act on his behalf. In the Westminster Bench serjeants seem to have enjoyed total freedom in deciding whether or not they would act for a particular litigant in any particular case. This was qualified only by their obligation to provide 'advice and assistance' to those paying them annual pensions for this purpose. The court would not force them to act for such clients; but if they failed to do so the court would hold the client justified in refusing payment of the pension. A much greater degree of restraint on the individual serjeant's freedom of contract seems to have existed in the Dublin Bench for litigants in this court seem to have been able to go to the court to ask the justices to assign them a serjeant. Four different entries from plea-rolls now lost of various dates between 1312 and 1336 transcribed in the Record Commission calendars show serjeants who had been assigned to litigants by the court asking for their 'salary', their fee for their professional services, to be 'taxed' or set by the court[6] or taking steps to recover a 'salary' which had already been 'taxed' for such services.[7]

Most litigants in the Dublin Bench seem, however, to have been able to obtain the services of a serjeant without invoking the court's assistance in this way. Agreements between serjeants and clients in the Dublin Bench (as in the Westminster Bench) seem to have taken a variety of forms. A serjeant might agree to act for a litigant in one particular piece of litigation only. Such agreements probably lie behind a majority of assignments of damages to serjeants recorded on the plea-rolls. But many litigants made longer-term agreements with their serjeants. Some appear to have been of indefinite duration and were perhaps terminable at the will of either party. We hear of one such agreement (between the serjeant Henry of Beningbrough and the general attorney of Thomas of Moulton) in litigation in 1308. The litigation was brought by Henry to recover arrears of a fee of one mark a year owed him for acting as Thomas of Moulton's serjeant in the Dublin Bench. This agreement was probably not recorded in writing; and this may have been common in agreements of this kind.[8] More commonly the serjeant agreed to serve the client (and

6. For examples see PROI RC 8/6, pp. 406–7, 436 and RC 8/19, pp. 478–80.

7. PROI RC 7/12, p. 380.

8. PROI RC 7/13/3, p. 130.

sometimes the client's heirs) for the remainder of his life. Such agreements were normally (perhaps invariably) recorded in writing and the terms of several of them were subsequently recorded on the plea-rolls of the Bench and of the justiciar's court, either because they were cited in the course of litigation or because one of the parties (perhaps generally the serjeant) had them enrolled soon after they were made as a safeguard against possible loss of or damage to the deed concerned. Fortunately the Record Commission calendars contain full transcripts of several of them. The earliest such deed to be enrolled is one of 1297 between the serjeant William of Bardfield and Robert Mansel, which was enrolled on a Bench plea-roll in 1299.[9] Under its terms Robert agreed to pay William an annuity of twenty shillings a year and to give him each year a robe of the same value, in return for William's 'praiseworthy service' for the remainder of his life ('pro laudabili servicio michi quamdiu vixerit impendendo'). If payments were in arrears it was agreed that William could distrain Robert's manor of 'Moyglas' in Co. Limerick to enforce payment. It is, however, only our knowledge of William's career as a serjeant which makes it clear that the 'praiseworthy service' here referred to must be service to Robert as his serjeant. Also enrolled in the same year was a deed recording an agreement made in 1299 between the same William of Bardfield and Nicholas son of John of Inkbarrow ('Inteberge').[10] This agreement is much more precise and refers rather more directly to the nature of the service which William was expected to provide. Under its terms Nicholas agreed to pay twenty shillings a year to 'his' serjeant William of Bardfield for his 'service, advice and aid in the king's court' ('pro servicio, consilio et auxilio suo in curia regis'). If the twenty shillings was not paid William was to be entitled to distrain Nicholas' manor of 'Rathdrum', Co. Tipperary. The serjeant's obligation was a qualified one: it was 'service, advice and aid in the king's court, *where I find him*' ('ubi eum invenio'). A similar phrase occurs in other such agreements[11] and seems to mean that William is only obliged to act on behalf of Nicholas in whatever royal court (be it Dublin Bench, eyre or justiciar's court) he is working when Nicholas makes a request for his services. If he is then working as a serjeant in the eyre Nicholas cannot require

9. PROI RC 7/6, p. 53.

10. PROI RC 7/6, p. 63.

11. E.g. PROI RC 7/6, p. 45 ('ubi invenitur'); RC 7/10, pp. 528–9 ('ubicumque in curia regis fuerit inventus'); RC 8/17, pp. 513–16 ('ubicumque ipsum Johannem presentem esse contigerit').

him to travel to Dublin to act for him there (nor vice versa). The deed also contains one further qualification: 'saving the service of the king, and his other prior lords before the making of the present deed' ('salvo servicio regis et aliorum primorum dominorum suorum ante confeccionem presencium'). Again similar phrases are found in other such deeds.[12] They seem to mean that if Nicholas becomes involved in litigation with the king or with any of the clients whom William has taken on in return for a similar annuity before the making of this agreement then those clients and the king have a prior claim to William's services. William had been retained as a serjeant by the king since 1297.[13] In other such deeds involving serjeants not in the service of the king no such reservation is made in his favour, though commonly to the reservation in favour of prior clients is added one in favour of the serjeant's own relatives.[14] Later agreements are all with one exception of the same general form but with a number of minor variations in their wording. The exception is an undated agreement enrolled on the plea-rolls of the justiciar's court in 1333 between the otherwise unknown serjeant Adam de la Galeye and William de Launeye.[15] Under its terms William granted Adam an annuity of twenty shillings a year for life, secured on his manor of 'Turvylauneyston' in Co. Dublin. This annuity was simply said to have been granted in return for Adam's service to William and his heirs 'in the office of serjeant' ('in officio narratoris').

Serjeants who made agreements of this sort seem commonly in England to have had to sue for arrears of their annuity or to have had to distrain for it; and behind many such suits and distraints may have lain disputes between serjeant and client as to whether the serjeant had forfeited his right to the annuity by failing to provide the client with the service to which he was entitled. The surviving Record Commission transcripts of the Bench plea-rolls, however, only provide hard evidence of a single such dispute involving a serjeant of the Dublin Bench, and that in the form of a memorandum recording the terms on which it was settled.[16] The

---

12. E.g. PROI RC 7/6, p. 45 ('salvo servicio aliorum primorum suorum habitorum ante confeccionem presencium'); RC 7/10, pp. 528–9 ('exceptis primis dominis suis'); *Reg. St John, Dublin*, pp. 18–19 ('salvis personis quibus idem Rogerus ante confeccionem presencium exstiterat obligatus per sacramentum').

13. Richardson & Sayles, *Admin. Ire.*, p. 174.

14. E.g. PROI RC 7/10, pp. 528–9 ('exceptis ... consanguinitate et affinitate'); RC 8/18, pp. 202–15 ('exceptis ... proximis affinibus suis et sanguine suo').

15. PROI RC 8/17, pp. 328–9.

16. PROI RC 7/11, pp. 426–7.

dispute was between the serjeant Robert of Dalinghoo and one rather special client of his, Walter of Kenley. By the time the settlement was reached Walter had himself become a justice of the Dublin Bench. The settlement was made in 1306. Walter had granted Robert an annuity of two marks a year for life in return for his services but claimed that Robert had failed in their performance ('occasione servicii ipsius Roberti eidem Waltero minus plene facti'). Robert now renounced the annuity and agreed to make satisfaction to Walter by giving him a palfrey worth £40. Robert also agreed to continue performing his obligations to Walter under their agreement. These obligations are spelled out in some detail. Robert was to act as Walter's serjeant and also to be his adviser ('consiliator') as best he knew how ('in quantum sciverat') in all matters belonging to his 'office' ('in omnibus que ad officium ipsius Roberti pertinent'). This is of particular interest for it seems to indicate that the serjeant was expected not just to plead in court on his client's behalf but also when required to give general legal advice to his clients.

Two cases (of 1299 and 1306) suggest that it may have been possible at this time to obtain the services of a serjeant in the Westminster Bench for a single case for as little as forty pence; and in the mid-fifteenth century it could still be argued that in the absence of any specific agreement in advance to the contrary a fee of forty pence was payable to a serjeant 'as of common right'. Other late thirteenth and early fourteenth-century evidence, however, shows Westminster serjeants being paid much larger sums and it remains unclear how many serjeants were in practice willing at this time to act for so small a sum. The lowest recorded payment to a serjeant of the Dublin Bench is the half mark (or twice forty pence) assigned to three (or perhaps four) serjeants from damages in a case of 1306.[17] The lowest 'salary' awarded to a serjeant whom the court had assigned to a litigant was the one mark adjudged to John of Grantchester for his services in a case of 1312.[18] This is matched by the total of five marks shared between five serjeants from damages awarded in a case of 1308.[19] Twenty shillings,[20] forty shillings[21] and even sixty shillings[22] are the sums

17. PROI RC 7/11, pp. 275–9. There is no direct evidence that the fourth man (Thomas de Balymore) was a serjeant though this seems quite probable.

18. PROI RC 8/6, pp. 406–7.

19. PROI RC 7/13/3, p. 76.

20. E.g. PROI RC 7/9, pp. 275–6; RC 7/10, p. 103; RC 8/11, p. 175.

21. E.g. PROI RC 7/9, p. 299; RC 7/10, pp. 103, 112–13; RC 7/13/2, p. 4.

22. E.g. PROI RC 7/9, p. 299; RC 8/2, p. 174; RC 7/10, pp. 112–13.

more commonly assigned to serjeants for their services from damages. The two lower sums (and in one case, as much as fifty shillings each for two serjeants) are also found as 'salaries' awarded to serjeants in other cases where they were assigned to clients by the court.[23] The highest payment of all for services in a particular case seems to be the ten pounds assigned to Roger of Ashbourne from damages awarded in a case of 1304.[24]

The sums most commonly paid to serjeants of the Westminster Bench by way of retainer were twenty shillings and forty shillings, though retainers of one mark and of two marks are not uncommon. The lowest sum paid to a serjeant of the Dublin Bench as an annuity was twenty shillings.[25] Two marks and forty shillings are also commonly mentioned.[26] The highest annuity known to have been paid to a serjeant of the Dublin Bench (though not specifically for his services as a serjeant) was the five marks and one robe payable to Simon fitzRichard by the archbishop of Armagh which is mentioned in litigation in the justiciar's court in 1318.[27] Some Irish serjeants (like their English counterparts) are known to have accumulated large numbers of annuities. According to a petition of William Bardfield of 1321 his appointment as a royal justice (in 1308) had led to the loss of no less than £32 in fees and robes from such agreements.[28]

The fees which could be charged by individual serjeants for their services must have been affected and were perhaps even largely determined by the amount of competition that existed between those offering their services as serjeants. By the end of the thirteenth century there seems to have existed a regime of restricted competition in the Westminster Bench, which conferred on a small group of professional serjeants the sole right to offer

23. Twenty shillings: PROI RC 8/6, p. 436; forty shillings: PROI RC 7/12, p. 380, RC 8/19, pp. 478–80, *Cal. justic. rolls, Ire., 1305–7*, p. 16 (for service in the justiciar's court); fifty shillings: RC 7/13/2, pp. 9–10 (for services in the Drogheda eyre).

24. PROI RC 7/10, p. 175.

25. For some examples see: *Cal. justic. rolls, Ire., 1305–7*, p. 378; PROI RC 7/4, p. 481; RC 7/6, pp. 53 (plus one robe worth twenty shillings), 63; RC 7/10, p. 539 (plus one robe worth at least twenty shillings); RC 7/11, p. 136; RC 8/11, pp. 395–6 (plus one robe worth twenty shillings); RC 7/13/2, p. 7 (plus one robe worth twenty shillings).

26. For some examples see: (i) for two marks: PROI RC 8/2, pp. 281–2; RC 8/5, pp. 27–8; RC 7/10, pp. 528–9; (ii) for forty shillings: PROI RC 7/6, pp. 14, 45; RC 7/13/2, p. 6; Sayles, *Affairs of Ire.*, p. 53; *Cal. justic. rolls, Ire., 1305–7*, p. 54 (with additional robe worth two marks).

27. PROI RC 7/12, p. 161.

28. Sayles, *Affairs of Ire.*, 103–4.

their services on a regular basis to those with business in the courts. Entry into this group came, in the later fourteenth century, to be controlled by the crown; but this was clearly not the case earlier and then it was probably simply a matter for the court's own justices, perhaps with some advice from the existing serjeants. It is probable that a good knowledge of the law and a mastery of the skills of the serjeant were necessary qualifications for admission to the group; but they may not have been sufficient. It seems possible, even probable, that the size of the group was kept artificially small in the interests of its existing members. A similar situation seems also to have obtained in the Dublin Bench, though the evidence for this is no more than circumstantial. In 1306 and 1333 we find suggestive references to the exercise of the 'office' of serjeant.[29] The existence of a recognised corps of professional serjeants from which individuals could retire (or be expelled) would also explain why and how William of Athy, who was then still alive, could be referred to as being 'late serjeant pleader' in litigation in the justiciar's court in 1305.[30] The most likely context for the liability of a serjeant to be assigned to a litigant by the court is that this was some sort of *quid pro quo* for official 'recognition' of the serjeants and of their monopoly. As early as 1316 we find Nicholas of Snitterby bringing litigation in the Bench by bill specifically as a serjeant, further presumptive evidence of a degree of official recognition of the serjeants by the court, since the privilege of initiating litigation in the Bench by bill was probably restricted to those who were in some sense 'officials' of the court.[31]

How did the would-be professional serjeant set about acquiring the knowledge and technical skill required to enter and succeed in his profession? In England we know that by the 1270s at latest elementary lectures on the common law were being given for students and that by the end of the thirteenth century reports of cases were also being used for teaching purposes (though probably only for the instruction of rather more advanced students). Would-be serjeants were also by then in regular attendance at the court and picked up part of their knowledge both of the serjeant's technical skills and of current law by listening to the arguments of serjeants and justices. Their presence in the court was actively encouraged by the justices; and by the early years of the reign of Edward II there was even a 'crib', a special enclosure set aside for

29. Above, p. 27, notes 15 and 16.

30. *Cal. justic. rolls, Ire., 1305–7*, p. 35.

31. PROI RC 8/11, pp. 827–8.

them, in the court. It is probable that it is to these listeners that we owe the Year Book reports, which were perhaps reports compiled by them for their own instruction and use. By the late 1280s the law students attending the Bench for educational reasons were a sufficiently well-established group to have acquired a distinctive name, 'apprentices of the Bench'.

There is some evidence of men from Ireland going to London for training in the law during this period. In 1287 Robert de St Michael of Ireland was staying at Westminster with the king's permission 'for the purpose of learning in the Bench'. This we learn incidentally from royal letters patent allowing him to be represented by a permanent attorney in Ireland for the whole of the ensuing year.[32] As it happens this is also the earliest specific reference known to a student of the common law. The next (and only other) reference to a law student from Ireland in England prior to 1350 comes from a 1344 inquisition into an affray in the city of London. This mentions two Irish apprentices of the Bench (Richard of Cardiff and John Barry) as involved and as being common malefactors lying in wait at night to rob passers-by of their belts and purses.[33] The two men had an English colleague in their wrongdoing; and it should be added that many other early references to apprentices of the Bench are also to the offences committed by such apprentices.

There is also, however, other evidence to suggest that some instruction in the common law may have been available in Ireland. The early legal treatise known as *Natura Brevium* which survives in a number of different manuscripts seems to be derived from lectures and (as I have noted elsewhere) it (or they) seem to have been 'written or altered with a specifically Irish audience in mind'.[34] This is clear from a passage in the treatise on the action of wardship which is concerned with the problem of claims to the wardship of lands held by socage tenure by lords who are relying on the custom of the lordship of Ireland for their title. It envisages the use of action by bill before the chief justiciar as a way of recov-

32. PRO C 66/106, m. 11: 'Consimiles litteras de attornato habet Robertus de Sancto Michaele in Hibernia qui de licencia regis causa addiscendi in Banco regis apud Westm' moram fecit sub nomine Ade Clythyn clerici per unum annum duraturum, presentibus etc. Teste Edmundo comite Cornub' consanguineo regis apud Westm' xxviij Junii' (calendared in *Cal. pat. rolls, 1281–92*, p. 269). I owe this reference to the kindness of Dr David Higgins.

33. *Calendar of the plea and memoranda rolls of the city of London, 1323–64*, ed. A.H. Thomas (Cambridge, 1926), p. 213.

34. See below, p. 465 n. 6.

ering such a wardship.[35] I have also noted elsewhere that one of
the two main manuscript traditions of the pleading manual *Novae
Narrationes,* while apparently using precedents drawn from cases
heard in the English courts, 'hibernicises' those precedents by the
substitution of Irish place–names and personal names for the
English originals.[36] The manual clearly played a part in the education of future serjeants. It is conceivable that it only ever circulated in written form; though equally likely that it too derives from
lectures. What is important, though, is that the 'hibernicisation' of
the treatise indicates that the C manuscript tradition of the manual
derives either from lectures given in Ireland or from a manuscript
of the manual which was extensively revised with an Irish audience
in mind. Nor were the Irish personal names used in the treatise
drawn entirely at random. The name most commonly used in the
treatise in this manuscript tradition is that of John Plunket;[37] and
it can be no coincidence that John Plunket was a prominent
serjeant of the Dublin Bench in the early fourteenth century.[38]
Other serjeants of the period whose names are used in the treatise
are Richard le Blund, John of Cardiff and John Keppok.[39]

35. In Harvard Law Library MS. 162 (at ff. 166r-v) this passage reads: 'Et si cel
    bref face mencioun de service de chevalier et poet estre qe le tenant ne tient
    pas ceux tenemenz par service de chevalier mes par altre service auxi com par
    rente ou siute de court, dount ne seit acordaunt al bref, le deforceour purra
    transverser le bref e le counte par la resoun de les services de chevalier mes par
    altres services auxi com par rente etc., e issint abatre son bref a cele foyz solom
    le dit des asqunes gentz. Et sil velt la garde aver donc covent qil purchase un
    altre bref qe face nent mencioun de service de chevalier mes dautre service
    solom la coustume qest usee (in the version in Cambridge University Library
    MS. Hh. 3. 11 at f. 152v this reads 'solom le custome de Irlaund') et qe le bref
    die 'si come renablement purra moustrer etc. Et sil ne poet nent aver bref de
    cele fourme saunz service de chevalier donc covent qil plede par bille devant
    chef Justice si come il pert e semble a asqune gentz com avunt est dit'.

36. See below, p. 460.

37. His name appears in the main manuscript tradition of C96 and his wife's
    name in C55. His name also appears in two manuscripts in place of the
    initials found in the other manuscripts in C41, C45, C46, C53 and C262.
    These two manuscripts are probably reproducing faithfully the original text
    of the C tradition here. All references are to the edition of *Novae Narrationes*
    edited by E. Shanks and S.F.C. Milsom (Selden Society, vol. 80 (1963)).

38. See below, p. 38.

39. Richard le Blund: C 53 (in three manuscripts in place of the anonymous
    initials of the other MSS.); John of Cardiff: C 26–27 (in a single manuscript
    and in the distorted form 'Kerdyke'); John Keppok: C 53 (in a single
    manuscript in place of John Plunket). For Richard le Blund and John of
    Cardiff see below, pp. 37, 40. John Keppok was a serjeant at law (and royal
    justice) in Ireland in the second half of the fourteenth century.

III

It is possible to compile a fairly complete list of all serjeants practising in the Westminster Bench from the early 1290s onwards. There are two sources of evidence for the compilation of such a list which fortunately complement each other. One is the plea-roll entries recording the proffer of payments for permission to make final concords, formal agreements made under the court's auspices mainly about land. From mid-October 1293 these normally include a clause noting that the parties to the final concord have the chirograph, the formal document recording their final concord, 'through' (*per*) a certain named individual, 'their' serjeant. The other is the Year Book reports which record serjeants in their more characteristic activity of pleading in court on behalf of their clients and which begin to survive in much larger quantity from this time onwards. Between them these two sources of information indicate that during the sixty-year period from 1290 to 1350 around 150 serjeants practised at some time or other in the court.[40] Unfortunately there are no surviving reports of cases from the Dublin Bench; and the new Westminster enrolment practice associating the making of final concords with particular serjeants does not seem to have been extended to (or been copied by) its Dublin counterpart. From such evidence as does survive it is possible to compile a list of around 35 serjeants who are known or who can reasonably be assumed to have practised in the Dublin Bench during the same sixty-year period.[41] Such a list can have no pretensions to completeness; indeed, there is no way even of knowing what proportion of the total number of serjeants active in the Dublin Bench during this same period they may represent. All that can be said is that given the pattern of survival of the evidence it is possible that it is much closer to being complete in the case of the serjeants practising in the earlier part of this period than in the later.

Some of the serjeants on the list are little more than just names. Of Michael of Sutton ('Sotton'), for example, we know that he is mentioned in passing as a serjeant in a plea-roll entry of 1291. The successful litigant in the case (William Fokeram) is recorded at the end of the entry as acknowledging that he had granted 'his' serjeant ('narrator') Michael one half of the eighty acres at Rathcon, Co. Tipperary which he had recovered through litigation from

40. I have calculated this figure from the material contained in John Baker's *Order of serjeants at law* (Selden Society, supplementary series vol. v (1984)).

41. See below, Appendix.

Walter Uncle.[42] Michael also appears once as an essoiner in the surviving Bench plea-roll of Easter 1290 and is mentioned twice on the rolls of the justiciar's court in 1297, once as the assign of five shillings out of total damages of fifteen shillings, once as enforcing a debt of forty shillings owed to him.[43] Nicholas of Snitterby is described as a serjeant ('serviens narrator') when bringing litigation in the Bench in Michaelmas term 1316 against a man and his wife who had allegedly assaulted him in St Patrick's street by Dublin.[44] From his surname it seems likely that Nicholas was a relative of Thomas of Snitterby, a justice of the Dublin Bench between 1295 and 1307.[45] It is possible that the serjeant is the same man as the Nicholas of Snitterby who served as a baron of the exchequer, justice of the Bench and justice of the justiciar's bench at various dates between 1337 and 1357.[46] He may, however, simply be a namesake and relative of an earlier generation since it was common for the same Christian name to be used by members of a family in successive generations.

It is usually possible, however, to say a little about the man's background, and thus at the very least to distinguish between those serjeants whose immediate origins were English and who only came to Ireland in the course of their careers and those who belonged to English families which had been settled in Ireland for one or more generations. John 'de Ponte' (whose surname should probably be anglicised as 'of Bridgwater') belongs to the first group.[47] John acted as king's serjeant in Ireland from 1292 to 1300 and unlike most king's serjeants seems only to have acted for the king. It may be for this reason that he received a higher fee.[48] John had acted as Edward I's attorney in two cases in the English court of king's bench in 1269 and 1270 before Edward became king.[49] He is then found in the service of Edward's wife

42. PROI RC 7/3, pp. 169–70.

43. BL, Add. Roll 13598, m. 7; *Cal. justic. rolls, Ire., 1295–1303*, pp. 93, 125.

44. PROI RC 8/11, pp. 827–8.

45. Richardson & Sayles, *Admin. Ire.*, pp. 150–2.

46. Richardson & Sayles, *Admin. Ire.*, pp. 109–12, 160, 163, 171.

47. Richardson & Sayles, *Admin. Ire.*, give his surname as 'de Ponz'. For evidence of his property acquisitions in Bridgwater (in Latin simply *Pons*) see *Somerset fines*, ed. E. Green (Somerset Record Society, vol. 6 (1892)), pp. 230, 264.

48. He was paid twenty marks a year when other king's serjeants were paid ten marks a year. For evidence of his activity on the king's behalf in the Irish courts down to 1300 see *Cal. justic. rolls, Ire., 1295–1303*, pp. 29, 102–3, 142–3, 238, 316–7; PRO C 260/18, no. 10, m. 2; PROI RC 7/6, pp. 441–2.

49. PRO KB 26/192, m. 2 and KB 26/197, m. 18.

Eleanor acting as her bailiff in Somerset, as her constable of Leeds castle in Kent and (in 1289) as her under–steward.[50] He seems to have come to Ireland when a promising career in Eleanor's service was ended by her death. Much less is known about the antecedents of John's contemporary, John de Neville, who was also employed by the king as one of his serjeants between 1293 and 1297.[51] It is, however, clear that he also was English by origin. In 1295 he received a protection in respect of property he held in England; and when in 1302 Christ Church priory, Dublin obtained a quitclaim from him of the life interest he possessed in land at Clonturk in Co. Dublin it was dated at York, presumably because he had by then returned to England.[52] William of Bardfield, king's serjeant from 1297 to 1308, whom we have already encountered accumulating annuities for his services as a serjeant to private clients, was of English origin too.[53] William appears to have come from either Great or Little Bardfield in Essex and is to be found acting as an attorney in the Westminster Bench between 1279 and 1284.[54] In 1290 he stood surety for the future chief justice of the Dublin Bench, Simon of Ludgate, when Simon was in trouble in England for obtaining a papal bull whose contents were deemed unacceptable by the king.[55] At some date between 1286 and 1289 William married Katherine, one of two sisters of John of Bayfield. John had been chief clerk to Hamon Hauteyn the senior justice of the exchequer of the Jews between 1273 and 1284 and the marriage brought William property interests in the counties of Norfolk and Middlesex which Katherine had inherited from her brother.[56]

50. *Cal. close rolls, 1279–88*, p. 88; *Cal. close rolls, 1288–96*, p. 113; *Chronica Johannis de Oxenedes*, ed. H. Ellis (Rolls Series, 1859), p. 273.

51. Richardson & Sayles, *Admin. Ire.*, p. 174.

52. *Cal. pat. rolls, 1292–1301*, p. 138; *Calendar to Christ Church deeds* (ed. M.J. McEnery) in *P.R.I.rep.D.K.*, no. 20 (1888), Appendix 7, pp. 36–122, no. 23 (1891), Appendix 3, pp. 75–152 and no. 24 (1892), Appendix 8, pp. 100–94 (continuous enumeration throughout) [hereafter cited as *Cal.Ch.Ch. Deeds*], no. 172. For land acquired by a John de Neville (possibly the Irish serjeant) in Yorkshire in 1300 see *Yorkshire feet of fines, 1300–14*, ed. M. Roper (Yorkshire Archaeological Society, record series, vol. 127 (1965), p. 12, no. 59.

53. Richardson & Sayles, *Admin. Ire.*, p. 174; above, p. 20.

54. PRO CP 40/28, m. 80; /29, mm. 81, 82; /39, mm. 72, 76d; /41, mm. 87, 87d; /42, mm. 154d, 155, 161; /44, m. 91; /51, m. 111d; /52, m. 67d.

55. PRO E 159/63, m. 13d.

56. PRO JUST 1/578, m. 45; CP 40/79, m. 16; JUST 1/544, m. 10; CP 40/109, m. 117.

These English property interests explain why William obtained a protection in England in 1298 and appointed general attorneys to act for him there in 1308, 1311, 1314 and 1318.[57] Henry of Beningbrough, who is to be found acting as a serjeant in the Dublin Bench, the justiciar's court and in eyres during the first decade of the fourteenth century, was also probably of English origin. Beningbrough is close to York; and one John the chaplain of York is mentioned as being one of his executors in 1312 litigation brought to recover the arrears of an annuity owed by one of his clients.[58] Of serjeants active in the second quarter of the fourteenth century only Thomas of Dent (king's serjeant from 1331 to 1334) seems to have been of English birth. Thomas probably came from Dent in Yorkshire. He too appointed general attorneys to act on his behalf in England though only after he had been appointed a justice in Ireland (in 1337, 1344 and 1347).[59] Thomas also seems to have acquired property in Ireland, however, for after his return to England he is to be found (in 1361) appointing general attorneys to act on his behalf in Ireland.[60]

A majority of the Irish serjeants of this period, however, seem to have been of Anglo-Irish origin. Several came from a Dublin bourgeois background. Roger of Ashbourne, active as a serjeant from at least the 1290s up to the time of his death (in 1307/8) for example, had been one of the bailiffs of the city in 1287 and was clearly related to the Roger of Ashbourne who was mayor of Dublin in the 1260s and 1270s (who was probably his father).[61] Roger held significant amounts of property in the city as well as in the county of Dublin. He also acquired property in Co. Kildare and in the suburbs of the city of Cork but later disposed of them.[62] Robert of Bristol, who was active as a serjeant from the late thirteenth century through to the early 1320s (when he was

57. *Cal. pat. rolls, 1292–1301*, p. 358; *Cal. pat. rolls, 1307–13*, pp. 80, 354; *Cal. pat. rolls, 1313–7*, p. 159; *Cal. pat. rolls, 1317–21*, p. 193.

58. PROI RC 8/6, pp. 375–6 (cf. RC 7/10, pp. 528–9).

59. Richardson & Sayles, *Admin. Ire.*, pp. 160, 162, 177; *Cal. pat. rolls, 1334–8*, p. 519; *Cal. pat. rolls, 1343–5*, p. 318; *Cal. pat. rolls, 1345–8*, p. 416.

60. *Cal. pat. rolls, 1361–4*, p. 130.

61. *P.R.I.rep.D.K. 37*, p. 25; *Chartul. St Mary's, Dublin*, vol. I, p. 455 and n.

62. For his property in the city of Dublin see: *Cal. justic. rolls, Ire., 1295–1303*, p. 314; *Reg. St John, Dublin*, no. 34 (pp. 18–9); PROI RC 7/9, pp. 297–8. For his lands in Co. Dublin see: PROI KB 1/1, m. 47; RC 7/10, pp. 78, 281, 340–1; RC 7/11, pp. 464–5, 501; RC 7/13/2, pp. 6–7; RC 7/13/4, p. 50. For his lands in Co. Kildare see: *Cal. justic. rolls, Ire., 1305–7*, pp. 329–30. For his lands in the suburb of Cork see: PROI RC 7/8, pp. 399–400; RC 8/2, pp. 278–9.

appointed a justice of the Bench) was a citizen of Dublin and held property there and in Co. Dublin.[63] He was the son of William of Bristol, another former mayor of the city.[64] John of Grantchester, a serjeant from at least 1312 until his appointment as a baron of the Dublin exchequer in 1326, is probably to be identified with the John son of Ralph of Grantchester who was a citizen of Dublin and who in 1318 was granted an exemption from serving in public offices in the city or county of Dublin against his will.[65] He married Alice, the daughter of Geoffrey of Morton, yet another former mayor of Dublin, and in her right held various properties in the city of Dublin and in Co. Meath.[66] He also acquired further property in the city and lands in Co. Kildare.[67] John seems also, however, to have held lands in England, since in 1330, 1331 and 1334 he appointed attorneys to act for him there and in 1334 obtained an exemption from serving in public offices there against his will.[68] The Philip of Carrick who is mentioned as a serjeant in the justiciar's court in 1305 may also have come from a similar background. A Philip of Carrick, perhaps the same man, is found as bailiff of Dublin in 1297 and is also mentioned in connection with affairs in the city in 1306 and 1307.[69]

An even larger group of serjeants came from the eastern seaboard counties of Ireland, mainly from the area later to be known as the English Pale. Richard le Blund of Arklow was king's serjeant from 1297 to 1322 and acted as a serjeant for others as well during that period.[70] His name indicates that he came from Arklow though there seems to be no other direct evidence to connect him with the town. Richard can be shown to have been a tenant of lands in the city and county of Dublin and in Co. Louth.[71] His

---

63. *Anc. rec. Dublin*, vol. I, p. 111; PROI RC 7/3, p. 316; RC 7/4, pp. 479–80; RC 8 /11, pp. 269–70.

64. *Cal. justic. rolls, Ire., 1295–1303*, pp. 262–3; PROI RC 7/3, p. 316.

65. PROI RC 7/12, pp. 497–8.

66. *Rot. pat. Hib.*, p. 23b, nos. 105–6; *Cal. pat. rolls, 1321–4*, pp. 330–1; PROI RC 8/10, pp. 791–4; RC 7/12, pp. 434–5; RC 8/17, pp. 516–8.

67. PROI RC 8/15, pp. 64–5; RC 8/19, pp. 563–4; RC 8/11, p. 174; RC 8/17, pp. 316–9, 344–5, 366–9; PRO KB 27/283, m. 155.

68. *Cal. pat. rolls, 1330–4*, pp. 4, 227; *Cal. pat. rolls, 1334–8*, pp. 14, 28.

69. *Cal. justic. rolls, Ire., 1305–7*, pp. 98, 229; *P.R.I.rep.D.K. 38*, pp. 34–5; *Cal. doc. Ire., 1293–1301*, nos. 391 (p. 181) and 408 (pp. 190–1).

70. Richardson & Sayles, *Admin. Ire.*, pp. 174–6; PROI RC 7/6, p. 11; RC 7/8, pp. 151–2; RC 7/9, pp. 266, 275–6, 299; RC 7/10, p. 103; RC 7/11, pp. 275–9; RC 7/13/3, p. 76; RC 8/2, p. 174.

71. *Reg. St John, Dublin*, p. 371; PROI KB 2/7, p. 48; *Ormond deeds, 1172–1350*, nos. 324, 464; PROI RC 8/17, pp. 224–5; *Cal. pat. rolls, 1307–13*, p. 63.

wife seems to have brought him lands in Co. Tipperary and perhaps in Co. Dublin as well.[72] William of Athy was probably active as a serjeant throughout the 1280s and 1290s. By 1305 although still alive he was described as a former serjeant.[73] He is known to have held lands in Co. Kildare close to Athy as well as in Co. Dublin.[74] He was probably a younger son of the John of Athy who may himself have been a serjeant in the 1260s and was the deputy seneschal of the liberty of Kildare in the early 1270s.[75] William of Sully was active as a serjeant during the first decade of the fourteenth century. He is also known to have acquired and held lands in Co. Kildare.[76] In 1296 and 1304 he is to be found seeking lands further west in Co. Limerick, claiming that these had belonged to his grandfather Luke of Sully earlier in the thirteenth century (in the reign of King Henry III).[77] He also appears to have retained some links with the country from which his family had come to Ireland, Wales.[78] The John of Carmarthen who was active as a serjeant in the first and second decades of the fourteenth century seems to have been the eldest son of Adam of Carmarthen who had held lands in the counties of Kilkenny, Dublin and Limerick and property in the city of Dublin.[79] John forfeited all these lands when he adhered to the Bruces in company with Walter and Hugh de Lacy.[80] John Plunket, active as a serjeant from the end of the first decade of the fourteenth century to perhaps the fourth decade of the century, belonged to a

72. PROI CB 1/1, mm. 1d, 6; RC 7/10, p. 410; *Red Bk Ormond*, p. 73; *Registrum Prioratus Omnium Sanctorum juxta Dublin*, ed. R. Butler (Irish Archaeological Society, 1845), p. 125; PROI RC 8/11, pp. 433–4.

73. *Cal. justic. rolls, Ire., 1295–1303*, p. 218; Sayles, *Affairs of Ire.*, p. 53; BL, Add.MS. 4790, f. 141r; PROI RC 7/6, p. 14; *Cal. justic. rolls, Ire., 1305–7*, p. 35.

74. *Cal. justic. rolls, Ire.,1295–1303*, p. 155; *Red Bk Ormond*, p. 16; PROI RC 7/7, pp. 421–2, RC 7/9, pp. 268–9; RC 7/4, pp. 27, 40, 79, 162–4.

75. Below, p. 44 and notes 145–7. For evidence that John's heir was a son named Nicholas see PROI RC 7/3, p. 5; RC 8/1, p. 65; *Cal. doc. Ire., 1254–84*, no. 1862; and for this William being called William son of John of Athy see *Cal. doc. Ire., 1252–84*, no. 1448 and PROI KB 2/5, p. 1.

76. For evidence of William of Sully as a serjeant see *Cal. justic. rolls, Ire., 1305–7*, pp. 16, 69; *Cal. justic. rolls, Ire., 1308–14*, pp. 5–6; PROI RC 7/10, pp. 112–3. For his lands in Co. Kildare see *Cal. justic. rolls, Ire., 1305–7*, p. 151; PROI RC 7/10, pp. 208–9, 362–3, 563–4; RC 7/13/2, pp. 19–20.

77. PROI RC 7/4, pp. 79, 198; RC 7/10, p. 108.

78. *Cal. justic. rolls, Ire., 1305–7*, pp. 768–9.

79. *Cal. justic. rolls, Ire., 1305–7*, pp. 321–3; PROI RC 8/11, p. 175; PRO C 47/10/18, no. 11; *P.R.I.rep.D.K. 42*, p. 19.

80. *Rot. pat. Hib.*, p. 22, no. 33 and p. 24b, no. 126; *P.R.I.rep.D.K. 42*, p. 19.

family which since his grandfather's time had held land in Dublin but which in his father's time had also acquired property in Co. Louth close to Drogheda.[81] His wife Alice brought him further lands in the same county centered on the manor of Beaulieu where they founded a new parish.[82] He also acquired lands in counties Dublin, Meath, Louth and Kildare.[83] Simon fitzRichard seems to have been a serjeant by 1317 and was king's serjeant in Ireland from 1322 to 1331 (before becoming a royal justice).[84] He seems to have come from Co. Louth where he is known to have held and acquired land while a serjeant.[85] He is probably to be identified with the man who had been to Flanders in the company of John fitzThomas in 1298, was sheriff of Co. Roscommon in 1309–10 and in 1317 was sub-escheator in Co. Louth.[86] John Gernoun was king's serjeant from 1327 to 1330 and again from 1334 to 1338.[87] The annuity he was being paid as a serjeant by the seneschal of Christ Church in Dublin in 1343 (at a time when he was chief justice of the Bench) presumably had its origin in an earlier period of service to the priory.[88] The various Irish John Gernouns of the period are difficult to distinguish; there was also at least one contemporary English namesake who appears to have had no connection with Ireland.[89] The John Gernoun who was a serjeant probably belonged to a family who held lands in counties Louth and Meath and himself acquired lands in Co. Louth.[90]

81. P. Brand, 'The formation of a parish: the case of Beaulieu, county Louth' in *Settlement and society in medieval Ireland: studies presented to F.X. Martin*, ed. J. Bradley (Kilkenny, 1988), p. 261 and n. 15.

82. Ibid., p. 265.

83. In Co. Dublin: PROI RC 7/13/3, pp. 107–8; RC 8/15, pp. 179–80. In Co. Meath: RC 8/17, pp. 203–4; RC 8/19, pp. 164, 418; RC 8/20, pp. 6–7. In Co. Louth: RC 7/12, pp. 209–13; *Registrum de Kilmainham: register of chapter acts of the hospital of St John of Jerusalem in Ireland, 1326–1339*, ed. C. McNeill (Irish Manuscripts Commission, 1932), pp. 20–1, 29–30. In Co. Kildare: RC 8/20, pp. 44–8.

84. PROI RC 7/12, pp. 139–41; Richardson & Sayles, *Admin. Ire.*, p. 177.

85. PROI RC 7/12, p. 137; *P.R.I.rep.D.K. 42*, p. 35.

86. *Rot. pat. Hib.*, p. 5, no. 15; *P.R.I.rep.D.K. 39*, p. 27 (and note he was also under consideration as sheriff of Meath in 1313: PROI RC 8/9, p. 6); RC 7/12, pp. 138–9.

87. Richardson & Sayles, *Admin. Ire.*, pp. 176–7.

88. *Account roll of Holy Trinity, Dublin*, pp. 45–6.

89. Robin Frame (in *English lordship in Ireland, 1318–1361* (Oxford, 1982), p. 247) identifies our John with the John Gernun who held property in Essex but cites no evidence to support this improbable identification.

90. *P.R.I.rep.D.K. 39*, pp. 36, 42; *Rot. pat. Hib.*, pp. 75b–76, no. 109; *Dowdall deeds*, no. 125.

His wife Maud was the widow of William of Nottingham who belonged to a prominent Dublin merchant family.[91] John of Cardiff was perhaps already a serjeant in 1317 and was certainly king's serjeant from 1327 to 1330.[92] His father and namesake seems to have held lands in counties Dublin, Meath and Waterford in the reign of Edward I, but the future serjeant spent at least part of his childhood in England to which he was taken by his guardian Guy Cokerel.[93] Hugh Brown was king's serjeant from 1331 to 1346 and is known to have received an annuity as a serjeant from Christ Church priory in Dublin.[94] When he died in 1360 he possessed various lands in Co. Meath, and he probably came from that county.[95]

A minority of serjeants came from more remote areas of the country. Master David le Blund, active as a serjeant in the first decade of the fourteenth century, seems to have held lands in Co. Cork and to have come from this county.[96] His title suggests that he may have possessed a university degree, apparently a unique qualification for a serjeant during this period in either England or Ireland. Richard Locard was active as a serjeant during the same period but by 1313 had been murdered.[97] His property interests lay in counties Cork and Tipperary and it was at Cashel that he was killed.[98] In the late 1280s he had been a clerk in the household of the treasurer Nicholas de Clere and in 1292 served as sheriff of Co. Dublin.[99] In Reginald Macotyr of Co. Tipperary, active as a serjeant in the justiciar's court during the first two decades of the fourteenth century, we even find one serjeant of

91. PROI RC 8/19, pp. 108–15, 487; RC 8/20, pp. 326–330.

92. PROI RC 8/11, p. 175; Richardson & Sayles, *Admin. Ire.*, p. 177.

93. PROI RC 7/4, pp. 39–40; RC 7/11, p. 234; RC 7/13/4, pp. 32–3; RC 8/14, pp. 551–2.

94. Richardson & Sayles, *Admin. Ire.*, p. 176; *Account Roll of Holy Trinity, Dublin*, pp. 46, 93, 103–4, 108–9.

95. *Rot. pat. Hib.*, p. 88, no. 17.

96. For evidence of his career see: PROI RC 7/10, pp. 367–8; RC 7/11, pp. 25–6, 441; RC 7/13/3, p. 76; RC 8/2, pp. 278–9. For evidence of his lands see: PROI RC 7/11, pp. 60–1; RC 8/2, pp. 171, 278–9; RC 8/11, pp. 673–4; CB 1/1, m. 7; *Cal. justic. rolls, Ire., 1305–7*, pp. 367–70, 459.

97. *Cal. justic. rolls, Ire., 1305–7*, pp. 116, 371–2, 393; *Cal. justic. rolls, Ire., 1308–14*, pp. 62, 302–3.

98. PROI RC 7/7, p. 325; RC 7/11, p. 92; *Cal. justic. rolls, Ire., 1308–14*, pp. 108–10, 132–3.

99. *Cal. doc. Ire., 1252–84*, nos. 558, 595, 709, 969, 1148; *P.R.I.rep.D.K.37*, p. 49.

the period who was of native Irish (or more correctly Hiberno-Norse) origin.[100]

The first serjeants of the Westminster Bench to be appointed as justices of the king's courts in England were Richard of Boyland and Alan of Walkingham who were appointed as justices in eyre in 1279. By 1300 such appointments had become common and by 1350 only serjeants were being appointed to the two main royal courts (the Bench and king's bench). A significant number of the serjeants active in the Dublin Bench were likewise appointed as justices of the king's courts in Ireland. When William of Athy and John of Horton were appointed as justices in 1294 it was only for them to act as temporary substitutes for the chief justice of the Bench (Robert Bagod) while he was ill[101] but John of Bridgwater, while still a king's serjeant, was being appointed to hear assizes and deliver gaols all over Ireland and he became a justice of the Bench and sat in various eyres between 1300 and 1306.[102] Subsequently William of Bardfield became a justice of the Bench from 1308 to 1312 and again from 1316 to 1320;[103] Master David le Blund was a justice of the justiciar's court and a justice in eyre from 1308 to 1310 and again in 1317–8 and also an assize justice;[104] Robert of Bristol acted as a justice of the Bench from 1322 to 1324;[105] Richard le Blund of Arklow, who (like John of Bridgwater) heard assizes while still king's serjeant became a justice in eyre and justice of the Bench from 1322 to 1325;[106] John of Grantchester became a baron of the exchequer and then a justice of the Bench and of the justiciar's court between 1326 and 1334;[107] Simon fitzRichard acted as a justice of the Bench from 1331 to 1341;[108] John Gernoun acted as

100. *Cal. justic. rolls, Ire., 1308–14*, pp. 7, 10; PROI KB 1/1, mm. 6, 37, 75, 75d; KB 2/5, pp. 20, 34, 89; KB 2/6, p. 41; KB 2/9, pp. 35, 82, 117; KB 2/10, p. 31; RC 8/5, p. 76.

101. BL, Add. MS 4790, f. 141r.

102. For Bridgwater as an assize and gaol delivery justice see: *Cal. justic. rolls, Ire., 1295–1303*, pp. 9, 15, 19, 55–6, 72, 97, 150, 175, 215, 221–2, 225, 231–2, 236, 244–5, 280–2, 324, 341, 359; PROI RC 7/3, p. 442; RC 7/4, pp. 116–8, 216; RC 7/7, p. 183. For Bridgwater as a Bench and eyre justice see: Richardson & Sayles, *Admin. Ire.*, pp. 142–5, 151, 153 (and for evidence that he may have served earlier as a Bench justice see *Cal. justic. rolls, Ire., 1295–1303*, p. 318).

103. Richardson & Sayles, *Admin. Ire.*, pp. 153, 155.

104. Richardson & Sayles, *Admin. Ire.*, pp. 145, 167–8; PROI RC 8/7, p. 53.

105. Richardson & Sayles, *Admin. Ire.*, p. 155.

106. Richardson & Sayles, *Admin. Ire.*, pp. 147, 155, 157; PROI RC 7/11, p. 298; RC 7/12, pp. 209–13.

107. Richardson & Sayles, *Admin. Ire.*, pp. 107, 156, 169.

a justice of the Bench between 1338 and 1344 and again from 1348 to 1355;[109] Thomas of Dent acted as a justice of the Bench from 1334 to 1336 and again from 1344 to 1358;[110]William Petit was a temporary justice of the justiciar's bench from 1347 to 1348 and again in 1359;[111] and Robert of Preston was a justice of the Bench from 1358 to 1378.[112] The serjeants of the Dublin Bench did not, however, succeed in securing a monopoly of judicial appointments in Ireland. Partly this was because English serjeants were eligible for appointment to the Irish bench and were sometimes appointed to it. Thus Richard of Willoughby and Henry of Hambury, both long-serving serjeants of the Westminster Bench, were appointed chief justice of the Dublin Bench in 1324 and 1325 respectively; and Robert of Scarborough, another Westminster serjeant, was appointed chief justice of the Dublin Bench in 1332 and of the justiciar's court in 1334.[113] More puzzlingly it seems also to have remained possible to appoint men who seem to have had no experience as a serjeant in either country, men such as Thomas of Montpellier, who served as a justice of the Dublin Bench between 1335 and 1341.[114]

Other ties also existed between the serjeants of the Dublin Bench and the Irish judiciary. Nicholas of Snitterby was surely related to the Bench justice Thomas of Snitterby; and beside him we can place the serjeant Robert of Preston, son of Roger of Preston, a justice of the justiciar's court and of the Bench[115] and Roger of Ashbourne, father of the Bench justice, Ellis of Ashbourne.[116] Although it is not now possible to trace the family tree in detail it seems clear that the early fourteenth-century serjeant John Plunket was related to the many members of the family of that name who later became serjeants and justices in Ireland. Nicholas of Edgefield, a serjeant active in the first decade of the fourteenth century, was not directly related to any member of the Irish judiciary but is known to have married the widow of the former Bench justice, Simon of Ludgate.[117]

108. Richardson & Sayles, *Admin. Ire.*, pp. 156, 158, 160.

109. Richardson & Sayles, *Admin. Ire.*, pp. 160, 163.

110. Richardson & Sayles, *Admin. Ire.*, pp. 158, 160, 162.

111. Richardson & Sayles, *Admin. Ire.*, pp. 171 n. 2, 172.

112. Richardson & Sayles, *Admin. Ire.*, pp. 162, 164.

113. Baker, *Order of serjeants at law*, pp. 516, 535, 545.

114. For his career see Frame, *English lordship in Ireland*, pp. 105–6.

115. Ibid., p. 95.

116. PROI KB 1/1, m. 47; RC 7/13/2, pp. 66–7; RC 7/13/4, p. 50.

117. *Cal. justic. rolls, Ire., 1305–7*, pp. 231, 261.

IV

Such information as we possess about the functions performed by attorneys in the Dublin Bench seems congruent with them performing much the same functions as their much better-documented English counterparts. The basic, primary function of the attorney was simply to attend court on the client's behalf; to come forward to the bar of the court when the client's name was called out by one of the criers of the court and show that his client was present through his attorney. If his client was the plaintiff in the case several such appearances in successive terms would normally be necessary before the court's procedures secured the appearance of the defendant and the case could be pleaded. Even after that several more such appearances were commonly required before final judgment was given. If a plaintiff was not present either in person or through his attorney at any of the days appointed by the court for the hearing of his case and failed to make his excuse for absence in proper form, the case would be dismissed and his sureties for pursuing the case would be amerced and he would have to start the case all over again. If his client was the defendant the attorney had fewer appearances to make. He had simply to attend the court as and when the client required him to do so for the pleading of the case. By the later thirteenth century these basic functions had attracted to themselves certain other subsidiary ones. The plaintiff's attorney seems commonly to have seen to the acquisition of the appropriate writ for the initiation of the litigation. He seems also to have become responsible (at the purely procedural stages of litigation) for ensuring that his own appearance and the defendant's absence were recorded on the plea-rolls of the court by one of the court clerks and for ensuring that the appropriate judicial writ authorising the next stage of process against the defendant was issued and delivered to the appropriate local sheriff. At the pleading stage the attorneys on both sides had the ultimate power to avow or disavow what had been said by the serjeants. They may also commonly have engaged those serjeants on behalf of the client and have 'briefed' them on the main facts of the case.

A much greater degree of formality attached to the appointment of an attorney than to the authorisation of a serjeant. All appointments of attorneys were supposed to be recorded on the plea-rolls of the Bench. What was recorded, however, was the purely oral authorisation of the attorney. Litigants did not have to draw up any kind of written document giving the attorney authority to act on their behalf. Originally both litigant and attorney had to

appear before the court during term-time for such an appointment to be made; but it seems probable that by this date the
requirement had been relaxed in Ireland as it is known to have
been in England, where it was possible to appoint an attorney out
of term before a justice of any of the royal courts or even one of
the senior clerks of the Bench in any locality which they visited.

Such appointments must, of course, have been preceded by
agreements between litigant and attorney as to the terms on
which the attorney was willing to act. In the Westminster Bench
these varied very considerably: from agreements to act in one
particular case to longer term agreements to act for a particular
client until further notice or for life. There were also variations as
to the remuneration agreed. Very little evidence survives about
the terms of such agreements in the case of attorneys appointed to
act in the Dublin Bench. A surviving transcript, however, does
give us the terms of one agreement made between the attorney
John le Blound of Gowran, Co. Kilkenny, and the abbot of
Monasteranenagh, which was confirmed by the successor of the
abbot who had made the original agreement in 1317. Under its
terms John received an annuity of twenty shillings for the services
done by him for the abbey in the Dublin Bench. The annuity
presumably also paid for his future service as well.[118]

It clearly remained possible throughout this period for a litigant
in either of the Benches to appoint as his attorney a friend or
relative with no pretensions to any professional expertise. Both
Benches did, however, recognise the existence of the professional
attorney at least to the extent of applying special measures
against him if found guilty of professional misconduct (including
debarring such an attorney from practice in the court). In the
Westminster Bench there appears even to have been an unsuccessful attempt in 1292 to confine regular paid practice as an
attorney in the court to a closed group of around one hundred
and forty members chosen by the justices of the court. No such
measure is known to have been attempted in the Dublin Bench;
and it is probably correct to assume that a regime of wholly free
competition obtained in the court.

It is quite difficult even in England to identify for certain the
professional attorneys who practised in the Bench. There are no
sources comparable to those which make it so easy to identify the
professional serjeants who practised there. A few professional
attorneys can be identified from the litigation brought against
them by dissatisfied clients but most can only be identified by the

118. PROI RC 7/12, pp. 322–3.

laborious process of searching through those sections of the plea-rolls which are devoted to recording the individual appointments of attorneys in particular cases and looking for names which recur with sufficient frequency to suggest that the individuals in question are professionals. The loss of almost all the plea-rolls of the Dublin Bench renders a comparable exercise looking for professional attorneys quite impossible; and we are therefore dependent for the most part on occasional passing references and the comparatively few appointments of attorneys which are recorded in the Record Commission calendars for the identification or possible identification of professional attorneys active in the Dublin Bench. The surviving Bench plea-roll for Easter term 1290 does, however, allow us to identify at least two possibly professional attorneys then practising in the Bench. About Alexander Giffard nothing more seems to be ascertainable.[119] Maurice Honne or Houne, however, can be traced in the calendars being appointed as an attorney down to 1309;[120] and some indication of his possible place of origin is provided by litigation of 1306 between him and Leticia daughter of Andrew Honne/Houne which shows him claiming lands at 'Balyhokyn' in Co. Dublin.[121] Confirmation of his professional status, if not of his professional skill, comes from a case of 1301 in which his negligence as an attorney caused his clients to lose their case.[122] He was committed to gaol for that negligence, a punishment suitable for a professional but not for an amateur. Other professional attorneys who can be identified as such from the surviving evidence include John le Blound of Gowran (whom we have already encountered) who was active as an attorney from 1308 to at least 1318 (and perhaps till his death in 1331).[123] John is known to have sued the abbot of Monasteranenagh and the archbishop of Armagh for arrears of annuities of twenty shillings a year each (and the former was certainly for his services in the Bench).[124] He is also known to have sued two other probable clients for arrears of annuities of

---

119. BL, Add. Roll 13598, mm. 2, 2d (seven appointments).

120. For his seven appointments as an attorney in Easter term 1290 see ibid. (and for his activity as an essoiner in the same term see ibid., m. 7). For subsequent appointments see PROI RC 7/3, p. 332; RC 7/5, p. 139; RC 7/9, pp. 384–5; RC 7/10, p. 519; RC 7/13/4, p. 71.

121. PROI RC 7/11, p. 466 (though the surname is here transcribed as Howe).

122. PROI RC 7/8, pp. 107–8.

123. PROI CB 1/1, mm. 26, 26d; RC 8/11, pp. 202–216, 442–53, 857–65; RC 7/12, pp. 400–1. For the date of his death see *P.R.I.rep.D.K.44*, p. 54.

124. PROI RC 8/11, pp. 426, 599; RC 7/12, p. 367.

one mark each.[125] John Gothemund, probably from Cashel, is described as an 'attorney in the (king's) bench at Dublin' after his murder in 1314. This suggests that he too was a professional attorney of the court.[126] At least two other possible professional attorneys of the period seem to have come from Co. Tipperary. One was Peter 'de Halleton' whose name occurs with some frequency in the surviving lists of attorneys in the Record Commission plea-roll calendars between 1317 and 1336.[127] The second is Roger de Sancta Brigida. He only occurs as an attorney on the plea-rolls between 1299 and 1305 but was specially authorised in 1302/3 by Nicholas of Inkbarrow (Inteberge) to surrender an advowson to the hospital of St John the Baptist in Dublin and in 1315 sued the archbishop of Cashel for five years arrears of a forty shilling annuity, which may have been granted him for his legal services.[128] Roger is known to have held property at Knockgraffon in Co. Tipperary.[129] Nicholas of Tintagel occurs as a Bench attorney in 1325, 1332 and 1336.[130] In 1336 he was seeking land in his own right in Co. Cork, seeking land in right of his wife (as the dower of a previous husband) in Kildare town, and also suing for an alleged assault against himself at Oxmantown.[131] Richard Manning was the king's attorney from 1313 to 1328 but is found acting for others at various dates between 1305 and 1327.[132] He is known to have held lands in Co.

125. PROI RC 8/15, pp. 130, 144–5.

126. *Cal. justic. rolls, Ire., 1308–14*, p. 313. For evidence linking him with Cashel see PROI KB 1/1, m. 34 (=*Reg. St John, Dublin*, pp. 302–3); KB 2/5, p. 35.

127. PROI RC 8/11, pp. 442–53 passim, 730; RC 8/15, pp. 68–77 passim; RC 8/19, pp. 168–78 and 370–9 passim; KB 2/9, p. 124. For his connexions with Co. Tipperary see PROI RC 8/16, pp. 170–1; RC 8/19, p. 431; RC 8/20, pp. 282–3.

128. PROI RC 7/6, pp. 2, 60, 575–6; RC 7/7, pp. 132, 273–4; RC 7/8, pp. 202–3; RC 7/9, pp. 383, 477; RC 7/10, pp. 517–8; *Reg. St John, Dublin*, p. 309; RC 8/10, p. 318.

129. PROI RC 7/9, pp. 266–7; RC 8/17, pp. 52–3. For his attempts to recover land there see RC 7/5, p. 285; RC 7/10, pp. 185, 600–2.

130. PROI RC 8/14, p. 581 et seq.; RC 8/17, pp. 267–304 passim; RC 8/19, pp. 370–9 passim; RC 8/20, pp. 53–70 passim.

131. PROI RC 8/20, pp. 149, 153–4, 347–8.

132. Richardson & Sayles, *Admin. Ire.*, pp. 174, 176; *Rot. pat. Hib.*, pp. 16, no. 34, 18b, no. 143; *Cal. justic. rolls, Ire., 1305–7*, pp. 291–2; PROI RC 7/10, pp. 397, 519, 630; RC 7/11, pp. 102, 378, 380–1, 524, 563; RC 7/12, pp.185, 400–1; RC 7/13/4, pp. 71–2; RC 8/1, pp. 177–8, 202–16, 442–53, 857–65; RC 8/5, pp. 76–7; RC 8/15, pp. 5, 68–77; KB 2/11, pp. 2–3.

Kildare.[133] No more than names are the Martin le Reve who is commonly found as a Bench attorney between 1316 and 1336[134] and William of Woodworth who acted as the king's attorney from 1328 to 1334 but who had also previously acted for (and been rewarded by) the prior of the Hospitallers.[135]

V

Professional serjeants are also to be found at work in the court of the justiciar in Ireland. The surviving evidence, however, suggests that the court did not possess its own separate corps of serjeants. The same group of men appear to have practised indifferently in this court and in the Dublin Bench. In this feature the Irish legal profession again resembles its English counterpart. In England by 1300, if not before, the same group of serjeants seem to have acted both in the Bench and in king's bench. Combining practice in the two courts was, of course, quite easy when both were holding sessions in Dublin; but the justiciar's court often held its sessions elsewhere and we do not know how individual serjeants then decided which court to attend. There is a similar problem with the two courts in England. Professional serjeants may have enjoyed a qualified monopoly in the justiciar's court similar to that which they enjoyed in the Bench. On one occasion at least (in 1305) two of them (Henry of Beningbrough and William of Sully) were assigned by the court to the service of a litigant (the communities of the city of Drogheda) and it has already been suggested that this practice may be associated with such a monopoly.[136] It is possible that there were also professional attorneys practising in the court; but there seems to be no definite evidence to either prove or disprove this.

The king's serjeants acted for him in the eyre as well as in the Bench (and sometimes in other courts as well). In 1292–3 John of Bridgwater was paid for prosecuting and defending pleas and business on the king's behalf 'before the justices of the Bench, the

133. PROI RC 7/10, p. 318; RC 8/10, p. 299; RC 8/11, pp. 185–7.

134. See passim: PROI RC 8/11, pp. 202–16, 240–2, 442–53, 857–65; RC 8/14, p. 581 et seq.; RC 8/15, p. 200 et seq.; RC 8/17, pp. 267–304; RC 8/19, pp.168–78, 370–9; RC 8/20, pp. 53–70.

135. Richardson & Sayles, *Admin. Ire.*, p. 176; *Reg. Kilmainham*, pp. 2–3, 11–2; *Cal. justic. rolls, Ire., 1305–7*, p. 50; *Cal. justic. rolls, Ire., 1308–14*, p. 47; PROI RC 7/10, pp. 517, 631; RC 7/11, p. 337; RC 8/4, p. 7.

136. *Cal. justic. rolls, Ire., 1305–7*, p. 16.

justices in eyre and the barons of the exchequer' and in 1295–6 John de Neville was paid for acting as the king's serjeant for his pleas 'in all places in Ireland'.[137] William of Bardfield is known to have pleaded on the king's behalf in the 1301 eyres of counties Louth and Cork as well as in the Bench, the justiciar's court and the exchequer; Richard le Blund of Arklow in the 1301 eyre of Co. Louth as well as in the Bench, the justiciar's court and the exchequer.[138] Other evidence of serjeants' activity in the eyre is disappointingly sparse. We do hear of Robert of Bristol and William of Bardfield being adjudged one hundred shillings in the 1307 Tipperary eyre for services to John de Cogan in the previous eyre held by the same justices in Co. Meath.[139] We also know that both John Plunket and John of Staines were present at the 1322 Meath eyre, where they stood surety for the prior of Llanthony Secunda (and presumably also acted in a professional capacity as serjeants).[140] In England reports of cases heard in the eyres in this period show that the serjeants who practised in the eyre were largely (but not exclusively) drawn from those who practised in the Bench. The same was very probably also true in Ireland. There is no certain evidence of professional attorneys practising in the eyre in Ireland.

There were certainly professional lawyers practising in the lower courts of the Irish lordship as well. As early as 1272 William Picot was complaining of being unable to obtain a 'narrator' or 'consultor' (by which he clearly means a serjeant) for litigation in the court of the city of Dublin because of the influence of his opponent in the case, Richard of Exeter, a justice of the Bench.[141] This suggests that already by this date there may have been a small group of professional serjeants practising in the court whose

---

137. PRO E 372/139, m. 9; E 372/144, m. 28.

138. Bardfield: (i) in eyres: PROI RC 7/8, pp. 61, 215; (ii) in the Bench: RC 7/5, pp. 441–3; RC 7/6, pp. 15–6; RC 7/9, pp. 379–81, 441; RC 7/10, pp. 136, 602–3; RC 7/11, pp. 309–10, 353–5; RC 7/13/2, p. 1; RC 8/2, p. 168; (iii) in the justiciar's court: *Cal. justic. rolls, Ire., 1295–1303*, pp. 383–5, 445; *Cal. justic. rolls, Ire., 1305–7*, pp. 155, 162, 302–4, 305; (iv) in the exchequer: PROI RC 8/2, p. 136. Blund: (i) in the eyre: PROI RC 7/8, pp. 9, 13–4, 215 and PRO C 47/10/17, no. 2; (ii) in the Bench: PROI RC 7/5, p. 367; RC 7/7, pp. 216, 509; RC 7/8, pp. 98, 163; RC 7/9, p. 311; RC 7/10, p. 273; (iii) in the justiciar's court: *Cal. justic. rolls, Ire., 1295–1303*, p. 411; *Cal. justic. rolls, Ire., 1305–7*, pp. 10, 101–3; PROI KB 1/1, m. 48; (iv) in the exchequer: PROI RC 8/4, pp. 450–1; RC 8/9, pp. 591–2.

139. PROI RC 7/13/2, pp. 3–4, 9–10.

140. PRO C 260/43, no. 10.

141. PRO C 47/10/13, no. 8. (cited by Hand in *Eng. law in Ire.*, at p. 139).

services a litigant could normally expect to obtain. There is also a provision in the custumal of the city of Dublin, which seems to belong to this period, as to the penalty to be imposed when someone was 'disavowed' in litigation. The person disavowed is here specifically called 'un countour'.[142] It is not possible to be sure whether or not this is a reference to a professional serjeant rather than just 'one who makes a count for someone else'; but the former seems the more likely. In England we know that there were professional serjeants practising not just in the city courts in London but also in the courts of smaller towns such as Shrewsbury, King's Lynn and Oxford. It would be surprising if Dublin did not also have its own professional serjeants.

Reports of cases heard in the Warwickshire county court in the early fourteenth century indicate that there were then at least five or six professional serjeants practising in the court; and it is possible to show that there were also professional serjeants in a number of other English county courts. In Ireland it is only the fortuitous survival of a single piece of evidence which allows us to see that in 1306 there were already professional serjeants practising in at least one county court, that of Co. Louth.[143] A lessee had been distrained for arrears of the rent owed by his lessor to that lessor's feudal lord. He asked the lessor to take appropriate steps to deal with the matter. The lessor claimed that the rent had been paid and told the lessee to contest the justice of the distraint through an action of replevin in the county court. He would himself, he said, pay for the litigation and find a serjeant. However, when the case came on for hearing at the county court the lessor failed to provide a serjeant and the lessee was non-suited in his plea for lack of one. The reference is surely to a professional serjeant. If there were professional serjeants in the county court of Co. Louth by this date then it seems reasonable to assume that professionals were also by then active in other Irish county courts though not necessarily in all.

By 1300 there seems also to have been a group of professional serjeants practising in the court of the liberty of Kilkenny. In 1302 John son of William de Poer complained that when his father William had assigned a debt of £100 owed him by John to Master Thomas of Quantock, chancellor of Ireland, and Master Thomas had brought litigation in the court to secure payment of his debt John had been unable to get 'right, grace and favour' or even a

---

142. Above, note 5.

143. *Cal. justic. rolls, Ire., 1305–7*, pp. 182–3.

serjeant in the court because of the influence of his opponent.[144]
There were presumably professional serjeants by this date in the
other liberty courts of Ireland as well.

VI

In England the evidence for the existence of professional (or
perhaps more precisely proto-professional) lawyers goes back to
the early thirteenth century. Doris Mary Stenton noticed that
some fourteen men occurred on the plea-rolls of the king's courts
during the reign of King John with sufficient frequency as
attorneys and sureties to suggest that they may have been
professional lawyers; and we know that at least one of these men
(John Bucuinte) also on occasion acted as a serjeant. It is of
interest to note that at least two of the fourteen men (Roger
Huscarl and Richard Duket) also went on subsequently to serve
as justices in Ireland: thus the link between the English legal
profession and the Irish judiciary was one forged very early in the
history of both institutions.

During the following reign (that of Henry III) we first get clear
evidence of a distinct group of professional serjeants active in the
Westminster Bench and by the end of the reign it is clear that the
normal assumption is that litigants in the court will have professional serjeants speaking on their behalf. It is also during the latter
part of the same reign that we first begin to get evidence pointing
to the existence of professional lawyers in Ireland. The Record
Commission calendars show John of Athy, father of the later
Bench serjeant William of Athy, suing on behalf of the king in the
1260 eyre of Co. Cork and the 1261 eyre of Co. Dublin.[145] In the
early 1270s we find the same man acting as deputy seneschal
of the liberty of Kildare.[146] John is also to be found *c*.1258–64
witnessing a confirmation of a grant to the abbey of St Thomas in
Dublin in company with two royal justices (Wellesley and Exeter)
and *c*.1260–5 witnessing a quitclaim to the archbishop of Dublin in
company with the same two justices and the treasurer of Ireland.[147]

144. *Cal. justic. rolls, Ire., 1295–1303*, pp. 392–3 (and transcribed in full in PROI
      RC 7/9, pp. 514–8).

145. PROI RC 7/1, pp. 248, 260, 323, 327.

146. *P.R.I.rep.D.K.36*, p. 23.

147. *Register of the abbey of St Thomas, Dublin*, ed. J.T. Gilbert (Rolls Series,
      1889), pp. 52–3; *Alen's reg.*, p. 138.

There is no definite proof here that he was a professional lawyer; but the evidence is at least suggestive of such a conclusion. Clearer evidence is provided by a petition of Roger Oweyn dating from the 1270s.[148] In it Roger claimed that he had been appointed to act as serjeant for the king (then the lord Edward) at the time when Richard de la Rochelle was justiciar of Ireland and Fromund le Brun chancellor (between 1261 and 1266). Despite the promises which had been made to him, he said, he had received no payment for his services. If he had not been in the king's service, he went on to assert, he could have received large fees from the magnates of Ireland ('ubi dictus Rogerus magnum sallarium de magnatibus Hibernie potuit recepisse'). Roger is himself clearly a professional serjeant, though apparently a disappointed one.[149] What he has to say suggests that there were also other professional serjeants in practice in Ireland. It was presumably the large salaries which they had received from the Irish magnates which led Roger to talk of the large salaries which he could have received if he had not been in the king's service. And the most likely context for the lord Edward retaining a serjeant full-time to act on his behalf in the first place is a well-established practice of other litigants utilising the services of other professional serjeants for their litigation. This evidence suggests, therefore, that by the early 1260s at latest professional serjeants had become a normal feature of the Irish courts.

In England it is the reign of Edward I (1272–1307) which first brings much fuller evidence of the existence and activities of professional lawyers; and some of that evidence entitles us to begin describing them as members of a legal profession. The same period also brings much fuller evidence of the existence and activities of professional serjeants in Ireland. In addition to the serjeants retained by the king (Roger Oweyn and his successors Robert of St Edmund's and John fitzWilliam)[150] we also find during the 1280s a number of serjeants being paid by the earl of

---

148. PRO C 47/10/13, no. 6 (printed but with several errors and omissions in Richardson & Sayles, *Admin. Ire.*, p. 230).

149. For evidence of his activity on behalf of Edward in the 1269 and 1278 Dublin eyres see PROI RC 7/1, pp. 427, 473, 475, 480–1; RC 8/1, p. 31. For evidence that he was retained by at least one private client (the chapter of St Patrick's cathedral in Dublin) see *Crede Mihi: the most ancient register of the archbishop of Dublin before the reformation*, ed. J.T. Gilbert (Dublin, 1897), p. 113, no. cxxii.

150. Richardson & Sayles, *Admin. Ire.*, pp. 174–5. For evidence of annuities paid to Robert of St Edmund's by private clients see PROI RC 7/4, p. 53.

Norfolk for their services in the Irish courts: William of Weston, Eliis of Ibstone and David of Pembroke.[151] A note of material from the now lost Bench plea-roll of Trinity term 1282 shows the same William of Weston and an otherwise unknown Richard Basset being amerced half a mark for 'chattering and speaking foolishly' but being pardoned the half mark, apparently in return for providing breakfast for the clerks of the court.[152] There is a marginal annotation opposite the entry 'castigatio narratorum' ('punishment of serjeants'), and the entry clearly relates to some kind of unacceptable behaviour on the part of the two serjeants which the court subsequently forgave. The earl of Norfolk also made a single payment of sixty shillings to the English serjeant (and future chief justice of the English court of king's bench) Gilbert of Thornton during the same period. This was for his service in the earl's litigation with Philip of Stanton. Philip was claiming the manor of Old Ross but the litigation ended (in part, at least, thanks to Gilbert's assistance) with the earl retaining the manor.[153] Gilbert had been sent over to Ireland in the autumn of 1284 to act for the king in *quo warranto* proceedings in the Dublin Bench against Thomas fitzMaurice. These concerned the shrieval-ties of the counties of Waterford, Cork and Kerry and the lands of Decies and Desmond.[154] Gilbert's return to England in June 1285 (to resume his role as king's serjeant on one of the English eyre circuits) created a major problem in the Decies and Desmond proceedings. When the litigation started it had been envisaged that Gilbert would remain in Ireland until the plea was over. The justiciar had therefore given permission for 'all the good serjeants of Ireland' ('quasi omnes bonos narratores Hibernie') to act for Thomas. He had then retained them to act for him and thus all of them knew his strategy for the litigation ('qui sciunt totum consilium predicti Thome in hac parte'). When Gilbert left Ireland before the litigation ended it was no longer possible to engage any of them to act on the king's behalf in his place. The solution eventually adopted, perhaps the only solution possible in

151. PRO SC 6/1239, nos. 1–9. David of Pembroke was only paid once, and then for not acting against the earl in a particular case. The earl also paid the king's serjeant, John fitzWilliam, for his assistance during the same period.

152. RIA, MS. 12.D.12, p. 9.

153. PRO SC 6/1239, no. 4.

154. *Cal. pat. rolls, 1281–92*, pp. 134, 136; PRO C62/60, m. 2; *Cal. doc. Ire., 1252–84*, nos. 2310, 2319; PRO C 47/10/14, no. 22 (printed in *Anal Hib*, no. 1 (1930), 209–12).

the circumstances, was for the case to be transferred to England. This case suggests that as yet, in the mid-1280s, the number of expert professional serjeants in Ireland may have been quite small, no more than a handful of men. It also suggests, in the way that these professionals are described as 'serjeants of Ireland', that already as later these serjeants could probably be found acting for clients in any of the main Irish royal courts, the Dublin Bench, the justiciar's court and eyres.

We have already seen that there were probably professional attorneys in the Dublin Bench by 1290 but apparently in much smaller numbers than in the Westminster Bench.[155] It is of course possible that there were more professional attorneys than the two identified but the amount of business coming to the court suggests that there cannot have been many. The earl of Norfolk's Irish accounts of the 1280s record payments to attorneys, but none of them seem to be professional attorneys practising in the main Irish courts. Some are men sent over from England by the earl and paid expenses in crossing the channel and two pence a day while in Ireland.[156] Others seem to be officials of the administration of the earl's liberty of Carlow or their close relatives.[157] These arrangements suggest that there may not as yet have been many professional attorneys practising in the Irish courts whom the earl could engage on his behalf. The real development of professional attorneys in Ireland probably only came after 1290; even then they were probably always much less numerous than their counterparts in England.

VII

By 1300 there was a legal profession in Ireland whose members provided specialist legal assistance to those with litigation in the courts of the lordship of Ireland. That legal profession seems to have borne a close resemblance to the legal profession which had recently emerged in England. It too was split into two separate branches (serjeants and attorneys) and the members of those two branches appear to have performed much the same services for

155. Above, p. 45.

156. E.g. Richard Faucun and Ardern sent to Ireland for the Old Ross case in 1284: PRO SC 6/1239, no. 3.

157. E.g. Ralph Wade, probably a relative of Thomas Wade the treasurer of Carlow, and William Cadel, seneschal of Carlow, both paid for acting as attorneys in different cases in 1284–5: PRO SC 6/1239, no. 4.

their clients as their English counterparts. A sizable minority of the Irish serjeants of the late thirteenth and early fourteenth centuries themselves came from England; and there is evidence suggesting that others as well received part of their professional education in England (though there is also evidence pointing to the availability of some legal education in Ireland). The two legal professions were, however, distinct entities. There is no evidence of professional lawyers practising on a regular basis in both countries or of them transferring their practice from one country to the other; and the promotion of English serjeants to the Irish bench was a one-way phenomenon. There were, moreover, certain distinctive features of the Irish legal profession which are not paralleled in England: the courts' ability to require individual serjeants to act for clients who sought the court's assistance (presumably a by-product of the relatively small number of serjeants); the failure of the Irish serjeants to gain a monopoly over appointments to the higher judiciary; and (probably) the relatively small size of the 'lower branch' (attorneys) in proportion to the number of serjeants in Ireland. The Anglo-Irish legal profession in its early years bears a close resemblance to its English counterpart, but they are by no means identical twins; and for the historian the differences between them are perhaps at least as instructive as the resemblance.

APPENDIX

Irish serjeants, 1290–1350

This list contains the names of all persons who are specifically described in official records of the period as being serjeants. Each entry gives the earliest and latest dates at which they are to be found so described (though their careers as serjeants must in many cases have been much longer than those here given) and also the sources for this information.

Ashbourne, Roger of: serjeant, 1299–1307: PROI RC 7/6, p.11; *Cal. justic. rolls, Ire.*, *1305–7*, p.392.

Athy, William of: lately a serjeant, 1305: *Cal. justic. rolls, Ire., 1305–7*, p.35.

Bagod, Thomas: serjeant, 1318 (but only in the court of the justiciar): PROI KB 2/10, p.46.

Bardfield, William of: king's serjeant, 1297–1308: PRO E 372/144, m. 28d; PROI RC 7/13/2, p.1.

Barford, Edmund of: king's serjeant, 1347–60: Richardson & Sayles, *Admin. Ire.*, p.178.

Beningbrough, Henry of: serjeant, 1302–1308: *Cal. justic. rolls, Ire., 1305–7*, p. 406 (and PROI RC 7/9, p. 299); PROI RC 7/3/3, p. 130.

Blund, Master David le: serjeant, 1303–5: PROI RC 8/2, pp. 278–9; PROI RC 7/11, pp. 25–6.

Blund, Richard le, of Arklow: king's serjeant, 1297–1322: Richardson & Sayles, *Admin. Ire.*, pp. 174–6.

Bridgwater (Ponte), John of: king's serjeant, 1292–1300: PRO E372/ 139, m.9; *Cal. justic. rolls, Ire., 1295–1303*, pp. 238, 316–17.

Bristol, Robert of: serjeant, 1303–9: PROI RC 7/13/2, pp. 9–10 (though not specifically described as such); PROI RC 7/13/4, p. 56.

Brown, Hugh: king's serjeant, 1331–46: Richardson & Sayles, *Admin. Ire.*, p. 176.

Cardiff, John of: king's serjeant, 1327–30: Richardson & Sayles, *Admin. Ire.*, p. 177.

Cardiff, Nicholas of: serjeant, 1317 (apparently in the court of the justiciar): PROI RC 7/12, pp. 139–41.

Carmarthen, John of: serjeant, 1306: *Cal. justic. rolls, Ire., 1305–7*, pp. 321–3 (but only in the court of the justiciar).

Carrick, Philip of: serjeant, 1305: *Cal. justic. rolls, Ire., 1305–7*, pp. 67–70 (but only in the court of the justiciar).

Chaumflour, Nicholas de: serjeant, 1317 (apparently in the court of the justiciar): PROI RC 7/12, pp. 139–41.

Dallinghoo, Robert of: serjeant, 1299–1306: *Cal. justic. rolls, Ire., 1295–1303*, pp. 319–321: PROI RC 7/6, p. 11; PROI RC 7/11, pp. 426–7.

Dent, Thomas of: king's serjeant, 1331–4: Richardson & Sayles, *Admin. Ire.*, p. 177.

Edgfield, Nicholas of: serjeant, 1307: *Cal. justic. rolls, Ire., 1305–7*, p. 361 (but only in the court of the justiciar).

FitzRichard, Simon: serjeant, 1317: PROI RC 7/12, pp. 139–41; and king's serjeant, 1322–31: Richardson & Sayles, *Admin. Ire.*, p. 177.

Forester, Henry: serjeant, 1317 (apparently in the court of the justiciar): PROI RC 7/12, pp. 139–41.

Forester, Simon: serjeant, 1336: PROI RC 8/19, pp. 478–80.

Galeye, Adam de la: serjeant, 1333: PROI RC 8/17, pp. 328–9.

Gernoun, John: king's serjeant, 1327–30 and 1334–8: Richardson & Sayles, *Admin. Ire.*, pp. 176–7; and serjeant, 1343: *Account roll of Holy Trinity, Dublin*, pp. 45–6.

Gerveys, John: serjeant, 1317–8 (but only in the court of the justiciar): PROI KB 2/9, p. 22; PROI KB 2/10, p. 55.

Glen, Roger of: serjeant, late Edward I: *Cal. justic. rolls, Ire., 1308–14*, pp. 42–3.

Grantchester, John of: serjeant, 1312–8: PROI RC 8/6, pp. 406–7; PROI RC 7/12, p. 380.

Hanwood, Matthew of: king's serjeant, 1310–5: Richardson & Sayles, *Admin. Ire.*, p. 175; PROI RC 8/10, p. 546.

Horton, John of: serjeant, 1299: *Cal. justic. rolls, Ire., 1295–1303*, p. 267 (but only in the court of the justiciar).

Kinton, John of: serjeant, 1344: *Account roll of Holy Trinity, Dublin*, p.44.

Laffan: see Lessayn.

Lenfaunt, Robert: serjeant, 1313: PROI KB 1/1, m. 42 (but only in the court of the justiciar).

Lessayn, William: serjeant, 1318: PROI KB 2/10, p. 55 (but only in the court of the justiciar) and note that PROI KB 2/9, pp. 107 and 120 suggest that Lessayn may be a misreading for Laffan.

Locard, Richard: serjeant, 1305–8: *Cal. justic. rolls, Ire., 1305–7*, pp. 337–8; *Cal. justic. rolls, Ire., 1308–14*, p. 62 (but only in the court of the justiciar).

McCotyr, Reginald: serjeant, 1312–3: PROI KB 1/1, mm. 6, 37 (but only in the court of the justiciar).

Neville, John de: king's serjeant, 1293–6: PRO E 372/139, m. 9; PRO E 372/144, m. 28.

Petit, William: king's serjeant, 1334–48: Richardson & Sayles, *Admin. Ire.*, pp. 177, 179.

Plunket, John: serjeant, 1310–17: PROI RC 8/5, p. 251; PROI RC 7/12, pp. 139–41.

Ponte, John de: see Bridgwater.

Preston, Robert of: king's serjeant, 1348–58: Richardson & Sayles, *Admin. Ire.*, p. 179.

Reading, John of: serjeant, recently murdered in 1316: PROI KB 2/7, p. 63 (not associated with any particular court).

Snitterby, Nicholas of: serjeant, 1316; PROI RC 8/111, pp. 827–8.

Staines, John of: king's serjeant, 1319–27: Richardson & Sayles, *Admin. Ire.*, pp. 176–7.

Staines, Nicholas of: serjeant, 1312: PROI RC 8/6, pp. 443–4.

Sully, William of: serjeant, 1305: *Cal. justic. rolls, Ire., 1305–7*, p. 16 (but only in the court of the justiciar).

Sotton, Michael de: serjeant, 1291: PROI RC 7/3, pp. 169/70.

Stapenhill, William of: serjeant, 1344: *Account roll of Holy Trinity, Dublin*, p. 103.

Threekingham, Hugh of: serjeant, 1307: *Cal. justic. rolls, Ire., 1305–7*, p. 413 (but only in the court of the justiciar).

Vincent, Walter: serjeant, 1313: PROI KB 2/5, pp. 108, 109 (but only in the court of the justiciar).

3

Courtroom and Schoolroom: The Education of Lawyers in England Prior to 1400

IN A WELL-KNOWN passage in his *De Laudibus Legum Anglie* written in about 1470 Sir John Fortescue talks of the *studium pupplicum* in the suburb of London where English law is taught.[1] He does not use the term 'university' for this institution; indeed, the context is an attempt to explain why the common law of England is not studied in English universities although Roman and canon law are. 'University' was a word with a precise technical meaning. The *studium pupplicum* of which Fortescue was speaking was not an institution of higher learning recognized by the Church and not one which awarded its own degrees. Nor did its constituent parts have any formal organizational links with each other. What Fortescue was also concerned to show, however, was that in certain important respects this *studium pupplicum* was the equivalent of a university. Instruction was given in it on a regular basis to those wishing to master English law; and the 'degree' of serjeant at law obtained by those who had studied and taught there was, he asserted, the equivalent of a university doctorate.

This institution consisted, Fortescue wrote, of ten or more lesser inns known as inns of chancery ('hospicia cancellarie') where students learnt the first elements of their subject and four greater inns known as inns of court ('hospicia curie') to which they proceeded once they had mastered those basics. Fortescue is disappointingly vague on the details of the teaching of law in the inns in his day; but scholars have been able to reconstruct the main outlines of this from other contemporary sources. The core of the curriculum in the inns of chancery appears to have been the study of original writs, the writs obtained from the royal chancery to initiate civil litigation.[2] The teaching was probably intended to equip the young law student not just with a knowledge of the formulae of the more common standard writs but also with an understanding of the types of circumstance in which each was the appropriate way of seeking redress. It was also in the inns of chancery that the student began his acquaintance with the English system of oral pleading, learning the standard basic formulae for making counts (the formal statement of claim or complaint that had to be made at the beginning of all litigation) and for making defences to them.

The law student's education in the inns of court was intended to give him practice in extemporary oral argument as well as a detailed knowledge of English

---

[1] Sir John Fortescue, *De Laudibus Legum Anglie*, ed. S. B. Chrimes (Cambridge, 1942), pp. 113–20.

[2] *The Reports of Sir John Spelman*, ed. J. H. Baker (Selden Soc., xciii, xciv, 1977–8), ii, introduction, pp. 127–9; J. H. Baker, 'Learning exercises in the medieval inns of court and chancery' in his *The Legal Profession and the Common Law* (1986), at pp. 16–19 (I am indebted to Dr. Baker for allowing me to see this article before publication); A. W. B. Simpson, 'The source and function of the later year books', *Law Quart. Rev.*, lxxxvii (1971), 94–118, at 103–6.

law.[3] These ends were served through such learning exercises as 'putting the case', a regular daily argument after dinner between students about a point of law suggested by a senior member of the inn, and 'moots', mock trials where two of the most junior members of the inn were required to play the part of the serjeants making the formal count and defence and two less junior members argued over the one or more points of law raised by the pleadings. Students seem also to have been expected to be in regular attendance at the law courts at Westminster to listen to litigation there: indeed, Fortescue specifically mentions it as one of the advantages of the teaching of English law in a *studium pupplicum* close to Westminster that it allowed students to attend the courts and listen to the 'disputations' conducted there and the judgments given at their conclusion by men who were 'viros graves, senes, in legibus illis peritos et graduatos' (an implicit comparison is again being made here with the formal disputations conducted in the universities and attended by students).[4] One other important element in the education curriculum of the inns of court was the 'reading'. This was a combined lecture and seminar course given by a senior member of the inn three or four mornings a week for three or four weeks in each of the two 'learning vacations' (in Lent and preceding Michaelmas term). In his reading the lecturer expounded a particular piece of legislation clause by clause, using individual clauses as a springboard for a more general discussion and exploration of associated legal topics. The readings covered each of the main thirteenth-century statutes from Magna Carta to the statute of Westminster II in turn as part of a cycle which by the later fifteenth century took as long as ten or twelve years to complete.

Scholars seem to be in general agreement that the *studium pupplicum* as it existed and functioned in Fortescue's day was a fairly recent creation. The inns of chancery are generally held to have come into existence only in the latter part of the reign of Edward III when certain senior chancery clerks began to provide instruction for their juniors who resided in inns under their charge. Law students who wanted to learn about writs soon began to attend these inns as well and for a period they and the junior clerks received instruction side by side. The *Ordinaciones Cancellarie* of 1389 attempted to prevent this infiltration of the inns of chancery by law students; but they were unsuccessful. By around 1400 the chancery clerks were abandoning or had already abandoned the inns of chancery and they had become institutions for the training (and housing) of law students.[5]

A note in a manuscript of the Year Book for 12 Richard II to which Dr. John Baker has drawn attention gives the inns of court to which those who were newly created serjeants in 1388 belonged. This is the earliest clear evidence for the existence of a society of lawyers at Gray's Inn (from which two of the serjeants came); the earliest evidence also for separate inns of court in the Inner Temple

[3] *Reports of Spelman*, ii, introduction, pp. 131–5; Baker, 'Learning exercises', pp. 10–11, 19–22.
[4] Fortescue, p. 116.
[5] T.F. Tout, 'The household of chancery and its disintegration' in *Essays in History presented to Reginald Lane Poole*, ed. H. W. C. Davis (Oxford, 1927), at pp. 46–85, also reprinted in *Collected Papers of T. F. Tout* (3 vols., Manchester, 1932–4), ii. 143–71; E. W. Ives, *The Common Lawyers of Pre-Reformation England* (Cambridge, 1983), pp. 39–40. But for a somewhat different view see Baker, 'Learning exercises', p. 7.

(from which five of the serjeants came) and the Middle Temple (one of the serjeants came from this Inn).[6] Lawyers were, however, certainly living in the Temple prior to 1388. Over thirty years before one had been given a pardon for the death of a kitchen servant of the manciple of the New Temple; two chroniclers mention the damage done by the rebels to the lawyers living there and to their property in 1381; and in the prologue to the Canterbury Tales Chaucer writes of the manciple to a 'Temple' and makes clear that this 'Temple' is a group of lawyers living together, suggesting that one or more inns had been established in the New Temple for some time prior to the late thirteen-eighties.[7] The fourth inn of court, Lincoln's Inn, seems to have been founded after the other three inns of court. There are no references to it predating its own earliest internal records; and it seems likely that it came into existence not long before 1422.[8] The practice of communal living by law students and practising lawyers in inns may well, however, predate the existence of the four great inns of court. The earliest clear evidence for this seems to be in 1344 when we find Isabel widow of Robert de Clifford leasing or granting a messuage in the parish of St. Dunstan in the West to a group of apprentices of the Bench for a rent of ten pounds a year.[9]

Professor Thorne and, more recently, Dr. Ives have argued that the provision of legal education at the inns of court was a development of the fifteenth century.[10] The inns for lawyers which had existed in the London area in the fourteenth century were, Dr. Ives writes, 'in all probability, little more than group arrangements among lawyers from the provinces who needed accommodation in London during the law terms, and they lasted no longer than it suited those concerned'. Professor Thorne explains that it was 'easier, cheaper, and safer and more comfortable' for lawyers 'to band themselves together and rent a house, hire a cook and a manciple, engage a servant or two and be assured of bed and a reasonable dinner' than to have to live with friends and relations or find rooms individually elsewhere. The transformation of one of the inns, Lincoln's Inn, into an educational institution can, Ives and Thorne argue, be traced in the Black Books of the inn. When these started in 1422 there were already certain vacation residence requirements imposed on new entrants to the inn but they were solely concerned with ensuring the attendance of such new members at the inn's Christmas festivities. It was not until 1442 that all new entrants were required to attend the learning vacations, though these had by then clearly already been in existence for some time. Over the same two decades we can also see a process of experimentation in the

---

[6] J. H. Baker, 'The inns of court in 1388', *Law Quart. Rev.*, xcii (1976), 184–7 and reprinted in *The Legal Profession and the Common Law*, at pp. 3–6.

[7] R. F. Roxburgh, 'Lawyers in the New Temple', *Law Quart. Rev.*, lxxxviii (1972), 414–30.

[8] Baker, 'The inns of court in 1388', pp. 185–6. But see also R. F. Roxburgh, 'Lincoln's Inns of the 14th century', *Law Quart. Rev.*, xciv (1978), 363–82.

[9] *Calendar of Inquisitions Post Mortem*, viii, no. 531 (p. 385).

[10] S. E. Thorne, 'The early history of the inns of court with special reference to Gray's Inn', *Graya* 1 (1959), 79–96; *idem*, *Essays in English Legal History* (1985), at pp. 137–54; E. W. Ives, 'The common lawyers' in *Profession, Vocation and Culture in Later Medieval England: Essays Dedicated to the Memory of A. R. Myers*, ed. C. H. Clough (Liverpool, 1982), pp. 181–217, especialy pp. 199–208; Ives, *Common Lawyers of Pre-Reformation England*, pp. 39–43.

arrangements made to ensure the attendance of more senior members of the inn at these learning vacations to supervise and assist their juniors. The earliest surviving texts of readings at the inns of court belong to the third decade of the fifteenth century. These were short, elementary and anonymous and seem to show that readings were repeated with little alteration by successive readers. Only in the fourteen-sixties did readers begin to cover statutes in much more detail and with a greater degree of originality and the surviving manuscripts of readings begin to attach names to particular readings. 'It is hard', writes Dr. Ives, 'to avoid the conclusion that we are witnessing a new educational method in the process of evolution'.

The common law was already by 1300 a sophisticated and highly technical legal system; and by that date there had come into existence also an English legal profession. If the system for the training of common lawyers that we find in operation in Fortescue's day had been in existence for less than a century there is an obvious problem. How did the legal profession get its education before the inns of chancery and inns of court took up this function? Dr. Ives has suggested that training for lawyers prior to 1400 was simply 'a matter for the courts, where students had a place reserved for them ("the crib") and judicial comment was at least partly for their benefit'.[11] Professor Thorne is willing to go a little further than this. Plucknett had, he notes, drawn attention to some small tracts belonging to the twelve-sixties and seventies which were 'evidently used for teaching purposes'. They consisted of almost a hundred stock cases stated very briefly which were 'doubtless put by the instructor to his class year after year'. The tracts also gave their stock answers and a number of one-sentence rules of law (maxims) which the students had to commit to memory. He seems to envisage that these continued in use up to the late fourteenth century. More advanced students, he agrees, gained their education from listening to litigation in court.[12]

There can be little doubt that attendance at the courts, and more particularly at the Bench (the main royal court for the hearing of civil litigation), did form an important part of the education of the common lawyer from at least the later thirteenth century onwards. The earliest references to a student of the common law in official records seems to be one of 1287 to a man from Ireland who was staying at Westminster in order to study in the Bench; and the semi-official name given to law students from the late thirteenth century onwards, a name first encountered in official records in 1289 (when two such students were indicted for a robbery committed at Boston fair), was 'apprentice of the Bench', rather than 'apprentice of the common law'.[13] The name alone suggests that these students were present in court with some degree of official toleration, even encouragement; and we may find further evidence of such an attitude in a provision in the abortive scheme of

---

[11] Ives, *Common Lawyers of Pre-Reformation England*, p. 39.

[12] Thorne, 'Early history of the inns of court', p. 88. The 'tracts' referred to here are the various different versions of *Casus Placitorum* which are further discussed below.

[13] *Calendar of Patent Rolls 1281–92*, p. 269 (I wish to thank Dr. David Higgins for drawing my attention to this entry); Public Record Office, JUST 1/1286, m. 15.

1292 to restrict practice as a professional attorney in the Bench to county quotas of attorneys which stipulated that those selected by the justices to make up these quotas were to be drawn 'de melioribus et legalioribus et libentius addiscentibus'. That it was specifically the apprentices that the king and his council had in mind is confirmed by the fact that the relevant entry on the parliament roll refers to itself as being concerned with apprentices as well as attorneys. The intention was probably to ensure that room be found in the county quotas for those apprentices who needed to support themselves by acting as attorneys.[14] Official encouragement certainly also took the form of the provision of special accommodation in the court for the apprentices (the 'crib') and of helpful comment for the apprentices from the justices. The earliest evidence for the latter that this author has seen comes from 1302 when a year-book report specifically notes the chief justice of the Bench, Ralph de Hengham, at the end of a case explaining a legal point raised by the case for the benefit of the apprentices, and the same thing seems also to have been done on occasion by his successors.[15]

There is, however, also a considerable body of evidence for the organized education of common lawyers outside the courtroom as well long before 1400. Take first the evidence of a 'treatise' to be found in a manuscript in the British Library, Lansdowne MS. 467.[16] This contains a good basic introduction to common law litigation. It starts with a general analysis of the different kinds of civil proceedings, and then looks in turn at each of the more common of these, explaining the kinds of claim or complaint that could be made through them, giving the wording of the appropriate original writ (translated into French, the language of the treatise) and then going on to reproduce a specimen count (one of the limited number of forms of words which could be used in a claim or complaint initiated by the writ) and a specimen defence to this particular count. The first action to be dealt with is the writ of right for land; and the treatise uses this as a suitable place to discuss matters relevant to other types of action also such as essoins (excuses for non-attendance given by litigants) and exceptions. One striking feature of the work is the use of *casus*: stories illustrating factual situations where the use of particular writs is appropriate, and what seems to be reports of actual cases showing particular types of action being used by litigants. It seems clear from a whole series of asides and connective passages that what we are dealing with here is a student's report of a series of lectures given by a teacher. Thus we find the teacher telling the class that the count in the action of *nuper obiit* claimed that the demandant's ancestor was seised of the land being claimed as of fee, right and demesne and this for two reasons that he was unable now to explain (evidently the teacher was running out of time or had temporarily forgotten what they were);[17] and at the end of the section on essoins we find him saying that he could say much more on the subject but had

---

[14] *Rotuli Parliamentorum*, i. 84 (no. 22).

[15] British Library, Stowe MS. 386 fos. 125v–126; *Year Books 5 Edward II*, ed. W. C. Bolland (Selden Soc., xxxi, 1915), p. 90; *Year Books 10 Edward II*, ed. M. D. Legge and W. S. Holdsworth (Selden Soc., lii, 1934), p. 96; *The Eyre of Northamptonshire, 1329–30*, ed. D. W. Sutherland (Selden Soc., xcvii, xcviii, 1983–4), i. 478.

[16] Brit. Libr., Lansdowne MS. 467 fos. 143–58.

[17] *Ibid*. fo. 143.

run out of time.[18] At the beginning of that part of the treatise which deals with writs of entry we can again hear him speaking to the class, explaining that he was now about to tell them about writs of entry and then telling them about the first kind of writ of entry and reassuring them that it was the easiest of the various kinds.[19] We also seem to see the teacher forgetting to give the form of the writ of right of wardship and the count and defence on this writ at the proper place in his lectures, later remembering this and interrupting the flow of his lecture to repair the omission.[20] The teacher obviously made use of visual aids in his teaching. The student not only took them down but also recorded what the teacher had said to the class about them.[21] In another passage we see the interruption or involvement of an eager student. The teacher has set up a very complicated factual situation and invited the class to consider what action other than the writ of right can be used by the two claimants to recover their land, and begins to explain the problem to the class. A student interrupts with a possible solution. The teacher then explains why this solution would not work.[22] Internal evidence allows the dating of these lectures. They must have been given some time between June 1276 and August 1278.[23]

Fortunately there also survive two apparently almost identical manuscripts recording lectures given by the same teacher for a few years later.[24] This student (or these students) wrote down much less of the connective material that shows that the 'treatise' started life as the lectures of a teacher but the similarities not just in general outline but also in detailed treatment of various topics indicate that these manuscripts also derive from lectures given by the same teacher.[25] What is interesting is that this second version of the lectures shows definite signs of revision, for they incorporate reports of cases from eyres of the Northern eyre circuit heard during 1278 and 1279; and the section on writs of entry has been revised to take account of the changes made by the statute of Gloucester in 1278.[26] This was clearly a competent teacher and to all appearances a conscientious one.

The way in which the second student wrote up what clearly started out as lecture notes, transforming them in the process into something difficult to distinguish from a 'treatise', an instructional work written only in order to be read, suggests that various other works which now look like treatises may have started life as lectures.

---

[18] Brit. Libr., Lansdowne MS. 467 fo. 145v.

[19] *Ibid*. fo. 151.

[20] The writ should have appeared on fo. 154 of the manuscript with the lesson on wardship. Instead it is given on fo. 154v between the material on debt and replevin.

[21] Brit. Libr., Lansdowne MS. 467 fos. 156, 158, 158v.

[22] *Ibid*. fo. 148v.

[23] The date limitations are consistently as altered by c.39 of the statute of Westminster I of 1275. This chapter did not come into operation until June 1276. There is no reference to any of the changes made by the statute of Gloucester of 1278.

[24] Harvard Law School, MSS. 24 and 33. Extracts from these MSS. are printed in *Brevia Placitata*, ed. G. J. Turner and T. F. T. Plucknett (Selden Soc., lxvi, 1951), at pp. 183–216.

[25] Both use recognizably the same story for the *casus* in the writ of right section; both give in the same order the possible reasons for challenging an essoin; both use the same *casus* for the writ of intrusion; both use the same 'marvellous' replevin *casus* though do not give it the same outcome.

[26] *Brevia Placitata*, pp. 196, 198, 210–12, 212–14.

Of particular importance in the present context is *Brevia Placitata*. Like the lectures just mentioned the core of this work was a general survey of the types of action in most common use in the royal courts: giving for each a French translation of the writ used to initiate the action and a specimen count and defence, though without any general guidance as to the circumstances where the use of the writ was appropriate. Nor is there any direct equivalent either to the *casus* which are used to introduce (and make palatable?) the teacher's other material on each of the forms of action, though something of the same function seems to be performed by the dialogue found in greater or lesser length in the various different manuscripts, continuing the court scenes set by the initial count and defence, sometimes in very vivid dialogue.[27] If it is right to see *Brevia Placitata* as in origin the product of lectures—and there is also some internal evidence in the work to support such a hypothesis[28]—then we can take the tradition of teaching a basic course on common law remedies back to at least 1260.[29]

Casus Placitorum also needs to be fitted into our picture of basic legal education in the third quarter of the thirteenth century.[30] This is a collection of notes arranged in no obviously discernible order; indeed, the notes are arranged in a different order in each of the twenty or so manuscripts that contain them. To add to the confusion, although there is a common core to the different collections they also vary greatly in length.[31] High claims have been made for this work. Its editor (W. H. Dunham junior) suggested that it represented 'a text-book made for the learner by a teacher' and so 'enable[d] one to find out what law the lawyer learned in the last half of the thirteenth century and to some extent how he learned it'.[32] Plucknett agreed that *Casus Placitorum* '. . . positively reeks of chalk and duster and ink. There is no other work on English law which gives us so strong an impression of being in a medieval class-room'; and he believed that the common ancestor of all the different collections was probably not a written text but 'the lessons of some anonymous teacher'.[33] Many of the notes in these collections are probably ultimately derived from the teaching of one, or possibly a number, of teachers at work in the twelve-fifties or early sixties, but while it may possibly be true that an earlier generation of teachers than our teacher of the twelve-seventies and the man or men responsible for *Brevia Placitata* gave lessons that followed no discernible pattern of arrangement and took the form of a series of unconnected paragraphs strung together, this seems unlikely. It seems more probable that what we have in the notes in *Casus Placitorum*

---

[27] For examples see *Brevia Placitata*, pp. 7–8 (cf. 48–9, 159–60), 9–10 (cf. 52, 162), 19–20 (cf. 64–5, 147–8, 172–3).

[28] See, for example, the warning of the serjeant about the count in the writ of right at pp. 4, 46, 128, 158; and the use of the instructional second person plural in the note on the count for the writ of dower *unde nichil habet* at pp. 5, 46, 77.

[29] *Brevia Placitata*, pp. xviii–xix.

[30] *Casus Placitorum and Reports of Cases in the King's Courts, 1272–8*, ed. W. H. Dunham, jr. (Selden Soc., lxix, 1952), pp. 1–44.

[31] The shortest has 56 items; the longest has 222, though there are also some duplicates contained in this. Dunham thought that the common matter comprised from two-thirds to three-quarters of each manuscript (*Casus Placitorum*, pp. xxviii–xxix).

[32] *Casus Placitorum*, p. xi.

[33] T. F. T. Plucknett, *Early English Legal Literature* (Cambridge, 1958), pp. 90, 91.

are no more than extracts from lectures taken out of their original context; perhaps only those parts of lectures where the teachers departed from the standard format of the common law remedies course of translated writ, count and defence to say something more, something thought worth recording in itself, which then circulated separately from the record of their common-form teaching (*Brevia Placitata* or its immediate forerunners).[34] Such a hypothesis would also explain why there is comparatively little here about the making of counts. This was something which was the subject of the unrecorded common form instruction. *Casus Placitorum* may well be derived from teaching in the class-room, but it is probably positively misleading as to the nature and quality of the education available there.

There is no evidence that our anonymous teacher of the twelve-seventies had any direct successors giving a similarly comprehensive beginner's course in common law remedies; but at least two different treatises offering a basic introduction to the most common types of remedy were composed in the twelve-eighties and at least one of these almost certainly does go back to a teacher's spoken lectures. *Modus Componendi Brevia* was composed in Latin *circa* 1285.[35] It provides a brief analysis of the various kinds of action about title to land and advowsons and explains the circumstances in which they were appropriate; discusses the uses of the actions of replevin, *ne vexes* and customs and services and gives a short account of the various different remedies available in the case of disputes over pasture rights. It concludes with a brief introduction to the various different types of exception. What the treatise does not give is either the writs themselves or the counts and defences appropriate to such writs. It purports to be the work of a senior chancery clerk writing for the instruction of his junior colleagues.[36] It may indeed be the work of such a clerk but it certainly reads as though it was composed with the needs of the law student as well as the young chancery clerk in mind. It is normally found in manuscripts in the company of other legal treatises; and it must be significant that it makes a specific cross-reference in its concluding passage to the more detailed treatment of exceptions contained in a separate treatise on this subject.[37] Exceptions were a matter of some interest and importance to the law student but of little relevance to the chancery clerk. All surviving manuscripts of the treatise seem to descend from a version prepared for circulation in written form, though it is possible that behind this stood originally some kind of spoken text. The second treatise, *Natura Brevium*, is in French and much more obviously derives directly from spoken lectures.[38] It was composed a little later, but not long after 1285, and

---

[34] Most manuscripts of *Brevia Placitata* do include some additional didactic material. Manuscripts C and E include large amounts of such material and it seems to be interchangeable with that found in *Casus Placitorum*.

[35] *Modus Componendi Brevia* was edited by G. E. Woodbine in *Four 13th Century Law Tracts* (New Haven, Conn., 1910), at pp. 143–62.

[36] See, for example, the opening words of the treatise (at p. 143 of the printed text); and the passage introducing the section on exceptions (at p. 161).

[37] *Four 13th Century Law Tracts*, p. 162.

[38] Manuscripts containing this treatise include Harvard Law Library, MS. 162 (at fos. 156v–168); Cambridge University Library, MS. Hh.3.11 (at fos. 149–53); Brit. Libr., Additional MS. 22708 (at fos. 39v–45v), Harley MSS. 673 (at fos. 117–28) and 5213 (at fos. 184v–194v).

took the form of a general introduction to the functions of the most common types of writ and to the mesne process appropriate to each. Again it does not reproduce the writs themselves (even in translation) or the appropriate counts and defences. Its treatment of the basic common law remedies is much more comprehensive and, in addition, much more useful than that contained in the *Modus Componendi Brevia*.

The *Register of Writs* also needs to be fitted into the early history of legal education. The late Derek Hall, in his introduction to the Selden Society volume of *Early Registers of Writs* of which he was joint editor, noted that one of the obvious uses to which registers of writs might be put was that the practising lawyer

might, as a beginner, use the Register with other books to learn his law; *Glanvill*, the statutes, the smaller tracts of the late thirteenth and early fourteenth centuries, and *Novae Narrationes* are often bound up with Registers, and this corpus of literature would provide the elements of instruction.[39]

He seems to have envisaged a process of transmission for the register that was entirely written, and to have seen registers as forming one element in a process of individual self-education through reading. What this article would like, however, to suggest is that by 1300 registers may well normally have been transmitted orally and in the context of an organized educational course run by senior chancery clerks which was geared to the needs not just of junior clerks but also of others who wanted to gain a knowledge of original writs as a first step in acquiring a more general expertise in English law, the same two groups for whom the *Modus Componendi Brevia* seems to have been composed.

Take the early fourteenth-century register of writs in the British Library manuscript, Harley MS. 408.[40] It was the practice in the writ of right to mention the service by which the demandant claimed to hold the land he was seeking. In the section of this register covering the writ of right various possible types of service that can be specified at this point in the writ are mentioned and then it simply says 'hec dicta sufficiunt causa exempli'.[41] These words sound like the spoken words of an instructor. Such an instructor is also to be heard in a number of connective passages in the same register. In the passage preceding the section on prohibitions, for example, we read:

Sequitur modus prohibicionum tam illarum que sunt de cursu quam aliarum que formantur in suis casibus que quidem multipliciter habent fieri eo quod omnia placita regni nostri spectant ad dignitatem domini regis exceptis placitis de testamento vel matrimonio et de decimis que quartam partem ecclesie non attingunt (si vero agatur in curia christianitatis inter duas personas ecclesiasticas de decimis unius ecclesie que quartam partem ejusdem ecclesie attingunt tunc est locus prohibicionis de indicavit). Primo quidem dicendum est de prohibicione de advocacione ecclesie medietatis, tercie partis, vel quarte partis ecclesie et eodem modo de advocacione; deinde de forma indicavit de advocacione ecclesie vel capelle; et de prohibicione de layco [feodo] et de catallis et de decimis[42] que non sunt de testamento vel matrimonio, unde due sunt forme, una scilicet quam omnes

---

[39] *Early Registers of Writs*, ed. E. de Haas and G. D. G. Hall (Selden Soc., lxxxvii, 1970), p. cxxv.
[40] Brit. Libr., Harley MS. 408 fos. 67–137.
[41] *Ibid*. fo. 69.
[42] Recte: *debitis*.

volentes possunt impetrare et altera in nomine regis et non nomine alterius ut privilegium et dignitas domini regis non derogetur et ne clerici videantur convalescere[43] mittendum est sub nomine domini regis judici ne procedat et parti ne sequatur. Item de prohibicionibus formatis in suis casibus cum attachiamentis contingentibus ad singulas prohibiciones. Sed primo de advocacione ecclesie prohibicione.[44]

This kind of detailed sketching out of the territory to be covered sounds characteristic of a lecturer explaining what is to come next and some of the basic ground-rules involved, not the kind of thing someone adding connective material to a written text would produce. Half-way though the section on writs of novel disseisin we find another connective passage. Again it sounds like an instructor talking:

Dicendum est ucusque de formulis brevium nove disseisine de tenementis quot modis ea fieri contingit; nunc dicendum est de disseisina de accidentibus ad tenementa. Primo scilicet de hiis de quibus assise fiunt et postea de aliis que coram vicecomitibus comitatuum placitantur sine assisa et terminantur et vocantur parva brevia de disseisina et alia que placitantur cum assisa vocantur magna brevia de disseisina.[45]

These connective passages could simply have been added to the written text of the register at appropriate points but they sound like someone speaking and giving instruction, not like someone writing for a reader. Similar connecting passages are found in most later registers and generally in much the same words.

That the teaching which accompanied the dictation of the formulae of writs was intended to be of use not just to young would-be chancery clerks but also to apprentice lawyers is clear from the context of some of the rules and notes which accompany the writs and record that teaching. We may perhaps disregard some of the advice found in registers as early as the beginning of Edward I's reign as given in an excess of zeal or informativeness to clerks who were going to be meeting those who came to chancery to purchase writs,[46] but the amount and content of such notes in registers from the end of Edward I's reign onwards leaves little room for doubt that this teaching was consciously framed with the beginning lawyer as well as the future chancery clerk in mind. Let us take for example again the register in Harley MS. 408. In this register the chancery writ notifying the justices of the Bench of the appointment by a litigant of two attorneys to represent him in litigation provides the excuse for a long excursus on the powers and responsibilities of such attorneys once appointed, a matter of little interest to the chancery clerk but of major importance to the would-be lawyer.[47] Elsewhere in the register accompanying the formulae of writs of darrein presentment we find the following note:

Nota breve de ultima presentacione et breve de utrum in placitando sequentur naturam brevis mortis antecessoris excepta prescriptione temporis: quia in istis duobus brevibus,

---

[43] Followed by a blank in the manuscript.

[44] Brit. Libr., Harley MS. 408 fo. 80v.

[45] *Ibid*. fo. 120.

[46] See, for example, the passage on the *pone de nativis* in a register of the beginning of Edward I's reign, Brit. Libr., Harley MS. 323 fos. 69–87v (at fo. 77v).

[47] Brit. Libr., Harley MS. 408 fo. 75v.

videlicet de utrum et ultima presentacione nulla est presccripcio: brevi mortis antecessoris manifeste tamen continetur. Nec obstat similiter si papa vel delegati aud loci diocesanus per lapsum temporis aud per quamcunque necgligenciam patroni ecclesiam contulit quin non obstante hujusmodi collacione patronus recuperabit presentacionem suam per assisam vel ultime presentacionis, quia per collaciones non sunt patroni in tali casu exclusi nec sicut advocati presentaverint et sic quia non patroni sic labitur cum tempore potestas qua lapsa non nocet hujusmodi collacio in dominico . . .[48]

This is clearly material intended for the instruction of lawyers not chancery clerks.

In another British Library register, this time from near the end of the reign of Edward II, Cotton MS. Titus D. xxiii, we find the following note on the action of naifty:

En le brief de nativis il covient qe le seignur meigne prove du saunk ove lui de qui il est seisi; e si il ne soit seisi de nul de saunk il ne dereignera rien si le villein nad conu en court qe port record lui estre son vilein. Et si deux parceners porterent bref de neifte e lun soit nonsuy le bref irra tut a la terre in favore libertatis.[49]

Again this is clearly instructional material intended for lawyers. In the same register we also find the following note:

Si un homme soit oblige a un homme e sa femme en une dette e le baron devie la femme serra soule respondue saunz les executours le baroun e ceo fust agarde en leire de Kent e ceo est pur ceo qe lei suppose qe la femme feust cause del obligacion; mes sil soit oblige a deux autres e lun devie laccion demoert en commune a ses executors e lautre.[50]

Once again obviously a note for the future lawyer. These are only a selection of notes from two registers, but they are not unrepresentative of the normal run of registers of writs of this period. It appears—and the subject needs much fuller investigation—that later registers indicate that subsequent teachers did not discard the notes added by their predecessors but did continue to add new notes of their own. The end result, as we can see it in the printed *Register of Original Writs*, was to produce something that in some ways resembles the glossed texts of the learned law; with the authoritative original text of writs surrounded by different layers of rules and notes of various dates.

If this is a correct reading of the evidence of the registers, the pre-history of the inns of chancery goes back to at least 1300. By 1300 there was already formal teaching probably by more senior chancery clerks which transmitted the register of writs to new generations of chancery clerks, but also allowed it to be copied down by young lawyers and the presence of the young lawyers was beginning to have a marked effect on the content of the rules and notes which accompanied the formulae of the writs. There may well not have been as yet separate inns where senior chancery clerks lodged and presided over their juniors and educated them, but the teaching tradition later represented by the inns of chancery had, it seems, already been established.

---

[48] Brit. Libr., Harley MS. 408 fo. 77r–v.
[49] *Ibid*., Cotton MS. Titus D. xxiii fo. 50v.
[50] *Ibid*. fo. 78r–v.

There is also evidence that suggests that by about 1300 there was some provision for education in the common law of a more advanced nature. Take first the early year-book reports, unofficial accounts in French of what was said and done in the courts, principally in the Bench at Westminster. G. J. Turner argued long ago that the year-book reports were compiled 'for the instruction of those who were studying law and legal procedure'.[51] This seems unlikely; it seems much more probable that these reports were compiled initially by the reporters for their own information. But there was some evidence to support Turner's argument. Many year-book reports certainly were used for instructional purposes, if not originally compiled with such purposes in mind.[52]

One indication of this is the fact that in many reports there is an explanation of the factual situation underlying the dispute either at the beginning or at some other relevant point in the report. This was certainly not the work of a listener simply taking down what he had heard in court. Information of this kind was the one thing which did not emerge clearly in most cases; when it did it would normally be only at a later stage in the proceedings when the jury gave its verdict, a stage at which the reporters were normally absent. Editorial matter of this kind has to be the work of someone who felt it necessary or desirable to supplement the information to be gleaned from what was said in court in order to explain what happened there and why the pleading took the form it did: and this looks like the work of a teacher trying to explain matters to his class. More conclusive, perhaps, is the use of a report to make some specific point not made by counsel or judge in the course of the litigation being reported. Take, for example, a report of a replevin case of 1296 where the defendant's counsel has avowed a distraint made to enforce the attendance at a seignorial court of an alleged debtor, and the report goes on to say:

> Et sciendum qe si la partie qe demande la dette die qil fu tenuz a luy par divers contracts qil covent dire en le avowement qe par chescon contract fist il un attachement e qe la partie demandant trova plegges a chescon attachement; e issint fit il ceste avowerie.[53]

Also characteristic of the teacher's technique is the gathering together at the end of a report of all the various points which can be gleaned from it. At the end of a case of 1298, for example, the report goes on to say that 'En ceo play plussors choses pount estre notez' and then to give seven of them.[54]

Such features as these appear commonly but not invariably in reports of cases from the twelve-nineties onwards, and to all appearances the manuscripts which contain them belong themselves to a not much later date. They seem, then, to indicate that already by the early fourteenth century reports of cases were being used in the teaching of law.

It is fairly certain that it was the apprentices of the king's court who were being taught; what is less clear is just who was doing the teaching. There are some possible indications to be found in the series of notes interspersed among year-book reports

---

[51] *Year Books 4 Edward II*, ed. G. J. Turner (Selden Soc., xlii, 1936), pp. xl–xli.
[52] cf. *Year Books 12 Edward II*, ed. J. P. Collas and T. F. T. Plucknett (Selden Soc., lxx, 1953), p. lxv.
[53] Brit. Libr., Add. MS. 5925 fo. 35v.
[54] *Ibid*. fo. 40v.

of cases in two closely related manuscripts now in the British Library, Harley MS. 25 and Additional MS. 35116.[55] These notes show a law student early in the reign of Edward II recording information of legal interest given to him,[56] following up particular points which have puzzled him when he has been listening to litigation in the Bench[57] and seeking out opinions on various points of difficulty in the law such as the availability of a particular kind of exception in the assize of mort d'ancestor[58] or whether a lessee can carry off a crop sown during his lease after the lease has expired.[59] Sometimes the note simply gives us the answer he receives but attaches no names to it[60] or despairingly records that he had never been able to find two serjeants of the same opinion on the matter.[61] More commonly the note-taker attributes the opinions and explanations he has received to particular, named individuals. Those who assisted him with advice and information include a number of men who were clearly already in practice as serjeants in the Bench when their opinions were recorded, men such as Edmund of Pashley and John le Claver (who had both become serjeants before the end of Edward I's reign),[62] several others who became serjeants early in the reign of Edward II but who may still have been senior apprentices when their views were being recorded, such as John of Deanham and his brother William, William of Midgley, John of Ingham and John of York (all of whom became serjeants in 1309) and Peter of Wallingford (who became a serjeant in 1311),[63] others who were certainly only senior apprentices when their opinions were recorded but who later became serjeants, such as Richard of Aldbrough (who became a serjeant in 1313) and John of Shardlow (who became a serjeant only in 1318)[64] and at least one man who was probably an apprentice but who never did become a serjeant, John of Lancaster.[65] If we are looking for the kind of men who taught the more junior apprentices through the year-book reports this seems a very promising group: men who were sufficiently senior to be capable of grasping the often complex points raised in litigation; men who had themselves a direct interest in recording the cases for their own information but who were not yet themselves in practice as serjeants or who had only recently become serjeants and who there-fore had the time as well as the ability to explain the cases to their more junior

[55] Brit. Libr., Add. MS. 35116 seems to be a rearranged fair copy of Harley MS. 25 and of no independent value other than for those sections of Harley 25 that are now lost. In subsequent footnotes Harley 25 is referred to as H; Add. MS. 35116 as A. For discussion of the notes in A (in which some of them are printed) see *Year Books 3 Edward II*, ed. F. W. Maitland (Selden Soc., xx, 1905), pp. xxi–xxv; *Year Books 4 Edward II*, pp. xxxv–xxxix; *Year Books 6 Edward II*, ed. P. Vinogradoff and L. Ehrlich (Selden Soc., xxxviii, 1921), pp. xiii–xiv.

[56] See, for example, *Year Books 3 Edward II*, p. xxiv.

[57] See, for example, H fo. 26v (= A fo. 101).

[58] *Year Books 3 Edward II*, p. xxiv.

[59] H fo. 187 (= A fo. 244).

[60] See, for example, H fo. 185v (= A fo. 142).

[61] *Year Books 3 Edward II*, p. xxiii.

[62] H fo. 105v (= A fo. 142); H fo. 12v (= A fo. 156v).

[63] For opinions of both John and William of Deanham, for example, see H fo. 12v (= A fo. 156v).

[64] For opinions of Richard of Aldbrough see, for example, A fo. 57v and H fo. 48v (= A fo. 92). For an opinion of John of Shardlow see H fo. 187 (= A fo. 244).

[65] A fo. 57v; H fo. 12v (= A fo. 156v).

colleagues. Our law student may well have asked his questions of these men and expected and got an answer because they were his teachers.

At least one of the questions asked by the compiler of Harley MS. 25 revealed a real disagreement among the more senior lawyers to whom it was addressed[66] and another seems to have sparked off a lively discussion between them.[67] The compiler of Harley MS. 25 also records a number of other arguments between senior lawyers which do not seem to be taking place in the context of a court case and which may perhaps have been stimulated by the questions of our compiler or one of his fellow-students.[68] These reported arguments are probably to be distinguished from an apparently closely related form, the *questio* or *questio disputata*. Some twenty of these are to be found in as many as six different early fourteenth-century manuscripts.[69] They generally conform to a single basic format: an initial statement of facts (sometimes labelled a *casus* or *cas*) followed by a question of law arising out of those facts, followed by alternate paragraphs of arguments for two contrary viewpoints on this question of law prefaced by such introductory phrases as 'videtur quod sic' or 'dicitur quod sic' and 'dicitur quod non' or 'dicitur aliter' or the like. In a minority of *questiones*, however, we are given only one side of the argument.[70] Such *questiones* resemble year-book reports of real litigation in some respects but can be distinguished from them in that they never give names to the 'parties' involved (other than A and B); give no names to the places concerned and no other circumstantial details; are generally concerned with a single question of law and never cover more than three closely related points (in the year-book reports cases almost always raise a number of unrelated points); and never tell us of a presiding judge's opinion expressed during the course of the argument or of his final judgment on the disputed point (always of interest to the reporter in real cases). In the minority of *questiones* where we seem to be getting only one side of the argument what we may be hearing is the voice of a teacher, perhaps again one of our year-book report teachers,[71] but in a majority we seem to be hearing a real argument between two or more people and it would seem both from the artificial nature of the disputation and from the way it is reported that we must be dealing with some sort of academic learning exercise.

Three of the *questiones* are concerned with the interpretation of one particular statute, the statute of Westminster II, cap.1 (de Donis).[72] This suggests a possible

---

[66] H fo. 187 (= A fo. 244).

[67] *Year Books 3 Edward II*, p. xxv.

[68] See, for example, A fos. 62v–63; *Year Books 3 Edward II*, p. xxii.

[69] Counting H and A as a single manuscript for this purpose. The manuscripts are Brit. Libr., Add. MS. 31826 (at fos. 119v, 188v, 226v, 227, 318v), A (at fo. 49), H (at fos. 70v–71 (= A fo. 104r–v) and fo. 146v (= A fo. 171)), Harley MS. 408 (at fos. 176v–177), Stowe MS. 386 (at fos. 118v, 147v); and Lincoln's Inn, Hale MS. 188 (at fo. 49r–v) and Misc. MS. 87 (at fo. 30). The largest number in any one manuscript is the 12 of Hale MS. 188 fo. 49r–v.

[70] Brit. Libr., Add. MS. 31826 fos. 226, 227; Lincoln's Inn, Misc. MS. 87 fo. 30 and Hale MS. 188 fo. 49(11) (two reports of same *questio*); Lincoln's Inn, Hale MS 188 fo. 49(3); A fo. 49.

[71] The reported *questio* found in Lincoln's Inn, MSS. Misc. MS. 87 fo. 30 and Hale MS. 188 fo. 49(11), for example, seems very close in form to some parts of the teaching of our teacher of the 1270s.

[72] Brit. Libr., Add. MS. 31826 fo. 119v; Lincoln's Inn, Hale MS. 188 fo. 49v(12); H fos. 70v–71 (= A fo. 104r–v).

connection between these *questiones* and the *Questiones Compilate de Magna Carta et Aliis Statutis* found in two Cambridge University Library manuscripts and discussed by Judge Morris Arnold and Dr. John Baker.[73] The basic format of the *questiones* in these two collections is to state a question of law connected with the interpretation of a particular chapter of one of the major Henrician or Edwardian statutes and to give an authoritative answer to this question, sometimes with the name of a particular individual attached to it. One manuscript (MS. Hh.2.8) seems to be mid fifteenth century in date and arranges the *questiones* by statutes but not in chapter order; the other (MS. Ll.4.17) looks earlier in date, has much the same *questiones* as the other manuscript though arranged in chapter as well as statute order, but breaks off after the *questiones* belonging to the statute of Westminster I. Judge Arnold and Dr. Baker agree in seeing the *Questiones Compilate* as deriving from some kind of learning exercise: Baker dating it to around 1342, Arnold to around 1350. It seems, however, that it is more likely that the *questiones* transcribed in this collection were propounded (and quite possibly argued, in disputations which the compiler of the collection was not concerned to transcribe) and authoritative solutions offered to the questions in learning exercises held over a number of years. This would explain why in these *questiones* we find Pulteney, presumably the John de Pulteney who became a serjeant in 1342, and died in 1344, rubbing shoulders with three persons who are probably to be identified with men who became serjeants only in 1354—Fyncheden, Fyffyd' and Knyvett', presumably William de Fyncheden, William de Fifhide and John Knyvet respectively. These *questiones* in turn look to be forerunners of the *questiones* posed by the readers in the inns of court in the fifteenth century during the course of their readings and offered for discussion, which were also specific arguable points related to the particular chapter of the statute which the reader was then expounding.

But is there any evidence of lectures on the statutes taking place before 1400 with which the mid fourteenth-century *Questiones Compilate* or the *questiones disputate* of around 1300 could be linked? Dr. John Baker discusses a text in a Bodleian manuscript which looks like an early reading on Magna Carta and which seems to date from not long after 1374, a good half century and more older than the earliest readings on the statutes hitherto known.[74] He also mentions the *Tractatus super statutum Westmonasterii secundi* which is to be found in British Library, Additional MS. 22552 and which he says 'may well be a reading of the same period'.[75] The latter does indeed seem to be an early reading on the statute of Westminster II, but from the way it cites decided cases mainly of early years of Edward III, and in no instance later than Hilary term 18 Edward III (1344), this author would suggest that it probably belongs to a date not much after 1344, at least a quarter of a century earlier than the Bodleian text. There is even some fragmentary evidence to indicate that lectures on the statutes may have been going on already around 1300: at least two

---

[73] Cambridge University Library, MSS. Hh.2.8 fos. 115–120v and Ll.4.17 fos. 219–222v. Discussed in *The Old Tenures c.1515 and The Old Natura Brevium c.1518*, ed. M. Arnold (Classical English Law Texts, 1974), introduction, note 50; and in Baker, 'Learning exercises', p. 14.

[74] Baker, 'Learning exercises', p. 14.

[75] Brit. Libr., Add. MS. 22552 fos. 51v–54v: discussed in Baker, 'Learning exercises', pp. 14–15.

manuscripts contain expository material related to the statute of Westminster II, cap.1 (de Donis) which looks as though its natural home would be in such a lecture.[76] If these really are fragments of lectures on the statute, then the link between at least some *questiones* and lectures on the statutes is something that can be taken back to the very beginning of the fourteenth century, since the three *questiones* concerned with statutes also happen to be related to precisely this particular statute.

Both the lecture taking the form of a commentary on a work of authority (in the case of common law instruction the lectures on the statutes) and the *questio disputata* are reminiscent of techniques used in the teaching of the learned laws (Roman and canon law) in the universities and suggest some degree of influence by the learned law tradition on the educational methods of the common lawyers.[77] This is hardly surprising. As Ralph Turner has shown, the practice of the king employing university graduates (including graduates in the learned laws) as royal justices goes back to the reign on Henry II and can be traced through to the second quarter of the thirteenth century.[78] The tradition was continued during the latter part of the reign of Henry III in the persons of Master Simon of Walton, who was almost certainly by training a canonist[79] and William Bonquer, who was fairly certainly either a canonist or a civilian.[80] The early years of Edward I's reign saw the appointment as justices of the Bench of Master Roger of Seaton and Master Ralph of Farningham, both of whom seem to have been canon lawyers,[81] and the appointment of another possible canonist, Master Thomas of Siddington, as one of the king's itinerant justices.[82] The last representative of this tradition seems to be Master John Lovel, a royal justice in the early twelve-nineties, who had been an advocate in the court of Arches before entering the king's service.[83] Such men could well have been the channel for the transmission to the common law of the educational institutions of the learned lawyers. There is, however, also another possible line of communication. A number of the serjeants of Edward I's reign though never described as

[76] Brit. Libr., Add. MS. 31826 fos. 226v–227 (and *ibid*. fo. 227v); H fos. 71, 71v (and perhaps fos. 78v, 83v) (= A fo. 104v (and fos. 109, 112v)).

[77] The literature on the teaching of the learned laws is extensive. One fairly recent summary account is contained in W. Ullmann, *Law and Politics in the Middle Ages* (1975), pp. 86, 175 (and references cited there).

[78] R. V. Turner, *The English Judiciary in the Age of Glanvill and Bracton, c.1176–1239* (Cambridge, 1985), pp. 35–8, 94–8, 150–4, 226, 233.

[79] For evidence suggesting he was a trained canonist see *Cal. Pat. Rolls 1232–47*, pp. 173, 261, 265; *Cartulary of Oseney Abbey*, ed. H. E. Salter (Oxford Hist. Soc., lxxxix, xc, xci, xcvii, xcviii, ci, 1929–36), iii. 42, no. 1176 (and cf. no. 1175).

[80] For his career and evidence to suggest that he was a civilian or a canonist see J. B. Whitmore in *Notes and Queries*, cc (1955), 324–7, 418–21; and C. A. F. Meekings in *ibid.*, cci (1956), 54–6.

[81] For evidence to suggest that Seaton was a trained canonist see *Registrum Palatinum Dunelmense*, ed. T. D. Hardy (4 vols., Rolls Ser., 1873–8), i. 336–7; and for similar evidence about Farningham see *Cal. Pat. Rolls 1258–66*, p. 29; *Cal. Pat. Rolls 1266–72*, p. 140; *Calendar of Liberate Rolls 1267–72*, no. 1298; *Calendar of Close Rolls 1272–9*, p. 117.

[82] In 1270 he was given a dispensation to study either canon law or theology for one year (*Register of Bishop Godfrey Giffard*, ed. J. W. Willis Bund (2 vols., Worcestershire Hist. Soc., 1902), i. 40).

[83] For evidence that Lovel had been an advocate in the court of Arches see P.R.O., CP 40/123, m. 40.

magistri can be shown to have had some knowledge of the learned law and it must be presumed that this was gained through university attendance where they too would have become aware of university teaching methods. Such knowledge can be demonstrated not just for William de Bereford, the future chief justice, a serjeant in the twelve-eighties and early twelve-nineties,[84] but also for William Inge,[85] Henry le Scrope[86] and Edmund of Pashley.[87]

It would in any case be wrong to exaggerate the distance separating the common law and learned law traditions in England. In *Bracton* we see one attempt made during the first half of the thirteenth century to integrate the two. Plucknett thought that this was a work 'addressed to English lawyers who had been brought up in the clerical tradition and expected a law-book to be built upon the plan of contemporary civilian and canonical works ...' but that in the second half of the thirteenth century this public 'was rapidly being replaced by another whose tastes were very different. The academic Roman, Latin and clerical tradition had no attraction for the new men who were insular, French and lay ...'.[88] *Bracton* was, however, clearly being read during the last two decades of the thirteenth century by men belonging to the lay legal tradition. We can be fairly certain that Gilbert of Thornton, a serjeant in the twelve-seventies and eighties before becoming chief justice of King's Bench, was the owner of a *Bracton* since he produced his own epitome and commentary on the text;[89] and another owner was the Matthew of the Exchequer who also acted as a serjeant in eyre in the twelve-eighties and is the most probable author of a second epitome and commentary on Bracton known as *Fleta*.[90] When in 1294 Chief Justice Mettingham advised counsel who voiced a doubt about a particular matter to look it up in *Bracton* ('Alez a vostre Bruton' e yl vous ensegnera') he was clearly assuming that any well-read serjeant would have ready access to a copy and (perhaps) would know where in *Bracton* to look.[91]

There is also evidence of some teaching and writing in the universities or on their fringes which concerned itself with the common law. Some of this at least was the work of men who were also acquainted with the learned law tradition. The treatise *Divisiones Brevium*, apparently composed between 1275 and 1285, is a treatment in survey form of the basic property writs and covers the writ of right,

---

[84] For Bereford's knowledge of the maxims of Roman law see Brit. Libr., Hargrave MS. 375 fo. 43v; Cambridge University Library, MS. Ee.6.18 fo. 11; Brit. Libr., Harley MS. 25 fo. 186v; *Year Books 2 & 3 Edward II*, ed. F. W. Maitland (Selden Soc., xix, 1904), pp. 173–8.

[85] Lincoln's Inn, Misc. MS. 738 fo. 62.

[86] See the dialogue between him and Pashley reported in Brit. Libr., Egerton MS. 2811 fos. 101v–102v.

[87] Staunton J. even describes Pashley in one passage as being 'legister', a civilian (*Year Books 33–35 Edward I*, ed. A. J. Horwood (Rolls Ser., 1879), p. 471).

[88] Plucknett, *Early English Legal Literature*, p. 96.

[89] T. F. T. Plucknett, 'The Harvard manuscript of Thornton's Summa', *Harvard Law Rev.*, li (1938), 1038–56; S. E. Thorne, 'Gilbert de Thornton's Summa de Legibus', *University of Toronto Law Jour.*, vii (1947), 1–23, also reprinted in *idem*, *Essays in English Legal History*, pp. 111–36.

[90] R. J. Whitwell, 'The libraries of a civilian and canonist and of a common lawyer, An. 1294', *Law Quart. Rev.*, xxi (1905), 393–400; N. Denholm-Young, 'Who wrote "Fleta"?', *Eng. Hist. Rev.*, lviii (1943), 1–12; *idem*, 'Matthew Cheker', *ibid.*, lix (1944), 252–7. G. O. Sayles, the modern editor of *Fleta*, still rejects Matthew of the Exchequer as the author of the treatise (*Fleta*, iv (Selden Soc., xcix, 1984), pp. xx–xxv).

[91] Lincoln's Inn, Misc. MS. 738 fo. 121v.

writs of entry and other possessory actions about land.[92] The language of the treatise sounds academic (the writ of right, for example, is called 'breve expressum recti') and its treatment of its topics certainly is. In discussing the writ of right it starts by asking what it is before going on to ask such typically academic questions as 'que natura brevis'; 'quis modus in brevi et in processu ejus'; 'que causa'; 'quis titulus'; 'que intentio' and 'quis effectus'. Certain of the phrases used in this brief treatise suggest that it probably began as a lecture. Of even greater interest is a treatise on charters written apparently in about 1300 and to be found in a single manuscript now in the Free Library of Philadelphia.[93] This contains a general academic discussion of charters covering such matters as the elements necessary to a charter; the numbers of types of charter; whether only one kind of opening is possible in a charter; how specific a charter ought to be in mentioning the property conveyed, and other similar questions. The writer shows a familiarity with Roman law not just in the civilian tags he reproduces[94] but also in some of his arguments.[95] But the author also frequently cites English legislation and various common law treatises, so he really does seem to span the two legal traditions.[96] In the same manuscript is part of what seems to have been a quite separate work on the fee tail.[97] This could have come from another lecture on the statute of Westminster II, c.1; but the fact that it is in Latin and that it shows a particular concern with the charters associated with the conveyance of fee tail estates suggests that it probably belongs to one of those lectures on charters given on the fringes of the university, perhaps in that Oxford business school to which H. G. Richardson long ago drew attention.[98]

These treatises show that by around 1300 English law was being taught and learnt in schoolrooms not just in London and Westminster but also at Oxford (or, much less likely, Cambridge). It is, however, clear that most of the education in the common law that was being provided in 1300 was being provided in and around London, and that it was available both at a level appropriate for beginners (*Brevia Placitata*, our teacher's lectures of the twelve-seventies, *Natura Brevium*, the teaching given with the register of writs) and at the rather more sophisticated level associated with the utilization of year-book reports for teaching purposes, with the learning exercises that produced the *questiones disputate* and perhaps even some lectures on the statutes. Other evidence points to the second half of the thirteenth

[92] Manuscripts of this treatise include Brit. Libr., Add. MS. 18600 fos. 163–5; Add. MS. 22708 fos. 30–31v; Harley MS. 1120 fos. 146v–148; Harley MS. 1208 fos. 137–9; Lansdowne MS. 467 fos. 172v–173v; Royal MS. 10.A.v fos. 147v–149v.

[93] Philadelphia Free Library, MS. LC 14.3 fos. 205v–207v.

[94] E.g. 'quia dicitur in lege "quis plus quam in se est alteri concedere non potest" ' (fo. 206v); and 'quia alteri per alterum non debet iniqua condicio afferri nec res inter alios acta aliis debet prejudicare' (fos. 205v–206).

[95] E.g., when the writer discusses the number of witnesses that should be put in a charter, he says 'duo sufficiunt de jure civili quia in ore duorum vel trium existit omne verbum. Dico tamen quod quinque ponantur ad minus' (fo. 206).

[96] The treatises cited are *Bracton*, *Magna Hengham*, *Parva Hengham*; *Fet Asaver*, *Summa de Arte Levandi Fines et Concordias in curia domini regis* and the Register of Writs. The statutes mentioned are Magna Carta, De Bigamis, Marlborough, Westminster II and Quia Emptores.

[97] Philadelphia Free Library, MS. LC 14.3 fos. 149v–150.

[98] H. G. Richardson, 'Business training in medieval Oxford', *American Hist. Rev.*, xlvi (1941), 259–80.

century as the period when an English legal profession emerged; the evidence discussed in this article indicates that it is in this same period that we can also find the beginnings of a system of proper professional legal education. The courtroom certainly was an important part of the training of any English lawyer in the later thirteenth and fourteenth centuries, but it was by no means the only place where law was learnt. Courtroom and classroom were already both playing a part in the education of the common lawyer in 1300 just as they did in Fortescue's day.

4

'Multis Vigiliis Excogitatam et Inventam': Henry II and the Creation of the English Common Law

1989 has been a great year for anniversaries. In France they have been celebrating the 200th anniversary of the French Revolution and the 100th anniversary of the Eiffel Tower. In England, if Mrs. Thatcher had known a little more (or perhaps a little less) history, we might have been celebrating the 300th anniversary of our own Declaration of Rights. In both countries (and elsewhere in Europe), we have been remembering (celebrating is clearly not the right word) the 50th anniversary of the outbreak of the Second World War. But the two connected anniversaries which will, I think, mean most to members of the Haskins Society are the 800th anniversary of the death of Henry II (on 6 July 1189) and the 800th anniversary of the coronation of Richard I (on 3 September 1189).

The second of these two dates is also, surprisingly, a date of some significance for English lawyers. It remains possible to prove title to rights of common, rights of way, and other easements in England by showing continuous and peaceable possession of such rights since 'time out of mind,' and this (at least in theory) means showing continuous and peaceful possession ever since 1189, when legal memory begins.[1] The limit of legal memory was first fixed at 1189 over seven centuries ago. Chapter 39 of the first Statute of Westminster of 1275 appears to establish only that in future no litigant bringing an action of right may base his action of the seisin of an ancestor or predecessor during any reign prior to that of Richard I (hitherto litigants had been able to go back to the reign of Henry II but no further).[2] But the legislation probably altered the limit of legal memory for other purposes as well. There were certain kinds of custom or customary right on which a party to litigation could rely only if he could show that they had been followed, observed, or enjoyed since 'time out of mind.' A case heard in 1247 seems to indicate that by the middle of the thirteenth century this was understood to mean that the party concerned had to be able to show continuous seisin or observance of them, not literally since time

---

[1] *Halsbury's Laws of England*, 6, ed. R. Peter Moore, 4th ed. (London, 1974), 219 and 14: 39. I would like to record my thanks to Professor Robert C. Palmer of the University of Houston and the Humanities and the Professions Program at the University of Houston for encouragement and support.

[2] *Statutes of the Realm*, 1 [ed. Alexander Luders, et al.] (London, 1810), 36.

out of mind, but simply since the limitation date then in force for the writ of right (the beginning of the reign of Henry II).[3] By the later thirteenth century, 'time out of mind' was regularly being given a similar meaning (though now the relevant limitation date had changed to 1189).[4]

It is ironic that for over seven centuries the limit of legal memory has been fixed in such a way as to exclude from the memory of the law and of lawyers the reign of the one king of England who has most claim to be regarded as the founder of the English Common Law, Henry II. But it is hardly surprising. The memory of Henry II's contributions to the making of English law disappeared surprisingly quickly. *Glanvill*'s treatise, completed towards the end of Henry II's reign, has references to many of the legislative ordinances of the reign which helped to create the Common Law and some general references in the prologue to the man (though none which specifically name Henry himself).[5] The treatise which we call *Bracton*, written less than half a century later, knows nothing of Henry's legislation apart perhaps from a distant memory that the assize of novel disseisin had been thought out and contrived after many night watches, though even here the author does not tie this down to the reign of Henry II or the work of Henry and his advisers, and the phrase itself is one borrowed from Justinian's code.[6] *Bracton*'s only specific reference to Henry II (as far as I can see) is not to the man, but to his reign: as a period during which a litigant's ancestor may be said in a count to have been in seisin of property.[7] Henry III and Edward I were both known to many generations of later lawyers through their legislation, which was copied and lectured on throughout the later Middle Ages and into the early modern period. Henry II was forgotten because texts of his legislation did not survive as part of the living professional tradition of the lawyers.

The rediscovery of Henry II's importance in the history of the Common Law appears to have begun only in the second half of the seventeenth century with the work of Sir Matthew Hale, the first lawyer in England to write a coherent history of the Common Law,[8] and was made possible through the work of sixteenth-century editors in producing texts of Howden and *Glanvill*.[9] In this paper I want to follow in the tracks of Hale and Hale's many successors in assessing the contribution made by Henry II and his advisers to the creation of the English Common Law, by looking in particular at their contribution to the development of the English legal system.

[3] *Abbot of Kirkstead* v. *Warner Son of Eudo*, P.R.O, JUST 1/81, m. 6.

[4] See the 1292 annual rent case of *Hugh de la Penne, rector of Staunton* v. *Hugh de Clifford, rector of la More*, P.R.O, CP 40/96, m. 114 and the 1294 detinue of chattels case of *Master of the Templars* v. *Executors of Master John of Grantham*, P.R.O., CP 40/104, m. 105.

[5] *Glanvill*, ed. G.D.G. Hall (London, 1965), xxxiv–vi, 1–3.

[6] *Bracton*, ed. George E. Woodbine and translated with revisions and notes by Samuel E. Thorne (Cambridge, 1977), fol. 164b (III, 25).

[7] Ibid., fols. 318b, 372b, 373 (IV, 23; IV, 169; IV, 170).

[8] Matthew Hale, *The History of the Common Law of England*, 3rd ed. (London, 1739), 88–93.

[9] May McKisack, *Medieval History in the Tudor Age* (Oxford, 1971), 64–65; *Glanvill*, lxii–lxiii.

Here begins the treatise on the laws and customs of the kingdom of England composed in the time of King Henry the Second, when justice was under the direction of the illustrious Ranulph de Glanvill, the most learned of that time in the law and ancient customs of the kingdom; and it contains only those laws and customs which are followed in the king's court at the Exchequer and before the justices wherever they are.

Thus runs the opening rubric of *Glanvill*, the earliest treatise on the English common law in one of the two main manuscript traditions of that treatise, Beta.[10] And what the Beta rubric has to tell us is both true and important: the English Common Law at this early stage in its existence (at the very end of the reign of Henry II) was primarily the law and custom followed and being developed by the king's courts and more especially by two particular king's courts or types of king's court: the king's court at the Exchequer and the king's court held before the justices in eyre, the justices of the general eyre. Despite some earlier forerunners, both courts were essentially creations of the reign of Henry II and owed their existence and functioning as law courts to Henry II and his advisers. Thus the institutional basis for the creation of the English Common Law was itself created only during Henry II's reign and on the initiative of Henry and his advisers.

Scholars have commonly located the beginnings of the general eyre in the reign of Henry I.[11] There can be little doubt that the later part of Henry II's reign did see the appointment of justices by the king with the power to hear a range of pleas in several different counties.[12] But the sessions held by these royal justices differed in at least two important respects from the sessions held by the justices of the general eyre of the later twelfth and thirteenth centuries. One was pointed out by Prof. William T. Reedy, Jr. in an article of 1966.

[10] *Glanvill*, 1, n. b; *Glanvill*, ed. George E. Woodbine (New Haven, 1932), 23, 183. Woodbine's insertion of a comma after 'curia regis' is unnecessary and destroys the obvious sense of the passage: cf. Ralph V. Turner, 'The Origins of Common Pleas and King's Bench,' *American Journal of Legal History* 21 (1977): 238–54 at 241 and n. 12, 243.

[11] E.g., Doris M. Stenton, *English Justice between the Norman Conquest and the Great Charter, 1066–1215* (Philadelphia, 1964), 65: '. . . all this shows that before 1130 the conception of a general eyre had been translated into fact.' *Pleas before the King or His Justices, 1198–1212*, 3, ed. Doris M. Stenton, Selden Society 83 (1966), xlviii: '. . . no convincing evidence survives of an earlier date than the Pipe Roll of 1130 that the practice has been established of sending groups of royal officers to act as judges throughout the land. The evidence of this roll, ample as it is, is not sufficient of itself to show the point of the reign when Henry I began to send out regular judicial eyres. . . .' R.C. Van Caenegem, *The Birth of the English Common Law* (Cambridge, 1973), 20: 'It really began under Henry I when from the *curia regis* some *curiales* were sent on occasional eyres . . . through a certain number of counties to hold pleas. . . . the essentials of the general eyre were there: a broad scope *ratione materiae* and officials sent *a latere regis* to *inter alia* judicial work on an eyre through several counties. . . .'

[12] William T. Reedy, Jr., 'The Origins of the General Eyre in the Reign of Henry I,' *Speculum* 41 (1966): 688–724 at 698–716; Stenton, *English Justice*, 61–65; C. Warren Hollister and John W. Baldwin, 'The Rise of Administrative Kingship: Henry I and Philip Augustus,' *American Historical Review* 83 (1978): 867–905, esp. 882–85; Judith Green, *The Government of England Under Henry I* (Cambridge, 1986), 108–10.

Sessions of the general eyre in individual counties in the later twelfth and thirteenth centuries were normally planned (though not necessarily executed) as part of a countrywide scheme of visitations bringing royal justice to the whole country on a county by county basis within a particular limited period of time. There is no evidence that sessions of the itinerant justices of the reign of Henry I were ever planned to form part of such countrywide visitations.[13] The other and even more significant difference lay in the internal structure and functioning of these courts. Sessions of the general eyre in the later twelfth and thirteenth centuries were run by the royal justices whom the king appointed to the circuits concerned. They did not simply preside in these courts. They also made any judgments that were to be made there. This does not appear to have been the case with the sessions held by the itinerant royal justices of the reign of Henry I, who seem only to have presided over the courts they held and not to have made judgments there.

We know for certain that when royal justices were commissioned on an ad hoc basis by kings in the later eleventh and early twelfth centuries to hear particular pleas, these justices functioned only as presiding officers, and not as judges at the sessions they held. Judgments at such sessions were made by those who regularly attended and made judgments at the county court of the county concerned (or in some instances the hundred court in question). The distinction between these two roles is made clear by a royal order of Henry I's reign addressed to Swein of Essex. This orders him to respect the bishop of London's freedom from various dues as the bishop had proved by charters and writs at Writtle before the king's justices (*ante justiciarios meos*) at a session where Swein himself had been one of the 'judges' ('ubi tu ipse fuisti unus ex judicibus').[14] A later reference to the plea between the bishop of Worcester and abbot of Evesham, which the bishop of Coutances was commissioned to hear sometime between 1079 and 1083, describes the plea as being heard before the commissioner and others, but 'with the whole county judging and attesting';[15] and what seems to be a contemporary report of the trial on Penenden Heath, which the bishop of Coutances was ordered to hear, speaks of the whole county being ordered to meet for the plea, of the whole county being kept there for three days, and of the judgment in the archbishop's favor being 'agreed and adjudged' by 'the whole county.'[16] The same was also true of the courts of the local justiciars.[17] This we can deduce

[13] Reedy, 'Origins of the General Eyre,' 690; Green, *Government of England*, 109. The difference is noted but discounted by Van Caenegem, *Birth of the English Common Law*, 20.

[14] *Early Charters of the Cathedral Church of St. Paul, London*, ed. Marion Gibbs, Royal Historical Society, Camden Third Series 58 (1939), 17, no. 17. The calendared version in *Regesta*, 2: no. 429a elides the difference by calling Swein one of the 'justices.'

[15] *Regesta*, 1: no. 221.

[16] John Le Patourel, 'The Reports of the Trial on Penenden Heath,' in *Studies in Medieval History Presented to F.M. Powicke*, ed. R.W. Hunt, W.A. Pantin, and R.W. Southern (Oxford, 1948), 15–26.

[17] For the local justiciar, see H.A. Cronne, 'The Office of Local Justiciar under the Norman Kings,' *University of Birmingham Historical Journal* 6 (1937): 18–38; Stenton, *English Justice*, 65–68.

from the charter from the very end of Stephen's reign in favor of Robert of Chesney, bishop of Lincoln, granting him the office of local justiciar within the county of Lincolnshire and in Lincoln.[18] The charter makes it clear that, although it is the bishop who will decide when he is going to hold sessions, it is the men of Lincoln and Lincolnshire who will attend those sessions 'to hold the king's pleas and make the king's judgments' ('ad placita mea tenenda et judicia mea facienda'); and the writ suggests that this had also been the practice in the reign of Henry I. Those who attended such sessions were probably much the same as those who attended sessions of the county court: indeed the *Leges Henrici Primi* suggests that sessions over which the justiciar presided could simply be described as sessions of the county court.[19]

Such evidence as we have about the activities of the 'itinerant justices' of the reign of Henry I seems to indicate that these justices also merely presided over the courts which they held, but that judgments in them were made by others, probably the judges or suitors of the counties which they were visiting. Thus in 1116 we find the royal justice Ralph Basset presiding over the session at Huntingdon where Bricstan was convicted of usurping buried treasure, which as treasure trove belonged to the king, and of lending it out at interest;[20] but the actual judgment against Bricstan, though 'ordered' by Ralph Basset, was not apparently made either by him alone or by him and colleagues and was most likely given by the leading men of the area whom we are told had been summoned to the session 'as was customary in England.' Another piece of evidence pointing in the same direction is the reference in the *Peterborough Chronicle* to the 'Hundehoge' session in 1124 at which 40 thieves were hanged and six mutilated. The chronicler is not very exact in his references, but he talks of the session as taking place before Ralph Basset 'and the king's thegns.'[21] The reference may simply be to unnamed judicial colleagues, but it sounds more like a reference to the leading men of Leicestershire; and again it seems likely that they were there to give judgment in a session at which Basset presided. Among the deeds associated with the king's scribe Bernard are two witnessed by three men (Robert Arundel, Durand de Moion, and Herbert de Alneto), who are specifically described in one of the deeds as 'justices of the lord king' (*justiciarii domini regis*), but who probably also witnessed the other deed in the same capacity. Both deeds record the outcome of litigation, and it is reasonable to suppose that they appear among the witnesses to these deeds because they had presided in the courts at which the plea had been heard whose settlement was being recorded. Both deeds speak of 'judgment' as having been given in the case in question. But in neither is the judgment said to have been given by the royal justices. In one, judgment is said to have been given by the county court of Devon; in the other, by the court

---

[18] *Calendar of Charter Rolls*, Public Record Office, 6 vols. (London, 1903–27), 4: 139.

[19] *Leges Henrici Primi*, ed. L.J. Downer (Oxford, 1972), 168 (53, 1).

[20] Orderic, 3: 346–61.

[21] *The Anglo-Saxon Chronicle: A Revised Translation*, ed. Dorothy Whitelock, D.C. Douglas, and S.I. Tucker (London, 1961), 191.

of the bishop of Exeter.[22] It was perhaps because all they were required to do at their sessions was to preside, rather than make judgments, that there were so few itinerant justices under Henry I. In Henry II's reign, itinerant justices acted in large groups of up to eight justices at a time. Such evidence as we have for these itinerant justices of the reign of Henry I suggests that they were sometimes just a single individual, sometimes two individuals and never more than three.

The fact that royal itinerant justices of the reign of Henry I only presided and did not make judgments in the counties they visited was more than just a technicality. Each county court had its own customs.[23] It seems likely that it was these customs which the judges of the county court followed and applied even when giving judgment in a court presided over by royal justices. As yet, then, the sessions presided over by these royal justices were not local sessions of a national royal court (there seems, indeed, to be no evidence that such sessions were even described as sessions of the king's court), but merely special sessions of the county courts or other courts concerned.

During the early years of his reign, Henry II did no more than revive the practice of his grandfather in sending out individual justices or groups of justices to particular counties, making no attempt to ensure that their sessions covered the whole of the country within a particular period of time;[24] and the smallness of the groups concerned may mean that these justices (like their predecessors in the reign of Henry I) simply presided at their sessions and did not themselves act as judges at them. The earliest visitation to be planned on a countrywide basis (with the country being divided up into a number of separate circuits in order that the inquiry be completed within a limited timespan) appears to have been the Inquest of Sheriffs of 1170. But the commissioners of this inquiry were instructed simply to seek presentments of official misdeeds and not to determine those presentments or punish those involved, and they did not hear or determine any other kind of business. So this countywide visitation cannot be regarded as anything more than at most a very distant forerunner of the general eyre.[25] The Pipe Rolls appear

---

[22] J.H. Round, 'Bernard the King's Scribe,' *EHR* 14 (1899): 422, no. 16; 421–22, no. 15.

[23] This was still the case according to *Glanvill* at the end of Henry II's reign: *Glanvill*, ed. Hall, 147. The differences are also noted by the author of the *Leges Henrici Primi* who ascribes them to the 'rapacity and evil and hateful practices of lawyers': *Leges Henrici Primi*, 99 (6, 3a).

[24] Stenton, *English Justice*, 68–69; *Pleas before the King or his Justices*, 3: l–lii.

[25] *Historical Works of Gervase of Canterbury*, ed. William Stubbs, 2 vols. (London, 1879–80), 1: 217–19. Lady Stenton believed that the earl of Essex and Richard de Lucy visited most of England enforcing the Assize of Clarendon in 1166 and suggested that other counties escaped visitation only because of the earl's death in October of that year (*English Justice*, 71–72), but J.C. Holt has argued convincingly that the two justices only visited counties in the eastern half of England (J.C. Holt, 'The Assizes of Henry II: The Texts,' in *The Study of Medieval Records: Essays in Honour of Kathleen Major*, eds. D.A. Bullough and R.L. Storey [Oxford, 1971], 85–106, esp. 103–06).

to indicate that the very first countrywide visitation (by two groups of two justices) dealing with both civil and criminal business took place in 1175 (or possibly in 1174–75).[26] The small numbers of justices assigned to this visitation suggests, however, that these justices may only have presided at their sessions and not also made judgments there.

We need have no such doubts about the visitation of 1176 (which continued into 1177 and perhaps into 1178). From chronicle evidence we know that a countrywide judicial visitation was planned at a meeting of the king and his council at Northampton in late January 1176 and that it was there that the country was divided up into six circuits each to be visited by a group of three justices.[27] The instructions given to these justices show that they were authorized to deal with all three kinds of business later characteristic of the work of the justices of the general eyre: civil and criminal pleas and inquiries into matters of concern to the king.[28] These instructions also make clear that the justices were to be in full control of proceedings and were to make judgments at their sessions themselves. They were, the instructions state, to determine litigation brought by writ of right where the tenement in demand was half a knight's fee or less, unless the case was so great that it could not be determined without the king or such that the justices report on it to the king or those in his place because of their doubts (*pro dubitacione sua*).[29] Surviving final concords from the same visitation also make clear the dominant role played by the king's justices. In almost all it is only the royal justices (who are so described in the fines) who are specifically named as constituting the court.[30] One final concord mentions other barons as also being present, but it does not name them and does not give the impression that they are there as constituting the county court or as persons playing any significant role in the functioning of the court.[31] A second final concord from the same visitation records that it was made, not just before the two royal justices named, but also before five other individuals, who seem to be prominent landowners of the county where the session was being held (Yorkshire), together with other unnamed barons of the lord king.[32] This fine is perhaps the work of a scribe who had not yet adjusted to the new realities; but it is noticeable that even he does not imply

[26] Ranulf de Glanvill and Hugh de Cressy visited some 15 counties; William de Lanvaley and Thomas Basset, 14: *Pleas before the King or His Justices*, 3: lvi.

[27] *Gesta Regis Henrici Secundi*, ed. William Stubbs, 2 vols. (London, 1867), 1: 107–08. The Pipe Roll and final concord evidence for the visitation is summarized in *Pleas Before the King or His Justices*, 3: lvii–lix.

[28] *Gesta Regis Henrici Secundi*, 1: 108.

[29] Assize of Northampton, c. 7 (above, n. 28).

[30] P.R.O., C. 260/186, no. 1C; *Final Concords of the County of Lincoln*, 2, ed. C.W. Foster, Lincoln Record Society 17 (1920), 311; *Magnum Registrum Album*, ed. H.E. Savage, William Salt Archaeological Society (1924): 104, no. 224; J.H. Round, *Feudal England* (London, reset edition of 1964), 389; B.L., Harley MS. 3640, fol. 113v.

[31] Round, *Feudal England*, 388.

[32] *Yorkshire Deeds*, 2, ed. William Brown, Yorkshire Archaeological Society, Record Series 50 (1914), vi–vii.

that the landowners are representing or acting for the county or that the final
concord is being made at a session of the county court. It is, moreover, also the
only surviving final concord from this visitation which does not either directly
or indirectly state that it had been made at a session of the king's court: directly,
by stating that they had been made in the king's court at the place the sessions
were being held; indirectly, by saying that the litigation now settled had been
heard in the king's court. Even this one rogue final concord perhaps implies
the same thing because it says that it was made at York *ad asisam*.

The general eyre rapidly became established as a regular part of the English
legal system. Pipe Rolls and final concords indicate that there were seven
further visitations of the general eyre before the end of Henry II's reign,
so that on average during the later part of the reign there was an eyre
visitation of the whole country every other year. The precise arrangements
seem to have varied from visitation to visitation. Two groups of justices
covered the whole country in the visitations of 1178–79 and 1181–82,
with four justices being assigned to each circuit for the first, and three or four
to each circuit in the second.[33] More commonly the country was divided up
into four circuits. In 1179 three of the four circuits were assigned five justices
and the fourth (which was also to accompany the king to hear complaints
made to him), six;[34] in 1184–85 the circuits were assigned between four
and seven justices each;[35] in 1185–86, only three or four justices each;[36]
while in 1187–88 the circuits seem to have been assigned between three
and five justices each.[37] The final visitation of the reign in 1188–89 saw
the number of circuits rise to five and also apparently a more generous
assignment of justices to each circuit (as many as seven, eight or nine justices
per circuit).[38]

The surviving final concords from these visitations (like those from the
1176–78 visitation) are virtually unanimous in continuing to ascribe to the
king's justices the dominant role in proceedings. In almost all the surviving
fines, it is only the royal justices who are specifically named as constituting
the court. A number of fines also mention other barons of the king (or other
barons and lieges or other barons and knights) as being present, but they do not

---

[33] *Pleas before the King or His Justices*, 3: lx–lxi, lxv–lvii. But note that no final concords survive from
the visitation of 1178–79.

[34] *Gesta Regis Henrici Secundi*, 1: 238–39; *Pleas Before the King or His Justices*, 3: lxi–xiv.

[35] Ibid., lxviii–lxix. Where only Pipe Roll evidence survives for the activity of a circuit, we cannot be
certain that this gives us the names of all the justices active on the circuit. Where final concords survive
as well, these do give us the names of all the justices.

[36] Ibid., lxx–lxxi.

[37] Ibid., lxxii–lxxiv.

[38] Ibid., lxxv–lxxviii.

name them and do not give the impression that they are playing any significant role in the functioning of the court.[39] There are only two final concords of the period which differ significantly from this norm. One is a fine of 1179 which describes itself as being made by the permission of named royal justices and before them, but also before the (unnamed) justices and nobles of the county ('permissione . . . justiciarorum domini regis et coram eis qui tunc ibi aderant et justiciis et viris nobilibus de comitatu . . .').[40] The second is a fine of 1183 which describes itself as recording an agreement made before three royal justices and the sheriff of Gloucestershire in the presence of the county of Gloucestershire ('. . . coram justiciariis domini regis . . . et coram . . . tunc vicecomiti . . . presente comitatu de Gloucestr').[41] Neither concord seems necessarily to imply any kind of active role for the justices and nobles of the county or for the county court in the process of adjudication, however, and both are perhaps best seen as representing no more than a non-standard variant on the common formula as to the presence of other barons and lieges in the court.

Also relevant here is the discussion in *Glanvill* of what happens when a litigant sues for the enforcement of a final concord made before justices itinerant, and his opponent challenges the genuineness of the alleged concord.[42] There was, of course, as yet no official copy of the final concord in official custody (these were kept only from 1195 onwards). *Glanvill* tells us that it was not the justices itinerant alone who were summoned to bear record of how the original litigation had been determined. Discreet knights were also summoned to make a record of the outcome 'ex parte tocius comitatus.' The writ of summons for these knights does, nonetheless, make clear that the joint record is of how the plea remained 'in'the king's court' (*in curia mea*), not in the county court, and the record is to be of how the case was determined 'coram justiciis,' not 'coram comitatu.'[43] This makes it clear that the knights are being summoned as witnesses of what had been done at the session of the Eyre, not as full participants in the session.

These same final concords confirm that the individual sessions of the general eyre held in each county during the later years of Henry II's reign were regarded

---

[39] For examples of fines which only mention the king's justices, see *Final Concords of the County of Lincoln*, 2: 335–36 (1179) and *Feudal Documents from the Abbey of Bury St. Edmund's*, ed. David C. Douglas, British Academy, Records of Social and Economic History 8 (1932), 185, no. 227. For fines which mention other barons and lieges as well, see, for example, *Final Concords of the County of Lincoln*, 2: 310 (1187) and 312 (1179); B.L., MS. Harley 236, fols. 24r-v (1184). For two fines which mention other barons and knights of the king see B.L., Harley MS. 3688, fol. 173r (1184) and *Final Concords of the County of Lincoln*, 2: 330 (1185).

[40] B.L., Lansdowne MS. 415, fol. 24r.

[41] *Historia et Cartularium Monasterii Sancti Petri Gloucestriae*, ed. William H. Hart, 3 vols. (London, 1863–67), 1: 234–35.

[42] *Glanvill*, ed. Hall, 98–99.

[43] The writ given in *Glanvill*, ed. Hall, 99, for securing the record of knights from the county does, indeed, speak of the case as being 'in comitatu tuo,' but it looks as though the treatise's author is using an inappropriate writ at this point, perhaps because he has had difficulty finding the writ with the appropriate formula.

as sessions of the king's court. Many specifically say that they are recording an agreement made in the king's court at a named place; and almost all the others imply the same thing by stating that the litigation now being settled had been heard in the king's court (clearly a reference to the session itself). The only final concords not to do either are the two non-standard final concords of 1179 and 1183 to which I have already referred.[44] The fact that sessions of the general eyre were regarded as sessions of the king's court and that judgments were made there by the king's justices was of major importance. It meant that judgments at sessions of the general eyre could be made (and were made) in accordance, not with the local custom of each county, but with a more general custom of the king's court, which was of nationwide applicability.

An older generation of scholars traced the origins of the Common Bench, the most important royal court for the hearing of civil litigation throughout the later Middle Ages and beyond, back to arrangements made by Henry II in 1178, appointing two clerks and three laymen of his household to hear and redress complaints from all over England.[45] More recent scholarship has shown that the Common Bench developed gradually out of the Exchequer, forming an institution wholly separate from the Exchequer only some time in the mid 1190s.[46] But when did the Exchequer first begin acting as a general court of justice as well as a financial institution? Some scholars have suggested that the Exchequer was already acting as such in the reign of Henry I;[47] but, even assuming that we can speak of the Exchequer as an institution rather than just as an occasion at this time,[48] the evidence for the Exchequer or persons at an Exchequer session hearing litigation unconnected with the Exchequer's financial functions during Henry I's reign is very exiguous. A

---

[44] Supra, nn. 40 and 41.

[45] For references, see Turner, 'Origins of Common Pleas and King's Bench,' 240 and nn. 6 and 7; Ralph V. Turner, *The English Judiciary in the Age of Glanvill and Bracton, c. 1176–1239* (Cambridge, 1985), 21.

[46] Turner, 'Origins of Common Pleas and King's Bench,' 241–45; Brian Kemp, 'Exchequer and Bench in the Later Twelfth Century – Separate or Identical Tribunals?,' *EHR* 88 (1973): 559–73; Turner, *English Judiciary*, 21, 68–73.

[47] E.g., Stenton, *English Justice*, 59: 'Before 1108 the Exchequer was in being. The integration of this permanent financial bureau into the fluctuating group of ministers through whom the King governed England is the outstanding achievement of Henry's reign. Long before its close, the barons of the exchequer were acting as a court of justice and their rolls were providing the king with a yearly record of the state of his finances.'; H.G. Richardson and G.O. Sayles, *The Governance of Mediaeval England from the Conquest to Magna Carta* (Edinburgh, 1963), 188: 'A few writs survive which leave us in no doubt that the court of the justiciar under Henry I was very much what it was to be under Henry II. Its functions in regard to matters of justice and finance – if indeed these were conceived as distinct issues – were seemingly identical at both periods, and the evidence that the "justiciarii tocius Anglie" sat at the Exchequer to adjudicate upon financial issues is sufficient to establish that some of them would be present when the court adjudicated in civil actions. Indeed it is inconceivable that they should have adjudicated upon all manners of pleas in the country and not in the central court.'

[48] Cf. Hollister and Baldwin, 'Rise of Administrative Kingship,' 879.

royal precept of 1108 × 1127 orders the bishop of London to 'do full right' to the abbot of Westminster concerning the men who had broken into his church of Wennington with arms at night and instructs the 'barons of the Exchequer' (*barones mei de Scaccario*) to take action if the bishop fails to do so.[49] A second writ of c. 1130–33 notifies the men of the counties of Middlesex and Sussex that Herbert, abbot of Westminster, had proved his title to lands at Parham in Sussex and Mapleford in Middlesex against Herbert son of Herbert in litigation before the barons of the Exchequer.[50] These two writs constitute the sole evidence for believing that the Exchequer was acting as a general court of law in Henry I's reign; and they can scarcely be said to constitute sufficient proof that the Exchequer so acted on a regular basis. It may be significant that the abbot of Westminster was involved in both cases.[51] It must surely be significant that no other religious house seems to preserve records of ordinary litigation determined or compromised at the Exchequer during the reign. I think it is reasonable to conclude that, while ordinary litigation may have been heard at Exchequer sessions from time to time in Henry I's reign, it was not being heard at such sessions on anything like a regular basis.

Ordinary litigation was certainly being heard in a royal court at Westminster by the mid 1160s,[52] and it is from shortly after this that there come the first final concords recording the settlement of litigation heard there.[53] Enough concords or copies of concords survive from the archival collections of the parties concerned for Henry's reign to show that by the later 1170s (if not before) ordinary civil litigation was being heard at Westminster on a regular

---

[49] *Regesta*, 2: no. 1538.

[50] Ibid., 2: no. 1879.

[51] It was also the abbot of Westminster who, according to a charter of Wiliam Rufus, proved his right to certain lands before a group of the king's barons consisting of no more than five named and prominent individuals (rather than the more usual much larger group of royal barons who made up the *curia regis* at this time.): *Regesta*, 1: no. 370; in full in J.A. Robinson, *Gilbert Crispin Abbot of Westminster* (Cambridge, 1911), 136. However, it may be relevant here that the abbot seems to be proving his right to land that the king himself holds and which the abbot claims to have been given by William the Conqueror.

[52] For a quitclaim made at the Exchequer at Michaelmas 1165 after litigation there, see *Westminster Abbey Charters*, eds. Emma Mason, Jennifer Bray and Desmond J. Murphy, London Record Society 25 (1988), 139–40 (and for the background to the quitclaim see *Gesta Abbatum Monasterii Sancti Albani*, ed. Henry T. Riley, 3 vols. [London, 1867–69], 1: 134). For payments made for the removal of litigation to the king's court at the Exchequer during the late 1160s and early 1170s, see *P.R. 14 Henry II*, 197; *P.R. 15 Henry II*, 66; *P.R. 17 Henry II*, 73. For a royal confirmation of a fine made at Westminster before the king himself, Richard, archdeacon of Poitou, William, earl of Gloucester, Robert, earl of Leicester, and Roger Picot in 1163 × 1166 see B.L., MS. Cotton Galba E. II, fol. 31b (and 62b) (noted in Round, *Feudal England*, 389–90).

[53] The earliest final concords made before the court are themselves undated, but their approximate date can be ascertained from the names and titles of the court personnel mentioned in them. One such concord in B.L., Cotton MS. Otho D. III, fol. 73v seems to come from around 1170 as does another printed by J.H. Round (in 'The Earliest Fines,' *EHR* 12 [1897]: 300–301) and Lady Stenton (in *Pleas before the King or His Justices, 1198–1202*, 1, Selden Society 67 [1953], 365–66). The earliest dated final concord made in the Exchequer belongs to Easter 1173: B.L., Lansdowne MS. 415, fol. 22v (first Easter after the coronation of Queen Margaret, daughter of the king of France).

basis and that this practice continued for the remainder of the reign.[54] There can be no doubt at all that the court at which this litigation was heard was a royal court. The final concords recording the settlement of litigation heard in this court normally call it 'the king's court at Westminster'; and even the minority of final concords which do not contain this form of words still clearly imply that it is a royal court which has been hearing the litigation or before which the litigation has been settled.[55] The final concords are rather less clear about the relationship between this king's court at Westminster and the Exchequer. All the final concords made in the king's court at Westminster prior to 1179 also specify that they are being made 'at the Exchequer' (*ad Scaccarium*). This is probably still primarily a reference to an occasion rather than to an institution or place, as a final concord of 1178 with its reference to the *scaccarium Pasche* suggests;[56] but the occasion was rapidly turning into an institution, and it seems clear that these final concords do indeed record the work of that institution.[57] After 1179 (and more particularly after 1181), it became uncommon for final concords to refer in any way to the Exchequer, though a minority of final concords continued to do so down to 1186.[58] But there are no observable differences between the personnel of the king's court at Westminster in the majority of the concords and the personnel of the king's court at Westminster at the Exchequer in the minority, and the former like the latter continued to number among its more regular members the king's treasurer Richard Fitz Neal, the most readily identifiable of all the officials of the Exchequer. It seems clear therefore that the king's court at Westminster continued (whatever the

[54] The final concords show litigation being settled in the king's court at Westminster during periods which seem to correspond to the Easter and Michaelmas sessions of the Exchequer each year from 1179 to the end of Henry II's reign except for Easter 1180 (though there is a final concord said to have been made in the king's court at the Exchequer shortly prior to Easter), Easter 1184, Michaelmas 1186, Easter 1187, and Easter 1188.

[55] For examples, see the final concord of c. 1170 in B.L., Cotton MS. Otho D. III, fol. 73v, which describes the concord as having been made 'apud Westm' ad Scaccarium,' but specifies also that it was made before named men 'et ceteris justiciariis regis qui tunc aderant' and the final concord of 12 November 1177 printed in *Final Concords of the County of Lincoln*, 2: 329–30 which is said to have been made 'apud Westm' ad Scaccarium' and which concerned property 'unde placitum fuit inter eos in curia domini regis. . . .'

[56] *The Thame Cartulary*, ed. H.E. Salter, Oxfordshire Record Society 26 (1948), 131; cf. B.L., Lansdowne MS. 415, fol. 22v: '. . . ad Scaccarium ad proximum Pascha . . .'(final concord of 1173).

[57] Richard Fitz Neal, the treasurer, is the most readily identifiable member of the new institution. He appears in a majority of these fines.

[58] For final concords of the period 1180–86 which specifically stated that they have been made 'ad scaccarium sancti Michaelis,' see *Early Yorkshire Charters*, ed. W. Farrer, 3 vols., Yorkshire Archaeological Society Record Series, Extra Series (1914–16), 2: 494 (no. 1220) and B.L., Cotton MS. Otho D. III, fol. 29b; 'ad scaccarium in festo sancti Michaelis,' see B.L., Cotton MS. Domitian A. X, fols. 184v–85r; 'ad scaccarium Pasche,' see B.L., Harley MS. 2110, fol. 114r; B.L., Egerton MS. 2827, fol. 282r; *Early Yorkshire Charters*, 2: 239–40 (no. 895); 'in scaccario Pasche,' see B.L., Harley MS. 3656, fol. 99d; and just 'ad scaccarium,' see *The Cartulary of Oseney Abbey*, 4, ed. H.E. Salter, Oxford Historical Society (1934), 478 (no. 439); B.L., Harley MS. 3697, fol. 132v; *Manuscripts of the Duke of Rutland Preserved at Belvoir Castle*, 4 vols., Historical Manuscripts Commission (1888–1905), 4: 22; *Final Concords of the County of Lincoln*, 2: 311.

changes in scribal practice) to be the same institution as the Exchequer down to the end of Henry II's reign.[59]

The general eyre had been called into existence by a deliberate act of will on the part of Henry II and his advisers. No such act of will was needed to create the Exchequer, for it already existed as a functioning financial institution before it began to take on the additional burden of hearing ordinary litigation. The Exchequer may have begun to take on these additional responsibilities because of the justiciar's special position and responsibilities there.[60] Litigation is known to have been heard in courts headed by justiciars, but sitting away from Westminster, prior to the mid 1160s;[61] and it may be that all that happened was that the justiciar began to hear cases while he was presiding over the Exchequer at Westminster as well and naturally took as his colleagues those who were his colleagues in the Exchequer. But if this is the explanation, it is clear that the actual presence of the justiciar in the court fairly quickly ceased to be a necessity: that the Exchequer soon began to hear such litigation whether or not the justiciar was actually present in the court. As early as c. 1170, we find a final concord being made in the court which does not name the justiciar as one of those present for the making of the concord (and, we may presume, for the prior hearing of the case or the hearing of other cases at the same time) and this makes clear that the Exchequer was perfectly competent to act in his absence.[62] It may indeed be wrong to connect the Exchequer's additional responsibilities too closely with the justiciar's presence in the court. There were clearly advantages to having a royal court functioning on a regular basis while the king was out of the country, and the decision may have been taken in the mid 1160s that it was the Exchequer that should perform this function.

These new royal courts possessed a number of distinctive characteristics which seem to have been wholly new and to have made them quite different in nature from any pre-existing English court. The first is one to which I have already referred. A common feature of all of the courts of Anglo-Norman England had been a division of responsibility between a presiding officer and a group (perhaps in many cases a large group) of 'suitors' who actually made judgments in the court, with the latter being drawn from the substantial landowners subject to the jurisdiction of the same court, but possessing no special expertise in its law and custom. This was true not just of the

---

[59] Cf. Kemp, 'Exchequer and Bench in the Later Twelfth Century,' 560, 563–70.

[60] Francis West, *The Justiciarship in England* (Cambridge, 1966), 41–42, 45–46, 57–58.

[61] Ibid., 42–44.

[62] Round, 'The Earliest Fines,' 300–1; Stenton, *Pleas before the King or His Justices, 1198–1202*, 1: 365–66.

hundred[63] and county courts,[64] but also (as we have already seen) of the courts held by the various types of royal justice or justiciar,[65] and even of the king's court proper.[66] It was also true of seignorial courts, though here the picture

[63] For evidence suggesting that a duty of regular attendance at the hundred was incumbent only on the more substantial landholders resident in the hundred, see the writ of William II to all *judices*, sheriffs and officials on behalf of the abbey of Bury St. Edmund's, ordering, among other things, that no tenants of the abbey were to be forced to attend the hundred court (or the county court) other than those 'qui tantum terre habent unde digni fuissent tempore regis Edwardi ire ad schiras vel ad hundreda': H.W.C. Davis, 'The Liberties of Bury St. Edmund's,' *EHR* 24 (1909): 417–31, esp. 424 (calendared in *Regesta*, 1: no. 393). For further evidence suggesting that those who made judgments in the hundred were drawn simply from those who attended it on a regular basis, see the writ printed by Davis in 'The Liberties of Bury St. Edmund's,' 427–28 (calendared in *Regesta*, 2: no. 1812): precept of Henry I to all barons and men who hold land in the eight and a half hundreds of the abbot of Bury St. Edmund's in Suffolk ordering them 'quod veniatis ad placita de viij hundredis et dimidio per summonicionem abbatis sancti Edmundi et ministrorum ejus ad faciendam justiciam et recta mea tenenda' as they had previously done; and the precept of Stephen printed by Davis in 'The Liberties of Bury St. Edmund's,' 430 (calendared in *Regesta*, 3: no. 753): precept to all the barons of same hundreds ordering them 'ut ita bene veniatis per summonicionem abbatis sancti Edmundi et ministrorum ejus ad curiam suam tenendam et ad judicia et recta sua perquirenda et facienda' as they had done in the time of Henry I. It was probably only later that a link developed between suit to the hundred court and the holding of specific tenements. It seems likely that in the twelfth century as in the thirteenth, it was the hundred bailiff who normally presided over meetings of the hundred court, though in private hundreds this was sometimes done by the lord's steward: H.M. Cam, *The Hundred and the Hundred Rolls* (London, 1963), 185.

[64] The *Leges Henrici Primi* suggests that in the early twelfth century those who gave judgment in the county court were the 'barons of the county', who held free lands there: *Leges Henrici Primi*, 130 (29–29, 1a). This group seems to be the same as the 'lords of lands' who were required to attend meetings of the county court (*Leges Henrici Primi*, 98 [7,2]). Additional confirmation that regular attendance was required from those who held landed property of a certain (but unstated) minimum value is provided by a royal writ of the reign of William II concerning the attendance of tenants of the abbey of Bury St. Edmund's at county (and hundred) courts; Davis, 'The Liberties of Bury St. Edmund's', 424 (calendared in *Regesta*, 1: no. 393). It was the sheriff who presided at meetings of the county court.

[65] Supra, p. 80-82.

[66] The king's court (*curia regis*) of the Anglo-Norman period was the court over which the king himself commonly (though not invariably) presided. For a particularly clear reference to the king presiding in his own court in 1086, see *Regesta*, 1: no. 220 (in full in appendix, no. xxxii at 127), and for evidence that even in the king's own court it might be someone other than the king who pronounced judgment, see *Regesta*, 2: no. 880. Judgments in the court were normally made, not by the king and not by royal justices, but by the king's barons, the tenants-in-chief of the crown, a practice which is reflected in chapter 11 of Henry II's Constitutions of Clarendon which claimed it as part of the custom of Henry I's day that: 'Archiepiscopi, episcopi et universae personae regni qui de rege tenent in capite et habent possessiones suas de domino rege sicut baroniam . . . sicut barones ceteri debent interesse judiciis curie domini regis cum baronibus usque perveniatur in judicio ad diminiucionem membrorum vel mortem': *Gervase of Canterbury*, 1: 180. In some cases the records themselves stress the size and comprehensiveness of the group who made the decision; see, for example, the royal writ of around 1081 which gave the result of litigation between Bishop Herfast of Thetford and Baldwin, abbot of Bury St. Edmunds, about the bishop's claim to the church and town of Bury itself, in which it is said that by the king's order 'archiepiscopi et episcopi, abbates et comites aliique mei proceres judicium . . . tenuerunt et juste judicaverunt et assenserunt unanimiter. . . .': *Memorials of St. Edmund's Abbey*, ed. Thomas Arnold, 3 vols. (London, 1890–96), 1: 350 (calendared in *Regesta*, 1: no. 138). See also the report of a case heard probably in 1108 between Abbot Peter of Gloucester and Bishop Reinhelm of Hereford before Henry I, Archbishop Anselm, Robert, count of Meulan, and 'many bishops, abbots and *proceres*' about their rival claims to the body of Ralph Fitz Askitill: *Historia et Cartularium Monasterii Gloucestriae*, 1: 13 (calendared in *Regesta*, 2: no. 880). More commonly, however, we hear only of the case having been heard before the king and his barons and thus have no way of knowing how many barons were present for the hearing of the plea other than a minimum figure derivable from the witness list to the royal writ concerned. Sometimes the king's writ does not even specifically refer to the barons as participants in the work of the court, but we can deduce the participation of barons in the proceedings from their appearance in the relevant witness list.

was further complicated by the practice of reinforcing the judges for hearing difficult cases with outsiders who were not themselves subject to the jurisdiction of the court.[67] In the new royal courts, comparatively small groups of royal justices not only presided, but also made judgments, uniting these two hitherto separate functions; so that judgment-making was, for the first time, in these courts in the hands of men directly appointed (and directly removable) by the king.

Although we know little with certainty about how non-professional land-owning judges reached their judgments, it must be significant that the author of the *Leges Henrici Primi* advised litigants, when they had a choice as to whether they should plead or put off a plea, to exercise that choice in accordance with who was present in court that day. A litigant should see how many of his friends were present and how many of his enemies were absent.[68] The clear implication is that it is the presence of friends and absence of enemies that is one of the key factors, if not the crucial factor, in obtaining a favorable judgment: so that judgments in these courts were more a matter of politics and influence than of law. Putting the judicial function in the hands of small groups of men appointed directly by the king created for the first time the possibility (though clearly not always the actuality) of courts being run on more purely legal lines by men whose chief qualification for judicial office was their knowledge of and expertise in the law and custom of the court.

And we can, I think, see Henry II and his advisers deliberately using their powers of appointment in the new royal courts to build up a 'core' group of expert judges with long periods of regular service in the courts, a phenomenon Prof. Ralph Turner has already noted. At least 70 different individuals are known from the evidence of the final concords to have sat in the Exchequer as justices at some stage between Michaelmas 1165 and the death of Henry II.[69] Half of these men are recorded as sitting in the court on one or two occasions only and clearly never became regular justices there. But beside

[67] That the lord's tenants might be reinforced (perhaps particularly in the more contentious cases) by other neighboring landowners or friends of the lord invited to the court for this purpose is mentioned in two passages in the *Leges Henrici Primi*: at 136–37 (33, 1) and 262–63 (86, 1). There also seems to be independent evidence of this in the record of the case of Modbert and Bath Priory heard in the court of the bishop of Bath in 1121, where the case was heard, not just by the bishop's barons, but also by his *amici* (though they seem to have been present to celebrate a feast day rather than specifically to hear the case): Thomas Madox, *The History and Antiquities of the Exchequer* (London, 1711), 75, n. 1. So also in the Charwelton case, heard in the court of the abbot of Thorney c. 1107–11, we see the judgment being given by a group of named men plus the men of the saint. The distinction seems to be between outsiders called in to help make the judgment and the abbey's own tenants: Stenton, *English Justice*, 138–39. It was the lord himself who normally presided in his court: F.M. Stenton, *The First Century of English Feudalism* (Oxford, 2nd. ed., 1961), 77.

[68] *Leges Henrici Primi*, 162–63 (49, 2–49, 2a).

[69] The following figures are derived from the final concords listed in *Pleas before the King or His Justices*, 3, ed. Stenton, liii–lxxvii, plus such other final concords and other related records of the period as I have been able to find.

them we also find a much smaller group of regular and generally long-serving justices. The justiciar(s) of the day (Robert, earl of Leicester, and/or Richard de Lucy to 1168; Richard de Lucy from 1168 to 1179; Rannulf de Glanville from 1179 to 1189) is recorded as a justice of the court in around 88 per cent of the fines and related documents. The figure is high enough to demonstrate that he did normally sit in the Exchequer, not so high as to suggest that his presence ever became a fiction.[70] Another royal official who sat ex officio was Richard Fitz Neal, the treasurer, although he appears only in around two-thirds of the surviving documents. Richard of Ilchester, archdeacon of Poitou and then bishop of Winchester, was as assiduous as the justiciar in his attendance between 1165 and 1184; and after Richard's retirement, Hubert Walter came close to equalling his record in the last five years of the reign, appearing in around three-quarters of fines dating from this period. Four other justices (Geoffrey Ridel, archdeacon of Canterbury and later bishop of Ely; John of Oxford, bishop of Norwich; Rannulf of Gedding; Hugh Bardulf) appear in over half the fines and other documents made during the periods they were active as justices;[71] while another five men (William Basset, Roger Fitz Reinfrey, Robert of Wheatfield, Godfrey de Lucy and Michael Belet) occur in over one-third of the documents produced during the period of their activity as Exchequer justices and may also perhaps be regarded as outer members of this core group.[72] Between them these 12 individuals and the justiciar of the day account for about two-thirds of the total number of appearances of named justices of the Exchequer in the surviving records. The existence of this small group of core justices, three of whom served in the court for 20 years and more and four more for ten years or over, must have played an important part in the shaping of the court and of the law which it enforced. Such men had time to become expert in the hearing of litigation and are likely to have ensured that the Exchequer court retained consistency over time in its decision-making, an important factor in the development of a coherent body of custom associated with the court.

A similar phenomenon is also observable in the Eyre, though here it is less

---

[70] West is in error in stating that Glanvill is named at the head of the justices in all final concords of the period of his justiciarship (West, *Justiciarship in England*, 60). For final concords from this period in which he is not named see B.L., Cotton MS. Domitian A. X, fols. 184v–85r; B.L., Cotton MS. Otho D. III, fol. 66r; *The Cartulary of Newnham Priory*, ed. Joyce Godber, Bedfordshire Historical Record Society 43 (1963–64), 153; Douglas, *Feudal Documents of the Abbey of Bury St. Edmund's*, 186–87 (no. 229); *Feet of Fines of the Reign of Henry II and of the First Seven Years of the Reign of Richard I, 1182–1196*, P.R.S. 17 (1894), 3–4; *Sibton Abbey Cartularies and Charters: Part Four*, ed. Philippa Brown, Suffolk Records Society 10 (1988), no. 492.

[71] Geoffrey Ridel appears in around 65 per cent of the relevant documents between 1165 and 1189; John of Oxford, in around 66 per cent between 1177 and 1189; Ranulf of Gedding, in about 56 per cent between 1181 and 1185, and Hugh Bardulf in around 55 per cent between 1185 and 1189.

[72] William Basset occurs in 48 per cent of the final concords and other documents of the period between 1169 and 1185; Roger Fitz Reinfrey, in 37 per cent of the same between 1178 and 1189; Robert of Wheatfield, in 38 per cent between 1181 and 1189; Godfrey de Lucy, in 36 per cent between 1182 and 1189, and Michael Belet, in 33 per cent between 1180 and 1189.

easy to quantify and perhaps also less marked. A majority of the men who are known to have acted as justices in eyre during Henry II's reign (46 out of 84 justices) acted only on a single eyre visitation, and a further 20 justices acted only in two visitations. This leaves a fairly small group of just 18 justices (just over 20 per cent of the total number of justices) who were active on three or more eyre visitations; of whom two (Roger Fitz Reinfrey and Michael Belet) served on as many as six visitations.

It is important to note that there was also a significant degree of overlap between the 'core' justices in eyre and the 'core' justices of the Exchequer. Just under half of the 18 'core' justices (seven out of 18) were also 'core' justices of the Exchequer, and they included two eyre justices (Roger Fitz Reinfrey and Michael Belet) who served on the largest number of visitations. This overlap played a significant role in ensuring that a uniform and general 'custom of the king's court' developed and was observed both in the Exchequer and in the general eyre. But the 1176 instructions to the justices in eyre already discussed suggest another mechanism: reference by the justices of the general eyre of difficult cases (the cutting edge of new rules and customs) to the king and those in his place (perhaps a reference to the justiciar and the Exchequer court), thereby allowing such decisions to be taken centrally.[73] We should also not underestimate the amount of specific instruction given in legislation and communicated to all the justices of the king's courts.

By the thirteenth century, a second significant difference was clearly observable between the older courts which had been created prior to Henry's reign and the new-style royal courts created in that reign or on a similar model subsequently. All the former were periodic courts holding sessions lasting for one day or less at regular intervals: seignorial courts and hundred courts at three weekly intervals;[74] county courts at intervals of one month or more.[75] The Common Bench and King's Bench, by contrast, did their business in terms: holding daily sessions for several weeks during each of four terms every year. The general eyre was different. Only for visitations of major counties during the reign of Edward I did the justices of the general eyre adopt the practice of sitting for whole terms in a particular county. But they too seem normally to have held daily sessions in each of the counties they visited, until they had dealt with the business of the county and were ready to move on.

This difference was probably already observable (though in a less marked form) during Henry II's reign. The older rule had been the hundred courts should meet only once every four weeks, and this may still have been the

---

[73] See supra, p. 83.

[74] This was the maximum frequency laid down for such courts by legislation of 1234, though prior to this they may have met more frequently, perhaps as often as once every two weeks: *Close Rolls, 1231–34*, Public Record Office (London, 1905), 588–89.

[75] This was the maximum frequency laid down by c. 42 of the 1217 reissue of Magna Carta (c. 34 of the 1225 reissue): *Select Charters and Other Illustrations of English Constitutional History*, ed. William Stubbs, 9th ed. rev. by H.W.C. Davis (Oxford, 1921), 343, 350.

case in Henry II's reign (though in the thirteenth century it was believed that hundred courts were then meeting as often as once every two weeks).[76] The pre-Conquest practice with regard to county courts seems to have been that they should meet only twice a year, but allowed for additional meetings where this was necessary; and the author of the *Leges Henrici Primi* evidently still regarded twice yearly meetings as the norm. Legal historians, however, have generally thought it probable that by the early twelfth century county courts were meeting more regularly and on a monthly basis, and this was perhaps also the practice in Henry II's reign.[77]

The patchy survival of final concords prior to 1195 makes it difficult to be certain about the sessions held by royal courts in Henry II's reign. When in 1179 we find final concords being made before the itinerant justices visiting Lincolnshire as early as 30 June and as late as 18 July, it may well be that they were hearing business continuously between those two dates.[78] In 1187 we can certainly track another group of itinerant justices through final concords hearing cases at York on 4, 8, 16, and 22 July, hearing cases at Carlisle on 29 August, hearing cases at Doncaster on 17 September and then hearing them at Lincoln on 8, 9, and 17 October.[79] The Exchequer is even more problematic: for here we can be fairly certain that its justices were not dealing continuously with legal business, since they also had financial business to conduct at the same time. But we can see that the court must at certain times have been dealing with ordinary legal business on almost a daily basis. Thus in 1182 we find final concords being made at the Exchequer on 10 October and on 15, 16, and 21 October as well;[80] in 1186 we find final concords being made there on 27 April and on 6, 9, and 17 May;[81] and in 1188 we final final concords being made there on 29 October, 5, 13, 18, and 29 November and 5 December.[82] Continuous sessions meant, of course, that royal courts could deal with more business than was feasible for the older courts; and they were only made possible by the fact that these courts were run by men who were (for a period of time at least) full-time judges in the king's service, not local landowners like the judges of the older courts whose commitment to the legal system was only a part-time one.

---

[76] A meeting every four weeks is mentioned in the tenth-century Hundred Ordinance. The *Leges Henrici Primi* envisages that the hundred court will normally meet twelve times a year: *Leges Henrici Primi*, 100 (7, 4). For evidence that it was believed in 1234 that in Henry II's reign hundred courts had met every two weeks, see *Close Rolls, 1231–34*, 588–89.

[77] Frederick Pollock and Frederic William Maitland, *The History of English Law before the Time of Edward I*, 2nd ed. 2 vols. (Cambridge, 1898), 1: 540, n. 2; Cam, *Hundred and Hundred Rolls*, 10–11. But Palmer is non-committal: Robert C. Palmer, *The County Courts of Medieval England* (Princeton, 1982), 3–4.

[78] *Pleas before the King or His Justices*, 3: lxii.

[79] Ibid., 3: lxxii–lxxiii.

[80] Ibid., 3: lxvi–lxvii; *MSS. of Duke of Rutland at Belvoir*, 4: 22.

[81] *Pleas before the King or His Justices*, 3: lxxi.

[82] Ibid., 3: lxxv–lxxvi; B.L., Additional MS. 50121, fol. 41r.

There were other respects too in which the new king's courts differed from all existing courts. Hitherto courts had not kept any kind of written record of cases that they had heard: we know of particular pieces of litigation generally only through records drawn up by one of the parties or through royal writs drawn up at the end of the litigation to record the outcome and enforce the decision reached. The earliest surviving Plea Roll of one of the king's courts comes from 1194, and it has recently been suggested that Hubert Walter was responsible, as chief justiciar, for beginning the practice of keeping a permanent official record of litigation.[83] There is, however, enough evidence to show that this is mistaken and that the practice of keeping Plea Rolls to record all the litigation heard in the king's courts (and all the preliminary stages prior to the hearing of such litigation) does in fact go back to the reign of Henry II. A membrane from a Plea Roll of Michaelmas term 1207 reproduces a number of entries from older Plea Rolls, and these include one from an Exchequer Plea Roll of Hilary term 1181;[84] and Brian Kemp in 1973 printed an entry from the cartulary of Forde Abbey which reproduced an entry from an Exchequer Plea Roll of 34 Henry II (1187–88).[85] In Trinity term 1200 it was believed that there were still in existence rolls from the time when Richard de Luci was justiciar (that is, from before 1178), and a memorandum records the decision to search them for information relating to a final concord produced by one of the parties to a case.[86] But there is no record of what was found and thus no proof that there was a roll to search, so the question of whether or not Plea Rolls were being compiled in Richard de Lucy's time must remain open. No specific references have so far been found to Plea Rolls recording business heard before itinerant justices during Henry II's reign, but Richardson and Sayles have argued that we can deduce that they had come into existence by 1179 from references in the *Dialogus de Scaccario* to the extraction of individual debts from the rolls of the itinerant justices. Although the two passages cited are ambiguous, their interpretation is probably correct.[87] They may also be right in suggesting that 1176 (when the Pipe Rolls first begin to talk of *rotuli* rather than *brevia* containing the amercements of individuals before royal justices) marks the date when full Plea Rolls and not simply lists of amercements began to be kept by the justices.[88] If so, the change is one that coincides almost exactly with two other changes we have already discussed: the beginnings of a fully nationwide system of general

---

[83] Michael T. Clanchy, *From Memory to Written Record* (London, 1979), 74, 122; followed by John Baker in 'Records, Reports and the Origins of Case Law in England,' in *Judicial Records, Law Reports and the Growth of Case Law*, ed. John H. Baker (Berlin, 1989), 15–16.

[84] *Curia Regis Rolls*, Public Record Office, 16 vols. (London, 1923–79), 5: 76. This entry was also noted by Maitland, *Select Pleas of the Crown*, ed. F.W. Maitland, Selden Society 1 (1888), esp. xxvi.

[85] Kemp, 'Exchequer and Bench in the Later Twelfth Century,' 573.

[86] *Curia Regis Rolls*, 1: 208 and cf. the much less informative parallel versions of the same entry at pp. 227 and 245.

[87] Richardson and Sayles, *Governance of Mediaeval England*, 185; *Select Cases in the Court of King's Bench under Edward I*, 2, ed. G.O. Sayles, Selden Society 57 (1938), xv–xvi.

[88] Richardson and Sayles, *Governance of Mediaeval England*, 185.

eyres and the transformation of the royal justices who held sessions in counties from being merely presiding officers at those sessions to being the judges who determined litigation there.[89]

The keeping of a full written record of proceedings in the king's courts was an essential tool in the efficient running of those courts. If the king's courts were to keep track of the cases they were hearing, it was essential that they keep a record of the appearance and non-appearance of litigants before the court and of the orders the court itself then issued to the local sheriff. If those same courts were to ensure that the judgments they had given really were final judgments and the litigants not able to reopen the same cases on a subsequent occasion (something we know to have been a concern of Henry II and his advisers from the so-called 'Assize of Essoiners' which may belong to 1170),[90] then it was essential that the courts keep a permanent official record of such judgments. The only real puzzle here is how other courts had managed for so long to do without their own regular records.

There was also one other characteristic of the new royal courts which marked them off from all existing courts. There was by 1154 a long tradition of litigants bringing royal writs to initiate litigation, and this tradition continued and was reinforced in those older courts during Henry II's reign; but there is no suggestion (and there was still no suggestion in 1189) that any of these courts was limited to hearing only litigation initiated in this manner. The new royal courts, as soon as we can see them in operation, and probably from the very beginning of their existence, were limited to hearing only such litigation as they had been authorized to hear by royal writ; and the Eyre was probably also from the first limited to hearing only such other business (pleas of the crown and inquiries on the crown's behalf) as was specifically authorized in the articles of the eyre which the justices had received when they set out on their circuit. In practice the king was not willing (and perhaps not able) to make his courts available to litigants, whatever the litigation they were bringing, and followed a policy of admitting only certain specific categories of litigation there. Closely connected with this policy, indeed the outward manifestation of the policy, was the fact that most of the litigants were allowed to initiate litigation only through one of a limited number of standard forms of writ available from Chancery, each of which corresponded to a particular type of litigation which the king's court was willing to hear. By the end of Henry II's reign, to judge from *Glanvill*, there were in all some 30 original writs available.

The fact that royal courts were only competent to hear such litigation as they had been specifically authorized to hear by individual royal writs was probably of major importance in helping to foster the growth of legal argument there. It opened up to litigants and the legal advisers they came to employ whole new areas of possible argument. Defendants could now

[89] See supra, 80-86.
[90] See *Pleas before the King or His Justices*, 1: 151–54.

for the first time attempt to show that the plaintiff should not be answered because there were technical defects in his writ (so that, for example, the writ's form did not correspond with the standard form), or factual errors in the writ (for example, that the land sought was in another village than that named in the writ), or even simply spelling errors in it. They could also attempt to show that the plaintiff should not be answered because the plaintiff's count (his oral statement of claim or complaint made in court) did not correspond in one or more material particulars with his writ and was therefore not 'warranted' by it: for example, by showing that the quantities of land sought through the count differed from the quantities specified in the writ or that the plaintiff had called himself by one name in the count and by another in the writ. And naturally plaintiffs and the legal advisers they came to employ were given the opportunity of rebutting the arguments put forward on behalf of the defendant. We can already see litigants making these kinds of argument in the earliest surviving Plea Rolls; and there is every reason to suppose that the practice goes back to Henry II's reign. The use of standard forms of writ was important because it helped to point judges and lawyers in the direction of conceptualizing English law in terms of a series of discrete forms of action, each corresponding to one particular type of writ, each offering a particular type of remedy for particular constellations of factual circumstance, each following its own procedural rules and having its own distinct rules about proof. This was long to prove an effective obstacle to any broader conceptual thinking either about rights or about the law of proof.

In the final section of this paper I want to look at the various measures undertaken by Henry II and his advisers which began the process of integrating the older courts into a single legal system with these new royal courts. By the end of Henry II's reign, as we learn from *Glanvill*, there existed a rule that 'no-one is bound to answer concerning any free tenement of his in the court of his lord unless there is a writ from the lord king or his chief justice.'[91] Legal historians have disagreed and continue to disagree about the origins of this rule,[92] but there is no disagreement that it was a rule by 1189 and that its effect was to ensure that any litigation about title to free land brought in

---

[91] *Glanvill*, ed. Hall, 148 (XII, 25). The same rule is stated in slightly different terms at ibid., 137 (XII, 2).

[92] Maitland thought the rule was statutory in origin (Pollock and Maitland, *History of English Law*, 1: 147) and was inclined to associate it with the origins of the assize of novel disseisin and to date it to 1166 (*Select Pleas in Manorial Courts*, ed. F.W. Maitland, Selden Society 2 [1888], liv–lv). Lady Stenton also thought that the rule was 'statutory' and believed that it belonged to the period shortly after Henry II's accession: Stenton, *English Justice*, 26–29. R.C. Van Caenegem, however, thought that it was simply a common practice which had hardened into a customary rule: *Royal Writs in England from the Conquest to Glanvill*, Selden Society 77 (1958–59), 212–31; *Birth of the Common Law*, 25–28. S.F.C. Milsom argued that it was a simple statement of fact before it became a rule: S.F.C. Milsom, *The Legal Framework of English Feudalism* (Cambridge, 1976), 57–64. His view is followed, but modified in detail by Robert Palmer: 'The Origins of Property in England,' *Law and History Review* 3 (1985), 1–50, esp. 19–24.

lords' courts had to be initiated by royal writ.[93] *Glanvill* indicates that there were three types of writ which could be used for this purpose. One was for use by the lord himself when his tenant had committed a purpresture against him by occupying part of the lord's demesne and was addressed to the sheriff. It ordered the sheriff to ensure that the tenant appeared in the lord's court to answer him for purpresture.[94] The other two, the principal writ of right and the writ of right of dower, were both addressed to the lord himself and instructed him to do full right without delay ('precipio tibi quod sine dilacione plenum rectum teneas . . .') to the demandant in the case.[95] In effect, then, any lord hearing land litigation in his court (other than in the case of purpresture litigation, which was probably rare) was now being treated as a royal justice or royal commissioner. He could only act if he had specific royal authorization to do so, and that authorization came in the form of a royal order addressed to him. In land litigation, therefore, the lord's court had in some sense been turned into a 'royal' court by 1189.

This was largely a symbolic matter. Of greater practical significance in promoting the integration of seignorial courts into the English legal system was the creation of two routine mechanisms for the removal of litigation out of seignorial courts into other parts of the court system. The first of these was the procedure known as tolt. This allowed a plaintiff in land litigation initiated by royal writ to have that litigation removed into the county court on the basis that the lord's court had failed to do justice to him in his suit; an allegation that the court had failed to entertain his case or had unduly delayed it, rather than that it had given an unjust judgment determining it. Some legal historians have thought that the procedure was already in existence by the reign of Henry I, but the better opinion is that it was created early in Henry II's reign, perhaps shortly before 1164, though modified in detail thereafter.[96] The second allowed the removal of litigation only at a much later stage, was initiated by the defendant rather than the plaintiff, and secured the transfer of litigation into the king's court (normally the eyre), rather than the county court. This mechanism was called into play when, after the plaintiff had made his claim to land and offered battle to prove his right, the defendant denied that right and opted to support that denial, not by battle, but by putting himself on the

---

[93] The reference to the order of the chief justiciar refers to writs issued in the name of the chief justiciar rather than of the king during the king's absence. For writs of right of this kind issued shortly after the end of Henry II's reign, see *Pleas before the King or His Justices*, 1: 417–18 (nos. 3552–54).

[94] *Glanvill*, ed. Hall, 114–15 (IX, 11–12).

[95] *Glanvill*, ed. Hall, 61, 137–38 (VI, 5 and XII, 3–5).

[96] Joseph Biancalana, 'For Want of Justice: Legal Reforms of Henry II,' *Columbia Law Review* 88 (1988): 433–536, esp. 452–463; Mary Cheney, 'A Decree of King Henry II on Defect of Justice,' in *Tradition and Change: Essays in Honor of Marjorie Chibnall*, eds. D. Greenway, et al. (London, 1985), 183–193. The alternative view will be found in Stenton, *English Justice*, 57 and n. 13; R.C. Palmer, 'The Feudal Framework of English Law,' *Michigan Law Review* 79 (1981): 1130–64, esp. 1141–42, and *County Courts of Medieval England*, 144–45. For the procedure followed by the end of Henry II's reign, see *Glanvill*, ed. Hall, 139 (XII, 7) and cf. ibid., 61 (VI, 6) for the availability of the same procedure in the writ of the right of dower.

grand assize. Once he had done this, he needed to go to the king's chancery and secure a writ of peace addressed to the local sheriff and instructing him to prohibit the lord of the court from hearing the case any further. It was then up to the plaintiff to take the appropriate steps to ensure the choice of twelve local knights to give a verdict in the king's court as to which of the litigants had 'greater right' in the land concerned.[97] In fact, as *Glanvill* makes plain, this procedure was not confined to litigation about land. It was also available to the tenant in litigation between lord and tenant about feudal services claimed by the lord even though such litigation had not been initiated by royal writ.[98] This mechanism was almost certainly created when the grand assize itself was created (in 1179) and represents a careful and balanced compromise between the claims of lords and king.[99] Lords were to keep their jurisdiction over land pleas and over pleas about services. Jury trial was to become available (though not compulsory) in such pleas. The king was to retain his monopoly of the right to put free men on oath. These seemingly incompatible goals were to be reconciled by litigation continuing to be initiated in the lord's courts, but being removed out of them into the king's courts, if (but only if) the defendant chose the grand assize.

The integration of seignorial courts into a common legal system was also promoted in a number of other ways. Although *Glanvill* is not very clear on the matter, it seems probable that any allegation of 'false judgment' against a seignorial court was in his day a matter for the king's court and had been for most, if not all, of Henry II's reign.[100] Such allegations amounted to a claim that the court had wrongly decided a case, and so could have been a way in which the proceedings of such courts were measured by common external standards. But it seems unlikely that they were as yet an important channel contributing to legal uniformity. *Glanvill*'s discussion suggests that at the end of Henry II's reign it was still the normal practice for such cases to be decided by battle (preferably, he says, between the man who actually pronounced the judgment and the complainant), rather than by argument about the judgment and its relationship to the pleadings.[101] *Glanvill* also tells us of what happens when a case is being heard in a seignorial court and some legal difficulty arises which the court feels itself unable to determine. In such an eventuality, what happens is that the lord 'puts his court in the king's court' (that is, secures the

---

[97] The procedures followed at the end of Henry II's reign are described in *Glanvill*, ed. Hall 29–33 (II, 7–15).

[98] Ibid., 29–30 (II, 9); ibid., 105 (IX, 1).

[99] For the origins of the grand assize in legislation enacted at Windsor in 1179, see J.H. Round, 'The Date of the Grand Assize,' *EHR* 31 (1916): 268–69.

[100] For a discussion of the earlier twelfth-century practice with regard to false judgment, which seems to have involved immediate rehearing before another court locally, see Biancalana, 'For Want of Justice,' 456–58. By 1178–79 the justices in eyre were imposing amercements for false judgment (see *P.R. 24 Henry II*, 77, 99), but this did not necessarily mean that they were hearing individual pleas of false judgment, since such amercements could have been imposed on the basis of material revealed through presentments.

[101] *Glanvill*, ed. Hall, 110 (VIII, 9).

transfer of the case to the king's court), so that he may get the counsel and assent of the king's court as to what his court should do. Once he has got the advice, the case goes back to his court for determination. Interestingly, *Glanvill* does not regard this as a matter of grace or favour on the king's part, but as a duty that the king owes his barons. [102] Although elsewhere in the treatise, the author excuses his failure to discuss what happens in seignorial courts when litigation is brought there by writ of right partly on the grounds that the customs of such courts are 'so many and so varied that they cannot be written down,'[103] the implication of this procedure seems to be quite different: that there is already a 'common custom' of England that is shared by the king's courts and those of his barons, a common corpus of customs and rules applied in all courts.

Henry II's reign also saw the introduction of a series of procedures whose effect was to promote the integration of county courts into the national court system. Sheriffs were, of course, with few exceptions appointed by the king and so any cases over which they presided in the county court were in one sense being heard in a court presided over by a royal commissioner. But by the end of Henry II's reign, as we learn from *Glanvill*, sheriffs were also being directly and specifically commissioned by royal writs of set form to hear litigation there as well. [104] This made them even more directly and clearly royal commissioners for the hearing of such cases. What it did not do (though many distinguished historians have thought the contrary) was to authorize the sheriff to act on his own, without the suitors of the county courts, as though a single new-style royal justice. [105]

More important, perhaps, in terms of the integration of county courts into an overall system which also included the king's courts were the various procedures available for the removal of cases out of the county court into royal courts. Land or service litigation might be removed out of the county court (in much the same way as it was removed out of the lord's court) if the defendant in the case put himself on the grand assize. [106] Of greater importance in the present context was the writ *pone*, which (according to the account given in *Glanvill*) could be issued by the king at the request of either party or of both to remove a case from the county court into one of the king's courts, without the party concerned having to show that the county court had failed to do justice

---

[102] Ibid., 102–3 (VIII, 11).

[103] *Glanvill*, ed. Hall, 139 (XII, 6).

[104] Ibid., 53–54, 68–69, 80–81, 113, 116, 142–43 (V, 1; VI, 18; VII, 6–7; IX, 9–10, 14; XII, 12–14).

[105] Palmer, *County Courts of Medieval England*, 189–98. To the historians noted by Palmer as holding this view should be added Lady Stenton: see *English Justice*, 81–82.

[106] This is nowhere explicitly stated by *Glanvill* probably because its author considers the grand assize primarily in the context of litigation being initiated directly in the king's court. He does then, however, consider the procedure applicable where litigants put themselves on the grand assize in a seignorial court: see e.g., *Glanvill*, ed. Hall, 29–30 (II, 8–10). For evidence that defendants were getting the writ of peace after putting themselves on the grand assize in the county court before the end of Richard's reign, see *Curia Regis Rolls*, 1: 12. This had probably been the procedure ever since 1179.

to him, indeed, apparently without having to show any particular reason for wishing this to be done.[107] A variant form was apparently also available for litigation to be removed out of the county at the county's own request, where some legal difficulty had arisen which it was unable to resolve.[108] When this occurred, the litigation was removed permanently into the king's court and final judgment given there; it was not sent back to the county court (in contrast to what happened when it was a lord's court that asked for advice).

The author of *Glanvill* is even more insistent in the case of the county court than he is in the case of seignorial courts on the differences in custom between different county courts,[109] but the existence of such a mechanism for deciding difficult legal questions, and the comparative ease with which litigants could have cases transferred from the county court into the king's court, suggests that such differences may not have been too substantial and that there must already have been a considerable pressure for the homogenization of rules and procedures by the end of Henry II's reign. Thus already by 1189, considerable progress had probably been made towards creating a single legal system, embracing not only the king's courts, but also the county courts and (though only to a more limited extent) seignorial courts as well.

'Henry II and his advisers did great things; but they did not reach out from their own world.'[110] Such is the verdict of one recent and very distinguished legal historian, Prof. S.F.C. Milsom. I have argued in this essay that great things were indeed done in Henry II's reign and that these were in many cases the result of careful and deliberate changes made by the king and those who advised him; but I have also tried to show some of the ways in which it seems to me that Henry II and his adviser's were indeed 'reaching out' from their own world and consciously attempting to create something quite new and very significantly different from anything which had existed before. This they did when they created a system of regular countrywide judicial visitations and a central royal court for the hearing of civil litigation; when they ensured that judgments in these courts would be made by judges appointed by the king and that there would be sufficient continuity in the core personnel of these courts to allow the creation of a coherent body of national custom; when they decided that these courts were to keep a full record of their business; when they ensured that these courts would only do such business as the king specifically authorized; and when

---

107 *Glanvill*, ed. Hall, 62 (VI, 8). Palmer (*County Courts*, 149) implies that the tenant in *Glanvill*'s day had to show cause to secure a *pone*, but this view is not warranted by anything in *Glanvill*'s text. There are good reasons for thinking that the restriction was imposed after 1200. For the two forms of *pone* given in the treatise, see *Glanvill*, ed. Hall, 61–62 (VI, 7) (writ of right of dower) and 54 (V, 2) (*de libertate probanda*). *Glanvill* mentions the possibility of writs of right being so transferred but does not give the appropriate writ; ibid., 136 (XII, 1).

108 *Glanvill*'s discussion of this procedure is not very clear, but it would seem that it is the county court itself which has initiated the transfer, since both parties to the litigation are to be summoned when this occurs.

109 *Glanvill*, ed. Hall, 113, 147, 177 (IX, 10; XII, 23; XIV, 8).

110 Milsom, *Legal Framework of English Feudalism*, 3.

they began the process of integrating the various pre-existing local courts into a single nationwide legal system. It is difficult to resist the conclusion that Henry II and his advisers possessed a vision of the legal system they wished to create in England, a legal system that was radically different from the fragmented, localized and inefficient system they had inherited. How much this vision owed to Henry and how much to his advisers is not, I think, at all clear; but 1989 is as good a time as any for us to honor the memory of the creator (or perhaps the creators) of the Common Law.

5

Edward I and the Judges: The 'State Trials' of 1289-93

I

Edward I landed at Dover on 12 August 1289 after having spent over three years out of England. For the senior members of the judiciary who had run the main royal courts during Edward's absence, the year which followed his return proved to be traumatic. Four of the five justices of the Bench were dismissed from their posts. Its chief justice, Thomas Weyland, subsequently abjured all the territories under Edward I's rule and went into exile in France; the others were imprisoned in the Tower and then began the payment of large fines to the king for wrongdoing. All three judges of King's Bench were dismissed, and two similarly imprisoned and made to begin payment of substantial fines. One former justice of King's Bench agreed to pay a considerable sum to obtain a royal pardon. Death had already removed three of the five men who had served on a regular basis between 1286 and 1289 as justices of the 'Northern' eyre circuit; of the two survivors, one was imprisoned and fined in 1290, though the other survived unscathed. All four surviving regular justices of the 'Southern' eyre circuit were imprisoned and started paying large fines for misconduct.

This purge of senior royal judges and of their clerks was not an entirely isolated phenomenon. Complaints of misconduct during the king's absence were made at the same time against certain other senior royal officials and at least two of them (Adam of Stratton, one of the chamberlains of the Exchequer, and Master Henry de Bray, escheator south of the Trent) were dismissed from office and punished for wrongdoing. A large number of local officials were also the subject of complaints, and between 1290 and 1293 about 40 of these were imprisoned and made to pay fines for their misconduct.

The dismissal and punishment of individual royal officials, even quite senior ones, for misconduct was by no means unknown prior to 1289; and investigations into, and punishment of, the misdeeds of local officials had a long history stretching back at least as far as the Inquest of Sheriffs of 1170. But the making of complaints against so many royal judges and the punishment of so many of them was quite unprecedented. Henry of Bath, the senior justice of the court of King's Bench, had been dismissed and punished for misconduct in 1251, but he was the only judge to be disgraced at this time.[1] Master William of

---

[1] This episode is discussed by the late C. A. F. Meekings, *King's Bench Justices, 1239–1258*, scheduled for publication in the Selden Society's supplementary series. Unless otherwise stated, all manuscript references are to documents in the PRO.

Watford, a justice of the Jews, had been dismissed and convicted of misconduct in 1272 and subsequently outlawed, when he failed to surrender to his bail; but again he was the only justice directly implicated in wrongdoing.[2] The closest precedent to the events of 1289 – 90 lies in the disgrace of Hamon Hautayn and Robert of Ludham in 1286 for misconduct in the running of the Exchequer of the Jews. But the justices of the Jews can hardly be counted as members of the higher judiciary and again the scandal was confined to a single court.[3]

The downfall of so many royal judges certainly made a considerable impression on contemporaries. All the chroniclers mention it. It inspired a biblical parody, the 'Story of the Passion of the Justices' (*Narracio de Passione Justiciarorum*) and a short poem.[4] It is also something mentioned in almost all modern textbooks on the period as well as in some more specialised works on the history of English law and legal institutions. There is, however, only one detailed 'modern' account of this episode, that by Tout and Johnstone.[5] A reappraisal of all the relevant evidence, including some material not known to Tout and Johnstone, indicates that much of their account is in need of revision. In this paper I will try to indicate some of the more serious errors in this standard account and sketch out the main outlines of a revised interpretation of the whole episode.

II

'For three years', wrote Tout and Johnstone, 'the country had been free from [Edward I's] personal supervision' and,

> from his justices and officials of trust, down to the humblest of his subordinates, all apparently had seized the opportunity of their master's absence to extort money, pervert justice, use their official position to serve their private ends.

It was hardly surprising, therefore, that a 'universal outcry' had 'greeted him on his return'. The king's response had been the appointment in mid-October 1289 of a group of commissioners, headed by John de Pontoise, bishop of Winchester, 'ad audiendum gravamina et injurias si que per ministros illata fuerint quibuscunque personis regni'. These commissioners, the *auditores querelarum*, had then been at work at Westminster for the next three years, and a record of their proceedings still survived in two plea rolls now in the Public Record Office (JUST 1/541A and 541B). It had been as an 'immediate result' of their work that there had occurred the 'gradual removal of the

---

[2] The relevant records are printed and discussed in Brand, 'The Exchequer of the Jews, 1265 – 90', to appear as the introduction to Vol. VI of the Jewish Historical Society's edition of the Plea Rolls of the Exchequer of the Jews.
[3] *Select Cases in the Court of King's Bench*, I ed. G. O. Sayles (Selden Soc., lv, 1936), clv – lix.
[4] *State Trials of the Reign of Edward the First, 1289 – 1293*, ed. T. F. Tout, H. Johnstone (Camden Soc., 3rd ser., ix, 1906), 95 – 9. There is a second version of the poem in BL MS Stowe 386, f.201v.
[5] *State Trials*, introduction.

greatest offenders'. Thomas Weyland, 'the first to suffer', had been 'starved into submission after an ignominious flight, and finally by his own choice abjured the realm'. Ralph de Hengham, William of Brompton, John de Lovetot, and others 'were imprisoned and fined'. The 'permanent character of [Thomas Weyland's] punishment', his 'notable disgrace and banishment', indicated that he had been 'more deeply involved than his colleagues' in wrongdoing; and the 'enormous sum of 7,000 marks reported as the amount of [Hengham's] fine would seem to imply serious guilt' on his part as well. In both cases the punishment imposed reflected a general judgment on the extent and nature of each man's wrongdoing, but some of the fines paid by the other judges were, Tout and Johnstone suggested, of an entirely different character. Once the worst offenders had been punished, the king's rigour could 'abate for a money consideration'. In their cases, the fine was no more, in effect, than a bribe to the king to pardon their offences.[6]

A first important correction concerns the downfall of Thomas Weyland. The precipitating cause of Weyland's downfall was a murder which took place in July 1289. Within two months justices had been appointed to enquire into the killing, and by mid-September 1289 Weyland had been indicted for having harboured the two killers. He was subsequently arrested but managed to escape and take refuge at the Franciscan friary at Babwell. It was while he was still a fugitive that he was suspended from office, and that suspension was a direct consequence of his indictment and flight. Eventually Weyland was starved out and taken under safe-conduct to London. Although a number of complaints of official misconduct had by then been made against him, the only charges he faced at his trial were those of having been an accessory after the fact to murder and of prison breach (for having escaped from custody). In advance of the trial Weyland was offered a choice between ordinary jury trial on these charges, perpetual imprisonment and abjuration. He chose the latter. Arraignment was, therefore, merely the formal prelude to Weyland's admission of guilt and his abjuration. The *auditores querelarum* played no part in Weyland's downfall. His indictment preceded their appointment by almost a month, and it was this indictment which led to his arrest and flight and his consequent suspension (and eventual dismissal) from office. His 'trial' was before three specially appointed justices of gaol delivery, none of whom was an *auditor querelarum*. Weyland's eventual abjuration was the 'punishment' for two specific offences of felony, neither of which had any connection with his duties as a royal justice. It was not the consequence of any general judgment of just how deeply Weyland had been involved in official wrongdoing while the king had been abroad.[7]

It is doubtful whether the *auditores querelarum* really were, as Tout and Johnstone supposed, appointed in response to a stream of complaints received by Edward I on his return to England. Admittedly, this is what the Dunstable annalist tells us, and John of Oxnead even suggests that they were appointed because of the many complaints the king had received while he was still abroad. The Osney annalist, however, is equally clear that it was the

[6] *State Trials*, xiii, xxix – xxx.
[7] Thomas Weyland's downfall is discussed in greater detail with full references below, pp. 113, 131–3.

appointment of the commission which provoked the complaints and not *vice versa*; and the wording of the writ notifying sheriffs of the appointment of the *auditores* and ordering them to publicise it gives as the king's motive for so doing his 'heartfelt desire for the tranquillity of our kingdom and people' and speaks only of 'any complaints . . . there might be'. This does not sound like a king reacting to a stream of complaints already received.[8] Moreover, an eyewitness present at Westminster on 12 November 1289, the day and place appointed for the receiving of complaints, tells us that only a few people actually brought complaints on that day; and other evidence suggests that many of the complaints against the judges, and against others too, were only submitted later: in the judges' cases, probably only *after* their dismissal and punishment.[9]

The timing of the appointment of the *auditores querelarum* suggests that it could have been a reaction to the news of the indictment and flight of Thomas Weyland. Edward I might have begun to wonder whether others of his senior judges and officials had been involved in serious wrongdoing during his absence. Inviting those with grievances against them to submit complaints was one way of discovering the truth. But the timing may well have been fortuitous. The wording of the writ to sheriffs telling them of the establishment of the *auditores querelarum* does not suggest any particular concern with the misdeeds of senior royal officials or judges, and may well indicate that when it was drafted it was expected that it would be local officials who would be the main, and perhaps the only, object of complaints. The appointment of the *auditores querelarum* should, then, perhaps be seen as yet another Edwardian expedient for dealing with the persistent problem of misconduct by local officials — in succession to the Hundred Rolls enquiry of 1274 – 5, the abortive plans for special justices set out in the statute of Ragman and the delegation to the justices in eyre (as from 1278) of powers to hear complaints against local officials. This time the king and his advisers were trying a centralized solution, deputing the receipt of complaints and the holding of preliminary hearings into them to what amounted to a subcommittee of the king's council, but reserving to the council itself the giving of judgment on them. Edward certainly had good reasons for embarking on a fresh attack on the problem of local government corruption. He was short of money.[10] Almost inevitably some, quite possibly many, of his local officials would be convicted of misconduct in any fresh enquiry and would then be compelled to make fine with him for their offences. Encouraging such complaints, and redressing the grievances of the complainants, might also turn out to be helpful when he came to seek the consent of parliament to taxation. On this hypothesis, it was no part of the original plan to provide a forum for complaints against senior royal officials and justices. It was largely a matter of chance that the remit of the commissioners was sufficiently wide to allow them to entertain such complaints as well as those against local officials.

Tout and Johnstone were, in any case, wrong to suppose that it was the *auditores querelarum* appointed in mid-October 1289 who remained at work for the next three years. The original *auditores* were specifically commissioned

[8] *Ann. Mon.*, iii. 356; *Chronica Johannis de Oxenedes*, ed. H. Ellis (*RS*, 1859), 274; *Ann. Mon.*, iv. 319; *Foedera*, I, ii. 715.

[9] *HMC Report on MSS in Various Collections*, vol. i (1901), 256 – 7.

[10] M. C. Prestwich, *War, Politics and Finance under Edward I* (London, 1972), 202.

to receive complaints and to report on them to the next session of parliament; it was the king's council itself that was then to give judgment on them. Their work and their existence came to an end at the Hilary parliament of 1290.[11] What the two surviving plea rolls (JUST 1/541A and 541B) identified by Tout and Johnstone as a record of proceedings before the original group of *auditores* actually record, for the most part, are proceedings subsequent to the Hilary parliament of 1290 before two separate groups of *auditores* with jurisdiction over greater and lesser offenders respectively, and with power to give judgment on the complaints that were made to them. These two separate, though not wholly independent, groups seem to have been appointed at the same parliament. That which dealt with great offenders was again led by the bishop of Winchester and contained five of the original seven *auditores*; that which dealt with lesser offenders was led by Master Thomas of Scarning. The appointment of these two separate groups was presumably a reaction to the volume of complaints that had by then been received against the great offenders. After Michaelmas term 1291, these two groups in turn seem to have been merged under a single new head, Peter of Leicester.

Tout and Johnstone give the impression that it was the *auditores querelarum* who alone conducted all the 'State Trials' of 1289–93, and alone imposed punishment on the major offenders. They seem, however, to have played only a very limited part in the proceedings which led to the imprisonment and fining of the judges. Weyland's colleagues were convicted of misconduct in proceedings initiated by a complaint which seems to have been submitted directly to the king's council at the Hilary parliament of 1290; and judgment on it was certainly given by the council during the course of that parliament. The complaint seems to have been directed solely against Thomas Weyland. It was only during the course of the proceedings that it was decided that the alleged misconduct of the chief justice also implicated the court's chief clerk and all of Weyland's colleagues in the Bench, other than Beckingham.[12] Solomon of Rochester and his colleagues of the 'Southern' eyre circuit seem likewise to have been convicted of wrongdoing as the result of a complaint made directly to the king's council at this parliament and in this case, too, judgment seems to have been given by the council itself during the course of the parliament.[13] The original group of *auditores querelarum* did at least process the complaint which eventually led to the downfall of Ralph de Hengham, but again the actual judgment in the case seems to have been given by the king's council in the Hilary parliament of 1290.[14] Hengham's colleague, William of Saham, seems also to have been convicted of wrongdoing as a result of the same complaint, but the judgment against him was probably given by the 'great offenders' group of *auditores querelarum*.[15] He seems to have been the only justice whose initial conviction was before this group. Other justices were brought before these commissioners to answer complaints against them, but only after their initial convictions for wrongdoing. In several cases complainants did succeed in securing redress as a result of their complaints against

[11] *Foedera*, I, ii. 715.
[12] CP 40/81, m.102.
[13] SC 8/263, no. 13125; *Rot. Parl.*, i. 56; KB 27/124, mm.42d – 43.
[14] *State Trials*, 27 – 40.
[15] *State Trials*, 27 – 40.

justices being heard by the commissioners, but in only one do the commissioners seem to have given a further judgment against a royal justice, ordering his renewed imprisonment pending his agreement to pay a second fine to the king.[16]

And what of the supposed shift in the king's attitude towards offenders during the course of the 'State Trials'? Weyland's 'punishment', as we have seen, was not imposed for judicial corruption, and its apparent harshness merely reflects the seriousness of his offence. The other judges were, with one exception, all treated in much the same way: a brief period of imprisonment preceding the agreement of the offender to pay a sizable fine to the king. The imprisonment was analogous to that suffered by defendants in ordinary civil litigation when they had been convicted of a trespass, not a punishment in itself but simply a way of ensuring that the defendant consented to pay a sum 'agreed' with the king for his release and found adequate sureties to do so. The amount of the fine must in all cases have reflected the offender's ability to pay rather than any considered judgment on the extent and gravity of his wrongdoing, since it was fixed while other charges of wrongdoing were still pending and did not subsequently increase even when the offender obtained a royal pardon of all wrongdoing committed while in the king's service or was again convicted of wrongdoing.[17] It seems clear that Hengham's fine was so large not because he was the worst offender but because he was the wealthiest. Only in the single case of Nicholas of Stapleton is it possible to see any softening of the king's attitude, for Nicholas was allowed to pay his fine for a pardon before he had been convicted of any wrongdoing.[18] But this hardly amounts to a major shift in royal policy.

It is also clear that Tout and Johnstone were wrong in asserting that *all* of the king's justices had taken advantage of the king's absence to 'extort money, pervert justice and use their official position to serve their private ends'. This is not to deny that there is some fairly substantial evidence of judicial corruption during the period the king was out of the country. In his complaint against Thomas Weyland, Hugh of Gosbeck alleged that the chief justice had been responsible for the alteration of part of an entry on his plea roll, the main official record of all business done in the court, to Hugh's detriment. The roll had originally recorded Hugh as denying the claim of a demandant to be the rightful heir of the relative on whose seisin he had based his title to a rent-charge in two Suffolk villages and the submission of this issue to a jury. Weyland had erased this part of the entry and substituted for it a passage recording that judgment had been given against Hugh on the grounds that he had left the court before the conclusion of the hearings in contempt of court. Weyland's plea roll has indeed been erased at the relevant point, and after his

---

[16] *State Trials*, 5 – 11; but there is no evidence that Boyland paid a second fine. He had previously been convicted of wrongdoing with Rochester and the other members of the 'Southern' eyre circuit.

[17] There is only one piece of evidence to suggest that fines might have been increased after their initial 'agreement'. A schedule to one of the membranes of JUST 1/541B (printed at *State Trials*, 39) puts Hengham's fine at 8000 *m.*, though he is known to have paid well over 9000 *m.* and perhaps as much as 10,000 *m.* Only John de Lovetot is known to have been made to pay a second fine for wrongdoing, and he is known to have protested vigorously at being made to do so; E 159/66, m.26. It may not have been for wrongdoing while in the king's service.

[18] *CPR 1281 – 92*, 389; *CFR 1272 – 1307*, 284; *State Trials*, 84.

fall he is to be found in possession of a rent-charge in the two villages concerned of exactly the same value as that at stake in the litigation. Presumably he had been given some sort of interest in it as the price of his assistance.[19] It also seems certain that Henry Gerard of Guildford, the clerk of John de Lovetot, had received a bribe from Gilbert of Dunmow for his assistance in procuring a favourable jury at a gaol delivery session to acquit him of a charge of homicide, and quite possible that part of the bribe was destined for Henry's master. In the course of proceedings before the *auditores querelarum* both Gilbert and Henry admitted the transaction.[20] There is also fairly strong circumstantial evidence of wrongdoing by Nicholas of Stapleton and William of Brompton.[21] It should be noted, however, that in the case of each of these justices convincing evidence of corrupt behaviour exists only for a handful of cases at the most, a minute proportion of the total number of cases which the justices had heard during these years, and this notwithstanding the fact that the appointment of the *auditores querelarum* and the downfall of the justices gave those with grievances against corrupt justices an excellent opportunity to seek redress. If there was corruption it seems to have been on a much smaller scale than Tout and Johnstone seem to imply.

Moreover, as we have already seen, at least two of the justices who had served the king during this period survived the 'State Trials' entirely unscathed; one (Ellis of Beckingham) retaining his position as a justice of the Bench, the other (John of Mettingham) becoming chief justice of the same court.[22] It also seems probable that a further three justices who were convicted of wrongdoing in 1290 were not in fact guilty of any serious misconduct. Roger of Leicester, one of the justices of the Bench, was only convicted of wrongdoing in a single set of proceedings. The complaint appears to have been directed solely against Weyland, and it seems to have been the king's council which concluded that Leicester and all of Weyland's other colleagues (apart from Ellis of Beckingham, who only escaped responsibility because for the one term in question he was not sitting in the Bench) were guilty of misconduct simply because the plea rolls made for them were in agreement with the chief justice's plea roll in their recording of the case. This was harsh treatment because in so doing they were simply following the established practice of the court, under which the rolls of the other justices 'followed' that of the chief justice and were copied from it, probably some time after it was written. It looks even harsher when we remember that it may well be that it was only Weyland himself who actually knew what had really happened in the case.[23] Leicester was only involved in one other set of proceedings: those arising out of a complaint made against Richard of Boyland in his role as an assize justice for Cambridgeshire. In the course of these proceedings Boyland requested that Leicester be summoned to answer with him as his fellow justice in hearing the assize. Both men seem to have been cleared of any wrongdoing in the matter.[24] Walter of Hopton, one

---

[19] CP 40/73, m.86d; E 372/139, m.8d.

[20] *State Trials*, 53 – 61.

[21] I hope to discuss this in detail elsewhere.

[22] It should, however, be noted that Mettingham did become involved in several of the proceedings against his colleagues.

[23] CP 40/81, m.102; JUST 1/541B, mm.5,10d,12,24d,33; *Bartholomaei de Cotton Historia Anglicana*, ed. H .R. Luard (*RS*, 1859), 173; *CR 1251 – 3*, 372.

[24] JUST 1/540B, m.5d.

of the justices of the 'Southern' eyre circuit, was also convicted of wrongdoing only in a single case. In a subsequent petition he made out a convincing case for exoneration from all responsibility. The petition was initially rejected, but it may ultimately have been successful for there is no trace of the fine being paid or of measures being taken to make him pay it.[25] There are no other complaints alleging misconduct by him. Master Thomas of Siddington was convicted of misconduct in the same proceedings. He was not able to make a similarly convincing case for escaping liability but his responsibility was probably only formal and does not reflect any real culpability on his part. In any case, for him too, this seems to have been the only set of proceedings in which he was involved.

There was, then, certainly some corruption during the king's absence, though by no means all the justices were involved in it, and the actual extent of it may have been comparatively small. It does not follow that even this small amount of corruption was in any way facilitated by the king's absence. There is no real reason to suppose that when he was in the country the king was able to exercise so tight a control over his judges or other royal officials as to exclude entirely all possibility of corruption on their part. It may well be that the amount of corruption revealed by the 'State Trials' of 1289 – 93 did not differ greatly from that which was normal when the king was in the country; and it may well be that all that was exceptional in 1289 – 93 was that the king created the most favourable conditions possible for individuals wronged by corrupt justices to complain of their grievances.

Tout and Johnstone put a specific figure on only four of the fines which the judges were induced to agree to pay: those of Hengham, Brompton, Rochester and Saham, amounting in all to some 20,000 m.[26] In fact fines for misconduct, or in Stapleton's case for a pardon, were made by a total of some ten justices; and, although we cannot be certain of the exact amount in every case, the total seems to have been in excess of 30,000 m. Tout and Johnstone also tabulated the amounts actually paid by eight of the judges, a grand total of just under £15,000.[27] Unfortunately their figures are incomplete, for they do not take into account any payments made after Hilary term 1294. The total actually paid by or on behalf of the eight judges was in excess of £19,127 6s. 8d. and to this figure should be added the £200 paid by a ninth judge, Nicholas of Stapleton. To reach a total for the profits made from the trials of the judges by the king we must also add in the £350 received by the king from the forfeiture of the chattels of Thomas Weyland and from one year's profits from his lands.[28] The king's total profit from the trials thus came to just under £20,000, not much under one year's normal Crown income.

Tout and Johnstone noted only one instance of the rehabilitation of one of the disgraced justices: that of Ralph de Hengham, appointed a member of the king's council in 1300 and as chief justice of the Bench in 1301.[29] But Hengham was not the only one. By 1300 William of Brompton had sufficiently regained the king's confidence to be employed overseas on negotiations concerning the

---

[25] SC 8/263, no.13125; *Rot. Parl.*, i. 56.

[26] *State Trials*, xxix – xxxii.

[27] *State Trials*, xxxviii.

[28] E 372/139, mm.8d,5d. Most of his chattels and most of the profits from his lands went to the prior of Ely and the abbot of Bury St. Edmund's.

[29] *State Trials*, xxx.

dower of the king's daughter Elizabeth, countess of Holland, and in 1302 he was appointed a justice of the Cornish eyre.[30] Master Thomas of Siddington was sent on the king's service to Scotland in 1298 but died the following year.[31] Most of the other judges did not survive long enough to be rehabilitated. The earliest to die was William of Saham. By 1296 Boyland, Lovetot and Stapleton were dead as well.[32] The only justices to live beyond 1300 and not be rehabilitated were Hopton and Leicester. Even Thomas Weyland enjoyed a measure of rehabilitation. In 1292, while in Paris, he was one of the legal experts consulted by an emissary of Edward I about the Scottish succession question, and later he was given a pardon allowing him to come home to England, so that it was in Essex that he died early in 1298.[33]

III

In this paper I have followed conventional usage in referring to the various proceedings involving judges, clerks and other royal officials heard between 1289 and 1293 as 'State Trials'. The term is a convenient and, in some respects at least, an apt one. The defendants were all royal officials, and in most cases what was being alleged against them was misconduct in an official capacity. In certain other respects, however, the term is misleading. As we have already seen, Thomas Weyland's indictment and trial were for wrongdoing wholly unconnected with his official duties, and the same seems also to have been true of the two trials of Adam of Stratton.[34] More importantly, there is little trace, even in those proceedings where official misconduct was alleged, of the proceedings being seen as 'state trials'. There was no use of the procedures of presentment or indictment characteristic of legal proceedings concerned with offences against the king or the public interest, no use other than in one wholly exceptional case of criminal appeal procedure.[35] Nor was there even an attempt to maintain the theory that complainants were suing in the name of the king, or in the king's name as well as their own.[36] Judicial corruption and other forms of official wrongdoing were treated simply as matters of private grievance, of concern only to those who had directly suffered as a result of

---

[30] *CPR 1292 – 1301*, 102; *Records of Antony Bek, Bishop and Patriarch, 1283 – 1311*, ed. C. M. Fraser (Surtees Soc., clxii, 1953), 76 – 8,85; *CPR 1292 – 1301*, 494; *CPR 1301 – 07*, 57,64.

[31] *Documents Illustrating the Crisis of 1297 – 98 in England*, ed. M. C. Prestwich (Camden Soc., 4th ser., xxiv, 1980), 157,158,n.1; CP 40/124, m.38; *CIPM.*, iii. no. 551.

[32] E 159/65, m.15d; *CIMisc.*, iii. no. 365; *CIPM*, iii. no. 207; City of London Record Office, Hustings Deeds and Wills, Roll 22, no. 2.

[33] Above, n. 7.

[34] Stratton's first conviction early in 1290 was for felony and he was probably tried like Weyland before specially appointed commissioners. No records of this trial have so far been discovered. His second conviction for the forgery of charters was in proceedings in the Exchequer early in 1291; E 368/62, m.12.

[35] *State Trials*, 40 – 5.

[36] Except in the proceedings brought against Nicholas of Stapleton by Thomas of Goldington and his wife, where the fiction that they had been suing on the king's behalf was invoked when Stapleton acquired a royal pardon after the joinder of issue to halt further proceedings: *State Trials*, 81 – 4. But this was only possible because the original proceedings in which the alleged miscarriage of justice had occurred were themselves conducted at the king's suit.

them. Complainants were, therefore, free to withdraw from their complaints as they saw fit and so be able to make out of court settlements with those they accused. Admittedly, the king did receive fines from offenders on conviction; but even this, as we have already noticed, was also characteristic of other purely private types of litigation. It could well be argued that one of the most interesting aspects of the whole episode, though one which has been obscured by the label conventionally attached to these proceedings, is that in certain important respects these were not 'State Trials' at all.

6

Chief Justice and Felon: The Career of
Thomas Weyland

On 20 February 1290, at a special gaol delivery session held at the Tower of London, Thomas Weyland took an oath of abjuration, promising to leave England and not to return to it nor to enter any of Edward I's other territories without special permission from the King. He was assigned Dover as his port of embarkation and given nine days to reach it. Despite the time of year, Weyland, like other abjurors, had to make his journey barefoot and without any covering for his head. He was assigned specific places to reach each day en route to Dover but he was not allowed to leave the highway when he reached them to take shelter for the night. The places assigned are, as might be expected, all on Watling Street, the main route from London to Dover; and the stages assigned to each day of the journey were fairly easy ones. The furthest Weyland was expected to travel in any one day was about nine miles. We are told that he was in a weak condition when starting out and that he was deliberately given an easy journey for this reason.

Just under nine months before this enforced winter walk, Thomas Weyland had still been in office as one of the most senior of Edward I's judges. In Trinity term 1289 Weyland had presided over the Bench at Westminster, the main royal court for the hearing of civil litigation, as its chief justice, and as late as 18 July 1289 was still sitting as an assize justice at Waltham Cross in Hertfordshire. How had this dramatic downfall come about? And who was Thomas Weyland? What were his origins and background? What do we know about his career as a royal justice? And what happened to him after his downfall?

This paper on the life and career of Thomas Weyland is part of a much larger long-term study of the Edwardian judiciary as a whole. For most of its history the common law has been the product of a complex interaction between lawyers, judges, and the world outside the court room. One essential preliminary to the understanding of that interaction in any period of its history is the accumulation of reliable information about the judges: to see from what social class or group they were drawn; what kind of experience and training they had acquired prior to their appointment; how they actually functioned within their courts; what the norms of judicial behaviour were both in theory and in practice; what was the status enjoyed by members of the judiciary; what were the terms on which they held their posts.

The reign of Edward I (1272-1307) is the first period in which we can begin to give satisfactory answers to many of these questions. It is the first period for which we possess detailed information about what was actually said and done in the King's courts in the form of unofficial reports of cases heard there, written in the Anglo-Norman French that was the language used by judges and lawyers. For earlier periods we possess only the formal and often summary reports of litigation contained in the Latin plea-roll enrolments, the official record of business done in the court, which are much less informative. We can, for the first time, in Edward's reign begin to see in detail the ways in which the common law was being shaped and developed and the contribution which was being made to that process by individual judges. It is also the first period for which relevant sources survive in sufficient quantity to make it possible for us to acquire detailed information on the background of all the members of the higher judiciary. Comparatively little work has, however, been done on the judges of Edward I, and scholars who have worked on them have generally used only a small part of the surviving sources relevant to such a study.[1]

Thomas Weyland, for example, has attracted the attention of a small number of scholars. In the mid-nineteenth century his life was briefly reviewed by Lord Campbell as part of his series of *Lives of the Chief Justices of England*, and Edward Foss similarly gave a short account of it in his comprehensive prosopographical work, *The Judges of England*. Thomas Weyland was also sufficiently well-known (or, rather, notorious) for T. F. Tout at the end of the nineteenth century to have written a fresh account of his life for the *Dictionary of National Biography*. Much more recently, his life and career have again been

---

[1] The only comprehensive study of the justices of Edward I is that contained in the third volume of Edward Foss's *The Judges of England* published in 1851. G. O. Sayles, writing in 1936, noted that 'The lives of the judges as set forth in the pages of Foss clamour for re-editing and amplification, but the task is formidable and not likely to be faced for many years': *Select Cases in the Court of King's Bench*, vol. 1, ed. G. O. Sayles, Selden Soc. lv, 1936, xlix. The only general study of any kind devoted to the Edwardian justices published since then has been that by Sayles himself in the same volume. This was, however, confined to King's Bench justices and was intended only to provide a 'skeleton outline' of their careers.

discussed by Professor Anne Spitzer.[2] Each of these scholars, however, used only such materials bearing on the life and career of Thomas Weyland as were already in print. They made no use of the extensive material relevant to both which survives in manuscript in the Public Record Office, nor of the many unprinted Year Book reports of cases heard in the Bench during the period of his chief justiceship, sources of major importance for our knowledge of Thomas Weyland's life and career.

Using these new sources, I will demonstrate that Weyland's origins and early career were not as supposed by earlier biographers; make a fresh appraisal of his work as a royal justice; and show the need for a major revision of the hitherto accepted view as to the chronology and causes of his dramatic downfall in 1289. I will also hope to demonstrate the need for a reassessment of the traditional view of Thomas Weyland as a clearly and notoriously corrupt justice and conclude by filling in some of the hitherto unknown details of just what happened to him after his disgrace.

1

Tout's biographical note on Thomas Weyland in the *Dictionary of National Biography* asserts that he was born into a 'respectable' Norfolk gentry family, which drew its name from 'Weyland, a wood near Watton, which [also] gives its name to a Norfolk hundred' and that he was probably a younger son of William de Weyland, escheator of England south of the Trent in the early 1260s and a justice of the Bench in 1272-3. In fact, Thomas Weyland was the third son of Herbert and Beatrice Weyland and William Weyland was an elder brother, and there is no reason to suppose that either of his parents belonged to the gentry.[3] Herbert Weyland certainly did not come from the Norfolk gentry family of Weyland, for no such family existed at this time. He was probably from a local peasant family.[4] Thomas's mother, Beatrice, was one of six daughters and coheiresses of Stephen of Witnesham, who had been a minor landholder in

[2] J. Campbell, *The Lives of the Chief Justices of England*, vol. 1, London 1849, 77-78; Foss, vol. 2, 170-2; T. F. Tout in the *D.N.B.* sub Weyland; Anne L. Spitzer, 'The Legal Careers of Thomas Weyland and Gilbert of Thornton', *Journal of Legal History* vi, 1985, 62-83.

[3] F. Blomefield, *An Essay towards a Topographical History of the County of Norfolk*, vol. 6, London 1807, 173 note 4; *Cal. Fine Rolls, 1272-1307*, 22; CP 25(1)/214/27, no. 24; E 159/34, m. 4d.; *Cal. Fine Rolls, 1272-1307*, 21.

Witnesham, a Suffolk village some four miles north-east of Ipswich, and in two other neighbouring villages, Westerfield and Akenham.[5] The family surname of Weyland is not toponymic in origin but is probably derived from the personal name Wayland. It was only as Thomas and his brothers began to rise in the world that they began to add the locative 'de' to their name, perhaps with the deliberate intention of suggesting that it was a toponymic and thus disguising the lowliness of their origins.

The comparative obscurity of Weyland's beginnings is typical of a majority of the higher judiciary of the reign of Edward I. Of the thirty-eight men who served as justices of the Bench or King's Bench during his reign only five seem to have come from knightly or baronial families.[6] Most justices, like Weyland, came from the ranks of the lower free tenantry; and at least one senior royal justice, Ellis of Sutton, a justice of King's Bench from 1285 to 1287, was of servile birth.[7] Thomas Weyland is a typical figure in another sense, too. No less than five of the twenty-five Bench justices of the reign of Edward I came from his home county of Suffolk, more than from any other county.[8]

---

[4] The authority vouched by Tout for his statement that the manor of Oxburgh in Norfolk had been in the possession of the Weyland family in the early thirteenth century is the Black Book of the Exchequer, as printed by Walter Rye in *Norfolk Antiquarian Miscellany*, vol. 1, Norwich 1877. This, however, contains extracts from an account of an aid collected in 20 Edward III (1346-7). The manor only passed into the possession of members of the Weyland family around 1270 when the future chancellor Robert Burnell settled it on Thomas's elder brother William, William's illegitimate son Nicholas and Nicholas's wife Juliana: KB 27/49, m. 21. For the earlier history of the manor see Blomefield, vol. 6, 168-71. The manor continued to be held by the descendants of Nicholas.

[5] CP 25(1)/213/16, no. 78; CP 25(1)/213/18, no. 30.

[6] Of the justices of the Bench, Gilbert of Preston (chief justice in 1273) was the eldest son and inherited the lands of a Northamptonshire knightly family which can be traced back to the time of Domesday Book; John of Cobham (justice 1273-5) was the eldest son and inherited the lands of a former Bench justice who had become a member of the Kent gentry; John de Lovetot (justice 1275-89) was the younger son of one of the coheirs of the Huntingdonshire barony of Southoe. Of the justices of King's Bench Walter of Hopton (justice 1274-8) was probably the eldest son and inherited the lands of a Shropshire knightly family; Robert Malet (justice 1290-5) was the eldest son and inherited the lands of a minor Buckinghamshire knightly family. Fuller details and references will be found in my forthcoming study of the judges of Edward I.

[7] Ellis was manumitted in 1269 by the archbishop of York at the request of Gilbert of Preston: *Register of William Wickwane*, ed. W. Brown, Surtees Soc. cxiv, 1907, 334.

[8] His brother William Weyland; John of Mettingham; William of Gisleham and Hervey of Stanton. No other county produced more than two.

Thomas Weyland was born in, or not long before, the year 1230.[9] Little has so far come to light about the first forty years or so of his life, the period prior to his first appointment as a royal justice at the very end of Henry III's reign. During this time he must have been accumulating the experience that rendered him eligible for appointment as a royal justice, but it is not clear what the nature of that experience was.

Foss states that Thomas Weyland had been 'brought up to the study of the law . . .' and that he owed his initial appointment as a royal justice in 1272 to the eminence he had by then obtained in the legal profession.[10] This appears to have been no more than guess-work on Foss's part, a conjecture for which he cites no evidence and which seems to have been based on an error made by Dugdale. The latter deduced from a writ of 1275 ordering that Weyland be paid his expenses that he was at that time a King's serjeant, and thus a leading member of the legal profession. In fact, the payment was one made to him for his services as a justice of the Bench not as a King's serjeant, and there is no evidence that Thomas Weyland was ever a serjeant, still less a King's serjeant.[11] It is possible to identify many, if not all, of the Bench serjeants of the latter part of the reign of Henry III. Thomas Weyland is not one of them. In any case, at the time of Weyland's initial appointment as a royal justice (in 1272), the serjeants of the Bench had not yet become a significant source of justices. The first justices to be appointed from their ranks seem to have been Richard of Boyland and Alan of Walkingham, who became justices in eyre in 1279; and it was only in and after 1290 that Bench serjeants began to be appointed as justices of the Bench itself and of the court of King's Bench.[12]

Service as a clerk in one of the King's courts was certainly seen at this time as one good way of acquiring the expertise in law and legal procedure needed in a royal justice; and many of the men appointed as

[9] In Easter term 1251 he acted as the attorney of his eldest brother John for the making of a final concord: CP 25(1)/214/22, no. 72. It seems probable that all attorneys were required to be of age.

[10] D. Crook, *Records of the General Eyre*, P.R.O. Handbooks 20, 1982, 134, 140, 141; *Select Cases . . . King's Bench*, vol. 1, cxxxv.

[11] The *liberate* was for twenty pounds 'in subvencionem expensarum suarum quas fecit in servicio regis': C62/51, m. 2.

[12] The bench serjeants appointed as justices of the Bench were Robert of Hartforth (Hertford) (1291-4); William of Gisleham (1290-3); William of Barford (Bereford) (1292, 1294-1326); and William Howard (1297-1308). The only Bench serjeant appointed a justice of King's Bench was Gilbert of Thornton (1290-4) but William of Ormsby had been an eyre serjeant.

royal justices during Edward I's reign can be shown to have been promoted from the ranks of these clerks.[13] Thomas's eldest brother John was just such a clerk. From the frequency of references to his minor property transactions on the plea rolls and his frequent use of final concords it seems clear that he was a clerk of one or more of the justices of the Bench from at least 1244 onwards and by the time of his death (in either 1259 or 1260) he had become sufficiently senior to enter the King's own service.[14] His career had brought him a degree of material prosperity as well, allowing him to make several purchases of land in his own area of Suffolk and at least one major acquisition, the Suffolk manor of Brandeston, for which he paid in excess of one· hundred pounds.[15] Thomas Weyland may have followed him into clerical service in the courts. Such clerks were normally in clerical orders and it is known that at some fairly early period in his life Thomas was ordained a subdeacon.[16] But there is no positive evidence that Thomas Weyland was ever a court clerk and the balance of probabilities seems to be against this, for as early as the 1250s he was in a position to spend sums much larger than those available to his brother on property acquisition. In 1256 he paid one hundred marks to purchase the Suffolk manor of Chillesford and only three years later he was able to pay a further three hundred marks to buy another Suffolk manor, that of Blaxhall.[17] By the mid-1260s, moreover, he had in effect laicised himself. It was at this time that he married his first wife Anne; and by 1270, at the latest, he had received the honour of a knighthood, a status incompatible with clerical orders.[18]

The other main career pattern typical of a substantial number of Edwardian judges was service to one or more of the great magnates as

[13] Examples from the justices of the Bench include Ralph de Hengham (1273-4, 1301-8); Roger of Leicester (1276-89); William of Brompton (1278-89); Ellis of Beckingham (1285-1307); Lambert of Threekingham (1300-1316); Henry the Marshal of Guildford (1305-6); and Harvey of Stanton (1306-13). King's Bench justices who had once been clerks include Ralph de Hengham (1274-90); Martin of Littlebury (1273-4); Walter of Wimborne (1276-89); and Ellis of Sutton (1285-7). Fuller details and references will be included in my study of Edwardian justices.

[14] KB26/133, m. 5d; BL Additional Charter 5898; KB26/160, mm. 35d, 39d, 54; *Cal. Charter Rolls*, ii, 20-21.

[15] Above note 14; CP 25(1)/214/20, no. 23; CP 25(1)/214/22, no. 72; CP 25(1)/214/21, no. 17; CP 25(1)/214/23, no. 28; CP 25(1)/214/26, no. 3 etc.

[16] *Registrum Epistolarum fratris Johannis Peckham archiepiscopi Cantuariensis*, vol. 3, ed. C. T. Martin, Rolls Series 1886, 968.

[17] CP 25(1)/214/24, no. 18; CP 25(1)/214/26, no. 2.

[18] *Cal. Close Rolls, 1288-1296*, 160; CP 40/24, m. 78; *Close Rolls, 1268-72*, 297-9.

an administrator and adviser.[19] There is some evidence to indicate that Thomas may have conformed to this pattern, though all of it comes from a brief period immediately preceding his appointment as a royal justice. In 1271 he was acting as one of the auditors of Roger Bigod, earl of Norfolk, and in that same year put in an appearance at the Exchequer on the earl's behalf in connexion with the debts of the earl's predecessor.[20] The earl was married to Alina, the daughter of the former royalist justiciar, Philip Basset. There is also some evidence to suggest that Thomas Weyland may have been for a period in the early 1270s in the service of John FitzJohn, the husband of Philip Basset's other daughter, Margery.[21]

Thomas's other elder brother, William Weyland, had pursued a career perhaps best seen as a variant on this. He first went to Ireland in 1248 in the service of Henry III's half-brother, Aymer de Lusignan, and probably acted during the 1250s as seneschal of the earl of Norfolk's Irish liberty of Ross. He then entered the King's service in Ireland on appointment in 1257-8 as a justice of the eyres of counties Limerick and Tipperary. After the death of his elder brother John, William returned to England and was appointed in 1261 escheator of England south of the Trent, a post he held until the triumph of the Montfortian party at the battle of Lewes in 1264.[22] He subsequently returned to Ireland and by 1269 was acting as seneschal of another of the great Leinster liberties, that of Kildare. By 1271 he was once more back in England and was appointed a justice in eyre; he served in a number of eyres at the very end of Henry III's reign and was appointed to the Bench at the very beginning of the reign of Edward

---

[19] Examples in the Bench are Stephen Heym (1273-4), in the service of Richard, earl of Cornwall, during the 1250s and 1260s; Walter de Heliun (1276-1281), in the service of Robert Walerand from 1260 to 1273 and of Edmund, earl of Cornwall in 1274-5 (and after his period as a justice of the Bench in the service of the earl of Lancaster); Peter Mallore (1292-1308), probably in the service of Ellis de Rabayne and then of the earl of Lincoln; John of Mettingham (1290-1301), in the service of the earl of Lincoln. Examples in King's Bench are Roger Brabazon (1290-1316), in the service of the earl of Lancaster from 1275 to 1290; and Robert Malet (1290-5), in the service of the earl of Cornwall during the 1270s.

[20] SC6/932/12; E159/45, m. 8d (I owe this reference to the kindness of Dr. David Crook).

[21] *Close Rolls, 1268-72*, 297-9; BL Additional Ms. 28024, ff. 40^{r-v}; *Cal. Close Rolls, 1272-79*, 122.

[22] *Cal. Pat. Rolls, 1247-58*, 19; J. H. Bernard, 'Charters of the Cistercian abbey of Duiske in co. Kilkenny', *Proc. Roy. Irish. Acad.* xxv section C, 1920-2, 95-6; G. J. Hand, *English Law in Ireland, 1290-1324*, Cambridge 1967, 220-1; A. Wood, *List of Escheators for England and Wales*, List and Index Soc. lxxii, 1971, 1.

I.[23] It is possible that Thomas was for part of this time in the service of his brother William. It would certainly have given him the relevant experience of administration, particularly legal administration. But there is no real evidence that he was.

2

Thomas Weyland was first appointed as a royal justice at the very end of the reign of Henry III. In 1272 he sat as a justice for the latter part of the Essex eyre and was appointed a justice of the next eyre on the same circuit in Hertfordshire, though this did not, in the event, take place because of the death of Henry III in November, which brought a halt to all the eyre visitations.[24] In Michaelmas term 1274 he was appointed to serve as one of the justices of the Bench. Although two terms separate his appointment from the death of his elder brother William, he appears to have been appointed as a replacement for him. He then sat as a junior justice of the Bench for almost four years until the chief justice of the Bench, master Roger of Seaton, retired from office, probably through ill-health, at the end of Trinity term 1278.[25]

Thomas Weyland was his successor and held office as chief justice until the end of Trinity Term 1289. In the following Michaelmas term Ralph of Sandwich took Weyland's place, but only on a purely temporary basis; his permanent replacement, John of Mettingham, was not appointed until January 1290. Weyland's eleven years in office are not as impressive a period of service as the almost thirteen years enjoyed by his successor, Mettingham, but they represent almost a third of the entire reign and comfortably exceed the periods during which each of the other chief justices of the Bench of Edward's reign held office – one year in the case of Gilbert of Preston, the first chief justice of the reign, almost five years in the case of Weyland's immediate predecessor, master Roger of Seaton, and a little over seven years (including the period he remained in office at the beginning of Edward II's reign) in the case of Ralph de Hengham.[26]

Five justices was the most common complement of the Bench during the reign of Edward I, and for just under two thirds of the period during which Weyland sat as chief justice he had four junior

[23] P.R.O., Dublin RC7/1, 484; Crook, 137, 139.

[24] Crook, 140; *Cal. Pat. Rolls, 1266-72*, 711.

[25] *Select Cases . . . King's Bench*, vol. 1, cxxxv–cxxxvii; *Annales Monastici*, vol. 3, ed. H. R. Luard, Rolls Series 1866, 272; *Registrum Epistolarum . . . Johannis Peckham*, vol. 1, 57-8, 100-1.

[26] *Select Cases . . . King's Bench*, vol. 1, cxxxv–cxxxix.

colleagues there. For the remainder of the period Weyland had only three colleagues, the minimum complement of the court during Edward's reign.[27] These numbers, however, represent only the theoretical membership of the court – its membership as recorded in formal documents associated with the court; not the number of justices actually present and active there. John de Lovetot was nominally a justice of the Bench during the whole of Weyland's period as chief justice and was paid as such for the whole period. He was, however, abroad on official business for a number of the terms when the final concords record him as being present in the court at Westminster. When he handed in his plea rolls in December 1289, Lovetot claimed to have no plea rolls for fourteen of the terms during which he had nominally been a Bench justice (around one third of the total number of terms during which Weyland was chief justice of the court) because he had been abroad in those terms.[28] He was certainly abroad for some of them, but his own assize rolls indicate that for others of them he was in England and probably did sit in the Bench.[29]

The earliest surviving Year Book style reports of cases pleaded in the Bench come from the period at the very end of the reign of Henry III when Martin of Littlebury was chief justice of the court, and over a dozen such reports survive from the four year period when master Roger of Seaton was its chief justice (1274-8). It is, however, only from Thomas Weyland's period of office onwards that they begin to survive in any real quantity.[30] I have succeeded so far in locating and identifying reports of around eighty cases belonging to this period. Many are to be found in more than one manuscript; and a significant number of cases are reported in more than one version. So far none of them has been printed.[31]

---

[27] *Select Cases . . . King's Bench*, vol. 1, cxxxv-cxxxvii.

[28] *Select Cases . . . King's Bench*, vol. 1, clx.

[29] For evidence, for example, that he was at Westminster during the Easter, Trinity and Michaelmas terms of 1281 see JUST 1/1256, mm. 3d, 7, 7d, 12 and 13.

[30] For reports from Littlebury's period as chief justice see *Casus Placitorum*, ed. W. H. Dunham jr, Selden Soc. lxix, 1952, 79-81 and perhaps 77-78; Cambridge Univ. Lib. Ms. Dd. 7. 14, ff. 387a-b. For reports from Seaton's period as chief justice see *Casus Placitorum*, 49, 72-3, 96-7, 99-110, 121-6; Lincoln's Inn Ms. Misc. 87, ff. 68ᵛ-69ʳ (and BL Ms. Harleian 1208, ff. 259ᵛ-260ᵛ); Cambridge Univ. Lib. Ms. Dd. 7. 14, ff. 40lb, 403b-404a; Lincoln's Inn Ms. Hale 174, ff. 20ᵛ, 83ᵛ

[31] Manuscripts containing such reports include BL Mss. Additional 5925, 31826, 32088, 35116, 37657; Egerton 2811; Harleian 835, 1208; Lansdowne 467; Royal 10. A. V; Stowe 386; Cambridge Univ. Lib. Mss. Dd. 7. 14 and Hh. 3. 11; Lincoln's Inn Mss. Hale 174 and 188; Misc. 87 and 738. I am preparing an edition of all the pre-1290 Bench reports for the Selden Society.

The reports suggest some interesting conclusions about the way in which the Bench organised its business during Weyland's chief justiceship. Roger of Leicester sat as a justice of the Bench for the whole of the period, but not one of the reports even mentions him. It may just be that he never had anything to say that was considered worth reporting, but it is probable that there is a quite different explanation for this absence. From incidental mentions on the plea rolls it is known that in Trinity term 1276 and again in Trinity term 1287 he was sitting apart from his colleagues making adjournments in cases where litigants had been essoined; and that in Michaelmas term 1287 he and his colleague Ellis of Beckingham were sitting by themselves when they awarded judgment on a default.[32] The real reason for his absence is probably that he regularly sat apart from his colleagues, by himself or with a single companion, to deal with routine procedural matters which were of no interest to the reporters. John de Lovetot is mentioned in comparatively few reports. It is possible that this simply reflects the fact that Lovetot was often absent from the court, but again it is more probably to be explained as a consequence of the way in which the court managed its business. Certainly, four of the six reports in which Lovetot does appear feature him alone of all the justices. This may mean that when he was in the court he too sat by himself for much of the time, though hearing a more interesting class of business than his colleague Leicester.

For the reporters it was clearly two of the justices, William of Brompton and Thomas Weyland himself, who formed the main focus of attention. Weyland occurs in fifty-three of the reports; Brompton in thirty-four. The reports suggest that both justices may have heard some cases on their own. In fourteen reports Brompton alone is mentioned and in thirty-five only Weyland. When the two justices did sit with another justice it was most commonly with each other. They appear together but without any other colleagues in fourteen reports. Only in some four reports do as many as three of the justices appear together.

It cannot, of course, automatically be assumed that the failure of the reporter to note any remark by a justice means that he was not sitting in the court; but the general pattern of evidence from the reports taken with occasional references on the plea rolls themselves suggests that by the 1280s the justices of the Bench did not normally, if ever, sit together as a single court, and that much of the Bench's business was

---

[32] CP 40/17, m. 123; JUST 1/541B, m. 32d; CP 40/70, m. 58d.

heard separately by individual justices or small groups of justices. The reports also indicate that it was Weyland and Brompton who heard the most important and interesting cases and suggest that these two men were the leading justices in the court.

The reports also allow us to form some sort of impression of Thomas Weyland at work as a justice. In one case Alice, Andrew's widow, brought an action of dower claiming one third of a carucate of land against Joan, the widow of Andrew's brother, Alexander. Joan's serjeant claimed that Alexander had been the elder of the two brothers and so had been in possession of the land before Andrew; she had therefore been endowed before Alice, and the latter was not entitled to a dower share of land already allocated as dower to Joan. Alice's serjeant, however, claimed that Andrew had been the older of the two brothers, and had held the land first and so she had a good claim to dower in that land. Aware, perhaps, of the weakness of his client's case, Joan's serjeant then went for a victory on technical grounds. Joan had previously herself brough an action of dower against Alice in the king's court, and, when she had done so, Alice in her defence had not claimed that she was the widow of the older of the two brothers and thus dower was not due, and Joan had then recovered dower against her. Alice was, therefore, he claimed, estopped from making this claim now. Weyland made short work of this. If Alice's serjeant had pleaded badly on a previous occasion, he said, that was no reason now for depriving her of her right of action to recover her dower. Joan was made to traverse Alice's claim that her husband was the first seised and the dispute submitted to a jury.[33]

In another case we can see Weyland deciding an important point of statutory interpretation. When a plaintiff brought the action of *cessavit per biennium* created by chapter 21 of the Statute of Westminster II (1285) to recover a tenement held of him by a tenant who had not performed the services owed for the tenement for two years, did he have only to prove that the services had not been performed for two years or should he also be required to prove that the tenement concerned had not been open to distraint during that two year period? Weyland was quite clear that the latter was the case, and his reasoning was based, interestingly enough, not on the specific wording of the chapter concerned but on the intent of the makers of the statute, which had been to provide a remedy only where the common law was deficient, that is to say where the lord was unable to exercise his

[33] Cambridge Univ. Lib. Ms. Dd. 7. 14, f. 375a.

common law remedy for securing arrears of service, distraint.[34] Weyland's sureness and clarity on this point remind us also that he was the chief justice of the Bench at the time of the enactment of the statute; and that he may well himself have played some part in its drafting.

In a third case heard in 1287, Henry de Pierrepoint and his wife Annora avowed a distraint for six years' arrears of a rent of ten pounds said to be owed them by Richard Barry for a tenement he held of them at Bassingfield in Nottinghamshire. They were unable to show any seisin of the rent either by themselves or by any of the ancestors of Annora, but claimed that this was because Annora's ancestor, James of Holm, had died shortly after granting the land to Richard's father and before the first instalment of rent had fallen due. It also emerged, however, in the course of pleading, and partly through the questioning of the two justices Weyland and Brompton, that Richard and his father had held the land for twenty-six years without paying any rent for it, and that Annora was only a distant relation of James, though by now his nearest surviving heir. Weyland's judgment in the case is a classic example of a particular type of early common law judgment. Yes, he agreed, there was a hardship to the defendants if they were not now able to recover the rent by distraint, for their lack of seisin would also lose them any action of customs and services they might bring for the rent. But, he said, there would be a still greater hardship to the plaintiffs (and to other plaintiffs too) if the defendants were to be allowed to distrain for the rent without showing seisin of the services enjoyed by themselves or their ancestors as title to the services; and thus on the balance of convenience he found for the plaintiffs.[35]

The one thing that is missing from these reports, unfortunately, is any kind of personal touch. For his successors as chief justice of the Bench, John of Mettingham and Ralph de Hengham, the reporters give us anecdotes and moral stories, even the occasional proverb, which help to bring these men close to us as individuals. We know that his colleague Brompton on at least one occasion quoted an

---

[34] BL Additional Ms. 35116, f. 120[r]. What seems to be a report of an earlier stage of pleading in the same case (in which several of the arguments employed in it are given an airing) is to be found in three manuscripts in closely related versions: BL Additional Ms. 5925, f. 94[r]; BL Additional Ms. 31826, f. 221[v]; BL Additional Ms. 35116, ff. 117[r-v].

[35] BL Additional Ms. 31826, ff. 58[v]-59[r]. Also reported in Lincoln's Inn Ms. Hale 188, ff. 24[r-v]; BL. Harleian Ms. 835, f. 2[r]. The plea roll enrolment of this case will be found on m. 97d of CP 40/69.

English proverb ('Won mon aveth mon, yenne aveth loverd to') but we have nothing of this sort for Weyland.[36] The nearest we come to a personal touch is in the report of a Bench case of 1289 where Weyland reminisces about how he had once been in a similar position to the plaintiff – the grantee of a wardship (in Weyland's case, one given or otherwise granted to him by the abbot of Bury St. Edmund's) against whom a widow had sought the body of an heir in an action of wardship, and how he had not been allowed to vouch the abbot because the voucher was contrary to law. The only other personal touch comes in a collection of reports where we have what may well be a caricature of Weyland's face in profile by a report of one of his speeches in a case, for it has what we are elsewhere told is Weyland's characteristic long beard.[37]

3

In his sketch of Weyland's life in the *Dictionary of National Biography* Tout claimed that, during his eleven years as chief justice of the Bench, Weyland '. . . had neglected no opportunity of furthering his own interest and building up a landed estate' and alleged that Weyland's conduct, which had always been 'questionable', had become 'exceptionally scandalous between 1286 and 1289, when the absence of Edward I and the chancellor Burnell on the continent removed the chief checks upon his action and that of his colleagues'.

It is certainly true that Thomas Weyland did make very substantial property acquisitions during the period he was chief justice of the Bench. These included at least seven manors or substantial property holdings in his home county of Suffolk, three manors or substantial holdings in Essex, and various other properties. From the purchase prices recorded in the associated final concords for some (though not all) of these acquisitions we know that he spent at least £1,150 on them, and perhaps half as much again: an average of some £150 a year. Clearly purchases on this scale could not have been funded from the £40 a year which Weyland received as his salary from the King for acting as the chief justice of the Bench.[38] But it is not necessary to

---

[36] Cambridge Univ. Lib. Ms. Dd. 7. 14, f. 401a.

[37] Cambridge Univ. Lib. Ms. Dd. 7. 14, ff. 239b-240a, 370b; *Bracton: On the Laws and Customs of England*, vol. 1, ed. G. E. Woodbine and S. E. Thorne, Cambridge, Mass. 1968, 83, note 2.

[38] C 62/55, m. 3, /56, mm. 6, 3, /57, mm. 9, 4, /59, m. 7, /60, mm. 4, 2, /61, mm. 8, 7, 1, /62, m. 3, /63, mm. 3, 2, 1, /64, m. 3, /65, mm. 4, 3.

assume that Weyland's acquisitions were wholly, or even largely, funded from the profits of judicial corruption, as Tout seems to imply. Thomas Weyland was in possession of property in England and Ireland worth at least £150 a year (and perhaps considerably more than that) *before* he became chief justice of the Bench. Of this about two-thirds had come to him by inheritance on the death of his elder brother William in 1274.[39] To this must be added the unknown, but apparently sizeable, income he derived from the two Essex manors (Brundon and Mashbury) held in dower by his second wife, Margery, of the endowment of her first husband, John of Moze, and profits of £20 a year from the lands at East Smithfield by the Tower of London which were owned by his stepson John of Moze, but whose income Weyland seems to have received up to the time of his downfall.[40] Such an income placed him, even in 1278, in the ranks of the upper gentry. More significantly, in the present context, it was also sufficiently large to have allowed him to finance many of his purchases out of current income and accumulated savings.

The only other evidence of Weyland's misconduct as a judge is the complaints made against him, as against almost all his colleagues in the judiciary, in 1289-90. In mid-October 1289 *auditores querelarum* were appointed to receive complaints of wrongs committed by the King's officials against his subjects during Edward I's absence in France. Three complaints seem to have been made to these *auditores* which alleged misconduct on the part of Weyland. Of these, the abbot of St. Évroult's complaint also named his fellow Bench justices as culprits but seems to be of an erroneous rather than a culpably and deliberately wrongful judgment. In any case it was not, apparently, successful.[41] William of Bardwell's complaint was directed mainly against Ralph de Hengham. Against Weyland it alleged only that he (and two other royal justices) had been in the court of King's Bench when a case brought by Bardwell had been heard there, and that all three of them had been there to give counsel and assistance to his opponent, the abbot of Bury St. Edmund's. Bardwell clearly thought such conduct improper; but, by contemporary standards, it would seem to have been at most on the borderline of acceptability.[42] In a

---

[39] The lands inherited from his brother were the Suffolk manors of Monewden and Brandeston, the Gloucestershire manor of Sodbury and the two Irish manors of Killoteran and Ballyconnery, both in county Waterford.

[40] CP 40/121, m. 209; *Cal. Inquisitions Miscellaneous*, vol. 1, no. 1505.

[41] *State Trials of the Reign of Edward the First, 1289-1293*, ed. T. F. Tout and H. Johnstone, Camden Soc. 3rd. series ix, 1906, 91-2.

[42] *State Trials*, 49-51.

different complaint of the same period which was directed principally against Weyland's colleague Brompton and alleged misconduct by him in the taking of the verdict of a jury in litigation in the Bench, Walter de Surdeval mentioned that John of Mettingham had been sitting on the bench with Brompton at the time of the alleged misconduct. In the course of the proceedings on this complaint, Mettingham is recorded as admitting that he had been in court, but as claiming that this was not in the role of justice but solely in that of a well-wisher (*benivolens*) to Surdeval's opponent, the prior of Sempringham. His reply seems to have been accepted by the *auditores querelarum* as a full and satisfactory answer, which entirely exculpated him.[43] The third complaint linked Weyland's name with those of Brompton and Hengham as bearing responsbility for the issuing of a writ of entry of novel form for the use of John Lovel in making a claim to an extensive holding at Stanford Rivers and Kelvedon Hatch in Essex as the remainderman under a settlement. The complainant, the tenant of these lands, John de Munteny, also complained that his exception against the writ had been wrongly disallowed and that the justices had wrongfully refused to seal the bill of exception to which he was entitled under the provisions of c. 31 of the Statute of Westminster II of 1285, which would record the exception he had put forward and the fact that it had been disallowed by the justices. Corruption was not alleged in this complaint; and what we seem to have here is a genuine conflict of opinion about whether or not the writ should have been made available to the plaintiff. Munteny seems to have had Chancery opinion on his side against the use of the writ, as also that of the post-1290 judiciary, but Hengham, Weyland and Brompton, the leading lights of the pre-1290 judiciary, seem to have thought otherwise. The refusal of a bill of exceptions was clearly wrong, but if Hengham had played some part in the authorisation of the issuing of the writ, it may well have seemed that there was little point in allowing such a bill.[44]

A further five complaints against Weyland were made directly to the King and his council in Parliament, as were many other of the complaints made against the justices at this time. That made by the bishop of Carlisle is easily dismissed. It is almost certain that the 'royal charter' which the bishop produced in a Bench case of 1287 concerning the right to present to the vacant church of Brough under Stainmore was only a letter of Richard I presenting a clerk to the

[43] JUST 1/541B, m. 36d.
[44] E 175/File 1, no. 7, m. 3; *Rot. Parl.*, vol. 1, 84-5.

vacant church and not a royal charter granting the advowson. The
bishop was probably, therefore, not justified in claiming that
Weyland and his colleagues had acted wrongly in not adjourning the
case on the production of this document pending consultation with
the king.[45] Margery and Violetta de Zoyn complained that Weyland
had arranged for two final concords to be levied in the name of their
now deceased brother John, while he was still a minor, one conveying
the Essex manor of Chignall Zoyn to himself and other members of
his family, the other conveying the Hertfordshire manor of Westmill
to John's guardian, Thomas of Lewknor. These fines were certainly
levied and the complaint sounds plausible.[46] The sisters, however,
failed to recover either manor, despite bringing litigation for that
purpose in the Bench in 1290 and 1294.[47] A third complaint by
Thomas de Verdun alleged that Weyland had assisted his brother-in-
law, William de Grey, in tricking him out of land worth £30 a year.
Verdun had arranged to marry Grey's daughter and had agreed to
grant this land to Grey, in order that Grey might then regrant it to the
new couple. The grant to Grey had taken place as planned and the
associated charter had been recorded on the Bench plea roll; Grey had
promised to regrant the land to Verdun and his daughter but this
agreement had not been put in writing or enrolled. The marriage had
not taken place and he had lost his land. It is difficult to know what
exactly to make of this story, since no defence to it is recorded. A
calculated fraud is possible but seems unlikely. Some kind of dispute
over marriage arrangements seems the most likely explanation.
Verdun does not seem to have recovered his land.[48]

The remaining two complaints provide the most credible evidence
for real wrongdoing on the part of Weyland. In one (which, formally
speaking, is not a complaint at all) Robert of Ufford tried to make out
a convincing case for being allowed an action of attaint to reverse the
verdict of a jury in an action of trespass. What had been at stake in the
action was the right to a ship which had been wrecked at Bawdsey in
Suffolk. It was the general rule not to allow the use of attaint to
reverse jury verdicts in actions of this kind, and in the event Ufford
did not succeed in having the rule waived in this particular case. What
Ufford alleged was that Weyland had taken the jury's verdict alone
and without a colleague; had charged the jury incorrectly; and had

---

[45] *Rot. Parl.*, vol. 1, 23–4; CP 40/68, mm. 10d, 78.
[46] *Rot. Parl.*, vol. 1, 56–7.
[47] CP 40/86, m. 43; CP 40/104, m. 134; CP 40/146, m. 75d.
[48] SC 8/256, no. 12796; *Rot. Parl.* vol. 1, 47, no. 25 (summary only).

subsequently entered judgment in the case in the Bench without calling the parties to hear their judgment. He ascribed Weyland's misconduct to undue favour for Robert's opponent, the earl of Norfolk, and attributed this to the fact that Thomas was one of the earl's followers ('*mesneng*') at that time and his chief counsellor.[49] It is not difficult to find other evidence showing that Weyland continued to act as one of the earl's advisers after his appointment as a royal justice.[50] Indeed, the connexion must have been well-known and does not seem to have been the subject of any kind of official disapproval. Weyland was even appointed by royal letters patent to act as one of the two attorneys for the earl in England during his visit to Ireland in 1279.[51] Such a connexion can, moreover, be parallel both in John de Lovetot's service during the 1280s to Queen Eleanor and in Lambert of Threekingham's service while a justice of the Bench in the early fourteenth century to successive archbishops of York and at least one bishop of Durham.[52] What cannot be proved, however, is that the connexion did lead to misconduct in this particular instance: for that we only have Robert of Ufford's word. If things had turned out differently and it had been the earl who had been making the complaint he too could have given reasons why Weyland might have favoured his opponents. The chief justice is known to have been a tenant of Ufford's co-defendant, the prior of Butley, and on sufficiently good terms with him to have deposited his deeds for safe-keeping in his priory; and some degree of friendship between Weyland and Ufford himself seems to be indicated by the appearance of Ufford high in the list of witnesses to two unrelated deeds, both in Weyland's favour, of 1286 and 1287.[53]

The remaining complaint was one made by Hugh of Gosbeck. It

[49] *Select Cases in the Court of King's Bench*, vol. 2, ed. G. O. Sayles, Selden Soc. lvii, 1938, cxxxviii; and cf. *Rot. Parl.*, vol. 1, 53, no. 90.

[50] SC 6/997, no. 2; SC 6/997, no. 5.

[51] *Cal. Pat. Rolls, 1272–81*, 319.

[52] JUST 1/836, mm. 1, 2, 6; JUST 1/542, m. 12; J. C. Parsons, *The Court and Household of Eleanor of Castille in 1290*, Toronto 1977, 81; CP 40/23, m. 38. For Threekingham see *Register of Thomas Corbridge*, part 1, ed. W. Brown, Surtees Soc. cxxxviii, 1925, 223–4; part 2, ed. W. Brown and A. H. Thompson, Surtees Soc. cxli, 1928, 32, 73, 77, 121–3, 126, 128, 131; *Register of William Greenfield*, part 1, ed. W. Brown and A. H. Thompson, Surtees Soc. cxlv, 1931. 199; part 4, ed. W. Brown and A. H. Thompson, Surtees Soc. clii, 1938, 270, 342; part 5, ed. W. Brown and A. H. Thompson, Surtees Soc. cliii, 1940, 162, 166; *Registrum Palatinum Dunelmense*, vol. 2, ed. T. D. Hardy, Rolls Series 1874, 866–8, 945–6.

[53] *Cal. Inq. Misc.*, vol. 1, no. 1493; SC 8/151, no. 7536; E 40/3374; KB 27/107, m. 11.

concerned proceedings brought in the Bench in 1288 by William (son of Roger) of Braham by writ of cosinage with the object of recovering a rent of fifty (or fifty-six) shillings at Trimley and Kirton in Suffolk. The defendant in the case, William of Aldborough, had vouched Herbert Weyland (almost certainly a relation of Thomas) and his wife Margaret to warranty for the rent. They had warranted and in turn vouched the complainant to warranty. He had, he claimed, appeared in the Bench in Trinity term 1288, warranted and then traversed the demandant's claim that he was the next heir of the 'cousin' on whose seisin he had based his claim, and this issue had then gone to a jury. After the case had been adjourned, however, Weyland had, he alleged, seen to it that the relevant part of the plea roll entry had been erased and had then substituted for it a record that the complainant had departed in contempt of court and so judgment had been given against him. For this allegation there is confirmatory evidence. We do know that King and council reversed the judgment in the case on the grounds of manifest (though unspecified) error in the Hilary Parliament of 1290 and sent the case back to the Bench to be reheard. Indeed it was because of their responsibility for the recorded judgment in the case along with Thomas Weyland that his fellow Bench justices Brompton, Lovetot and Leicester and the chief clerk of the Bench, Robert of Littlebury, were heavily fined and made to pay damages to the complainant. The remaining Bench justice, Ellis of Beckingham, seems to have escaped punishment simply because in this one term alone he did not sit in the Bench, having been appointed as one of the justices of the Dorset eyre.[54] We can also see from the surviving entry of the case on Weyland's plea roll that the relevant part of the plea roll has been erased and then written over.[55] And there is a third and even more damning piece of evidence, which provides a motive for Weyland's wrongdoing. At the time of his downfall, Weyland was in possession of a rent-charge of approximately the same value in just these two Suffolk villages, an area of Suffolk in which he possessed no other property.[56] This suggests that the successful demandant, the only beneficiary of his wrongdoing, granted him some sort of interest in the rent in return for his assistance.

Although in this one case there is fairly conclusive evidence of

---

[54] CP 40/81, m. 102; JUST 1/541B, mm. 5, 10d, 12, 24d, 33; *Bartholomei de Cotton Historia Anglicana*, ed. H. R. Luard, Rolls Series 1859, 172-3.

[55] CP 40/73, m. 86d.

[56] E 372/139, m. 8d.

corruption on Weyland's part and it seems possible that he was guilty of misconduct in other cases too, the volume of accusations against him is surprisingly small, far fewer than the accusations against his colleague Brompton or against the chief justice of King's Bench, Ralph de Hengham, it is possible that his abjuration meant that many complainants who would have complained against him complained against his colleague Brompton instead. What is clear, however, is that the surviving evidence does not support the assertion that Weyland was guilty of corruption on any very considerable scale. It was certainly not judicial corruption that led to his downfall in 1289.

4

It was probably on 20 July 1289 that two of Thomas Weyland's servants in his Suffolk manor of Monewden committed a murder at a fair.[57] The victim is named in the official record of Weyland's trial as William Carwel of Ireland; but in the special commission appointed to inquire into the murder he is called Carewel le Forester.[58] He was, then, from Ireland and quite possibly of native Irish origin. It is tempting to identify him with the Cearbhaill Ó Foirchtern who in 1281 received a safe-conduct to visit his kinsman, the earl of Norfolk, in England, and to suggest that he was back in England on a return visit, but this cannot be proved.[59] The murder may have been unpremeditated, the result of the kind of drunken brawl that was common at markets and fairs. But perhaps, in view of Thomas Weyland's own Irish connexions, the killing was part of some wider Anglo-Irish feud to which Weyland and his servants had become parties. There is also another possibility: that there was a link between the murder and the bitter rifts which took place within the household of the earl of Norfolk in the later 1280s, pitting Robert of Benhall and Geoffrey Atwater of Ditchingham against other members of the earl's *familia* and the earl himself.[60] There is some evidence at least to suggest that Weyland took the side of Robert and Geoffrey in these disputes.[61] The victim may, then, have been Irish but have been killed

[57] JUST 3/87, m. 1.

[58] C 66/108, m. 9d.

[59] R. Frame, 'The Justiciar and the Murder of the MacMurroughs in 1282', *Irish Historical Studies* xvii, 1972, 223, 230.

[60] KB 27/114, mm. 35, 50d; KB 27/116, mm. 15d, 23; KB 27/118, mm. 23, 24d; KB 27/123, m. 9; KB 27/124, m. 26; KB 27/125, mm. 2d, 46d; KB 27/126, m. 58; JUST 1/1282, m. 32d; CP 40/116, m. 42.

[61] *Cal. Close Rolls, 1288-96*, 59.

because he was a supporter of the earl.

Thomas Weyland's involvement in the murder seems to have been solely that of an accessory after the fact, through having failed to have his servants arrested when they returned to Monewden, despite the fact that he knew of the murder. Just possibly, he actively sheltered them from arrest after their return. On 4 September 1289, only just over a month after the killing, special justices were appointed to inquire into it, with power to determine any indictments they received. By 19 September, they had tried and hanged Weyland's two servants at a special gaol delivery session. At that same session Thomas Weyland himself was indicted for having harboured the two murderers, and orders were given for his apprehension. He was duly arrested one evening in his home village of Witnesham by a clerk of the sheriff of Suffolk. Weyland asked to spend the night at home before being taken to Ipswich and was then able to make good his escape under cover of darkness. He eventually reached the Franciscan priory at Babwell, just outside Bury St. Edmund's, where he took the Franciscan habit and resumed clerical tonsure. Once his presence in the priory had become known, the men of the neighbourhood were set to guard it and soon Robert Malet was appointed by the King to take charge of arrangements for guarding him and then starving him out of the priory. Eventually, in mid-January 1290, Weyland surrendered and was taken under safe-conduct to London; once there, he seems to have been offered a choice between standing trial, perpetual imprisonment and abjuration of all of the King's lands.[62] His choice of this last option led to the gaol delivery session at the Tower in late February 1290 which I mentioned at the beginning of this paper.

The standard account of the 'State Trials' of 1289-93, that given by T. F. Tout and Hilda Johnstone in their introduction to the Camden series volume of *State Trials* published in 1906, links Weyland's downfall with the appointment by Edward I on 13 October 1289 of *auditores querelarum* to receive complaints of misconduct by the king's ministers during his three year absence in France: 'the immediate result of this inquiry was the gradual removal of the greatest offenders. Thomas de Weyland, Chief Justice of Common Pleas [was] the first to suffer . . .'.[63] This view is, however, clearly quite mistaken. The gaol delivery session at which Weyland was indicted

<hr/>

[62] JUST 3/87, m. 1; *Bracton*, vol. 1, 83, n. 2; *Annales Monastici*, vol. 3, 356; *Liber Memorandorum Ecclesie de Bernewelle*, ed. J. W. Clark, Cambridge 1907, 225.
[63] *State Trials*, xiii.

preceded by almost a month the appointment of the *auditores querelarum* and preceded by almost two months their first sessions. If there was a connexion between the appointment of the *auditores querelarum* and the indictment of Thomas Weyland then it was of the reverse kind: it was Weyland's indictment that led to the appointment of the *auditores* and not vice versa.

5

What happened to Thomas Weyland when he reached Dover in late February 1290? Geoffrey Hand, in an article published in 1970, was the first to draw attention to evidence that Thomas Weyland had subsequently reached Paris and was still there in 1292 when an emissary of Edward I canvassed the opinions of a number of Parisian legal experts on the Scottish succession question.[64] Until recently that was the last that was known of him. However, Dr. Henry Summerson has kindly drawn my attention to an entry on the Exchequer memoranda roll for 1297-8 which contains a reference to the death of Thomas Weyland; and further investigation has provided evidence that Thomas Weyland in fact died not long before 20 January 1298, and not in exile but back in England, at his wife's dower manor of Brundon.[65] No pardon to him seems to have been enrolled on the patent roll, but one was almost certainly granted, for it would have been very foolhardy for him to have returned to England without one.[66] John Weever tells us that a Thomas Weyland was one of the persons buried in the Suffolk priory of Woodbridge (perhaps in the priory church, now the parish church of the town); and since Thomas Weyland, the chief justice, is known to have been a benefactor to the priory, this may well be a reference to him.[67] Wherever he may lie and whatever his sins *requiescat in pace*.

[64] G. J. Hand, 'The Opinions of the Paris Lawyers upon the Scottish Succession Question', *Irish Jurist* v, 1970, 149.

[65] E 368/69, mm. 59, 85, 116, 120d.

[66] Among the deeds delivered by Thomas's widow Margery in 1311 to her step-son John was 'unam cartam domini regis de restitucione pacis domino Thome de Weylund patri ejusdem domini Johannis': DL 25/1575. Edward may have substituted a fine of £1000 for the original sentence of exile for in 1303 John obtained a respite in the payment of just such a fine owed by his deceased father: E 159/76, m. 14.

[67] J. Weever, *Ancient Funerall Monuments*, London, 1631, 752-3.

7

Edward I and the Transformation of the English Judiciary

The reign of Edward I (1272-1307) was marked by the enactment of a series of major statutes, beginning with the fifty-one chapters of the first statute of Westminster of 1275 and ending with the statute of Carlisle and the statute of Fines and Attorneys enacted only a few months before Edward's death in 1307. These statutes made major changes in the English common law which were of fundamental importance in the shaping and reshaping of that law. Their significance has led to Edward I being described (albeit with some exaggeration) as 'the English Justinian' – 'a title which' (as bishop Stubbs wrote) 'if it be meant to denote the importance and permanence of his legislation and the dignity of his position in legal history, no Englishman will dispute'.[1] Stubbs was not the originator of the soubriquet. It can be traced back to Sir Edward Coke writing in the early seventeenth century: ' . . . all other the statutes made in the reign of this king may [also] be styled by the name of establishments, because they are more constant, standing and durable laws then have been made ever since: so as king E.I . . . may well bee called our Justinian'.[2] But it is important not to allow the sheer volume of Edwardian legislation to obscure the fact that there were also important developments taking place in the English legal system during this period which owed little or nothing to Edward's legislative activities. The particular developments which I wish to discuss in this essay are the emergence during the course of the reign of a much more recognisably 'professional' judiciary and the forging of the first direct connexions between that judiciary and the newly emerging English legal profession.

The Transformation of the Court System during Edward I's Reign

At the beginning of Edward I's reign there was only a single royal court which was wholly run by a permanent staff of royal justices. This was the Common Bench at Westminster, the main central royal court for the

---

[1] William Stubbs, *The Constitutional History of England* (2nd. edition, Oxford, 1877), ii. 105.
[2] Edward Coke, *The Second Part of the Institutes of the Laws of England* (London, 1809 edition), i. 156 (commentary on the statute of Westminster I).

hearing of civil litigation, which had gained its own full-time specialist staff
when it became separated from its parent body, the Exchequer, during the
last decade of the twelfth century.[3] All other royal courts either had no
permanent staff of their own (indeed had no permanent existence of their
own) or were dependent for their successful functioning on the assistance
and participation in their work of individuals whose primary responsibilities
lay elsewhere. The first aspect of the growing 'professionalisation' of the
English judiciary I want to discuss, therefore, is the addition of a number of
other courts to the tally of those possessing their own permanent staffs.

The Court of King's Bench

A court of King's Bench had existed since 1234 or perhaps a little before.
This was a court which travelled round the country with the king, so that
summonses to the court required litigants to appear on a specific day not at
some specific place but 'wherever we [the king] then shall be'. A royal court
accompanying the king round England had existed at times in the reign of
Henry II and was of considerable importance in John's reign, when for a
five-year period it in effect replaced the stationary Common Bench at
Westminster. There was, however, no direct institutional continuity
between these courts and the court created in Henry III's reign; and it
differed from them in a number of important respects. Unlike its predecessors this court, though in some senses still the king's own special court,
continued to function even when the king himself was out of the country.[4]
The new court possessed a jurisdiction which was much more clearly,
though still not totally, differentiated from that of the Common Bench at
Westminster. It had now to operate within the limitations imposed by clause
17 of Magna Carta which barred it from hearing 'common pleas' and so it
came to specialise in pleas that could plausibly be represented as ones of
special interest and concern to the king: pleas directly involving the king's
property interests; pleas that alleged a breach of the king's peace; pleas

---

[3] Brian R. Kemp, 'Exchequer and Bench in the Later Twelfth Century: Separate or
Identical Tribunals?', (1973) 88*EHR* 559-73, especially at 570-2; Ralph V. Turner, 'The Origins
of Common Pleas and King's Bench', (1977) 21 *American Journal of Legal History*, 238-54 at 243-
4; Ralph V. Turner, *The English Judiciary in the Age of Glanvill and Bracton* (Cambridge, 1985), 70-
4. But note that prior to 1250 the Common Bench shared its personnel with the eyre and this
necessitated the suspension of Common Bench sessions during eyre visitations: C.A.F. Meekings in *Crown Pleas of the Wiltshire Eyre, 1249* (Wiltshire Archaeological and Natural History
Society, Records Branch, vol.xvi, 1961), 11.

[4] On the origins of the Henrician King's Bench and its forerunners see Turner, 'Origins of
Common Pleas and King's Bench', 245-54; Turner, *English Judiciary*, 200-5; G.O. Sayles in
1*Select Cases in the Court of King's Bench* [hereafter *SCKB*], xi-xl and 4*SCKB*, xxvi-xxxviii; C.A.F.
Meekings in15*Curia Regis Rolls*, xxi-xxxvii.

where it was alleged that there had been an error in the judgment of another royal court.[5]

For certain periods during Henry III's reign (prior to 1240 and again from Michaelmas term 1251 to Easter term 1253) the court possessed only a single justice and its normal complement of justices during the reign was no more than two; but it appears that for most of the period the stewards of the royal household (two or three in number at any one time) made up the numbers in the court by sitting with its full-time staff of justices as required. These men can certainly not be classified as in any sense permanent royal justices, for their main responsibilities lay in the running of the king's household. During the period of baronial reform and more particularly between 1258 and 1265 the court was also afforced by holders of the revived office of chief justiciar who likewise (in view of their other political and administrative responsibilities) cannot be classified as full-time royal justices.[6] At the very beginning of Edward I's reign a decision seems to have been made to give this court a larger complement of justices who would suffice by themselves to do the work of the court. The number of justices sitting in the court thereafter never fell below two and the average complement of justices working in the court during the reign was three.[7] This did not at first wholly exclude the continuing participation of the stewards in the work of King's Bench; but this had apparently come to an end prior to 1290, a development perhaps connected with the creation of a new household court, the court of the Marshalsea, with which the stewards were closely associated.[8]

The General Eyre

Countrywide visitations (or what were planned as countrywide visitations) by royal justices with wide powers to determine civil and criminal pleas and to receive presentments on matters of interest to the king in each county they visited had commenced during the reign of Henry II.[9] But prior to Edward I's reign each eyre visitation was planned separately and there was no real continuity from one visitation to the next; and justices drawn from the Common Bench (and who subsequently returned to it) constituted a

---

[5] Turner, 'Origins of Common Pleas and King's Bench', 250-4; Turner, *English Judiciary*, 203-5; Sayles, 4*SCKB*, xxix-xxxviii.

[6] Meekings in 15*Curia Regis Rolls*, xxii; Sayles, 7*SCKB*, xlii-xliv; Meekings in *List of Various Common Law Records* (Public Record Office Lists and Indexes, Supplementary Series, no.1 (1970)), 36-70.

[7] 1*SCKB*, cxxix-cxxxiii. The numbers of justices varied between two and five.

[8] 3*SCKB*, lxxxvi-lxxxvii; 7*SCKB*, xliv-xlv.

[9] Doris M. Stenton, *English Justice between the Norman Conquest and the Great Charter, 1066-1215* (Philadelphia, 1964), 71-7; Turner, *English Judiciary*, 17-24; Meekings, *Crown Pleas of the Wiltshire Eyre*, 1-4.

core element in the judiciary assigned to the general eyre circuits.[10] All this changed during Edward's reign. In 1278 a decision appears to have been taken to establish two permanent groups of itinerant justices to conduct a continuous visitation of the whole country. The evidence for this is no more than indirect. Hitherto, it had been the normal practice to finish one nationwide visitation before embarking on the next: but between 1278 and 1294 we find a number of counties being visited a second time before other counties had received a first visitation, a practice consonant with the abandonment of the concept of discrete countrywide visitations.[11] When the Exchequer drew up an estimate of revenue in 1284, it apparently assumed that itinerant justices working in two circuits ('Northern' and 'Southern') would form a permanent part of the judicial landscape and bring in a regular income.[12] After 1278 there was for the first time a complete separation of personnel between the eyre and other royal courts and a substantial degree of continuity within the personnel of each of the two eyre circuits, at least down to 1289 (though the 'State Trials' then made a complete replacement of justices on both circuits a necessity).[13]

In practice, the 1278 decision did not establish two circuits of itinerant justices as a permanent feature of the English judicial system. The work of the itinerant justices was suspended as a result of the Welsh wars between 1282 and 1284 and again as a result of the king's absence and of the upheavals within the judiciary which followed his return between 1289 and 1292; and the general eyre was effectively brought to an end in 1294 on the outbreak of war with France (with only individual eyres thereafter in 1299 and 1302 and Edward's successors effectively abandoning the holding of regular eyres).[14] Here then the move towards the greater 'professionalisation' of the judiciary was ultimately abortive.

Assize Courts

The reign of Edward I also brought major changes to the arrangements made for the hearing of petty assizes (novel disseisin, mort d'ancestor) and related pleas (attaint, certification). Since the 1220s it had become increasingly common for such assizes to be heard locally before justices specially

---

[10] Meekings, *Crown Pleas of the Wiltshire Eyre*, 9-12.
[11] David Crook, *Records of the General Eyre* (Public Record Office Handbooks 20 (1982)), 144. Counties visited twice between 1278 and 1294 include: Hertfordshire 1278 and 1287; Wiltshire 1281 and 1289; Sussex 1279 and 1288; Dorset 1280 and 1288; Kent 1279 and 1293-4; Westmorland 1278-9 and 1292; Cumberland 1278-9 and 1292; Northumberland 1279-80 and 1293; Yorkshire 1279-81 and 1293-4. Worcestershire was not visited at all after 1278 though there had been an eyre there in 1275.
[12] Mabel H. Mills, 'Exchequer Agenda and Estimate of Revenue, Easter Term 1284', (1925) 40 *EHR*, 229-35 at 233.
[13] Crook, *Records of the General Eyre*, 144.
[14] Crook, *Records of the General Eyre*, 145-6, 171, 178-9.

commissioned for this purpose (and with separate individual commissions to hear each assize). Between 1220 and 1241 such commissions went most commonly to four men from the locality concerned (often four local knights); but thereafter it became the norm to commission a single justice with power to choose associates or two justices from the pool of central court justices or royal servants possessing some judicial experience. There were attempts in 1259 and 1271 to limit the number of individuals to whom commissions might be issued but these were effective only for short periods of time; and on neither occasion was there any attempt to assign those who were eligible for commissions to particular counties.[15] At the very beginning of Edward's reign (in July 1273, while Edward was still abroad) the decision was taken to divide England up into a series of circuits (initially six) and two justices were assigned on a permanent basis to each circuit as the justices who were to hear petty assizes in the counties of their circuit.[16] This marks an important stage in the development of the assize courts: the first time that something like permanent assize courts with their own justices and their own specific areas of jurisdiction were established in England.

As yet the system remained fluid. In 1274 the six circuits were reduced to four. Subsequent piecemeal alterations had raised the number of circuits by 1284 to eight or nine.[17] In 1285, chapter 30 of the statute of Westminster II attempted to make major changes in the new system. It envisaged a continuation of the existing practice of assigning specific justices to hear assizes in groups of counties (circuits) but stipulated that the two sworn circuit justices were in future to take one or two local knights as their associates in each of the counties they visited for the hearing of assizes in that county, a partial return to the pre-1241 arrangements. It also stipulated that in future assizes were to be heard only during three specific periods of the year (or three terms): between 8 July and 1 August; between 14 September and 6 October; and between 6 January and 2 February.[18] However, in practice the first of these changes remained a dead-letter though there was a substantial reorganisation of the circuits in August 1285. Nine circuits were established, each now manned by three or four justices.[19] The second change (limiting the period when assizes could be heard) does seem to have

---

[15] The most satisfactory treatment of these developments is that in C.A.F. Meekings' introduction to *Calendar of the General and Special Assize and General Gaol Delivery Commissions on the Dorses of the Patent Rolls, Richard II (1377-1399)* (Nedeln, Liechtenstein, 1977), 1-4.

[16] Meekings, *op. cit.*, 4; *CCR 1272-9*, 52 (July 1273 schedule). The justices of the new circuits still received individual commissions to hear each of the assizes concerned and in practice some individual commissions were still issued to royal justices who were not among the twelve assize commissioners.

[17] Meekings, *op. cit.*, 4; *CCR 1272-9*, 135-6 (November 1274 arrangements).

[18] 1*SR*, 85-6.

[19] *CCR 1279-88*, 365.

been effective though it remained possible to obtain authorisation for specific assizes to be heard at other times as well.[20]

A further reorganisation of the system took place in 1293. Eight of the twelve assize justices appointed in 1273 had been justices of the central courts, able to act only in the vacations. This had been reduced to just one in 1274; but the 1285 reorganisation had seen a return to the practice of using central court justices (plus central court clerks) on assize commissions. Of the thirty-four assize justices commissioned in August 1285 four were justices of the Common Bench; three were justices of King's Bench; nine were justices of one of the new permanent eyre circuits; two were barons of the Exchequer; and one was keeper of rolls and writs in the Common Bench; and the timing of the sessions laid down in the statute may have been fixed at least in part to allow the justices, barons and clerk to take assizes during their vacations. In 1293 it was decided to appoint full-time permanent justices with no other responsibilities to take assizes. This allowed a reduction in the number of circuits (to just four) and perhaps also allowed a reduction in the number of justices assigned to each circuit to two. In order to make full use of the services of these full-time justices the provisions of the statute of Westminster II about the timing of sessions was at the same time repealed.[21]

Chapter 3 of the Statute of Fines of 1299 made a major addition to the duties of these full-time assize justices by also giving them responsibility for gaol deliveries (trying criminal suspects in gaol or on bail) in each of the counties of their circuit.[22] Special gaol delivery sessions had formed part of the English judicial system since at least the 1220s, but for most of the thirteenth century commissions were issued separately for each gaol and the commissioners were drawn mainly from the local gentry.[23] Circuit panels of gaol delivery justices do not seem to have emerged before 1294 (twenty years later than the similar development of assize circuits). The merging of the assize and gaol delivery justices in 1299 was not in practice permanent and the link between them had been broken again by the end of the reign; but it prefigured and perhaps suggested the permanent merger of the two which took place early in the reign of Edward III.[24]

Nor was the establishment of full-time assize (and gaol delivery) justices itself permanent. The assizes did remain the province of an expert judiciary

---

[20] Meekings, *op. cit.*, 6.

[21] Meekings, *op. cit.*, 5. For the 1293 ordinance see 1*Rotuli Parliamentorum*, 99 and 1*SR*, 112. The commissions are calendared in *CCR 1288-96*, 319-20. The statutory provisions as to the timing of assize sessions were, however, reinstated (for reasons that are not at all clear) in May 1303 (*CCR 1302-7*, 89-90) and appear to have remained in force for the rest of the reign.

[22] 1*SR*, 29. If one of the assize justices was a cleric his colleague was to conduct the gaol delivery with the assistance of a local knight instead.

[23] The development of the gaol delivery system is discussed in Ralph B. Pugh, *Imprisonment in Medieval England* (Cambridge, 1970), chapters XII and XIII.

[24] Pugh, *Imprisonment in Medieval England*, 281.

working through a circuit system but the pattern which eventually emerged (by *c.*1340), and which then continued to the end of the middle ages and indeed well beyond, was for most of the personnel of the assize circuits to be provided by the main central courts with only a minority of assize justices drawn from king's serjeants and other serjeants of the Common Bench who held no other permanent judicial appointments.

Changing Career Patterns: The Growing Importance of Long-Serving Royal Justices within the Royal Courts

A second aspect of the growing 'professionalisation' of the royal courts during Edward I's reign was a significant growth in the proportion of royal justices who spent long periods of time serving as royal justices: men who were making a career or a profession out of working in a judicial capacity in the king's courts.

There certainly had been long-serving royal justices prior to Edward I's reign. As early as the second half of the twelfth century, for example, we find Richard fitz Neal acting as a royal justice for over thirty years (from around 1165 to 1196). But fitz Neal was hardly a full-time royal justice during this period for at the same time he was also acting as the king's treasurer and it seems likely that it was always his financial responsibilities that came first.[25] Among his colleagues we find two other justices who acted for over twenty years each: Michael Belet and Geoffrey fitz Peter. Michael Belet first acted as a justice in eyre in 1178 and acted in each main eyre visitation down to the death of Richard I: but (even taking into account his occasional presence in the Exchequer and Common Bench) his judicial activity does not seem to have been continuous and he seems to have combined this work with that attached to the position of hereditary butler to the royal household. Thus it is again doubtful whether he can be described as a full-time royal justice.[26] Geoffrey fitz Peter (justiciar 1198-1213) had a judicial career acting as a justice (or as the justiciar) spanning from 1189 to 1213; but again his position as justiciar gave him responsibilities wider than the merely judicial and thus his long career cannot be regarded as a wholly judicial one.[27] The first royal justice who does look something more like a full-time royal justice to have had a career of over twenty years was Simon of Pattishall, a justice of the Common Bench and of the eyre under Richard and of those courts and of the court coram rege under John, with a continuous judicial career of some twenty-six years (1190-1215). Here we do seem to be on much safer ground in hailing our first real long-serving career

[25] The earliest reference to him sitting in a judicial capacity in the Exchequer is in a quitclaim made at the Exchequer at Michaelmas 1165: Madox, *Formulare Anglicanum*, xix. For subsequent references see Stenton, *3PKJ*, lv-cxv.

[26] Turner, *English Judiciary*, 26, 48-9.

[27] F.J. West, *The Justiciarship in England, 1066-1232* (Cambridge, 1966), 97-177.

justice, though even he managed to combine this career with that of acting as a sheriff and briefly as a justice of the Jews.[28] Three justices active in Richard's reign likewise had careers of over ten years (master Thomas of Hurstbourne, Richard of Herriard and Osbert fitz Hervey); as did a fourth justice (John of Guestling) whose career began only under John. But in Richard and John's reigns these remained quite exceptional figures.

When we reach Henry III's reign long-serving justices become rather more common. In Gilbert of Preston we find a royal justice who served continuously in the Common Bench and eyres for over thirty years between 1240 and 1273.[29] The reign also produced three justices with careers lasting twenty years or more (Robert of Lexington, Roger of Thirkleby and Henry of Bath). Robert and Roger both seem to have served continuously as royal justices in the Common Bench and on eyre without combining this with other activity. Henry of Bath's career as a justice of the Common Bench, King's Bench and the Eyre between 1238 and 1260 was interrupted by a period of disgrace between 1251 and 1253 and he also managed to combine the earlier part of it with acting as sheriff in the counties of Northamptonshire and Yorkshire.[30] Even a continuous judicial career of more than ten but less than twenty years would mean that the justice concerned had spent a significant part of his lifetime as a judge and well before the end of his time as a judge would have acquired a considerable degree of legal knowledge and expertise simply in the course of carrying out his judicial duties. Henry III's reign managed to produce some eight judges with careers of this length.[31]

Edward I's reign, however, certainly produced proportionately a much larger number of long-serving justices, justices who were clearly making a professional career out of acting as a royal justice.[32] Two royal justices managed to follow judicial careers lasting for over thirty years. William of

---

[28] Turner, *English Judiciary*, 86, 105-6, 156.

[29] The following paragraph is based on the list of judges participating in Common Bench final concords of Henry III's reign compiled by Maitland for the first volume of his edition of *Bracton's Note Book* (London, 1887) at 139-45; on the listing of the judges participating in general eyres of the reign contained in Crook's *Record of the General Eyre* at 71-142; and on C.A.F. Meekings' account of King's Bench justices of the reign contained in his analysis of the rolls and writs of King's Bench in the *List of Various Common Law Records* at 38-46.

[30] *Crown Pleas of the Wiltshire Eyre, 1249*, 128-9.

[31] They are: Martin of Pattishall; Stephen of Segrave; William de Lisle; Thomas of Moulton; William of York; William of Raleigh; Alan de Wassand; Master Simon of Walton. I am excluding three justices (master Roger of Seaton, Robert Fulks and Thomas Weyland) who began judicial careers under Henry III as by far the largest part of their careers lay in the reign of Edward I.

[32] The following paragraph is based on the lists of royal justices of the Common Bench and King's Bench of the reigns of Edward I and Edward II compiled by G.O. Sayles for Appendixes I-IV of the introduction to 1*SCKB*; and on the listing of the judges participating in the eyres of Edward's reign contained in Crook's *Records of the General Eyre* at 142-80.

Bereford was continuously active as a justice in eyre and in the Common Bench from 1292 to 1326 (and became chief justice of the Common Bench in 1309). Ellis of Beckingham served as an assize justice from 1273 to 1285[33] and then as a justice of the Common Bench from 1285 to 1306. No less than four justices who began their careers under Edward I (or the major portion of whose career lies in Edward's reign) acted as royal justices for periods of twenty years or more (as compared with a total of only three for the much longer reign of Henry III): Ralph de Hengham, who was a royal justice in eyre, in the Common Bench and in King's Bench between 1271 and 1309 but whose career was interrupted by a period of disgrace between 1290 and 1301; John of Mettingham, who was an assize justice from 1274 onwards,[34] a justice in eyre from 1278 to 1289 and chief justice of the Common Bench from 1290 to 1301; Roger le Brabazun, a justice and then chief justice of King's Bench from 1290 to 1316; and Gilbert of Rothbury, a justice of King's Bench from 1295 to 1316 and of the Common Bench from 1316 to 1321. Edward I's reign also produced no less than fourteen justices whose careers spanned ten years or longer (as compared again with just eight justices whose careers lasted for a similar period produced by the much longer reign of Henry III).[35]

The effects of this change towards royal justices having much longer judicial careers, indeed towards them making a career of serving as a judge, are most clearly seen in the Common Bench, the one royal court not to be affected by the structural changes I discussed in the previous section of this essay. No more than twenty-six justices in total sat in the Common Bench during Edward's reign. This compares with some seventy-nine justices who are known to have sat in the same court at some point during the admittedly much longer reign of Henry III; or the forty-one justices who had sat in the same court during John's reign (though the court itself ceased to exist for part of that reign) and the fifty-seven justices who sat in the court (or in its forerunner, the Exchequer) during the reign of Richard I.[36] To make sense of these figures it is necessary to build in some sort of adjustment both for the different lengths of the various reigns and for the different numbers of

---

[33] *CCR 1272-9*, 52, 135-6; JUST 1/1229, 1252, 1257, 1270; C 62/52, m. 6.

[34] *CCR 1272-9*, 135-6; C 66/95, m. 36d; C 66/98, mm. 24d, 20, 19d.

[35] These are: master Roger of Seaton; Robert Fulks; Thomas Weyland; John de Lovetot; Roger of Leicester; William of Brompton; William of Saham; master Thomas of Siddington; Solomon of Rochester; Roger of Boylund; Peter Mallore; William Howard; Lambert of Threekingham.

[36] These figures are calculated from the lists of Exchequer and Common Bench justices for the reigns of Richard and John which are supplied by D.M. Stenton in *3PKJ*, lxxix-ccxciv and from the lists of Common Bench justices for the reigns of Henry III and Edward I supplied by the sources mentioned above in footnotes 29 and 32.

justices sitting in the court at different periods.[37] If we take these variations into account we find that the average length of career of a Common Bench justice under Richard I was little more than a year. Under John this rose to a little over two years and under Henry III to a little over three years. But under Edward I it doubled – to over six years. Appointment as a justice of the Common Bench had now become appointment to a post which the justice could expect to hold for a much longer period of time than had previously been the case.

The longer-serving justices also came under Edward I to play an even more predominant role in the Common Bench than had previously been the case. Over the reign of Henry III as a whole the longer-serving justices (those whose careers lasted for ten years or more) between them accounted for around 60 per cent of all judicial service in the Common Bench. Thus already a fairly small group of long-serving justices had become dominant in the court. But the figure for Edward I's reign shows them not merely dominant but predominant. During Edward's reign they accounted for around 85 per cent of all judicial service there.

The Payment of Royal Justices

A third area in which there is clear evidence to support the overall thesis of a growing 'professionalisation' of the English judiciary during the reign of Edward I relates to the regular payment of salaries to members of the judiciary. Individual payments of varying amounts at irregular intervals and alternative methods of payment (through such means as gifts of ecclesiastical livings or of wardships in the king's hands) point to a relatively 'unprofessional' view of the individuals to whom such payments were made: they are not seen as doing a regular and skilled job for which fixed and regular remuneration is the appropriate reward. It is only when the king begins to pay his judges fixed salaries at regular intervals that we can see that he and his advisers now view the judges as 'professionals', doing a regular job for which a fixed payment is the appropriate method of remuneration. Thus the change from one form of payment to the other marks an important stage in the 'professionalisation' of the judiciary.

Single payments had been made to individual royal justices by Henry II, Richard and John, and those kings had also rewarded their justices in other ways through grants of ecclesiastical livings and of wardships and mar-

---

[37] The average number of justices sitting in the court during Richard I's reign was seven and in John's reign it was still as high as six. It went down to an average of only four in Henry III's reign but rose again to an average of five under Edward I.

riages,[38] but it is not until the reign of Henry III that we find any evidence of regular salaries being paid to royal judges. In January 1218 the three junior justices of the Common Bench were paid £5 each and in the following July a similar sum was paid to the same three plus a fourth companion who had just been appointed to the court. This second payment is specifically said to have been made in respect of the term of the Advinculation, apparently indicating that the money was part of an annual salary payable on certain specific days of the year.[39] The same four men were also paid a further sum in November or December of the same year though this time the amount was £6.[40] There is no evidence that similar payments were made to them in 1219[41] but in 1220 one of these justices received further payments for his services, which show that he was being paid an annual salary of £20 receivable at four terms of the year.[42] Evidence for royal justices being paid regular salaries then disappears.[43] Individual payments continued to be made on an ad hoc basis (in 1227 as many as nine justices received them) but none clearly and indisputably fits into a pattern of regular salary payments.[44] In 1235 evidence for the payment of regular salaries resumes: but this appears to show that such salaries were being paid only to a very small minority of the judges in the king's service. Adam fitz William was granted a salary of £20 a year during pleasure in 1235 and from 1237 to 1241 William of Culworth was in receipt of a regular annual salary of the same amount.[45] During the 1240s at least two justices of the Jews

---

[38] Turner, *English Judiciary*, 51, 54, 108-9, 177.

[39] 1*Rot. Litt. Claus.*, 350, 365.

[40] *Ibid.*, 381b, 382b, 383b.

[41] The only payment to a judge recorded in 1219 was a single ad hoc payment to the eyre justice Maurice de Turville: *ibid.*, 385.

[42] *Ibid.*, 411, 422, 444. In April 1220 the sheriff of Huntingdonshire was notified that Stephen of Segrave, another of the justices, had been given custody of the manor of Alconbury 'to support himself in the king's service during pleasure': *ibid.*, 415b.

[43] Turner, *English Judiciary*, 245 is in error in saying that 'By 1221 Stephen of Segrave's semi-annual payment had quintupled to twenty-five pounds, and the next year Ralph Hareng's salary jumped from 100 shillings to one hundred marks'. The payment to Segrave was as keeper of the Tower of London not as a royal justice; the payment to Hareng was a single payment, not an instalment of a regular salary, and may explain why he ceased to be paid a regular salary.

[44] For the 1227 payments see: *Cal. Liberate Rolls, 1226-1240*, 13, 17, 23, 44, 48-50, 59-60. Robert of Lexington was paid twenty marks in two instalments in 1221 and 1223 and forty marks in one instalment in 1225: 1*Rot. Litt. Claus.*, 461, 468b, 551, 576b. This would fit a regular annual salary of twenty marks (paid in 1225 in respect of 1224 and 1225). What would not fit are the payments to him in 1226 and 1227 of fifty marks and forty marks respectively: *Cal. Liberate Rolls, 1226-1240*, 11 (and 44), 48.

[45] *Cal. Pat. Rolls, 1232-1247*, 87; *Cal. Liberate Rolls, 1226-1240*, 255, 295, 325, 376, 437, 460, 498; *Cal. Liberate Rolls, 1240-5*, 50. Although the king only granted Culworth the salary during pleasure in 1237 (*Cal. Pat. Rolls, 1232-47*, 204) the first payment was in respect of his services in 1235-6 (20 Henry III).

were in receipt at different times of annual salaries.[46] Most justices, however, continued to be paid only on an ad hoc basis.[47]

It is only in the 1250s that for the first time most royal justices came to be paid regular salaries. In 1253 six royal justices (plus a justice of the Jews) were paid them;[48] in 1254 eight.[49] Between 1255 and the end of Henry III's reign the overwhelming majority of payments to royal justices were by way of salaries and it became rare for justices to be paid on an ad hoc basis.[50] From 1253 all (or almost all) justices of King's Bench were being paid regular annual salaries. In the Common Bench it was only in 1259 for the first time that all the justices were in receipt of annual salaries and in several subsequent years some of the justices (though never a majority) seem not to have received them. An overwhelming majority (though never quite all) of the justices in eyre were paid annual salaries during eyre visitations only as from 1262. There was also a considerable degree of standardisation in the salaries actually paid. The lowest annual salaries were those of forty marks a year paid to Roger of Whitchester, William of Cobham and William of Englefield as justices in eyre between 1256 and 1258 and again to Geoffrey de Lewknor, Richard of Middleton, Richard of Hemmington and Walter of Berstead as justices in eyre in 1261-2.[51] The standard salary was forty

---

[46]   Thomas of Newark: *Cal. Liberate Rolls, 1240-5*, 98, 190; *Close Rolls, 1242-7*, 34, 227. John de Wyville: *Cal. Liberate Rolls, 1245-1251*, 23, 89, 127, 151, 182, 209, 232, 256. Wyville continued to be paid the same annual salary down to 1256 when it was raised to sixty marks on his becoming a Common Bench and eyre justice. He was paid at the new level till 1263.

[47]   Thus Gilbert of Preston was paid (or allowed in his debts) £20 in 1240, 1241, 1243, 1244, 1246 and 1248, 20 marks in 1245 and 40 marks in 1247: *Cal. Liberate Rolls, 1226-1240*, 487; *Cal. Liberate Rolls, 1240-5*, 51, 169, 241, 315; *Cal. Liberate Rolls, 1245-51*, 71, 124, 214. Henry of Bath was paid in 1241, 1245, 1247 and 1248; Roger of Thirkleby in 1241, 1243, 1244, 1245, 1246, 1247 and 1248.

[48]   Roger of Thirkleby, Henry de la Mare and Henry of Bath were all paid at the rate of one hundred marks a year (*Cal. Liberate Rolls, 1267-72*, no. 2297J; *Cal. Pat. Rolls, 1247-58*, 215; *Cal. Liberate Rolls, 1251-1260*, 158); Gilbert of Preston and Nicholas de la Tour both at the rate of sixty marks a year (*Cal. Liberate Rolls, 1267-1272*, no. 2297H; *Cal. Pat. Rolls, 1247-1258*, 215; *Cal. Liberate Rolls, 1251-60*, 152); Henry of Bratton at the rate of fifty pounds a year (*Cal. Liberate Rolls, 1251-60*, 159); and John de Wyville (as a justice of the Jews) at the rate of forty marks a year (*Cal. Liberate Rolls, 1251-60*, 127, 150).

[49]   *Cal. Liberate Rolls, 1251-60*, 170, 171, 174, 181, 182, 184, 185, 188. Ad hoc payments were still being paid to as many as seven other royal justices: *Cal. Liberate Rolls, 1251-60*, 185-6.

[50]   However, the number of justices in receipt of annual salaries varied from year to year, partly as a consequence of political disturbances, partly as a reflection of the king's need for justices. Only two justices received salaries in 1264 and three in 1265 during a period of major political upheaval, but as many as seventeen justices received salaries in 1268 and 1272 when major eyre visitations were in progress. Indeed some salaries were specifically said to be payable only so long as the justice was serving as a justice in eyre: see for example the payments made to Roger of Whitchester and William of Cobham in 1256: *Cal. Liberate Rolls, 1251-60*, 326, 328.

[51]   *Cal. Liberate Rolls, 1251-60*, 281, 293, 326, 328, 329, 364, 376, 400, 401, 416, 431; *Cal. Liberate Rolls, 1260-7*, 41, 77-8, 83, 109.

pounds a year: and on one occasion at least (in 1256) a royal justice seems to have been successful in making representations to the king to the effect that this was the minimum sum needed for the honourable support of a justice in the king's service, getting his salary raised from forty marks to forty pounds as a result.[52] Senior justices in the latter part of Henry's reign were paid at the more generous level of either one hundred marks or one hundred pounds a year.[53]

The payment of regular salaries to an increasing proportion of royal justices from the early 1250s onwards seems to have been part of a more general movement taking place at around this time towards putting the king's servants on regular salaries payable by the Exchequer. When the office of chief justiciar was revived by the baronial reformers in 1258 its holder was given a salary of 1,000 marks a year.[54] At around the same time the king's chancellor was given a salary of 400 (later 500) marks a year to maintain himself and the clerks of chancery[55] and the treasurer, paid 100 marks for the support of himself and his clerks.[56] At a less exalted level the clerk who was keeper of rolls and writs in the Bench was in receipt of a regular annual salary from 1246 onwards,[57] as was the king's remembrancer in the exchequer from 1251 onwards.[58] Thus this aspect of the 'professionalisation' of the judiciary was not an exclusively legal phenomenon but part and parcel of a more general change in the conditions of service of members of the bureaucracy.

That even by the end of Henry III's reign the payment of regular judicial salaries was not firmly established as a practice is, however, shown by the sequel. For the first six years of Edward's reign no regular salaries were paid to any of the royal justices, though many received ad hoc payments of varying amounts during this time.[59] In 1278 a decision was made by the

[52] *Cal. Liberate Rolls, 1251-60*, 317 (Nicholas of Hadlow).

[53] Henry of Bath was granted a salary of one hundred pounds a year in 1250 till the king provided more bountifully for him in wardships or escheats: *Cal. Pat. Rolls, 1247-58*, 61 and at least one instalment of this salary was paid: *Cal. Liberate Rolls, 1245-51*, 310. From 1254 to 1260 he was paid at the rate of one hundred marks a year: *Cal. Liberate Rolls, 1251-60*, 170, 181, 204, 238, 279, 367, 404, 431, 441, 468, 479, 500, 535. Gilbert of Preston was paid one hundred marks a year from 1262 to 1272 and Roger of Thirkleby from 1256 to 1260; Henry de la Mare in 1254; Robert de Briwes and Richard of Middleton in 1268-9. William of Wilton was granted a salary of one hundred pounds a year in 1261 (*Cal. Pat. Rolls, 1258-66*, 194) and payments of this salary can be traced in 1262-3 (*Cal. Liberate Rolls, 1260-7*, 86, 120).

[54] *Cal. Liberate Rolls, 1260-7*, 2, 4, 60, 87, 110, 121.

[55] *Cal. Liberate Rolls, 1260-7*, 9, 31, 60, 88, 110, 169, 210, 239, 272, 293 etc..

[56] *Cal. Liberate Rolls, 1260-7*, 88; *Cal. Liberate Rolls, 1267-72*, no. 2367.

[57] The first holder of the post to be paid the salary was Roger of Whitchester: see C.A.F Meekings, 'Roger of Whitchester (+ 1258)', *Archaeologia Aeliana*, 4th. series xxxv (1957), 100-28.

[58] David Crook, 'The Early Remembrancers of the Exchequer', (1980) 53*Bulletin of the Institute of Historical Research*, 11-23.

[59] For payments to justices of the Common Bench see C 62/49, m.4; /50, m.6; /51, m.2; /52, m.6; /54, m.2. For payments to justices of King's Bench see 1*SCKB*, lxxi-lxxii, cxxix-cxxx. For payments to the justices of the 1275 Worcestershire eyre see C 62/52, m.8. Only master Thomas

king's council to return to the system of regular payment of justices in all the major royal courts (Common Bench, King's Bench and both eyre circuits). The most senior justice of each court or each circuit was to be paid sixty marks a year (less generously than their counterparts in Henry III's reign); the next most senior justice in King's Bench and the northern eyre circuit and two next most senior justices in the Bench (but no justice of the southern eyre circuit) were to receive fifty marks a year; and the other junior justices of all courts were to receive forty marks a year.[60] Thereafter the justices were paid salaries on these scales on a regular basis down to 1294 (though with some interruption in 1282-3 due to the Welsh wars and in 1289-90 due to the large-scale removal of members of the higher judiciary); and although the salaries thereafter were only paid much in arrears the principle of regular payment of the justices of the Bench and King's Bench on these fixed scales was maintained.[61] Under Edward I, moreover, the principle also became established within at most a few years after 1278 that all the justices in these courts were to be paid the regular salaries: not just a majority but all the justices serving in these courts.[62]

The practice of paying regular judicial salaries was first tried during Henry III's minority but seems soon to have been abandoned. It was resumed from the mid-1230s in the case of a small number of royal justices but only really became established for most, though still not all, royal justices in the later 1250s and early 1260s. But the principle of such payment and for all the justices of the two highest royal courts and of the eyres was only firmly established under Edward I.

Judicial Ethics

A fourth area where there is evidence for the increasing 'professionalisation' of the English judiciary during the reign of Edward I is in the field of

of Siddington seems to have been paid for his part in the London and Bedfordshire eyres of 1276-1277: C 62/52, m.7; /53, m.6.

[60]   1*Parl. Writs*, 382.

[61]   These conclusions are drawn from a detailed study of the unpublished liberate rolls for the reign. The same source indicates that although some assize justices were being paid for their work from the very beginning of the reign the principle that such justices should be paid a regular salary was still not clearly established in 1307, though those justices who were paid in the latter years of the reign did receive a fixed salary of either twenty pounds or twenty marks a year for their work.

[62]   The most junior justice of the Common Bench (William of Brompton) was not provided for under the 1278 scheme but was in fact paid as from Michaelmas 1279. At the same time, however, payment to his senior colleague Walter de Heliun seems to have ceased. It was only after Heliun's retirement in 1281 that all the justices of the Common Bench were paid. No provision was made under the 1278 scheme for payment of John des Vaux, the senior justice of the northern circuit, but in practice he was regularly paid the appropriate rate for chief justices. Only one piece of evidence (or absence of evidence) might suggest that the principle of universal payment of eyre justices was still not fully accepted as late as the 1290s. There seems to be no evidence that four of the six justices of the southern eyre circuit of 1292-4 (Berewick, Normanville, Mallore and Cave) were ever paid for their work.

professional ethics. This evidence relates partly to the enunciation of much clearer and more explicit professional standards for members of the judiciary; partly to the more rigorous enforcement of those standards.

The Enunciation of Standards:
Judicial Oaths and Statutory Provisions

It seems likely that royal justices took some kind of oath on taking office from at least the later twelfth century onwards; but the earliest judicial oath we have is that given in *Bracton*. This is the form of oath taken by justices of the General Eyre and is probably the form which was in use in the late 1220s or early 1230s.[63] It is remarkably unspecific in nature. Of its three main clauses, two simply bind the justice to perform the duties entrusted to him: by 'keeping the assize' according to the chapters and doing 'all matters of justice belonging to the king's crown' (probably references to the criminal and civil jurisdiction the justices were to exercise respectively).[64] Only a single clause binds the justice to any standard of conduct in the exercise of the jurisdiction entrusted to him and his colleagues: he swears to do right justice ('*rectam justiciam*') to the best of his ability ('*pro posse suo*') in the counties in which he is to sit and to do this both to rich and to poor (a rather vague and unspecific reminder that he is not to favour either rich or poor in his judgments). The justice does not, Bracton tells us, take an oath to act for the profit of the king; but immediately after taking his oath he is instructed to keep this in mind.

The next specific evidence we have about the wording of the oath taken by royal justices comes from 1257. The Burton Annals for that year contain the wording of the oath taken by the bishops of London and Worcester when they became members of the king's council. The text of the oath appears to have been reworked on this occasion; and it is noted that one of the clauses (though not the remainder) was also to be sworn both by the justices and by the barons of the exchequer. By this they were specifically to promise not to receive either directly or through an intermediary any gift or service from anyone they knew had business in the king's court by reason of that business (though apparently food and drink were to be excepted). A specific punish-

---

[63] *Bracton*, f. 109 (II, 309).

[64] These clauses of the oath are very reminiscent of the formulation of the instruction to the justices contained in chapter 7 of the so-called Assize of Northampton of 1176 under which the justices were to do all 'justitias et rectitudines spectantes ad dominum regem et coronam suam' by the writ of the king on fees of half a knight and below unless the case was too grand or one they needed to report back for doubt and were to make the assize ('faciant . . . assisam') on thieves and malefactors and were also reminded to ensure the king's profit: *Stubbs' Select Charters* (9th. edition revised by H.W.C. Davis), p. 180. The formulation of the justices' oath may thus in part at least go back to 1176.

ment was, moreover, stipulated for anyone breaching this rule: removal from the king's service (and loss of one year's income from their lands).[65]

The Close Roll for 1278 contains a form of oath to be taken by justices in eyre which bears little resemblance to the form given by *Bracton*. The justices were now to swear in the first place (and in rather more general terms than in the Bractonian oath) to serve the king well and loyally in the office of justice in eyre. A second clause contained a much more explicit (and much lengthier) promise about the conduct of the justice in the exercise of his duties: he was to do justice to the best of his ability to all as well poor as rich; he was not to disturb or respite justice against right or against the law of the land either for the great or the rich, nor for hatred nor for favour nor for the estate of anyone nor for a benefit, gift or promise given or to be given to him nor in any other way; but loyally do right to all according to law and custom. A third clause extended and made more general the promise first introduced in 1257: the justice was also to promise not to receive anything from anyone.[66] It is possible that the presence of the entry on the Close Roll indicates that the oath was entirely reworked in 1278 when the eyre system itself was being reorganised to put it on a permanent and continuing basis; but it should be noted that there is little in the oath that is specific to the justices in eyre and this raises the possibility that this form of oath was not in fact new in 1278 but had already been taken on previous occasions by other royal justices and that its enrolment on the Close Roll in 1278 is simply the result of a quirk in the system of recording material of peripheral importance like judicial oaths. Either way, however, it seems certain that the oath form belongs either to the later years of the reign of Henry III or to the early years of the reign of Edward I; and the precise chronology is less important than the changes in the oath which made it much more specific.

When we next hear of an oath taken by royal justices it is in the aftermath of the removal of a large proportion of the higher judiciary and while many of them were facing charges early in 1290. The oath given is closely related to the oath taken by the justices in eyre in 1278 but represents a further refinement and development of that oath.[67] It is also now absolutely clear that this is a general form of oath for royal justices and not just the oath of justices in eyre (indeed there were early in 1290 no justices in eyre to take

---

[65] 1 *Annales Monastici*, 395-6. Sayles (1*SCKB*, lxiv) suggests that the text envisages that the whole of the councillor's oath is to be taken by royal justices, but although this is suggested by the annalist in introducing the text of the oath, the internal evidence of the text of the oath indicates this not to be the case.

[66] C 54/95, m. 1d.

[67] E 368/61, m. 10; E 159/63, m. 10. It is printed from the former text in Ehrlich, *Proceedings against the Crown*, 222.

the oath). The new form does not (unlike its predecessor) make royal justices promise not to receive anything from anybody, but substitutes for this a promise not to receive anything without the king's permission (and the enrolment of the oath indicates that the king made a general standing concession to the justices who were swearing the oath allowing them to accept food and drink for the day).[68] A new clause was added at the end which is clearly a direct result of the evidence that was beginning to emerge about judicial wrongdoing during the king's absence between 1286 and 1289. The justices had now also to swear not to assent to any wrongdoing ('malice') on the part of their judicial colleagues but to attempt to prevent it if this was possible and to promise that if they were unable to do this that they would report the wrongdoing to the king's council and if they failed to take appropriate action would report it to the king.

A second way in which the standards expected of the king's justices came to be further developed during Edward's reign was through legislation. In 1275 chapter 25 of the statute of Westminster I for the first time laid down a firm rule that no officer of the king (and officer in this context certainly included the king's justices) was to 'maintain' pleas, suits or other matters in the king's courts concerning lands, tenements or other things in person or through a third party in return for a share of the property at stake in litigation or any other reward; and stipulated that the appropriate punishment for any convicted of this was punishment at the king's will.[69] More broadly, in 1285 chapter 49 of the statute of Westminster II included the king's justices among the group of royal servants (whose other members included the Chancellor, the Treasurer, members of the king's council, members of the king's household and clerks of chancery, exchequer and the justices or others) who were prohibited from acquiring or receiving churches or advowsons, lands or tenements whether in fee or to farm by gift or purchase while they were the subject of litigation in any of the king's courts. Again anyone who breached this prohibition was to be punished at the king's will.[70] But neither of the statutory provisions was concerned solely with royal justices; in both cases the legislation also applied to various

---

[68] A similar clause was included in the counsellors' oath recorded in Michaelmas term 1294 ('e qe rien ne prenderont saunz congie du Roy si ceo ne seit mangier e boyvre qant a la jornee'): E 159/68, m. 64. In a later version of the counsellors' oath associated with the Carlisle parliament of 1307 a similar but more elaborate clause is said to be taken only by the judicial members of the king's council ('Et sil deyve estre justice soit chargez del darein point'): 'Et qe rien ne prendrez de doun de nulli pur pled ne pur autre chose qil eit a fere devant vous si ce ne soit manger e bevire a la jornee'): 1*Rotuli Parliamentorum*, 218-9.

[69] 1*SR*, 33.

[70] 1*SR*, 95.

other categories of royal servant as well. They did not therefore make any real contribution to the development of a distinctive professional ethic for the judiciary.

The Enforcement of Ethical Standards

Edward I's reign also marked a significant advance in the actual enforcement of standards of professional conduct among the higher judiciary. Hitherto there had been only one occasion when one of the members of the higher judiciary had been dismissed and punished for misconduct in the execution of his professional duties. In 1251 Henry of Bath, the senior justice of the court of King's Bench, had been dismissed and punished for wrongdoing, though his disgrace did not last for long and he was reinstated as a justice of the same court in 1253.[71] Edward I's reign, by contrast, saw dismissal and punishment of members of the higher judiciary for misconduct on a large scale. In 1289-90 all three justices of King's Bench (Ralph de Hengham, William of Saham, and Walter of Wimborne) were dismissed from office.[72] Subsequent proceedings alleging misconduct while in office were brought against two of the three (Hengham and Saham),[73] resulting in the conviction of both justices and leading to their payment of very substantial fines (perhaps as much as 10,000 marks in the case of Hengham

---

[71] Bath's dismissal and punishment are discussed in C.A.F. Meekings, *King's Bench Justices, 1239-1258* (scheduled for future publication by the Selden Society). In 1272 master William of Watford, a justice of the Exchequer of the Jews, was dismissed and convicted of misconduct (and later outlawed when he failed to surrender to his bail) but the justices of the Jews were as much administrators as judges and cannot be considered members of the higher judiciary. The episode is discussed in my forthcoming introduction to volume VI of the Jewish Historical Society's edition of the *Plea Rolls of the Exchequer of the Jews*.

[72] Wimborne was the first to be dismissed. That he was still sitting in the court during the early part of Michaelmas term 1289 is shown by JUST 1/541B, m. 21d; that he was no longer one of the justices of the court by the end of Hilary term 1290 is shown by KB 27/118, m. 12d. Hengham and Saham seem to have remained in office till the end of Hilary term 1290: 1*SCKB*, xlv-xlvi. A fourth justice (Nicholas of Stapleton), who had been a King's Bench justice in 1273-4 and again between 1278 and 1287 seems also to have sat in King's Bench during Michaelmas term 1289 (JUST 1/541B, m. 21d; KB 27/121, m. 13; CP 25(1)/249/5, no. 15) but not thereafter.

[73] For proceedings against Hengham for alleged misconduct (i) *as chief justice of King's Bench* see *State Trials of the Reign of Edward the First, 1289-1293*, ed. T.F. Tout and H. Johnstone (Camden Society, 3rd. series, ix, 1906), 27-40, 46-8, 49-51; E 175/ File 1, no. 7, mm. 1, 3, 4; JUST 1/541B, mm. 21d, 22, 22d, 27 (printed in full as part of subsequent proceedings in 2*SCKB*, 97-112), 31d; KB 138/4, no. 81 (partly transcribed in 1*SCKB*, cxlvi-cxlviii); SC 8/42, no. 2080; 1*Rotuli Parliamentorum*, 52, nos. 82, 84; (ii) *in other judicial capacities* see JUST 1/541B, mm. 25, 34.

For proceedings against Saham (i) *as a justice of King's Bench* see *State Trials*, 27-40; (ii) *as a justice in eyre* see *State Trials*, 71-7; JUST 1/541B, mm. 9d, 11d; (iii) *as an assize justice* see JUST 1/542B, mm. 8, 29d, 46; (iv) *in a capacity that is unclear* see JUST 1/541B, m. 34d.

and 3,000 marks in the case of Saham).[74] At about the same time four of the five justices of the Common Bench (Thomas Weyland, William of Brompton, John de Lovetot and Roger of Leicester) were also dismissed from their positions;[75] proceedings for misconduct while in office were brought against all four.[76] All were then convicted of misconduct, leading to three of the four (Brompton, Lovetot and Leicester) paying substantial fines (6,000 marks in Brompton's case; £1000 in Lovetot's case; and 500 marks in

[74] Hengham was only actually convicted of misconduct in a single case (*State Trials*, 27-40) though in a second case his judgment was apparently quashed (JUST 1/541B, m. 22d). His judgments were specifically upheld in at least four other cases (*State Trials*, 46-8; JUST 1/541B, mm. 21d, 22, 25) and in at least two cases the plaintiff making the complaint was subsequently non-suited (E 175/ File 1, no. 7, mm. 1, 3). Tout and Johnstone (*State Trials*, xxx, xxxviii) give 7,000 marks as the fine payable by Hengham (though the passage they cite actually gives 8,000 marks as the figure payable) but suggest that he only paid a little over £4,000. This latter figure, however, as I have pointed out elsewhere (above p. 110) ignores (as do those for his fellow-justices) payments made after Hilary term 1294 and also grossly understates the amount paid by Hengham prior to this date and when both these are taken into account the total amount paid by Hengham comes to 9,360 marks. Since most fines were fixed in round numbers it seems likely that some unrecorded payment or payments (or one which I have overlooked) bring the sum up to 10,000 marks.

Saham was also convicted of misconduct in the same case as Hengham (*State Trials*, 27-40) though this is clear only from the sequel, proceedings brought by Saham against Hengham's clerk, John of Cave, and the Common Bench justice, William of Brompton (*State Trials*, 40-5). His judgment was also quashed in two other cases and the possibility raised in one of them (though the sequel to this is unclear) of the aggrieved party recovering damages against him (JUST 1/541B, mm. 9d, 46). In at least one case against him the complainant was non-suited at a late stage in the proceedings (JUST 1/541B, m. 11d). Tout and Johnstone (*State Trials*, xxxi-xxxii) note the view that Saham's fine was as high as 3,000 marks but suggest on the basis of the Receipt Rolls that he only paid £1,666 13s 4d; but they have overlooked two payments amounting in all to 500 marks which bring the total up to 3,000 marks.

[75] Brompton, Lovetot and Leicester were all sitting in the Common Bench as justices throughout Michaelmas term 1289 (1*SCKB*, cxxxvii) and Brompton was still described as a royal justice when witnessing a deed of 2 January 1290 (*CCR 1288-96*, 116); but all three men had probably been dismissed by 14 January when orders were given for the seizure of their lands and chattels (*CFR 1272-1307*, 268-9). Their replacements were appointed on 15 January (*CPR 1281-92*, 336). Chief Justice Weyland, by then a fugitive from justice, did not sit in the court in Michaelmas term 1289, but he was only suspended from acting as chief justice and not permanently dismissed. His permanent replacement was not appointed until January 1290: see above, p. 120.

[76] For the proceedings against Weyland see above, pp. 126-31.

For proceedings against Brompton (i) *as a justice of the Common Bench* see *ibid.* and *State Trials*, 1-5, 18-23, 33; JUST 1/541B, mm. 10d, 32d, 33d, 35, 36d; SC 8/107, no. 5338; SC 8/263, nos. 13105, 13143; (ii) *as an assize justice* see: JUST 1/541B, mm. 6d, 14d, 36d, 46d; (iii) *as a royal justice*: see *State Trials*, 27-40; JUST 1/541B, m.34d. Several of the proceedings against Brompton as a Common Bench justice were nominally against all the justices of the court but only he is recorded as answering the complainants and his other colleagues seem to have played no part in them at all.

For proceedings brought against John de Lovetot (i) *as a Common Bench justice* see above pp. 126-31 (ii) *as a gaol delivery justice* see *State Trials*, 53-61; (iii) *as an assize justice* see *State Trials*, 62-7; JUST 1/541B, mm 8, 35; (iv) *as a royal justice* see *State Trials*, 49-51; JUST 1/541B, m. 11d.

For proceedings brought against Roger of Leicester (i) *as a Common Bench justice* see above pp. 126-31; (ii) *as an assize justice* see JUST 1/541B, m. 5d.

Leicester's case).[77] Chief Justice Weyland suffered the heavier penalty of abjuration (exile from all the territories of the king) with loss of all his lands and chattels: but this was for being an accessory after the fact to a murder committed by his servants.[78] There were also proceedings against four men who had served as justices in eyre in the southern eyre circuit during the 1280s (Solomon of Rochester, Richard of Boyland, Walter of Hopton and master Thomas of Siddington),[79] and all four were convicted of misconduct, though only three subsequently paid substantial fines (4,000 marks in the case of Rochester; over 1,000 marks in the case of Boyland; and probably 2,000 marks in Siddington's case).[80] Nicholas of Stapleton, a

[77] All four Common Bench justices were convicted of misconduct in the case discussed, see above pp. 129-31. Brompton was also convicted of misconduct in a second case: *State Trials*, 27-40; and for cases in which Brompton's judgment was annulled but no penalty imposed on him see JUST 1/541B, mm. 32d, 36d, 46d. For other complaints in which Brompton was exonerated see *State Trials*, 1-5; JUST 1/541B, mm. 14d, 33d, 36d. Lovetot's judgment was annulled in a second case but no penalty imposed on him for it: see *State Trials*, 62-7.

Tout and Johnstone (*State Trials*, xxxi) note Brompton as only paying £3666 13s 4d of the fine of 6,000 marks attributed to him; but in fact payments made by him in June 1294 which are not noted by them bring his payments up to the full 6,000 marks. So too in Roger of Leicester's case, the failure to note payments made after Hilary term 1294 leads Tout and Johnstone (*State Trials*, xxxviii) to record a lower total than that eventually paid. In Lovetot's case Tout and Johnstone's table of fines paid (*State Trials*, xxxviii) overstates the amount paid by John de Lovetot since it includes the first payments (in 1294) of a second fine which was probably not connected with his judicial career or functions: E 159/66, m. 26; E 159/67, m. 16d.

[78] See above, pp. 113, 131-2.

[79] For a fifteenth-century transcript of the record of proceedings on a complaint against Rochester, Boyland and Hopton see BL Additional Roll 14987. Hopton subsequently denied involvement in the wrongdoing (see SC 8/263, no. 13125 and 1*Rotuli Parliamentorum*, 56) and may ultimately have cleared his name. For other proceedings (i) against Rochester (and Boyland, Hopton and Siddington) see: SC 8/177, no. 8816; (ii) against Rochester, Boyland and Siddington see: *State Trials*, 67-70; (iii) against Rochester and Boyland see: *State Trials*, 11-14 (and 14-17); JUST 1/541B, m. 12; (iv) against Rochester and Siddington see: JUST 1/541B, m. 12; (v) against Rochester (and William of Brompton) see 1*SCKB*, cxliv-cxlv; (vi) against Rochester alone see: *Select Cases before the King's Council, 1243-1482*, ed. Leadam and Baldwin, 2-5; SC 8/42, no. 2077; 1*Rotuli Parliamentorum*, 46, no. 10; 58-9, no. 160; SC 8/115, no. 5744; (vii) against Boyland alone: see *State Trials*, 5-11; JUST 1/541B, m.34; E 207/1/1, no. 1; (viii) against Boyland and Roger of Leicester (as Assize Justices) see: JUST 1/541B, m. 5d.

[80] Rochester, Boyland and Hopton (and the clerk Robert of Preston) were all apparently convicted of misconduct in the case recorded on BL Additional Roll 14987; but Hopton later denied that he had been present in the eyre at the time the alleged misconduct was committed (SC 8/263, no. 13125 and 1*Rotuli Parliamentorum*, 56) and this may later have led to the quashing of the judgment against him (and note that it is Rochester, Boyland, Siddington and Preston who are recorded as paying fines to be released from the Tower after their conviction for misconduct in BL Additional Roll 14987). Boyland alone was also convicted of misconduct in another case: see *State Trials*, 5-11. Rochester and various of his colleagues were cleared of any misconduct in three cases: see *State Trials*, 67-70; JUST 1/541B, m. 12 (bis); Boyland of misconduct in another case: *State Trials*, 14-17; and Boyland and Leicester in yet another: JUST 1/541B, m. 5d.

former King's Bench justice, was also accused of wrongdoing while acting as an assize justice and as a special commissioner appointed to determine a homicide case[81] but he was allowed to purchase a pardon for 300 marks before being convicted of any specific act of wrongdoing.[82]

Although these were the only actual convictions for misconduct of members of the higher judiciary during Edward's reign, they clearly established an important precedent and the possibility of further convictions must have influenced the behaviour of both justices and litigants. In 1293 we hear of Eustace and John de Parles defaming the royal justice William of Bereford in the king's hall in the presence of the magnates of England by claiming that he had maintained parties pleading before him and given them his counsel in the recent Staffordshire eyre and done other things there contrary to oath. Clearly they had not made a formal accusation against Bereford, for the record specifically mentions the fact that they had open to them the remedy of making a plaint to the king against Bereford (by way of explaining why their conduct was not acceptable); but the charge must have led to some sort of investigation into Bereford's conduct because the record also notes that the accusation has been found to be false. Both men were as a consequence sent to the Tower.[83] Again in 1306 after Ralph of Hengham had been rehabilitated and appointed chief justice of the Common Bench we hear of him being summoned before the king to answer for his refusal to seal a bill of exception, when a defendant made an exception which he had refused to allow or have enrolled. Hengham clearly gave a satisfactory answer for he continued to act as chief justice of the Common Bench till the end of the reign and beyond.[84]

The trials of the judges in 1289-90 show that Edward I's reign was not just a period when professional standards were increasingly made explicit, but also one where those standards were (perhaps for the first time) being enforced: though the conviction of so many justices for professional misconduct suggests that as yet their standards were not very high. In any case the actual enforcement of such standards is at least as important as their

Tout and Johnstone (*State Trials*, xxxi, xxviii) again underestimate the amount of the fine paid by Rochester because they do not take account of the money paid by his executors after Hilary 1294 (and miss one earlier payment). The same is true of Boyland's fine which was still being paid by his son and his widow in instalments as late as 1302; as also in the case of Siddington (whose recorded payments amount to 1, 975 marks and who can be presumed to have paid the whole of the 2,000 marks fine recorded in BL Additional Roll 14987).

[81]   For the proceedings against him as an Assize Justice see: JUST 1/541B, mm. 33, 36. For the proceedings against him as a special commissioner see: *State Trials*, 81-4. For evidence that he sat as a King's Bench justice in Michaelmas term 1289 see above, n. 72.

[82]   *CPR 1281-92*, 389; *CFR 1272-1307*, 284; *State Trials*, 84. The fine was paid in full in three instalments, the last on 16 October 1291. Stapleton pleaded the pardon to prevent further proceedings in one of the cases brought against him: *State Trials*, 81-4.

[83]   1*Rotuli Parliamentorum*, 95a-b.

[84]   *YB 33-35 Edward I*, 137-9; LI Misc. 738, f. 47r.

enunciation in demonstrating another significant aspect of the 'professionalisation' of the English judiciary.

Changes in the Pattern of Recruitment to the Higher Judiciary

'Before the middle of the fourteenth century', noted G.O.Sayles, 'the Bench
and the Bar had joined themselves together in an intimate and inseparable
association . . . No one could become a justice of the central courts of law,
that is the king's bench and the common bench, unless he had previously
been a serjeant-at-law' (that is, one of the small group of professional
lawyers who acted as advocates for clients in the Common Bench).[85] The
final major development of Edward I's reign that I want to discuss here is
the beginnings of the change in the pattern of recruitment to the higher
judiciary which was to culminate in this small segment of the legal profession gaining a monopoly over all appointments to the higher judiciary in
England.

As Professor Ralph Turner has recently pointed out, those scholars like
Maitland, Plucknett and Dawson who had 'assumed that clerics predomi-
nated among the royal justices until laymen began to be recruited from the
ranks of professional lawyers by the time of Edward I' had ignored the fact
that from as early as the reign of Henry II (that is, from the very beginnings
of the creation of a system of regular royal courts) a substantial proportion
of the judiciary were laymen.[86] There was, therefore, already a long
tradition of appointing laymen to the higher courts in England by the
beginning of Edward I's reign. What there was not was any real tradition of
appointing laymen who were also professional lawyers. It has been suggested that the first professional lawyer was appointed to the bench (as a
justice of the King's Bench and the Common Bench) as early as the reign of
John: one Roger Huscarl. The suggestion was first made somewhat hesit-
antly by H.G. Richardson, and his suggestion subsequently endorsed by
Lady Stenton and by Professor Ralph Turner.[87] But as they have all
recognised the evidence for this assertion is extremely slim. If we re-
examine the twenty-six references to his activity in the courts between 1199
and 1209 collected by Lady Stenton we find that ten of these are to his own
litigation; and the remaining sixteen show him acting as an attorney or in
some other capacity in no more than eight cases. In two of these eight cases

---

[85] Sayles, *7SCKB*, xxviii.

[86] Turner, *English Judiciary*, 291.

[87] H.G. Richardson, 'William of Ely, the King's Treasurer, 1195-1215' (1932) 15 (4th.
series)*TRHS*, 67; Stenton, *3PKJ*, cccxvi-cccxvii; Stenton, *English Justice*, 86, 98; Turner, *English
Judiciary*, 153-4; R.V. Turner, 'Roger Huscarl, Professional Lawyer in England and Royal
Justice in Ireland, *c.* 1199-1230', (1981) 16(new series)*The Irish Jurist*, 290-8.

we find him acting as no more than a surety.[88] Six cases hardly suffice to make Huscarl a professional lawyer. Nor do we find professional lawyers being appointed as justices in the king's courts during Henry III's reign. Some, though by no means all, of the professional lawyers who were active in the Common Bench, the Eyre and King's Bench during the reign of Henry III, can be identified.[89] Not one of them became a royal justice apart from Laurence del Brok, king's attorney (and serjeant) from 1247 to 1262 (who also seems to have enjoyed an extensive private practice as a serjeant). Laurence acted as a justice of King's Bench but only on a temporary basis and probably only in Easter term 1271.[90]

It was Edward I's reign that saw the first known appointments of professional lawyers, more specifically of professional serjeants, as regular justices of the king's courts. The honour of being the very first such appointee belongs to Richard of Boyland. Richard is to be found speaking as a serjeant in the Common Bench in a report that can be dated *c.* 1268-72 and acted as one of the king's serjeants in the Exchequer, in King's Bench and in the Common Bench between 1272 and 1278.[91] He was appointed a justice of the southern eyre circuit in May 1279 and acted in every eyre on that circuit down to 1289 (and also participated in the 1287 Gloucestershire eyre

---

[88] Stenton, *3PKJ*, cccxvi-cccxvii. Lady Stenton also suggests that the royal justice Ralph Hareng was drawn from the ranks of professional lawyers (Stenton, *3PKJ*, xl) but most of the references she prints (*3PKJ*, cccxiii-iv) are to his activities as a litigant in his own right or as a juror, not as the legal agent of others.

[89] In chapter 4 of my *The Origins of the English Legal Profession* I identify over twenty professional serjeants or probable professional serjeants of the period.

[90] For full details concerning Brok's career see Brand, *The Origins of the English Legal Profession*, 64-5. He is not mentioned as a justice of King's Bench by C.A.F. Meekings in his *List of Various Common Law Records*, 36-70; but for proof that he was sitting in the court with master Richard of Staines in Easter term 1271 see BL MS. Additional 50121, f. 47r (Lilleshall Cartulary). Evidently he did not remain a justice for long. Plucknett's reference to him becoming a justice in 1268 (*Concise History*, 239) is based on the entry in Foss, which only notes his being commissioned to take assizes in that year; he had in fact received occasional judicial commissions since 1249.

[91] *Casus Placitorum*, Collection I, no. 21 at 79. He is described as a king's serjeant in a pardon issued at his request in 1272 (*CPR 1266-72*, 653) and there is evidence on the Common Bench plea rolls of his acting on the king's behalf in a series of suits between 1273 (CP 40/2B, m. 7) and 1277 (CP 40/19, mm. 10d, 41). For evidence of his acting for the King in the Exchequer and King's Bench see E13/2, m. 11 and Donald Sutherland, *Quo Warranto Proceedings in the Reign of Edward I* (Oxford, 1963), 20, n. 1. During the 1260s he was in receipt of a pension of one mark a year from Ramsey abbey (*3Cartularium Monasterii de Ramesia*, 322-6) and in 1269 sued the dean and chapter of Chichester for five years arrears of a pension of twenty shillings a year (KB 26/180, m. 20). Both pensions were probably granted him for his legal services.

on the northern eyre circuit).[92] A second professional lawyer, Alan of
Walkingham, was just embarking on a career as a royal justice when he died.
Alan is known from reports to have acted as a serjeant in the Common
Bench in 1275 and 1276. He was paid for his services as one of the king's
serjeants between 1275 and 1281 and is known to have acted in that capacity
in the Common Bench in 1277 and 1278 and in both the 1276 Bedfordshire
and the 1279-81 Yorkshire eyres.[93] Alan was associated with the justices of
the Devon eyre of 1281-2 and sat as a justice at the very end of the eyre. He
was also commissioned to take part in the succeeding Cornwall eyre but had
died before its delayed start took place.[94]

No further appointments of professional lawyers to the higher judiciary
then took place until 1290. In that year Gilbert of Thornton was appointed
initially as a junior justice and then on Hengham's downfall as chief justice
of the court of King's Bench and he remained chief justice of this, the
highest regular royal court, until his death in August 1295.[95] Thornton had
been active as a serjeant in the Common Bench and in eyres from at least
1272 onwards; and had acted as king's serjeant on the eyres of the northern
circuit between 1280 and 1287 (apart from a period in 1284-5 when he was
on the king's service as a serjeant in Ireland).[96] His appointment as chief
justice of King's Bench in 1290 brought a professional lawyer for the first
time to the highest judicial office in England. At about the same time

---

[92] Crook, *Records of the General Eyre*, 156-70.

[93] *Casus Placitorum*, Collection I, no. 2 at 48-9; Collection II, nos. 6A at 101-2, 6B at 102-4
and 15 at 121-2; C 62/57, m. 10 (and *CCR 1279-88*, 39); CP 40/21, mm. 16d, 95; CP 40/27, m.
52; JUST 1/10, m. 44d; *PQW*, 187-199 passim. In 1275 he was one of the Common Bench
serjeants retained by the bishop of Hereford: *Reg . . . Thome de Cantilupo*, 22. Final concords
made by him in the Common Bench show that he was present in the court in 1262, 1265, 1270,
1274, 1275, 1277, 1282 and 1283.

[94] Crook, *Records of the General Eyre*, 160; *CPR 1281-92*, 10; *2CIPM*, no. 535. Walkingham
had earlier been one of the justices of the bishop of Durham's 1279-80 Durham eyre: Crook,
Records of the General Eyre, 147-8.

[95] KB 27/118, m. 12d; *1SCKB*, cxxxi-cxxxii; BL Campbell Charters XXI, 4; *Book of Prests*,
201.

[96] The earliest evidence for his activity as a serjeant is in a case in the 1271-2 Lincolnshire
eyre (CUL MS. Dd. 7. 14, ff. 370v-371r) and he is also known to have been present and to have
stood pledge for a litigant in the 1272 Warwickshire eyre (JUST 1/955, m. 33d). The earliest
securely dated Common Bench case in which he is known to have participated is one heard in
Hilary term 1275 (LI MS. Misc. 87, ff. 68v-69r and BL MS. Harley 1208, ff. 259v-260v, which
are reports of CP 40/8, m. 41d). He can be traced thereafter acting as a Common Bench serjeant
in 1276, 1277, 1279, 1282, 1283, 1285, 1286 and 1287 (full references will be found in my
forthcoming Selden Society volume of pre-1290 Common Bench reports). In the Yorkshire
eyre of 1279-81 Alan of Walkingham was the main king's serjeant but in at least one quo
warranto case it was Thornton who spoke for the king (*PQW*, 198). Thornton was also
subsequently paid for his services in the 1280 Nottinghamshire eyre (C 62/58, m. 2). His
subsequent career in the king's service can be traced both in the quo warranto pleas and in
payments made to him. In the 1287 Gloucestershire eyre William Inge seems to have been
much more active as king's serjeant than Thornton, but he did appear in some quo warranto
pleas there (*PQW*, 257, 259). For references to his Irish trip see *1SCKB*, lvii and for his activity
while there see: *1Analecta Hibernica*, 209-12; SC 6/1239, no. 4. For his activity as king's serjeant

William of Gisleham was appointed as one of the junior justices of the Common Bench, a position he retained until his death in mid-February 1293.[97] Gisleham was Thornton's counterpart as king's serjeant in the eyres of the southern eyre circuit from 1279 to at least 1287[98] and is also known to have acted on the king's behalf in the Common Bench in 1280, 1283, 1284, 1287 and 1289.[99] The reports show him acting as a serjeant in the Common Bench for other litigants in 1284 and 1285 as well.[100] Robert of Hartforth (Hertford) was also appointed a junior justice of the Common Bench at the same time and he retained that post until Easter term 1294, when he left the court to accompany the earl of Lincoln to Gascony.[101] Hartforth had not been a king's serjeant but there is some evidence to suggest that he had acted as a serjeant for other litigants in the northern eyre circuit in the late 1270s and early 1280s and that he may also have acted as a serjeant in the Common Bench in the late 1280s.[102] It is, however, probable that Hartforth spent part of this time in the service of a succession of great lords, so there is some doubt about whether he should be classified as a regular professional serjeant.[103] Hartforth does nonetheless have some

in the Common Bench in 1283, 1286 and 1287 see: CP 40/48, m. 15; CP 40/63, m. 39d; CP 40/64, m. 122d; CP 40/66, m. 67.

[97] *CPR 1281-92*, 336; 1*SCKB*, cxxxvii; *CPR 1292-1301*, 44; SC 1/27, no. 191.

[98] Sutherland says that he 'seems to have represented the crown in every eyre of the southern eyre circuit from 1278 to 1289' (Sutherland, *Quo Warranto Proceedings*, 37) but there seem to be no positive evidence that he was active in the 1278 Hertfordshire eyre or in the 1288 Sussex and 1289 Wiltshire eyres.

[99] CP 40/33, m. 10; /49, m. 4d; /51, m. 59d; /52, m. 35; /68, m. 78; /76, m. 42d.

[100] Full references and identifications of these cases will be found in my forthcoming volume of pre-1290 Common Bench reports.

[101] *CPR 1281-92*, 336; 1*SCKB*, cxxxvii; *CPR 1292-1301*, 115, 116. But note that his replacement, William de Bereford, was not formally appointed until 22 August 1294.

[102] In 1278-9 he was of five serjeants paid, probably for their services in the 1279 Northumberland eyre, by the bursar of Durham priory: 2*Durham Account Rolls*, ed. J.T. Fowler (Surtees Soc., vol. 100), 488; and in 1281 was one of five serjeants paid for their services in a plea between Isabel de Forz and Peter d'Eyncurt (perhaps a plea in the 1279-81 Yorkshire eyre): SC 6/824/12, m. 3. (cited in Denholm-Young, *Seignorial Administration*, 37). He is also probably the 'Hertf' found in reports of a nuisance case from the 1281-4 Lincolnshire eyre (Roger de Huntingfield *v.* John de Warenne earl of Surrey: BL MS. Additional 31826, f. 61v) and the 'Hertford' of a mort d'ancestor case from the same eyre (Neal *v.* bishop of Lincoln: Trinity College Cambridge, MS. 0.3.45, f. 38v). The 'Hert' or 'Hertford' who appears in two out of three reports of a Common Bench case of 1286 (acting for the earl of Richmond) and the 'Hert' who appears in another Common Bench report of a case of 1289 are also probably him, as is the 'Herford' or 'Herfort' who appears in an undentified Common Bench case from the 1280s (for full references see my forthcoming volume of pre-1290s Common Bench reports).

[103] In 1283 he was one of two general attorneys appointed by Robert of Tattershall to act on his behalf while he was overseas: *CPR 1281-92*, 109. In 1284 John of Brittany, earl of Richmond, appointed him as his general attorney for five years while he was overseas (*CPR 1281-92*, 146) and it was perhaps as a result of his reponsibilities in the earl's service that we find Hartforth acting as steward of Boston fair in 1286 (C 255/11/1, no. 4; SC 1/30, no. 177). He had perhaps entered the service of the earl of Lincoln by 1289 when he was given a judicial

claim to being the first professional lawyer who had not been employed in the king's service to be appointed a member of the higher judiciary. With Roger Brabazon, appointed a junior justice of King's Bench in 1290 (probably at the same time as Thornton became chief justice of the court), and who became chief justice of the court on Thornton's death, we are on much shakier ground.[104] Our evidence indicates that he had been in the service of a single magnate, the king's brother Edmund of Lancaster, from at least 1275 onwards, and shows him as specialising in Edmund's legal business.[105] On one occasion at least we can find him acting as a serjeant – in a case in the 1281 Derbyshire eyre: but this was on behalf of one of Edmund's men to whom Edmund had given the land which was the subject of the litigation.[106] It seems doubtful whether we can properly classify Roger Brabazon as a professional lawyer: for it seems likely that his duties for Edmund also included more general administrative tasks. Certainly he was not a professional lawyer in the same sense as Thornton, Gisleham or even Hartforth, for there is no evidence that he ever acted as a serjeant of the Common Bench.

Others of the justices appointed to the two central courts in 1290 were also fairly certainly not professional lawyers in origin. John of Mettingham, who was appointed chief justice of the Common Bench in 1290 and who remained its chief justice till his death in 1301, had been a justice in eyre on the northern eyre circuit from its beginning in 1278, apparently specialising in hearing quo warranto and other related pleas until he became chief justice of the circuit in time for the 1288 Dorset eyre.[107] Between 1274 and

commission to enquire into the taking of trees from one of the earl's woods (1*Cal. Inq. Misc.*, no. 1490) and certainly had by 1291, when (although also at this time a justice of the Common Bench), he was one of two general attorneys appointed by the earl to act for him during his absence overseas on the king's business (*CPR 1281-92*, 410). He had stood surety for the earl's essoiner in 1281 in the Lincolnshire eyre (JUST 1/501, m. 68d).

[104] 1*SCKB*, cxxxii-cxxxiv.

[105] For evidence of Brabazon acting as attorney for Edmund's general attorneys or directly as his attorney between 1275 and 1290 see: CP 40/11, m. 134; CP 40/18, m. 7d; CP 25(1)/123/36, no. 144; CP 40/69, m. 51d; CP 25(1)/183/16, no. 106. He is also to be found acting as the attorney of men going abroad with Edmund in 1276 and 1281 (*CPR 1272-81*, 157, 441). In 1285 he was among those commissioned by the king at Edmund's request to enquire into the misdeeds of his bailiffs and stewards (*CPR 1281-92*, 207); in 1287 one of those commissioned by the king to hold a forest eyre in Edmund's Lancashire forest (*CPR1281-92*, 263-4) and in 1287 is described in a charter as seneschal of the honour of Tutbury: BL MS. Stowe 879, f. 6r (and also in a charter the editor dates to c. 1295: *Cartulary of Tutbury Priory*, 243, no. 334). He is also later described as having been in the 1280s one of the leading men of Edmund's council and as having made a decision that the abbot of Burton was not obliged to find a tithingman for the wapentake of Wirksworth for a deserted vill: SC 8/95, no. 4737.

[106] BL MS. Harley 3640, ff. 26r-v.

[107] *CPR 1281-1292*, 336, 1*SCKB*, cxxxvii-cxxxviii; *Cal. Chancery Warrants*, i. 135; Crook, *Records of the General Eyre*, 146-57; Sutherland, *Quo Warranto Proceedings*, 35; *CCR 1272-9*, 479, 509.

1278 he had acted as an assize justice on one of the new assize circuits.[108] Prior to that the details of his career are unclear. Reports of a case heard in the Common Bench very early in the reign of Edward I appear to show him acting as a serjeant for one of the parties; but his clerical status would almost certainly have debarred him from practising as a serjeant on a regular basis.[109] The Hundred Rolls enquiry appear to show him acting as a local official of the earl of Lincoln in Norfolk in 1274-5.[110] But in a sense this does not matter: his appointment as chief justice of the Common Bench presumably came because in 1290 he had over sixteen years of experience as a royal justice in other courts. We can be even more certain that master Robert of Thorp, appointed as one of Mettingham's junior colleagues at the same time, and who served in that position only until Michaelmas term 1291, was not a professional common lawyer: for there is no evidence to link him with the common law courts prior to his appointment as a justice of the Common Bench.[111] As for Thornton's third colleague in the court of King's Bench, Robert Malet, who appears to have sat as a justice of that court until his death in 1295, again there seems to be no evidence of his being a professional lawyer.[112] As Sayles noted, there is evidence of his having acted as a gaol delivery, oyer and terminer and assize justice prior to his appointment (though not on a regular basis); and he is also probably to be identified with the man who was sheriff of Bedfordshire and Buckinghamshire for a few months in 1285.[113] It is also known that he had been steward of Edmund of Cornwall's honour of Wallingford.[114] But this evidence is not enough for us to class him as a professional lawyer. Thus although three (or just possibly) four of the men appointed as justices to the central courts were professional lawyers, an equal number of the new appointees certainly were not. Professional lawyers had begun to move in on judicial appointments; but they had certainly not gained anything like a monopoly of them.

A further seven men were appointed as justices of the Common Bench between 1290 and 1307 (the end of Edward I's reign), though one of these (Henry of Guildford) was appointed only on a temporary basis and will

---

[108] *CCR 1272-9*, 136; *CPR 1272-81*, 237-8; JUST 1/1223, 1228, 1231.

[109] Full references to the reports of the this case will be found in my forthcoming volume of pre-1290 Common Bench reports.

[110] 1*Rotuli Hundredorum*, 517.

[111] *CPR 1281-92*, 336; 1*SCKB*, cxxxvii.

[112] 1*SCKB*, lix, cxxxi-cxxxii.

[113] 1*SCKB*, lix.

[114] E 36/57, f. 31v. He also appears among the witnesses to several deeds in favour of Edmund of Cornwall: E 36/57, ff. 3v (of 1274/5), 20v, 52r.

therefore be disregarded here.[115] Two of these six (Lambert of Threekingham and Hervey of Stanton) are known to have served as clerks in the
courts before their appointment;[116] as had Ralph de Hengham, appointed
chief justice of the court in 1301, though in the more immediate past he had
spent two years as a junior justice of the Common Bench and sixteen years
of chief justice of King's Bench before his dismissal and disgrace in 1290.[117]
Peter Mallore, appointed a justice in 1292,[118] may appear in a single
unidentified report of an assize of mort d'ancestor and in another unidentified report of a pre-1292 quare ejecit case from the Common Bench or the
Eyre as a serjeant. These suggest that he might have been a professional
lawyer prior to his appointment.[119] But other evidence points to his having
been an administrator in magnate service: serving Ellis de Rabayne and his
wife Maud until after Ellis' death when he himself married Maud[120] and
then perhaps entering into the service of Henry de Lacy earl of Lincoln.[121]
The remaining two Common Bench justices certainly were professional

---

[115] *CPR 1301-7*, 408-9; *CCR 1302-7*, 300; 1*SCKB*, cxxxix. But note that there is evidence
that he may already have been sitting in the Common Bench in Trinity term 1305 (when many
adjournments are noted as being authorised by him) and in the following Michaelmas term
(when he gave a litigant permission to withdraw from his writ): CP 40/153, m. 141). In the latter
term he is also mentioned among the justices of the court in reports: *YB 33-35 Edward I*, 65-7,
73-7.

[116] Lambert of Threekingham, appointed a justice in 1300 (1*SCKB*, cxxxvii-cxl) was already
serving as a clerk in the 1281-4 Lincolnshire eyre when he is to be found suing in the king's
name in three pleas (JUST 1/510, m. 43d) and having a debt to himself enrolled on the plea roll
(JUST 1/492, m. 81d). He is also perhaps the 'dominus Lambertus' who acted as a clerk of the
justices and served as an intermediary in the 1286 Cambridgeshire eyre (*Liber Memorandorum
Ecclesie de Bernewelle*, 159). He certainly appeared before the Treasurer and Barons of the
Exchequer in Easter term 1293 as a clerk of John of Mettingham to attest the appointment of an
attorney (E 13/18, m. 29d). It was presumably as Mettingham's clerk that he was authorised to
receive the appointment of attorneys prior to Michaelmas term 1293 and again in Easter term
1294 (CP 40/102, m. 290; /104, m. 162d); and his relatively senior status as Mettingham's clerk
is probably reflected in the fact that he appears in 1295 as witness to a settlement which is also
witnessed by the justices of the Common Bench and the keeper of rolls and writs in the court
(CP 40/108, m. 153).

Hervey of Stanton was appointed a justice in 1306 and served as such till 1313 (1*SCKB*,
cxxxix-cxl). In 1297 he was pardoned a fine proffered for licence to concord as a clerk of the
Common Bench ('*quia clericus de banco*') (CP 40/119, m. 100); but the Year Book references to
interventions by 'Hervy', 'Hervy le Clerk' and 'Staunton' take his career in the court back to at
least Trinity term 1293 (for the earliest such reference se *YB 21 & 22 Edward I*, 241-5); and we
can find debts being acknowledged to him in the Common Bench (as Hervey de Staunton
clerk), something commonly associated with activity as a clerk of the court, as early as Easter
term 1293 (CP 40/100, mm. 8, 50).

[117] See below, pp. 468-9.

[118] *CPR 1281-92*, 507; 1*SCKB*, cxxxvii-cxxxix.

[119] BL MS. Hargrave 375, ff. 81v-82r; BL MS. Egerton 2811, f. 102v.

[120] JUST 1/207, m. 30; *CPR 1272-81*, 447; *CCR 1279-88*, 537; *CCR 1288-96*, 150.

[121] He occurs among the witnesses to confirmations by the earl in January and march 1292
in favour of Thornton priory, Kirkstead abbey, and a canon of Wells: 2*CChRolls*, 412; BL
Cotton Vespasian E xvii, ff. 228v, 229v-230r; *CPR 1281-92*, 481.

lawyers. William of Bereford first became a justice of the Common Bench for three terms in 1292 and returned to the court two years later after an intermission spent serving as a justice on the southern eyre circuit. He then remained a justice of the court right through to 1326, becoming chief justice on Hengham's retirement in 1309.[122] William had been a serjeant of the Common Bench between 1281 and 1290, appearing in some thirty-seven identifiable Common Bench reports of that period (plus reports of a further sixteen cases which belong to the period Thomas Weyland was chief justice of the court), a total which far exceeds that of any other serjeant of the period.[123] Although never retained on a regular basis by the Crown he is also to be found suing on its behalf in a number of cases in the Common Bench from 1279 onwards.[124] William Howard first became a justice of the Common Bench in 1297 and then served there continuously till 1308.[125] He is known to have acted as a serjeant in a number of the eyres of the southern eyre circuit during the 1280s[126] and again in all the eyres of the southern eyre circuit of 1292-4.[127] He is also to be found acting as a Common Bench serjeant in reports which can be identified as those of cases of 1291, 1292, 1294, 1295 and 1296.[128]

[122]   *CCR 1288-1296*, 219; *CPR 1292-1301*, 115; 1*SCKB*, cxxxvii-cxli; Crook, *Records of the General Eyre*, 175-8.

[123]   The earliest identifiable report in which he appears is BL MS. Royal 10.A.V, ff. 112v-113r (report of case enrolled on CP 40/42, m. 110d); the latest is BL MS. Additional 35116, ff. 148v-149r (report of case enrolled on CP 40/86, m. 232d). Full details of the other cases will be given in my edition of the pre-1290 Common Bench reports.

[124]   CP 40/28, m. 30d; /38, mm. 18, 59; /39, m. 2; /46, m. 66d; /61, m. 55d; /69, m. 148d. He is also to be found suing on behalf of the Crown in at least one King's Bench case: KB 27/114, m. 20.

[125]   *CPR 1292-1301*, 319; 1*SCKB*, cxxxviii-cxxxix.

[126]   He is known to have acted for the prior of Little Dunmow in a case heard in the 1285 Essex eyre (BL MS. Harley 662, f. 16r) and to have acted for Robert of Horford in a case in the 1286 Norfolk eyre (BL MS. Stowe 386, ff. 94r-95v: report of JUST 1/578, m. 47). He also appears in seven reports of cases which appear to come from the 1289 Wiltshire eyre: LI MS. Hale 188, f. 40r (and LI MS. Misc. 738, f. 23r; BL MS. Additional 37656, ff. 92r-v; CUL MS. Dd.7.14, ff. 406r-v) (reports of JUST 1/1011, m. 12); BL MS. Additional 37657, ff. 117r-v (and CUL MS. Dd.7.14, ff. 409r-v) (reports of JUST 1/1011, m. 27); BL MS. Hargrave 375, f. 42v (and CUL MS. Dd.7.14, f. 402r); CUL MS. Dd.7.14, f. 408r; CUL MS, Dd.7.14, f. 403r; CUL MS. Dd.7.14, f. 408v.

[127]   He is one of the three most commonly occuring serjeants in reports of the 1292 Herefordshire eyre (*YB 20 & 21Edward I*, 3-207); one of the two most commonly occurring serjeants in reports of the 1292 Shropshire eyre (*ibid.*, 211-93); the most commonly occurring serjeant in reports of the 1293 Staffordshire eyre (*ibid.*, 373-479); the most commonly occurring serjeant in reports of the Kent eyre of 1293 (BL MS. Additional 37657, ff. 67v-79v); and one of the two most commonly occurring serjeants in reports of the 1294 Middlesex eyre (*YB 21 & 22 Edward I*, 301-9, 317-37, 339-53).

[128]   For the 1291 case see LI MS. Hale 188, f. 34v (and three other reports of the same case) (identifiable as reports of the case enrolled on CP 40/90, m. 50); for the 1292 cases see *YB 20 &21 Edward I*, 321-9 (identifiable as CP 40/92, m. 36d), 343-9 (identifiable as CP 40/92, m. 124); for the 1294 case see *YB 21 & 22 Edward I*, 311-7 (identifiable as CP 40/105, m. 78d); for the 1295 cases see BL MS. Additional 5925, ff. 44r-45r (and seven other reports of the same case)

In King's Bench the story is a similar one. Four justices were appointed to the court between 1290 and the end of the reign. Of these one (master John Lovel) appears to have sat in the court for less than a year and his appointment is therefore to be seen as only temporary; and he will be disregarded here.[129] Gilbert of Rothbury was a justice of King's Bench from 1295 to 1316 (and then a justice of the Common Bench from 1316 to 1321).[130] He had probably been a clerk in the courts before his appointment in 1290 as clerk of the king's council and clerk of parliament.[131] But his two colleagues (William of Ormsby and Henry Spigurnel) both seem to have been professional lawyers before their appointment. William of Ormsby acted as a justice of King's Bench during 1296 and again between 1298 and 1303.[132] His immediate background experience prior to appointment to King's Bench was as a junior justice in the northern circuit eyres of 1292-4.[133] Prior to that, however, he seems to have been a professional lawyer: not a serjeant of the Common Bench but a professional lawyer whose activity seems to have been confined to his own home county of Norfolk.[134] Henry Spigurnel was appointed a justice at the very end of the reign and continued in this post through to 1323.[135] Again the immediate background to his

(identifiable as CP 40/109, m. 11), BL MS. Additional 37657, ff. 99r-v (identifiable as CP 40/109, m. 67d), BL MS. Additional 37657, ff. 105r-v (and five other reports) (identifiable as CP 40/109, m. 19d) and BL MS. Additional 5925, ff. 38r-v (and six other reports) (identifiable as CP 40/110, m. 152); for the 1296 cases see BL MS. Additional 5925, ff.36r-37r (and four other reports) (identifiable as CP 40/112, m. 91), BL MS. Additional 5925, ff. 34v-35v (and seven other reports) (identifiable as CP 40/112, m. 128), BL MS. Additional 5925, ff. 37r-v (and three other reports) (identifiable as CP 40/115, m. 108), BL MS. Additional 5925, ff. 37v-38r (and two other reports) (identifiable as CP 40/115, m. 68d), LI MS. Hale 188, f. 35r (identifiable as CP 40/115, m. 38), BL MS. Stowe 386, ff. 97r-98r (and three other reports) (identifiable as CP 40/115, m. 51); BL MS. Additional 31826, f. 96v (and two other reports) (identifiable as CP 40/115, m. 143d).

[129] 1*SCKB*, lx.

[130] 1*SCKB*, lx-lxi, cxxxii-cxxxiv, cxl-cxli.

[131] For evidence that he was at Lincoln in November 1281 during the Lincolnshire eyre and witnessed a deed with various serjeants and other court clerks see JUST 1/501, m. 49. In 1293 Gilbert was one of the executors of Anger of Ripon (CP 40/101, m. 81). Anger had been the chief clerk of the northern eyre circuit of the 1280s and Gilbert's nomination as one of his executors suggests that Gilbert may have worked with him. For his career after 1290 see 1*SCKB*, lx-lxi.

[132] 1*SCKB*, lxi-lxii, cxxxii.

[133] Crook, *Records of the General Eyre*, 171-4, 179.

[134] In 1283 he was receiving a fee of one mark (presumably for his services) from the prior of Norwich: 19*Norfolk Archaeology*, 281. In the 1286 Norfolk eyre he is to be found acting as a surety for a debt on an agreement with Howard (JUST 1/578, m. 3); being paid for acting there as a serjeant for the earl of Norfolk (SC 6/935/44) and is among the serjeants mentioned in the report of a case from the eyre in BL Stowe 386, ff. 94r-95r. In 1288 he is to be found with Howard and another local serjeant, Colney, witnessing a deed at Norwich: 2 *Norwich Cathedral Deeds*, no. 362.

[135] 1*SCKB*, lxiii, cxxxiii-cxxxiv.

appointment was service as a justice in eyre (in the 1299 Cambridgeshire and 1302 Cornwall eyres) but to this was added (in Spigurnel's case) service as a regular assize justice from 1295 onwards and a brief period in 1301 as a substitute King's Bench justice.[136] Prior to this, however, and also continuing alongside it, was his career as a professional serjeant. He is known to have acted as such in a number of the eyres of the 1280s and appears in reports of a few Common Bench cases from the same decade.[137] He appears as a serjeant of the Common Bench in reports of cases of the period 1290-2 and 1295-8 and is found between 1292 and 1294 acting as one of the serjeants of the southern eyre circuit.[138]

The overall picture at the end of Edward I's reign then was that professional lawyers, and more particularly the serjeants of the Common Bench, had become established as a source of justices for the two major royal courts, King's Bench and the Common Bench, but that they had not yet established a monopoly of appointments to those courts. It was only during the following reign, that of Edward II (1307-27), that the serjeants of the Common Bench established their predominance over new appointments to the two highest royal courts (King's Bench and the Common Bench); and by about 1330 the serjeants of the Common Bench had in practice gained a monopoly of permanent appointments to the Common Bench and King's Bench, though it still remained possible to appoint non-serjeants to these courts on a temporary basis and one was appointed as late as 1364.

It can be no coincidence that the first justices to be appointed to the higher judiciary in England who were professional lawyers were lawyers who had previously been employed in the king's service, and who had thus provided the king (and his advisers) with proof not just of their professional competence but also of their assiduity in the promotion and protection of the king's

---

[136] Crook, *Records of the General Eyre*, 179-80; C66/114, m. 6d (appointment as an assize justice) and JUST 1/1309, 1311 (records of circuit); 1*SCKB*, xlviii, lxiii.

[137] He appears in one of three reports of the 1285 Northants eyre case of master William de Henhore v. Richard fitz John (JUST 1/622, m. 30d), that in BL Lansdowne 467, ff. 119v-120r, and in the 1287 Gloucestershire eyre he stood surety for a champion (an office frequently undertaken by serjeants) (JUST 1/278, m. 11). He also appears in the report of a case apparently from the 1289 Wiltshire eyre in CUL MS. Dd.7.14, f. 403r. In the Common Bench he acted in a case heard in Michaelmas term 1287 which is reported in Gonville and Caius MS. 715/721, f. 43v (and enrolled on CP 40/69, m. 129d) and in two other unidentified cases from the period Weyland was chief justice of the court: LI MS. Miscellaneous 87, f. 49r and BL MS. Lansdowne 467, ff. 121r-v.

[138] The references to him as a Common Bench serjeant are too numerous to give in full. Spigurnel is one of the three serjeants most commonly mentioned in reports of the 1292 Herefordshire eyre (*YB 20 & 21 Edward I*, 3-207); the serjeant most commonly mentioned in reports of the 1292 Shropshire eyre (*YB 20 & 21 Edward I*, 211-93); one of two serjeants most commonly mentioned in reports of the 1293 Staffordshire eyre (*YB 20 & 21 Edward I*, 373-479); one of the three serjeants most commonly mentioned in reports of the 1293 Kent eyre (BL MS. Additional 37657, ff. 67v-79v) and the serjeant most commonly mentioned in reports of the 1294 Middlesex eyre (*YB 21 & 22 Edward I*, 301-9, 317-37, 339-53).

interests. Laurence del Brok was the first lawyer retained in the king's service; he was also the first professional lawyer appointed to the bench (if only on a temporary basis). As soon as there were professional lawyers in the king's service, they began to be appointed to the judiciary. Such men were clearly much better qualified than the non-professional laymen with no record of service to the Crown who had been a significant element in the judiciary prior to this point. But from 1290 onwards we also find professional serjeants who had not been employed by the king appointed as justices (initially Robert of Hartforth; later William of Ormsby, William Howard and Henry Spigurnel). The initial impulse to go outside the ranks of those hitherto considered eligible may have been provided by the circumstances of 1290, when so many of the existing justices had been dismissed and disgraced; but it may also be significant that both Robert of Hartforth (appointed to the Common Bench in 1290) and Peter Mallore (appointed to the Common Bench in 1292) are known to have had connections with Henry de Lacy earl of Lincoln prior to their appointment and that de Lacy was one of Edward I's closest confidants, and it seems possible that de Lacy in some way vouched for their competence and loyalty. William of Bereford's appointment in 1292 may be explicable in terms of his service to the Crown on an ad hoc basis prior to 1290; but may also owe something to the sponsorship of Edmund of Cornwall, whose service Bereford appears to have entered in 1290, and who was also close to Edward.[139] Other serjeants who had not become king's serjeants but who were appointed royal justices during this period such as William Howard and Henry Spigurnel were given a chance to prove themselves through service as assize justices before their appointment to one of the central courts.

The subsequent development, the emergence of the serjeants of the Common Bench as the predominant (though still not exclusive) source of justices of the central courts during Edward II's reign, is probably to be associated with changes in the structure of the English legal profession which had taken place by the end of the reign of Edward I.[140] By 1307 a relatively small group of about thirty individuals had gained a monopoly of practice on a regular basis in the Common Bench and the same individuals also offered their services in King's Bench (and in the eyres) as well. It seems likely that admission to this group was gained on the basis of proven technical competence; hence the formation of a group of 'apprentices', learners present in the court and hoping to qualify for future admission to the ranks of the serjeants. Thus by 1307 there existed a clearly defined

---

[139]   For deeds of Edmund of Cornwall of dates between December 1290 and September 1291 in which William de Bereford appears as first or second witness see E 36/57, ff. 29v, 62r, 65v-66r, 66v; *Monasticon Diocesis Exoniensis*, 32-3. Bereford was also later named as one of Edmund's executors: CP 40/135, m. 208.

[140]   These developments are discussed in Brand, *The Origins of the English Legal Pofession*, where full references will be found.

group with a certified competence and practising in the very courts to which appointments were being made. Such men obviously had a very good claim to be considered for appointment as justices; a much better claim than any other possible lay candidates. The real problem, however, is to explain how and why the serjeants also then managed to exclude from appointment to the higher judiciary the leading clerks in the courts. These men had as much opportunity as the serjeants to acquire an expertise in the law administered in the courts in which they served, and the yearbooks of the reign of Edward I show them intervening in legal proceedings in a way that clearly demonstrates that expertise. Judges were still being appointed from their ranks in the later years of Edward I and at least one justice of the reign of Edward II (John Bacun) was appointed from their ranks. Perhaps in the long run it was their inability to participate fully in the administration of the criminal justice system (as clerics they were unable to give judgments which led to the shedding of blood) which led to their exclusion; for it became the practice to make use of the justices of the central courts in running the assize system and it was clearly a disadvantage to have judges who were able to act as an assize judge but not also to act as gaol delivery justices. Only with this group of clerical experts out of the way was the stage set for the serjeants to gain a monopoly of judicial appointments.

Conclusions

Historians have often written as if there was a professional judiciary in England from the reign of Henry II onwards or at latest by the beginning of the thirteenth century.[141] I believe this view to be mistaken, for what I believe we can see during Edward I's reign is a movement towards the 'professionalisation' of the judiciary in the higher royal courts, a judiciary which in a number of important respects had not been fully professional

---

[141] Thus Maitland speaking of the most durable and fruitful of the results of Henry II's work says that ' . . . the whole of English law is centralized and unified by the institution of a permanent court of professional judges . . . ' (Pollock and Maitland, 1*HEL*, 138); Lady Stenton writing of the early thirteenth century says ' . . . it is obvious that the judges are but the leading figures in what was becoming an elaborately organized profession . . . ' (D.M. Stenton, *English Justice*, 86); and John Baker notes that 'by about 1200 . . . a new distinction is perceptible at the centre. The typical justices of the Bench were no longer politicians, administrators and men of public affairs, but professional judges spending most of their time on the administration of the nascent common law . . . ' (J.H. Baker, *An Introduction to English Legal History* (2nd. edition, London, 1979), 17). Professor Ralph Turner in his recent study of the English judiciary in the last quarter of the twelfth century and first four decades of the thirteenth century (R.V. Turner, *The English Judiciary in the Age of Glanvill and Bracton, c. 1176-1239* (Cambridge, 1985) has discounted the use of the term 'professional' for the judges of Henry II's reign but is willing to describe the judges of Richard I's reign as 'professionals' or at least 'proto-professionals'. He has no hesitations about describing the judges of the early part of Henry III's reign as professionals.

hitherto. There were at least four separate strands to this development: a substantial addition to the number of royal courts which existed on a permanent basis and were run by their own full-time staff of justices; a significant change in the pattern of service of members of the judiciary, which shows that a higher proportion of royal justices were becoming career justices; the beginnings of regular payment of all justices serving in the higher royal courts; the enunciation (through judicial oaths and legislation) of much more explicit norms of professional conduct for members of the judiciary and a real attempt for the first time to enforce those norms. However, what eventually developed in England was not a separate 'judicial' professions as such, but a professional higher judiciary that formed part of a much wider English legal profession. Here too the reign of Edward I marks one of the crucial turning-points for it was, as we have seen, only during that reign that professional lawyers first began to be appointed as justices of the king's courts. Edward I's reign should certainly be remembered for the great Edwardian statutes; but it ought also to be given its due importance as a period of major significance in the development of the English legal system.

8

Medieval Legal Bureaucracy:
The Clerks of the King's Courts in the Reign of Edward I

In Michaelmas term 1290 Walter of St. Edmund's, one of the clerks of the Bench, brought a plaint in that court against Robert of Upton alleging defamation.[1] Walter was the clerk assigned to enter appointments of attorneys in the main plea roll of the court (the chief justice's roll). Robert had apparently accused the clerk of making a back-dated entry in the plea roll of the preceding Easter term as though an attorney had been duly appointed for a particular piece of litigation during that term. Walter asked to have the matter enquired into so that he could prove his innocence. If he was guilty, he should be punished in an appropriate fashion. But if he was innocent, then Robert should be punished for making an allegation that touched his personal honour and the reputation of the court. The attorney whose appointment was recorded in the entry also joined in the suit and claimed that Robert had defamed him too by alleging that he had procured the making of the entry. There was, however, a significant difference between the two complaints. The attorney's complaint alleged not that Robert had said that the entry had wrongly been backdated but that the attorney's principal had never appeared before a justice in the court or elsewhere to make the appointment (and thus that he had never been validly appointed). Robert of Upton was present in court and was asked by the justices if he wished to bring suit against them for misconduct. He declined and denied having made any such allegations. He put himself on a jury of men of the court ('*probos et legales homines istius curie*') to clear himself. He was careful, however, to ensure that the jury should not include any of the clerks of the court. Walter, the complainant, was a clerk and their colleague ('*clericus est et socius curie*') and clerical solidarity might bias them against him. The jury found that he had indeed made the allegations. The court also inspected the relevant membrane of the plea roll for Easter term and found the relevant entry half way down the membrane with no indication that it had just been written and nothing else about the entry that gave rise to any suspicion. It did not, however, proceed to punish Robert. Evidently, it was thought best

---

[1] CP 40/86, m. 258.

to consult the king and his council before doing so for he was simply required to find mainpernors to appear before king and council or in the Bench (as required) to receive judgment. What punishment he eventually received is not known.

This case is of particular interest because it is one of the few pieces of evidence from the later thirteenth century which shows a named clerk of the Bench at work performing one of the main functions of such clerks, the writing of plea rolls. There are a small number of others. The proceedings following a complaint made against the former Bench justice William of Brompton in 1290 tell us that another Bench clerk, Simon of Harrowden, had been responsible for making a particular entry recording an essoin in Michaelmas term 1286;[2] and an entry on the plea role for Hilary term 1294 recording proceedings against a professional attorney (John Sturmyn) shows Henry of Lichfield as the Bench clerk to whom John had handed over a schedule recording an adjournment allegedly made at the request of both parties to litigation to enter on the plea roll and thus show a third Bench clerk at work.[3] But these three cases really tell us very little. They give us no idea of how many Bench clerks were engaged on the writing of plea rolls or how the work was divided between them.

Such information first becomes available in the final years of the reign of Edward I. In Easter term 1305 the Bench adopted the practice of having its clerks append their names at the bottom of the membranes which they had written.[4] This shows us that at least thirty-two clerks were at work in the court writing plea roll membranes in Easter term 1305. It also indicates that the work was not evenly distributed between them. Some clerks wrote many more membranes than others.[5] Analysis of these membranes also makes it clear that as yet there was no attempt to make particular clerks responsible for the business from particular counties.[6] The plea rolls of subsequent

---

[2] JUST 1/541B, m. 33d.

[3] CP 40/103, m. 159d.

[4] A few membranes do not have 'signatures' but the vast majority do. A minority of membranes are signed by more than one clerk.

[5] The following is a list of clerks who sign membranes with the number of membranes each signed in brackets: Scothowe (19); Melles (16); Wiclewode (16); Elmham (11); Langhale (11); Tameworth (11); Baketon (9); Eton (9); Suthwerk (9); Gislingham (9); Elingham (8); Wrattyng (8); Cantebr' (7); Garboldesham (7); Repinghale (7); Hampton (6); Hengham (6); Poynton (6); Haukedon (5); Thweyt (5); Chaumbre (4); Keleby (4); Redenhale (3); Hauville (2); Aringworth (1); Friseland (1); Horneby (1); Lodne (1); Neuport (1); Pevenese (1); Wykewane (1); Normanby loco Hengham (1) (presumably this is an under-clerk signing a membrane in the absence of his superior; some of the other signers of single membranes may also be under-clerks). There are also membranes signed by both Scothowe and Eton; Scothowe and Fincham; Suthwark and Fincham; Scothowe and Simkyn; Scothowe and Pevenese; Poynton and Friseland.

[6] It is however clear that a single clerk (Melles) with a particularly fine and distinctive hand was responsible for the enrolment of a disproportionately large share of the cases in which there was intricate and interesting pleading both in this and in later terms.

terms show that the number of clerks active in writing Bench plea rolls varied from term to term but that overall the numbers were gradually rising between 1305 and 1307. By the last term of Edward I's reign (Trinity term 1307) there were as many as forty-three clerks writing plea roll membranes in the court.[7]

The second major task for which the clerks of the Bench were responsible was the writing of judicial writs: writs running in the name of the king but attested by the chief justice of the court, which, among other things, set in motion the various stages of mesne process necessary to secure the appearance of defendants and jurors and ordered the execution of other judgments rendered by the court. Two cases heard during the 1290s show the clerks of the court performing this function out of court and after the main meal of the day ('*post prandium*'), probably after the court had risen. In the first, which refers to an incident which occurred while the court was still at Westminster, the clerks of the court were said to have been writing out judicial writs in the lodgings ('*hospicium*') of the chief justice, John of Mettingham;[8] in the second, referring to an incident which occurred while the court was in York, the clerks were said to have been writing judicial writs in the church of St. Andrew within the priory of the Sempringham order in York.[9] The clerks of the Bench began signing their names to the judicial writs which they had written more than a decade before they started signing plea roll membranes. The practice can be dated precisely (it began on 1 May 1292) and was clearly required by some kind of specific regulation.[10] Surviving Bench writ files from the last fifteen years of the reign of Edward I indicate that there were at least twenty different clerks writing judicial

---

[7] The following is a list of clerks who sign membranes separately with the number of membranes signed in brackets: Eton (23); Wiclewode (20); Melles (17); Langhale (15); Tutyngton (14); Elmham (13); Garboldesham (12); Wrattyng (12); Marlingford (10); Poynton (10); Athelingfleet (9) (this is the same man as the Chaumbre of Easter term 1305); Gislingham (9); Elingham (8); Tameworth (8); Catefeld (7); Hampton (7); Haukedon (7); Repinghale (7); Baketon (6); Gotham (6); Haxay (6); Lodne (6); Scothowe (6); Cantebr' (5); Keleby (5); Surlingham (5); Suthwerk (5); Fincham (4); Hengham (4); Thweyt (4); Wolvernehampton (4); Pevenese (3); Rotheley (3); Gra (2); Ludington (2) (and one Ludington loco Hengham); Wynneferth (2); Beverl' (1); Brecles (1); Bussh (1); Norwiz (1); Warr' (1); Wakedene (1); Olton loco Hengham (1). Thirty-two further membranes are shared by two or three clerks. A further five clerks appear only on these membranes: Aringeworth; Broun; Purefey; Somerby; Wykewane.

[8] CP 40/90, m. 57d.

[9] CP 40/124, m. 22d.

[10] In practice not all judicial writs issued after this date were 'signed' but signatures are sufficiently common to indicate that this was intended to be the general rule. Some signatures may have been trimmed off writs prior to the sealing of the writ.

writs in 1292;[11] that the number had risen to at least thirty-two by 1296[12] and to a minimum of thirty-five by 1303-4.[13]

During the final years of the reign it becomes possible to compare the clerks whose signatures appear on judicial writs and those clerks whose signatures appear on plea rolls. In Easter term 1306 some nineteen clerks are to be found engaged in both activities; seventeen clerks only writing plea roll membranes; and six clerks only writing writs.[14] A larger degree of overlap occurs in the following term (Trinity term 1306) though here the combined total of clerks also rises from forty-two to forty-seven. Of the forty-seven, twenty-four are found performing both functions, thirteen only writing plea roll membranes and ten only writing writs.[15]

[11]   Their names are taken from a writ file for the quindene of Trinity and a writ file for the octave of Michaelmas. Many are given only in abbreviated form but can be extended with the aid of later writ files or other evidence. The names are: Antingham, Blund, Brokedys, Costesy, Couton, Fincham, Fulks, Harpley, Hath', Hek', Helpringham, Hoperton, Hunsingore, Ickworth, Nor' (?=Norwich), Pokelington, Redenhal, Sandwiz, Singleton, Wymondham.

[12]   Their names are taken from writ files for the quindene of Trinity and the morrow of Martinmas 1296. The names (again extended where necessary and possible with the aid of other evidence) are: Antingham, Aylesham, Baketon, Brokedys, Costesy, Couton, Elingham, Fincham, Ford', Hath', Hek', Hoperton, Ickworth, Keleby, Kelshale, Kendale, Langhale, Lust', Mells, Morton, Nor' (?=Norwich), Oltone, Pokelington, Redenhale, Russel, Silham, Sutton, Trobridge, Wamberge, Wyke (?=Wykewane), Wymondham.

[13]   Their names are taken from two writ files for one month and five weeks after Easter 1304. The names (again extended where necessary and possible with the aid of other evidence) are: Aringworth, Aylesham, Baketon, Brokedys, Cantebr', Costesy, Elingham, Elmham, Eton, Garboldisham, Giff', Gislingham, Hampton, Hau', Horneby, Jernemue, Kel' (?=Keleby or Kelshale), Langhale, Lodne, Luch', Mells, Poynton, Redenhale, Repinghale, Rotheley, Scothowe, Suthwerk, Swyneford, Tameworth, Thweyt, Wals', Wiclewode, Wyke (?=Wykewane), Wymondham, Wratting.

[14]   The clerks signing judicial writs are taken from the surviving writ files for the quindene of Michaelmas 1306. Those found signing both are: Cantebr', Chaumbre, Elingham, Elmham, Eton', Gislingham, Gotham, Hampton, Kelleby, Langhale, Lodne, Melles, Poynton, Repinghale, Scothowe, Tamworth, Thweyt, Wiclewode, Wratting. Those found only on the plea roll are: Brampton, Brun, Enges, Fincham, Garboldisham, Gra, Haukedon', Haxay, Hengham, Ludington, Neuport, Norwiz, Rotheley, Somerby, Suthwerk', Tutyngton', Wykewane. Those found only on writs are: ?Aringworth, Carleton, Chesterfield, Friseland, Pyk', J de Thrill'.

[15]   The clerks signing judicial writs are again taken from the surviving writ files for the quindene of Michaelmas 1306. Those found signing both are: Baketon', Cantebr', Chaumbre, Elingham, Elmham, Eton', Garboldisham, Gislingham, Gotham, Hampton, Haxay, Kelleby, Langhale, Lodne, Ludington, Melles, Norwiz, Poynton, Repinghale, Scothowe, Tamworth, Thweyt, Wiclewode, Wratting. Those found only on the plea roll are: Brampton, Enges, Fincham, Gra, Hath', Haukedon', Neuport, Pevenese, Rotheley, Somerby, Suthwerk', Tutyngton', Warr'. Those found only on writs are: ?Aringworth, Aylesham, Brecles, Pyk', Redenhale, Rushes, Seleby, Truston, Wykewane, Wym'.

There were also a number of other, more senior clerks attached to the Bench and performing particular specific functions there. There had been a *keeper of rolls and writs* in the Bench since at least the middle years of the reign of Henry III.[16] He was responsible for the compilation of a plea roll recording proceedings in the court, the plea roll which during Edward I's reign bore at the top of each membrane the word '*Rex*' where the chief justice's roll bore the chief justice's name. Prior to 1253 this was apparently the main record of the court; but thereafter it became a subsidiary one and was perhaps copied from that compiled for the chief justice.[17] Despite his title, the keeper of rolls and writs did not have custody of the plea rolls compiled for the chief justice, only of those compiled for himself or his predecessors in office, and that only until they were handed in to the Exchequer for safekeeping in the Treasury.[18] But the keeper did have official custody of all original and judicial writs returned into the court, at least until he in turn surrendered them into the custody of the Exche-

[16]   The holders of this office can only be traced with certainty from the point (in 1246) when Roger of Whitchester started receiving a payment from the king for carrying out the duties of the office but there may well have been previous holders of the post who were not so remunerated. Certainly when a separate Irish chancery was established in 1232 it was provided that the Irish chancellor should have a clerk at sessions before the justiciar who would keep his own roll and the court's writs and this was said to be as the chancellor had in England: *Close Rolls, 1231-4*, pp. 112-3. This looks like a description of the office of keeper of rolls and writs. Meekings noted that the Bench clerk William of York who appears in the Bench from 1219 onwards was closely tied to the chancellor and might well have been a forerunner of Roger of Whitchester: see his 'Martin Pateshull and William Raleigh' in his *Studies in 13th Century Justice and Administration*, art. XI, pp. 175-7. For a list of holders of the post between 1246 and 1307 see Margaret Hastings, *The Court of Common Pleas in fifteenth Century England* (Ithaca, 1947), pp. 271-3 (and for some additions to the corrections of that list see C.A.F. Meekings, 'Roger of Whitchester (+ 1258)' in his *Studies in Thirteenth-Century Justice and Administration* at 108 and below, pp. 00-00).

[17]   Hastings, *Court of Common Pleas*, pp. 54-5, 121-3. But note that the passage in Bracton referring to the 'first' roll of the court as that of the protonotary probably predates this change and the protonotary referred to is probably the keeper of rolls and writs: see below, pp. 00, note 124.

[18]   In November 1289 Robert of Littlebury delivered into the Exchequer a complete set of plea rolls from 1266-7 (50 Henry III) onwards plus matching essoin rolls: 1*SCKB*, pp. clix-clx. These must have been the 'Rex' rolls for at around the same time Robert of Retford was handing over to Ellis of Beckingham a complete set of the rolls made for chief justice Weyland between 1277 and 1289 then being kept in the London church of St. Mary Somerset: CP 40/80, m. 94d (and see also E 159/63, m. 9d). Littlebury subsequently handed over what must have been the 'Rex' roll for Michaelmas term 1289 to his successor Master John Lovel: 1*SCKB*, p. clxii. In May 1292 Lovel handed over this roll and the plea and essoin rolls compiled by and for him since then to his successor, John Bacun: CP 40/93, m. 148d.

quer,[19] as also of various other documents connected with the running and the business of the court.[20]

The keeper of rolls and writs probably had at least a small staff of clerks of his own as well. The master Thomas of Quantock (Cantok) who was acting as lieutenant of master John Lovel (the keeper of rolls and writs) early in 1290 and who subsequently became chancellor of Ireland may well have been a senior clerk in Lovel's service; and one Thomas of Heydon is twice mentioned on the rolls in 1291 as Lovel's clerk when taking custody of deeds whose genuineness had been impugned in litigation (presumably in the absence of Lovel).[21]

A second specialist clerk was the *chirographer* who was responsible for drawing up all final concords levied in the court. John of Bradford was appointed chirographer of the Bench in March 1284 and reappointed in 1290 and again in 1307.[22] He was not the first holder of the office for at his appointment he was said to be replacing one Simon son of William le Cirographer[23] and who is probably to be identified with the Simon of Nottingham who had been appointed chirographer of the Bench in February 1284 in place of his father William of Nottingham but who evidently proved unsatisfactory.[24] Again it seems likely that John had other clerks working for him (the final concords of the period do not seem to be in a single hand); but who they were is not known.

---

[19]   In November 1289 Littlebury delivered into the Exchequer all the original and judicial writs which had been returned into the Bench since the beginning of the reign of Edward I (other than those writs which had been extracted from the files for transmission to Eyres): 1*SCKB*, pp. clix-clx. Early in 1290 he also delivered the writs from Michaelmas term 1289 to his successor, master John Lovel: 1*SCKB*, p. clxii. Early in 1290 master Thomas of Quantock as the deputy of master John Lovel received from Ellis of Beckingham Bench writs of the period 13-17 Edward I: E 159/63, m. 9d. Ellis of Beckingham may have retained other writs from the period of Weyland's chief justiceship. There is a reference in 1304 to writs of the Bench from this period having been in his custody before they passed to the Exchequer: CP 40/152, m. 158d. In May 1292 Lovel transferred custody of the writs returned into the Bench between Michaelmas term 1289 and Easter term 1292 to his successor John Bacun: CP 40/93, m. 148d.

[20]   These included notes of fines (agreements on the terms of fines to be levied in the court) and all writings produced in court whose genuineness was impugned by the opposing party ('*scripta dedicta*'). For fuller details see the two lists of documents handed over by Robert of Littlebury in 1289-90 and the list of documents handed over by master John Lovel in 1292: 1*SCKB*, pp. clix-clx, clxii; CP 40/93, m. 148d. Early fourteenth-century evidence indicates that it was also the keeper of writs and rolls who had custody of feet of fines once they were levied and before they were transferred to the Exchequer: CP 40/158, m. 4; /159, m. 69d. For the feet of fines transferred by Bacun to the Exchequer on a regular basis between 1293 and 1307 see *Antient Kalendars and Inventories of the Treasury of His Majesty's Exchequer, vol. III*, ed. F. Palgrave (Record Commission, 1836), pp. 100-3, 110-2.

[21]   E 159/63, m. 9d; CP 40/89, m. 47; CP 40/91, m. 89. For other evidence pointing to the existence of a staff of clerks in the service of master John Lovel see CP 40/91, m. 303d.

[22]   *CCR 1279-88*, p. 259; *CCR 1288-96*, p. 64; *CPR 1307-13*, pp. 7, 36. But later in 1307 he was replaced by Robert de Hauville: *CPR 1307-13*, p. 22.

[23]   *CCR 1279-88*, p. 259.

[24]   *CCR 1279-88*, p. 253. For a reference to William of Nottingham as the chirographer of the Bench in the early 1280s see BL MS. Harley 2148, f. 50r.

By the later years of the reign of Edward I it is also possible to discern a single senior clerk who can be described as the *chief clerk of the chief justice* of the court (what would later be called the protonotary of the court). Between 1293 and 1307 this position was held by Henry of Hales. The clearest indication of his status is that when damages were assigned by successful litigants to the clerks of the Bench during this period, and the clerks subsequently sued process to the appropriate sheriff to ensure they were levied, the clerks are regularly described as Henry of Hales and his colleagues.[25] As the chief justice's chief clerk Hales did not himself apparently write any of the judicial writs issued by the court or any of the plea roll membranes recording business in the court but he probably exercised a general supervision over the clerks performing both functions. One report indicates that Hengham's seal as chief justice was in his custody: this would have meant that all judicial writs issued by the court would have passed through his hands before sealing and would have given him ample opportunity for checking up on them.[26] Another report shows one of the clerks of the court consulting him in advance when in doubt about a particular judicial writ and him then going to seek the advice of chief justice Hengham.[27] His overall responsibility for the content of the plea rolls may be reflected in the fact that he was in a position to give assurances as to how judgments would be entered on the rolls.[28] He seems also to have born overall responsibility for the safe custody of the plea rolls made for the chief justice until they were transferred to the Exchequer. In Trinity term 1298 a Cornish attorney assaulted the man who was assigned to take care of the Bench plea rolls when he was denied immediate access to them in the York church where the clerks of the Bench were sitting with them after dinner, writing out judicial writs. The man who was assaulted was described in an enrolment as the servant not of the chief justice but of Henry of Hales.[29]

Henry's predecessor was probably Anger of Ripon who is likewise named as assign of damages with the keeper of rolls and writs and unnamed fellow-

---

[25]   There are many such references. For examples see CP 40/101, m. 7; CP 40/160, mm. 189d, 301.

[26]   BL MS. Hargrave 375, f. 118r: this report shows him consulting Bereford when in doubt about whether or not he should seal a particular writ in Trinity term 1305.

[27]   BL MS. Hargrave 375, f. 139v. We also find Hales checking up on writs before the court gives judgment or even after joinder of issue (but presumably before the appropriate judicial writ is issued): see *YB 33-35 Edward I*, pp. 153-5; *YB 32 & 33 Edward I*, pp. 157-9. For other comments which show his particular expertise in and particular responsibility for the making of judicial writs see: *YB 32 & 33 Edward I*, pp. 31-5, 305-17; BL MS. Hargrave 375, ff. 174v-175r.

[28]   BL MS. Hargrave 375, ff. 112r-v; *YB 33-35 Edward I*, pp. 293-5. Note also evidence of him showing an enrolment to the justices Howard and Stanton for their advice, possibly in Michaelmas term 1306: BL MS. Hargrave 375, ff. 162r-v.

[29]   CP 40/124, m. 22d.

clerks of the Bench in 1290 and 1292.[30] Anger's predecessor may have been Robert of Retford who in 1289 transferred custody of Weyland's rolls to Ellis of Beckingham.[31]

The chief justice's chief clerk evidently also played a part in the adjudication of cases in the Bench. Henry of Hales does not begin to feature in reports of cases heard in the Bench until Michaelmas term 1299;[32] but thereafter he appears in them on a regular basis down to the end of the reign of Edward I.[33] Often he is mentioned simply as giving an opinion or participating in the general argument in a case. He shows himself well-informed when making such interventions.[34] But we also find him engaged in a full range of other judicial functions as well: pressing parties towards the framing and acceptance of issues acceptable to the court;[35] rejecting particular exceptions;[36] adjourning parties after pleading has taken place and adjourning essoins[37] and even giving judgment on the court's behalf.[38] His predecessor Anger of Ripon can also be found assisting in the court's work in a quasi-judicial capacity in a small number of reported cases of the early 1290s.[39]

The *keeper of rolls and writs* also seems to have played a similar role. A report of a replevin case ascribed to Easter term 1293 shows John Bacun telling a defendant to answer over after making an exception, something we normally find justices of the court doing, and this in a report in which none

---

[30]　CP 40/86, m. 30; CP 40/92, m. 194.

[31]　CP 40/80, m 94d.

[32]　For a report of a case probably of that term in which he appears see BL MS. Additional 31826, f. 102v.

[33]　In Hilary term 1306 he is mentioned in reports of as many as thirteen different cases.

[34]　For examples see: BL MS. Additional 31826, ff. 142v, 343v, 366r; BL MS. Additional 37657, ff. 42r, 163r; *YB 30 & 31 Edward I*, p. 391; *YB 32 & 33 Edward I*, pp. 417-9, 451-5, 459-61; *YB 33-35 Edward I*, pp. 65-7, 143, 309-11, 459-61.

[35]　For examples see: *YB 33-35 Edward I*, pp. 145, 181, 517.

[36]　For examples see: BL MS. Hargrave 375, ff. 116r, 135v-136r, 166r; *YB 32 & 33 Edward I*, pp. 467-9.

[37]　For examples see: BL MS. Egerton 2811, ff. 103v-104r; BL MS. Additional 31826, f. 190v; BL MS. Hargrave 375, f. 138v; *YB 33-35 Edward I*, p. 539.

[38]　For examples see: BL MS. Additional 31826, ff. 102v, 397v; *YB 33-35 Edward I*, pp. 145-7, 181, 193-5, 215 (refusal to accept final concord).

[39]　These cases are: (i) *YB 21 & 22 Edward I*, pp. 589-91 (at 591): the case is misascribed to the 1294 Middlesex eyre but can be identified as a case heard in Michaelmas term 1291 (see CP 40/91, m. 81d). The editor has also misprinted his name as Auger; evidently his first name alone was quite sufficient to identify him; (ii) *YB 21 & 22 Edward I*, pp. 591-3 (at 593): again the case is misascribed to the 1294 Middlesex eyre but can be identified as a case heard in the same term (see CP 40/91, m. 80d). Again the editor has mistranscribed the name as 'Auger'; (iii) *YB 20 & 21 Edward I*, pp. 361-5 (at 363): this can be identified as the case of Hilary term 1292 enrolled on CP 40/92, m. 137. This time his name is correctly transcribed as Anger; (iv) *YB 21 & 22 Edward I*, pp. 489-91 (wrongly ascribed to the 1294 Middlesex eyre) (Anger here appears as 'Aug' [Inge?]); BL MS. Additional 31826, f. 215r.

of the justices of the Bench themselves appear.[40] He does not then appear again in a datable report until Michaelmas term 1300, when it is he who looks at the wording of chapter 35 of the statute of Westminster II when a writ of ravishment of ward is challenged. It was on the basis of his consultation of the statute that the court decided that the writ was good.[41] He subsequently appears in a number of other datable reports. In them we can see him on at least one occasion actually giving the judgment which adjourns a case sine die till one of the litigants involved comes of age (though only after consulting the chief justice, Ralph of Hengham).[42] In other cases we do not find him giving judgment but we do find him giving opinions on a number of legal points which arise in pleading just like the justices of the court[43] and like them pressing litigants on particular matters which arise in the course of pleading.[44]

Another senior clerk who evidently played a similar role in the adjudicatory process over a ten year period from 1293 onwards was the future Bench justice *Hervey of Stanton*.[45] It is rare for the reports to give him his full name or his surname. He is usually just called 'Hervy' or 'Hervy the clerk'; but there can be little doubt that it is Hervey of Stanton who is involved in all

---

[40] *YB 21 & 22 Edward I*, pp. 25-7.

[41] BL MS. Additional 37657, f. 31r. This may be connected with his responsibilities as keeper of rolls and writs for custody of the copies of statutes sent to the court. Certainly his predecessor, Robert of Littlebury, in 1289 possessed a hanaper containing statutes and shortly before dismissal delivered this into the Exchequer: 1*SCKB*, pp. clix-clx. It was also perhaps by virtue of his office that (perhaps in Hilary term 1307) we find him reading out a writ and the sheriff's return to the writ when this was requested by counsel for the defendants: BL MS. Additional 31826, f. 90v.

[42] *YB 33-35 Edward I*, p. 7.

[43] For examples see BL MS. Additional 37657, ff. 33v-34r (identifiable as a report of a case of Michaelmas term 1300: CP 40/130, m. 228); BL MS. Additional 37657, f. 120r (perhaps a report of a case of Easter term 1301); BL MS. Hargrave 375, f. 175v (perhaps a report of a case heard in Hilary term 1307). For an opinion given by him in out of court discussion with chief justice Hengham see LI MS. Misc. 738, f. 16v.

[44] For examples see BL MS. Additional 31826, f. 132r (perhaps a case of Easter term 1302); BL MS. Hargrave 375, ff. 116r-v (report of a case heard in Trinity term 1305: CP 40/156, m. 96); *YB 33-35 Edward I*, pp. 367-71; BL MS. Additional 31826, f. 327r (case heard during period Hengham was chief justice).

[45] Hervey of Stanton became a justice of the Bench in Easter term 1306: 1*SCKB*, p. cxxxix; *CPR 1301-7*, p. 428. He was first appointed an oyer and terminer commissioner in 1301 (*CPR 1301-7*, pp. 78-9), was a justice of the 1302 Cornwall eyre (*CPR 1301-7*, p. 57; *CCR 1296-1302*, p. 594) and was appointed a regular Assize justice in May 1303 (*CCR 1302-7*, pp. 89-90). The first unambiguous reference to him as a Bench clerk is in Trinity term 1297 when his proffer for a licence to concord was pardoned specifically on the grounds that he was a clerk of the Bench (CP 40/119, m. 100) but other plea-roll references suggesting that he was a Bench clerk go back to at least Easter term 1293 (when two debts were acknowledged to him on the Bench plea-roll: CP 40/100, m. 8, 50). It is possible that he is the Hervey le Clerk who was appointed as his attorney by the abbot of Colchester in Michaelmas term 1291 (CP 40/91, m. 341d). He never appears among the clerks signing Bench writs.

these cases.[46] In a majority of the cases where his contribution is reported he seems to be doing no more than participating in the discussion, though his comments show him to be well-informed on current law and practice.[47] In some, though, he can be seen acting in a definitely quasi-judicial capacity in pressing parties towards the framing or acceptance of issues acceptable to the court;[48] in rejecting particular exceptions made by defendants;[49] and even in giving judgment on the court's behalf.[50]

Much less is known of the clerical staffs of the other main royal courts

[46] For reports where he appears as plain 'Hervi' or 'Hervy' see LI MS. Hale 188, f. 20r; BL MS. Egerton 2811, ff. 106r-107r (and Inner Temple MS. Miscellaneous 1, ff. 39v-40v); Inner Temple MS. Miscellaneous 1, ff. 44r-v; BL MS. Additional 31826, f. 110r (and BL MS. Harley 2183, ff. 94v-95r); BL MS. Additional 31826, f. 113r; BL MS. Harley 25, ff. 72v-73r; LI MS. Miscellaneous 738, f. 98r; BL MS. Additional 37657, ff. 15r-v (and BL MS. Additional 31826, f. 105v); BL MS. Additional 31826, f. 163r (and BL MS. Egerton 2811, f. 125r); BL MS. Additional 31826, f. 167v; BL MS. Additional 37657, f. 14v; BL MS. Additional 37657, ff. 11r-v; BL MS. Additional 5925, f. 32v; BL MS. Additional 37657, f. 19v; BL MS. Additional 31826, f. 98v; BL MS. Stowe 386, f. 124v (and BL MS. Additional 31826, f. 396r, LI MS. Hale 188, f. 20v; IT MS. Misc. 1, f. 33r); BL MS. Additional 31826, f. 397v; BL MS. Additional 31826, f. 391r; BL MS. Additional 37657, f. 120r etc. etc. For reports where he appears as 'Hervey le Clerk' , 'Hervi clerc' or 'Hervi clerk' see: *YB 21 & 22 Edward I*, pp. 241-5 (he also appears here as just 'Hervy'); BL MS. Additional 37657, ff. 12r-v; BL MS. Additional 37657, ff. 11v-12r; BL MS. Additional 37657, f. 28v (but in LI MS. Hale 188, ff. 31r-v he is just 'Hervi'); BL MS. Additional 37657, f. 19r; BL MS. Additional 37657, ff. 18v, 21r; BL MS. Additional 37657, f. 21r; BL MS. Additional 37657, ff. 22v-23r. For reports where he appears as 'Staunton' or 'Stanton' see: BL MS. Stowe 386, f. 144v; Trinity College Cambridge, MS. 0.3.45, f. 56v. For a report where he appears as 'H de Stanton' see BL MS. Stowe 386, f. 124r.

[47] For examples see: *YB 21 & 22 Edward I*, pp. 241-5 (identifiable as a report of a case of Trinity term 1293 enrolled at CP 40/101, m. 48); BL MS. Stowe 386, f. 144v (identifiable as a report of a case of Michaelmas term 1297 enrolled on CP 40/121, m. 123d); LI MS. Hale 188, f. 20r and BL MS. Hargrave 375, ff. 59r-v (identifiable as reports of a case of Michaelmas term 1298 enrolled on CP 40/125, m. 125); BL MS. Harley 25, ff. 72v-73r (identifiable as a report of a case of Michaelmas term 1299 enrolled on CP 40/130, m. 54d); BL MS. Additional 5925, f. 32v (identifiable as a report of a case of Trinity term 1300 enrolled on CP 40/134, m. 115); BL MS. Stowe 386, f. 124r (report of an unidentified case perhaps of Michaelmas term 1300); BL MS. Additional 31826, f. 273v (report of an unidentified case perhaps of Easter term 1303).

[48] For examples see BL MS. Additional 31826, f. 110r (and BL MS. Harley 2183, ff. 94v-95r) (identifiable as reports of a case heard in Michaelmas term 1299 and enrolled on CP 40/130, m. 46d); BL MS. Additional 37657, ff. 18v, 21v (identifiable as a report of a case of Trinity term 1300 enrolled on CP 40/134, m. 99); BL MS. Additional 37657, f. 28v (and LI MS. Hale 188, ff. 31r-v) (identifiable as reports of a case heard in Trinity term 1300 enrolled on CP 40/134, m. 130).

[49] For examples see: Trinity College Cambridge, MS. 0.3.45, f. 56v (identifiable as a report of a case heard in Easter term 1299 enrolled on CP 40/127, m. 16d); BL MS. Additional 31826, ff. 81v-82r (though here he purports to be speaking on behalf of his 'masters' the justices of the court).

[50] For examples see: BL MS. Additional 37657, f. 14v (identifiable as a report of a case of Easter term 1300 enrolled on CP 40/133, m. 3d) (as Hervi); BL MS. Additional 37657, f. 19r (identifiable as a report of a case heard in Trinity term 1300 enrolled on CP 40/134, m. 12); BL MS. Additional 37657, f. 19v (identifiable as a report of a case of Trinity term 1300 enrolled on CP 40/134, m. 20d).

during the same period. For a brief period of two terms in 1290 some (though not all) of the membranes of the King's Bench plea-roll had the names of the clerks who had written them subscribed at the bottom of the membrane and this allows us to see at least eleven clerks at work in the court in this particular single year.[51] In 1276 William of Brompton (the future Bench justice) was appointed as keeper of rolls and writs in King's Bench by the king[52] but there is no evidence that he had predecessors or successors in this post and custody of the court's writs and of the chief justice's plea rolls appears normally to have been the responsibility of the chief justice's chief clerk.[53] It is possible to trace the succession of holders of this office from the mid-1280s onwards.[54] Allegations made against Hengham's chief clerk, John of Cave, during the so-called 'State Trials' of 1289-93, indicate that Cave as chief clerk was in a position to influence the content of an enrolment of a jury verdict of a case heard in King's Bench[55] as also to change that part of an enrolment which recorded the date to which the case had been adjourned.[56] These appear to indicate that, as in the Bench, the chief justice's chief clerk bore some kind of overall responsibility for the chief justice's plea roll. William of Saham's answer to the allegations made against him by Henry de la Leghe and Nicholas of Cernes during the same proceedings also suggests that the examination and the sealing of writs issued by the court was normally the responsibility of the clerk who had custody of writs returned into the court (the chief justice's chief clerk);[57] though in his own suit against John of Cave it emerged that when the chief justice himself was absent from the court and writs went out under the attestation of Saham as the most senior justice present in the court it was Saham himself who sealed them though still Cave who brought writs to him to seal.[58] There seems to be no clear evidence that Cave (or any of his successors) ever participated in the adjudicatory process like their counterparts in the Bench; but there is some evidence from the 'State Trials' to suggest that another of Hengham's clerks, John of Chester, may have done so. In their complaint Henry le Keu and his wife Agnes alleged, among other things, that John had sat alone on the bench at the taking of the inquest jury on their case without the presence of any of the justices. In his

[51] 1*SCKB*, p. lxxx.

[52] *CPR 1272-81*, p. 171.

[53] 1*SCKB*, pp. lxxxi, lxxxiv. But note that the Thomas de Chaunceus who is described as *custos rotulorum et brevium* early in 1302 does not seem to have been the chief justice's chief clerk.

[54] 1*SCKB*, pp. lxxxi-lxxxii.

[55] JUST 1/541B, m. 29. It is not clear whether or not the clerk making the entry was Cave himself. The claim may have been that Cave was able to ensure an omission from the verdict through his supervision of enrolments.

[56] *State Trials of the Reign of Edward I*, p. 40.

[57] *State Trials of the Reign of Edward I*, p. 34. But note that Saham appears to be talking of 'clerks' in the plural here.

[58] *State Trials of the Reign of Edward I*, p. 41.

defence John claimed that Walter of Wimborne, one of the junior justices of
the court, had been sitting on the bench when the verdict was taken, but did
not deny that he had been on the bench as well. It seems reasonable to
conclude that John of Chester may well have sat as, in effect, Wimborne's
colleague for the taking of the jury verdict.[59] This same complaint is also of
interest for what it tells us of the process of writing judicial writs in King's
Bench during the second half of the 1280s. Henry and Agnes alleged that
John had assaulted Agnes when they had gone to the church of St. Swithin,
Candlewick Street, in London, to secure the judicial writs they needed for
their suit from John who was then writing Hengham's judicial writs.[60] This
seems to indicate that just as in the Bench the writing of judicial writs was an
activity that took place out of court (and perhaps after court sessions were
over). It also gives us the identity of one (but only one) of the clerks of King's
Bench who were responsible for this part of the clerical work of the court.

No direct evidence survives of the size of the clerical staff of either of the
eyre circuits of the 1280s and 1290s nor of any of the individual eyres that
preceded and followed those eyre circuits, though the amount of business
done in the eyres suggests that they were probably quite substantial. What
we can do is to trace the succession of clerks who acted as *keepers of rolls and
writs* in the eyres of Edward I's reign from 1276 onwards.[61] Like their
counterparts in the Bench these clerks were among other things responsible
for compiling their own plea rolls (similarly marked as 'Rex' rolls). The
surviving evidence, however, appears to suggest that, despite their title, it
was only after 1284 that they gained custody of the writs returned before the
justices in eyre on their circuits.[62] One keeper of writs and rolls (Ellis

---

[59]   *State Trials of the Reign of Edward I*, pp. 26-7.
[60]   *State Trials of the Reign of Edward I*, p. 26.
[61]   Crook, *Records of the General Eyre*, pp. 143, 146, 157, 171, 175, 179-80. For evidence that
Roger of Whitchester, the keeper of rolls and writs in the Bench, also held that position in at
least one of the eyres of the late 1240s (while Bench sessions were suspended) see *ibid.*, p. 26.
[62]   When orders were sent out in 1284 for the surrender of writs from the eyres held since
1278 these were apparently addressed to the senior justices on each circuit. The keepers of
writs and rolls were asked only to surrender their rolls: *CPR 1281-92*, p. 131. That the keeper
of writs and rolls on the southern circuit gained custody of the writs thereafter is suggested by
the fact that in 1316 Robert of Retford (who had been keeper of writs and rolls on the circuit
between 1292 and 1294) was in the position to hand in writs from eyres from 1284 onwards
(presumably his predecessor John of Berwick had handed over the writs from the earlier eyres
to him on handing over office): *Antient Kalendars of the Treasury of the Exchequer*, vol. III, p. 116.
Retford also handed in at the same time writs from the 1299 Cambridgeshire and 1302
Cornwall eyres where he served in the same position: *ibid.* Berewick may at the same time have
gained custody of the feet of fines made on the circuit. In 1288 and 1292 his clerk John Bacun
handed in to the Exchequer feet of fines made in eyres between 1284 and 1289: *ibid.*, pp. 99-
100. The changeover may have taken place later on the northern eyre circuit. William of
Saham, the chief justice of the 1286 Ely eyre, was the person who handed in writs from that eyre
in 1289: 1*SCKB*, pp. clx-clxi. In 1305, however, it was William Gerberge, who had been keeper
of rolls and writs in the 1293-4 Yorkshire eyre, who handed in to the Exchequer the writs of
that eyre: 1*SCKB*, p. clxi.

of Sutton) on his appointment to the northern circuit in 1279 was specifically also given responsibilities for chirographs[63] but in 1292 we find a separate chirographer (Richard of Cornwall) being appointed on the same circuit.[64] We also know from a writ enrolled on the plea roll of the 1279 Kent eyre that the first keeper of writs and rolls on the southern circuit (John of Lushill) was given responsibility for chirographs on his circuit;[65] but whether or not his successors retained this additional responsibility is not known. Nor is it entirely clear whether or not there was a chief clerk of the chief justice of the eyre who fulfilled a similar function to that of his counterparts in the Bench and King's Bench. Certainly during proceedings on a complaint made by Robert de la Sale in the 'State Trials' we find a junior clerk, Henry of Shenholt, whom Robert accused (with a fellow-clerk, Robert of Preston) of having made an enrolment of a jury verdict on a plaint made against Robert in the 1287 Hertfordshire eyre which departed in material particulars from that jury's verdict, alleging that he had simply made the enrolment at the dictation of the same Robert of Preston as chief clerk 'as was customary'.[66] However, in a fifteenth-century transcript of proceedings in the 'State Trials' on complaints made by the burgesses of the city of Norwich and Robert Rose against the justices of the 1286 Norfolk eyre for failure to take proper action on presentments made there, we find Robert of Preston again mentioned (and a joint defendant with the justices) but this time specifically as the 'chief clerk of the Crown' in the eyre.[67] This may well mean that he was only responsible for overseeing and controlling the clerical side of that section of the eyre which dealt with crown pleas business. This would certainly not be inconsistent with the evidence relating to Preston's part in the 1287 Hertfordshire eyre for there he is described as having custody of the 'bills and verdicts' as well as other things pleaded before the justices and reading them: a form of words which would certainly fit his having been the chief clerk only of that section of the eyre which dealt with crown pleas and bills (though not the main civil pleas). Separate chief clerks for civil and crown pleas would certainly have made sense in view of the way in which such business seems normally to have been transacted concurrently in separate sections and the fact that clerks in clerical orders may not have wished (and may have felt themselves to be debarred) from playing any part in proceedings which might lead to the shedding of blood.

There is also a little evidence to suggest that eyre clerks may have played some part in the adjudication of cases in the eyres where they served. Reports of cases heard in the 'northern' eyre circuit of 1292-4 show that

---

[63] *CPR 1272-81*, p. 304.

[64] *CPR 1281-92*, p. 491. A Richard 'Cyrograffarius' occurs as early as 1274 as a litigant in cases connected with property in Cornwall and is also noted as a defaulter in the 1284 Cornwall eyre: CP 40/5, mm. 101, 105; JUST 1/112, m. 5.

[65] JUST 1/370, m. 2d.

[66] JUST 1/541B, m. 30.

[67] BL Additional Roll 14987.

'Fressingfield' was a participant in the adjudicatory process in this eyre circuit.[68] This must be the John of Fressingfield who was a clerk in the Bench in the early 1290s[69] but who by Hilary term 1293 had entered the service of Hugh of Cressingham, chief justice of this circuit[70] and who in 1295 departed for Ireland in the service of John Wogan, who had been a junior justice on the same circuit.[71] Another possible eyre clerk involved in adjudication is Henry of Guildford. He is to be found in reports of three separate cases heard in the 1299 Cambridgeshire eyre in what is clearly a judicial or quasi-judicial capacity, though he was not one of the justices appointed for this eyre.[72] This seems to be the Henry Marshal of Guildford who may have begun his career as a clerk in the service of the Bench justice master Ralph of Farningham[73] and then passed into the service of Solomon of Rochester, senior justice of the southern eyre circuit of the 1280s.[74] Henry may also have acted as a clerk in the southern eyre circuit of the 1290s.[75] It is not unreasonable to suppose that he was present in the Cambridgeshire eyre in a clerical capacity as well.

Sources of Clerical Income

Of the many clerks attached to the Bench only one is known to have been paid on a regular basis by the Crown: the keeper of rolls and writs. At the very beginning of Edward I's reign Roger of Leicester received two payments in 1274 and 1275 but these do not seem to be related to any particular annual fee for the office.[76] His successor William of Middleton was paid ten

---

[68]   BL MS. Additional 31826, f. 249r; LI MS. Hale 188, f. 53v; LI MS. Misc. 87, ff. 69v, 72v-73v.

[69]   *3SCKB*, pp. 9-11. For a comment made by him in the course of a case heard in the Bench in Michaelmas term 1291 see *YB 21 & 22 Edward I*, p. 541 (misascribed to the 1294 Middlesex eyre but can be identified as a report of the case enrolled on CP 40/91, m. 41).

[70]   CP 40/98, m. 117.

[71]   *CPR 1292-1301*, p. 167. For his subsequent clerical and judicial career in Ireland see Richardson and Sayles, *The Administration of Ireland*, pp. 144, 166, 167, 185; *CJR 1295-1303*, pp. 245, 266. In 1309 he was chief justice in an eyre of the Channel Islands: Crook, *Records of the General Eyre*, p. 192.

[72]   BL MSS. Stowe 386, ff. 103v, 108v; Additional 31826, f. 97r.

[73]   Some connexion with Farningham is suggested by his acting on Farningham's behalf in suing a prohibition plea in 1277 and in acting as one of the attorneys of a man and his wife making a final concord with master Ralph in 1276: below, note 158.

[74]   Below, note 159

[75]   Below, note 160.

[76]   *1SCKB*, p. cxlviii. He had however, been paid an annual fee of ten marks a year in 1264 (*Cal. Liberate Rolls, 1260-7*, p. 148), half-yearly instalments of the same fee in respect of Easter 1265 and Michaelmas 1266 (*ibid.*, pp. 255, 266); and for most terms between Easter 1267 and Easter 1272 (*ibid.*, p. 294; *Cal. Liberate Rolls, 1267-72*, nos. 294, 483, 687, 901, 1247, 1650, 1930). A similar annual fee was paid to his immediate predecessor John Blundel (see below, p.000, notes 143, 144) and to his predecessor Richard of Middleton: *Cal. Liberate Rolls, 1251-60*, pp. 331, 368, 402. Roger of Whitchester had been paid the more generous salary of ten pounds a year: Meekings, 'Roger of Whitchester', p. 106.

annual fee for the office.[76] His successor William of Middleton was paid ten pounds a year. Subsequent keepers were paid only ten marks.[77] There is also some evidence of Ellis of Sutton as keeper of writs and rolls of the northern eyre circuit being paid an annual fee of ten pounds a year between 1279 and 1284[78] and of at least one payment to his counterpart on the southern eyre circuit, John of Berwick, in 1283.[79] But there is no evidence of any other court clerks being paid by the Crown.

However, as Sayles has noted, there were a number of other sources of income open to the court clerks who were not paid by the Crown.[80] Clerks certainly charged fees for some of the tasks which they performed. An undated memorandum which perhaps comes from shortly before 1285 suggests that it had once been the practice that clerks did not charge at all for writing judicial writs but that they were now charging one penny for each such writ.[81] Chapter 44 of the statute of Westminster II in 1285 specifically authorised such a charge while prohibiting the levying of any higher fee.[82] Eyre clerks were likewise specifically authorised in 1275 by chapter 27 of the statute of Westminster I to charge presenting juries two shillings and no more for copies of the articles of the eyre for making their presentments.[83] Evidence from one of the complaints made in the course of the 'State Trials' indicates that litigants also had to pay for the record of proceedings in the Bench which was made and sent to *nisi prius* justices (via the local sheriff) when the jury stage of cases was heard locally;[84] and the same was probably also true of the records of litigation in the Bench which were made when litigation was adjourned from the Bench into the Eyre. From the same complaint we hear also of a clerk of the eyre justice Solomon of Rochester charging two shillings for searching for a writ on a file which had allegedly been deliberately misfiled there.[85] What is less clear is whether or not the clerks were able to charge for making entries on the plea-rolls. There seems to be no specific evidence that they did, though such a charge would not seem entirely improbable. The same undated memorandum of c. 1285 also says that the chirographer's fee for a chirograph used to be two

---

[77] 1*SCKB*, pp. cxlviii-cxlix. Although Beckingham's fee for Michaelmas 1279 is given on the Liberate Roll as ten pounds the actual writ (which survives) was for ten marks: C 47/35/15, no. 8.

[78] The actual pattern of payments and allowances however was an irregular one see E 159/59, m. 22; E 159/57, m.3d; E 159/58, m. 1.

[79] C 62/59, m.1 (twenty pounds).

[80] 1*SCKB*, pp. lxxxv-lxxxviii.

[81] SC 1/31, no. 135. But note that in 1283 the prior of Norwich seem to have paid twenty-one pence for three judicial writs (seven pence each): *Norfolk Archaeology*, xix, 282.

[82] *Stat. Realm*, i. 93.

[83] *Stat. Realm*, i. 33.

[84] 1*SCKB*, p. cxliv. This was not simply a copy made for private purposes as Sayles seems to suggest (*ibid.*, p. lxxxviii).

[85] 1*SCKB*, p. cxliv (not two pence as Sayles states at p. lxxxviii).

shillings but was now as much as half a mark and even one mark.[86] Westminster II, c. 44 fixed this fee at four shillings.[87] With final concords running at the levels they had reached by the early fourteenth century (303 in 1300 rising to as many as 744 by 1305) this made the chirographer's office in the Bench a very valuable one.[88]

A second source of income mentioned by Sayles is the assignment by successful plaintiffs to the clerks of a share in the damages they had recovered. As Sayles notes, this was as yet not a fixed proportion of the damages recovered and could vary between as little as one tenth and as much as the whole of the damages. Nor is it clear that any assignment at all was made in some such cases.[89] The assignment was perhaps in theory still voluntary but litigants, particularly wealthy litigants, who failed to 'grant' a share of damages to clerks may simply have had difficulty in getting any of the clerks of the court to write the necessary judicial writs to secure the levying of their damages.[90] From a writ sent to the justices of the southern eyre circuit during the 1280 Hampshire eyre we hear of elaborate arrangements for the collection and distribution of the income from payments for the articles of the eyre and damages assigned to the clerks. These were to be collected by two clerks in the service of junior justices of the eyre who were to be sworn to their duties and then to be distributed so that one third went to the chief justice's *hospicium* (perhaps here only his clerks) and the remaining two-thirds to be divided equally between Rochester's junior colleagues for the use of their clerks and the keeper of rolls and writs.[91]

It was also possible for clerks to supplement their income by offering various kinds of legal assistance to private clients. As Sayles notes, the clerks of King's Bench are prominent in the reign of Edward I in the ranks of those acting as attorneys in that court.[92] Their counterparts in the Bench appear to have been less prominent in this respect but can certainly be traced acting in a similar capacity.[93] Clearly litigants paid clerks for this service, presumably normally on an ad hoc basis. The legal expertise of the more senior clerks made them men worth retaining for 'advice and assistance' on a more regular basis through permanent pensions. Robert of Littlebury certainly acquired an impressive list of pensions even before he became keeper of

---

[86] SC 1/31, no. 135.

[87] *Stat. Realm*, i. 93.

[88] Totals for the number of chirographs made in the Bench are taken from the lists of feet of fines delivered into the Exchequer by the keeper of rolls and writs: *Antient Kalendars of the Treasury of the Exchequer*, vol. III, pp. 110-2.

[89] 1*SCKB*, p. lxxxv and note 5.

[90] A note on the Bench plea roll for Easter term 1277 notes 'quicumque de istis dampnis levandis breve fecerit anatema sit absque redempcione quia primo dedit medietatem clericis, novissime auferebat maliciose': CP 40/19, m. 65d.

[91] JUST 1/783, m. 5.

[92] Sayles, 1*SCKB*, pp. lxxxvi-lxxxvii.

[93] For examples see the appointments of William of Brockdish as an attorney in 1298 and 1300 on CP 40/122, m. 204; /123, m. 171; /125, mm. 285, 291d; /133, m. 194d; /131, mm. 369,

writs and rolls and while he was still just a senior clerk in the service of the royal justices Martin of Littlebury,[94] master Roger of Seaton[95] and Thomas Weyland.[96] At least nineteen 'clients' are known to have entered into obligations to pay him sums of between half a mark and five marks a year during this period, though generally we know of this only because they had then failed to keep up payments.[97] At least another two 'clients', and

372d, 378, 393d; the appointments of Thomas of Ellingham as an attorney in 1298 and 1300 on CP 40/123, m. 172d; /125, mm. 286, 286d; /134, m. 211d; the appointments of Bartholomew of Elmham as an attorney in 1295, 1297, 1298 and 1299 on CP 40/110, m 269; /116, m. 143d; /123, m. 178; /125, m. 298d; /127, m. 177. For the appointments of John of Redenhall as an attorney in 1297, 1298, 1299 and 1300 see CP 40/118, mm. 137, 137d; /121, m. 326; /122, m. 204; /123, mm. 171, 172, 172d, 176d, 178d; /125, mm. 285, 303d; /127, mm. 176, 176d, 177; /129, mm. 366, 369, 378, 379; /133, mm. 194d, 204d, 206; /134, m. 208; /131, mm. 369, 372d, 384d, 385, 394. Redenhall was sufficiently active as an attorney between at least 1298 and 1300 for him to look like a professional.

[94] For damages assigned to him in assizes heard before Littlebury see CP 40/8, m. 56 (and /10, m. 23; /13, m. 21d); and for damages assigned to him in King's Bench from the time Martin of Littlebury was chief justice of the court see CP 40/11, mm. 2, 86d; /13, m. 62d. In 1281 money was paid to him as the assign of the executors of Martin: CP 40/39, m. 66d.

[95] For damages assigned to him and his fellow-clerk Henry of Howden from an assize session held by Seaton see CP 40/9, m. 42d; and from the 1274 Middlesex eyre see CP 40/9, m. 46d. For damages assigned to him and fellow-clerks in the Bench in 1278-9 see CP 40/24, m. 12; /28, m. 2d. In 1276, 1277 and 1278 we find proffers for licences to concord pardoned at his request: CP 40/15, m. 106d; /20, m. 2; /21, m. 93d; /23, m. 7; /24, m. 19d. In 1277 we find him receiving money on behalf of master Roger: CP 40/20, m. 19.

[96] For a 1281 letter of archbishop Pecham to Weyland which refers to him as being Weyland's clerk see *Reg. Epp. John Pecham*, i. 169-70. For damages being assigned to him and fellow-clerks see CP 40/31, m. 152d; /33, m. 73. For proffers for licences to concord pardoned at his request in 1282 and 1284 see CP 40/45, m. 9; /46, m. 20; /53, m.13; /54, m. 23d. For a 1279 commission to him to tax Bench amercements see *CPR 1272-81*, p. 406. In 1283 he brought a number of judicial writs to the exchequer for sealing as the justices of the Bench had left the court: E 13/11, m. 7.

[97] See for pensions of (i) half a mark a year: E 13/27, m. 57 (administrators of goods suing Henry Wyger in 1305 for twenty-four years' arrears (since 6 Edward I) and deed acknowledged); (ii) ten shillings a year: CP 40/60, m. 84d (suing John son of John de Maundeville in 1285 for ten years' arrears); (iii) one mark a year: CP 40/60 and /62, m. 27d (suing John Wyger in 1285 for nine years' arrears which in 1286 he agrees he owes); CP 40/15, m. 42d and /64, m. 81 (suing William de la Mare in 1276 for three years' arrears; suing his heirs in 1286 for ten years' arrears which they acknowledge owing); CP 40/73, m. 24 (suing William de Turville in 1288 for twelve years' arrears which he acknowledges owing); CP 40/76, m. 17 (suing Adam de Ardern in 1289 for ten years' arrears which he acknowledges owing); E 13/27, m. 15 (administrators of goods suing Thomas son of Lambert of Moulton in 1304 for eighteen years' arrears and deed acknowledged); (iv) twenty shillings a year: CP 40/60, m. 84d (suing Hugh de Plessey in 1285 for five years' arrears); CP 40/63, m. 58 (suing John of Elsfield in 1286 for two years' arrears which he acknowledges owing); CP 40/73, m. 32 (suing the prior of Monks' Kirby in 1288 for six years' arrears which he acknowledges owing under deed of predecessor); CP 40/ 109, m. 118d (suing Richard of Chauton in 1295 for arrears under a deed of 1282 but Richard denies his deed); CP 40/106, m. 33d (suing abbot of Shrewsbury in 1294 for ten years' arrears which he acknowledges owing); E 13/26, m. 53 (administrators of goods suing John of Ladbrooke in 1304 for twenty-one years' arrears since 10 Edward I and deed acknowledged); E 13/26, m. 69d (administrators of goods suing Robert of Holland in 1304 for twenty-one years'

perhaps as many as eleven, are known to have entered into such obligations during the period when he was keeper of writs and rolls in the Bench between 1285 and 1289.[98] A complaint made in 1290 by the prior of Huntingdon alleged that the Bench justice William of Brompton had prevented the hearing of an assize of darrein presentment in the court until the prior had agreed to pay an annuity of one hundred shillings to his clerk, John of Chertsey.[99] We also know that in 1290 Gilbert son of Stephen alleged that he had granted an annuity of one hundred shillings a year to John son of Richard of Hadlow, a clerk of Solomon of Rochester, so that Solomon would be 'favourable' to him in the 1281-2 Devon eyre and that he alleged that this money was destined for Solomon himself.[100] Some clerical annuitites may then have been extorted from unwilling grantors or granted for improper judicial favours and not have been destined for the clerk concerned but for his master. But others do seem to have been granted for

arrears since 10 Edward I and deed acknowledged); E 13/27, m. 56 (administrators of goods suing Geoffrey de Camville in 1305 for twenty-two years' arrears since 9 Edward I and deed acknowledged); E 13/27, m. 5d (administrators of goods suing Roger de Bavent (as kinsman and heir of Peter de Skydemore in 1304 for twenty-seven years' arrears since 4 Edward I); (v) forty shillings a year: CP 40/64, m. 81 (suing Nicholas le Archer in 1286 for six years' arrears under grant by father and deed acknowledged); (vi) four marks: CP 40/31, m. 78 (suing Eustace de Hacche and wife Amice in 1279 for two years' arrears); (vii) five marks a year: CP 40/60, m. 73d; /62, m. 64d (suing Ralph de Trehampton in 1285 for six years' arrears which in 1286 he acknowledges owing).

[98] The two pensions known to have been granted during this period are: (i) one of twenty shillings a year granted by Ingram de Munceaus in 1286, for arrears of which the administrators of his goods sued in 1307 but which Ingram's son and heir claimed to have been discharged by provision to a benefice: E 13/29, m. 46d; (ii) one of five marks a year granted by Roger le Bigod earl of Norfolk in 1286, for arrears of which he was suing in 1294, and which the earl acknowledged owing: CP 40/105, m. 29d. The other nine pensions which may have been granted during this period (but which may have been granted earlier) are: (iii) the pension of one mark a year sixteen years in arrears (since 13 Edward I) for which the administrators of his goods were suing Gilbert de Umfraville in 1304 and which Gilbert acknowledged owing: E 13/27, m. 9d; (iv) the pension of twenty shillings a year four and a half years in arrears for which he was suing John son of Reginald fitz Peter in 1289: CP 40/78, m. 71d (though this obligation probably dates back to pre-1285); (v) the pension of forty shillings a year five years in arrears for which he was suing the community of the vill of Salisbury in 1293: CP 40/102, m. 14; (vi) the pension of forty shillings a year seven and a half years in arrears for which he was suing Warin de Sackville in 1293: CP 40/102, m. 14; (vii) the pension of forty shillings a year in arrears since 17 Edward I for which the administrators of his goods were suing Thomas of Moulton of Gilsland (as son of Thomas son of Thomas of Moulton) in 1306 and which he acknowledged owing: E 13/29, m. 27; (viii) the pension of five marks a year five years in arrears for which he was suing Matthew fitz John in 1293: CP 40/102, m. 14; (ix) the pension of five marks a year six years in arrears for which he was suing Ranulf son of John de Rye in 1294: CP 40/103, m. 109d; (x) the pension of five marks a year which he received from Westminster abbey between 1288 and 1293: Harvey, *Walter of Wenlock*, p. 32, n. 11; (xi) the pension of five pounds a year three years in arrears for which he was suing John bishop of Winchester in 1292: CP 40/93, m. 142.

[99] SC 8/263, nos. 13105, 13143; *Rot. Parl.*, i. 48, no. 37.

[100] SC 8/115, no. 5744.

legal assistance. One example is the annuity of forty shillings granted to Master Thomas of Quantock (Cantok) by master Robert de Wichio. In 1294 master Thomas sued master Robert for four years' arrears of the annuity.[101] Master Robert's defence was that he had granted the annuity for past and future service but that when he had been summoned to answer a debt plea in the Bench in Michaelmas term 1288, although master Thomas was present in Westminster hall, he had refused to give his advice as requested. Master Thomas, in reply, agreed that he had been asked to give advice but that he had had to withdraw from doing so once master Robert had proffered a deed purporting to attest payment of the debt which was challenged as false for he was in the king's service and the falsity of a deed was a matter of concern to the king as well as the opposite party. Master Robert claimed his refusal came still earlier before the plea had been heard but the jury subsequently found that he had given advice and assistance till he had himself detected the alteration of the writing proffered attesting payment of the debt. It seems clear then that master Thomas of Quantock was given this annuity in return for legal advice and assistance but that he was careful not to allow this to override his primary loyalty to the king.[102]

One further source of income for many, though not all, of the senior clerks of the courts was the ecclesiastical benefices that they held. Sayles long ago noted this was true of at least some of the clerks of King's Bench.[103] It can also be shown to be true of many of the senior clerks of the Bench. Thus Ellis of Beckingham, while keeper of writs and rolls in the Bench between 1278 and 1285, can be shown to have held the church of Uppingham in Rutland (to which he had been presented by the abbot and convent of

---

[101] CP 40/104, m. 82 (printed in *YB 4 Edward II* (Selden Society vol. xlii), pp. 199-201).

[102] It is impossible to be absolutely certain that master Thomas Quantock was a clerk of the courts at this date. In April 1288 he received a safe-conduct as a king's clerk for a mission to Scotland on the king's affairs (*CPR 1281-92*, p. 293) and in 1291 he was sent to Ireland to become chancellor. Clerks of the courts (other than the keeper of writs and rolls) were not normally described as king's clerks nor sent on such missions; nor is promotion to the Irish chancellorship the kind of promotion one might expect for such a clerk. But his presence in Westminster hall and the fact that his legal advice was valued both tend to point to a close connexion with the courts as does the fact that in 1286 he found the Bench chirographer John of Bradford and the future keeper of writs and rolls in the Bench, master John Lovel, as sureties to prosecute litigation (CP 40/64, m. 26). Moreover early in 1290 we find him acting as the lieutenant of master John Lovel in receiving the writs and rolls of the Bench (E 159/63, m. 90d). The balance of probabilities is that he was acting in late 1288 as a clerk in the Bench, perhaps in the service of the keeper of rolls and writs.

[103] Sayles, 1*SCKB*, p. lxxxvii. For benefices held by Hengham's chief clerk John of Cave see CP 40/24, m. 12d (rector of Grafton in Worcestershire in 1278); KB 27/57, m.34d and KB 27/96, m. 12 (rector of Narborough in Leicestershire in 1280 and 1286); CP 40/142, m. 207d (rector of Humber in Herefordshire presented in the reign of Henry III and recently resigned in 1302); E 368/62, m. 32d (orders given in 1290 for sequestration of ecclesiastical benefices at Narborough and Humber and of prebends at Exeter and Lincoln).

Westminster abbey) and then the church of Warmington in Northamptonshire (to which he was presented by the abbot and convent of Peterborough).[104] Henry of Hales, while chief clerk of the chief justice of the Bench
between 1292 and 1307, held the livings of Thrussington in Leicestershire
(to which he was presented by the prior and convent of Sempringham),
Stanford in Norfolk and possibly Church Stanton in Devon.[105] Hervey of
Stanton, while still a Bench clerk but playing a significant role in the
adjudicatory process, held the livings of Thurston in Suffolk and Warkton
in Northamptonshire and then added the church of East Dereham in
Norfolk.[106]

   This source of income was not available to all members of the clerical staff
of the courts. The Bench chirographer, John of Bradford, clearly qualifies
by virtue of his functions for membership of this group and is specifically
described as 'clerk' on his reappointment to the post in 1307.[107] He seems
nonetheless to have been (at least so far as the Church was concerned) a
layman and by 1294 at latest we find him engaged in land transactions with
his wife Isabel.[108] Another lay 'clerk' of the courts was Robert of Preston
who (as we have seen) appears to have been chief clerk of the crown on the
northern circuit of the later 1280s and who thus had good reason to remain
a layman.[109] He too appears to have been married[110] and cannot be found
in possession of any ecclesiastical benefice.[111] At least one of the senior
clerks of King's Bench may also have been a layman: for on the King's Bench
roll for Michaelmas 1302 we find Reginald of Ashbourne (presumably to be
identified with the clerk of the same name) bringing a trespass plea with his
wife Edith.[112]

---

[104] *Reg. Oliver Sutton*, ii. 10, 15.

[105] *Reg. Oliver Sutton*, viii. 47 (and *CPR 1292-1301*, p. 122); CP 40/126, m. 73; CP 40/141, m.
27.

[106] *Cal. Papal Registers*, ii. 19 (and 42, 43); *Suffolk Green Books*, p. 117. For his role in the
adjudicatory process see above, p.000.

[107] *CPR 1307-13*, p. 7.

[108] CP 40/103, m. 99d. The identification of this John of Bradford with the chirographer is
rendered virtually certain by the 1297 entry recording a fine proffered for licence to concord
by John and his wife which was pardoned by the justices at John's own request: CP 40/121, m.
14.

[109] Above, p. 000.

[110] For Surrey fines of 1283 and 1287 involving Robert and his wife Margaret see CP 25(1)/
227/24, no. 3; CP 25(1)/227/25, no. 4.

[111] It should however be noted that Ellis of Sutton, whom we have seen in the possession of
at least three livings, appears to have left a widow who sued his son for dower in 1288: CP 40/72,
m. 67. It was, however, not in the interest of either party to this litigation to deny the validity of
the marriage and a third party might have succeeded in doing so.

[112] KB 27/167, m. 59d.

Regulation of Conduct

The clerks of the king's courts performed, as we have seen, a variety of responsible functions within the legal system and were therefore of course open (and were clearly perceived to be open) to the temptation to abuse their position. Evidence of this perception is the wording of the oath provided for the clerks of the justices in eyre in 1278.[113] They were to promise to serve the king in their office well and loyally to the best of their ability and not to fail in their duty by reason of the greatness or riches of those with whom they came in contact nor out of hate or favour nor because of the power or position of anyone concerned nor for any benefit given or promised. They had also to promise not to receive any benefice or pension or other reward without the king's permission. It is not clear whether or not other clerks took a similar oath. We know that John of Bradford, the chirographer of the Bench, took an oath on entering office in 1284[114] but we do not what the oath was nor do we hear of oaths being taken by any of his colleagues, not even by the keeper of rolls and writs. In King's Bench Hengham's chief clerk, John of Cave, denied in proceedings brought against him in 1290 having taken any oath to the king; but judgment was given against him in part on the grounds that he had been at the material time the 'sworn chief clerk' ('*capitalis clericus juratus*') of the court. This suggests that he must have taken some sort of oath even if not one to the king.[115]

With the statutory regulation of the conduct of court clerks as evidence of the same perception we are on much firmer ground. We have already noted the statutory regulations enacted in 1275 and 1285 to regulate the amount clerks could charge for the articles of the eyre and the writing of judicial writs.[116] There seems, however, to be no evidence of any attempt as yet to lay down any more general scale of charges. The same statutes also laid down some rather more wide-ranging restrictions on their future behaviour. Chapter 28 of the statute of Westminster I of 1275 falls into two separate sections.[117] The first section prohibited any justice's clerk accepting presentation to any church whose advowson was the subject of litigation in the king's court unless he had the king's permission to do this. Other clerks in the king's service were also covered by the prohibition. The only punishment laid down was dismissal from the king's service (perhaps in the case of justice's clerks this should read dismissal from the service of their masters).[118]

---

[113] C 54/95, m. 1d.

[114] *CCR 1279-88*, p. 259.

[115] JUST 1/541B, m. 30.

[116] Above, p. 000.

[117] *Stat. Realm*, i. 33-4.

[118] The failure to make proper provision for the punishment of clerks who were not in the king's service may suggest that this part of the clause as originally drafted dealt only with king's clerks and that the inclusion of justices' clerks was a late addition.

The second section of the same chapter prohibits justices' clerks from 'maintaining' parties to litigation in the king's court or acting fraudulently in a way that delayed or prevented the doing of justice. Here too a second group of clerks was mentioned as well: this time those clerks who were in the service of local sheriffs. The punishment laid down was the same but with the proviso that if necessary a heavier one could be imposed. This clause forms part of a distinct section of the statute (running from chapter 25 to chapter 30) dealing with abuses in the legal system. Clearly it was thought desirable to have a general prohibition in statutory form of any behaviour on the part of clerks that delayed or prevented the doing of justice, even though such behaviour must already have been subject to punishment by the courts themselves. More obviously innovative were the prohibitions of maintenance and acceptance of presentation to litigious churches and in context it looks as though both prohibitions must have been intended to remove two obvious reasons for misbehaviour on the part of clerks. An alternative possibility is that, given that it might be difficult to prove misbehaviour on the part of clerks, the legislators decided that it would in future be sufficient merely to prove that they had good reasons for committing it (maintenance of a particular litigant; acceptance of presentation to a litigious church). The prohibition of maintenance may also be seen in the context of other later attempts to prohibit the same thing by other groups which seem to have been motivated by a desire to prevent unnecessary and vexatious litigation.

Chapter 49 of the statute of Westminster II went still further.[119] It prohibited any justice's clerk not merely from receiving presentment to any church but also from receiving as a gift or purchasing or taking to farm or taking any other kind of interest in any advowson, land or tenement that was the subject of litigation before the king or any of his ministers or taking any kind of reward. This time the punishment was to be at the king's will and punishment was to apply not just to the clerk but also to the person making the grant or bribe to him. Again it should be noted that this statute did not apply only to justices' clerks. They were simply part of a very wide group of officials in the king's service: a group which also comprised the chancellor, the treasurer, members of the king's council and the king's household and clerks of the exchequer. The underlying motive for the statute was probably much the same as those behind the comparable provisions of the 1275 statute: removing reasons for misbehaviour on the part of clerks (and others).

For evidence that clerks did abuse their positions of trust within the legal system we can turn to the various proceedings brought against them during Edward I's reign. During the so-called 'State Trials' of 1289-93 proceedings for various kinds of misconduct in the conduct of their official duties were

---

[119] *Stat. Realm*, i. 95.

brought against some eight clerks.[120] Although in 1297 it was believed that Robert of Littlebury, the keeper or rolls and writs in the Bench, had made his fine of £1000 in 1290 'for various great trespasses'[121] it is only possible to trace a single set of proceedings against him and in these he seems only to have been convicted of a single piece of misconduct: that of copying (or allowing to be copied) into the 'Rex' plea roll for which he was responsible the version of an enrolment of a case heard in the court in Trinity term 1288 as it had been altered by the chief justice Thomas of Weyland rather than the original and genuine version of the same enrolment.[122] Two sets of proceedings were brought against a second Bench clerk, Roger Savan of Bridgwater, a clerk of Thomas Weyland. One appears to be wholly unconnected with his official duties and concerned with a private dispute over the seizure of property in Yorkshire.[123] The second, however, alleged that Roger had 'maintained' the opponent of Gilbert de la Pitte in litigation in the Bench (behaviour clearly in contravention of the 1275 legislation) until bought off by a payment of six marks: it does not allege any other misconduct on his part. Here we have only the allegation and not any defence which Roger might have made to the charge for the case went without day on the production of a protection issued in his favour on his departure for Ireland in the service of the Justiciar.[124] It is not clear whether or not this should be treated as tantamount to a confession of guilt on his part. A third Bench clerk, John of Chertsey, who was a clerk not of the chief justice but of his senior colleague William of Brompton, was the object of a complaint by John son of Roger of Reed.[125] His complaint concerned a final concord made between himself and one Richard of Chertsey, evidently a relative of John of Chertsey and probably his brother, concerning property at Reed in Suffolk. John had leased this property to Richard and made him a charter of feoffment as surety for the term (to ensure he did not grant the land during the term to a third party). He had also levied the final concord in question. He was evidently trying to have the final concord quashed for

[120] For a recent discussion of the 'State Trials' which corrects some older misconceptions about their genesis, their conduct and the punishments of the main offenders and questions whether 'State Trials' is an appropriate term for them see above, pp. 103-112.

[121] E 368/69, m. 114d: this statement was made in a writ to the bishop of Bath and Wells for the sequestering of his benefices in order to more swiftly levy the remainder of the fine.

[122] This is no more than an inference from the surviving evidence. The actual record of the proceedings against Littlebury and Weyland and his colleagues does not survive: see above, pp. 129-31. But note that Littlebury had also been accused (though acquitted) of a murder in 1288 (1*SCKB*, 177) and in the 1288 Dorset eyre one of his servants (Walter of Barton) was accused of forging royal writs and the king's seal and receiving outlaws and other misdeeds (JUST 1/213, mm. 25d, 29, 29d, 46).

[123] JUST 1/541B, mm. 3, 7d, 10d, 12d, 23, 24d, 33, 43, 45d.

[124] JUST 1/541A, m.58d.

[125] *State Trials*, pp. 24-5. This case is of particular interest for the evidence that it provides that there were clerks who could be described as clerks of the Bench but who could also be described as clerks not of the chief justice but of one of his colleagues.

he now claimed that he had been a minor at the time the fine was levied and that John had been instrumental in ensuring the fine was levied without the justices examining the parties, without a writ and without even a proper summons (although John had been led before the justices at Westminster): a Bench clerk using his inside connexions to circumvent the safeguards built into the system and levy a fine without John knowing that this was happening. He also claimed that when he had learnt of the fine being levied he had got one of the serjeants of the court (John of Ramsey) to challenge it but said he did not know if his challenge had been enrolled, suggesting that John might again have used his connexions to ensure that this did not happen. John of Chertsey, however, denied the truth of John of Reed's allegations and claimed that the fine had been duly levied. Although no outcome is recorded to the case there is no trace of any punishment of John of Chertsey and so it seems probable that he managed to clear himself or settled out of court with John of Reed. Again, here, then we cannot be certain whether or not the allegations were true. It may just be that John of Reed was attempting to go back on the agreement he had made with Richard of Chertsey and was using these allegations as a way of doing so; it may be that the allegations were justified. A second allegation (in the form of a petition to the king) mentioned John of Chertsey only in passing: as the beneficiary of wrongdoing by his master William of Brompton who had allegedly obstructed the hearing of an assize of darrein presentment brought in the Bench by the prior of Huntingdon until the prior granted an annuity of one hundred shillings a year to him.[126] No answer is recorded to this allegation other than one recording the king's unwillingness to take any action. Three allegations were also made against Henry Gerard of Guildford, the clerk of another justice of the Bench, John de Lovetot. Of two of them we know no more than that they resulted in judgment being given against him and damages being awarded to the complainants.[127] The third (of which we have full details) shows Henry Gerard being convicted on his own admission of receiving money from prisoners indicted for homicide for giving them 'counsel and aid', to secure their release at a gaol delivery session over which his master had presided (aid which, it was alleged, took the form of rigging the jury to ensure it consisted of relatives of those indicted), as also for 'maintaining' some of them in an assize of novel disseisin heard before his master and other justices (contrary to the 1275 statute). Here at least we have clear evidence of misconduct admitted by the clerk concerned and the

[126] SC 8/263, nos. 13105, 13143. For other evidence that John had been granted the annuity see the litigation brought by him against the prior for arrears of it in 1285 and 1291 (CP 40/59, m. 72; /91, m. 41). On the second occasion the prior said he had discharged the obligation by presenting him to a suitable living.

[127] These are the cases brought by master John of Standon for which see JUST 1/541B, mm. 3, 3d, 4, 12d (and for earlier litigation brought by master John against Henry Gerard in King's Bench in 1288 which may be connected with this complaint see KB 27/104, m. 35d); and by Henry Carpenter for which see JUST 1/541B, mm. 4, 24.

misconduct was serious for it may have resulted in the wrongful acquittal of men accused of homicide (it is less clear that the 'maintenance' alleged in connexion with the assize was anything other than a breach of the statute).[128]

Two clerks of Ralph of Hengham, chief justice of King's Bench, were also the object of complaints. Only a single complaint was made against John of Chester though the complainants accused him of a number of connected misdeeds.[129] But Hengham's chief clerk John of Cave was the subject of some six or seven complaints. Of two of these we know only of their withdrawal early in 1290[130] and of a third only of process involving third parties also involved in the case.[131] In a fourth case it was alleged that out of favour for the complainants' opponent (the abbot of Osney) Cave had omitted from his enrolment of a jury verdict all mention of some of the chattels (books to the value of nineteen marks) which the jury had said the abbot had taken from them. Cave denied having been a clerk of the court when the case was heard but also denied the jury had mentioned the books concerned and it was apparently decided better to remedy the matter through a certification jury which the complainants had already begun suing in King's Bench.[132] Here again agnosticism as to the wrongdoing alleged seems to be the only sensible course. The case which led to Cave's imprisonment in the Tower, and then to a fine of 500 marks for trespass, was one brought by the preceptor of the Welsh Hospitaller preceptory of Slebech and accused Cave of receiving presentment to a litigious church (contrary to the provisions of the 1275 and 1285 statutes) and in essence of 'maintaining' an assize of darrein presentment, which the patron who had presented him to the church brought in the county court of Camarthen and subsequently in King's Bench and then once more (through a second writ) again in the county court and in King's Bench once more.[133] What the preceptor did not allege, however, was that Cave had actually used his position in King's Bench to pervert the court's processes in favour of his client. Perhaps he decided this was not necessary or would be too difficult to prove. By the time he was pursuing the complaint before the *auditores querelarum* the case had been decided in his favour and he had also reached and agreement with Cave's patron: so he was not concerned to upset the court's judgment. Perhaps if he had needed to do that he would have made some such allegations.

---

[128] *State Trials*, pp. 53-61.

[129] *State Trials*, pp. 25-7.

[130] KB 27/122, mm. 8 (Geoffrey de Wermewell), 30d (Richard de Punchardun). Both involved false imprisonment and other unspecified trespasses. Only the latter is known to have been brought before the *auditores querelarum*.

[131] JUST 1/541B, m. 33 (Margery de Ouvedale).

[132] JUST 1/541B, m. 29 (Thomas of Somerton and his wife Alice).

[133] JUST 1/541B, m. 30. For related material see 1*SCKB*, pp. 172-6; KB 27/114, m. 23; /121, m. 13.

The two remaining allegations were both part of the complex web of claims and counter-claims associated with the complaints of Henry de la Leghe and Nicholas de Cernes which seem to have defeated the efforts of the enrolling clerks to produce a lucid, comprehensive and comprehensible summary.[134] Although the main proceedings appear to take the form of a complaint solely against the King's Bench justices Ralph de Hengham and William of Saham and the Bench justice William of Brompton, it seems probable from adjournments given for judgment on the awarding of damages and arguments about their award that there had also been a complaint against Cave and judgment given against him as well.[135] What is known are the allegations made against Cave in the course of the same proceedings by William of Saham.[136] Saham seems to be suggesting that it had been Cave who had been responsible for changing the date of an adjournment on the plea roll and then sending out a writ under Hengham's attestation to produce a jury for the new date when a litigant's opponent had got the litigation adjourned without day on the non-suit of the litigant on the day to which the case had originally been adjourned: allegedly in return for a bribe from William of Brompton who was supporting the litigant concerned. Saham also said Cave had been responsible for a second writ which had required the appearance of the jury at a second return day (when it gave its verdict) and which was also ultimately authorised only by the changed enrolment (this writ had established Saham's guilt because he had attested it in Hengham's absence from the court). Cave's answer did not in fact deny any of the allegations concerned but did skilfully exculpate himself from any responsibility. He managed to get Saham to admit that it was he who had rendered the judgment which had adjourned the case without day and that he had nonetheless himself sealed the judicial writ which presupposed that the case had been adjourned to the later date. He also got Hengham to admit responsibility for the writ which had required production of the jury for the 'new' date (and investigation of the writ showed that it had been dated five weeks and more before the date the jury was to be produced not just a week as Saham had alleged). Cave also then managed to frighten Saham into withdrawing his allegations by offering to fight battle against him on them. All told, a very skilful operation on Cave's part but one which leaves one wondering whether Saham was not perhaps right in his allegations against Cave. The real truth underlying this very complex case is perhaps no longer recoverable.

Allegations were also made against three of the clerks who had served on the southern eyre circuit. Robert of Preston appears to have been convicted of wrongdoing along with Solomon of Rochester and some of his fellow-justices for failure to take any action on two presentments made against the

---

[134] *State Trials*, pp. 27-46.
[135] *State Trials*, p. 34.
[136] *State Trials*, pp. 40-5.

prior of Norwich at the 1286 Norfolk eyre as also failure to take any action on a further presentment against the abbot of St. Benet Hulme for obstruction of watercourses.[137] The chief clerk of the crown was clearly felt properly to blame along with his judicial superiors for such a neglect of matters within his province. Preston was also one of those accused (together with the justice Richard of Boyland and a more junior clerk, Henry of Shenholt) by a complainant who alleged among other things that it was these two clerks who had failed to enrol that part of a jury's verdict in which it had acquitted him of causing his opponent to lose an eye and found that any injury he had inflicted on his opponent had been in self-defence.[138] Shenholt claimed that he had been writing at the dictation of Preston and that the case had been enrolled in the presence of the justices (the implication being that it was they who, if anyone, ought answer for the judgment rendered in the case); and when both clerks were present in court they sheltered behind the finality of the court record and the fact that they were not responsible for its content. Again, it is difficult to know whether or not the doctrine of the finality of the court record and the responsibility of the justices for that record was simply a convenient defence for clerks who had been responsible for serious wrongdoing or whether they were simply the easiest and safest way of defending themselves on the charges made against them. A final complaint alleged that John son of Richard of Hadlow, a clerk of Solomon of Rochester, had been granted an annuity of one hundred shillings by the complainant's father in return for favourable treatment in the 1281-2 Devon eyre on the part of Solomon himself.[139] Solomon had been the real beneficiary of the pension rather than his clerk. The petition was clearly intended to secure the release of the complainant from the obligation; but we do not know if it achieved any success and whether or not the complaint was actually justified. In any case the real wrongdoer here, if anyone, was the justice rather than his clerk.

Apart from this group of cases brought in the exceptional circumstances of the 'State Trials' of 1289-93 there is comparatively little evidence of clerical wrongdoing or even alleged clerical wrongdoing. From the parliament roll of the Lent parliament of 1305 we hear of two accusations against John Bacun, keeper of rolls and writs in the Bench.[140] The first petitioner was non-suited in parliament; the second disowned the attorney who had sued the petition on his behalf and said that he had no wish to sue. The

---

[137]   BL Additional Roll 14987. It is less certain that he was found guilty of any responsibility for the alleged mishandling of a further presentment against the prior of Norwich which had led to proceedings in the eyre.

[138]   JUST 1/541B, m. 30.

[139]   SC 8/115, no. 5744. Interestingly the petition suggests that the granting of such pensions had been forbidden to both justices and their clerks both by the king (perhaps a reference to the 1278 oath of justices itinerant and their clerks: above, p. 000) and by the king's statutes (perhaps a reference to the 1285 legislation which is hardly specific on this point).

[140]   *Memoranda de Parliamento*, ed. F.W. Maitland (Rolls Series, 1893), pp. 166-8.

probability is that Bacun had been involved in serious wrongdoing but that he had managed to buy off both complainants. There is no evidence that he was punished.

An undated Year Book report tells us of proceedings which led to the Bench clerk Nicholas of Mells going to prison.[141] Judgment had been given by default in an action of dower in the Bench at the suit of the attorney Adam of Harrowden. Subsequently, however, Adam had agreed with the attorney of the defendant to waive the default and plead the case and the enrolment of judgment by default had been crossed through. When the case came on for pleading, but for reasons that are not wholly clear, the rolls had been searched and the deleted enrolment discovered. Mallore J. asked Adam who had given judgment and at whose suit and he said that it had been at his suit but that he could not say who had rendered judgment. Both attorneys were sent to prison for their attempt to undo a judgment already given (this presupposed that a judgment had been validly given); at the same time, however, Nicholas of Mells was also sent to prison because the judgment was found on one of his membranes and entered in his hand but was not 'recorded' by any of the justices, that is because none of the justices of the court said that they had made the judgment (this seems to presuppose that the judgment had never been validly given at all). What we seem to be seeing here is the beginning of the process by which routine judgments came to be given not by one of the justices of the court but simply by the clerk entering judgment on a roll; as yet, however, the court had evidently not accepted this process.[142]

The Promotion of Clerks to Become Royal Justices

We have already seen that the part some clerks played in the adjudicatory process indicates that senior clerks at least possessed a considerable amount of legal expertise. We have also seen that there is some evidence to show that such clerks made that expertise available to private clients in return for fees and pensions. Their legal expertise was also exploited in another way by the king. During the reign of Edward I substantial numbers of clerks were appointed royal justices.

The promotion record of the clerks who were keepers of writs and rolls in the Bench is perhaps the most impressive. Three of the six holders of this

---

[141] BL MS. Stowe 386, f. 174r.

[142] The dating of this case is problematic. The mention of Mallore J. shows that it must have taken place before 1308. Writ signatures indicate that Mells had been a clerk of the court since at least 1296 but the reference to the membrane of Nicholas of Mells appears to suggest that the case took place after Easter term 1305 when clerks began to append their signatures to membranes. There is, however, no break in Melles' signatures between Easter term 1305 and Trinity term 1307. Either the episode took place at the very beginning of Edward II's reign or it was quickly over and Melles then resumed his position in the court.

post ended up as justices of the Bench.[143] Of the remaining three, one (*William of Middleton*) subsequently held the semi-judicial post of baron of the exchequer and was one of the regular assize justices appointed in 1285;[144] another (*Robert of Littlebury*) was disgraced in 1290 but subsequently became a justice of the Dublin Bench and an itinerant justice in Ireland;[145] while a third (*master John Lovel*) became a justice of the northern eyre circuit in 1292-4 and was briefly in 1294 a justice of King's Bench.[146] Other clerks were promoted as well. *William of Brompton* appears to have been a clerk in the service of master Roger of Seaton, chief justice of the Bench and of the London and Bedfordshire eyres held in 1276[147] and then briefly keeper of writs and rolls in the court of King's Bench from 1276 to 1278[148] before becoming a justice of the Bench in 1278. *Lambert of Threekingham*, a justice of the Bench from 1300 to 1316 perhaps started out as a Bench clerk in 1277-8.[149] He seems then to have become a clerk of the 'northern' eyre circuit of 1278-88[150] but by 1293 had become a clerk of John

[143]   These were *Roger of Leicester*, keeper of writs and rolls from 1266 to 1276 and then a justice of the Bench from 1276 to 1289; *Ellis of Beckingham*, keeper of writs and rolls from 1278 to 1285 and then a justice of the bench from 1285 to 1307; and *John Bacun*, keeper of writs and rolls from 1292 to 1313 and a justice of the Bench from 1313 to 1320.

[144]   Middleton was keeper of rolls and writs from 1276 to 1278. He was a baron of the exchequer from 1285 to 1290 (C 62/62, mm. 2,3,4; /63, m. 3; /64, mm. 3,4; /65, m. 3; /67, m. 5) and an assize justice during the same period (*CCR 1279-88*, p. 365).

[145]   Littlebury was keeper of rolls and writs from 1285 to 1289/90. For his brief judicial career in Ireland between 1300 and 1303 see Richardson and Sayles, *Administration of Ireland*, pp. 142-5, 150-1.

[146]   Lovel was keeper of rolls and writs from 1290 to 1292. For his career as a justice in eyre see Crook, *Records of the General Eyre*, pp. 170-4; and as a justice of King's Bench see 1*SCKB*, p. cxxxii.

[147]   For evidence of his activity as a Bench clerk under Seaton in 1275-6 see: CP 40/8, m. 50d (Hilary 1275: authorises adjournment); CP 40/9, mm. 1, 2d (Easter 1275: debts acknowledged to him); CP 40/11, m. 21d (Michaelmas 1275: debt acknowledged to him by keeper of writs and rolls with annotation in other hand that then comes 'et scripsit manu sua et cognovit quod ei satisfactum est'); CP 40/13, m. 47 (Hilary 1276: debt acknowledged to him); CP 40/13, m. 78 (Hilary 1276: pardoned proffer for licence to concord). For evidence that he was acting as a clerk in the London eyre of February-March 1276 see the enrolment of the terms of an agreement he had made with a debtor who had mortgaged land in Northumberland to him on the London eyre plea roll: *London Eyre, 1276*, nos. 492, 497. In Seaton's Bedforshire eyre of 1276 he was appointed keeper of rolls and writs: *CPR 1272-81*, p. 160.

[148]   *CPR 1272-81*, p. 171.

[149]   Hence the acknowledgment of a debt to him on the Bench plea roll for Trinity term 1277 (CP 40/20, m. 7) and his acting as an essoiner in a case there in Easter term 1278 (CP 40/24, m. 15d).

[150]   Hence his suing on the king's behalf at the Michaelmas 1281 session of the 1281-4 Lincolnshire eyre in three adjourned pleas (JUST 1/501, m. 43d) and the acknowledgment of a debt to him at the Easter 1284 session of the same eyre (JUST 1/492, m. 81d). He is also perhaps to be identified as the *dominus Lambertus* who was a clerk of the justices and acted as an intermediary in ensuring a settlement of litigation in the 1286 Cambridgeshire eyre: *Liber Memorandorum Ecclesie de Bernewelle*, p. 159.

of Mettingham and returned to service in the Bench.[151] *Hervey of Stanton* was a third Bench clerk who subsequently became one of its justices.[152]

Other clerks became regular assize justices. *Robert of Littlebury* became a regular assize justice in 1285 while still acting as keeper of rolls and writs in the Bench.[153] *Robert of Retford* became an assize justice in 1294 after a career as a clerk in the Bench and as keeper of writs and rolls on the 'southern' eyre circuit of 1292-4, but was later again appointed keeper of writs and rolls in the 1299 Cambridgeshire and 1302 Cornwall eyres.[154] *Henry Marshal of Guildford* was an assize justice between 1297 and 1300,[155] a justice in eyre in the Channel Islands in 1304[156] and a temporary justice of the Bench itself in 1305-6.[157] His previous experience seems to have been as a clerk in the Bench in the late 1270s[158] and then on the 'southern' eyre circuit both of the

[151] In Easter term 1293 he is described as a clerk of Mettingham in an enrolment on the Exchequer plea roll which records his appearance in the Exchequer to attest the appointment of an attorney (E 13/18, m. 29d) and in the same term a shorter than normal adjournment in the Bench is recorded as having been made at his request (CP 40/100, m. 129). In Michaelmas term 1293 and Easter term 1294 he is recorded as having been authorised to receive the appointment of certain attorneys (something which only the most senior clerks were normally authorised to do): CP 40/102, m. 290; CP 40/104, m. 162d. His status as one of the senior clerks of the Bench is also shown by the fact that in Easter term 1295 he is recorded as one of the witnesses to an agreement settling litigation in the Bench with the justices of the court and John Bacun, the keeper of writs and rolls: CP 40/108, m. 153.

[152] Above, pp. 177-8.

[153] *CCR 1279-88*, p. 365.

[154] C 66/113, m. 16d. For evidence that he had been a clerk in the Bench between 1279 and 1290 see CP 40/28, m. 33; /30, m. 51d; /31, m. 152d; /109, m. 118d; /64, m. 26; /67, m. 55d; /80, m. 94d. For his appointments as keeper of rolls and writs see *CPR 1281-92*, p. 485; *CPR 1292-1301*, p. 392; *CPR 1301-7*, p. 57.

[155] He was first appointed to the northern assize circuit in October 1297 (C 66/117, m. 4d) but was removed and replaced in January 1300 (C66/120, m. 31d).

[156] Crook, *Records of the General Eyre*, p. 192.

[157] He is to be found authorising a number of briefer than usual adjournments in Trinity term 1305. In Michaelmas term 1305 he is to be found giving a litigant permission to withdraw from prosecuting his writ (CP 40/153, m. 41) and also participating in discussions recorded in the reports (*YB 33-35 Edward I*, pp. 65-7, 73-7)). He is only to be found in the feet of fines in Hilary term 1306 (Sayles, 1*SCKB*, p. cxxxix). His formal appointment on a temporary basis was made only 22 November 1305 (*CPR 1301-7*, pp. 448-9 and *CCR 1302-7*, p. 300).

[158] He is presumably the Henry Marshal who sued nominally for the king in an *ex relatu plurium* prohibition case involving the Bench justice master Ralph of Farningham in Trinity and Michaelmas terms in 1277 (CP 40/20, m. 28; /21, m. 64d) and who had previously (in Trinity term 1276) been appointed the attorney of litigants making a final concord with master Ralph (CP 40/15, m. 115). He is also probably the Henry Marshal to whom debts were acknowledged in Michaelmas term 1277 (CP 40/21, mm. 17, 23) and certainly the Henry Marshal of Guildford who was suing for a small debt in the same term (CP 40/21, m. 37) and to whom a debt had been acknowledged in Michaelmas term 1276 (CP 40/17, m. 54d).

1270s and 1280s[159] and of the 1290s as well.[160]

At least one court clerk became a justice of King's Bench. This was *Ellis of Sutton*, a justice of the court between Michaelmas term 1285 and Easter term 1287.[161] Ellis may have been a clerk of Gilbert of Preston, a royal justice in the Bench and in eyres for over thirty years from 1240 till his death late in 1273.[162] He was certainly appointed keeper of writs and rolls on the 'northern' eyre circuit in 1279 and seems to have served in that position down to 1285.[163] *Gilbert of Rothbury* was a justice of King's Bench between 1295 and 1316 (and then a justice of the Bench from 1316 to 1321).[164] There is some evidence to suggest that he too may have been a clerk in the courts before becoming clerk of the council and clerk of parliament in 1290.[165]

Were the Court Clerks Members of the English Legal Profession?

It is the legal expertise of some of the senior clerical staff of the main royal courts which constitutes the main grounds for considering the group as a whole as possible candidates for membership of the nascent English legal profession. There are, however, a number of reasons for rejecting them as

---

[159] When a brief adjournment was made in the Bench in Easter term 1287 he was described as the clerk of Solomon of Rochester, the chief justice of the circuit: CP 40/67, m. 30d. Debt acknowledgments made to him indicate that he was present on the circuit (presumably in a clerical capacity) from at least the 1280 Somerset and Hampshire eyres onwards: JUST 1/758, m. 34d; JUST 1/788, mm. 6, 48. His senior status among the clerks of the circuit is indicated by his appointment as one of the justices to hear pleas of the banlieu of Bury St. Edmund's in 1287: KB 27/125, m. 57.

[160] For evidence that he was present (presumably as a clerk) in the 1292 Herefordshire eyre where he was able to stand surety for the bailiff of the abbot of Reading and to act as the proctor and attorney of the *domus conversorum* for the levying of deodands see JUST 1/303, mm. 4, 38. For evidence that he was present, presumably in a similar capacity, at the 1293 Kent eyre see JUST 1/375, mm. 5, 63d, 72. In the interim between the end of the 1280s circuit and the resumption of eyres in 1292 he may have acted as a clerk in the Exchequer: see E 13/14, m. 14.

[161] Sayles, 1*SCKB*, p. xlv. Ellis was also appointed an assize justice in 1285: *CCR 1279-88*, p. 365.

[162] Ellis seems to have been manumitted by the archbishop of York at Gilbert's request in 1269: *Reg . . . Wickwane*, p. 334, no. 913. He was suing Gilbert's widow for arrears of an annuity in 1281: JUST 1/1068, m. 21.

[163] Crook, *Records of the General Eyre*, p. 146.

[164] Sayles, 1*SCKB*, pp. cxxxii-cxxxiv, cxl-cxli.

[165] For his appointment and functions as clerk of the council and of parliament see Sayles, 1*SCKB*, p. lxi; Richardson and Sayles, 'The King's Ministers in Parliament, 1272-1307', *EHR*, xlvi (1931), 529-550 at 537-42. For evidence that he may have acted as a court clerk see JUST 1/501, m. 49 (where he is one of the witnesses to a quitclaim made to the archbishop of York by Parnel widow of Herbert Miller of Beverley at Lincoln in 1281 with the leading clerk Anger of Ripon: but note had he had previously been appointed her attorney: *ibid.*, m. 48d). It may also be significant that in 1293 he was one of the executors of Anger of Ripon: CP 40/101, m. 81. As we have seen Anger had been a leading clerk on the 'northern' eyre circuit before becoming a

full members of that profession and for suggesting that they are best seen as a separate, although closely connected, professional group.

The first is the fact that whatever might have been true about a few senior clerks a majority of these clerks appear to have been engaged on duties best characterised as essentially scribal and bureaucratic in nature and which required very little by the way of real legal knowledge or expertise. Some certainly did engage in activity as attorneys, the work of the legal profession, but this was always secondary to their primary work in the service of the court and their judicial masters. A few clerks were legal experts, many more had some legal knowledge; but the principal duties of a majority of clerks were not such as to require the employment of that knowledge.

A second reason for seeing the clerks of the courts as a separate group is that in practice there seems to have been almost no movement between the clerical staff of the courts and the ranks of the professional lawyers. It is just possible that one court clerk in the reign of Edward I did make such a move. Nicholas of Laver (Laufare) is found as the assign of damages awarded before John of Battisford and William Howard as Assize justices in 1293 and again in 1295, which suggests that he was a senior clerk in the service of one of these justices.[166] A man of the same name (who does not occur prior to this among the attorneys of the Bench unlike most of his fellow serjeants) occurs between 1301 and 1316 as a Bench serjeant. I have not found it possible to prove that they are the same man but it may well be that they are. Other clerks did not make the move. At the lower levels of the legal profession there was perhaps little reason for them to do so anyway. At the higher levels they were probably prevented from doing so by reason of their clerical status. A majority of the senior clerks in the courts seem to have been in clerical orders and to have held benefices. Canon law forbad clerks and priests to act as advocates in secular courts other than in their own cases or in the cases of *miserabiles persone* (hardly the clients a professional lawyer was looking for).[167] Transfer to the ranks of serjeants would have meant renouncing the regular income of ecclesiastical benefices for the speculative possibility of future income at the bar; and the prospect was clearly not sufficiently attractive for most clerks to take it. Movement in the opposite direction was perhaps barred for other reasons, among them a tradition that clerks in the courts were generally in clerical orders. This would have debarred most professional lawyers (and certainly almost all serjeants) from seeking any such transfer for their acquisition of wives and children had ruled out any possibility of acceptance into the clergy.

A third reason for seeing the clerical staff of the courts as a group distinct from the legal profession lies in their treatment in the legislation of Edward

---

Bench clerk: above, pp. 175-76. Appointment as Anger's executor suggests that they may have once been colleagues.

[166]   CP 40/103, m. 46; JUST 1/1306, m. 30.

[167]   James A. Brundage, 'Legal Aid for the Poor and the Professionalization of Law in the Middle Ages', *Journal of Legal History*, ix (1988), 169-79 at 170-1.

I's reign establishing special rules as to their conduct.[168] Although some of the rules established resemble those laid down for members of the legal profession the fact remains that these statutes treated court clerks not as part of that profession but as part of the royal bureaucracy, part of a single group which embraced other royal clerks and officials.

Contemporaries certainly did not see them as part of the legal profession; nor should we. But they remain an interesting sub-group in the legal world: well worth our interest and attention in their own right as playing an important part in the running of the English legal system, both as bureaucrats, compiling and keeping documents, and in the case of the more senior members of the group helping in the performance of the adjudicatory functions of the courts.

---

[168] Above, pp. 189-90.

9

The Origins of English Land Law: Milsom and After

My theme in this essay is the beginnings of English land law. My concern is with what English customary land law was like before the reign of Henry II and with the principal mechanisms of change created during Henry's reign, the purposes behind their creation, and their longer-term effects. I want to concentrate on the ideas and theories which Professor S.F.C. Milsom has been developing over the last twenty years in a series of stimulating, but often difficult and allusive, works.[1] I will also be saying something about the views of Professor Robert C. Palmer.[2] Professor Palmer is a 'Milsomian', a scholar who in the main accepts the views of Professor Milsom, but who has suggested some interesting alternative interpretations and ideas for some of the phenomena discussed by Professor Milsom. My main aim in this essay is to provide a clear exposition of the views of Professors Milsom and Palmer. In the final section I will, however, indicate what seem to me to be some of the more obvious objections to these 'Milsomian' theories about the beginnings of English land law.

I will start by looking at Professor Milsom's view of what English land law (to use an anachronistic but useful phrase) looked like before the transformation effected by the legal reforms of King Henry II.

His starting-point is not very different from that of previous legal historians; jurisdiction in questions of land law was at this time a matter for feudal courts, the court which each lord held for his tenants; since there was

---

[1] A first statement of some of the relevant arguments appeared in 1968 in his 'Introduction' to the reissue of Pollock and Maitland's classic *History of English Law (Before the Time of Edward I)* (hereafter cited as *Introduction*). A much fuller exposition of his views and the supporting arguments for them appeared in 1976 in *The Legal Framework of English Feudalism* (a published version of his 1972 Maitland lectures) (hereafter cited as *LFEF*). A summary of those views (but one which constituted in some important respects also a further revision of them) appeared in 1981 in the relevant sections of the second edition of his *Historical Foundations of the Common Law* (hereafter cited as *HFCL*).

[2] These are to be found in a review article on *The Legal Framework of English Feudalism* in the 1981 *Michigan Law Review* entitled 'The Feudal Framework of English Law' as also in an article entitled 'The Origins of Property in England' which appeared in the Spring 1985 issue of *Law and History Review*.

at this time no mechanism for regular royal interference in the affairs of these courts each was able to function as a sovereign and independent body.[3] But where Milsom does depart radically from older views is in his notion of how these courts operated. The traditional view had seen these courts as essentially private, local versions of the king's court as we see it in the thirteenth century: the lord and his tenants sitting as impartial judges deciding questions of title to land for all land held of the lord. Milsom insists that in this older 'seignorial' world we must start by thinking of the lord as being the 'owner' of all the land held of his fee and in total control of his lordship.[4] The lord wanted services and was willing to pay for them by allocating land to a man for his lifetime in return for their performance.[5] But the tenant did not thereby acquire anything like an independent right or entitlement to the land, and certainly not anything resembling ownership over it. His rights remained entirely dependent on his relationship with the lord and he was in the land only by the lord's allocation.[6] Milsom deduces from this that there were only two kinds of question which could arise for decision in the lord's court: about the beginning and about the ending of a tenant's tenure. Who should get the land when a tenant died? Had the tenant who was in possession so acted, so neglected to fulfil his obligations, as to justify his being disseised by the lord?[7] Provided the tenant in

---

[3] *Introduction*, p. xxxv: 'within a single lordship the lord and his tenants formed an almost sovereign body'; *LFEF*, p. 66: 'In the seignorial world a grant or an inheritance as well as the judgment ending a dispute were final decisions of a sovereign body applying the only law there was'.

[4] *LFEF*, p. 39: 'if we are to think of either as owning anything, it must be the lord as owning the whole of his fee. But this is not some real result of conditions outside: outside he too is somebody's tenant. It is something postulated inside the fee, the internal plenitude of control which the historian like the tenant himself must accept'; *HFCL*, p. 100: 'rights are dependent upon a lord seen as having total control of his lordship . . . The lord was in our language . . . the owner of wealth'.

[5] *LFEF*, p. 39: 'the lord rather than the tenant . . . should be imagined as the buyer in some initial transaction. He is the buyer in the sense that he is the owner, he is the one with the wealth, the only form of capital wealth there can be . . . he buys services and pays directly in land. But of course the land is not transferred out-and-out: the basic purchase is of a life's service for a life tenure. He buys a man.'; *HFCL*, p. 100: 'The lord was in our language also the owner of wealth; and since there was no other form of wealth from which he could derive an income to pay for whatever services he desired, he paid directly in land'.

[6] *HFCL*, p. 100: 'Ownership belongs to a flat legal world in which rights in land or other forms of wealth are dependent upon no authority except the state . . . Tenure belongs to a smaller world in which there is no need and no room for abstract ideas like ownership. Rights are dependent upon a lord as having total control of his lordship. A tenant is in by the lord's allocation. He can have no more by way of title, unless it is some obligation on the lord to keep him in, or to admit his successors'; *LFEF*, p. 40: 'as between tenant and lord and within the lordship there is hardly room for any deeper proprietary concept. Seisin itself connotes not just factual possession but that seignorial acceptance which is all the title there can be.'

[7] *LFEF*, p. 41: 'It was only about the beginning and ending of the relationship that decisions had to be made: who should be seised in the first place; and has the man seised so acted as to justify his being disseised?' But note that elsewhere Milsom speaks as though decisions will also

possession was fulfilling his obligations it was impossible for the question of title to his tenement to arise: the lord's court on principle would not entertain such litigation. It was, therefore, impossible for a third party to make a claim to a tenement against a sitting tenant.[8]

How did feudal courts decide the questions that did come up? Milsom suggests that feudal courts possessed a considerable degree of flexibility and discretion in their decision-making, as not at all hidebound by decisions they had made in the past: and this simply by virtue of the fact that they were independent sovereign courts. Previous decisions on similar matters were a factor, but only one factor, in their decision-making process.[9] But he suggests that it was in fact practical considerations that were decisive in determining whether courts followed previous custom flexibly or inflexibly. As long as lords really needed the services of their tenants as fighting men, feudal courts had been flexible in their following of previous custom so as to ensure that the outcome of their decision was one best calculated to provide the lord with what he needed; once this requirement declined in importance custom tended to become less flexible.[10] Milsom suggests that custom was

---

have to be made when a lord succeeds: *LFEF*, p. 121: 'So long as William had only a title for life he could give only for his life. Even if he gave to Thomas and undertook that he and his heirs would warrant Thomas and his heirs, that created only an obligation; and when the time came William's heir would have to decide whether to honour it or not. In making that decision, he and his court would have to consider his other obligations: to William's widow, to William's other grantees, and above all the overriding obligation to Ralph'; *LFEF*, p. 131: 'The ancestor made an allocation from his inheritance, and undertook as a matter of obligation that he and his heirs would maintain it. When he died, his heir had to decide whether to honour that obligation, or rather his court had to decide whether circumstances were such that he was not bound to honour it'.

[8] *LFEF*, p. 41: 'In such a world the lord's court would police against wrongful invasions and encroachments, and would sometimes have to decide whether, for example, these acres belonged to this tenement or that. But the question of title to a tenement would not arise during the tenure of a tenant fulfilling his obligations'; *LFEF*, p. 66: '. . . so long as it regularly applied its own customs, he enjoyed the certainty which we associate with registered title, and which was long enjoyed by the copyhold successors of unfree tenants: the man accepted was by definition the man entitled'. But note that Milsom sounds more hesitant on this point in *HFCL* (at p. 100): '. . . he cannot by himself engage in dispute about the land: in principle the lord must decide who is to be his tenant. And if, like the theatre management which has sold a numbered seat twice over, the lord has incurred obligations both to the tenant now in and to a third party, there are two valid "titles" and the most that one "owner" can hope for is compensation.'

[9] *HFCL*, pp. 1–2: 'Factually the human and sometimes supernatural pressures to do the same thing again may be strong. But if the body is sovereign in the matter and its decision final . . . what matters is the present decision, the choice made now. That is guided or not by the past, but cannot be "wrong" because of it. It is the past that must give way, and then the present will have refined or modified the custom . . . What we did last time is just a factor in our decision; we do not have to do the same thing again; nor, if we decide not to do the same thing again, do we thereby reopen last time's decision'.

[10] *HFCL*, p. 2: 'It is easy to see how such customs can become more "binding". They must be formed by economic needs: when people generally die young, eldest sons are most likely to be fit to take over. But equally it is the economic need that makes for flexibility: the feeble-minded eldest son will never be fit. If the managerial requirement recedes, the custom is more likely to

beginning to harden in England from the time of the Norman Conquest onwards. Individual tenants were not normally required to provide military service directly for their lords (except perhaps during the Anarchy); the normal requirement was simply to provide part of the lord's contingent or quota for the king's army; and in practice even the king came to prefer money payments to an army 'composed of fighting men whose obligation might be limited both geographically and by the number of days they would serve in one year'.[11] These were optimum conditions, he suggests, for the hardening of feudal custom. His general view seems to be that by the mid twelfth century (though he is not very specific about dates in all of this) there were customs that were fairly uniform throughout the whole of England;[12] and that these customs were generally observed.[13] Milsom is insistent, however, that so long as customs operated within the context of feudal lordships, they were not and could not be the same as rules, for they could still be disregarded with impunity by lords (and by those lords' courts).[14] His overall conclusion, again apparently speaking about the mid twelfth century, is that questions still 'presented themselves to lords' courts not in the terms of ownership of property but in those of management' and that 'the customs of such a court were more like good managerial practices than rules of law'.[15]

What were the customs that Milsom thinks were generally followed by the

---

be seen as a somehow binding rule. In England this may have happened as the superior tenures ceased to be seen as having much to do with the provision of fighting men, so that except at the lowest levels the feudal structure lost touch with the economic reality that had once shaped it.'

[11]   *HFCL*, p. 103.

[12]   Milsom seems to have changed his mind over the years as to just how much variation there was between the custom followed in different courts. In his 1968 *Introduction* he wrote as if even on such critical matters as heritability there might well have been differences from court to court: 'A recent view has suggested a date near 1200 for the full heritability of the superior tenures, over a century after Maitland's. But neither the real nor the conceptual stages of the process are ever likely to be established. The customs of one lordship may have been clear, and different from the equally clear customs of another . . . ': *Introduction*, p. xxxiv. In *HFCL*, however, he seems to envisage a much more uniform development of custom, with individual lordships differing only over comparatively minor points of custom e.g. as to whether the eldest surviving son should be preferred for inheritance purposes to the heir of a predeceased elder son: *HFCL*, p. 107.

[13]   *LFEF*, p. 170: 'However regular the succession had been in fact, and however powerful the custom binding the lord to make a new grant, it was still only by a grant from the lord that each heir entered . . . '; *HFCL*, p. 122: 'the change in what actually happened may not at first have been great: the customs were no doubt generally followed . . . '

[14]   *HFCL*, p. 3: 'more is needed before abstract rights of property could come into being. So long as the allocations made by authority cannot be questioned, the customs can only be criteria for a present decision'; *HFCL*, p. 100: 'This court acted in accordance with customs which were thought to have some independent existence, but there was no external enforcement. Any obligations resting upon the lord, upon the management of the lordship, were therefore determined by rules which were within the management's ultimate control'.

[15]   The quotation is from his 'The Past and Future of Judge-Made Law', as reprinted in his *Studies in the History of the Common Law* (London, 1985), p. 209.

mid twelfth century in the two areas where feudal courts did have to make decisions: about what should happen when a sitting tenant died; and about whether it was right that a sitting tenant should be disseised for failure to fulfil his obligations. There has, of course, long been controversy among legal and social historians about exactly when free tenants in England acquired a full heritable interest in land, entitling their heirs to succeed them. Milsom follows what can best be described as a version of the Thorne thesis in these matters. Strictly speaking, even as late as the mid twelfth century, no tenant had anything more than a life interest in his land.[16] But when a lord took his tenant's homage he was by custom regarded as promising not just to allow that tenant possession of his tenement for his life-time but also to admit that tenant's heir after his death. In practice, therefore, land would normally be inherited from generation to generation, though only by virtue of a series of such grants.[17] The difference between this and full heritable right in land was more than just theoretical. Before the grant to the heir was made the heir had only a claim against the lord to be granted the land; and if he died before it was made, it was not his heir that had a claim to be admitted but the next heir of the tenant who had died in possession, and they were not necessarily the same person.[18] If, for what-

[16] *HFCL*, p. 169: 'If we ask whether in the twelfth century there were life estates other than dower and curtesy, we ask a question which is real but would have made no sense at the time. Even the tenant who had done homage could not hold longer than for his life'; *HFCL*, pp. 105-6: 'When the tenant died his seisin came to an end and the lord would, at any rate in principle, take the tenement into his own hand. He would then make livery of seisin to a new tenant, who would hold as the dead man had, and so the sequence would begin again. To the extent that seisin was a proprietary entity and tenure a proprietary relationship, the property right, the "freehold", could not outlast the tenant's lifetime'.

[17] *Introduction*, p. xxxvi: 'In [the truly feudal world] we must not think of a grant to one "and his heirs" as a once and for all matter. When that grantee died, his heir would become seised by the action of the lord; and this was a new grant to the heir "and his heirs" even though the lord had bound himself to make it . . .'; *LFEF*, pp. 170-1: ' . . . the case shows how inheritance must have looked when there was only the lord's law and the lord's court. However regular the succession had been in fact and however powerful the custom binding the lord to make a new grant, it was still only by a grant from the lord that each heir entered'. In *HFCL* he sounds more doubtful and is perhaps suggesting that something like true heritability had been established by custom (but he is maddeningly imprecise about dates): 'Within feudal custom, the force appears to have come from the homage which a lord took from his tenant. The original effect of that homage may have been first to oblige the lord's heir to honour the tenant's tenure; then to oblige the lord to admit the tenant's heir; and it seems that the force flowing from any particular act of homage was spent when both parties to it were dead. But though homage was in fact done at every devolution on either side, the idea grew that one act of homage created a relationship which would extend to an indefinite series of heirs. The obligation was already beginning to have a proprietary look . . .': *HFCL*, p. 106.

[18] *LFEF*, pp. 170-171: 'Before it was made, the heir could not think of himself as "owner". He had just his right, a claim *in personam* against the lord to be granted the land. If he died before this was done, for example, the tenement was never his, and his own heir as such had no right to be granted it. The person who now had that right was the next heir of the dead tenant; and only after the *casus regis* was out of the way and representation finally accepted would he normally be the same person'; *HFCL*, p. 106: 'But the matter is strictly one of obligation. Until

ever reason, the heir was in fact passed over, neither he nor his heirs would have any claim to the tenement when it next became vacant or on any other future occasion: for the right to succeed now lay in the heir of the tenant whose homage the lord had taken.[19] Milsom also suggests that in this earlier feudal world it may well have been possible for a living tenant to determine to whom his land should go after his death, thereby in effect allowing what English land law of the late twelfth century (and later) specifically prohibited: testate succession to land. Since succession to a tenement was a matter wholly for the lord and the court they might as a favour to the tenant agree to accept his beneficiary rather than his heir as his successor.[20] When intestate succession did occur it was the custom of each lordship that would determine who was to succeed.[21]

Milsom seems to have been the first legal historian to emphasise the importance of what he calls the 'disciplinary jurisdiction' exercised by feudal courts. He suggests that in the 'truly feudal' world the tenant's obligations to his lord were rather more extensive than those of his thirteenth-century successor. Certainly he owed specific services and was liable to pay relief and rightful aids (just like his thirteenth-century counterpart). But he was also obliged by virtue of his homage to do nothing (to use *Glanvill's* formulation) 'which works to the disinheritance or bodily dishonour of the lord';[22] and this was a large and flexible category.[23] Milsom further suggests (again on the basis of a passage to this effect in *Glanvill*) that the appropriate punishment for any breach of these obligations was disseisin.[24] Custom had, however, he

the lord makes livery to him the heir has no seisin, no freehold, no proprietary right at all; and if for example he dies before he is admitted, the person now entitled will not be his heir but the next heir of the dead tenant.'

[19]   *LFEF*, pp. 180-1: 'Suppose the heir is passed over; the lord does as Henry I once did and accepts a younger son because he is the better knight. It is done. Isaac should have blessed Esau, but cannot recall his blessing of Jacob. John and not Arthur is the crowned king. The elder son had a claim to be chosen, but he had not and has not a right. The inheritance was never his, and in that seignorial world it now never will be. He is disappointed, has been passed over unjustly; but he cannot by litigation seek the ouster of the one preferred.'

[20]   *LFEF*, p. 109: 'the heir became entitled by force of the lord's acceptance of himself, not by force of the grant to his ancestor. It is therefore no surprise that we find substitutions using the language of inheritance. Instead of asking his lord to accept a substituted tenant now, the present tenant may try to "make" an heir for the lord to accept after his death . . . So long as there was only the lord's court, this arrangement had presumably been effective and land to that extent devisable.'

[21]   *LFEF*, p. 41: 'Suppose a sovereign lordship to have its customs of inheritance . . .'; *HFCL*, pp. 106-7: 'In England it was not settled until the thirteenth century was well advanced that the son of a dead elder son was entitled as against the living younger son. For political reasons that particular doubt survived within the king's court. But it arose because customs had differed, so that some lords' courts had preferred the nephew, others the uncle . . .'

[22]   *Glanvill*, ed. Hall, IX, 1 (p. 104).

[23]   For Milsom's discussion of some of the actions which might be regarded as falling within this category see *LFEF*, pp. 26-7.

[24]   *LFEF*, p. 39: 'If later the man fails in his service, not just the render but also the devotion required by his homage, the lord will disseise him.'

suggests, by the mid twelfth century come to impose certain restraints on the way lords exercised this power. In general it could only be exercised on the authorisation of the lord's court; and that court could, he suggests, only give its authorisation in one of two kinds of situation.[25] One was where the tenant has been summoned to the lord's court to answer for a breach of his obligations and refused to appear; here it was necessary that the court should have followed a uniform customary process prior to the eventual judgment that he be disseised.[26] The other was where the tenant had appeared in court and the lord had proved a breach of obligation to the satisfaction of his court.[27] Milsom seems to suggest that in this 'truly feudal' world there were no mechanisms for the enforcement of the tenant's obligations other than the threat of disseisin or disseisin itself.

In 'The Feudal Framework of English Law', his first article reviewing Milsom's *Legal Framework of English Feudalism*, Professor Palmer seems willing generally to accept Milsom's picture of what the 'truly feudal' world had looked like,[28] though I think I detect a rather different emphasis in Palmer's account on the lord's continuing discretionary power. Palmer seems to regard it as an essential characteristic of this world, Milsom almost as an anomalous survival in a world where custom had come to be increasingly fixed.[29] By the time he came to write 'The Origins of Property' Palmer had moved rather further away from the Milsomian view. Decisions about

[25] Milsom's account does not always clearly distinguish these two different kinds of situation; but clearly they are conceptually quite distinct.

[26] *HFCL*, p. 104: 'there were three stages of increasingly stringent process: summons, distraint by chattels, and sequestration or ultimately confiscation of the land itself . . .'; *LFEF*, p. 9: 'A number of accounts survive from the years around 1200, surprisingly similar in different parts of England: and since they are given in law-suits by persons concerned to show that they have acted rightly they tell us at least what ought to happen when Thomas fails to do his services. He is summoned to Ralph's court: summoned by equal tenants, once again, and a third time. If by the fourth court day he has not come, the court orders that he be distrained by chattels taken on the land; and this is also ordered three times. If that fails, the tenement itself is taken into Ralph's hands, and held if necessary until a third set of three court days has passed. After that, the theory seems to be that the court can order the forfeiture of all Thomas's rights in the tenement to Ralph, who can allocate it to another . . .'

[27] *HFCL*, p. 104: '[the tenant's] holding is in some sense conditional upon his performance of the services due. He has tenure in the same sense as a professor or judge today. He is in and can only be put out for cause established by due process, namely the judgment of his fellow-tenants, his peers, in the lord's court . . .'

[28] Palmer has reservations with regard to Milsom's view of feudal courts as totally sovereign and independent. Palmer pointed to the existence of *tolt* procedure for the removal of litigation out of the lord's court into the county court, but he did not think that this would have been a serious blow to the autonomy of seignorial courts since 'the county court was dominated by the lords of the county': 'Feudal Framework of English Law', pp. 1141-2. A more serious difference between them seems to be that Palmer does at least allow for the possibility of the lord's court admitting a suit against a sitting tenant though he thought that the lord's court 'may not in fact often have been impartial': 'Feudal Framework of English Law', pp. 1161-2.

[29] 'Feudal Framework of English Law', p. 1135: 'Obligation, simplicity of title, discretion, and seignorial control characterized the truly feudal world . . .'.

the disseisin of a particular tenant were not, he suggests, governed by custom, but were essentially political in nature; and the result of such cases 'probably varied according to the prestige of the lord, the reputation and past history of the man, and the needs of a particular group at the time, in addition to the facts involved in a given dispute'.[30] And the establishment of heritability should also, he suggests, be seen in political terms. The lord wanted loyal knights; loyalty would only come from those 'fairly treated and fairly bought'; and 'the price of the man' was 'maintenance for life and provision for survivors: both his heir and his widow'. In any case the lord would usually want the heir simply because 'he was at hand, loyal and familiar'.[31]

Milsom suggests that this 'truly feudal world' was destroyed or transformed largely as a consequence of the introduction of three standard forms of legal remedy during the reign of Henry II. I will first look briefly in turn at each of them to see what they were and to see what Milsom suggests was the intention which lay behind their introduction. I will then look at how Milsom suggests they were able to achieve what he considers to have been their unintended longer-term effects.

The first in time was the writ of right. This, as we see it in the first textbook of the English common law written at the end of the reign of Henry II (*Glanvill*), is a form of royal writ addressed to the lord of whom a plaintiff claims to hold a tenement which ordered the addressee to 'do full right' without delay to the claimant with respect to a specified quantity of land in a particular village which he claims to hold of the addressee (for a specified service) and which another named individual is withholding from him. The writ goes on to stipulate that if the addressee fails to do as ordered then the sheriff of a specified county (the appropriate county) is to do so instead. *Glanvill* does not tell us what kinds of claim are appropriate to this writ; but it is generally assumed that it was the appropriate remedy when the plaintiff wanted to make a claim based on ancestral seisin, asserting that a particular ancestor had been in seisin of the tenement claimed at some time in the past and that the tenement ought by right to have descended to the plaintiff. Legal historians before Milsom had generally believed that this kind of claim was nothing new, indeed that it was the kind of claim that litigants had made before royal writs were needed to initiate litigation, and that litigants started to use royal writs of right to initiate litigation in which such a claim was made early in the reign of Henry II simply because of the imposition of a rule requiring the use of writs in the case of litigation about free tenements.

Milsom does not believe in the existence of such a traditional form of claim. Nor does he believe that the writ (initially at least) could be used to initiate a claim of this sort. He believes that the original context for the introduction

---

[30] 'The Origins of Property', p. 5.
[31] 'The Origins of Property', pp. 5-6.

of the writ of right was the peace made in 1153 at the end of the Anarchy between King Stephen and Duke Henry (the future Henry II).[32] The agreement between them, as we now have it, covers only succession to the kingdom of England; but, says Milsom, there is chronicle evidence for supposing that the original agreement was in somewhat wider terms than this and provided that all those who had been disinherited during the Anarchy should be restored to the rights which they had possessed in the reign of Henry I. The writ of right started, so Milsom suggests, as the mechanism for giving effect to this part of the agreement. The evidence for this lies in the kind of title that some demandants still made in actions initiated by the writ at the end of the twelfth century. By the time of the earliest plea rolls, many demandants were claiming on the seisin of their ancestors in the reign of King Henry II or King Richard, and when they did so, no further specification of a particular time within the reign of either king was necessary. But a substantial proportion of demandants made their claims on the seisin of their ancestors in the reign of Henry I, and when they did it was necessary for them to be more specific. For such a claim it was necessary to say that the ancestor had been seised 'in the year and on the day that the king was alive and dead'. It is in claims made in this form that Milsom sees preserved what had once been the only kind of claim which could be made through the writ, the kind of claim for which the writ was originally designed and intended. The implication seems to be that demandants were originally restricted to making a claim based on seisin at this one moment of time alone specifically to exclude a reopening of claims concerning disseisins during Henry I's reign, to ensure that the action was only allowed to undo disseisins which had taken place during the Anarchy.[33] In *The Legal Framework of English Feudalism* Milsom concedes that it was possible that the action was from the beginning intended to be a little more general than this: that it was intended to allow a general enforcement of the hereditary principle (as opposed to the general and widespread custom of inheritance) though he thought it more likely that 'no general change was intended': that the original intention was simply that 'lands lost during the anarchy were . . . to be restored'.[34] By the time he came to write the revised version of *Historical Foundations of the Common Law* he was more confident in his rejection of this hypothesis:

> a possible interpretation . . . is that the writ manifests a royal policy of enforcing the customs of inheritance. It has been suggested that such a policy was prompted by events during the Anarchy after the death of Henry I . . . On this view the desire for political stability caused regularity of inheritance to be perceived as itself a desirable goal. But the perception of the time was probably less ample and

[32] *LFEF*, p. 178; *HFCL*, p. 129.

[33] In *HFCL* at p. 129 he also suggests that there is a reminder of the origins of the action in the requirement that the demandant say that his ancestor was seised in time of peace.

[34] *LFEF*, p. 183.

less abstract; and in ordinary times, even in lords' courts and without any coercion from the king, inheritance was already the regular thing.[35]

It was merely accidental, he argues, that the writ of right was commonly used from the beginning to enforce claims based on the seisin of an ancestor. Many of the dispossessed must have been dead by the time the settlement was made and so it had to be their heirs who were restored but 'the original concern was with the restoration rather than with inheritance . . . '.[36]

The second was the assize of novel disseisin. As we see it at the end of Henry II's reign (in *Glanvill*) this was a royal writ by which a plaintiff could initiate proceedings in the king's court in which a jury of the neighbourhood would appear to answer a single question: had the defendant(s) unjustly and without a judgment disseised the plaintiff of his 'free tenement' in a particular village since a particular date? If the jury so found the plaintiff would be put back in possession of the land concerned. It appears to be an appropriate remedy whenever a plaintiff had been in possession of a tenement but has been wrongfully dispossessed of it. Legal historians prior to Milsom had generally seen the assize as having been invented for the purpose it was apparently already serving by the time of *Glanvill*: the general one of the protection of possessors against wrongdoers. Such a view was, however, difficult to reconcile with the Milsomian picture of the kind of world in which the assize had been born: an intensely seignorial world where lords were in real control of their lordships. Viewed in this context, the assize made, Milsom argued, much better sense as having been originally intended specifically for the use of tenants against their lords: 'The lord is not an unnoticed spectator, worrying if at all about a royal encroachment upon his jurisdiction. He is the defendant, and he is being made to answer for an abuse of his power'.[37] The assize was intended to provide additional sanction for the existing customary right of the tenant not to be disseised by his lord except for cause and after due process.[38]

Milsom (here following Professor Van Caenegem) believes that the 1166 Assize of Clarendon created only 'what we should call a "criminal" offence', imposing on local people 'a duty to present recent disseisins to the justices in eyre'. The regular 'civil' remedy (allowing an individual plaintiff to bring proceedings) he believes was a later development, perhaps not much predating the composition of *Glanvill* itself.[39] He nonetheless believes that there are several traces of the original purpose of the assize in the wording

[35] *HFCL*, pp. 128-9.
[36] *HFCL*, p. 129.
[37] *LFEF*, p. 11. Earlier Milsom had been more cautious: 'May not novel disseisin like mort d'ancestor have been in its inception a specific rather than a general remedy, and directed primarily against lords? Like mort d'ancestor, it from the beginning probably had a wider use . . . ': *Introduction*, p. xli.
[38] *HFCL*, p. 140.
[39] *HFCL*, pp. 138-9; cf. *Introduction*, p. xxxix.

of the assize writ itself. In the writ the plaintiff is said to have complained that he had been disseised not simply unjustly but 'unjustly and without a judgment'. Milsom argues that this makes real sense only against a lord because only a lord could disseise lawfully by judgment.[40] The sheriff is also told in the writ to 'see that the tenement was reseised of the chattels which were taken in it'. Milsom argues that this too makes no sense in the case of a casual wrongdoer who would consume or dispose of chattels, but that it makes good sense in the context of 'disciplinary' action by a lord against his tenant, since the first stage of process in such an action was regularly distraint by chattels, and it was likely that they would still be in his custody.[41] A third piece of evidence is that the tenement which the demandant is seeking does not need to be specified in the writ 'in acres or virgates as in every other writ concerning land'. The implication seems to be that this is because both lord and tenant know well the tenement they are talking about; and the tenant will have been disseised of all of his tenement.[42] A final piece of evidence relates to the order to the sheriff contained in the writ to summon the defendant 'or his bailiff if he himself cannot be found'. Milsom argues that this was not in origin as it later became 'a kindly arrangement whereby an absent defendant could be represented' but 'a regular order for the attachment of one whose existence is assumed, the lord's local agent'.[43] He finds additional confirmation of his view of the original orientation of the assize in the requirement in the writ that the plaintiff should have to complain that he had been disseised of his 'free tenement'. This made good sense, he argues, if the original context had been a measure to control the behaviour of lords towards their tenants; much less if that context was a police measure against casual wrongdoing.[44]

The third was the assize of mort d'ancestor. As we see it at the end of the twelfth century this was a writ by which a plaintiff could secure the appearance of a jury in the king's court to answer a series of questions: had a specified individual (a close relative of the plaintiff) died seised in his demesne as of fee of a specified quantity of land in a particular village; had he died since a particular date; and was the plaintiff his closest heir? If favourable answers were given to all these questions the plaintiff recovered against the current tenant of the land. A plaintiff would use the assize, therefore, when his claim was that a close relative had died seised of a heritable interest in land but that he had not been allowed to succeed him in

[40] *LFEF*, p. 11; cf. *Introduction*, p. xli: '. . . in a feudal world it could have a more obvious and factual sense: had the holding been taken into hand or allotted to another without a judgment of the lord's court?'

[41] *LFEF*, p. 12.

[42] *LFEF*, pp. 12-13.

[43] *LFEF*, p. 13; cf. *Introduction*, p. xlii: 'at first it meant what it said, that the bailiff was the obvious representative because the lord was the obvious disseisor. If the lord was simply taking the holding into his own hand, indeed, the bailiff might play a more active part . . .'

[44] *LFEF*, p. 13.

this land. Legal historians have long known from the text of the assize of Northampton of 1176 which introduced the assize that initially it was envisaged that it would be lords who would be the particular target of the assize: there has been little doubt, therefore, about the specifically seignorial orientation of the assize when it first came into existence. Milsom insists that we should take this evidence more seriously. The assize, he says, should not simply be seen as legal historians have tended to see it as 'an action for the recovery of property which happened at first to be aimed against only one possible class of defendant'.[45] The purpose was to '[protect] one party to a relationship against the other';[46] it was aimed at 'an order in which lords might abuse their customary powers of control'.[47] This does, of course, simply take up some of Milsom's themes about the way inheritance worked, and about how in the earlier, 'truly feudal' world the heir did not have an independent 'right' to his tenement, merely a claim to be accepted by the lord. Milsom also has interesting suggestions about the mischief at which the assize was aimed. It was of course intended for use against the occasional lord who really did try not to admit an heir; but, Milsom suggests, it may have been as much intended to prevent lords trying to charge more than the customary relief (and retaining land as a means of ensuring that the heir paid it).[48]

For Professor Milsom other provisions of the assize of Northampton were as important, if not more important, than the introduction of the assize of mort d'ancestor itself. These provisions prevented the lord, when it was an adult heir who was succeeding to a tenement, from taking the land concerned into his hands 'in any real sense'; and in the case of an infant succeeding to a tenement required the lord to take the infant's homage before taking possession of his land as 'a public and inviolable acknowledgment' of the capacity in which he was holding the tenement. He conceded that 'in practice even before the enactment an adult heir living in the tenement may not have been disturbed on the death' but insisted that formally to 'prohibit the lord from taking an actual possession, even for the purpose of making a routing livery to the heir', was 'to alter the look of inheritance . . . .'.[49]

It is important to notice how insistent Milsom is that there was no underlying anti-feudal policy behind any of these innovations. There was a royal policy but it was no more than to compel lords and their courts to

---

[45] *LFEF*, p. 166.

[46] *LFEF*, p. 166.

[47] *HFCL*, p. 135.

[48] *LFEF*, p. 166: 'its initial thrust may have been as much against improper exactions as against simple misappropriation'; *HFCL*, p. 135: 'If, as is suggested by the references to homage and wardship, the enactment was concerned with military tenures, probably few lords would be so hardy as simply to repudiate their obligations to heirs; and the common abuse may have been in demanding more for livery of the land than the customary relief.'

[49] *HFCL*, p. 135.

follow their own custom. As he writes in *Historical Foundations of the Common Law*: 'The actions came into being in a framework in which lords were still in control of their lordships, and in which therefore the king's court could seek only to control the doings of lords. The purpose of this control was not, and could not be, in any sense "anti-feudal": it was to prevent and correct departures by lords' courts from the accepted body of feudal custom'. But, he went on to say, 'The unintended effect was to deprive lordship of any legal reality . . .'.[50]

For Palmer, Milsom was right in connecting the origins of the writ of right with the Compromise of 1153; but wrong in detail as to what that compromise actually decided and therefore also wrong about the exact function the writ of right was intended to perform. Palmer suggests that when the land had been taken away from a tenant by his lord during the Anarchy and granted out to a third party, the Compromise protected the new tenant in possession for the remainder of his lifetime (a very Milsomian kind of assumption this, emphasising the strength of title of the lord's accepted tenant) but required that the dispossessed tenant or his heir be accepted by the lord when the new tenant died. The writ of right started out as a writ to allow such a claimant to make his claim under the terms of the Compromise against a lord who was refusing to accept him.[51] Palmer does not accept Milsom's view of the origins of the assize of novel disseisin. In the 'Feudal Framework of English Law' he rehearsed (and accepted) the arguments made by Donald Sutherland against viewing the assize as intended solely for use against lords and suggested that the true context for the assize might well again be the enforcement of the 1153 Compromise, though here that part of it which left the lord's accepted tenant in possession for the remainder of his lifetime. The assize was intended to provide protection for the tenant against the claimant who was not willing to wait until he died (or against a lord who was also not willing to wait). Palmer argued that the Compromise was perhaps intended to produce some sort of individual compromise between tenants in possession and claimants (by which the claimant got some land at once in return for allowing the tenant in possession to pass some of the land on to his heirs) and thought that lords might be particularly likely to act against recalcitrant tenants refusing such a compromise.[52] In the 'Origins of Property' he again suggested that the assize of novel disseisin was connected with the 1153 Compromise but this time only in its earlier form of a quasi-criminal public presentment procedure and suggested that it was intended to protect tenants against being disciplined for actions prior to 1153 (which the Compromise said were to be forgiven and forgotten) and also against dispossession if they refused to

---

[50] *HFCL*, p. 124.
[51] 'Feudal Framework of English Law', pp. 1143-5; 'Origins of Property', pp. 8-11.
[52] 'Feudal Framework of English Law', pp. 1145-6, 1149-53.

compromise in advance with a claimant.[53] The assize of novel disseisin as a private remedy he now dates only to shortly before 1188 and argues that from the first this was a general remedy for persons dispossessed unjustly and without judgment.[54] In the 'Origins of Property' he also develops for the first time an ingenious theory about the origins of the assize of mort d'ancestor which attempts to link these origins with contemporary political circumstances. The immediate context, he suggests, was the war between Henry II and the young King Henry in 1173-4 and the assize was 'designed . . . to inhibit the magnates' power to prepare for hostilities'. His suggestion is that the assize of Northampton was not concerned with ensuring the succession of adult males, solely with ensuring the succession of heiresses and minor heirs. The only reason lords had for intruding strangers or more distant relative in place of heiresses and minor heirs was that they wanted a tenant immediately capable of fighting. Protection of heiresses and minors against such intrusions was, therefore, a way of ensuring that lords did not maximise their fighting forces.[55]

For Milsom, it was the introduction of the writ of right, however limited the intention behind this move, that was 'the first and perhaps the decisive step in bringing down the seignorial world'. This was because in proceedings under the writ for the very first time the lord's acceptance of the tenant, his admission of the tenant to the tenement, was no longer regarded as conclusive, as excluding any possibility of litigation.[56] The writ of right did not have this effect in the court of the lord to whom it was addressed: here things continued as they always had done. What was crucial was the clause allowing the claimant to have his case removed out of the lord's court and into the county court (and ultimately, if he wished, into the king's court), which effectively gave jurisdiction over his claim to one of those other courts: for those other courts would entertain his claim and act on it.[57] By the end of the twelfth century there were a variety of ways in which a claimant could attack a sitting tenant and the writ of right was only one of them. Milsom's point is that it was the writ of right that was the first and

---

[53] 'Origins of Property', p. 12.

[54] 'Origins of Property', p. 22.

[55] 'Origins of Property', p. 13-17.

[56] *LFEF*, p. 183; cf. *LFEF*, p. 185: 'All this may have been inevitable from the first interference of the writ patent. Controlling jurisdictions have a habit of taking over the functions they control.'

[57] *LFEF*, p. 181: 'The conclusiveness was the important thing that the writ of right was to destroy. The lord has in fact accepted somebody other than the heir, and taken his homage. The question is not longer closed. It is still closed in the lord's own court, and hence the king's writ with its provision for removal. In the county or the king's court the heir makes his claim, essentially against the lord, as though the question was still open and the tenement still vacant. That it is not vacant is the lord's business: by taking homage he has conferred warranty on the present tenant. But this warranty now carries only a right to compensation if the heir wins: it is no longer the conclusive title to this tenement'.

therefore the most crucial breach in the absolute security the sitting tenant had hitherto enjoyed. But the writ of right went deeper than that. When, as would commonly be the case, the claimant was claiming as heir to an ancestor who had been dispossessed during the Anarchy, this claim was necessarily asserting that the canons of inheritance (the customary rules about who should inherit a tenement) were more than just rules that helped to determine a particular choice of heir by the lord's court: it transformed them into general rules which possessed retrospective force and so determined how the 'right' to a tenement ought to have descended.[58] Here too the effects of the writ of right were crucial and far-reaching. There was a third side-effect, similarly unintended but equally far-reaching. In *Glanvill* we find a rule that no one is obliged to answer for his free tenement without a royal writ and (as will be seen) Professor Milsom suggests that the application of this rule was to have important consequences of its own. Legal historians prior to Milsom had debated whether this rule was of legislative or merely customary origin. Milsom, however, suggests that this was not in origin a rule at all but simply a statement of fact. The lord's court would not hear a case against a sitting tenant, but a claimant who had got a writ of right could have his case removed into a court that was not immovably partial against him and would hear his claim.[59] So it was the writ of right and the way that it worked that gave rise to the rule.

Milsom also thinks that in the longer term the assize of Northampton (and the assize of mort d'ancestor which it created) played a major part in the creation of a full independent hereditary right to land: a right in tenants to succeed to land that is no longer seen as dependent on each successive heir's renewal of his homage and admission to the tenement by the lord and his court. This was partly, of course, because the heir could now enforce his right to succeed against a recalcitrant lord through the assize; but as important was the fact that under the rules of the assize of Northampton in most successions the heir would now take possession of the land for himself and did not have to wait for the lord to regrant him his ancestor's land.[60] It is also mainly to the assize that he ascribes the ending of the possibility of testate succession to land, for as he says in *The Legal Framework of English Feudalism:* 'royal justice has made the position of the natural heir extremely

---

[58] *LFEF*, pp. 180-2; *HFCL*, p. 129.

[59] *LFEF*, pp. 57-9.

[60] *LFEF*, p. 109: 'The lord was edged out of the ideas which had grown up around him in consequence of being edged out of his real part. Now the heir does not have to be put in: he goes in by himself, and becomes seised as though the lord had seised him. He begins to look like an owner taking what is already his, rather than just person having some claim that it should be granted to him. His relief begins to look like an irrational tax, and not the premium for a renewal which could thinkably be withheld. And his homage, once the compact from which flowed the obligations of a relationship, becomes a formality consequent upon the automatic devolution of some abstract title . . .'

strong, indefeasible if the original tenant dies seised'.[61] Once the assize of mort d'ancestor was in operation the arrangements made between lord and tenant in the lord's court to the benefit of a third party are no longer proof against the claims of the tenant's heir, for if the tenant has died seised of his tenement the assize on the facts will have to find in his favour. Milsom seems again to regard this as an unintended side-effect of the assize.

It was mainly the assize of novel disseisin that in Professor Milsom's view came eventually to destroy the lord's disciplinary jurisdiction and with it all possibility of the lord resuming the tenant's tenement for a breach of his obligations. The assize was certainly effective, he believes, in its primary purpose of preventing lords dispossessing their tenants at will or without due process. But in practice it went further than that. The first thing to disappear was the lord's ability to disseise the tenant permanently simply for failure to appear and answer the lord's case against him.[62] It is not very clear why he thinks this happened but he seems to regard it as an accidental consequence of the 'rigour' with which the king's courts enforced on seignorial courts 'their own ancient customs of due process'.[63] The disappearance of permanent dispossession as a possibility even after due process and conviction was more complex. In part, he suggests, it was a consequence of a longer-term change in the strength of the homage bond. It came to be seen as inappropriate to punish a tenant by loss of his tenement for certain types of action which had once been seen as good cause for this.[64] But also important was the 'misunderstanding' that came to prevail about the need for a writ before a tenant could be made to answer for his free tenement. By the early thirteenth century this had come to be seen as a rule which could be enforced through the assize of novel disseisin. It was this which ultimately destroyed the lord's right to take 'disciplinary' action against his tenant even for arrears of service, for it came to be held that any action which might be accounted a claim to additional services was something which affected the tenant's free tenement (since it lessened the value of his tenement) and therefore required a writ; and no writ was available which brought such a dispute to the lord's own court.[65] But this did not in practice leave the lord wholly impotent to enforce his right to services other than through the royal writ of customs and services; for what he came to enjoy in the thirteenth

---

[61] *LFEF*, p. 109.

[62] *HFCL*, p. 142: 'Avowed disseisin as an ultimate sanction quickly disappears, and process stops short at some formal sequestration of the tenement'.

[63] 'Past and Future of Judge-Made Law', p. 210: 'The power to get rid of a tenant, for example, finally disappeared because the king's courts would interfere at his instance to enforce upon lords' courts their own ancient customs of due process; and the enforcement was so rigorous that lords contented themselves with lesser means of securing what were now just fixed economic rights in the nature of servitudes.'

[64] *LFEF*, p. 28.

[65] *LFEF*, pp. 29-30.

century was a right of extra-judicial distraint on chattels for services instead, a small recompense for the loss of his 'disciplinary jurisdiction'.[66]

Palmer is not inclined to attribute nearly as much importance to the writ of right as Milsom does. Palmer's view is that the regularisation of the writ was 'an innovation which would have but did not in fact destroy' the truly feudal world. His reasons for this conclusion are not entirely clear. One argument seems to be that the writ did not directly interfere with how the lord's court conducted itself, leaving it free to act as it had always acted; another that the writ long remained a special remedy, solely for those enforcing rights under the 1153 Compromise and without wider uses or implications.[67] In the 'Origins of Property' at least (though not in the earlier article) he is inclined to place much more weight on the assize of mort d'ancestor as initiating the 'regular supervision of feudal courts', though not apparently seeing it (as Milsom does) as doing more than that, helping to break down the network of legal ideas and assumptions characteristic of the truly feudal world.[68] Palmer does, however, agree with Professor Milsom in seeing the origins of the rule that no one is obliged to answer for his free tenement without a royal writ in the factual situation created by proceedings initiated by the writ of right, though he sees it as passing through the stage of being a 'legal custom' before it became a 'rule of law'.[69] And he sees as a crucial moment in the decline of the feudal world the moment (already noticed by Milsom and connected by him with Countess Amice's case in 1200, though not I think given by him the same importance) when it ceases to be possible for a lord, even at the time of succeeding to a lordship, to question the title of the sitting tenants who hold of the lordship in his own court because he needs a writ to do this and such a writ has to go to his own lord.[70]

Milsom has, I think, almost certainly overestimated the degree of independence actually enjoyed by feudal courts prior to the reign of Henry II. From the surviving writs (which can only be a small proportion of those originally issued) and from the evidence of the sole surviving pipe roll of the reign we can be certain that there was a considerable amount of royal interference in the affairs of these supposedly sovereign jurisdictions as early as the reign of Henry I; and surviving writs show the same thing happening though perhaps on a lesser scale in the reigns of his two predecessors also. The *Leges Henrici Primi* shows that 'unjust judgment' as well as 'failure of justice' were already by the middle of Henry I's reign regarded as royal rights, as giving rise to royal jurisdiction; and it seems quite possible that cases were by then

---

[66] *LFEF*, pp. 34-5.
[67] 'Feudal Framework of English Law', pp. 1135-6; 'Origins of Property', p. 13.
[68] 'Origins of Property, p. 18.
[69] 'Origins of Property, pp. 19-21.
[70] 'Feudal Framework of English Law', pp. 1137-40; 'Origins of Property', pp. 22-3.

regularly being transferred to the jurisdiction of local justiciars on the basis of such allegations. It is also worth remembering that Sir Frank Stenton, to whom Milsom acknowledges his indebtedness for the vision of each feudal lordship as a sovereign state in miniature, himself suggested (in *The First Century of English Feudalism*) that decisions which were made in the king's court are likely to have exerted a significant influence on the development of feudal custom generally[71] and noted the existence of legislation on matters of feudal interest which was of general application.[72]

Milsom cites no contemporary evidence to support his view that the tenant at this time enjoyed absolute protection against rival claims during his tenure of a tenement. He suggests that the security of the later copyholder merely preserves what had once been a general rule applicable to all tenants, but it is questionable whether we can really safely look to copyhold tenure to provide us with a privileged insight into the workings of this much older world. Copyhold tenure must have been massively influenced by the introduction and large-scale use of written records; and the security that the copyhold tenant later enjoyed must in part have been the consequence of the existence of the written record of his admission. It also seems likely that the copyholder was ironically the beneficiary of the legal theory that regarded him (and any rival claimant) as at most tenants-at-will of the lord from whom they held; much more theoretically rightless than the free tenant ever was. Nor do I think Milsom can be correct in his suggestion that the admission of a tenant was regarded as conclusive because it was thought of as a judgment of the lord's court; and such judgments were final and irreversible. The finality of a 'judgment' which the court gave after litigation between parties seems to come from the 'judgment of God' that precedes the judgment (for how can God change his mind?). The admission of a tenant did not involve any such method of proof. There was also another good reason for distinguishing between such an admission and a final judgment. A final judgment was normally only given after two parties had litigated over the matter for a period of time and had thus given any third party ample opportunity to put in a claim. This was not the case with the admission of a tenant.

---

[71] Stenton, *First Century of English Feudalism*, p. 33: 'On innumerable occasions in the Norman period the king must have been compelled to consult with his barons about the disposal of escheated fiefs, the marriage of heiresses, or the settlement of conflicting claims to large estates. The lines along which he acted must have governed the whole of English feudal practice . . .'

[72] Stenton, *First Century of English Feudalism*, p. 37: 'It was only with the consent of a body similar to this in composition, though far more numerous, that the king could legislate on matters of feudal interest. It is not strange that traces of such legislation are hard to find . . . within the sphere of feudal law, the men who had approved a definition or an innovation were themselves immediately responsible for carrying it into effect. No decision affecting, for example, the rules of succession to lands held by military tenure could have been reached in the king's court without the consent of the baronage as a whole, nor could it have been carried out

Nor does there seem to be any real reason for supposing that the custom of such courts, just because it was custom, was necessarily weaker or less binding on those courts than the rules of law of the 'law and custom of England' later proved to be for the king's courts: both were in effect unwritten systems of customary law, able perhaps as a consequence to change and develop more easily than a fully written system, but no less binding for their flexible nature. And it seems unlikely that lords had a free choice as to whether they would or would not observe custom. Here indeed political realities must have played a part (though not quite as large a part as is assigned to them by Professor Palmer). Any display of will that simply disregarded the customs was a threat to all the lord's other tenants and might be expected to incur the disapproval of the lord's neighbours as well.

The argument that it was only the survival of a view of inheritance which saw it as a series of renewable life estates that can explain the failure of the representative principle in inheritance to become established in England before the late twelfth century ignores the fact that there are other equally good explanations for this. It might also be said that, even when the fully heritable fee simple had on Milsom's view become established, it remained true that for various purposes the only heir who really 'counted' was the heir who actually inherited. This we can see, for example, in the rules about inheritance by the half-blood which formed part of the canons of inheritance down to the nineteenth century.

The evidence of contemporary charters suggests that Milsom is wrong in supposing that there was only disseisin or the threat of it to act as a weapon to enforce the fulfilment of obligations in the twelfth century. Charters show quite clearly that distraint (both by chattels and by land) existed as an independent, free-standing mechanism for the enforcement of services and other obligations in the twelfth century; and that disseisin was more of an ultimate sanction and only applicable in certain kinds of extreme situation than a regular threat. And it seems to me that the uniform customary process which we see *c.* 1200 is as likely to be a recent product of royal interference (or even of legislation) as an independent creation of customary law.

I turn now to the mechanisms of change and their supposed purpose. If the original purpose of the writ of right was to put back in those dispossessed during the Anarchy one might reasonably expect some evidence of this on the face of the writ itself, some trace of it in the very words of the writ (if only the kinds of trace that Milsom thinks he sees in the writ of novel disseisin). But there is none. The wording of the writ suggests that it was framed with a general, not a specific, purpose in mind. Nor is the evidence of the form of count that speaks of an ancestor's seisin in the reign of Henry I on the day that king was alive and dead convincing evidence about the original purpose for which the writ was invented, for it looks as though the count in this form

unless individual barons had been prepared to apply it to concrete cases in the courts of their respective honours . . . '

was in fact a recent introduction at the time of the earliest plea-rolls and a consequence of a recent change in limitation dates. If we look at the two counts in *Glanvill* in actions which allow the plaintiff to base his claim on ancestral seisin (those in the writ *precipe* for land and in the writ *precipe* for an advowson) (there is no count given for the writ of right itself), we find that the author in both cases allows the plaintiff to make a claim simply on the seisin of his ancestor in the reign of Henry I (as well as in the reign of Henry II).[73] Many of the counts on the earliest plea-rolls, as enrolled, also simply speak of seisin in the reign of Henry I; and it may well be that some or all of these were in cases which had been started before a change in limitation date and to which the new rule (which did not allow the plaintiff to go back beyond the death of Henry I) did not therefore apply.

In any case, neither Milsom nor Palmer explain how what they see as a remedy intended originally solely for the use of those who had been put out during the Anarchy came to be used much more widely than this. Its use for claims based on seisin during Henry II's reign on their view of the origins of the writ of right represents a major extension and major transformation of the purview of the remedy. Any such extension must surely have been the product of a conscious decision to that effect. Even if we accept their view of the writ's origins it must still have been this decision (which in effect turned the action of right into a permanent feature of the legal landscape), rather than the decision to introduce a form of litigation that gave a remedy to those ejected during the Anarchy (which constituted at most a temporary irruption into the otherwise sovereign world of the feudal lordship), which was the crucial one in bringing an end to the world of the sovereign lordship; and it is this crucial decision which remains unexplained. It seems much more likely that the writ of right from its very inception as a standardised form of writ (and remedy) was intended to be used in a much wider range of circumstances: perhaps for a wide variety of kinds of claim made in lords' courts and not even exclusively for claims based on ancestral seisin. It seems likely that it became fixed as part of the legal landscape early in Henry II's reign: perhaps accidentally through the prevalence of temporary measures protecting seisin while the king was out of the country which excluded from the kinds of disseisin forbidden those authorised by royal writ, perhaps more deliberately and directly through the imposition of a requirement of a royal writ in land litigation.

Nor are the arguments for an exclusively seignorial original orientation of the assize of novel disseisin wholly convincing. The first point is a negative one, about what the writ does not say. The writ does not say that the plaintiff has complained that he has been disseised of the 'free tenement which he holds or claims to hold of the defendant (or one of the defendants)', although such a phrase could easily have been inserted if this was indeed the case, the situation for which the remedy was invented. This is in marked

---

[73] *Glanvill*, ed. Hall, II, 3; IV, 6 (pp. 23, 46).

contrast to the writ of right, which does indeed specify that the plaintiff claims to hold the land of the addressee of the writ. 'Unjustly and without a judgment' is not a phrase that points exclusively to the lord as chief or sole defendant: and indeed on Milsom's reading of this phrase the 'unjustly' would be superfluous, since for him the real target was lords who disseised without obtaining a proper judgment. And in a world that was not as wholly seignorial as Professor Milsom suggests there were surely others as well as lords who could disseise by judgment. It seems more probable that the phrase was intended simply to ensure that the assize was not used to remedy supposedly unjust judgments: for them some separate form of action specifically alleging a false judgment had been given was to continue to be necessary. The order to the sheriff to reseise the tenement of the chattels taken in it certainly would have made sense in the context of proceedings in a seignorial court where there had previously been distraint by chattels and the chattels were still in the lord's custody (though the wording of the writ suggests a reference to chattels taken at the time of the disseisin or since rather than chattels taken beforehand as Milsom's argument requires); but it is equally likely to make sense in the case of a dispute between neighbours where the disseisor might well have taken crops off the land to store in his own barn or taken animals to keep with his. Only the possessor in really bad faith, the land thief, is likely to have disposed of the chattels or immediately consumed them, and the assize was clearly intended to deal with other kinds of disseisor as well as him. The failure to specify the amount of land involved in the writ (which is not unique to novel disseisin, since it is also a feature of the writ of dower *unde nichil habet*) can be interpreted as Milsom interprets it; but can equally well (and perhaps rather better) be seen as a feature intended to ensure that the remedy is as non-technical and favourable to the plaintiff as it is possible to make it. He is not to be denied a remedy for failure to specify the correct quantity of land in his writ (and may even be able to use the same writ to seek a remedy for a disseisin which has taken place between the date of getting the writ and hearing of the assize). As for the provision in the writ for the summons of the bailiff if the lord cannot be found, it is rather surprising (on Milsom's understanding of the significance of this clause) that the bailiff is not invariably to be summoned along with his master. And again the more likely explanation of the clause seems to be that indeed the assumption was that the defendant might well have a bailiff (as did many, perhaps most, landowners); but that the main reason he is mentioned is because of the speed with which it was intended hearings should take place, which rendered it desirable that an absent defendant should regularly have someone who might answer for him. Nor am I any happier with Professor Palmer's views on the original purpose of the assize. It seems to me highly unlikely that it started as a specific remedy against disseisins that violated the 1153 Compromise (indeed I'm not entirely convinced that the latter had any private law component or consequences).

I think it to be more likely that the underlying purpose of the assize of novel disseisin was from the first a public order one and that it was confined to 'free tenements' and 'free tenants' because this marked the limit of the area within which serious public order considerations might arise as also the limit of the area within which it was felt that the king might reasonably undertake measures. To undertake to police disseisins of unfree tenants was to interfere in an area beyond the king's competence. It is also significant that the king offered litigants a remedy which offered them from the first and automatic right to trial by jury as well as a swift hearing of their case. Both features were attractive to litigants, and it is difficult not to see the king as engaged in a policy of deliberately attracting litigation to his courts, perhaps not so much as a hostile act against feudal courts, undercutting their power and influence, as a deliberate attempt to build up the business of royal courts, for the prestige and authority this brought him. It also seems not unreasonable in the light of other measures during the reign to see the king and his advisers as embarking on a deliberate policy of expanding the areas where jury trial, as opposed to trial by battle and compurgation, was the method of proof to decide litigation: attempting gradually to extend the areas where more rational methods of proof prevailed.

With the assize of mort d'ancestor my main queries are about the underlying motivation of the changes. It is difficult to believe that the assize of Northampton had drastic, but quite unintended effects on the way inheritance worked. There are two possibilities here: that genuine inheritance was already in practice established prior to 1176, so that the changes in the procedures by which the tenant entered his tenement when he was an adult already in the tenement changed nothing but the legal form; or (and I think this is less likely) that the assize really did change what happened in a significant way and that it was intended to. Reducing the lord's role in inheritance cannot have been a major change that was accidental and unintended. There must also be some significance in the fact that the king was here again offering a remedy that in practice brought business to a royal court; and was offering jury trial as the automatic mode of proof. Palmer's views seem to be based on a strained and implausible reading of the assize of Northampton which exclude the adult heir from its provisions and also on unrealistic suppositions about the likelihood of most tenants by knight service being willing to turn out and fight for their lords.

In general I find it much less difficult than Professors Milsom and Palmer do to see Henry II as a man who may have had an underlying anti-feudal bias. Historians have had no difficulty in seeing him as having one when it comes to the control of castles; why not in the matter of legal jurisdiction? A king who was simply interested in ensuring that feudal courts operated according to their own assumptions and customs would surely have simply made it easier for plaintiffs to remove litigation (or decisions) out of lords' courts into royal courts. He would not have acted (as he did in the case of the two assizes) to ensure that litigants had to initiate litigation in the king's court.

Milsom's suggestion as to the origins of the rule about no tenant being obliged to answer for his free tenement without the king's writ does not convince either. The rule in its earliest known form is not quite as broadly formulated as Milsom seems to suggest. As stated by *Glanvill* (the earliest known statement of the rule; subsequent statements give it in a more general form) it says that no one is obliged to answer *in the court of his lord* for his free tenement without a writ of the king or his chief justiciar. It was almost certainly true, of course, that no litigant would answer without such a writ elsewhere, but this was because it was the general rule that no litigation of any kind could be initiated in the king's court without a royal writ. But the precise formulation of the rule as given in *Glanvill* clearly envisages that provided the plaintiff has a royal writ the defendant will answer *in the lord's court* rather than elsewhere; so, assuming that *Glanvill's* formulation preserves the rule in its original form, we can be certain that it cannot have started as a simple factual statement about the fact that the lord's court will not entertain such litigation and that the king's writ is needed to ensure that the defendant has to answer the plea elsewhere.

Nor I think can Milsom be right in suggesting that the destruction of the power of testation with regard to land by the assize of mort d'ancestor was accidental for we know from *Glanvill* that there was legislation to exempt land held by burgage tenure in towns from the purview of the assize.[74] The most likely explanation of this exemption is that it was intended to preserve that feature which is characteristic of burgage custom in the thirteenth century, a more or less extensive ability to leave land by will.

This essay has examined only some of the main ideas of Professor Milsom. There are several other topics on which Milsom and Palmer both have interesting ideas e.g. on the origins of writs *precipe* and writs of entry which equally merit discussion. But I hope that in this essay I have made comprehensible (and not in the process too badly distorted) what I take to be some of the major themes of more general interest in their work. I hope I have also shown why, although Milsom and Palmer have to be read and taken seriously, it would be wrong to suppose that they are necessarily right, that their work represents a new orthodoxy to which all English legal historians interested in the beginnings of the common law must now subscribe. Their vision is a compelling one and one that has the merit of great internal consistency; but it must be doubted whether that vision necessarily corresponds in its entirety to the twelfth century reality.

---

[74] *Glanvill*, XIII, 11 (ed. Hall, p. 155).

10

Formedon in the Remainder before De Donis

It was over three-quarters of a century ago that the great legal historian F. W. Maitland first showed that there were good reasons for suspecting that the then orthodox doctrine (a doctrine whose origins dated back at least to the time of Coke, if not beyond) that it was only after the enactment in 1285 of cap. 1 of the statute of Westminister II ("de donis conditionalibus"), and as an indirect result of the reduction effected by that statute of the estate of the tenant granted land to hold to himself and the heirs of his body from a "fee simple conditional" to a "fee tail", that it became possible to create legally valid remainders after such conditional fees, was mistaken. The evidence on which he relied was, however, all of an indirect kind: the fact that such a remainder had come before a court as early as 1220 and that the court had to all appearances not been shocked by it; Bracton's word that a grant could be made to A and the heirs of his body and on failure of such heirs to B and the heirs of his body, and on failure of such heirs to C and the heirs of his body, and, elsewhere, that a remainderman in possession will have an "exception" to protect his seisin, and that a remainderman out of seisin will have a special writ (which, however, he fails to give) to recover his seisin, founded on the form of the gift; the fact that final concords purporting to create remainders after conditional fees were comparatively common as early as the late 1260s, and that the draftsmen of such concords must have known what they were doing, and cannot be thought to have been "devising futilities"; the fact that as soon as the Year-Books begin, in the early 1290s, such remainders were already being treated as a very natural thing, and that by the first decade of the fourteenth century, the remainderman was enjoying as full a measure of protection under the statute as the reversioner. Maitland had, however, to admit that direct evidence for the acceptance of the validity of such remainders before 1285 had eluded him: he had "looked through a good many plea rolls" but found no instance of a writ of formedon in the remainder being brought before 1285. Although quite certain that the action, when it developed, was "the outcome of pure common law doctrine and the practice of conveyancers", and nothing to do with the statute, the conclusive evidence to prove his point eluded him (*1*).

(*1*) F. Pollock and F. W. Maitland, *History of English Law,* 2nd edition (Cambridge, 1898), ii. 21-29. See also F. W. Maitland, "Remainders after Conditional Fees", in his *Collected Papers,* vol. ii (Cambridge, 1911), 174-181.

Subsequently, in 1941, W. H. Humphreys printed in the *Cambridge Law Journal* a specimen writ from a register of writs that dated from a few years before 1285 that he took to be a writ of formedon in the remainder; and this seemed to provide the evidence that had eluded Maitland to prove that there had existed a remedy for the remainderman at common law before the statute of 1285 (*2*). Almost immediately, however, doubt was cast on whether the writ Humphreys had printed really was intended for the use of a remainderman after a conditional fee, the suggestion being that it may have been intended for the use of the survivor of two joint tenants in tail (*3*); and subsequent writers on the subject seem to have shared this initial sceptical reaction, at least to the extent of not regarding the matter as definitively settled by the writ in question (*4*).

More recently, S. F. C. Milsom, in a wide-ranging article on the use of the various types of formedon writ before 1285, has again argued for the existence of formedon in the remainder before 1285, though this time on the basis of passages in *Casus Placitorum, Britton* and *Fleta*; but he too, like Maitland, was forced to admit that he had found no actual examples of actions of formedon in the remainder being brought in the courts before 1285, the only really conclusive evidence that the interest of the remainderman was protected at common law before that date (*5*).

The four plea-roll entries here printed (*6*) at last supply the missing evidence, and show how the action developed. The first two entries, of cases from 1257 and 1262, show remaindermen being allowed by the courts and by chancery to use the formulae of the writ of formedon in the reverter, historically the oldest of the formedon writs, to make their claims. The next case, from 1279, shows a remainderman being allowed, equally incongruously, to use the writ of formedon in the descender. The final case, also from 1279, shows the eventual emergence, two decades after the first action brought by a remainderman, of a writ specially framed for his situation, the writ of formedon in the remainder.

I

Just/1/567 m. 42: Norfolk eyre, 1257

Radulfus de Richild et Idonea uxor ejus petunt versus Petrum de Musters et Cristianam uxorem ejus unum mesuagium et sexdecim acras terre cum pertinenciis in Randeworth, Pinkesford et Pestewyk (*7*) ut jus

---

(*2*) W. H. Humphreys, "Formedon en Remainder at Common Law", *Cambridge Law Journal,* vii, 238-242.

(*3*) S. J. Bailey, "Warranties of Land in the Thirteenth Century", *Cambridge Law Journal,* viii, 274-299 at 275 n. 7.

(*4*) S. F. C. Milsom, "Formedon before *De Donis*", *Law Quarterly Review,* lxxii (1956), 391-397 at 391; T. F. T. Plucknett, *Concise History of the Common Law,* 5th edn. (1956), 561, n. 2; G. D. G. Hall in *Early Registers of Writs,* Selden Soc. vol. lxxxvii (1970), p. cxxxv.

(*5*) Milsom, *art. cit.,* 391-2.

(*6*) These transcripts of Crown-copyright records in the Public Record Office London appear by permission of the Controller of Her Majesty's Stationery Office.

(*7*) Ranworth, Panxworth, and Postwick, Norfolk.

ipsius Idonee (*8*) etc., que idem Petrus dedit Reginaldo filio Margerie et heredibus de corpore suo procurandis (*9*), et que ad ipsam Idoneam (*10*) reverti debent post mortem predicti Reginaldi per formam donacionis quam dictus Petrus eidem Reginaldo inde fecit. Et unde predicti Radulfus et Idonea dicunt quod cum dictus Petrus dedisset predicto Reginaldo predicta mesuagium et terram, ita quod si predictus Reginaldus obiisset sine herede de se, vivente predicta Idonea, idem mesuagium et terra reverti debent ad predictam Idoneam habenda et tenenda eidem Idonee et heredibus suis inperpetuum per cartam ipsius Petri quam profert et que hoc testatur, predictus Petrus contra formam donacionis sue post mortem predicti Reginaldi intrusit se in predictam terram etc.

Et Petrus et Cristiana veniunt et dicunt quod non possunt ad hoc breve respondere, quia dicunt quod non tenent (*11*) integre predicta tenementa versus eos petita. Dicunt enim quod quedam Alicia que fuit uxor Reginaldi filii Radulfi tenet medietatem predicti mesuagii et tenuit die quo breve suum fuit inpetratum. Et Radulfus et Idonea (*12*) non possunt hoc dedicere. Ideo consideratum est quod predicti Petrus et Cristiana inde sine die; et Radulfus et Idonea nichil capiant per breve istud et sint in misericordia pro falso clamore. Et perquirant sibi per aliud breve si voluerint etc (*13*).

II

Just/1/912A m. 6: Sussex eyre, 1262

Alicia filia Johannis de Bradbrig' petit versus Willelmum de Brade-brig' duas acras terre cum pertinenciis in Bradebrig' (*14*), quas Johannes de Bradebrig' dedit Edeline de Wyntreburne (*15*) et que ad ipsam Aliciam reverti debent post mortem ejusdem Edeline per formam donacionis quam dictus Johannes eisdem Edeline et Alicie inde fecit etc. Et unde dicit quod predictus Johannes de Bradebrig' dedit predictam terram cuidam Rogero Eldkinge (*16*) in liberum maritagium cum predicta Edelina de Wyntreburne habendam et tenendam eisdem Rogero et Edeline tota vita ipsorum Rogeri et Edeline (*17*), et post mortem utriusque ipsorum Rogeri et Edeline

---

(*8*) Interlined above *Jordani,* marked for deletion.

(*9*) *Sic.* in Ms. for *procreandis.*

(*10*) Followed in Ms. by *pertinet,* marked for deletion.

(*11*) Ms. *tenentar,* with the last two letters marked for deletion.

(*12*) Interlined above *Cristiana,* marked for deletion.

(*13*) In the next eyre on the same circuit, the Suffolk eyre of 1257-8, the same demandants brought a further action by an unspecified writ against the same tenants for two-thirds of a messuage and fourteen acres in the same three villages, and the tenants sought a view of the land claimed (Just/1/820 m. 32). They were subsequently non-suited in what seems to be the same case in the Bench at Michaelmas 1258 (K.B. 26/160 m. 29d).

(*14*) Broad Bridge, in Bosham, Sussex.

(*15*) Ms. *Wynteburne.*

(*16*) Ms. *Eldkingt.*

(*17*) It seems reasonable to assume that the grant, like other grants in frankmarriage, was one to Roger and Edelina and the heirs of their bodies, and that it was only if and because they failed to have such heirs that they held only for their lives.

reverterentur predicte due acre terre cum pertinenciis cuidam Nicholao filio predicti Johannis de Bradebrig' et predicte Alicie sorori ejus (*18*) que nunc petit habende et tenende ipsis Nicholao et Alicie et heredibus suis de legitimo conjugio (*19*) procreatis inperpetuum. Et dicit quod predictus Nicholaus frater ipsius Alicie obiit sine herede de se, et ea racione petit ipsa predictam terram per formam donacionis predicte. Et profert quamdam cartam sub nomine predicti Johannis de Bradebrig' que formam donacionis predicte ut predictum est testatur etc.

Et Willelmus venit; et concordati sunt per licenciam. Et est concordia talis quod predictus Willelmus recognoscit predictam terram esse jus ipsius Alicie et illam ei reddidit. Et pro hac etc. eadem Alicia dabit eidem Willelmo unam marcam, unde reddet ei ad Pascha anno quadragesimo septimo dimidiam marcam et ad festum sancti Michaelis proximo sequens dimidiam marcam. Et nisi fecerit concedit quod vicecomes faciat de terris etc.

III

Just/1/1066 m. 34d: Yorkshire eyre, 1279-1281 (Trinity term 1279)

Cumbr'. Theophania filia Avicie Werry et Margareta soror ejus petunt versus Willelmum de la More et Agnetem uxorem ejus viginti acras terre cum pertinenciis in Bampton' (*20*), quas Johannes Werry dedit Willelmo Werry et heredibus de corpore suo exeuntibus et que post mortem ipsius Willelmi ad prefatas Teofaniam et Margaretam descendere debent per formam donacionis predicte, eo quod predictus Willelmus obiit sine herede de (*21*) corpore suo exeunte etc. Et unde dicunt quod predictus Willelmus fuit seisitus de predictis tenementis in dominico suo ut de feodo et jure per feofamentum predicti Johannis tempore pacis tempore domini Henrici regis patris domini regis nunc, capiendo explecia ad valenciam etc., et qui obiit sine herede de corpore suo exeunte; et ea racione descendere debent istis Theophanie et Margarete. Et inde producunt sectam etc.

Et Willelmus et Agnes veniunt; et defendunt jus suum quando etc. Et petunt judicium desicut in brevi specificatur quod quia predictus Willelmus obiit sine herede de se predicta tenementa descendere deberent ipsis Theophanie et Margarete per formam donacionis predicte, et in narracione sua dicunt quod predicta tenementa eis descendere debent quia predictus Willelmus obiit sine herede de se et non per formam donacionis predicte, petunt judicium de variacione brevis et narracionis etc. Et si hoc non sufficit dicent alia.

Dies datus est eis a die sancti Michaelis in unum mensem de audiendo judicio suo (*22*).

(*18*) The last two words are interlined.
(*19*) Followed by *matrimonio* deleted.
(*20*) Kirkbampton, Cumberland.
(*21*) This word is supplied.
(*22*) On the next membrane (m. 35), the same demandants bring an almost identical action against the same tenants for land at Farlam in Cumberland, and the tenants make an almost identical objection to the count used. In this case, however, the

IV

Just/1/1075 m. 18: Yorkshire eyre, 1279-81 (Michaelmas 1279 session) *(23)*

Johannes de Ferlington' petit versus Ricardum de Brewosa et Aliciam uxorem ejus et Willelmum filium eorum manerium de Wyltone in Pykeringelyth' *(24)* cum pertinenciis exceptis quatuordecim bovatis terre in eodem manerio quod Johannes Maunsell' dedit Claricie sorori ejus et heredibus de corpore suo exeuntibus, et quod post mortem ipsius Claricie prefato Johanni de Ferlington' remanere debet per formam donacionis predicte eo quod predicta Claricia obiit sine herede de corpore suo exeunte etc. Et unde dicit quod predictus Johannes Maunsell' fuit seisitus de predicto manerio exceptis predictis quatuordecim bovatis terre in eodem manerio in dominico suo ut de feodo et jure tempore pacis tempore Henrici regis patris domini regis nunc, capiendo inde explecia ad valenciam etc. Et quod idem Johannes dedit predicte Claricie sorori sue et heredibus suis de corpore suo exeuntibus, ita quod si predicta Claricia obieret sine herede de corpore suo procreato vivente predicto Johanne, predictum manerium cum pertinenciis reverteretur predicto Johanni Maunsell' tenendum tota vita ipsius Johannis, et post decessum ipsius Johannis predictum manerium remaneret Sarre uxori Henrici de Ferlington' et heredibus suis *(25)*. Et quia predicta Claricia supervixit predictum Johannem et obiit sine herede de corpore suo procreato *(26)* descendit jus predicti

---

land is said to have been settled by John Werry on one Nicholas Werry and the heirs of his body. On the same membrane is also to be found an action of detinue of charter brought by the two sisters against the prior of Lanercost for the charter by which John Werry had settled the Farlam land on Nicholas "tenendum ipsi Nicholao et heredibus suis de corpore suo exeuntibus, et si idem Nicholaus obierat sine herede de corpore suo exeunte, quod post mortem ipsius Nicholai predicta tenementa descenderent ipsis Theophanie et Margarete", which he is said to be detaining. The prior, however, says he possesses no charter in which they are named, only a charter by which he had enfeoffed Nicholas of the land to himself and his heirs. This issue then goes to a jury. No final outcome is recorded for any of these cases.

(23) Because of its length the county civil pleas of the Yorkshire eyre of 1279-81 as well as the foreign civil pleas were recorded in separate terminal sections on the better-organized rolls. Just/1/1075 is the roll of the chief justice, John de Vaux, and its ascription of this case to Michaelmas 1279 is confirmed by a similar ascription on the roll of one of the other justices, William de Saham, Just/1/1065 m. 21d.

(24) Wilton in the parish of Ellerburn, Yorkshire.

(25) This settlement was effected through a final concord made in the Bench in Easter term 1253 between John Maunsel and his sister Clarice, here called Clarice de Childewyk': see *Feet of Fines for the County of York, 1246-1272*, ed. J. Parker (Yorkshire Archaeological Society, Record Series, lxxxii (1932)), pp. 90-91. This fine also shows that Sarah was John Maunsel's niece. For the career of Maunsel, one of Henry III's most important and influential counsellors and servants, see *D.N.B. s.v.* Maunsel.

(26) On Maunsel's death the manor was seized into the king's hands, but restored to Clarice by a royal mandate to the sheriff of Yorkshire of 16 November 1265 which cited not only the fine but also a subsequent royal confirmation of it: *Close Rolls, 1264-1268*, p. 220. Clarice and her husband, Geoffrey de Childewik', had then lost the manor by default in the Yorkshire eyre of 1268 to Richard de Braose and Alice, who were impleading them by a writ of escheat. This default was not collusive, for Clarice and Geoffrey did their best to heal it: Just/1/1056 mm. 10d. 53.

manerii predicte Sarre per formam donacionis predicte, et de predicta
Sarra isti Johanni qui nunc petit ut filio et heredi. Et inde producit sectam
etc.

Et Ricardus et Alicia et Willelmus per attornatum ipsius Alicie
veniunt. Et predictus Willelmus dicit quod ipse tenet predictum manerium
de dono predictorum Ricardi et Alicie, et vocat eos inde ad warantum;
qui eis warantizant. Et defendunt jus ipsius Johannis de Ferlington (27)
etc. Et dicunt quod idem (28) Johannes nichil juris clamare potest in
predicto manerio per formam donacionis predicte, quia dicunt quod
predicta Claricia nuncquam aliquam seisinam habuit de predicto manerio
per predictum donum sibi factum per predictum Johannem, nec idem
Johannes uncquam statum suum mutavit. Et de hoc ponunt se super
patriam. Et Johannes similiter. Ideo fiat inde jurata.

Juratores de consensu parcium electi dicunt super sacramentum
suum quod predictus Johannes Maunsell (29) nuncquam se demisit de
predicto manerio nec statum suum inde mutavit, ita quod predicta
Claricia liberum tenementum vel separalem seisinam in eodem manerio
habuit. Et ideo consideratum est quod predicti Ricardus et Alicia inde
sine die; et Johannes nichil capiat per juratam istam set sit in misericordia
pro falso clamore (30).

---

(27) The last four words are interlined above *suum quando* which are marked for deletion.
(28) This word is interlined above *predictus,* which is marked for deletion.
(29) This word is interlined.
(30) A *postea,* subsequently added to the roll, records a royal mandate to the justices,
dated 4 December 1280, ordering them to send the record and process in this case
to two other royal justices, Nicholas de Stapleton and John de Reygate, and the
justices' compliance with this mandate. Subsequent evidence suggests that this
was probably connected with a writ of attaint which the demandant subsequently
brought against the jurors in this case, which was terminated by agreement between
the parties under which the demandant quitclaimed any right he might have to the
land: C.P. 40/70 m. 21. However, in Trinity term 1285, the tenants were again
impleaded for the manor, this time by Roger Bigod, earl of Norfolk, who claimed
that at his death John Maunsel, who had been a bastard and died without heirs
of his body, had held the manor of Roger's dead uncle, and namesake, also earl of
Norfolk, whose heir he was, and that it should therefore have escheated to him. The
Braose family in defence claimed that the manor had in fact been granted to John
Maunsel by Alice's grandfather, whose heir she was, and that he had died her
tenant. The verdict of the jury, given a year later, was that it was indeed true that
Maunsel was originally enfeoffed by Alice's grandfather, but that he had been
impeded from taking seisin of the manor until he had agreed to hold the land under
a new charter, under which he was to hold the manor directly of the earl, Alice's
grandfather's lord, and that at the time of his death he was holding the manor
directly of the earl: C.P. 40/59 m. 81d. An attempt by John de Ferlington in Hilary
term 1288 to recover the manor from the earl, relying on the fine of 1253 for his
title, failed: the earl successfully pleading the verdict of the jury in the 1279 case
that Clarice de Childewyk', the supposed grantee under the fine of 1253, had never
been seised of the manor, and also John's subsequent quitclaim to the Braoses:
C.P. 40/70 m. 21. An attempt by the Braoses in the Yorkshire eyre of 1293-4 to
reverse the 1286 verdict was also unsuccessful: Just/1/1090 m. 13.

11

The Control of Mortmain Alienation
in England, 1200-1300

My object in this paper is to examine the different methods used during the century between 1200 and 1300 for the control of the alienation of land into mortmain:[1] that is to say, to control the sale or gift of land and other forms of real property[2] by laymen to religious houses (such as abbeys, priories and hospitals) or to the incumbents or holders of ecclesiastical dignities or benefices (such as archbishops, bishops, canons, rectors of parish churches, and chantry priests), when such grants were made to themselves and to their ecclesiastical successors.[3] My concern will be with the different types of control exercised originally by lords, and subsequently jointly by lords and the Crown, over alienations into mortmain which took the form of subinfeudations, grants under which the ecclesiastical grantee became the feudal tenant of the grantor and only a sub-tenant of that grantor's lord: since, although it is clear that it was possible by the early thirteenth century for such an alienation to be by way of substitution rather than subinfeudation, the grantee becoming a tenant of the grantor's lord rather than of the grantor himself, it seems virtually certain that transactions of this nature always required the active co-operation of that lord in order to become effective, and were therefore always under their full and effective control.[4]

---

1 For previous discussion of this subject see, in particular, F. Pollock and F.W. Maitland, *History of English Law before the reign of Edward I* (2nd ed., Cambridge, 1898), i, 329-49; T.F.T. Plucknett, *Legislation of Edward I* (2nd ed., Oxford, 1962), 94-102; J.M.W. Bean, *The Decline of English Feudalism* (Manchester, 1968), 40-66.

2 E.g. advowsons, rent-charges, or rights of common.

3 Alienation by sale or gift to such secular ecclesiastics in a private capacity — grants to them and their heirs, rather than to them and their successors — were not regarded as alienations in mortmain, since they were indistinguishable in legal consequences from grants to laymen.

4 Alienation by way of substitution was already in use in John's reign, and Bracton specifically states that a lord can be forced to accept the homage and service of such a substituted tenant: Pollock and Maitland, *History of English Law*, i, 345. Later evidence, however, suggests that the lord could not be forced to accept the homage of such a substituted tenant, and could continue to avow for services on his original tenant if he had not accepted homage from the substitute: see *Bissemede* v. *Bordelys* (1277) CP 40/23, m.19d; *Alinchecote* v. *Aumale* (1286) CP 40/63, m.55. Note also the clear statement made in 1256 in the court of the abbot of Ramsey to a tenant who wished to make just such an arrangement: 'quod non potest ita homagium suum et tenementum predictum

It is reasonably clear that in the twelfth century it was a generally accepted customary rule in England that no alienation of real property of any importance (and almost all mortmain alienations would belong to this category) could or should be made without obtaining the consent of the lord of whom that property was held.[1] This may simply reflect the close social relationship which still existed between most lords and their tenants in this period: it was socially, as much as legally, unthinkable for a tenant to act in such a matter without the advice and consent of his lord and also of his fellow tenants, meeting together in the lord's court. It may, however, also reflect a very real fear that without such consent being obtained the lord might decide to disseise both grantee and grantor of the property in question, might even take steps to deprive the grantor of his other lands for an action which had tended to the disinheritance of his lord.[2]

What is much less clear is just how far such customary controls over mortmain alienation were still being exercised at the beginning of the thirteenth century. Certainly when in 1203 the prior of Kenilworth impleaded the abbot of Stoneleigh for 'entering his fee' (that is, acquiring land held of the prior by one of his tenants) without his assent and against his will, he claimed that such an action was 'contrary to the custom of the realm',[3] and in 1212 the king's court was willing to entertain litigation brought by William de la Basoche against the prior of Lincoln Hospital for entering his fee without his assent, as also against Adam d'Iseny for selling land of his fee to

---

remittere nec alium loco suo ponere ad homagium faciendum nec ad alia facienda que ad dominum abbatem pertinent sine assensu ipsius abbatis' (*Court Rolls of the Abbey of Ramsey and of the Honour of Clare*, ed. W.O. Ault (New Haven, 1928), 34). Although unambiguous evidence on the point seems lacking from earlier in the century, it is significant that there are no known cases of lords being forced to take the homage of substitute tenants; and, indeed, there seems to have been no form of action by which this could have been achieved. There is no tenant's equivalent to the lord's *per quae servicia* for the attornment of services conveyed by a final concord.

1 Pollock and Maitland, *History of English Law*, i, 343. Maitland notes that Anglo-Norman custom seems to have started from 'some such idea as this, that the tenant may lawfully do anything that does not seriously damage the interests of his lord. He may make reasonable gifts, but not unreasonable. The reasonableness of the gift would be a matter for the lord's court'.

2 Glanvill, ix, 1. Glanvill states that any action on the tenant's part tending to the lord's disinheritance could, as of right, lead to the total disinheritance of the tenant. In 1260 a lord described an alienation in mortmain in exactly these terms: *Prior of Alvecote v. Basset* (1260) JUST 1/456, m.3, Cf. Glanvill, xii, 15, which suggests that it is doubtful whether a tenant could give lands more freely than he himself held them.

3 3 *CRR* 69 (1203). Cf. 2 *CRR* 282 (1203).

the prior without his assent,[1] as if the customary rule was still generally in force. King John's mandate of 1204 in favour of the bishop of London, ordering sheriffs and other local officials to assist the bishop in ensuring that none enter the fee of himself or of his church without his consent, can also, perhaps, be seen merely as lending royal assistance to an old faithful royal servant for the enforcement of a customary right which was by no means obsolete.[2] These are, however, only isolated pieces of evidence and, in so far as they show lords seeking royal assistance for the enforcement of controls, would tend to indicate that purely seignorial controls were breaking down — something that would fit in with other evidence that one of the by-products of Henry II's legal reforms was a general weakening of the powers exercised by lords and their courts.[3]

Some indication of just how far seignorial control of alienation had in practice been weakened by the end of John's reign is provided by two of the clauses added to Magna Carta at the time of its second reissue in 1217.[4] Clause 39 laid down that in future no man was to alienate so large a portion of his tenement that he was unable to perform the services due for the tenement as a whole from the resources left to him in the portion of the tenement which he retained. This was, of course, particularly but not exclusively aimed at alienations in mortmain, since such grants normally reserved only nominal services to the grantor from the grantee.[5] Clause 43 enacted that in future no man was to alienate land to a religious house on condition that the religious house should then grant it back to him — the point of such a transaction being, apparently, to contrive that the grantor's lord's incidental rights would be exercised solely over a valueless seignory, with the religious house enjoying the valuable

---

1 6 *CRR* 342-3 (1212).

2 *Rotuli Litterarum Patentium*, ed. T.D. Hardy (London, 1835), 47. The prohibition was cited in *Bishop of London* v. *Theodoric, son of Edric of Aldgate, and others* (1219) 8 *CRR* 138-9, though it was found not to be applicable as the defendants had purchased the land in question from a sub-tenant rather than a tenant of the bishop. Cf. *Rotuli Litterarum Clausarum*, ed. T.D. Hardy (London, 1833), i, 467.

3 F.W. Maitland, *Select Pleas in Manorial Courts* (2 *SS* 1888) lii-lx; D.W. Sutherland, *The Assize of Novel Disseisin* (Oxford, 1973), 77-86.

4 *Select Charters*, ed. W. Stubbs (9th ed., Oxford, 1913), 343; J.C. Holt, *Magna Carta* (Cambridge, 1965), 356.

5 This clause was rarely cited in pleading, as far as can be discovered from the surviving records. There was an action explicitly based on it brought in the court *coram rege* in Trinity 1273: *Bigge* v. *Maylord* (1273) KB 27/5, m.10. The clause was misquoted in pleading in *Prior of Bricett* v. *Tateshale and others* (1238/39) 3 *BNB* 263-4: 1248.

incidental rights arising out of the demesne tenancy.[1] Alienations of both these kinds were clearly transactions which would have been prevented by any lord who was exercising any real control over his tenants' alienations, so the fact that legislation was now being enacted with the avowed purpose of preventing such alienations clearly indicates that by 1217 there were some lords at least who no longer possessed the power to control them.

It was in the period between the enactment of these two clauses and the enactment of the first general legislation on mortmain alienations in 1259 that Bracton was writing his treatise. This contains the most extreme expression of the movement of judicial opinion favouring freedom of alienation: of what Maitland described as the tendency of the king's justices to concede to every tenant the fullest possible power of dealing with his land.[2] Although in the treatise Bracton acknowledges[3] the constraints on the tenant's freedom to alienate that had been introduced in 1217, and the further constraints introduced by legislation of 1228 prohibiting mortmain alienations by the king's tenants in chief,[4] these are the only constraints that he does recognise as valid. The tenant's alienation may, he says, cause his lord loss but it is not wrongful, not actionable. The condition on which land is granted to a tenant − the motive for the gift expressed in the charter of feoffment − is that the tenant shall perform homage and specified services for the land. As long as these are done the lord has no right to complain if, as a result of an alienation, the incidents of tenure are less valuable than they had been when the land was first granted to the tenant.[5] The treatise does, however, provide indirect evidence that even at the time Bracton was writing lords were attempting in various ways to protect their interests against damaging alienations. One such way was to prevent the alienee from ever taking seisin of the land he had been granted:[6] a method which, as long as the lord acted immediately at the time of the attempted transfer of seisin and was always prepared to return the land to its previous tenant, was in

---

1 Maitland, however, thought that the point of the transaction was to allow the tenant in question to claim immunity under the charters of a favoured religious body from various burdens, not necessarily from services as such: Pollock and Maitland, *History of English Law*, i, 333, n. 6.

2 Ibid., 344.

3 Bracton, iii, 35, 37 (ff. 168v, 169v).

4 *CR 1227-31*, 88. This legislation is discussed in Bean, *Decline of English Feudalism*, 58.

5 Bracton, ii, 140-2 (ff. 45v-6). Cf. iii, 274 (f. 263v).

6 Bracton says this is wrongful because the lord has no right to enter the land (which he must do to prevent the new tenant gaining seisin): ii, 141 (f. 46).

practice recognised as being a valid exercise of seignorial power by the king's courts from 1247 onwards.[1] The other method, for which there is also some, rather later, evidence (from the honour court of Lewes in 1266),[2] was that of summoning the alienee to the lord's court to show why he had entered his fee without his permission and to his damage: a procedure presumably intended to secure, at the least, some pecuniary compensation from the unlicensed alienee.[3] There is also further evidence from this period of the king helping lords to control alienations within their fees. In 1235 Westminster Abbey received a royal charter including a clause prohibiting anyone entering the abbey's fee save with the abbot's assent,[4] and the abbot may have been entitled to the assistance of royal officials in enforcing this. From 1243 onwards there are enrolled on the Close Rolls various prohibitions issued on behalf of favoured religious houses or individuals against all other (or sometimes only named other) religious houses entering their fees without their permission. These specifically authorise sheriffs and other royal officers to assist them in enforcing the prohibition.[5] That such prohibitions could, if necessary, be enforced not only by local executive action but also by litigation in the king's court, is shown by a writ on the Close Rolls in 1256 summoning the prior of Luffield to answer in the court *coram rege* for the breach of such a prohibition in purchasing land held of the Hospital of St John the Baptist, Oxford.[6] This writ is of particular interest not only because it is noted on the roll as having been authorised by, among others, Bracton himself,[7] but also because it appears to refer to general

---

1 See the cases cited by Sutherland, *Assize of Novel Disseisin*, 90-4; and *Prior of Caldwell* v. *Swynheved* (1247) JUST 1/4, m.5 (Bedfordshire eyre).

2 *Records of the Barony and Honour of the Rape of Lewes*, ed. A.J. Taylor (64 Sussex Record Soc., 1939), 25. Cf. ibid., 29, 33. The entry records the attachment of the prior of Sele to answer the lord of the court, Earl Warenne, for having entered the earl's fee without his consent.

3 Bracton, ii, 141-2 (f. 46). See also 12*CRR*, no. 1137.

4 *Calendar of Charter Rolls*, i, 209.

5 E.g. *CR 1242-7*, 50-1 (a prohibition in favour of the abbot of Westminster against the abbot of Pershore, 1243); ibid., 377 (a general prohibition on behalf of the abbot of Westminster, 1245); ibid., 404 (a prohibition on behalf of the abbot of Reading against the abbot of Boxley in connection with the abbot's fee at Hoo, Kent, 1246); *CR 1251-3*, 498 (a prohibition on behalf of William FitzHerbert while on the king's service in Gascony, 1253).

6 *CR 1254-6*, 400. The prohibition involved is probably that of 1255 (ibid., 124) which specifically forbade the entry of the prior of Luffield or any other religious into the hospital's fee. It was the last of a series of such prohibitions: *CR 1251-3*, 52, 106, 478.

7 The fact that neither the case nor the principle involved are referred to by Bracton in his treatise is relevant to a consideration of the dating and authorship of that treatise.

legislation already then in existence requiring all mortmain alienations to religious houses to have the consent of the lord of whom the land in question was held.[1] There is, however, no other evidence for this legislation.[2]

Such legislation, if indeed it ever existed, and the other controls exercised by lords, were clearly considered inadequate by those responsible for clause 10 of the Petition of the Barons of 1258, which sought a remedy not against mortmain alienations generally but more specifically against alienations in mortmain to religious houses made without lords' consent and which led to losses of wardships, marriages, reliefs and escheats.[3] That the complaint was limited to mortmain alienations to religious houses is evidence that the objection was not just economic or financial in origin, but was also symptomatic of a more general prejudice against the further accumulation of wealth by the old-established religious houses.[4] This complaint led, in 1259, to the enactment (as clause 14 of the Provisions of Westminster) of legislation requiring that all religious houses[5] in future should have the consent of the lord of whom lands were held before entering their fee — the first general mortmain legislation.[6]

Somewhat surprisingly, perhaps, the legislation seems to have been cited very little during the next three years, the period during which it was nominally in force: it was used once in an action by plaint in the special Warwickshire eyre of 1260,[7] and once cited by the justices in making a judgment in an assize of novel disseisin the same year.[8] Thereafter no use was made of it and it is difficult to resist the conclusion that this was because in practice, for political reasons, it was regarded as of no effect. It was also for political reasons (Henry III's need for the support of the Church) that it alone of the twenty-four clauses of the Provisions of Westminster was dropped when the Provisions were re-enacted by the king, now once again in

---

1 '. . . cum . . . provisum est et communiter statutum in regno nostro quod nullus vir religiosus feodum alicuius ingrediatur sine assensu et voluntate sua'.

2 Bean, *Decline of English Feudalism*, 61, suggests that this is a distorted reference to clause 43 of the 1217 Magna Carta. Alternatively, it might refer to the common usage of the realm rather than to specific legislation.

3 *Select Charters*, ed. Stubbs, 375.

4 Cf. S. Wood, *English Monasteries and their Patrons in the Thirteenth Century* (Oxford, 1955), 80.

5 The phrase 'viris religiosis' is probably intended to exclude secular clergy.

6 *CR 1259-61*, 149.

7 *Clinton* v. *Preceptor of Temple Balsall* (1260) JUST 1/953, m.6d. The legislation is not specifically cited in this case.

8 *Prior of Alvecote* v. *Basset* (1260) JUST 1/456, m.3.

control of the country, in January 1263; and kept it out of the subsequent re-issues of the Provisions, by the king in June 1263,[1] by the Montfortian regime in December 1264,[2] and by the king again in 1267 as part of the Statute of Marlborough.[3]

It is of some interest to note that, although tacitly repealed in 1263, clause 14 of the Provisions of Westminster appears to have enjoyed a vigorous after-life. In November 1264 it was cited by a litigant in an assize of novel disseisin and accepted, both by his opponent and by the justices hearing the case, as still being in force.[4] This was under the Montfortian 'baronialist' regime which ruled England after the battle of Lewes and before the re-issue of the Provisions in December 1264 which omitted this clause: that is, during a period when it would have been quite plausible to have argued that it was the original baronial Provisions of 1259 (which included the relevant clause) that were in force, rather than the revised royalist version of the Provisions as re-issued in 1263 (which omitted it). Much more curiously, there is a case on the Bench plea-roll for Michaelmas 1277,[5] which was brought allegedly under a clause of the Statute of Marlborough whose wording is identical to that of clause 14 of the 1259 Provisions, and the writ used in this case was enrolled the following year on the Close Roll.[6] Nor is this an isolated phenomenon. In a case heard during the course of the Yorkshire eyre of 1279-81, probably in Trinity term 1279, the Abbot of Whitby was summoned to answer one Adam de Levynthorpe for breach of the same rule.[7] However, the writ as enrolled on the plea-roll does not state whether or not the rule is statutory in origin, and the abbot does not demur on the existence of the rule but pleads successfully that he had found his church seised of the land in question on succeeding to the abbacy (and therefore had not *himself* entered the land). In a further case, from the same eyre, and this time certainly heard in Trinity term 1279,[8] the

---

1   1 *SR* 8-11, and footnotes; the two texts were identical.

2   *Registrum Malmesburiense*, ed. J.S. Brewer and C.T. Martin (*RS*, 1879), i, 42-50.

3   1 *SR* 19-25.

4   *Prior of Barnwell* v. *Master of the Templars, and others* (1264) JUST 1/1191, m.15.

5   CP 40/21, m.58d.

6   *CCR 1272-79*, 500-01. The Close Roll writ alone is noted and discussed by Bean, *Decline of English Feudalism*, 51.

7   JUST 1/1055, m.83. Cf. JUST 1/1062, m.17.

8   JUST 1/1074, m.19d. Because of the length of the eyre, the civil pleas were divided into separate terms. This roll contains only cases heard in Trinity term 1279.

Master of the Templars was summoned to answer Roger d'Eyville for a breach of this rule, the rule being stated on this occasion to have been statutory in origin, though no particular statute is mentioned. Unlike the abbot, the master at once demurred to the writ on the grounds that no such legislation as that cited in the writ had ever been published either by the present king or by his predecessors. The justices answered that similar writs had previously been issued by the Chancery and that the writs, and therefore presumably also the presupposition of the statute's existence, had thereby received royal approval.[1] The defendant persisted in his objections, only shifting his ground slightly to argue that legislation such as that cited in the writ had never been agreed to by the magnates of the realm nor published with their consent. He asked that the judges stay judgment on this objection until the king's will on the matter was known.

It was but a matter of months after the hearing of this last case that, at the Michaelmas parliament of 1279, the Statute of Mortmain was enacted.[2] The statute was published on 14 November 1279[3] by a writ sent to the justices of the Bench and also, almost certainly (although no evidence of this survives), like other thirteenth-century legislation, by writs sent to the sheriffs of every county. It was drastic in scope. All alienations in mortmain were henceforth to cease — not only alienations to religious houses but also all alienations to other ecclesiastical tenants, and any attempt at an infraction of the statute was to be punished by the forfeiture of the land concerned. The lord of whom the land was held was to be given a year within which to claim the land for himself by entering in the event of forfeiture. The statute is, however, unclear about what was to happen if he failed to act: as if two different and mutually irreconcilable schemes had been proposed and the legislators had not been able to make up their minds which to adopt. The statute says that each of the superior lords of the fee was in turn to be given six months to claim the land by entering it, but it also says that as soon as the year had elapsed the king was to be allowed to enter it and enfeoff a new tenant, who was to hold the land

---

1 The justices may have been referring to the fact that this writ was issued while the king himself was in France, 11 May to 19 June 1279.

2 1 *SR* 51.

3 That the date given in the Close Roll version of the statute (14 November) rather than that given in the Patent Roll (15 November) is the correct one, is indicated by the evidence of a case heard in the Bench in Easter term 1284, in which the court (presumably still in possession of the writ sent to it) said the statute had been published on 14 November: *Prior of the Hospitallers* v. *Pocklington* (1284) CP 40/53, m.20. It is also the date given to the Statute in a Close Roll enrolment of 1291: C 58/108, m.5d.

of its original lord for the services due, and also to perform additional services directly to himself.[1]

In practice, despite the statute, there was not a complete ban on alienations in mortmain after 1279. Within six months of the passing of the statute the king began to grant licences allowing alienations in mortmain 'notwithstanding the statute'. The earliest of these is dated 26 May 1280.[2] Although the very earliest licences seem to have been granted without any preliminary investigation into the proposed alienation, such preliminary enquiries (through inquisitions *ad quod damnum*) were being made from as early as February 1281.[3] By 1284 at the latest, if not indeed from 1281, such an inquisition seems to have been an essential preliminary to the granting of a licence, since in that year an inquisition was held into a proposed alienation by no less a person than the queen mother.[4] The inquisition *ad quod damnum* was authorised by royal writ which was normally addressed to the relevant sheriff or to some other royal official and sought the verdict of twelve jurors, of the locality where the land to be alienated was situated, on a series of questions: whether the proposed alienation was prejudicial or damaging to the interests of the king or others; of whom the land was held and by what service; and what the land was worth. Additional questions sometimes asked were: how many mesnes there were between the intending alienor and the king; and whether the alienor was retaining enough lands to perform in full the services he owed and to sustain various other specified duties whose dereliction would be prejudicial to his neighbours.[5] The inquisition and authorising writ would then be returned to Chancery, which would, it seems, normally forward them to a session of the king's council for consideration by king and council before a licence was granted. The evidence for this lies not only in the annotations commonly found from 1284 onwards of the council's comments on returned inquisitions, but also in the dating of licences: which are heavily concentrated in the periods during and just after sessions of the Great Council or of Parliament.[6]

---

1 Cf. Bereford C.J.'s suggested solution of this problem in Mich. 6 Edw. 2 (34 *SS*, 1918), 75, pl. 20.

2 C 66/99, m.17 [*CPR 1272-81*, 372].

3 C 143/5/17. This is a transcript of the original writ, preceding the returned inquisition.

4 C 143/7/1.

5 This last question is only found in full from June 1290 onwards, and subsequently becomes a standard feature of the writ.

6 I propose to discuss elsewhere the evidence on which the conclusions in this paragraph are based.

An entry on the Parliament Roll for January 1292 notes, among other things, that henceforth no requests for permission to alienate in mortmain will be considered without evidence of the consent of the lord of whom the land was held being produced.[1] Historians have generally seen this as marking a radical change in the licensing system.[2] There is, however, some evidence from as early as 1281, and plentiful evidence from 1285 onwards (from which date the endorsed annotations on inquisitions *ad quod damnum* frequently require evidence of such consent to be produced before the king's licence is given) which suggests that it had been the usual if not invariable practice even before 1292 to require evidence of the lord's consent before the king's consent was given. The memorandum also requires that the potential donor keep some of his lands, that the returned inquest be accompanied by the authorising original writ, and that the writ itself contain all the articles included in the 'new form' of writ (that is, the writ as altered in June 1290). It is in form neither a petition nor the answer to a petition, and the most plausible explanation is that it is an internal, administrative memorandum, intended simply to ensure that the king and his council are not bothered by having to consider inquisitions *ad quod damnum* which stand no chance of success, by allowing Chancery clerks or others working at a fairly low level of discretion to sift the inquisitions before they ever reached the king's council.

Two views have been put forward in recent years concerning the motives behind the statute. Plucknett[3] suggested that the Statute of Mortmain was a 'very dubious piece of political legislation' to which the lay lords present at the 1279 Parliament had been tricked into assenting by 'the bribe of statutory forfeitures' and the 'soft words of the final clause', the provision safeguarding the lord's right to services and feudal incidents even where the king had entered in the lord's default and enfeoffed a new tenant. It was, however, Edward I's intention by means of the statute to acquire 'by a single stroke . . . the sole prerogative of amortization' and Edward had soon

> revealed his plan by issuing when he saw fit his letters of licence to alienate into mortmain. The implication [was] that the king's consent [was] necessary, and that the king's consent [was] sufficient. The flow of property to the Church continued much as before, but from every gift the king took such toll as he could get.

More recently, Bean[4] has suggested that the motives behind the

1   1 *RP* 83, no. 13.
2   Bean, *Decline of English Feudalism,* 64-5.
3   Plucknett, *Legislation of Edward I,* 98, 99.
4   Bean, *Decline of English Feudalism,* 53, 64.

statute were primarily political, the intention being to employ the statute 'as a threat which would bring the clergy to heel'. The Crown had, he argued, only a marginal financial interest in the control of mortmain alienations in the fees of mesne lords: the reason it consented to legislation in 1279 was that it needed the support of the lay magnates against the Church to force the new Archbishop of Canterbury (Pecham) to withdraw certain decisions of his first provincial council which were considered to be prejudicial to the Crown's authority. The threat implied by the statute proved an immediate success, Pecham being 'forced to agree to [the] royal demands at the very parliament at which the statute of Mortmain was promulgated'. Even after the immediate crisis was over, however, the Crown embarked on a policy of licensing alienations instead of agreeing to a total repeal of the statute, since 'the threat of a future policy whereby the Church would be forbidden to acquire land' was thought 'a useful weapon against the recalcitrant clergy'.

Both these views are, I think, mistaken. Against Plucknett it can be argued that it seems to have been much the same group of lay lords who in practice consented to the issuing of licences as had consented to the original legislation. There was therefore no trick involved in the licensing system; and, far from gaining the sole prerogative of amortization as a result of the legislation, in practice what the king got was a share in the control of amortization with the lord of whom the land to be amortized was held. That the Crown's motives were not merely financial is shown not only by the detailed questions answered in inquisitions *ad quod damnum* and the care taken to improve and expand the list of questions asked — all of which show more concern with the control of alienations in the common good than desire for financial return — but also by the fact that a system of fines for licences to alienate does not seem to have come into operation until as late as 1299, when Edward I and his advisers were desperately seeking new sources of finance.[1]

Against Bean it can be argued that it is difficult to see why, if the statute was merely a threat, Edward I should nonetheless have gone on to publish it on 14 November, when its main object (the withdrawal by Pecham) had been achieved at some date between 9 and 11 November? The threat of the statute once enacted seems in fact to have been ineffective in cowing the clergy, who the following year produced a lengthy catalogue of grievances and in 1281 even re-enacted three

1 W. Ryley, *Placita Parliamentaria* (London, 1661), 478.
2 *Councils and Synods,* ed. F.M. Powicke and C.R. Cheney (Oxford, 1964), II, ii, 832.

of the five canons withdrawn by Pecham in 1279, without any cessation of the granting of licences.[1] Nor was Pecham the man to be cowed into submission by a threat to the Church's ability to acquire more lands. He himself had been a noted proponent of the Franciscan theory of poverty, and only ten years previously had launched a scathing attack on the wealth both of the secular clergy and of the monastic orders.[2]

If we are looking for the motives behind the statute, we need look no further than the statute's own words. Lay lords were worried about the damaging effects of such alienations on their income from feudal incidents. The king was worried about the effect of the transfer of landed wealth from laymen to the Church on the number of knights, the military potential of the kingdom.[3] It is possible that at first a complete prohibition of all further alienations was intended, but even if it was not seen from the start, it must soon have become clear that the interests of both mesne lords and king could be adequately safeguarded by a system of licensing. And if we are to look for what precipitated the legislation, we need look no further than the case involving the Master of the Templars which was heard in the Yorkshire eyre of 1279.[4] The case had involved an important political, even constitutional, point. It also involved an important defendant. What more natural than that the case should have been discussed at the Michaelmas parliament of 1279, particularly as some of the justices from the Yorkshire eyre were present at the parliament?[5] Once the specific point had been raised — whether there did exist legislation against mortmain alienations to religious houses — is it not easy to see how this could have led to a more general discussion of mortmain alienations, and thus to the enactment of the statute? May not the otherwise apparently gratuitous reference to the earlier legislation, which the Statute of Mortmain defiantly insisted and affirmed was still in force, be a clue to the origins of the statute in a discussion about whether such legislation did or did not exist?

1   Ibid., 887, 906-7.
2   D.L. Douie, *Archbishop Pecham* (Oxford, 1952), 26-31.
3   I propose to discuss this elsewhere.
4   Above, p. 240.
5   G.O. Sayles, *Select Cases in the Court of King's Bench*, i (55 *SS*, 1936), 51: 39.

12

King, Church and Property: The Enforcement of Restrictions on Alienations into Mortmain in the Lordship of Ireland in the Later Middle Ages

I

The statute of mortmain was enacted at a session of the king's parliament of England held at Westminster in the autumn of 1279. It prohibited all transactions which led to land or other forms of real property passing 'into mortmain'. The statute's preamble makes it clear that this covered the transfer of property into the possession of regular religious orders and individual religious houses; from the sequel it seems clear that it also covered the transfer of property into the possession of secular ecclesiastics, that is to say, the holders of ecclesiastical dignities and benefices, such as bishops, canons and the rectors of parish churches.

The statute could simply have declared void any transaction having such an effect. It did not do so. It declared that any such transaction undertaken in the future would render the property concerned liable to forfeiture. The feudal lord of whom the property was held was to be allowed one year to take possession of the forfeited property. If he failed to act, each in turn of the superior lords of the property was to be given six months to do so. An al-

ABBREVIATIONS AND CONVENTIONS. The Calendars of the English Charter, Close and Patent Rolls published by HMSO have been abbreviated CChR, CCR and CPR respectively. The Reports of the Deputy Keeper of Public Records in Ireland and the Calendar of the Justiciary Rolls have been abbreviated DK Rep Ire and CJR respectively. References (by class and piece number) to the Public Record Office, Dublin, are as follows: CB 1 = Original plea rolls of the Irish Court of Common Pleas; KB 1 = Original plea rolls of the Justiciar's Court; RC = Calendars made for the Irish Record Commissioners (RC 7 = Plea Rolls, RC 8 = Memoranda Rolls). References to materials in the Public Record Office, London, are as follows: C 47 = Chancery: miscellanea; C 81 = Chancery: warrants for the great seal; C 143 = Chancery: inquisitions *ad quod damnum*; C 260 = Chancery files: record; JUST I = Justices itinerant: plea rolls etc.; SC 1 = Ancient Correspondence; SC 9 = Parliament Rolls (Exchequer series).

ternative and incompatible provision allowed the king to take possession of the property if the immediate lord failed to act within a year. The provisions of the statute were officially communicated to the justices of the Bench at Westminster by a royal writ of 14 November 1279. They were also probably communicated to the sheriffs of each of the counties of England at the same time, as was the normal practice on the enactment of new statutes.[1]

Within six months of the statute's publication, the king's chancery had begun to issue licences for property in England to pass into mortmain 'notwithstanding the statute'; and before long an elaborate licensing system had been created. A preliminary inquiry (inquisition *ad quod damnum*) had to be held locally into the possible adverse consequences; the applicant had to produce written evidence of the lord's consent and (from 1299) the applicant had to pay a fine to the king. A permanent, total ban on property passing into mortmain was probably never envisaged, and was certainly never a practical possibility. The licensing system allowed lay donors of property to continue their endeavours to secure the salvation of their souls in the next world through the pious endowment of ecclesiastical bodies in this world. It also allowed lay vendors of property to continue to sell property to religious orders and secular ecclesiastics as well as to other laymen. It also ensured, however, that the feudal lords would not suffer material loss from their tenants' grants. By giving them a right of veto over such grants, it allowed them to insist on compensation for their losses. The licensing system also allowed the king and his advisers to prevent or mitigate the effects of transactions with damaging consequences for the Crown or the local community and gave the Crown a new source of revenue.[2] The statute of mortmain had not envisaged the creation of a licensing system, and certainly did not provide direct authority for its operation. The system was, nonetheless, dependent for its effective operation on the statute remaining in force. The controls only worked because in theory no alienations into mortmain at all were allowed and the provisions of the statute continued to be directly applicable, if and when property passed into mortmain without a licence.[3]

Two further pieces of legislation were passed by the English parliament

---

[1] The authoritative text of the statute is that given in A. Luders and others (ed), *Statutes of the realm* (Record Commission 1810–22) i 51. It has been reprinted many times, most recently in Sandra Raban, *Mortmain legislation and the English church, 1279–1500* (Cambridge 1982) 193–4. For the background to the enactment of the statute see above, pp. 233–244 and Raban, *Mortmain*, chapter 1.

[2] For the beginnings of the licensing system, see above, pp. 241–4; and for its later working see Raban, *Mortmain*, chapter 3.

[3] On the enforcement of the statute see Raban, *Mortmain*, chapter 3.

during the later medieval period relating to alienations into mortmain. In 1285, chapter 32 of the statute of Westminster II made it clear that the statutory ban on mortmain alienations also applied to the 'recovery' of property by default in collusive litigation in the royal courts. A new procedure was henceforth to apply. Before the court awarded possession of the property to the demandant a jury was to be summoned to give its verdict as to whether or not the demandant had a good title to it.[1] In 1391 chapter 5 of the statute of 15 Richard II tackled the problem of evasion through the 'use'. The statute established that in future property granted to lay 'feoffees to uses' who held to the use of an ecclesiastical *cestui que use* was to be considered as having been granted into mortmain, even though the legal title to the property remained in the lay feoffees. The same chapter also brought within the scope of the statutory ban the acquisition of property by guilds and fraternities and by town and borough communities and their officials.[2]

It is the purpose of the present paper to investigate the impact of this English mortmain legislation upon the Anglo-Norman lordship of Ireland – to discover when, and how, that legislation came to be regarded as part of the law of the lordship and to see what evidence survives for its direct enforcement. The evolution of the mortmain licensing system as it operated in the lordship in the later medieval period is too large a subject to be dealt with here: I hope soon to discuss it elsewhere.[3]

II

The proper procedure in the later thirteenth century for ensuring that English legislation was extended to Ireland seems to have been for a text to be sent to the Irish administration with an order for its publication, and for it then to be 'published' in Ireland.[4] Unless and until this procedure had been followed, the legislation was not properly part of the law of the lordship.

---

[1] *Statutes of the realm* i 87.

[2] *Statutes of the realm* ii 79–80. On the development of the use during the period after 1279 see J. L. Barton, 'The medieval use', *Law Q Rev* 81 (1965) 562–77 and cf. J. M. W. Bean, *The decline of English feudalism, 1215–1540* (Manchester 1968) chapter 3.

[3] The subject has received little attention from historians of the Anglo-Norman lordship and its institutions. The most satisfactory discussion is that to be found in G. J. Hand, *English law in Ireland, 1290–1324* (Cambridge 1967) 164–66.

[4] This was the procedure followed as early as 1236: H. F. Berry (ed), *Statutes and ordinances and acts of the parliament of Ireland: king John to Henry V* (Dublin 1907) 29, 31–2 (hereafter *Stat Ire, John–Hen V*). It was also the procedure used in 1285 and 1299: ibid., 47, 221–7. Full publication may already in 1279 have required, as it certainly did later, proclamation locally in each county and liberty, and proclamation centrally in the king's courts of the lordship. For an order of 1324 spelling out what full publication then meant, ibid., 297.

There is no evidence in any contemporary source to indicate that a text of the statute of mortmain was sent to Ireland in 1279, and there is also the almost contemporary testimony of the Irish chancellor, master Thomas of Quantock in 1296 that the statute had never been formally published in Ireland.[1] This makes it virtually certain that the statute of mortmain did not become part of the law of the lordship in 1279.

The reasons are far from clear. A deliberate decision may have been taken in England at the time of the statute's enactment that the statute should not be extended because it was in some way inappropriate to Irish conditions. This seems unlikely. Land tenure within the lordship had been 'feudalized' along English lines; and Irish land law was virtually identical to English land law. Within a few years, moreover, it had come to be believed in English official circles that the legislation was in force in Ireland: an improbable development if such a decision had been made only a few years before. It seems more probable that there was at this time some doubt on the general matter of principle–as to whether or not English legislation should continue to be extended as a matter of course to Ireland by royal mandate alone, especially as there was a separate Irish parliament passing legislation of its own.[2] It was not the only English legislation of the earlier part of Edward I's reign not to be extended to the lordship – this was also true of the statutes of Westminster I (1275) and Gloucester (1278), though in their case the omission was remedied in 1285.[3] At the Irish end there certainly seem to have been doubts as to the application of English legislation within the lordship.[4] Similar doubts may also have existed in England, though they must have been resolved prior to 1285, when use of the traditional procedure was resumed, leaving the two parliaments, in effect, to share legislative power over the lordship. The omission may have been simply the result of bureaucratic oversight, the justiciar's name having somehow come to be omitted from the list of officials to whom copies of new statutes were to be sent.

Within a few years it had nonetheless come to be assumed by several officials of the English and the Irish administrations that the statute was part of the law of the lordship. As early as February 1283 an anonymous letter-writer, possibly the English chancellor, Robert Burnel, was writing to Walter

---

[1] CCR 1296-1302, 3-4.

[2] It is from precisely this period that the earliest series of enactments from an Irish parliament comes: H. G. Richardson and G. O. Sayles, *The Irish parliament in the middle ages* (Philadelphia 1952) 290-93. [3] *Stat Ire, John-Hen V*, 46.

[4] The memorandum of the legislation enacted in the 1278 Irish parliament (see above, n.2) contains a clause, unfortunately heavily damaged in the original, concerning the application of English statutes in Ireland. It seems to indicate that there was some doubt on this matter and that the doubt had yet to be resolved.

of Odiham, a senior clerk of the English chancery, instructing him to write in the king's name to the justiciar of Ireland, telling him to stop bothering the abbey of Furness in connection with land which the abbey held on lease 'since it was not contrary to the king's statute that lands be leased to the religious...'[1] The reference must be to the statute of mortmain and shows the writer believed the statute to be in force in Ireland. It also suggests that the justiciar thought the same. In the following year the mayor and bailiffs of Dublin were ordered, by a writ issued by the English chancery, to allow the Augustinians to acquire lands adjacent to their friary 'notwithstanding the statute of mortmain'[2] – though the earliest mortmain licence seems not to have been issued until October 1289.[3] Late in the same year (December 1284) the English chancery sent a further writ to the justiciar on behalf of the priory of Llanthony Secunda. It ordered him to restore certain lands which had been seized because they had been acquired in contravention of the statute, but which the priory claimed to have acquired prior to its enactment. In his return the justiciar claimed to have made the seizure not under the statute's terms but at the request of an Irish religious house (the priory of Duleek) of whom the property was held, to assist that house in preventing a damaging alienation by its tenants.[4] The use of this older common-law method of preventing alienations in mortmain suggests that both the prior of Duleek and the justiciar believed that the statute of mortmain was not yet in force in Ireland, but the writ itself again demonstrates the contrary belief current in the English chancery.[5] By the later 1280s, this view had spread

[1] This letter is transcribed in the appendix as document 1.

[2] CCR 1279–88, 298. In June 1280 the Carmelite order had received a royal licence to enclose and inhabit three messuages in Dublin. This property had, however, been acquired prior to the enactment of the statute and the 'licence' was needed to overcome opposition from the citizens of Dublin and not to dispense the friars from the operation of the statute: CPR 1272–81, 379. For the background to this 'licence' see G. O. Sayles (ed), *Documents on the affairs of Ireland before the king's council* (Dublin: Irish Manuscripts Commission (IMC) 1979) (hereafter *Doc King's Council*) 24–25; C 143/5, no 6; W. Prynne, *The history of king John, king Henry II, and the most illustrious king Edward I* iii (London 1670) 1228–29.

[3] CPR 1281–92, 325. Five further licences were issued between 1290 and 1292 (CPR 1281–92, 365 (two), 379, 380, 397) but then no others until 1299 (CPR 1292–1301, 422–23). Two letters close issued in 1296 and 1297 were, however, the equivalent of licences: CCR 1288–96, 492–93; CCR 1296–1302, 53.

[4] The return, which incorporates a copy of the writ, is transcribed in full in the appendix as document 2.

[5] cf. 235–8. It might be argued that the extension to Ireland in 1285 of chapter 32 of the statute of Westminster II (above, p 251) also demonstrated the existence in England of the belief that the statute of mortmain was already in force in the lordship. The argument is a weak one. Several other clauses of this long and

to Ireland as well. An inquisition held in 1287 by a deputy to the escheator of Ireland found that property had been acquired by the priory of Llanthony Secunda 'contrary to the king's statutes'– evidently a reference to the statute of mortmain;[1] and by 1289, at latest, property was being seized into the king's hand as having been alienated into mortmain 'contrary to the statute'.[2]

Some still remembered that the statute had never been properly extended to Ireland. When the justiciar seized property acquired by the hospital of St John and the priory of St Patrick at Downpatrick, the heads of the two houses protested to the king in England – and it was their protests which led to the attestation by the Irish chancellor, already noted in the English parliament of autumn 1296, confirming that the statute had never been properly published within the lordship.[3] The property was conditionally restored to the two religious houses, pending further discussion of the matter at the English Easter parliament of 1297. The two houses were probably allowed to keep the property, and steps seem now at last to have been taken to have the statute formally published in Ireland. In proceedings in the Irish parliament in 1302, the escheator certified that various lands at Kells in Ossory had been seized because they had been acquired by the prior of Kells after the enactment of the statute of mortmain; he also certified, however, that on the day that they were acquired, the statute had not been published and was not known in Ireland.[4] The implication seems to be that by 1302 the statute had been published in Ireland. Again, in the course of litigation in the justiciar's court in 1306, mention was made of an inquisition into the alleged acquisition of property by the prior of Duleek contrary to the statute, and its finding that the property had been acquired long before the statute was promulgated in Ireland.[5] The words were clearly carefully chosen. The acquisition had been made *after* the enactment of the statute, but *before* the complex statute were clearly not applicable in Ireland, and the true explanation seems to be that no one thought to look through the legislation to weed out inapplicable clauses before sending it to Ireland.

[1] E. St J. Brooks (ed), *The Irish cartularies of Llanthony Prima and Secunda* (IMC 1953) 230-31. The lands included some of the lands previously seized, but the inquisition now found that all the property had been acquired in 1284. It is not clear whether this led to a renewed seizure of the lands. Matters may have been settled by the undated quitclaim by Duleek to the priory of Llanthony Secunda also copied into the cartulary: ibid., 321-22.

[2] (i) For a seizure made in 1289 see 38 DK Rep Ire, 89 and 42 DK Rep Ire, 69. (ii) For another seizure made in or before 1289 see CPR 1281-92, 325.   [3] above, 248 n 1.

[4] CJR 1295-1303, 386. This statement stands almost alone in its implication that 'common knowledge' of an English statute would be enough to make it applicable in Ireland.

[5] CJR 1305-7, 173-74. For other references in the early fourteenth century to the promulgation or publication of the statute in Ireland, as contrasted with the date of its enactment in England, see Hand, *English law*, 166.

date when it was promulgated in Ireland. In 1329, the abbot of St Mary's abbey in Dublin, in a petition sent to the king in England, claimed that a surrender of property made to his predecessor in the liberty court of Trim in 1290-1 was made before the statute was published in Ireland – once more clearly distinguishing that date from the date of the statute's enactment.[1] There is, moreover, no evidence after 1296 of any doubts being expressed as to whether or not the statute was in force in Ireland. Such doubts could only have been laid conclusively to rest by its formal publication.

The extension to Ireland of chapter 32 of the statute of Westminster II took place in 1285 when the statute as a whole was sent for publication and enforcement.[2] The legislation of 1391 is more problematic. There is no direct evidence of its extension either by royal order or through confirmation or re-enactment by the Irish parliament.[3] Indirect evidence, however, strongly suggests that it was extended in one of these ways or – just possibly – simply came to be regarded as in force in Ireland without any formal authority. As early as 1395, property which had been left by will to a fraternity in Dublin had been confiscated by the king as having been granted into mortmain without a licence, and was re-granted by him.[4] It was only the legislation of 1391 which brought alienations to fraternities within the scope of the statutory ban. There are also several fifteenth-century licences for guilds and fraternities to acquire property 'notwithstanding the statute of mortmain', which clearly reflect the extension of the scope of the legislation on mortmain effected by the act. It must also be significant that the Irish Close Roll of 4 Henry IV (1402-3), now destroyed, contained a transcript of this single item of English legislation.[5] The legislation was perhaps formally extended to Ireland in 1402-3, or its operation within the lordship was confirmed at that time.

III
(i)

The statute of mortmain appears to have envisaged that enforcement would be a matter, primarily, for the lords of whom the property alienated was held. There seems, however, to be comparatively little evidence in England of such lords taking possession of property claimed to be forfeit;[6] and

---

[1] CCR 1327–30, 444. See also below, 260–1.

[2] *Stat Ire, John-Hen V*, 46.

[3] A. G. Donaldson, The application in Ireland of English and British legislation made before 1801 (unpublished PhD thesis, Queen's University of Belfast 1952) 412.

[4] E. Tresham (ed), *Rotulorum patentium et clausorum cancellarie Hiberniae calendarium* (Irish Record Commission 1828) (hereafter *Rot Canc Hib*) 152b, no 50 (fraternity of St Katherine in church of St Michael in the High Street, Dublin).

[5] ibid., 168a, no 17.   [6] Raban, *Mortmain*, 72–73.

the much smaller body of Irish material supplies only two instances of lords taking possession of property on such grounds.[1] The introduction of the licensing system is a partial explanation. Most mortmain alienations made after 1279 seem to have been made only after a licence had been obtained; and this provided protection not only against royal seizures but also against seizures made by lords. A sizeable minority of alienations, however, were made without prior royal licence; and it is more difficult to see why they should commonly have led in both England and Ireland to royal seizures but only rarely have led to seignorial ones. This may in part be a trick of the evidence. This comes mainly from royal records which are likely to provide a much more complete picture of royal seizures than of seignorial ones. There may, however, also be other explanations. In several instances, the unlicensed grantee was also the lord of whom the property was held: here, a royal seizure was the only seizure likely to occur. In other cases, the parties may have secured the consent of the lord to the transaction but not a royal licence in the not unreasonable belief that they might evade the notice of the king's officials, but could not reasonably expect to evade the notice of the immediate lord. The lord was only given a comparatively short period of time within which to make his seizure, and would need to be quite certain that an unlicensed alienation had taken place if he was to avoid the penalties of conviction for disseisin. For the king there was no such time limit and no such penalty awaited him or his officials if they made an unjustified seizure.

Seizure of property into the king's hands could and did occur in a number of different ways. In England, it was the escheators and their deputies, royal officials responsible for the enforcement of the king's feudal prerogatives, who were most commonly responsible.[2] There was only a single escheator for the whole of Ireland for most of the later medieval period and he, too, made a number of such seizures. A local jury answering a general questionnaire on matters relating to the king's feudal prerogatives submitted to them by a deputy of the escheator in 1287 drew his attention to a number of mortmain alienations in their locality, but it is not clear whether or not this led to the seizure of the property concerned.[3] In 1289 the Irish escheator certainly did seize property allegedly alienated in mortmain to the archbishop of Cashel;[4] and he and his successors can be shown to have made a number of further seizures on various occasions between 1297 and 1392.[5] Property was

---

[1] KB 1/1 m 3d; RC 7/12 p 195–96, 228–30.   [2] Raban, *Mortmain*, 73–88.
[3] above, 250.   [4] above, 250 n 2(i).
[5] (i) CJR 1295–1303, 226 (abbey of St Mary, Dublin); (ii) ibid., 386 (priory of Kells in Ossory); (iii) C47/10/19, no 14 (archbishop of Armagh); (iv) CPR 1301–7, 117 (Carmelites of Ardee); (v) 42 DK Rep Ire, 21 (hospital of St John, Waterford); (vi) ibid., 26 (hospital of St Leonard, Waterford); (vii) ibid., 58 (priory of St John, Kilkenny); (viii) CCR

also seized into the king's hands in England by the justices in eyre. The earliest such seizure, in 1280, seems to have been prompted by a jury verdict on an article of the eyre which was not specifically intended to uncover such alienations;[1] the first seizures resulting from jury verdicts on an article specifically asking about mortmain alienations seem to have been in the 1293 Northumberland and 1293-4 Yorkshire eyres.[2] The new article, however, appears not to have been included in the articles of the eyre of the contemporary 'southern' circuit, or in subsequent eyres prior to the Kent eyre of 1313.[3] In Ireland seizures are known to have been made made by the justices in eyre who held the Co Louth eyre of 1301,[4] the Co Cork eyre of the same year,[5] and the Co Tipperary eyre of 1305-7.[6] It seems probable that these seizures were prompted by information given by local juries in response to an article of the eyre specifically concerned with mortmain alienations. That article may well have been included in the articles of these eyres because the justiciar, John

1327-30, 444 (abbey of St Mary, Dublin); (ix) RC 8/17 p 536-38 (priory of Llanthony Prima); (x) *Rot Canc Hib* 71a, no 103 (hospital of St Cross, Limerick); (xi) ibid., 71b, no 114 (abbey of Furness); (xii) ibid., 77b-78a, no 45 (priory of Llanthony Secunda); (xiii) CCR 1346-49, 459 (abbey of Furness); (xiv) J. T. Gilbert (ed), *Chartularies of St Mary's Abbey, Dublin*, Rolls Series 80 (1884-5) i 316-25 (abbey of St Mary Dublin); (xv) J. Graves (ed), *Roll of proceedings of the king's council in Ireland, 16 Richard II*, Rolls Series 69 (1877) 63-66 (Carmelites of Ardee). It is only rarely that we hear of the circumstances behind a particular seizure, but for one example of a private initiative lying behind such a seizure see CJR 1305-7, 173-74 (priory of Duleek).

[1] JUST 1/783 m 22d.

[2] JUST 1/653 m 31; JUST 1/1098 m 4, 8d, 9d, 27d, 42d, 62.

[3] W. C. Bolland and others (ed), *Year book, eyre of Kent, 6 and 7 Edward II* i (Selden Society Year Book ser 5 (1909) 31. A mortmain alienation was presented in the 1299 Cambridgeshire eyre, but not in response to such an article: JUST 1/95 m 60d.

[4] (i) RC 7/8 p 4-5 (Augustinians of Drogheda); (ii) ibid., p 7 [= ibid., p 23] (priory of St John, Ardee); (iii) ibid., p 8 [= ibid., p 23 and C260/13, no 21, m 2 (1st entry)] (archb. of Armagh); (iv) RC 7/8 p 8-9 [= ibid., p 23-24 and C 260/13, no 21, m 2 (2nd entry)] (archb. of Armagh); (v) RC 7/8 p 9-10 [= ibid., p 25-27] (archb. of Armagh); (vi) RC 7/8 p 10-11 (archb. of Armagh); (vii) RC 7/8 p 11-12 [= ibid. p 27-28 and C260/13, no 21, m 2 (3rd entry)] (archb. Armagh); (viii) RC 7/8 p 12-13 [= ibid., p 28] (archb. Armagh); (ix) ibid., p 13-14 (abbey of Mellifont); (x) ibid., p 14 [= ibid., p 29-30] (abbey of Navan); (xi) SC 9/25 m 2 and CPR 1301-7, 148 (priory of St Mary, Louth).

[5] (i) RC 7/8 p 48 (Franciscans of Buttevant); (ii) ibid., p 59-60 (bishop of Cloyne); (iii) ibid., p 61-62 (priory of Bridgetown); (iv) ibid., p 62 (priory of Bridgetown); (v) ibid., p 62-63 (priory of Bridgetown); (vi) ibid., p 63-64 (priory of Bridgetown); (vii) ibid., p 68 (abbot of Tracton).

[6] (i) RC 7/11 p 194 (Franciscans of Cashel); (ii) ibid., p 194-95 (priory of Athasssel); (iii) ibid., p 195-96 (priory of Athassel).

Wogan, had been a justice of the English eyres of Northumberland and York-shire in 1293–4, in which the article was used for the first time. There is also evidence in the late thirteenth and early fourteenth centuries of seizures having been made by the justiciar himself. The earliest such seizure was one made by William de Vescy in or before 1292; and John Wogan is known to have made further seizures of property acquired by various religious houses in Ulster and in Co Kildare in 1296–97.[1] Seizure by the justiciar could come about simply as a result of it emerging, in the course of litigation in his court, that an unlicensed alienation had taken place. In an assize of novel disseisin heard in that court in 1307, seizure was only averted by the further dis-covery, just in time, that the bishop's acquisition of the property concerned had been in a purely personal capacity.[2] In the fifteenth century, on at least one occasion, a seizure is known to have been made by the barons of the Dublin Exchequer as the result of an inquisition which they had held.[3]

When property was seized in one of these ways, it was essential that it also be ascertained just when the unlicensed alienation concerned had taken place – since the king was held to be entitled to the net annual value of the property for the whole of the period which had elapsed between alienation and seizure. In England, the king can be shown to have been in receipt of such 'mesne issues' from at least 1293–4;[4] in Ireland somewhat earlier, from at least 1290–91.[5]

The property seized into the king's hands lay in various different parts of the lordship–in the city and county of Dublin, and in the counties of Louth, Meath, Kildare, Kilkenny, Wexford, Waterford, Tipperary, Cork, Limerick, and Kerry.[6] It ranged from houses and small plots of land

[1] (i) C143/15 no 26 (priory of Athassel); (ii) CCR 1288–96, 492–93 and CJR 1295–1303, 87–88, 100 (abbey of Saul); (iii) CCR 1296–1302, 3–4 (priory and hospital of St John, Downpatrick); (iv) CJR 1295–1303, 171 (Dominicans of Athy); (v) ibid., 174 (Franciscans of Kildare).

[2] CJR 1305–7, 439. For an earlier case where the land was seized but was subsequently restored, as of grace, to the grantor, see CJR 1295–1303, 252–53.

[3] H. F. Berry (ed), *Statute rolls of the parliament of Ireland, Henry VI* (Dublin 1910) 779–83 (hereafter *Stat Ire Hen VI*). In the fifteenth century justices were also specially commissioned on several occasions to enquire into various matters, including infractions of the statute of mortmain, but no seizures are known to have resulted from their work: *Rot Canc Hib* 229b–230a, no 110; 232a–b, no 40; 238a, no 109.

[4] JUST 1/1098 m 4, 8d.

[5] Above, 250 n 2(i). For other references to the king's right to 'mesne issues' in Ireland see C 47/10/19, no 14 and above, 253 n 4(iii, iv, vii, ix).

[6] *Dublin city*: CJR 1295–1303, 165 (Carmelites of Dublin) and above, 251 n 4, 252 n 5(i).

Dublin county: (i) 53 DK Rep Ire, 38 (hospital of St John the Baptist, Dublin); (ii) E. St J. Brooks, *Register of the Hospital of St John the Baptist, Dublin* (IMC 1936) (here-after *Reg SJB Dublin*) 204–5 (= CJR 1305–7, 235) (hospital of St John the Baptist, Dubin towns and cities, sometimes specifically stated to have been acquired for the extension of the premises of an existing religious house,[1] to extensive holdings of land in the country.[2] Rent-charges[3] and advowsons[4] were also seized. In the vast majority of cases, the grantor of the property was, as might be expected, a layman but there are a few examples of grants by the

lin); (iii) *Chart St Mary's Dublin,* i 291-93 (abbey of St Mary, Dublin).

Louth: (i) CPR 1338-40, 85 (archbishop of Armagh); (ii) C143/94, no 27 (hospital of St Leonard, Dundalk); (iii) RC 8/17 p 536-38 (priory of Llanthony Prima); and above, 252 n 5(iv), 253 n 4.

Meath: (i) *Rot Canc Hib* 37b, no 166 (hospital of St John, Kells); (ii) CCR 1327-30, 444 (abbey of St Mary, Dublin); (iii) 44 DK Rep Ire, 31 (priory of Holmpatrick); (iv) 45 DK Rep Ire, 47 (light before cross in church of St Columba, Kells); (v) *Rot Canc Hib* 45a, no 67 (abbey of Furness); (vi) ibid., 71b, no 114 (abbey of Furness); (vii) ibid., 77b-78a, no 45 (priory of Llanthony Secunda); (viii) CCR 1346-49, 459 (abbey of Furness); (ix) *Chart St Mary's Dublin,* i 282-86 (abbey of St Mary, Dublin); (x) ibid., i 316-25 (abbey of St Mary, Dublin); (xi) 43 DK Rep Ire, 22 (abbey of St Thomas, Dublin). Nos (ii), (iii), (ix), (x) concern property in the present Co Westmeath.

Kildare: (i) 43 DK Rep Ire, 22 (hospital of St John, Naas); (ii) CJR 1295-1303, 165 (Carmelites of Kildare); (iii) ibid., 171 (Dominicans of Athy); (iv) ibid., 174 (Franciscans of Kildare); (v) *Rot Canc Hib* 45a-b, no 72 (abbey of St Thomas, Dublin); (vi) *Stat Ire, Hen VI,* 779-83 (priory of Great Connell); (vii) CPR 1313-17, 33 (priory of Christchurch Dublin).

Kilkenny: (i) C143/49, no 9 (priory of Kells in Ossory); (ii) N. B. White (ed), *Irish monastic and episcopal deeds, 1200-1600* (IMC 1936) (hereafter *Ir Mon and Ep Deeds*) 13-14 (abbey of Jerpoint); (iii) CJR 1295-1303, 386 (priory of Kells in Ossory); (iv) 42 DK Rep Ire, 58 (priory of St John, Kilkenny).

Wexford: (i) 44 DK Rep Ire, 29-30 (priory of St John, Wexford); (ii) CPR 1281-92, 325 (nunnery of Taghmon).

Waterford: (i) 42 DK Rep Ire, 21 (hospital of St John, Waterford); (ii) ibid., 26 (hospital of St Leonard, Waterford); (iii) 44 DK Rep Ire, 58 (rector of Dungarvan).

Tipperary: (i) RC 7/11 p 195-96 (priory of Athassel); (ii) C143/15, no 26 (priory of Athassel); (iii) 42 DK Rep Ire, 69 (archbishop of Cashel).

Cork: (i) 42 DK Rep Ire, 37 (bishop of Cloyne); (ii) Oxford, Bodleian Library, MS Rawlinson B 502, f 16r (Carmelites of Kinsale); and above, 253 n 5.

Limerick: (i) CPR 1334-38, 330 (bishop of Limerick); (ii) 43 DK Rep Ire, 19 (Augustinians of Hospital); (iii) ibid., (Trinitarians of Adare); (iv) *Rot Canc Hib,* 71a, no 103 (hospital of St Cross, Limerick).

Kerry: 47 DK Rep Ire, 63 (bishop of Ardfert).

[1] For examples see above, 251 n 4, 252 n 5(xi), 254 n 6: Dublin city, Louth (iii); Meath (i); Kildare (ii)-(iv); Waterford (i); Limerick (ii)-(iv).

[2] For examples see above, 253 n 4(v, ix, x); 254 n 6: Dublin county, Meath (ii, iii, v-xi); Kildare (i, v, vi); Kilkenny, Wexford, Tipperary (i, ii); Cork (i, ii); Kerry.

[3] For examples see above, 252 n 5(i); 253 n 4(iii, vi, viii, xi); 253 n 5(iii, v); 254 n 6: Louth (i); Meath (iv); Tipperary (iii); Cork (i).

[4] For examples see above, 253 n 4(iv), 254 n 6: Kildare (vii).

heads of religious houses to other religious houses leading to seizures.[1] The grantees who suffered a seizure of their property included the Irish abbeys of St Mary Dublin, St Thomas Dublin, Saul, Mellifont, Navan, and Jerpoint and the English abbey of Furness; the Irish priories of St Mary Louth, Bridgetown, Kells in Ossory, Downpatrick, Athassel, St John Kilkenny, St John Wexford, Holmpatrick, Christ Church Dublin, Great Connell, St John Ardee, and the English and Welsh priories of Llanthony Secunda and Llanthony Prima; the Irish hospitals of St John Downpatrick, St John the Baptist Dublin, St Leonard Dundalk, St John Kells, St John Naas, St John Waterford, and St Leonard Waterford; and the Irish nunnery of Taghmon. The religious orders from which seizures were made included the Trinitarians, the Carmelites, the Franciscans, the Augustinians and the Dominicans. Property was also seized from a number of secular ecclesiastics including the archbishops of Armagh and Cashel, the bishops of Ardfert, Cloyne and Limerick, and the rector of Dungarvan; and from the fraternity of St Katherine in the church of St Michael in the High Street of Dublin. Property alienated into mortmain remained liable to seizure even if subsequently re-granted out of mortmain to a lay grantee: a small number of seizures, therefore, were of property in the hands of lay tenants.[2]

(ii)

Most, possibly all, of these seizures were 'warranted' by prior jury verdicts finding that the property concerned had been alienated into mortmain without a licence. Such jury verdicts were, however, not regarded as conclusive or irreversible, and it was, therefore, not uncommon for such seizures to be challenged. If the seizure had been made as the result of a presentment made in the course of an eyre, it was probably the accepted procedure for the property to be restored to the ecclesiastical owner from whom it had been taken as soon as a request was made for this, but on condition that they answer the Crown, whenever required, in litigation about the property – and for such litigation then to lead to a second jury verdict and judgment for or against the ecclesiastical tenant in question. A similar procedure probably also obtained when seizures were made as the result of presentments made in the justiciar's court. Aggrieved ecclesiastical tenants are also known, on occasion, to have sought a remedy against what they considered to be unjustified seizures through petitions to the king in his parliament of England[3] or through petitions to the parliament of the lordship of Ireland.[4] The more

[1] For examples see above, 254 n 6: Meath (iii); Waterford (i).
[2] above, 254 n 6: Kildare (v); Limerick (iv).
[3] CCR 1296-1302, 3-4; CCR 1327-30, 444; and perhaps also CCR 1346-9, 459.
[4] *Stat Ire, Hen VI*, 779-83; J. F. Morrissey (ed), *Statute rolls of the parliament of Ireland*

common procedure, however, seems to have been for the ecclesiastical tenant to challenge the seizure by suing a royal writ to the escheator for him to
certify the Irish chancery as to the reasons for the seizure which he or his predecessor had made – and then counterpleading the certificate in a competent
court – the court of the justiciar,[1] the Exchequer of Ireland,[2] and perhaps the
Irish Chancery itself.[3] An analagous procedure seems also to have been in use
in England during the same period.

Seizures were challenged on a variety of different grounds. Some challengers claimed that the property concerned had not passed into mortmain at
all. This was, almost certainly, one of the arguments advanced by the archbishop of Cashel c. 1337 against being held accountable for property seized
from one of his predecessors; and certainly the jury in these proceedings
found that the property concerned had been acquired by the predecessor in
a personal capacity and not for his see.[4] In 1344-45 another seizure made by
the escheator was challenged. The escheator's certificate appears to have indicated that the seizure had been made on the grounds that a previous tenant
of the property had been a feoffee to uses, holding to the use of the abbey of
St Thomas, Dublin, and that the property had thereby passed into mortmain
– a striking anticipation of one of the main provisions of the 1391 mortmain
statute. The current tenant of the property seems to have counterpleaded
this certificate by asserting that the abbot had not acquired the property –
and thus it had not passed into mortmain. Our knowledge of the litigation
comes solely from a calendared version of a related enrolment on an Irish
close roll which no longer survives. It does not make clear – and, indeed, the
original enrolment may not itself have made clear – whether the tenant's
argument was one of law or of fact. He may have been arguing that, in law,
the acquisition of a beneficial interest in property through an enfeoffment
to uses did not constitute an acquisition of the property, and so did not in-
fringe the statute. He may have been arguing that, in fact, the tenant in question had not held the property to the use of the abbey. The use of a jury to

---

12-22 Edward IV (Dublin 1939) 397-9 (hereafter *Stat Ire, Ed IV, pt II*); *Ir Mon and Ep Deeds*, 13-14.

[1] CJR 1295-1303, 386 may be an early example of this: CJR 1305-7, 235 certainly is.
For later examples see RC 8/17 p 536-38 (which gives the relevant writs in full) and *Chart St Mary's Dublin*, i 316-25.

[2] above 254 n 6: Meath (ix). A rather different procedure was used in another case of the
same year where the property had long passed out of the king's hands, but where a
successor was being held accountable for its issues: 42 DK Rep Ire, 69.

[3] above, 254 n 6; Meath (v, vi, vii); Kildare (v); Limerick (iv); but some of these, at
least, may refer to proceedings in the justiciar's court.

[4] 42 DK Rep Ire, 69 (but this was only one of the reasons for exonerating the archbishop)
See also above, 254 and n 2.

determine the issue seems to indicate that the argument advanced was one of fact, not law. It is to be noted, however, that the jury then found that the property had been held to the abbey's use, but that the court subsequently gave judgment in favour of the tenant. The tenant may have hoped to secure the restoration of property by victory on the issue of fact - but then done so by victory on the point of law involved.[1] A similarly successful challenge was mounted in 1358. Here the certificate indicated that seizure had been made on the grounds that the property had once been granted to a feoffee to uses, who had held the property to the use of the hospital of St Cross, Limerick - and that this grant had constituted an infringement of the statute. On this occasion, however, it is clear that the current tenant succeeded in his challenge because he was able to demonstrate to the satisfaction of the jury that the tenant in question had held the property to his own use and not to the use of the religious house.[2]

Others challenging seizures did at least concede that the property in question had passed into mortmain. They asserted, however, that this had taken place before the enactment of the statute[3] or, less commonly, before the statute had been published in Ireland.[4] Alternatively, they claimed that the acquisition had been made with a royal licence and produced the relevant licence. This would normally bring proceedings to an end;[5] but there was always the possibility that it did not cover all the property acquired and seized[6] or that it might be claimed that the property had been acquired by some transaction other than that specified in the licence.[7] Other challengers attempted to show that their unlicensed acquisition of property had not been in breach of the statute. Thus one religious house which had 'recovered' land in litigation by the default of its opponent, but had then had that land seized, asserted that the default had not been collusive - and was in the position to produce a record of the jury verdict given in the Bench under the provisions of chapter 32 of the statute of Westminster II to support that assertion.[8] Another religious house seems to have secured the reversal of a seizure on the grounds that the property concerned had been acquired from one of the *hibernici* - the unfree, native tenants - of the religious house concerned; and that at common law the property held by a *Hibernicus* (like the property

---

[1] above, 254 n 6(v); and see also *Rot Canc Hib* 47b no 137 and 47b no 170.

[2] above, 254 n 6: Limerick (iv).

[3] above, 253 n 4(iv, ix); 253 n 5(iii, v, vi); 254 n 6: Dublin country (ii, iii); Louth (iii); Meath (v, vi, viii, ix, x).   [4] above, 245 n 2; 250 n 4.

[5] CJR 1295–1303, 84 and above, 253 n 4(i, vi); 253 n 6(i).

[6] above, 253 n 4(v); 253 n 6(ii).

[7] above, 254 n 6: Kildare (vi); Kilkenny (ii) and CPR 1334–38, 224 and CPR 1340–43, 52–4.   [8] above, 253 n 4(x).

held by a villain in England) was already the property of the lord of the unfree tenant concerned.[1] A third religious house was successful in its claim
that it was entitled to accept the surrender of a tenement held of it by a free
tenant but it seems to have been significant that in this case the value of the
tenement did not exceed the value of the rent previously paid for it.[2] In another case in the same year and in the same eyre a religious house which
simply claimed to have 'satisfied' its tenant for his holding, but did not assert
that the surrender was the result of the tenant's poverty or show that the
rent equalled or exceeded the value of the holding, found its justification rejected as being insufficient.[3] There seems also to have been some doubt as to
whether or not it was permissible under the statute to 'redeem' a rent-charge
charged on the property of the religious house or secular ecclesiastic concerned. The archbishop of Armagh argued in the 1301 Co Louth eyre that
such a redemption was allowed under the statute, but had his argument rejected.[4] A similar claim by the prior of Bridgetown in the succeeding eyre of
Co Cork was adjourned for judgment.[5]

Success in securing the restoration of property seized into the king's hands
might however be only temporary, and the property be seized several more
times before its owner was finally left in peace. In 1332 the English abbey of
Furness, which already had various Irish possessions, received a licence to acquire all the Irish property of the Norman abbey of Beaubec.[6] In 1336, Furness' tenure of Beaubec's lands was challenged on the grounds that Furness
had entered the lands by virtue of a twenty-year lease made prior to the
granting of the licence – but the king confirmed the abbey in possession of the
lands notwithstanding this.[7] In 1343-44 twenty acres of land in Beaubec,
part of the lands acquired, were again seized – this time on the grounds that
the abbey of Beaubec had acquired them from the community of Drogheda-

---

[1] above, 254 n 6: Meath (vii). The English position is discussed by Raban, *Mortmain*, 31–
33. The position in Ireland was not altogether clear. The same religious house had obtained a licence in 1311 for the acquisition of property in the same area from one Robert
O'Kelly, perhaps also one of its *hibernici* (CPR 1307-13, 84); and when an inquisition *ad
quod damnum* was held in 1337 into the restitution of properties seized from the predecessors of the archbishop of Armagh, these included property acquired by archbishop
Nicholas Mac Maoil Íosa from Richard Macslybir *hibernicus suus* (C 47/10/19 no 14).

[2] above, 253 n 4(ii). [3] above, 253 n 4(ix).

[4] above, 253 n 4(vii). [5] above, 253 n 5(iv).

[6] CPR 1330-34, 383. The grant by Beaubec to Furness is printed by W. Dugdale, *Monasticon Anglicanum* (1846 edition) vi 1129.

[7] CPR 1334-38, 224. The Pipe Roll calendar suggests that the manor of Beaubec was in
the king's hands from 28 September 1336 to 8 February 1337, even though a royal mandate not to molest the abbey in its possession of the manor had been issued on 27 February 1336: 47 DK Rep Ire, 73.

in-Meath without a licence after the enactment of the statute of mortmain;
but the land was restored when a jury found that it had not been acquired
after the enactment of the statute and had not belonged to the community.[1]
In or before 1348, the manor of Beaubec was retained in the king's hands
when the rest of the abbey's Irish lands were restored after the election of a
new abbot of Furness, apparently because of doubts as to whether or not the
acquisition of the manor had contravened the statute of mortmain; and the
abbot had to secure a royal mandate to the Irish escheator to secure its restoration.[2] Yet again, in or before 1358, forty acres of land at Beaubec were
seized into the king's hands on the grounds that it had once been the common land of the burgesses of Drogheda-in-Meath, and had been acquired of
them by the abbot of Beaubec without a licence. Once more the seizure was
counterpleaded by the abbot of Furness who claimed that the land had been
granted to Beaubec by Walter de Lacy long before the enactment of the statute of mortmain. The escheator was instructed to investigate this claim.[3]
Nor was Furness abbey's experience unique. In 1287 the abbot of St Mary's
Abbey, Dublin, had initiated litigation in the court of the liberty of Trim
against John de Ardern, claiming that he was entitled to a messuage, a carucate and a water-mill at 'Balycur' by way of escheat because of the outlawry
for felony of John's father, Reginald. The litigation was eventually compromised in 1291 with John acknowledging the abbot's right to the property,
and the abbot granting half of it to John.[4] In or before 1329 the land acquired by the abbot under this compromise was seized by the escheator; but
the abbot made representations to the king in England, claiming that the acquisition had been made in good faith and before the statute of mortmain
had been published in Ireland. The king ordered the chancellor of Ireland to
inspect the records relating to the litigation and instructed him that if he
found the concord between the parties had been made before the statute was
published in Ireland or that John's surrender had been made in good faith, he
was to cause a pardon to be issued, allowing the abbey to retain the land,
though only in return for a 'reasonable fine'.[5] We next hear of the abbey and
its holdings at 'Balycur' in 1337, when the abbot was summoned to the Exchequer to answer for issues to the value of five marks, in respect of the two
and a half years which had then elapsed since a further *ex officio* inquisition
before the escheator had found that the abbot had acquired two carucates of
land there from John de Ardern and his daughter Joan without a licence and
contrary to the statute of mortmain. The land had been seized but restored

[1] above, 254 n 6: Meath (v) (and *Rot Canc Hib* 47b no 170).
[2] CCR 1346–49, 459.   [3] above, 252 n 5(xi).
[4] *Chart St Mary's Dublin*, i195, 392–96. The place seems to be the modern Dysertale, Co
Westmeath.   [5] above, 251 n 1.

to the abbot on condition that he answer for the issues if the land was forfeit
to the Crown. The abbot claimed to hold the two carucates in question not
by the gift or surrender of John de Ardern and his daughter, but by the gift
of king John, as lord of Ireland, long before the statute. A jury verdict, taken
before a commissioner in the summer of 1337, confirmed that the two carucates had been granted to the abbey over a century earlier when 'Balycur'
had been known as 'Dissertale', though by Gilbert de Nugent and not by king
John. Possession was restored unconditionally to the abbey as a result.[1] It is
not clear whether the two carucates included the land surrendered by John
de Ardern in 1291. Two other carucates may be in question here; but it is
possible that the half carucate surrendered in 1291 (and perhaps also the
other half carucate retained by John then) were part of the two carucates;
had been part of the original grant to the abbey, been subinfeudated subsequently to an ancestor of John and then re-acquired by the abbey, but the
subinfeudation and subsequent re-acquisition had been passed over in silence
by the jury. In 1359 there was a further seizure of land in 'Balycur' belonging
to the abbey – this time of a messuage, a mill and eighty acres. There were
two reasons for the seizure – that the land had been acquired of Gilbert de
Nugent after the enactment of the statute without a licence; and that after a
previous seizure of the property made by a former escheator, the abbot had
re-entered the property without authority. The abbot counterpleaded the
escheator's certificate in the justiciar's court denying the intrusion, and
claiming that Gilbert had granted the land to his house over forty years before the enactment of the statute and that he and his predecessors had been
continuously seised of the land since then. Even before then, he claimed,
king Henry II had granted the same land to the abbey's mother house of
Buildwas. A jury confirmed the abbot's claim on both points.[2] It seems almost certain that his land was part of the land seized in 1337; and probable
that it also formed part or all of the land seized in or before 1329. If so, the
land had by 1359 been seized on three occasions within just thirty years.

(iii)

The alternative was for a religious house or order or secular ecclesiastic to
seek the restoration of property which had been seized into the king's hands
as of grace, not of right. Several written petitions of the early fourteenth century, sent to the king in England, and asking him to pardon the petitioners'
offence in having made a mortmain acquisition without a licence and to re-

---

[1] above, 254 n 6: Meath (ix); but for continuing problems over the issues see *Chart St Mary's Dublin*, i299–301.
[2] above, 252 n 5 (xiv). For transcripts of the charters of Gilbert de Nugent, king Henry II and king John, ibid., i79–80, 86–87, 88–89, 105–6.

store the property concerned to the petitioner, still survive.[1] Such petitions seem normally to have been discussed at meetings of the king's council or of parliament. The request seems also normally to have been investigated in detail by an inquisition *ad quod damnum*. The earliest known pardon and order for restitution issued in respect of property in Ireland dates from 1289;[2] like all other surviving pardons and restitutions of a date earlier than 1327, it was issued by the English chancery.[3] During the next twenty years such orders seem to have been issued both by the English and by the Irish chanceries.[4] No such pardons and restitutions of a date later than 1348 seem now to survive.

Restitution was sometimes obtained quite quickly. The 1289 restitution and pardon must have been of property seized within the previous ten years. Restitutions and pardons were issued in 1302 and 1303 for property seized during the eyres of 1301.[5] In other cases there was a much longer delay. It was only in 1338 that the archbishop of Armagh finally recovered properties, some of which had been in the king's possession since the Co Louth eyre of 1301, others of which had been in the king's possession since 1318-19.[6] An even longer period elapsed between the seizure of thirty-six acres at Collon, Co Louth, and their eventual restoration to the abbey of Mellifont. The original seizure was made in the Co Louth eyre of 1301.[7] The abbey's first attempt to secure their unconditional restoration was at the king's parliament of England in 1302 – and the recorded response to the petition indicates that there was no objection in principle to the restoration, only a practical problem about fixing what was an appropriate fine for the pardon, and that this was to be settled by an inquisition *ad quod damnum*.[8] The inquisition seems, however, not to have been held until 1312,[9] and no licence was

---

[1] SC 9/25 m 2, 2d; 20 DK Rep Ire, 69; *Docs King's Council*, 172.

[2] CPR 1281-92, 325.

[3] CCR 1296-1302, 53; CPR 1301-7, 57, 117, 148, 258; CPR 1313-17, 33.

[4] By the English chancery: CPR 1334-38, 330; CPR 1338-40, 85; CChR 1341-1417, 97-99. By the Irish chancery: *Rot Canc Hib* 37b, no 66; *Reg SJB Dublin*, 233-34; 44 DK Rep Ire, 58 and cf. CCR 1327-30, 444.   [5] CPR 1301-7, 57, 117, 148.

[6] CPR 1338-40, 85. The preliminary petition asking for restitution is *Doc King's Council*, 172 and the resulting inquisition is C47/10/19 no 14. As early as 1302 the archbishop had sued a certificate into the English chancery of the proceedings of the justices with regard to these and other properties which had been seized in connection with a petition for their restitution: C260/13 no 21. In 1309 an inquisition *ad quod damnum* was held into the restitution of the same properties: C143/75 no 1.

[7] above, 253 n 4(ix): the abbey was allowed to retain possession of the property, but had to pay a rental equal to its estimated annual value to the king.   [8] SC 9/25 m 2d.

[9] C143/86 no 20. An entry on the Memoranda Roll of 4-5 Edward II may explain the reason for the delay. This shows that the abbot of Mellifont was summoned to the Irish

then forthcoming. A further petition led to another inquisition *ad quod damnum* being ordered in 1338,[1] but again no licence was forthcoming. The land was only finally restored to Mellifont in 1348, as part of a general confirmation of charters to the abbey, which also included certain additional grants.[2]

On at least two occasions property seized by the king from one ecclesiastical tenant is known to have been subsequently granted to another ecclesiastical tenant. In 1324, the king granted to the prior of Bath a rent in Waterford which had been acquired without a licence by the hospital of St Leonard in Waterford:[3] in 1395 Richard II granted to the cathedral priory of Holy Trinity in Dublin property which had been left by will without a licence to a confraternity in St Michael's church in Dublin.[4]

(iv)

Chapter 32 of the statute of Westminster II specifically authorised the seizure of property into the king's hands when an ecclesiastical demandant was about to recover it in litigation by default, and its retention by the king until a jury verdict had been given as to whether or not the demandant had good title to the property concerned. It also specifically made the local sheriff responsible for the issues of the property while it was in the king's hands.

It is possible from surviving plea-rolls and calendars of plea-rolls now destroyed to show this procedure being applied in the lordship of Ireland in the late thirteenth and early fourteenth centuries:[5] it is also possible from the calendars of pipe-rolls now destroyed to show sheriffs being held accountable for the issues of lands seized in this way.[6] It is also possible to find at least one instance of property being retained in the king's hands when a jury found that a default was collusive and intended to circumvent the statute,[7] and at least one instance of a lord suing property out of the king's hands after such a verdict, again in accordance with the provisions of the statute.[8]

Exchequer in Trinity term 1311 to answer for being in occupation of the land. He claimed that the abbey had been in possession of the land when he was elected abbot, but said nothing of paying any rent to the king for it. The land was once more seized into the king's hands, but the abbot allowed to hold it as the king's farmer for a rent equal to its value: RC8/5 p 727-30.

[1] C143/247 no 53. The inquisition itself is no longer attached to the writ.
[2] CChR 1341–1417, 97–99.   [3] 42 DK Rep Ire, 46.
[4] *Rot Canc Hib* 152b no 50.
[5] The earliest reference to the statutory procedure takes its use in Ireland back to 1292: CJR 1308–14, 88–90. For other references to its use see RC 7/3 p 335 and CB 1/1 m 20.
[6] 42 DK Rep Ire, 12, 30; 47 DK Rep Ire, 19.
[7] RC7/11 p 193–94.   [8] CB1/1 m 20.

(v)

The statute of mortmain, as enacted by the king's parliament of England in 1279, was applicable only within the kingdom of England itself. No attempt was made at that time to extend the statute to the lordship of Ireland although there existed machinery which made such an extension a simple and easy matter. The omission is not likely to have been the result of any conscious decision to the effect that this legislation was somehow unsuitable for export to Ireland. Bureaucratic oversight is a possible explanation. If this is the explanation, then some not very flattering conclusions would have to be drawn as to the efficiency of the English governmental machine in this period; and also as to just how peripheral the lordship of Ireland was to the main concerns of English administrators. There is, however, an alternative explanation which has as much, if not more, to recommend it. This would see the omission as being the result of doubts as to the propriety of continuing to extend English legislation to Ireland in the customary manner, by royal mandate alone. If this is the explanation, it sheds a very interesting light on the Anglo-Irish constitutional relationship as seen from England at the beginning of the reign of Edward I, and indicates doubts where historians have hitherto seen only confident certainty.

It soon came to be assumed, at first only in England but subsequently in Ireland also, that the statute had been formally extended to Ireland and was in force within the lordship. This is not too surprising a development. There was no authoritative collection of statutes in force in Ireland to which reference could be made; at the time, there was no such collection in England either. The common law applied in the courts of the lordship was almost identical to that of England, and earlier English legislation had been extended to Ireland. It was natural to assume that the statute of mortmain had been extended to Ireland as well: that it had been integrated into the common law of the lordship in the same way that the English statute had been integrated into the English common law. This informal extension of the statute to the lordship did, however, come under challenge: there were those who remembered, and had good reasons for remembering, that the statute had never been properly extended to Ireland. Eventually, in the mid-1290s, the statute seems to have been formally extended to Ireland; and thereafter there were no doubts about its application within the lordship. The earlier history, however, continued for some decades to be reflected in the care taken in many circumstances to draw a distinction between the date of the enactment and the date of the publication of the statute of mortmain in Ireland.

In Ireland, as in England, there is comparatively little evidence for the direct enforcement of the mortmain legislation by feudal lords: much more evidence for its being enforced, on the king's behalf, by various types of royal official - escheator, eyre justices and justiciar, in particular. Again, as in England in the early fourteenth century, legal procedures were developed for challenging seizures made in the king's name, and litigation brought using these procedures shows the courts of the lordship tackling some interesting problems of interpretation posed by the statute of mortmain - for example, as to the legality of ecclesiastical lords 'acquiring' property from their own unfree tenants. Other such proceedings show that there may have been attempts in Ireland to anticipate part of the 1391 mortmain legislation - by treating enfeoffments to the use of ecclesiastical tenants as though they were alienations into mortmain under the terms of the 1279 statute. Two case histories traced indicate one of the main drawbacks to the procedures for challenging seizures - their lack of finality. Ecclesiastical tenants from whom property had been seized and to whom that property had then been restored could still find it being seized again - and on more than one occasion: the first restitution gave no protection at all against other subsequent seizures, particularly if the specific grounds for the seizure differed from those alleged on the previous occasion.

APPENDIX

These two transcripts of Crown copyright material in the Public Record Office, London, appear by permission of the Controller of Her Majesty's Stationery Office.

Document 1

Suo W de Odiham salutem. Mandetis per breve regis Justiciario Hibernie quod non distringat nec distringi permittat seu molestari ab aliquibus abbatem et conventum de Furneys pro terris suis quas habent ad firmam in Hibernia infra terminum suum, cum non sit contra statutum regis quod terre tam religiosis quam aliis ad terminum concedantur. Datum apud Rothelan, Non' Februarii.

Reference: C81/1684, no 48; this document was calendared by H. S. Sweetman in *Calendar of documents relating to Ireland*, ii no 2043.

Document 2

Excellentissimo principi domino Edwardo dei gracia illustri regi Anglie, domino Hibernie et duci Aquitanie, S. permissione ejusdem Waterford' ecclesie minister humilis Justiciarius suus Hibernie id parum quod potest obsequii reverencie et honoris. Litteras dominacionis vestre recepimus in hec verba: Edwardus dei gracia rex Anglie, dominus Hibernie et dux Aquitannie venerabili in christo patri S. eadem gracia Waterforden' episcopo Justiciario suo Hibernic salutem. Ex querela dilecti nobis in Christo prioris de Lanton' juxta Gloucestr' accepimus quod vos pretextu statuti nostri in Anglia nuper editi de terris vel tenementis in manum mortuam non ponendis octies viginti acras terre cum pertinenciis in Logher quas frater Johannes Wyther canonicus et procurator ipsius prioris in Hibernia diu ante edicionem dicti statuti emerat a Waltero le Jeovene et Alicia uxori ejus, Alexandro Barbedor et Isolda uxori ejus ad opus prioratus predicti et de qua quidem terra idem procurator per empcionem predictam per quinque dies extitit in plena et pacifica possessione cepistis in manum nostram et licet pluries vobis mandaverimus quod si ita esset tunc de eadem terra vos non intromitteretis tamen terram illam adhuc detinetis in predicti prioris et ecclesie sue predicte prejudicium et gravamen. Et quia nolumus quod eadem terra contra mandatum nostrum dicto priori detineatur indebite, vobis mandamus quod si ita est tunc permittatis quod predictus prior per procuratorem suum pristinam seisinam suam ejusdem terre recuperet hac vice de gracia nostra speciali, vel causam nobis significetis quare mandata nostra vobis alias inde directa exequi noluistis vel non potuistis; ita quod super hoc querelam non audiamus iteratam per quod manum correctionis ad hoc aliter apponere debeamus. Teste me ipso apud Bristoll' xxix die Decembris anno regni nostri terciodecimo. Nos preceptis vestris parere volentes in omnibus ut tenemur excellencie vestre tenore presencium duximus significandum quod predictas occies viginti acras terre cum pertinenciis non cepimus in manum vestram pretextu alicujus statuti vestri in Anglia nuper editi de terris vel tenementis in manum mortuam non ponendis set quia tenentur de abbate sancte Marie de Dyvelek et de dominio abbacie predicte cujus custodia tempore vacacionis ad vos pertinere dinoscitur eo quod idem abbas de vobis tenet in capite et prefatam intrusionem nobis conquerendo demonstravit et vos wardam et maritagium si medio tempore evenire contigerit amittetis si prefatus prior predictam terram per hujusmodi ingressum perpetuo possideat. Valeat vestra regia potestas per tempora longiora. Datum Dublin' xxv die Aprilis anno regni vestri terciodecimo. *Endorsed*: Domino regi Anglie domino Hibernie et duci Aquitanie per Justiciarium Hibernie pro priore de Lantony juxta Glovermiam.

Reference: SC1/17 no 189; this document was calendared by Sweetman in *Cal Doc Ireland*, iii no 39.

13

The Licensing of Mortmain Alienations in the Medieval Lordship of Ireland

The statute of Mortmain, prohibiting any transaction which led to land or other real property passing into "mortmain" (the possession of religious houses or orders or of secular ecclesiastics), was enacted in England in the autumn of 1279. Within six months of the enactment of the statute the royal chancery had begun to issue licences for property to be conveyed into mortmain "notwithstanding the statute" and an elaborate system was soon created to control and process the granting of such licences. As enacted, the statute only applied in England, but within a few years it had come to be assumed that the statute was also in force in the lordship of Ireland, and it seems probable that the statute was also formally extended to the lordship some time in the last decade of the thirteenth century (1). The first known example of a royal licence for an alienation into mortmain granted in respect of property within the lordship of Ireland was issued by the English chancery in 1289 (2). This article charts the story of the subsequent history of the licensing of mortmain alienations within the lordship of Ireland during the remainder of the Middle Ages.

(i)

During an initial phase of the operation of a mortmain licensing system in Ireland which lasted from 1289 to 1316, only the English chancery is known to have issued licences for property in Ireland to be alienated into mortmain. Thirty-four such licences were granted. Almost half gave permission for a specific alienation into mortmain which had not as yet taken place (3). A further quarter pardoned and confirmed an alienation which had already occurred and whose discovery had led to the seizure of the property in question (4). A small number of licences

---

(1) Paul Brand, "King, Church and Property: The Enforcement of Restrictions on Alienations into Mortmain in the Lordship of Ireland in the Later Middle Ages", above, 245-51.

(2) *Cal. Pat. Rolls, 1281-92,* p. 325.

(3) *Cal. Pat. Rolls, 1281-92,* pp. 379, 380; *Cal. Pat. Rolls, 1292-1301,* pp. 422-3; *Cal. Pat. Rolls, 1301-7,* pp. 45, 51, 157, 430; *Cal. Pat. Rolls, 1307-13,* pp. 84, 181 (bis), 345, 385, 518, 519; *Cal. Pat. Rolls, 1313-7,* p. 282. There is also an allusion to a licence granted to the Dominican house at Kilmallock in or before 1291 in P.R.O. London, C 47/10/14, no. 18.

(4) *Cal. Pat. Rolls, 1281-92,* pp. 325, 497 (but note that it is only P.R.O. London, C143/15, no. 26 that shows that the property had been seized); *Cal. Pat. Rolls, 1301-7,* pp. 57, 117, 148, 258 (but note that it is only P.R.O. London, C 143/49, no. 9 that shows that the property had been seized); *Cal. Pat. Rolls, 1313-7,* p. 33. All of these are pardons for specific acquisitions. There is also one more general par-

confirmed and pardoned an alienation which had already taken place but did not authorise the restoration of the property to the alienee, evidently because the property had not as yet been seized into the king's hands *(5)*. A fourth type of licence, the general licence, authorised the future acquisition of property up to a certain value by the licensee *(6)*.

An overwhelming majority of the licences went to existing religious houses *(7)*. Licences were issued in respect of property all over the lordship: as far north as Ulster *(8)*, as far south as counties Cork and Tipperary *(9)*, as far west as counties Connacht and Limerick *(10)*. Only a minority of the licences give any real information as to the nature of the transaction being licensed, but this can be supplemented to a limited extent by evidence derived from the inquisitions *ad quod damnum* held prior to the granting of such licences. There are a number of instances of the licensing of grants of property made for pious purposes such as the establishment of a nunnery at Cork *(11)*, of a chantry chapel for the earl of Ulster and his ancestors at either Loughrea or Ballintober *(12)* or for the erection of other new religious houses *(13)*. Some of the transactions licensed, however, clearly do not fall into such a category. These

don for all acquisitions made by the Carmelite order for the enlargement of their houses prior to 13 August 1297; *Cal. Cl. Rolls, 1296-1302*, p. 53. A further specific pardon in favour of Athassel priory is known only from a mandate addressed to the treasurer and barons of the Irish Exchequer which refers to it: P.R.O. Dublin, R.C. 8/4, pp. 665-6 (calendar of the memoranda roll of 3 Edward II).

(5) *Cal. Pat. Rolls, 1281-92*, p. 365 (bis); *Cal. Pat. Rolls, 1301-7*, p. 458; *Cal. Pat. Rolls, 1313-7*, p. 303.

(6) *Cal. Pat. Rolls, 1313-7*, p. 149; *Cal. Pat. Rolls, 1313-7*, pp. 317, 465, 541. There is also one general licence authorising the recovery of all property which had formerly belonged to the house concerned with no restriction as to the value of the property recovered: *Cal. Cl. Rolls, 1288-96*, pp. 492-3. Related entries on the justiciary rolls suggest that the licence was also taken as authority for the restitution of property acquired before the licence was issued which had been seized into the king's hands: *Cal. Just. Rolls, 1295-1303*, pp. 87-8, 100.

(7) But the licensees also include the rector of a parish church *(Cal. Pat. Rolls, 1281-92*, p. 379); an archbishop *(ibid.*, p. 365) and a college of chantry chaplains not yet in existence *(Cal. Pat. Rolls, 1301-7*, p. 430).

(8) *Cal. Pat. Rolls, 1301-7*, p. 430; *Cal. Cl. Rolls, 1288-96; pp. 492-3.

(9) For County Cork see *Cal. Pat. Rolls, 1301-7*, pp. 51, 57; *Cal. Pat. Rolls, 1307-13*, p. 181. For County Tipperary see *Cal. Pat. Rolls, 1281-92*, p. 497; *Cal. Pat. Rolls, 1301-7*, p. 458.

(10) For (the medieval) County Connacht see *Cal. Pat. Rolls, 1301-7*, p. 430. For County Limerick see *Cal. Pat. Rolls, 1307-13*, p. 385.

(11) *Cal. Pat. Rolls, 1301-7*, p. 51. The inquisition *ad quod damnum* and the petition filed with it (P.R.O. London, C 143/36, no. 10) make it clear that the nunnery was not as yet securely established and that the grants were needed for that purpose. They strongly suggest that the nunnery was at this time in no position to purchase the property.

(12) *Cal. Pat. Rolls, 1301-7*, p. 430.

(13) *Cal. Pat. Rolls, 1307-13*, p. 181 (the related inquisition *ad quod damnum* makes it clear that the house has not yet been established and that the land is to be used for this purpose: P.R.O. London, C 143/69, no. 5). For an inquisition *ad quod damnum* into a proposed grant of this kind which seems not to have led to the granting of a licence see P.R.O. Dublin, KB 1/1, m.46d.

include an exchange of property *(14)*; the purchase by a religious house of the holding of one of its tenants *(15)*; and the acceptance by another religious house of the surrender of their holdings by a number of the house's tenants *(16)*. There are also three instances of licences being given for a transaction which did not involve the transfer of property at all. Each licensed a religious house to appropriate to its own use a benefice (rectory or vicarage) whose advowson it already possessed: that is, to present itself to the benefice concerned as its permanent incumbent *(17)*. The framers of the statute of Mortmain are not likely to have intended to include such appropriations within the scope of the statutory ban, but by 1313 in both England and Ireland it was being held that the statute did apply to them, and that all appropriations needed a mortmain licence *(18)*.

The amount of property whose transfer into mortmain was authorised by these licences was comparatively small. The general licences allowed the acquisition of property up to a total value of one hundred and thirty pounds *(19)*. The other licences generally do not give a valuation of the property concerned, but in many cases it is possible to discover this from the associated inquisition *ad quod damnum*. These show that six of the licences were for the acquisition of property worth less than one pound *(20)*; five for the acquisition of property worth between one and five pounds *(21)*; and only five for the acquisition of property worth over five pounds *(22)*. Of the licences for which there is

---

(14) *Cal. Pat. Rolls, 1301-7,* p. 45 (but there were also political and military factors here); *Cal. Pat. Rolls, 1307-13,* p. 518. For other transactions which may have formed part of an exchange see *Cal. Pat. Rolls, 1281-92,* pp. 378-9; *ibid.,* p. 365.

(15) *Cal. Pat. Rolls, 1281-92,* p. 497. That the acquisition was by way of purchase is shown by the writ authorising the holding of an inquisition *ad quod damnum* into the transaction: P.R.O. London, C 143/15, no. 26.

(16) *Cal. Pat. Rolls, 1301-7,* p. 258. The related inquisition *ad quod damnum* tells us that the tenants concerned were poor and their services of the same value as the tenements surrendered: P.R.O. London, C 143/49, no. 9.

(17) *Cal. Pat. Rolls, 1307-13,* p. 519; *Cal. Pat. Rolls, 1313-7,* pp. 33, 282.

(18) In Michaelmas term 1312 there had been litigation in the Bench in England in which the king claimed an advowson as forfeit by reason of an unlicensed appropriation. This may have been regarded as a test case. Certainly the arguments of the defendant's counsel indicate that the king's claim was not as yet well-established: *Year Books 6 Edward II,* edd. P. Vinogradoff and L. Ehrlich (Selden Society vol. xxxiv (1917)), pp. 73-83.

(19) This, of course, excludes the general licence to acquire all property that had once belonged to a particular house: above, n. 6.

(20) *Cal. Pat. Rolls, 1301-7,* pp. 45, 117, 258, 458; *Cal. Pat. Rolls, 1307-13,* p. 181 (bis). The valuations are derived from the related inquisitions *ad quod damnum* in P.R.O. London, C 143/37, no. 9; /42, no. 14; /49, no. 9; /60, no. 18; /69, nos. 5, 7.

(21) *Cal. Pat. Rolls, 1301-7,* pp. 57, 148 (rents); *Cal. Pat. Rolls, 1281-92,* p. 497; *Cal. Pat. Rolls, 1292-1301,* pp. 422-3; *Cal. Pat. Rolls, 1307-13,* p. 345. The valuations for all but the first two transactions are derived from the related inquisitions *ad quod damnum* in P.R.O. London, C 143/14, no. 29; /15, no. 26; /79, no. 17.

(22) *Cal. Pat. Rolls, 1301-7,* pp. 51, 430; *Cal. Pat. Rolls, 1307-13,* p. 84; *Cal. Pat. Rolls, 1313-7,* pp. 33, 282. The valuations are derived from the related inquisitions *ad quod damnum* in P.R.O. London, C 143/37, no. 10; /40, no. 18; /53, no. 19; /96, no. 23; /101, no. 22.

no valuations six are for the acquisition of land for the building or extension of premises for religious houses: this is likely to have been of only small value *(23)*. This leaves only six licences where the value of the property to be granted is not now ascertainable. These are unlikely to materially change the overall picture of comparatively small-scale alienations being all that were licensed in this period.

The issuing of a mortmain licence was normally only the last stage in a fairly complicated process *(24)*. The first stage was the submission of a petition to the king in England, normally at a session of the great council or of parliament. If the petition was for a general licence and received a favourable response, the endorsed petition was the authority for the English chancery to issue the licence *(25)*. If what was requested was a specific licence the normal response was for the petitioner to be told to have the proposed acquisition investigated through an inquisition *ad quod damnum (26)*. Thirty-one writs authorising the holding of such inquisitions survive *(27)*. Two are addressed to the escheator of Ireland *(28)*; the remainder to the justiciar of Ireland or his deputy. Like

(23) Cal. Pat. Rolls, 1281-92, p. 380; Cal. Pat. Rolls, 1301-7, p. 157; Cal. Pat. Rolls, 1307-13, p. 385; Cal. Pat. Rolls, 1313-7, p. 303; Cal. Cl. Rolls, 1296-1302, p. 53; and the licence referred to in P.R.O. London, C 47/10/14, no. 18.

(24) For the preliminary stages in the licensing system in England see Sandra Raban, *Mortmain Legislation and The English Church, 1279-1500* (Cambridge, 1982), pp. 39-41; P. A. Brand, "The Control of Mortmain Alienation in England, 1200-1300" in *Legal Records and The Historian*, ed. J. H. Baker (London, 1978), pp. 29-40 at pp. 37-8 ; see above, pp. 241-42.

(25) For a successful petition see *Rotuli Parliamentorum*, i.277b (but note that the priory was only given permission to acquire property to the value of twenty pounds, not one hundred pounds as it had requested: see *Cal. Pat. Rolls, 1307-13*, p. 149). For an unsuccessful petition by the priory of St. Mary, Louth for a general licence to acquire property formerly held by the house see P.R.O. London, SC 9/25, m.2; and for another unsuccessful petition by the Dominican order in Ireland for a general licence to acquire land for the extension of their houses and to be allowed to receive legacies of land on condition they then sold them see *Documents on the Affairs of Ireland before the King's Council*, ed. G. O. Sayles (Irish Manuscripts Commission, 1979) [hereafter *King's Council Documents*], pp. 36-7.

(26) For examples of such petitions and their responses see P.R.O. London, SC 9/25, mm.2,2d; *King's Council Documents*, p. 58. For a petition not so answered but which seems to have resulted in a licence see A. Gwynn, "Documents Relating to the Medieval Diocese of Armagh", *Archivium Hibernicum*, xiii (1947), 15-6.

(27) The surviving original writs in the P.R.O. London (to which are normally attached the corresponding inquisitions *ad quod damnum*) are: C 143/14, no. 29; /15, no. 26; /30, no. 16; /31, no. 21; /37, nos. 2, 9, 10; /40, no. 18 [= *Cal. Just. Rolls, 1295-1303*, pp. 439-40]; /42, no. 14 [= *Cal. Just. Rolls, 1295-1303*, pp. 456-7]; /43, no. 25; /47, no. 1; /49, no. 9 (two writs); /53, no. 19; /60, no. 18; /69, nos. 5, 7; /75 no. 1; /79, no. 17; /87, no. 20; /94, no. 27 [= P.R.O. Dublin, KB 1/1, mm.20-20d]; /96, no. 23 [= P.R.O. Dublin, KB 1/1, m.7d]; /99, no. 2; /101, nos. 22, 24. Full copies of original writs and inquisitions which no longer survive in the original are to be found in P.R.O. Dublin, KB 1/1, mm.46d, 88d and in *Register of the Hospital of St. John the Baptist, Dublin*, ed. E. St. J. Brooks (Irish Manuscripts Commission, 1936) [hereafter *Reg. S.J.B. Dublin*], pp. 333-5 [= *Cal. Just. Rolls, 1308-14*], pp. 127-8. Calendared versions only of other writs and inquisitions which do not survive will be found in *Cal. Just. Rolls, 1295-1303*, pp. 154-5; *Cal. Just. Rolls, 1305-7*, pp. 96-7; *Cal. Just. Rolls, 1308-14*, pp. 129-32.

(28) P.R.O. London C 143/30, no. 16; /37, no. 2.

similar writs in England these writs normally specified a series of points on which information was required – whether the transaction would be prejudicial or damaging to the interests of the king or others; of whom the property was held and by what service; how much it was worth; and whether or not the grantor was retaining enough other property to perform in full the feudal services he owed and for him to continue performing other duties of a communal nature *(29)*. The addressee was instructed to acquire the requisite information on these points from a jury *(30)* and then to return this verdict (the inquisition *ad quod damnum*) with the covering writ to the king *(31)*.

About two-thirds of the surviving inquisitions of this period were taken by either the justiciar or his deputy; most of the remainder by third parties specially commissioned to do so *(32)*. Inquisitions were often taken within the county where the property to be alienated lay, but there was no necessity to do so, and almost as commonly inquisitions were taken elsewhere, apparently to suit the convenience of the official concerned *(33)*. Several inquisitions specifically state that no loss or damage will be caused to anyone as a result of the proposed alienation, and in some cases this does indeed seem to be true *(34)*. In others, however, it seems simply to reflect the partiality of the jury and their eagerness to return a favourable verdict rather than the truth of the matter *(35)*. A number of different types of possible loss or damage are mentioned in inquisitions. These include the loss to the lord of whom the property was

(29) Cf. Brand, "Control of Mortmain Alienation in England", 241. The two earliest surviving writs are of an earlier and more abbreviated form. Writs of a somewhat shorter form were also sometimes used later e.g. for an exchange (see C 143/37, no. 9) or for the recovery of property in the king's hands (see for example C 143/75, no. 1).

(30) In England, where such writs are normally addressed to the local sheriff, the writ normally specified that the jury was to be drawn from the same county. The writs sent to Ireland normally allowed the addressee to draw jurors from anywhere in the lordship, though in a minority of cases he was instructed to draw them only from the relevant county (see C 143/49, no. 9; /60, no. 18; /69, nos. 5, 7) and in one case from a particular locality (KB 1/1, m.46d).

(31) A few writs contain additional instructions. One (C 143/15, no. 26) orders the property concerned to be restored to the religious house until a specific date; another (C 143/30, no. 16) orders the inquisition to be returned in time for the next session of the English parliament and that the grantors be told to be there, to "do and receive" what the king's council ordered.

(32) See, for example, C 143/14, no. 29.

(33) Thus, for example, we find inquisitions being held at Dublin in respect of property in counties Kildare, Kilkenny, Louth and Meath, and inquisitions being held at Castledermot, County Kildare in respect of property in County Kilkenny and in Connacht and Ulster.

(34) E.g. C 143/15, no. 26 (where the property is held directly of the religious house itself); C 143/69, no. 7 (where the property is said to be of no value).

(35) In several instances the lord of whom the property was held was losing the possibility that the property might escheat to him, a possibility specifically mentioned as detrimental in other inquisitions. In one such case the lord seems also to have been losing any possibility of wadship: see C 143/37, no. 2. The favourable verdict in this last case may perhaps be connected with the fact that one of the donors was the justiciar.

held of the possibility of the property escheating on coming into that lord's hands by way of wardship *(36)*; the loss by the lord of relief payments *(37)* or of feudal services owed for the property *(38)*. Losses to others mentioned include the diminution for a feudal lord of whom the grantor held other property of the value of the right of marriage over the grantor's heirs *(39)* and (for the lord of the liberty in which property lay) the ending of the possibility of him profiting from the tenant's felony by confiscation of his chattels and wasting of his land *(40)*. Several inquisitions specifically mention the loss to the community from the fact that tenants of the property will no longer be liable to jury service *(41)*; and in two the jurors are careful to state that no damage will arise provided the new tenant continues to contribute to certain communal burdens *(42)*. In at least one inquisition we hear only of the benefits which will arise from the proposed exchange, that of a manor for the advowson of a church and a small area of land. The manor was currently lying waste and being used as a base by felons and thieves; its new lay owner seems to have been thought more capable of reducing it to order than its current ecclesiastical tenant *(43)*. More commonly we hear of benefits as some kind of set-off to the actual or potential disadvantages. Those mentioned include the educational opportunities which will arise from the foundation of a chantry college *(44)*; the spiritual benefits of a priory having additional chaplains to celebrate mass for the souls of the king's ancestors and all the faithful departed *(45)*; and the benefits to both knights and free men of that part of the country in making arrangements for the upbringing of their daughters from the establishment of a nunnery *(46)*.

In the few instances where we have any definite information on this point the inquisition seems to have been entrusted to the petitioner or his representative for transmission to England *(47)*. The petitioner would

---

(36) The loss of the possibility of escheat is mentioned, for example, in C 143/14, no. 29; the loss of both escheat and wardship in C 143/53, no. 19.

(37) The loss of relief payments is noted only in *Cal. Just. Rolls, 1295-1303*, pp. 154-5.

(38) It seems always to be assumed in the inquisitions that after the grant the property will be held in frankalmoin, though this was not a necessary concomitant of property passing into mortmain. The loss of services is mentioned in KB 1/1, m.46d and in *Cal. Just. Rolls, 1305-7*, pp. 96-7; the loss of a rent seck owed for the property in C 143/47, no. 1. Certain inquisitions make clear that arrangements have already been made to transfer the burden of service to other lands retained by the grantor: see, for example, C 143/42, no. 14.

(39) C 143/79, no. 17.

(40) C 143/49, no. 9.

(41) This is mentioned, for example, in C 143/14, no. 29. In some other inquisitions care was taken to explain why this would not happen; for example, because the grantor, being a clerk in the Dublin Exchequer, was not liable for jury service: see C 143/47, no. 1.

(42) *Cal. Just. Rolls, 1295-1303*, pp. 154-5; *Cal. Just. Rolls, 1308-14*, pp. 129-32.

(43) C 143/37, no. 9.

(44) C 143/53, no. 19.

(45) C 143/94, no. 27 [=KB 1/1, mm.20-20d].

(46) *Cal. Just. Rolls, 1295-1303*, pp. 154-5.

(47) KB 1/1, mm.46d, 71d, 88d; *Cal. Just. Rolls, 1308-14*, pp. 127-8, 129-32.

now have to submit a second petition to the king asking for a licence to be issued to him in the light of the findings of the inquisition *ad quod damnum (48)*. This would then normally be considered at a meeting of the great council or of parliament *(49)*. A sizeable minority of proposed alienations were vetoed at this point. Sometimes an endorsement explains why *(50)*; more often the reason has to be deduced from the returned inquisition. Refusal of a licence on one occasion did not preclude petitioners from trying to gain a licence for the same transaction on subsequent occasions *(51)*. There is no evidence of fines being charged for licences prior to 1299 *(52)*; but fines can be shown to have been charged for some licences after that date and probably became the norm. There seems to be no direct correspondence between the value of the property transferred and the fine charged for the licence. Petitioners from Ireland were evidently not always prepared for the fact that they would be required to pay a fine and so had to return later with the money submitting a further petition for the licence already promised them *(53)* or to seek permission to pay the money to the Exchequer in Dublin *(54)*.

Given the intricacies of the licensing system it is not surprising to find that the period taken to secure a licence could be quite lengthy. The first dateable point in the process is usually the issuing of the writ authorising the holding of the inquisition *ad quod damnum*. The shortest period between the issuing of this writ and the granting of a licence is three months *(55)*. In five other instances the process took under a year; but in nine it took over a year *(56)*. It was perhaps the length of time it took to secure a licence, and the possible hazards of doing so which led religious houses in Ireland as in England on occasion to use lay intermediaries to act as trustees for them, acquiring title from the real

---

(48) For examples see C 143/37, no. 10, m.1 and SC 9/25, m.2d.

(49) Cf. *King's Council Documents*, pp. 48-9.

(50) For examples see C 143/21, no. 21, m.2d (no licence because the donor retains no land) and C 143/37, no. 2, m.2d (no licence until the consent is obtained of the lord of whom the property is held).

(51) C 143/30, no. 16, for example, is an inquisition held in 1299 into a proposed alienation which had already been investigated once before in 1293 and then vetoed (C 143/31, no. 21). On the second occasion the jury were made aware of certain additional facts calculated to put the proposal in a more favourable light and duly incorporated them in its verdict but a licence was again refused.

(52) Brand, "Control of Mortmain Alienation", 243; Raban, *Mortmain Legislation*, pp. 55-60. A fee may however already have been payable for having the licence written and sealed.

(53) SC 9/25, m.2d.

(54) *King's Council Documents*, p. 59.

(55) C 143/96, no. 23 (writ issued 26 July and inquisition held 26 August 1313) and *Cal. Pat. Rolls, 1313-7*, p. 33 (licence issued 2 November 1313).

(56) Most commonly the process took just over a year, but in exceptional cases it might take as long as nine years: see C 143/14, no. 29 (writ issued 6 February and inquisition held 2 May 1290) and *Cal. Pat. Rolls, 1292-1301*, pp. 422-3 (licence issued 18 June 1299).

vendor and holding the property pending its eventual transfer to the real purchaser *(57)*.

(ii)

During a second phase of the operation of a mortmain licensing system in the lordship of Ireland, which lasted from 1317 to 1379, both the English and the Irish chanceries issued licences for property in Ireland to pass into mortmain. The English chancery is known to have issued fifty-four such licences; the Irish chancery twenty-three *(58)*. It is unclear on what authority, if any, the Irish chancery began to issue such licences. The only known specific delegation to the Irish justiciar of the power to grant such licences is a very limited one made in 1328. This gave him just for three years permission to license bishops to acquire lands in the marches of the lordship on condition that they then ensured that the lands were settled by inhabitants who would defend them against the native Irish *(59)*. In 1342 the justiciar and chancellor of Ireland were specifically forbidden to issue mortmain licences unless they had received prior authorisation to do so from the king in England under the English great, privy or secret seal *(60)*. This strongly suggests that they had been issuing licences without such authorisation and that there had been no permanent delegation of authority to them allowing them to do so. Licences continued to be granted by the Irish chancery after 1342. It is conceivable that all were issued only after specific authorisation had been received from England or that there was some more general delegation of authority to issue such licences within a few years of the 1342 prohibition. It seems more probable, however, that all that happened (after a decent interval had been allowed to elapse) was a resumption of the

(57) For the use in England by the abbey of Peterborough of Ellis of Beckingham, a royal justice, as such a trustee see Raban, *Mortmain Legislation,* p. 110. In Ireland the abbey of Furness seems to have used Robert of Willoughby, a citizen of Dublin, as its trustee when acquiring land at Colp, County Meath from William Whiterel. Inquisition *ad quod damnum* and licence show Willoughby as grantor: C 143/14, no. 29 and *Cal. Pat. Rolls, 1292-1301,* pp. 422-3. The abbey's own archives, however, show Whiterel quitclaiming the land to Willoughby ". . . ad usum et proprietatem abbatis et conventus monasterii de Furneys et successorum suorum in puram et perpetuam elemosinam inperpetuum convertendis . . .": *The Coucher Book of Furness Abbey,* ii, part iii, ed. J. Brownbill (Chetham Soc., new series, lxxviii (1919), p. 719, no. 5. In or before 1340 the land was seized into the king's hands as having been acquired of Whiterel and not of Willoughby: *Cal. Pat. Rolls, 1340-3,* pp. 52-4. Master John le Marshal, a canon of Kildare, may have acted in such a capacity for the hospital of St. John the Baptist, Dublin (*Reg. S.J.B. Dublin,* pp. 147-9); as may also on another occasion Simon of Tenby and Henry Rowe (*Ibid.,* pp. 333-9).

(58) The total for licences issued by the Irish chancery is likely to be a considerable understatement. Most of the relevant chancery rolls had been lost before they were calendared in the early nineteenth century: only ten, or about one-sixth of the total number of patent rolls originally compiled. Many of the Irish licences are known only through subsequent English confirmations enrolled on the English patent rolls.

(59) *Rymer's Foedera,* ed. A. Clarke and others (Record Commission, 1830-69), ii, part ii, p. 749.

(60) *Cal. Cl. Rolls, 1341-3,* pp. 409-10.

earlier practice of granting such licences without any specific authority for doing so.

The most common type of licence continued to be that authorising a specific alienation that had yet to take place. Just under half the licences issued by the English chancery are of this kind *(61)* and just under three-quarters of those issued by the Irish chancery *(62)*. Only a small number of licences were issued by either chancery to confirm an alienation that had already taken place *(63)*; but we do now also encounter for the first time a new variant on this type of licence, one confirming the union of two ecclesiastical benefices and the position of their current incumbent *(64)*. A quarter of the licences issued by the

(61) *Cal. Pat. Rolls, 1317-21*, p. 137; *Cal. Pat. Rolls, 1324-7*, p. 299; *Cal. Pat. Rolls, 1327-30*, pp. 179, 187, 456; *Cal. Pat. Rolls, 1330-4*, pp. 327, 383; *Cal. Pat. Rolls, 1334-8*, p. 44; *Cal. Pat. Rolls, 1338-40*, p. 16; *Cal. Pat. Rolls, 1348-50*, pp. 28, 94, 114, 150-1,564; *Cal. Pat. Rolls, 1350-4*, pp. 101, 256-7; *Cal. Pat. Rolls, 1354-8*, p. 418; *Cal. Pat. Rolls, 1358-61*, pp. 111, 477, 508; *Cal. Pat. Rolls, 1361-4*, p. 522; *Cal. Pat. Rolls, 1364-7*, p. 122; *Cal. Pat. Rolls, 1374-7*, p. 298; *Cal. Pat. Rolls, 1377-81*, p. 369. For licences which stipulate that the acquisition is to count as part of the property which the licencsee has been authorised to acquire under a previous general licence see: *Cal. Pat. Rolls, 1338-40*, p. 88 (repeated at *Cal. Pat. Rolls, 1340-3*, p. 177); *Cal. Pat. Rolls, 1354-8*, p. 30; *Cal. Pat. Rolls, 1364-7*, p. 190. On the requirement of such individual licences in addition to the general licence see Raban, *Mortmain Legislation*, p. 50. In each case the property acquired was to be taken for this purpose to be worth considerably in excess of the valuation put on it by the jurors of the inquisition *ad quod damnum*. A similar practice was followed in England: Raban, *Mortmain Legislation*, pp. 64-6. There is also one licence which authorises a specific acquisition but also gives general permission for the future acquisition of property up to a certain value: *Cal. Pat. Rolls, 1370-4*, p. 337.

(62) *Cal. Pat. Rolls, 1327-30*, p. 134; *Cal. Pat. Rolls, 1330-4*, p. 301 [= *Rot. Canc. Hib.*, p. 23b, no. 115]; *Cal. Pat. Rolls, 1345-8*, pp. 446, 451; *Cal. Pat. Rolls, 1348-50*, p. 100; *Cal. Pat. Rolls, 1388-92*, p. 419; *Rot. Canc. Hib.*, pp. 22a, no. 30; 22b, no. 73; 25a, no. 177; 25b, no. 178; 33b, no. 2; 64b, no. 1; *Cal. Ormond Deeds*, i.33-4; Bodleian Library, Oxford, MS. Rawlinson B 479, ff.53r-54v.

(63) For licences issued by the English chancery restoring property seized into the king's hands see: *Cal. Pat. Rolls, 1334-8*, p. 330 [= *The Black Book of Limerick*, ed. J. MacCaffrey (Dublin, 1907), pp. 138-9]; *Cal. Pat. Rolls, 1338-40*, p. 85. For a similar licence issued by the Irish chancery see *Reg. S.J.B. Dublin*, pp. 233-4; and there is an allusion to another such licence in *Rot. Canc. Hib.*, p. 37b, no. 166. There is also a licence issued by the English chancery pardoning and confirming an alienation and also giving the licensee permission for the acquisition of one messuage in Dublin or its suburbs and another in Drogheda or its suburbs as well as of waste land in the marches to the value of twenty pounds (and confirming other unrelated grants): *Cal. Ch. Rolls, 1341-1417*, pp. 97-9. For licences issued by the English chancery confirming appropriations of benefices that have already occurred see: *Cal. Pat. Rolls, 1317-21*, p. 12; *Cal. Pat. Rolls, 1327-30*, p. 171; *Cal. Pat. Rolls, 1338-40*, p. 83. For similar licences issued by the Irish chancery see: *Cal. Pat. Rolls, 1334-8*, pp. 402-3; *Rot. Canc. Hib.*, p. 22b, no. 60; *Cal. Pat. Rolls, 1354-60*, pp. 273-4. Both chanceries were also responsible for the issue of a licence restoring property seized but containing the additional stipulation that the acquisition was to count towards the total allowed under a general licence, in both cases at a discount: *Cal. Pat. Rolls, 1327-30*, p. 320; *Cal. Pat. Rolls, 1399-1401*, pp. 528-9.

(64) All the licences were issued by the English chancery. Two confirm permanent unions: *Cal. Pat. Rolls, 1343-5*, pp. 532, 537. One simply confirms the position of the current incumbent: *Cal. Pat. Rolls, 1374-7*, pp. 84-5. Two others confirm unions made only for the lifetime of the current incumbent: *Cal. Pat. Rolls, 1350-4*, pp. 101, 538. A sixth retrospectively pardons a union that has since been severed: *Cal. Pat. Rolls, 1348-50*, p. 499.

English chancery are general ones. Most allow the acquisition of property up to a certain valuation without any other restriction, but others convey only a more limited power of future acquisition *(65)*. The Irish chancery also granted a number of general licences of both these kinds *(66)*.

Religious houses continued to be the main recipients of licences, but the proportion of licences going to secular ecclesiastics increased significantly *(67)*. The licences issued by the English chancery still covered property as far north as Ulster *(68)*, as far south as County Cork *(69)* and as far west as County Clare *(70)*; but those issued by the Irish chancery were of more restricted geographical scope *(71)*. The licences issued during this period are rather more informative than their earlier counterparts as to the nature of the transactions being licensed. The pious grants licensed range from the property worth forty pounds which the earl of Ormond was licensed to grant to a Trinitarian house to be founded within his lordship of Carrick and property worth thirty pounds which the earl of Louth was licensed to grant to the priory of Ballyboggan of which he was patron *(72)* down to the plots of land which lesser donors were authorised to grant for the foundation of new religious houses *(73)*. Other pious or charitable grants licensed include eleven made for the

---

(65) The unrestricted licences are: *Cal. Pat. Rolls, 1317-21*, pp. 125 [printed in full in *Chartae, Privilegia et Immunitates* (Irish Record Commission, 1829), p. 49], 152, 197; *Cal. Pat. Rolls, 1330-4*, pp. 246, 327; *Cal. Pat. Rolls, 1334-8*, pp. 393, 413; *Cal. Pat. Rolls, 1338-40*, p. 96; *Cal. Pat. Rolls, 1358-61*, pp. 48, 188. The more restricted licences are: *Cal. Pat. Rolls, 1317-21*, pp. 152 (only property formerly belonging to the see of the licensee), 598 (only from a single donor); *Cal. Pat. Rolls, 1348-50*, pp. 197, 229 (only from a single donor and only of property in the city of Dublin); *Cal. Pat. Rolls, 1354-8*, p. 423 (only advowsons and alien priories and cells).

(66) The unrestricted licence is: *Rot. Canc. Hib.*, p. 147b, no. 10 [printed in full in *Chartae, Privilegia et Immunitates*, p. 88]. A general licence of the reign of Edward III mentioned in 1400 may also have been of this kind: *Irish Monastic and Episcopal Deeds, 1200-1600*, ed. N.B. White (Irish Manuscripts Commission, 1936), pp. 13-4. The restricted licences are: *Rot. Canc. Hib.*, pp. 21b, nos. 11-12 (only tenements held of the licensees and devastated in the recent wars); 25a, no. 162 (only vicarages and only given by their patron); *Cal. Ormond Deeds*, ii, 120 (and 344) (only from the founder).

(67) Just over one third of the licences issued by the English chancery went to secular ecclesiastics though less than one quarter of those issued by the Irish chancery.

(68) *Cal. Pat. Rolls, 1350-4*, p. 101; *Cal. Pat. Rolls, 1364-7*, p. 190.

(69) *Cal. Pat. Rolls, 1317-21*, p. 12.

(70) *Cal. Pat. Rolls, 1338-40*, p. 83.

(71) The Irish chancery issued licences in respect of property in three Munster counties (Cork, Limerick and Tipperary) and in all seven medieval counties of Leinster.

(72) *Cal. Ormond Deeds*, ii, 120 (and 344); *Cal. Pat. Rolls, 1317-21*, p. 598.

(73) *Cal. Pat. Rolls, 1348-50*, p. 28; *Cal. Pat. Rolls, 1354-8*, p. 418; *Cal. Pat. Rolls, 1358-61*, pp. 111, 477; Bodleian Library, Oxford, MS Rawlinson B 479, ff.53r-54v. Less certainly pious are the transactions by which existing religious houses acquired land for the extension of their premises: *Cal. Pat. Rolls, 1327-30*, p. 456; *Cal. Pat. Rolls, 1358-61*, p. 477; *Rot. Canc. Hib.*, pp. 22a, no. 30; 22b, no. 60; 33b, no. 2.

foundation or support of chantries *(74)*; three made for educational purposes *(75)*; one made for the erection of a new parish church *(76)*; and one for the enlargement of an existing church and of its churchyard *(77)*. Three licences for the acquisition of property by the English abbey of Furness speak of the property as having been given to support a monk celebrating daily for all the faithful departed or more generally for the support of divine service in the abbey *(78)*, but other evidence suggests that the property in question was in fact purchased by the abbey through its nominees who then "gave" it to the abbey *(79)*. During this same period Furness abbey also acquired the Irish lands of the Norman abbey of Beaubec, probably by purchase *(80)*; and it is likely to have been money that secured for the archbishop of Armagh the Irish cell of the French abbey of Lonlay at St. Andrew in the Ards and all its possessions *(81)*. Money is less likely to have been involved in the two instances in this period when one existing religious house was licensed to take over another house and all its property. In both cases the house being absorbed was said to be small and poor and appears to have been incapable of continuing an independent existence *(82)*.

Two of the general licences issued during this period contain no specific limitation as to the value of the property the licensee was allowed to acquire, though both imposed other restrictions on the property which

(74) *Cal. Pat. Rolls, 1334-8*, p. 413; *Cal. Pat. Rolls, 1345-8*, p. 446; *Cal. Pat. Rolls, 1348-50*, pp. 197, 229; *Cal. Pat. Rolls, 1354-8*, p. 30 (here the purpose of the grant is revealed only by the associated inquisition *ad quod damnum:* P.R.O. London, C 143/315, no. 16); *Cal. Pat. Rolls, 1358-61*, p. 508; *Cal. Pat. Rolls, 1370-4*, p. 337; *Cal. Pat. Rolls, 1377-81*, p. 369; *Cal. Pat. Rolls, 1388-92*, p. 419; *Rot. Canc. Hib.*, pp. 22b, no. 73; 64b, no. 1.

(75) *Cal. Pat. Rolls, 1348-50*, pp. 94, 114, 150-1; *Cal. Pat. Rolls, 1361-4*, p. 522. In each case the grantor was also to have the benefit of the associated chantry.

(76) *Cal. Pat. Rolls, 1327-30*, p. 134.

(77) *Cal. Pat. Rolls, 1348-50*, p. 564.

(78) *Cal. Pat. Rolls, 1334-8*, p. 44; *Cal. Pat. Rolls, 1338-40*, p. 16.

(79) Robert Normaund appears by himself as the "grantor" of a messuage and six shops in Drogheda to Furness abbey in 1334 and the inquisition *ad quod damnum* into the grant states that he has no other lands in Ireland: *Cal. Pat. Rolls, 1334-8*, p. 44; P.R.O. London, C 143/226, no. 20. Three years later, however, he is to be found with Laurence Russell granting two further shops in Drogheda to Furness. Again the inquisition finds that neither man has other lands in Ireland: *Cal. Pat. Rolls, 1338-40*, p. 16; P.R.O. London C 143/243, no. 10. The Furness archives contain various deeds relating to the second transaction, including quitclaims to Normaund and Russell made in 1336 by Richard of Preston, a burgess of Drogheda: *Coucher Book of Furness Abbey*, vol. ii, part iii, pp. 722-6. This suggests that Preston was the real vendor. For other evidence of the use of trustees in this period see a subsequent licence for Furness *(Cal. Pat. Rolls, 1350-4*, p. 101); the 1357 inquisition into a grant to the warden and college of vicars of St. Patrick's Cathedral, Dublin (P.R.O. London, C 143/333, no. 19); and the 1365 licence for a grant to the dean and chapter of St. Patrick's *(Cal. Pat. Rolls, 1364-7*, p. 122). In this last instance the grantors seem to have been acting as trustees of the deceased archbishop Bicknor who had granted them the land in 1349: *The "Dignitas Decani" of St. Patrick's Cathedral, Dublin*, ed. N. B. White (Irish Manuscripts Commission, 1957), pp. 71-4, 93-4.

(80) *Cal. Pat. Rolls, 1330-4*, p. 383.

(81) *Cal. Pat. Rolls, 1364-7*, p. 190.

(82) *Cal. Pat. Rolls, 1327-30*, p. 187; *Cal. Pat. Rolls, 1399-1401*, pp. 528-9.

could be acquired by virtue of the licence (83). The remaining general licences authorised the acquisition of property up to the value of seven hundred pounds. It is only rarely possible to discover the value of the property whose transfer was being authorised by specific mortmain licences issued by the Irish chancery (84). This is much more commonly possible in the case of licences issued by its English counterpart. Seven of the licences are for the transfer of property worth less than one pound (85); eight for the transfer of property worth between one and five pounds (86); and eight for the transfer of property worth over five pounds (87). The majority of the acquisitions licensed seem, then, still to have been comparatively small-scale as was the case in the first phase of the operation of the licensing system.

The submission of a petition probably continued to be the first step in the procedure for obtaining a licence (88). For those seeking a licence from the English chancery it was the king in England to whom the petition would be sent (89); for those seeking a licence from the Irish chancery, presumably the chief governor (90). It seems probable that in normal circumstances specific mortmain licences continued to be granted only after the holding of a preliminary inquisition *ad quod damnum,* though only twenty writs authorising the holding of such inquisitions

(83) *Cal. Pat. Rolls, 1317-21,* p. 152; *Rot. Canc. Hib.,* p. 21b, nos. 11-2.

(84) This is possible in the case of just four of the nineteen licences where the value is mentioned in the licence itself.

(85) The licences themselves give the valuation in *Cal. Pat. Rolls, 1358-61,* p. 477; *Cal. Pat. Rolls, 1370-4,* p. 337. The other licences concerned are: *Cal. Pat. Rolls, 1327-30,* p. 187; *Cal. Pat. Rolls, 1338-40,* p. 16; *Cal. Pat. Rolls, 1354-8,* p. 418; *Cal. Pat. Rolls, 1358-61,* p. 111. Here the valuations come from the corresponding inquisitions *ad quod damnum* now in the P.R.O. London, C 143/207, no. 26; /243, no. 10; /316, no. 1; /321, no. 9.

(86) The licences themselves give the valuation in *Cal. Pat. Rolls, 1348-50,* p. 94; *Cal. Pat. Rolls, 1338-40,* p. 88 (and *Cal. Pat. Rolls, 1340-34,* p. 177). The valuation of the property mentioned in *Cal. Pat. Rolls, 1354-8,* p. 30 is given in P.R.O. London, C 47/10/19, no. 14. The other licences concerned are: *Cal. Pat. Rolls, 1350-4,* pp. 256-7; *Cal. Pat. Rolls, 1364-7,* p. 122; *Cal. Pat. Rolls, 1374-7,* p. 298; *Cal. Pat. Rolls, 1377-81,* p. 369. Here the valuations come from the corresponding inquisitions *ad quod damnum* now in P.R.O. London, C 143/299, no. 9; /333, no. 18; /388, no. 16; /394, no. 1.

(87) The licences themselves give the valuation in *Cal. Pat. Rolls, 1338-40,* p. 83; *Cal. Pat. Rolls, 1348-50,* pp. 150-1; *Cal. Pat. Rolls, 1354-8,* p. 30. The other licences are: *Cal. Pat. Rolls, 1324-7,* p. 299; *Cal. Pat. Rolls, 1327-30,* pp. 187, 320; *Cal. Pat. Rolls, 1330-4,* p. 383. Here the valuations come from the corresponding inquisitions *ad quod damnum* now in the P.R.O. London: C 143/182, no. 14; /196, no. 6; /202, no. 21; /222, no. 19.

(88) For the procedure followed prior to 1317 see above, pp. 128-29.

(89) For three such petitions see *King's Council Documents,* pp. 104-5, 129-30, 172. Much of the wording of two other petitions appears to have been incorporated in the resulting inquisitions *ad quod damnum* see P.R.O. London, C 143/182, no. 14 (and note that the writ itself is authorised "per peticionem de consilio") and C 143/196, no. 6.

(90) No such petitions seem to survive from this period.

now survive *(91)*. The escheator of Ireland was the normal addressee of such writs during the second phase of the operation of the licensing system, not the justiciar as had been the practice during the first phase; and less than half the surviving writs specify the full list of points on which information was required that had become customary in the earlier period *(92)*. The overwhelming majority of surviving inquisitions were taken in person by the escheator and all but one were taken in the county where the property concerned was located *(93)*. As in the first period there are several examples of juries finding that no damage or loss will occur as the result of the transaction in question. Only in one instance does this seem to be true *(94)*. The types of loss mentioned are broadly similar to those mentioned in the earlier inquisitions, though we also hear for the first time of the possible loss to the local parish priest of the tithe payable on property alienated *(95)*. As in the earlier period there is at least one inquisition which speaks only of the advantages that will accrue to the king from the transaction proposed: in this case the acquisition by the priory of St. Thomas', Dublin of the priory of St. Katherine's by Leixlip *(96)*. In two other instances the jurors are careful to mention the advantages which will help balance the potential losses. The appropriation of the church of Clonard by the bishop of Meath will allow him to build a "residence" there which will assist the resistance against the native Irish and others attacking the town; the acquisition of additional lands by the hospital at Naas will help it perform its essential function of providing hospitality for those using the main road from Dublin to Munster *(97)*.

As earlier, it was probably necessary to submit a second petition at

(91) The surviving writs (and their accompanying returns, the inquisitions *ad quod damnum)* which are now in the P.R.O. London are: C 143/182, no. 14; /196, no. 6; /202, no. 21; /207, no. 26; /222, no. 19; /226, no. 20; /243, no. 10; /247, no. 23 (writ only); /296, no. 26; /299, no. 9; /315, no. 16; /316, no. 1; /321, no. 9; /323, no. 5; /330, no. 11; /333, nos. 18, 19 (writ only); /388, no. 16; /394, no. 1. An inquisition *ad quod damnum* which survives without its covering writ is C 143/191, no. 16. There is also an inquisition known only from the calendared version in *Rot. Canc. Hib.,* p. 34b, no. 29. A rather special writ for an enquiry into the proposed restoration of property to the archbishop of Armagh is P.R.O. London, C 47/10/19, no. 14. For licences which look as if they may have been issued without preliminary inquisitions see *Cal. Pat. Rolls, 1338-40,* p. 80 (where information as to the value of a manor seems to have been derived from oral testimony not from an inquisition) and *Cal. Pat. Rolls, 1361-4,* p. 522 (for a grant by the king's son, the duke of Clarence, and the property is "said" to be held in chief). It seems possible that the licences for the union of benefices were also issued without preliminary inquisitions.

(92) For writs which do require answers to the full range of questions see C 143/207, no. 26; /226, no. 20; /243, no. 10; /299, no. 9; /330, no. 11; /394, no. 1.

(93) The exception is an inquisition taken at Trim in respect of property in County Kildare: C 143/296, no. 26.

(94) C 143/222, no. 19 (transfer of the lands of Beaubec to Furness abbey). In four other cases the lord was losing the possibility of escheat; in a fifth the possibility of both escheat and wardship.

(95) C 143/207, no. 26. The licence issued was careful to safeguard his rights: *Cal. Pat. Rolls, 1327-30,* p. 456.

(96) C 143/196, no. 6.

(97) C 143/182, no. 14; C 143/191, no. 16.

this point before the licence was issued *(98)*. A number of requests for licences seem to have been rejected at this point *(99)*. When a licence was granted there was normally a fine payable for it, though we also find mention in the licences of a number of non-financial inducements for their being granted *(100)*. The shortest interval between the issuing of a writ authorising the holding of an inquisition *ad quod damnum* and the granting of a licence was again (as in the first phase) just three months *(101)* and in seven other cases it took less than a year. In seven others it took over a year; in exceptional cases as long as six or even ten years *(102)*.

(iii)

During the third phase of the licensing system, the century beginning in 1380, licences for the alienation of property in Ireland into mortmain were normally issued only by the Irish chancery *(103)*. At least fifty-nine such licences are known to have been granted *(104)*. Three were issued

(98)   Only one such petition seems to survive: *Coucher Book of Furness Abbey,* vol. II, part iii, 696-7.

(99)   For intended alienations investigated by inquisitions for which no licences were granted see C 143/296, no. 26; /323, no. 5; /333, no. 19. In two of these cases the property was held in chief of the king.

(100)   E.g. because of the good service to the Crown of grantor or grantee as in *Cal. Pat. Rolls, 1317-21,* p. 197 and *Cal. Pat. Rolls, 1338-40,* p. 83 (Roger Outlaw, prior of the Hospitallers); or because of a concession made to the Crown by the grantee as in *Cal. Pat. Rolls, 1317-21,* p. 137; or because of losses sustained by the licensee in the Bruce wars or from the attacks of the native Irish as in *Cal. Pat. Rolls, 1317-21,* p. 197 and *Cal. Pat. Rolls, 1358-61,* p. 188.

(101)   C. 143/196, no. 6 (writ issued 13 August and inquisition held 6 September 1327) and *Cal. Pat. Rolls, 1327-30,* p. 187 (licence issued 10 November 1327); C 143/222, no. 9 (writ issued 8 September and inquisition held 14 November 1332) and *Cal. Pat. Rolls, 1330-4,* p. 383 (licence issued 14 December 1332).

(102)   The exceptional cases are: C 143/333, no. 18 (Irish writ issued 8 October 1358 and inquisition held 3 April 1359) and *Cal. Pat. Rolls, 1364-7,* p. 122 (licence issued 18 May 1365); C 143/247, no. 23 (writ issued 26 March 1338; no surviving inquisition) and *Cal. Ch. Rolls, 1341-7,* pp. 97-9 (licence issued 28 September 1348).

(103)   Only two licences are known to have been issued by the English chancery during this period: *Cal. Pat. Rolls, 1405-8,* p. 178; *Cal. Pat. Rolls, 1413-6,* p. 169 [= *Rot. Canc. Hib.,* p. 204b, no. 3].

(104)   This total includes licences for whose issue there exists only the evidence of the penultimate stage in the licensing process, the act of the Irish great council or parliament authorising the issuing of a licence. It appears to be safe to use these as evidence of licences issued since acts which did not in the event result in the issuing of a licence seem to have been minuted to that effect: *A Roll of the Proceedings of the King's Council in Ireland, 16 Richard II,* ed. J. Graves (Rolls Series, 1877) [hereafter *Procs. King's Council Ire.*], pp. 152-4; *Statute Rolls of the Parliament of Ireland, 1-12 Edward IV,* ed. H. F. Berry (Dublin, 1914) [hereafter *Stat. Ire. Edw. IV, pt. I],* p. 189. Two-fifths of the Irish patent rolls of the period survived until modern times and were calendared for the Irish Record Commission. They came, however, overwhelmingly from the first half of this period; and this makes it all the more fortunate that it is possible to remedy their deficiencies during the second half of the period from these acts of the Irish parliament and great council. Such acts are first found recorded on the parliament rolls in 1450 and continue to the end of our period. The rolls themselves survived in an almost unbroken sequence until 1922 and full transcripts were made of them prior to their destruction. All have now been published.

during Richard II's first visit to Ireland in 1394-5 *(105)*; several others during the periods of office of chief governors who are known to have been given power to grant such licences *(106)*. Licences seem, however, to have been issued quite freely by the Irish chancery at other times as well; the only authority for this seems to have been established practice.

Licences giving permission for a specific alienation that had yet to occur ceased in this period to be the most common type. Only eleven of the fifty-nine licences are of this type (and almost half of these stipulate that the acquisition is to count towards the total amount of property the licensee was permitted to acquire under an existing general licence) *(107)*. There are just two examples of licences confirming and pardoning alienations that have already taken place *(108)* plus two licences pardoning and confirming a union of benefices that has already occurred *(109)*. The general licence is the most common form of licence. The most generous form of general licence, which is first encountered in this period, authorised the future acquisition of property by the licensee without restriction and specifically exempted the licensee from the requirement of suing out inquisitions *ad quod damnum* for such acquisitions. Only three licences of this exceptionally generous kind are known to have been issued *(110)*. More commonly general licences did impose a specific limit as to the amount of property which could be acquired by the licensee. There are sixteen general licences with such a restriction but which still

(105) *Rot. Canc. Hib.,* p. 153a, no. 54; *20 D.K.Rep.Ire.,* p. 85; *Stat. Ire. Edw. IV, pt. I,* pp. 125-9.

(106) Power to grant such licences was specifically given to John Stanley when he was appointed king's lieutenant for a six year term in 1413 (though in the event he was superseded in 1414): *Cal. Pat. Rolls, 1413-6,* pp. 53-4. It was also given to George, duke of Clarence when he was appointed king's lieutenant for a seven year term in 1462, and again when he was appointed for a twenty year term in 1471 (though in the event he was executed in 1478): *Cal. Pat. Rolls, 1461-7,* p. 142; *Cal. Pat. Rolls, 1467-77,* p. 243. No licences seem to have survived from the period when Stanley was empowered to grant them, though several do from the period when Clarence enjoyed such powers.

(107) Specific licences without the stipulation are: *Rot. Canc. Hib.,* pp. 126b, no. 184; 164a-b, no. 169; 204b, no. 37; *Procs. King's Council Ire.,* pp. 240-1; *Statute Rolls of the Parliament of Ireland, Henry VI,* ed. H. F. Berry (Dublin, 1910) [hereafter *Stat. Ire. Hen. VI*], pp. 405-7, 515. Specific licences which do contain the stipulation are: *Rot. Canc. Hib.,* pp. 152b, no. 51; 258a, no. 76; *20 D.K.Rep.Ire.,* p. 85; *Stat. Ire. Hen. VI,* pp. 393-7. There are also two licences for a union of ecclesiastical benefices for the lifetime of their incumbent that has not as yet occurred *(Rot. Canc. Hib.,* p. 120a, no. 33; *Procs. King's Council Ire.,* pp. 119-20) and one such licence for a permanent union of benefices *(Rot. Canc. Hib.,* p. 126a, no. 168). There is also a licence for the division of the endowment of a cathedral prebend *(Dignitas Decani,* pp. 46-9) and one hybrid licence allowing the appropriation of a specific church but also giving general permission for the future acquisition of property up to a certain value *(Rot. Canc. Hib.,* p. 255a, no. 98).

(108) Bodleian Library, Oxford, MS. Rawlinson B 502, f.16r.; *Stat. Ire. Edw. IV, pt. I,* pp. 125-9 (to count towards the acquisitions allowed under a general licence).

(109) *Rot. Canc. Hib.,* pp. 140a, no. 120; 173a, no 33.

(110) *Stat. Ire. Edw. IV, pt. I,* pp. 763-5; *Statute Rolls of the Parliament of Ireland, 12-22 Edward IV,* ed. J. F. Morrissey (Dublin, 1939) [hereafter *Stat. Ire. Edw. IV, pt. II*], pp. 27-9 (replacing the vacated entry at *Stat. Ire. Edw. IV, pt. I,* p. 731); *Stat. Ire. Edw. IV, pt. II,* pp. 897-901.

exempt the licensee from the need to sue out individual inquisitions *ad quod damnum* into each acquisition and allow the acquisition of property held in chief of the crown. Ten of these form part of more complex instruments which also authorise the creation or remodelling of a chantry or guild *(111)*; six stand by themselves *(112)*. A single licence authorises the acquisition of property up to a certain value without the need for inquisitions *ad quod damnum* but bars the acquisition of property held in chief: it is part of a more complex instrument authorising the creation of a new corporate body for the support of a non-parochial chapel *(113)*. A further nineteen general licences granted during this period did not exempt their grantees from the need to sue out individual inquisitions *ad quod damnum* for each of their acquisitions; but eleven of them did specifically allow the acquisition of property held in chief *(114)*.

Less than half of the licences went to individual religious houses or orders. Others went to secular ecclesiastics. This period saw a marked increase in the proportion of licences going to the chaplains of newly-created chantry chapels, and licences being granted for the first time to fraternities and guilds *(115)* and to the proctors of parish churches and non-parochial congregations *(116)*. The predominance of general licences in this period makes an analysis of the locations mentioned in licences of less value than in earlier periods. It is, however, noticeable that none of the licences refer to property in Ulster or in the west of Ireland *(117)*. The predominance of general licences also makes it impossible to analyse the motives of grantors other than in a few instances. Primarily religious motives probably lie behind the granting of property to newly-created chantries and to guilds created for the support of chantries *(118)*. Similar

(111) G. MacNiocaill, "Register of St. Saviour's Chantry, Waterford", *Analecta Hibernica,* 23 (1966), pp. 185-6 and and 211-3 (later, amended version); *Stat. Ire. Hen. VI,* pp. 509-13, 513 (bis.); *Stat. Ire. Edw. IV, pt. I,* pp. 245-9, 331-45, 457-61; *Stat. Ire. Edw. IV, pt. II,* pp. 327-33, 577-83, 769-85.
(112) *Stat. Ire. Hen. VI,* pp. 579-83, 733-5; *Stat. Ire. Edw. IV, pt. I,* pp. 155-9, 249-51; *Stat. Ire. Edw. IV, pt. II,* pp. 289, 403.
(113) *Stat. Ire. Edw. IV, pt. II,* pp. 171-3.
(114) For general licences which implicitly require the licensee to sue out inquisitions *ad quod damnum* for each acquisition see: *Cal. Pat. Rolls, 1405-8,* p. 178 (licence only allowing grants by the founder of the chantry); *Rot. Canc. Hib.,* pp. 153a, no. 54; 189b, no. 21; 258a, no. 76; *20 D.K.Rep.Ire.,* p. 85, no. 258; *Stat. Ire. Hen. VI,* pp. 205-7, 393-7; *Stat. Ire. Edw. IV, pt. I,* pp. 125-9, 331-45, 677-9; *Stat. Ire. Edw. IV, pt. II,* pp. 7-9, 123, 229-37. For licences which explicitly state that acquisitions are subject to this requirement see: *Rot. Canc. Hib.,* pp. 215b-216a, no. 24; *Stat. Ire. Hen. VI,* p. 207; *Stat. Ire. Edw. IV, pt. I,* pp. 323-331; *Stat. Ire. Edw. IV, pt. II,* pp. 223-5, 555-9.
(115) This was a consequence of the extension of the 1391 English statute of mortmain to Ireland: see Brand, "King, Church and Property", above, 247, 251.
(116) For examples see *Stat. Ire. Edw. IV, pt. II,* pp. 7-9, 123, 171-3.
(117) But note the act for granting a licence to the friars of Errew in Connacht which has subsequently been marked for deletion: *Stat. Ire. Edw. IV, pt. I,* p. 189; and the general licence for the proctors of the church at Kilmallock: *Stat. Ire. Edw. IV, pt. II,* pp. 7-9.
(118) Above, n. 111 and *Cal. Pat. Rolls, 1405-8,* p. 178; *Stat. Ire. Edw. IV, pt. I,* pp. 323-31, 331-45, 677-9; *Stat. Ire. Edw. IV, pt. II,* pp. 229-37.

motives can also be presumed in the case of grants to the proctors of parish churches and of a non-parochial chapel *(119)*. There is only one example from this period of the licensing of a clearly non-religious transaction, in this instance an exchange *(120)*.

Three of the general licences of this period, as already noted, contain no restrictions at all as to the value of property the licensee can acquire. The other general licences between them authorised the acquisition of property in excess of eight hundred pounds a year. In the absence of the appropriate inquisitions *ad quod damnum* little can be said as to the value of the acquisitions made under the specific licences *(121)*.

It seems to have remained the practice for those seeking mortmain licences to submit written petitions asking for them; and it now becomes possible to demonstrate that many, if not all, of the petitions that led to the issuing of licences by the Irish chancery were considered at meetings of the Irish great council or parliament. Three such petitions are to be found on a roll of 1392-3 recording proceedings before the great council *(122)*; many more such petitions are transcribed in full on the parliament rolls from 1450 onwards as incorporated into the individual acts authorising the issue of the relevant mortmain licences *(123)*. Other petitions are referred to incidentally in the licences which resulted from them *(124)*. Petitioners seem to have become increasingly precise in the framing of their petitions. By the second half of the fifteenth century we encounter petitions specifying the precise form of words that the petitioner wants to be used in his licence *(125)*.

Several of the licences issued during this period were issued without any fine being paid for them other than the standard fee for the writing and sealing of the licence *(126)*. For others only small fines were

(119) Above, n. 116.

(120) *Stat. Ire. Hen. VI*, pp. 405-7.

(121) No inquisition *ad quod damnum* of the period seems to survive, though there are a few incidental references to such inquisitions having been held: *Rot. Canc. Hib.*, pp. 152b, no. 51; 164a-b, no. 169; 255a, no. 98; *20 D.K.Rep.Ire.*, p. 85. The last of these references also indicates that as late as 1395 acquisitions made under a general licence but investigated by inquisition and also authorised by a special licence were being artificially inflated for the purpose of exhausting the general licence.

(122) *Procs. King's Council Ire.*, pp. 119-120, 152-4, 240-1.

(123) The earliest such petitions incorporated into acts in the printed edition of the rolls belong to 1450: *Stat. Ire. Hen. VI*, pp. 204-6, 209. The practice of passing acts of this form continued after 1480: *Stat. Ire. Edw. IV, pt. II*, pp. 897-901; S. G. Ellis, "Parliaments and Great Councils, 1483-99: Addenda et Corrigenda", *Analecta Hibernica*, xxix (1980), 102 and 107-8.

(124) *Rot. Canc. Hib.*, p. 120a, no. 33 (1385: by petition to the council, sealed by the lieutenant of Ireland); *Ibid.*, p. 255a, no. 98 (1432: by petition); *Stat. Ire. Edw. IV, pt. II*, pp. 555-9 (1446: by petition endorsed by the justiciar and sealed with his privy seal); *Analecta Hibernica*, xii, pp. 185-6 (1471: same) and 211-3 (1476: same).

(125) For examples see: *Stat. Ire. Hen. VI*, pp. 509-13; *Stat. Ire. Edw. IV, pt. I*, pp. 245-9; *Stat. Ire. Edw. IV, pt. II*, pp. 223-5.

(126) *Stat. Ire. Hen. VI*, pp. 405-7; *Stat. Ire. Edw. IV, pt. I*, pp. 323-31, 457-61; *Stat. Ire. Edw. IV, pt. II*, pp. 223-5, 229-37. The standard fee of twenty shillings for the writing and sealing of the licence is specifically mentioned and identified as such in a number of the acts of the Irish parliament: *Stat. Ire. Hen. VI*, pp. 405-7, 515,

payable *(127)*. The only substantial fine known to have been charged is twenty marks for a licence granted in 1413, and it is clearly no coincidence that this is one of the very few licences of the period to have been granted by the English chancery *(128)*. Again we hear of a number of non-financial inducements for the granting of licences: the good service of the licensee to the crown *(129)* or the fact that the religious house or ecclesiastic in question had suffered heavy losses, commonly ascribed to attacks from "English rebels and Irish enemies" *(130)*. The readiness of the Irish parliament to give permission for the foundation of fraternities, guilds and chantries and for those institutions to receive property must in part at least be connected with the sponsorship these institutions managed to attract from the great men of the lordship who were named among the founders or founder-members of the institutions concerned *(131)*. Less commonly the granting of licences may in part be ascribed to provisions made for the king to receive spiritual benefits from the foundation in question *(132)*.

(iv)

The main effect of the statute of Mortmain in the lordship of Ireland (as in England) was an indirect one: that of causing the emergence of a complicated bureaucratic system for controlling all alienations into mortmain and a number of other types of transaction which could be represented as falling under the statutory prohibition. At first, as we have seen, mortmain licences were issued solely by the English chancery and all requests for such licences had to go through the English licensing system, although the inquisitions *ad quod damnum* into proposed alienations were held locally in Ireland. From 1317 onwards the Irish chancery

579-83; *Stat. Ire. Edw. IV, pt. I*, pp. 323-31, 457-61; *Stat. Ire. Edw. IV, pt. II*, p. 403. It is probably the same as the twenty shillings payable to the hanaper mentioned in some other acts *(Stat. Ire. Edw. IV, pt. I*, pp. 155-9, 249-51, 763-5; *Stat. Ire. Edw. IV, pt. II*, pp. 223-5, 229-37).

(127) Six shillings and eight pence: *Stat. Ire. Edw. IV, pt. I*, pp. 155-9, 249-51, 331-45. Three shillings and four pence: *Stat. Ire. Edw. IV, pt. II*, p. 289 and the vacated entry in *Procs. King's Council Ire.*, pp. 152-4.

(128) *Cal. Pat. Rolls, 1413-6*, p. 169.

(129) *Rot. Canc. Hib.*, pp. 120a, no. 33; 126a, no. 168.

(130) *Stat. Ire. Hen. VI*, pp. 205-7, 515, 579-83; *Rot. Canc. Hib.*, pp. 153a, no. 54; 215b-216a, no. 24.

(131) The most impressive list of founders is that of the guild of English merchants trading to Ireland: *Stat. Ire. Edw. IV, pt. II*, pp. 769-85. This includes the chief governor of the lordship, the archbishop of Dublin, the chancellor, the treasurer, the chief justices of the courts of King's Bench and Common Pleas, the keeper of the rolls of chancery, the chief baron of the exchequer, the king's serjeant at laws and the attorney-general. The chief governor of the day is also given first place among the founders of chantries at Dunboyne, Dunsany, Dunshaughlin, Greenoge, and Piercetown and of fraternities or guilds of cordwainers at Dublin and of the parish of Skreen.

(132) *Cal. Pat. Rolls, 1405-8*, p. 178 (king and late wife apparently to be sole beneficiaries of chantry but fine still payable); *Stat. Ire. Edw. IV, pt. II*, pp. 171-3 (prayers to be said for the king, chief governor, chancellor and treasurer in the chapel).

began also to issue such licences though without having been given specific authority to do so; and so an Irish licensing system came to exist side by side with the English one. After 1380 it was the Irish chancery alone that normally issued such licences (though still apparently for most of the time without specific authority to do so); and requests for such licences were now normally processed through the Irish licensing system. These changes were of considerable significance. As long as the English chancery exercised sole power to grant mortmain licences it was the king in England, acting on the advice of his English advisers, who had the final say as to whether or not property should pass into mortmain in Ireland. There followed a period of dual control of mortmain alienations, when it may have been possible to obtain a licence from the Irish chancery through the Irish licensing system even when one had been refused in England (or vice versa); though, in the absence of fuller information about the working of the Irish system, it is perhaps unwise to speculate about how possible conflicts between the two licensing systems were resolved in practice. Eventually, after 1380, control over mortmain alienations in Ireland passed to the Irish administration in Dublin, to the chief governor and his advisors or (from 1450 onwards at least) to the Irish parliament. The change seems to have been part of a more general shift which took place during the same period of power and authority from the king in England to his chief governor in Ireland, from the English administration to the Dublin administration, though this shift was of course also accompanied by another, that which saw a marked decline in the size of the area which was effectively under the control of the rulers of the lordship: so that the Irish administration had more independent authority, but exercised it over a smaller area.

There were also significant changes over the period as a whole in the proportions of licences going to different types of licensee. In part these changes are no more than a reflection of changes in the purview of the licensing system. There was a marked increase in the proportion of licences going to secular ecclesiastics once it became necessary to obtain a mortmain licence for the union of two ecclesiastical benefices; and licences for the acquisition of property by guilds and fraternities are only to be found once such acquisitions came to require licences as a result of the extension of the English mortmain legislation of 1391 to Ireland. The decline in the proportion of licences going to religious houses does, however, also probably reflect the decline in popular support for these institutions during the later Middle Ages, in much the same way as the increase in the proportion of licences for the granting of property for the support of chantries reflects the increasing popularity of these institutions during the same period.

There were also important changes in the types of licence issued and the relative popularity of the different types. New types of licence or new variants on existing types had to be devised to meet new kinds of situation or transactions which were now for the first time being brought within the control of the licensing system. One obvious example of the former is the licence for the absorption of one existing religious house by another; of the latter the licence for the union of ecclesiastical benefices. More surprising are the changes in the relative popularity of the different overall categories of licence during the course of the period. Licences pardoning unlicensed alienations and restoring the property concerned to the licensee dwindle to insignificance during the course of the fourteenth century. This probably reflects a decline in the activity and vigilance of the royal officials responsible for monitoring such matters and also the increasing availability of legal remedies for challenging seizures rather than any decline in the number of unlicensed alienations *(133)*. In the final phase of the operation of the medieval licensing system, as we have seen, there was a massive increase in the proportion of general licences and evidence of the plentiful granting of general licences which exempted the licensee from the need to sue out individual inquisitions *ad quod damnum* into acquisitions made under the licence and even the occasional grant of licences of this kind which also allowed the licensee to make acquisitions without any restriction as to the value or nature of the property being acquired. The increased frequency of general licences and the introduction of these most liberal variants on the general licence seem to be connected phenomena. They seem to reflect a decreased commitment on the part of those who controlled the licensing system to any idea of exercising real control over property passing into mortmain. This decreased commitment seems, in turn, to be associated with the transfer of effective control over the licensing system from England to Ireland. The chief governor and his Irish advisers seem to have had no real interest in the control of mortmain alienations, not even for the money this would bring in, if one can judge from the smallness of the fines being charged for licences by the end of this period. Local control of the mortmain licensing system meant, in practice, no real control at all: merely a formality to be complied with, not any real obstacle to the acquisition of property by the Church. In 1480 it must have seemed that the mortmain legislation, if not yet a dead letter within the lordship, was well on the way to becoming such.

(133) See above, 256-61.

14

Legal Change in the Later Thirteenth Century: Statutory and Judicial Remodelling of the Action of Replevin

It has long been known that the reign of Edward I (1272-1307) was a period of major legal change. Indeed this is something that has probably never been wholly forgotten.[1] Yet so far only one modern scholarly study, T.F.T. Plucknett's *Legislation of Edward I,*[2] has attempted to look at the legal developments of the period in any kind of general way. Plucknett's pioneering work deserves our respect, but that respect should not blind us to the book's major weakness, its exclusive reliance on printed materials. Thus Plucknett's view of the background to the Edwardian statutes is drawn mainly from internal evidence they themselves provide and from plea rolls of the first half of the thirteenth century. His picture of the impact and interpretation of these statutes is derived solely from the printed Yearbook reports of the reigns of Edward I and Edward II.

This paper demonstrates how the use of other evidence, particularly the plea rolls of the reign of Edward I and the many Yearbook reports of the reign still in manuscript, can lead to conclusions regarding both the reasons for the enactment of Edwardian legislation and the changes it made in the existing law which are quite different from those reached by Plucknett. I will show how this evidence necessitates significant revisions in the story of how courts enforced and interpreted legislation during Edward's reign. I will also demonstrate that the same sources point to the conclusion that this was also a period when important non-statutory changes oc-

---

1. During the later Middle Ages knowledge of the major Edwardian statutes was an essential prerequisite for any practising lawyer. It seems probable that many of them possessed a book of the 'old' statutes, a large part of which contained the legislation of Edward's reign. In the fifteenth and early sixteenth centuries lectures on the legislation of Edward's reign formed a core element in the educational curriculum of the Inns of Court. As late as the early seventeenth century, Edward Coke's *Second Institutes,* dealing with the older legislation which a law student would have to master, was concerned mainly with legislation of this reign. In his introduction to the *Second Institutes,* Coke became the first to describe Edward I as 'our Justinian.'

2. T.F.T. Plucknett, *Legislation of Edward I* (revised ed. 1962). The first edition was published in 1949, and the book was based on Plucknett's Ford lectures of 1947.

curred in the common law, an aspect of legal development which Plucknett mentions only in passing.[3] Since I have been working for some time on a projected edition of the Yearbook reports and more significant plea-roll enrolments of replevin cases of the reign of Edward I for the Selden Society I will illustrate these points by reference to some of the changes which occurred during Edward's reign in this particular form of action.

(i)

The first section of chapter 2 of the statute of Westminster II (1285) began with an explanation of the problem it purported to remedy. The problem which the statute claimed to address was that lords distraining their tenants for services were often aggrieved by those tenants initiating an action of replevin in the county court or other lower court with replevin jurisdiction, and, when the lords came to avow the distraint, the tenants disavowing holding of them. This led to lords being amerced for unjust distraint and tenants going quit; but the disavowal had no further consequences since it had been made in a court which did not bear record (and so the lords were not able to bring an action of right to recover the tenements on the basis of the disclaimer). The remedy provided by the statute was to allow lords, as soon as they had been attached to appear at such a court, to have the case removed into a royal court, where any disavowal would be of record. The legislators added that this would not be a derogation from the common law rule that litigation could not be removed from lower courts to the king's court at the request of defendants, because in effect in such cases the lord was plaintiff, not defendant, anyway.[4]

---

3. Plucknett, *Legislation of Edward I*, at 9-10.

4. 'Quia domini feodorum distringentes tenentes suos pro serviciis sibi debitis multociens gravantur per hoc quod cum tenentes sui districcionem suam per breve vel sine brevi replegiaverint ac ipsi domini cum ad querimoniam tenencium suorum ad comitatum vel ad aliam curiam habentem potestatem placitandi placita de vetito namio per attachiamentum venerint et racionabilem et justam districcionem advocaverint, per hoc quod tenentes deadvocant nichil tenere nec clamare tenere de eo qui districcionem fecit et advocavit remanet qui distrinxit in misericordia et tenentes sui quieti quibus pro illa deadvocacione per recordum comitatus sive aliarum curiarum que recordum non habent pena infligi non potest. Decetero provisum est et statutum quod cum hujusmodi domini in comitatu vel hujusmodi curia justiciam de hujusmodi tenentibus suis consequi non possint quam cito attachiati fuerint ad sectam tenencium suorum concedatur eis breve ad ponendum loquelam illam coram justiciariis coram quibus et non alibi justicia hujusmodi dominis exhiberi poterit. Et inseritur causa in brevi "quia talis distrinxit in feodo suo pro serviciis et consuetudinibus sibi debitis." Nec per istud statutum derogatur legi communi usitate que non permisit placitum aliquod poni coram justiciariis ad peticionem defendentis; quia licet prima facie videbatur tenens actor et dominus defendens habito tamen respectu ad hoc quod dominus distringit et sequitur pro serviciis et consuetudinibus sibi a retro existentibus realiter pocius apparebit actor sive querens quam defendens.'

Plucknett accepted the explanation for the statute's enactment given by its framers, even though there are good *prima facie* reasons for scepticism.[5] It would have been perfectly possible for the statute to have provided that lower courts in future should bear record of disavowals in the same way as they bore record for certain other purposes.[6] The statute could also have prohibited disavowals in such courts. Either solution would have affected only those tenants wanting to make disavowals. The remedy chosen was one certain to have an effect on many tenants who had no such intention and to have the consequence of allowing any lord intending to avow for arrears of service to have his case removed into the Bench or Eyre. That this was indeed the real purpose behind the legislation is suggested by the sentence purporting to justify the change; this is, it will be noted, a justification for allowing the removal of any replevin case where a lord was intending to avow for services.

Further grounds for scepticism about the legislators' motives are provided by a cause célèbre heard not long beforehand. In the 1279-81 Yorkshire eyre the abbot of Thornton claimed that false judgments had been given in two replevin cases brought against him by Thomas of Flinton in the king's wapentake of Holderness. In these cases the abbot had avowed his distraint for service arrears and Thomas had denied holding the places where the distraints had been made of the abbot. The wapentake court had then awarded damages against the abbot for unjust distraint. The abbot claimed that he had been ready to show that he was in seisin of the services and that the places where the distresses had been taken were part of the tenements held of him, and alleged that a tenant's disavowal was not admissible where the lord was ready to prove a recent seisin of the services in question at the hand of the tenant as owed for the tenements concerned. The eyre justices upheld the judgment of the lower court, on the grounds that any tenant was allowed simply to disavow holding of his lord. They said that disavowal carried its own penalty, though as we have seen the framers of the statute asserted that such a disavowal in practice had no adverse consequences.[7] However, this was not the end of the matter. The case was subsequently removed into King's Bench, and there the abbot seems to have secured a return of the distresses.[8] Subsequently the whole case seems to have been repleaded there. The abbot avowed as

---

5. Plucknett, *Legislation of Edward I,* at 61-2.

6. R.C. Palmer, *The County Courts of Medieval England* 156-159 (1982). The author of *Hengham Magna* suggests that the county court does bear record of a disavowal made in the action of customs and services: *Radulphi de Hengham Summae* 12 (ed. W.H. Dunham jr. 1932).

7. JUST 1/1067, m.59d.

8. KB 27/64, m.38 (Trinity 1281).

before and Thomas was forced to answer the avowry. This time he simply said there were no arrears when the distraints were made and that he held less land than the abbot claimed. Eventually a jury gave its verdict in favour of the abbot.[9]

It was, then, the practice in at least one (and possibly other) local courts for replevin litigation to be decided automatically in the tenant's favour when he made a disavowal. The abbot's argument in these cases, however, suggests that this was not the general practice in *all* local courts prior to the statute.[10] The problem of fraudulent disavowals may not have been a general one after all. Indeed, the existence of this cause célèbre suggests the possibility that the legislation, far from being a response to a general problem that necessitated a statutory remedy, may have been the result of discussion sparked off by this single case. The case was taken as indicating the existence of a more general problem, which was used as the pretext for legislation giving lords the right to remove replevin cases into the Bench when their distraint had been for services. If this was so, it would not have been a unique occurrence. There are certainly other pieces of legislation of this period where it appears that the discussion of a single case was the catalyst which led to the drafting of the legislation.[11]

The statute is also misleading in its suggestion that prior to 1285 it was not possible for a lord to secure the removal from a lower court of a replevin case where he was intending to avow for arrears of services. As early as 1256 there existed a form of the writ *pone*[12] allowing the removal of a plea of replevin by a defendant who was intending to avow for arrears of service, and in Edwardian registers of writs we also find two other apparently pre-statutory forms of

---

9. KB 27/67, m.11d (Easter 1282).

10. It should be noted that another local court, the county court of Lincolnshire, had been amerced £100 in 1243 in a false judgment case for giving judgment on a disavowal in a plaintiff's favour in a replevin plea where the avowry had been to secure the plaintiff's appearance to answer a case in the court of the defendant's lord: KB 26/130, m.19.

11. Other probable examples include the second section of chapter 6 of the statute of Marlborough, the statute of Mortmain, and chapter 16 of the statute of Westminster II.

12. This was enrolled on the close rolls, perhaps as an exemplar: *Close Rolls, 1254-6*, at 411-2. The *causa* clause of the writ, explaining and justifying the reasons for its removal, ran: 'Quia predictus abbas cepit averia predicta pro quibusdam serviciis et consuetudinibus a predicta Matillide ei debitis ut dicitur.'

pone for the removal of replevin cases in similar circumstances.[13] It is not difficult to reconcile this with what we have already suggested were the real reasons for the making of the statute. The purpose behind the statute was to make routine and more readily and cheaply available a procedure that had hitherto been available only to a few defendants.

It is difficult to gauge precisely the effect of the statutory provision, since the enrolments of replevin cases do not tell us at whose request a case has been removed into the Bench; and the Bench writ-files do not survive in sufficient quantity to allow us to discover this information from them. What is certainly true is that there was a very marked increase in the number of replevin cases heard in the Bench in which defendants avowed for arrears of services after 1285. It seems likely that this increase should be attributed, at least in part, to the effects of the legislation.[14]

Yet the statute's effect was not limited to cases where the defendant avowed for services. The writs of *pone* and *recordari* authorized by the statute soon came to be used by defendants who were not intending to avow for services at all. By 1293 the use of such a writ by one who was intending to avow for arrears of a rent-charge was apparently so commonplace that it was not even challenged;[15] the only challenge which was made was to the writ being used by a defendant who was only the bailiff of the owner of the rent-charge. Even though the defendant was strictly outside the statute's provisions, the challenge was not successful. More surprisingly, in a case of 1292,[16] the Bench seems to have been unsympathetic to a plaintiff's challenge to an avowry for damage feasant by a defendant who

---

13. The *causa* clause of one ran: 'Quia predictus A averia ipsius B cepit pro servicio sibi debito et adjudicato per judicium curie sue de tenemento quod idem B tenet de feodo predicti A in N et idem B subterfugia querit quominus idem A consuetudines et servicia inde debita consequatur ut dicitur': *Early Registers of Writs*, edd. E. de Haas and G.D.G. Hall (Selden Soc., lxxxvii, 1970), CC 90, first version; also found in BL Lansdowne 467, ff.54v-55r (abbot of Peterborough and tenement in magna N) and at least eight other Mss. The *causa* clause of the other ran: 'Quia predictus talis averia sua replegiari procuravit querendo subterfugia ut servicium predicto A debitum de tenemento suo quod de eo tenet in N non fecerit ut dicitur': *Early Registers of Writs*, CC90, second version; also found in BL Lansdowne 467, f.55r and at least eight other Mss.

14. See Table [at end of footnotes].

15. *Roger de Lisle v. Nicholas de Segrave jr.*: CP 40/100, m.34. The case is reported in *Y.B. 21 & 22 Edward I* at 631-7, though it is misascribed there to the 1294 Middx. eyre.

16. *Hugh parson of Bilney v. William de Mortimer and wife Alice*: CP 40/96, m.61. There is also a note relating to this case in BL Ms. Stowe 386, f.142v.

had used the statutory writ to remove the plea into the Bench. The case was adjourned for judgment, and in a later term we find the plaintiff pleading to the avowry. Under the chief justiceship of Ralph de Hengham (1301-9), the man who had been chief justice of King's Bench when the legislation was enacted, a much stricter position was adopted. In 1304,[17] a defendant who had removed litigation into the Bench by a statutory writ made an avowry for the attendance of a tithingman at a view of frankpledge. When this was challenged by the plaintiff, the case was dismissed to the county court. An even sterner approach was taken in another case of the same year.[18] Again the defendant had secured the removal of the case out of the county court by the statutory writ, but avowed in the Bench for damage feasant. This time the plaintiff's challenge led to the defendant losing his case and the plaintiff recovering damages.

(ii)

The other statutory change I want to examine is the one made by the following section of the same chapter. This stated that it had been agreed that a distraint by a lord against a tenant (for services) could be avowed as reasonable if it was supported by seisin on the part of the lord's ancestors or predecessors since the limitation date for novel disseisin (currently fixed at 1242). The reason for this pronouncement was said to be so that the justices could be certain as to what kind of recent seisin would support such an avowry.[19]

Plucknett believed that by 1285 replevin was a well-established possessory action for litigation about services and so thought the legislation was of little importance. He considered that the legislation was made solely 'for the more precise information of the courts.'[20] In fact, the action of replevin had only recently become established as a common way of litigating about services, and the effects of the statute were much more significant than Plucknett

---

17. *Master John of Uphaven v. Henry Inthetoune*: CP 40/150, m.118. This case is reported in *Y.B 32 & 33 Edward I* at 83-5 and in BL Ms. Additional 31826, f.373v.

18. *William of Belsted v. Sibyl widow of Roger Loveday et al.*: CP 40/149, m.34. This is the case reported in *Y.B. 32 & 33 Edward I*, at 143. It is also reported in BL Ms. Additional 35116, f.185r (of which there is a copy in BL Ms. Harley 25, f.129r).

19. 'Et ut in certo sint justiciarii de qua recenti seisina poterunt domini advocare racionabilem districcionem super tenentes suos decetero concordatum est quod racionabilis districcio poterit advocari de seisina antecessorum vel predecessorum suorum a tempore quo breve nove disseisine currit.'

20. Plucknett, *Legislation of Edward I*, at 69. Naomi Hurnard, in an article reviewing Plucknett's book, hypothesized that the real point of the legislation was to bring the limitation date for replevin back into line with that applicable in the assize of novel disseisin, which had been changed in 1275: N.D. Hurnard, 'Did Edward I reverse Henry II's Policy upon Seisin?', 69 *Eng. Hist. Rev.*, 529, 547 (1954).

supposed. The pre-statutory rule on the kinds of seisin which could be used to support an avowry was a much more restrictive one, generally requiring a much more recent seisin. It was clearly stated in litigation of 1282.[21] The defendant had avowed her distraint on Robert fitz Roger for arrears of homage and fealty, and claimed that her father had been seised of homage and forinsec service at the hands of Robert's father. Robert joined with the plaintiff in answering and said that the defendant's father had been succeeded by his son George and that it was only on his death that she had succeeded to the seignory. George, he claimed, had never been seised of his homage, and so the distraint had been unjust since no-one was allowed to distrain for a service unless he had been in seisin of it or his immediate ancestor had died in seisin of it. The defendant did not deny that this was the rule. Instead, she claimed that her brother had been a minor when he had succeeded, and had distrained for the homage as soon as he had come of age, and had died while still distraining for the same. No judgment was given. A very similar rule can also be found in one of the Edwardian legal treatises, *Modus Componendi Brevia*, written between 1278 and 1285.[22] Most (though not all) avowries for service of the thirteen year period between the beginning of Edward's reign and 1285 seem to observe this rule.[23]

Therefore, the effect of the legislation was to legitimize the use of distraint by lords for arrears of services in a wider range of circumstances than had been the case prior to 1285. Except in the most exceptional cases, the legislation made it unnecessary for a lord to bring the action of customs and services when he wished to claim arrears of service. A majority of lords who made avowries for services after 1285 claimed to have been in seisin of the services for which they were distraining themselves; such a title would, of course, have been equally acceptable prior to the making of the statute.[24] However, in the remaining cases, we now find lords avowing on the seisin of an ancestor or predecessor without stating

---

21. *John Deen v. Milisent widow of Eon la Souche et al.*: CP 40/45, m.20d.

22. *Four Thirteenth Century Law Tracts*, 155 (ed. G.E. Woodbine 1910): each lord can avow distraints made within his fee 'pro arreragiis et serviciis suis, de quo fuit seisitus per manum tenentis, vel eciam si continuo post mortem antecessoris sui cujus heres ipse est pro servicio sibi debito districcionem illam in feodo suo fecerit, licet de eodem seisitus non extiterit'.

23. The defendant avowed his distraint on the basis of his seisin alone in 26 cases, on the basis of his own seisin and that of a predecessor in title in seven cases (in one case that of his father at his death and that of his guardian since, in another just that of his father and his guardian since). The apparent exceptions to the general rule, six in all, may all be explicable (e.g. because the service is an exceptional one of which the lord can only rarely be in seisin, or because the seisin enjoyed by the ancestor mentioned in the avowry was one which he still enjoyed at his death).

24. 395 out of 694 cases where a title is recorded (almost 57% of the total).

that this was at their death.[25] In a few cases, we can demonstrate that the ancestor or predecessor on whose seisin the defendant relied was not the immediate predecessor in title of the defendant.[26] When litigants took issue as to whether or not the lord's ancestor or predecessor had been seised, the jury would not be examined about whether or not that seisin had been since 1242. It did become possible to take issue specifically on this point,[27] though such pleas never became common.[28]

The first case to hold that there was one type of tenurial service, suit of court, to which the statutory provisions did not apply occurred in 1305.[29] In that case, the court decided that the provisions of c.9 of the statute of Marlborough of 1267, requiring those who distrained for suit of court to show either a specific requirement that suit be done in the charter of feoffment or seisin of the suit prior to 1230, had not been repealed by the legislation of 1285, and that they could be pled by the plaintiff not just in the special action created by the statute (*contra formam feoffamenti*), but also in the common law action of replevin. However, the plaintiff had to plead the provisions of the statute specially. If he did not do so, issue might still be taken on a later seisin.[30] The case is also of interest because it shows the short memory of the legal profession. In the course of pleading one of the serjeants claimed that the statute had been enacted because in replevin pleas prior to 1285 defendants had been avowing on seisins so old that juries were unable to have knowledge of them.[31] However, the limitation date did also come to be applied to avowries for certain types of obligation other than services. In 1287 we can see it being applied to the obligation of attendance at view of

---

25. The ancestor whose seisin is most commonly mentioned is the defendant's father—in 139 cases (20% of the total), but in 87 cases (over 12%) it is that of another relation. In some 73 cases (around 10%) it is that of an ecclesiastical predecessor.

26. See, e.g. *Prior of Shelford v. Thomas de Furnivall* heard in 1303 (CP 40/146, m.2d) where the defendant relied on the seisin of his great-grandmother, Maud de Lovetot. It can be shown that there had been two intervening tenants of the seignory concerned.

27. The earliest case in which issue was taken on this point was one of 1290: *Alan of Pennington v. Roger of Lancaster*: CP 40/86, m.71.

28. This issue was taken by an average of just one plaintiff a year between 1290 and 1307 (and between 1295 and 1300 not a single plaintiff took it). Only in one year (1292) do we find it being taken by as many as four plaintiffs.

29. *Nicholas de Alneto v. abbot of Tavistock*: CP 40/153, m.372. The case is reported in *Y.B. 33-35 Edward I*, at 79-83; in BL Ms. Additional 31826, f.333v and in LI Ms. Misc. 738, f.40r.

30. See e.g., *John fitzHugh of Ancaster v. prior of Wilsford et al.*: CP 40/158, m.176d (Hilary 1306); *Michael atte Rye v. John of Benefield et al.*: CP 40/164, m.181 (Trinity 1307).

31. *Y.B. 33-35 Edward I* at 83.

frankpledge,[32] in 1291 to suit to a hundred court,[33] and in 1302 we even find it being applied to a private toll on ships leaving a port.[34]

(iii)

To show that there were important developments in Edward's reign that were of a non-statutory origin I will conclude by looking at one such development, again in the action of replevin. Distraint by chattels had long been used by non-royal courts as a way of securing the appearance of defendants, and as a way of enforcing the payment of amercements, fines and judgment debts adjudged due by such courts. As early as 1194 we find a defendant in an action of replevin avowing a distraint made in order to enforce payment of an amercement adjudged due by his court. Thereafter, a number of replevin cases arose in which distraints were justified on similar grounds.[35] However, there is no indication prior to the reign of Edward I that plaintiffs were allowed to use the action of replevin as a way of challenging such judgments.

This changed early in Edward's reign. While the change cannot be associated with any particular leading case in which the decision was taken to allow this, we can note its occurrence and examine its consequences. Between 1273 and 1307 there were some seventy-seven cases where a distraint was avowed in order to secure the attendance of the plaintiff to answer in a lower court, most commonly a seignorial court, as a defendant.[36] Many of these cases did not involve a challenge to the judgment in the lower court: in eighteen of the cases, for example, the parties simply took issue as to whether there had been any such litigation when the plaintiff was distrained, or on whether or not the distraint had been authorized by the court. However, in fourteen other cases, the plaintiff admitted that there had been litigation, and that the distraint had been authorized by the court, but claimed there had been some error in the

---

32. *Master of Sandon hospital v. Agnes de Percy of Foston et al.*: CP 40/69, m.148d.

33. *Prior to Dodnash v. prior of Ely et al.*: CP 40/91, m.276. This case is reported in *Y.B. 21 & 22 Edward I*, 561-3.

34. *Robert of Walton et al. v. Robert of Tattershall et al.*: CP 40/141, m.50. This case is reported in BL Mss. Additional 31826, f.128r and Additional 37657, f.149r.

35. *Avice of Oakley v. William Basset*: *Pipe Roll Soc.*, first series, xiv, 26; *Geoffrey of Childwick v. abbot of St. Alban's*: KB 26/142, m.7 (Trinity 1250); *Roger de St. John v. Robert of Shelfanger*: KB 26/143, m.29 (Michaelmas 1250); *Richard of Seaton v. Robert le Eyr et al.*: KB 26/200C, m.34d (Michaelmas 1270).

36. Of these seventy-seven, sixty-three were to answer cases at fifty-nine different seignorial courts in twenty counties; two were for attendance to answer at county courts; three at borough courts; and nine at hundred courts.

preceding process which rendered the distraint wrongful: the earliest such case is one of 1281.[37] As early as 1284, we also find a case where a plaintiff claimed that a judgment ordering his distraint to answer a plea of debt had been invalid because of the constitution of the court concerned. The plaintiff alleged that the prior of Walsingham's court at Burnham in Norfolk was not able to hear the case against him because the court had no free suitors, and therefore its judgment would not be (as Magna Carta required) by his peers.[38] In a still earlier case of 1275, the earl of Norfolk alleged that the honor court of Wallingford had exceeded its jurisdiction by distraining him to answer a plea of rescue.[39] More commonly the plaintiff did not deny that the court had jurisdiction to hear pleas of the type in question, but he claimed that it had exceeded its jurisdiction by taking cognisance of this particular litigation. In a case which was heard in 1285 the plaintiff did not deny holding of the defendant's fee, but did say that he held his lands of a third party (the prior of Launde) who held a court for his own tenants with jurisdiction to redress wrongs done by them; he claimed, therefore, that he should not have been distrained to answer a case in the defendant's court.[40] The Bench, however, held that, as chief lord of the village, the defendant was entitled to make summonses and distresses (and thus by implication to hear litigation in his court) against all who held of his fee. A case of 1299 squarely raised the question of whether an overlord could claim jurisdiction for his court over litigation involving villein subtenants.[41] The defendant avowed a distraint on the grounds that two villeins of the prioress of Grace-Dieu, resident in her villeinage but within his fee, had been summoned to answer pleas of trespass in his court. They had then made several defaults, leading to the distraints now challenged. He claimed that the two villeins were justiciable in his court, as they and their ancestors had been justiciable there in the past. The prioress did not deny that this had been the practice in the past, but took the high ground of princi-

---

37. *Laurence Cole v. Hervey son of Geoffrey of Riseley et al.*: CP 40/33, m.18d; for another early case see *Agnes de la Dene et al. v. earl of Lincoln et al.*: CP 40/42, m.98.

38. *Simon Subburg' of Burnham v. prior of Walsingham*: CP 40/55, m.97d. The prior claimed the court had both free and villein suitors and so was competent to hear the litigation.

39. *Earl of Norfolk v. earl of Cornwall*: CP 40/11, m.76.

40. *William of Twyford, parson of moiety of church of Weldon v. Ralph Basset*: CP 40/59, m.14. The same term also saw litigation between the prior of Launde and Ralph Basset over other seignorial rights in the same village. This is also recorded on the same membrane of the plea roll.

41. *Prioress of Grace-Dieu v. Nicholas Musard*: CP 40/127, m.124. This case is reported in BL Ms. Additional 31826 at f.140v.

ple. The avowry had been made as though the two men were of free condition and owned the animals; no villein was justiciable by his chattels except in the king's court or the court of his lord. The case was then adjourned for judgment.[42]

Fewer litigants waited until final judgment was given to make a challenge: there were only thirty-six replevin avowries in the Bench of distraints made to enforce such judgments.[43] Again some cases did not really challenge the validity of the proceedings of the lower court, yet others certainly did. For example, in one instance, a plaintiff alleged that his case had been removed out of the court before the judgment was given;[44] in another a plaintiff alleged that one of the parties had died before judgment was given.[45]

Replevin also began to be used as a way of challenging proceedings at views of frankpledge and other franchisal courts, proceedings which had hitherto been quite unchallangeable. There are some fifty-two replevin cases of this period where the distraint is said to have been made by virtue of a presentment at such a court.[46] The plaintiff might simply challenge the distraint on the grounds that the defendant's court did not possess the jurisdiction he claimed,[47] or that the court did not possess jurisdiction over the plaintiff. The cases where the plaintiff's claim was that the court had exceeded its jurisdiction (e.g. by accepting a presentment of a purpresture which

---

42. According to the report, judgment was eventually given against the defendant by Chief Justice Mettingham on the grounds that 'vileins ne sunt pas amenables de dreit en nuly curt forqe en la curt lur seignur ou en la curt le rey'. No final judgment is recorded on the plea roll. There had also been previous replevin litigation between these same parties about an earlier distraint during the same litigation. This too had been won by the prioress, but on much narrower grounds which had not specifically confirmed her jurisdictional monopoly over her villein tenants: CP 40/121, m.153 (Michaelmas 1297). This case is reported in BL Mss. Additional 5925, f.43v and Stowe 386, f.143v, in LI Ms. Misc. 738, f.90v and CUL Ms. Ee. 2.19, f.139v.

43. Five concern the enforcement of the judgment of county courts; five the judgments of four hundred courts; one the judgment of a market court; twenty-six the judgments of seignorial courts.

44. *John of 'Yoldesthorne' v. William Trenchard*: CP 40/162, m.116d (Hilary 1307).

45. *Peter Pec of Morton v. John son of John of Rippingale*: CP 40/112, m.125d (Easter 1296).

46. This figure excludes distraints made by virtue of presentments for non-attendance at such sessions. Eleven of the presentments mentioned were at views held by lords of hundreds or wapentakes; thirty-seven at franchisal courts with view of frankpledge; four at other courts.

47. See e.g., *Hugelina of Ravendale v. prior of Ravendale*: CP 40/134, m.76d (Trinity 1300): presentment for breach of assize of ale, but plaintiff says can only claim as appurtenant to view of frankpledge which defendant does not have; *Henry le Bailiff v. Thomas Pridyas et al.*: CP 40/153, m.143 (Michaelmas 1305): plaintiff says defendants do not have view of frankpledge in village. For a report of this case see BL Ms. Additional 31826, f.332v.

damaged only a private individual[48]) or that the court had wrongly exercised a jurisdiction that it did possess (e.g. by distraining a plaintiff for not being in tithing when he was a scholar and in clerical orders[49]) are far more interesting than the simple challenges described above. The alleged error might also be in the manner in which a presentment was made. For example in a case of 1294,[50] the plaintiff claimed that an alleged presentment was invalid because it had been made by outsiders not tithingmen. It was also possible to claim that an error had been made at the next stage—after the making of the presentment. This might simply be that the distraint had been made on the wrong person or at the wrong place. In at least one case, a plaintiff claimed that the amercement which was levied was not the proper penalty for the offence concerned.[51] The defendant avowed as bailiff of the prior of Edith Weston for two amercements due from the plaintiff's wife for brewing ale contrary to the assize. The plaintiff, far from being relieved that his wife had incurred only a monetary penalty, claimed that such a punishment was incorrect, and that she should have suffered corporal punishment instead.[52]

(iv)

Re-examination of two pieces of Edwardian legislation in light of the manuscript evidence highlights the dangers of accepting at face value what the legislation itself says were the reasons for enactment, and the hints it gives regarding its intended effects. It also shows the possibilities that exist for detailed and accurate surveys of the actual effects of the legislation. The final section of this paper has shown that legal change in this period was not just a matter of statutes; there were also important non-statutory developments, a

---

48. *Prior of Holy Trinity London v. abbot of Lessness*: CP 40/96, m.166 (Michaelmas 1292). For reports of this part of the case see BL Mss. Additional 37657, f.147r and Additional 31826, f.130r.

49. *John son of master Robert of Rydemere v. Thomas Bardolf et al.*: CP 40/86, m.19 (Michaelmas 1290). This case is reported in *Y.B. 20 & 21 Edward I*, at 297-9.

50. *Ralph atte Legh v. Laurence of Messingham et al.*: CP 40/105, m.1 (Trinity 1294).

51. *William le Fraunchomme v. Thomas de Arderne*: CP 40/149, m.158d (Michaelmas 1304).

52. The report of this case in BL Ms. Additional 31826, f.127v, indicates that it was Howard, J. who initially made the argument ascribed to the plaintiff in the plea roll enrolment. It also shows that Hampton had then alleged the prior had no free court and no tumbrel, pillory or other forms of punishment, so that he could not have imposed corporal punishment anyway.

fact which Plucknett's work on the legislation has tended to obscure. It is only through such detailed work on the unpublished sources that we can begin to understand the ways in which the common law was evolving in this period.

Table of Bench Replevin Cases in which Defendant's Avowry is for Services, 1272-1307

§1273 total = 0 [out of 1 case]	1291 total = 64 [out of 151 cases]
§1274 total = 2 [out of 4 cases]	1292 total = 64 [out of 133 cases]
*1275 total = 13 [out of 24 cases]	*1293 total = 57 [out of 94 cases]
1276 total = 13 [out of 28 cases]	*1294 total = 63 [out of 106 cases]
1277 total = 6 [out of 14 cases]	*1295 total = 73 [out of 106 cases]
#1278 total = 9 [out of 20 cases]	1296 total = 33 [out of 72 cases]
1279 total = 5 [out of 25 cases]	*1297 total = 50 [out of 96 cases]
1280 total = 14 [out of 39 cases]	*1298 total = 41 [out of 73 cases]
1281 total = 9 [out of 23 cases]	1299 total = 41 [out of 86 cases]
1282 total = 9 [out of 19 cases]	*1300 total = 59 [out of 98 cases]
1283 total = 7 [out of 18 cases]	*1301 total = 42 [out of 78 cases]
1284 total = 7 [out of 28 cases]	1302 total = 36 [out of 88 cases]
1285 total = 12 [out of 39 cases]	*1303 total = 44 [out of 80 cases]
1286 total = 13 [out of 33 cases]	*1304 total = 45 [out of 81 cases]
*1287 total = 32 [out of 51 cases]	*1305 total = 56 [out of 99 cases]
*1288 total = 38 [out of 67 cases]	*1306 total = 68 [out of 116 cases]
1289 total = 35 [out of 85 cases]	*1307 total = 51 [out of 93 cases]
1290 total = 54 [out of 111 cases]	

---

* = years when replevin cases about services over half total no. of replevin cases.

§ = only one term's roll survives for this year.

\# = only three terms' rolls survive for this year.

15

Lordship and Distraint in Thirteenth-Century England

On 25 August 1290 William de Vernun and Robert de Frechenvill seized three cows belonging to the abbot of Darley at a place called 'Collesley' in the Derbyshire village of Ripley.[1] They then drove the animals to Ralph de Frechenvill's manor of Crich, some four miles away, and placed them in a pound. The purpose of this distraint was to bring pressure on the abbot to perform the homage and fealty which, Ralph claimed, the abbot owed him, and to pay the £10 relief appropriate to a holding of two knights' fees. We may presume that the distraint had been preceded by some sort of request to the abbot to perform these services, but there is no evidence that there had been any formal legal proceedings about them, either in Ralph's court or elsewhere. The abbot did not perform the services. Instead, he secured the conditional release of his animals by initiating an action of replevin in the Derbyshire county court, challenging the lawfulness of this distraint.[2] Subsequently, the litigation was removed out of the county court and into the Bench at Westminster. What happened in court in Trinity term 1291 was recorded both on the plea roll of the court (in Latin) and in at least two different unofficial Year Book reports (in French). The abbot's count gave details of the distraint, and alleged both that the initial seizure had been unjustified and that the defendants had then committed a further wrong by refusing to release the distresses that they had taken when they were offered 'gage and pledges' (suitable sureties) for them. In reality, this 'offer' was almost certainly a legal fiction. All plaintiffs had, for historical reasons, to make the allegation of such an offer and refusal when bringing the action of replevin, but it did not matter in practice whether or not such an offer and

---

1 Details of this distraint and of subsequent proceedings in the Bench come from the plea roll enrolment of the case: PRO, CP 40/90, m. 50; reports of the case in Lincoln's Inn, MS Hale 188, f. 34v; BL, MSS Egerton 2811, fos. 94v–95r, and Add. 31826, f. 64v; Cambridge Univ. Library, MSS Ee.6.18, fos. 10r–11r, and Mm.1.30, fos. 8r–8v. All these reports, other than that in BL, MS Add. 31826, appear to derive from a single archetype. The abbot's count in the Bench alleges that it was not only William and Robert but also Ralph de Frechenvill who had taken and driven away the animals, but other evidence from replevin cases of the same period indicates that this should not necessarily be taken literally and that it was normal practice to include the lord in whose name (and on whose orders) a distraint was made among those who were alleged to have made the distraint, even though he was not personally present when it was made. (Unless otherwise noted, all further citations of unpublished plea rolls are from those in the PRO.)
2 The enrolment of the abbot's count in the Bench replevin case is one of a minority of such counts in Bench replevin cases in 1291 which do not specify whether release was obtained by royal order or simply by action of the king's bailiff(s). The former normally indicates litigation initiated by royal writ; the latter, litigation initiated by plaint. However, one of the reports of this case (BL, MS Add. 31826) shows that the case was initiated by plaint, since it refers to the removal of the case into the Bench by a writ of *recordari facias*.

refusal had actually taken place, and in a case like this it is extremely unlikely that they had.[3] The abbot concluded his count by claiming damages of 40 s. in respect of both these wrongs. Ralph answered for all those involved and 'avowed' the distraint that they had made as lawful and justified. He claimed that the abbot held the tenement where the distraint had been made, together with other tenements, by homage and the service of two knights' fees. He had distrained the abbot for homage, fealty and the relief due on the death of Abbot Henry, his immediate predecessor. By way of title to make the distraint, he asserted that he had been seised of the scutage appropriate to a holding of two knights' fees at Henry's hands. Almost certainly he also made a formal denial of the refusal to release the animals in return for the offer of 'gage and pledge', though neither reports nor enrolment record this, and the second allegation then played no further part in the case. The abbot (or rather the Bench serjeant, Nicholas of Warwick, who was speaking on his behalf) challenged Ralph's avowry. It was necessary when avowing a distraint, he said, to show that the lord who was distraining, or one of his ancestors, had been seised of the services for which the distraint had been made; but Ralph had failed to show that he or any of his ancestors had ever been seised of homage, fealty or relief for this holding from the abbot or any of his predecessors. Roger of Higham, another Bench serjeant, answered for Ralph de Frechenville. Homage, fealty and relief were, he claimed, merely 'accessories' (incidents of tenure). A lord who could show that he had been seised of scutage was *ipso facto* entitled to distrain for them as well. The chief justice showed himself sympathetic to Ralph's argument, but judgment was adjourned and no eventual resolution of the case is recorded, either on the plea roll or in the reports.

This case is of specific interest because it is the earliest replevin case to raise (but not resolve) the question of when, and under what circumstances, ecclesiastical tenants by knight service were liable to pay relief.[4] But its significance in the present context lies in the fact that it is a typical replevin case: just one of almost 1250 replevin cases heard in the Bench during the reign of Edward I in which a plaintiff challenged a distraint and the defendant avowed it as having been made for arrears of services owed him by a tenant (often but not necessarily the plaintiff).[5] These cases indicate that lords in later thirteenth-century England were making relatively frequent use of a procedure (distraint, or more precisely extrajudicial distraint) which appears to amount to no more than a relatively primitive kind of self-help. Lords were compelling tenants to perform services or incidents of tenure, not by bringing litigation against them, but simply by seizing property belonging to the tenant (or the tenant's sub-tenant) and retaining it until the tenant did or paid what the lord claimed that he owed. These very cases are, however, also evidence of the degree to which the lord's use of this powerful weapon was subject

---

3 Below, 309-10.
4 The general rule had been that such tenants were exempt, though it was accepted that they could specifically oblige themselves and their successors to pay relief by deed: H.E. Salter, 'Reliefs "per cartam" ', *EHR* xlv (1930), 281-5. In Edward I's later years a determined attempt seems to have been made to challenge and alter the general rule, and thus to make ecclesiastical tenants by knight service liable to pay relief. On the relationship between Darley abbey and the Freche(n)ville family, see *The Cartulary of Darley Abbey*, ed. R.R. Darlington (Kendal, 1945), i. xvi ff.; and ibid. 557 for a 1240 final concord between Ralph's grandfather and the abbot's predecessor about the services owed for these tenements.
5 In about 60% of these cases the plaintiff appears to have been the lord's tenant; in the remainder, he is normally a sub-tenant.

by this date to routine, external control. In each, the lord's exercise of his power has been challenged by his tenant or sub-tenant. The lord is being made to justify his distraint in the king's court, and to show that it conformed to the rules which the king's court laid down about the making of distraints. These cases may, moreover, form only the tip of a much larger iceberg, for many replevin cases involving services were probably heard and determined in county courts; and there, too, lords were compelled to justify their use of the weapon of distraint. Of course, not every distraint for services will have been challenged in this way, but the very existence of a ready mechanism for doing so is likely to have influenced the behaviour of both lords and tenants, and must have ensured that most unchallenged distraints went unchallenged precisely because they could readily have been justified in the courts.

My intention in this paper is to put these cases — and what they tell us about the use and control of extra-judicial distraint in later thirteenth-century England — in context by looking at the development of the law and practice relating to the enforcement of services and the use of extra-judicial distraint for this purpose during the century or so prior to 1300. In the first section of the paper I want to look at the origins of the use of extra-judicial distraint in the enforcement of services, and to suggest that these are much older than most scholars have supposed. In the second section I will look at the rules about the use of distraint being enforced through the action of replevin during the first half of the thirteenth century, and look for reasons why these may have meant that extra-judicial distraint was much less common as a method of enforcing services during this period than it later became. In the third section I look at extra-judicial distraint in the context of other competing remedies for the enforcement of services that existed during the same period (litigation in the lord's own court and litigation initiated by the royal writ of customs and services) and will suggest reasons why the latter may have been particularly important and popular during this period. The fourth section deals with the main statutory and non-statutory changes in the workings of the action of replevin during the second half of the thirteenth century; while in the fifth section I will be looking at the effects of these changes in converting lords to the virtues of the use of extra-judicial distraint for the enforcement of services. I will conclude by looking briefly at the effects of the changes I have been examining on the relative power of lords and tenants within the lord-tenant relationship.

I

Historians have expressed differing views about when, how and why lords in England gained the right to distrain their tenants to perform services without the need for any prior judicial authorization. Maitland believed that in the twelfth century lords had needed the permission of a court before they could distrain, and that they could only distrain tenants to appear in their courts to answer for the withholding of services, not to perform those services. By the time 'Bracton' was written, lords no longer needed such permission and were able to distrain tenants directly to perform services, though some lords still followed the older practice of distraining their tenants to answer in their courts for arrears of service instead. Maitland's explanation for the change is characteristically allusive. The lord's right to distrain his tenant to come to his court to answer for arrears of service was easily transformed under favourable circumstances into a right simply to distrain the tenant to do services, and such favourable circumstances were provided by the changes which allowed the law relating to distraint to be shaped by royal justices who 'had no love for feudal justice'.[6] Plucknett likewise believed that there had been no extra-judicial distraint in the twelfth century, and he pointed to 'Bracton''s treatise as the earliest evidence for the acceptance of its use. But he differed from Maitland in suggesting that in the twelfth century the only legitimate use of distraint had been to enforce the performance of services after proceedings in the lord's court to settle any differences as to the services due, and he did not adopt Maitland's explanation for the subsequent change or provide any alternative explanation of his own.[7] Professor Milsom shares Maitland's view that in 'feudal' twelfth-century England distraint had been proper only if used to secure the tenant's attendance at his lord's court to answer for the withholding of services, and that this was still the position when 'Glanvill' was written at the end of Henry II's reign. He also seems to share Maitland's belief that such distraints were then normally authorized by the court concerned, since he sees distraint by chattels as simply forming an intermediate stage in the process for enforcing attendance at the lord's court, coming after summons but before distraint by the tenant's holding.[8] Milsom, indeed, suggests that one of the main functions of the royal writ of customs and services which we find in 'Glanvill' was to provide a remedy for those exceptional petty 'lords' who did not possess a functioning court and so could not use the process of that court to secure their services from their tenants.[9] It is not altogether clear whether he believes that extra-judicial distraint had become licit by the time 'Bracton' was written. He says that the treatise 'almost consistently' assumes that the lord has a court and is working through it, but the 'almost' is an important qualification here, as is also the further prefatory phrase 'whatever the realities are in his day'.[10] We may conclude that Milsom believes that extra-judicial distraint had made an appearance by the time the treatise was written, and that it was recognized as licit then or soon afterwards. Milsom also provides an alternative explanation for the emergence of extra-judicial distraint and hints at yet another. There had been, he suggests, in the period between 'Glanvill' and 'Bracton', a substantial increase in the number of lords who did not possess their own courts. If all had needed to bring the action of customs and services each time their tenants were in arrears, this would have placed an intolerable burden on the county court, to which the *justicies* writ of customs and services brought most such litigation. The only solution was to allow lords to distrain for services without a prior judgment, but to make such distraints subject to review through the action of replevin.[11] The alternative explanation would relate the change to a second major development which, Milsom believes, occurred during the same period — that by which seignorial courts lost the power to hear cases about services, if the tenant denied holding of the lord or if he simply denied owing the services that the lord claimed.

6 F. Pollock and F.W. Maitland, *The History of English Law before the Time of Edward I* (2nd edn. Cambridge, 1898), i. 353–4; ii. 574–6.
7 T.F.T. Plucknett, *Legislation of Edward I* (2nd edn. Oxford, 1962), 56.
8 S.F.C. Milsom, *The Legal Framework of English Feudalism* (Cambridge, 1976), 10–11.
9 Milsom, *Legal Framework*, 33.
10 Milsom, *Legal Framework*, 31.
11 Milsom, *Legal Framework*, 33–4.

Once the lord's court had lost its competence to hear and determine a substantial proportion of all litigation about services, it must also have ceased to seem important whether or not a court had actually authorized the lord to make a distraint.[12] Richardson and Sayles, as so often, dissent. Extra-judicial distraint, they argue, had always existed in England, and such evidence as appeared to point to the contrary had been misunderstood and was susceptible of other and better explanations.[13] It is my belief that they are right.

Our starting-point must be the passage in the early twelfth-century *Leges Henrici Primi* which seems to suppose that prior judicial authorization is required for all distraint, and has generally been taken to prove that this was the position in early twelfth-century England. However, this passage is only repeating a rule of Anglo-Saxon law and, like much else in that treatise, cannot be accepted as a reliable guide to contemporary reality without supporting evidence.[14] There is certainly some contemporary evidence to the contrary in an early twelfth-century episode related in the chronicle of Abingdon abbey. A burgess of Oxford who held a wick by Oxford bridge of the abbot of Abingdon detained his rent for a year. It was then the abbot himself, and not his court, who gave orders for the seizure of all movables found on the land at harvest time and for some kind of formal seizure of the land itself. Only after the seizure had taken place did the matter become one for the abbot's court. The burgess sent two intermediaries to the abbot to procure the release of the chattels in return for sureties to appear in the court and answer for the service.[15] The evidence of a number of royal writs of the reigns of Henry I and Henry II has also to be taken into account. These envisage lords taking action to enforce their right to services through distraint without any kind of prior authorization from their own courts.[16] However, it is not clear how common such writs were. Nor, more significantly, is it possible to be certain whether what they are doing is spelling out and reinforcing existing customary procedures or consciously authorizing departures from them. It seems likely, however, that they did play some part in accustoming men to the idea of extra-judicial distraint for services.

Our main source for later twelfth-century law is 'Glanvill', and two passages in book IX of the treatise concern the use of distraint. In the first, which is concerned with services generally, although it is said that the distraint is to secure the tenant's appearance in the lord's court to answer for withholding all or part of his service, nothing is said of this distraint being made by the judgment of the court, and responsibility for making the distraint is ascribed solely to the lord.[17] The second passage concerns the use of distraint to enforce payment of 'reasonable' aids. Here, distraint by chattels (or, if necessary, distraint by the tenant's holding) is said to be made with judicial authorization ('per iudicium curie sue') as though this was a necessary requirement.[18] It is possible that the second passage simply makes explicit what was implicit in the first, but there are also good reasons for different

12 Milsom, *Legal Framework*, 30–1.
13 *Select Cases of Procedure without Writ under Henry III*, ed. H.G. Richardson and G.O. Sayles (Selden Soc. lx, 1941), xciii, n. 1.
14 *Leges Henrici Primi*, ed. L.J. Downer (Oxford, 1972), 166 (51, 3), 359–60.
15 *Chronicon Monasterii de Abingdon*, ed. J. Stevenson (RS, 1858), ii. 140–1.
16 E.g. *Regesta Regum Anglo-Normannorum, II*, ed. C. Johnson and H.A. Cronne (Oxford, 1956), nos. 1387 (1123?), 1860a (1100–33); *Reading Abbey Cartularies*, ed. B.R. Kemp (Camden Soc., 4th ser. xxxi, xxxiii, 1986–7), i. no. 24 (1155).
17 *Glanvill*, ed. G.D.G. Hall (London, 1965), 105.
18 *Glanvill*, 111–12.

rules being applied in the two different kinds of situation. Reasonable aids were different from other types of service or incidents of tenure. The amount of service owed by a tenant was something fixed in advance. The amount payable to a lord as aid was, however, subject to negotiation between a lord and his tenants on each occasion that an aid was paid, and it may already have been established by 'Glanvill''s time that this was done by the lord calling his tenants together to agree a standard rate for all the lord's tenants.[19] Distraint would only be proper if the individual tenant had failed to pay the appropriate amount after this. Such a collective grant might well have been described as a 'judgment' of the lord's court. If so, all this passage would mean is that a distraint for 'reasonable' aids, though not for other services, would need prior authorization through such a grant. An alternative explanation would focus on the fact that in this passage, though not in the earlier one, the author of 'Glanvill' mentions the possibility of distraint by the tenant's holding as well as by his chattels. Distraint of the former kind, involving the disseisin of the tenant, certainly did require the authorization of a court, and the author may mention court judgment in this passage precisely because he is thinking of the employment of this kind of distraint as well as distraint by chattels.

For the legal position with regard to extra-judicial distraint in the late twelfth and early thirteenth centuries we also have the evidence of the small number of replevin cases on the early plea rolls. During this period plaintiffs often added to the standard count (alleging unjust distraint and wrongful detention against gage and pledge) a number of further allegations of related wrongdoing. Yet in not one of these cases do we find a plaintiff alleging that a distraint had been wrongfully made because it had been made without the prior authorization of the defendant's court. A possible explanation is that in practice lords only distrained after obtaining such authorization. But if that had been the case, one might still have expected that tenants would sometimes allege a lack of authorization, and have the claim refuted. A more likely explanation is that authorization was not a requirement for a valid distraint.[20]

Seignorial courts certainly did on occasion, in the late twelfth and early thirteenth centuries, specifically authorize the use of distraint by chattels as well as distraint by the tenant's holding.[21] It may be that prior authorization had been a requirement of the custom of particular lordships. Perhaps weaker lords preferred to have the backing of their courts in making distraints because this strengthened their hands in dealing with potentially recalcitrant tenants. A third possibility is that

---

[19] Cf. F.M. Stenton, *The First Century of English Feudalism, 1066–1166* (2nd edn. Oxford, 1961), 173, 277: agreement of 1183–4 between William fitzRichard and the monks of St. Andrew's, Northampton about the services owed for land which the monks held of him, which mentions the specific occasions when the monks are to contribute aid like William's other free tenants, but does not go on to specify the amount payable, merely noting their liability to pay at the level fixed as appropriate by the tenants as a group. For 13th-c. evidence of meetings of a lord's knights and free tenants to fix the level of aid owed to a lord (whose collection has been specifically authorized by the king), subsequently followed by distraint to enforce their payment, see *Bracton's Note Book*, ed. F.W. Maitland (Cambridge, 1887), pl. 1146 (1235–6); and KB 26/149, m. 15d (1253).

[20] For early replevin cases which involve services and where there is no hint that the distraint was made with the authorization of the lord's court, see *Memoranda Roll 10 John*, ed. R.A. Brown (Pipe Roll Soc., new ser. xxxi, 1955), 96–7 (1198); *CRR* x. 297 (1222), and 306 (1222); *CRR* xii. no. 192 (1225); *CRR* xiv. no. 936 (1230); *CRR* xv. no. 7 (1233).

[21] For service cases in which it is alleged that a court has specifically authorized the use of distraint by chattels, see e.g. *CRR* iii. 98, 133–4, 207–8.

lords sought such authorization when they envisaged having to proceed to distrain the tenant by his holding. By the early thirteenth century, and probably for half a century prior to that, it was the rule that distraint 'by the fee' (by the tenant's holding) required judicial authorization; and late twelfth-century custom certainly insisted that before such a distraint could be authorized it was necessary to have gone through the prior stages of summoning and distraining the tenant by his chattels to answer for the service claimed. It is certainly the case that in a majority of the instances where we do know of court authorization being obtained for distraint by chattels, the lord and his court then went on to make a distraint 'by the fee' as well.[22]

Our evidence suggests that even when a tenant was distrained without judicial authorization, he could still choose to appear at the lord's court to contest the justice of the distraint, and was entitled to have the distresses released once he had found sureties to do this.[23] But this does not mean that extra-judicial distraint was seen simply as part of the process of securing the tenant's attendance at the lord's court. The earlier twelfth-century evidence already discussed indicates that extra-judicial distraint was then seen primarily as a way of compelling tenants to perform services, and that lords could distrain without any prior summons or other warning to the tenant.[24] This seems also to be the position in 'Glanvill', which says nothing to suggest that distraint by chattels is proper only if it is preceded by the summoning of the tenant to the lord's court.[25] There is also other evidence to disprove Milsom's thesis, which sees the origins of distraint for services in the mesne process of seignorial courts. That thesis requires that distraint should originally have been 'personal' in nature, legitimate only when used to seize the chattels of the tenant who was being pressured to make an appearance in his lord's court.[26] This was certainly not the position in the thirteenth century, when lords were entitled to seize any chattels found within their fee, whether or not they belonged to

---

[22] Milsom, *Legal Framework*, 9. For evidence that may point to the imposition at some date prior to *c.* 1160–3 of a requirement that distraint by the fee be by judgment of the lord's court, see *Registrum Antiquissimum of the Cathedral Church of Lincoln*, ed. C.W. Foster and K. Major (Lincoln Rec. Soc. 1931–73), ii. 5 (no. 313).

[23] Refusal to release distresses in return for 'gage and pledge' (the more serious of the two allegations made in the action of replevin) in the case of a distraint made for services, as in the case of distraints made for other reasons, seems originally to have meant a refusal by the lord to release distresses in return for sureties that the tenant would do this. 'Bracton' explains 'gage and pledge' in the case of distraint for all reasons other than for arrears of service as a surety to come to court and stand to right; but in the case of services (though only where the services have been acknowledged as due) it talks of the surety simply as surety to perform the service with arrears: *Bracton: On The Laws and Customs of England*, ed. G.E. Woodbine, revised and trans. S.E. Thorne (Cambridge, Mass. 1968–77), ii. 440. In this we see the distorting effect of the seignorial court's loss of jurisdiction in cases where the tenant denies owing the services claimed: below, 14–15. But a little later in the same passage we see what I take to be a survival from an older world, where an offer of 'gage and pledge' meant an offer of sureties for appearance in the lord's court even where the distraint was for services, for 'Bracton' tells us that where it has been found that the lord has wrongfully detained distresses against gage and pledge the sheriff will release the distresses on such terms that the distrainee will come to his lord's court to answer for the service he acknowledges, and the arrears. For 12th-c. evidence of a tenant who did precisely this when he was distrained by his lord, see above, 305.

[24] Above, 305 and n. 16.

[25] *Glanvill*, 105, 112.

[26] By the later 13th c. it was clearly the case that any distraint intended to secure a defendant's appearance in court could only be made against his own chattels; and the rule has every appearance of being an old one.

their tenant. Milsom suggests that some customary rules and practices found in the early thirteenth century take us back into an earlier world where this had indeed been the position.[27] This evidence, however, is hardly conclusive, and there is other and stronger evidence to suggest that as early as the first half of the twelfth century it had been perfectly proper for a lord to distrain sub-tenants for services owed by his tenants. This takes the negative form of charters from lords to sub-tenants promising not to do this, for such charters contain no hint that what they are promising not to do would otherwise be wrong.[28] 'Glanvill', too, contains a writ which unmistakably assumes that distraint by the chief lord on a sub-tenant is only wrongful if the chief lord demands more than an appropriate amount of service from the sub-tenant.[29]

There was no major shift in the early or middle thirteenth century from a world where the only kind of distraint that was permissible was judicial to one where extra-judicial distraint for services became for the first time permissible; and there is thus no need to look for explanations as to why such a shift occurred. Extra-judicial distraint had long existed, but side by side with the judicial kind. However, as we will see, a related but distinct change probably did take place at about this time. Other legal developments made it increasingly uncommon in practice for lords to distrain with the prior authorization of their courts; and thus extra-judicial distraint became the main — indeed, in practice, virtually the only — kind of distraint commonly used by lords.

II

The main legal mechanism for control of the lord's use of extra-judicial distraint during the first half of the thirteenth century was the action of replevin, an action which had to be initiated in the county court. The best-known account of the working of this action during this period is that provided by Plucknett. He suggested that the action did not, at this time, provide tenants with adequate protection against lords misusing their right of distraint to usurp services to which they were not entitled. The action was, indeed, comparatively simple and easy for a tenant to bring. All he had to do was to purchase the appropriate royal writ and he would have the distresses restored to him pending the outcome of the case, thus freeing him from the pressure of the lord's distraint until the case was decided.[30] But all the lord needed to do in order to make a successful avowry, and thus to secure a judgment for the return of the distresses, was to show that he possessed a 'short, recent seisin' of the services for which he had distrained.[31] Plucknett believed that the application of this standard was particularly likely to lead to injustice in the

---

27 Milsom, *Legal Framework*, 113–14.
28 *Early Yorkshire Charters*, ed. W. Farrer and C.T. Clay (Yorks. Arch. Soc., Rec. ser., Extra Ser. 1914–65), iii. 244–5 (no. 1567), 274–5 (no. 1608); iv. 26 (no. 24); *Documents Illustrative of the Social and Economic History of the Danelaw*, ed. F.M. Stenton (London, 1920), 151–2 (no. 219), 280 (no. 376); *Cartae Antiquae Rolls 11–20*, ed. J. Conway Davies (Pipe Roll Soc., new ser. xxxiii, 1957), 57.
29 *Glanvill*, 143.
30 Plucknett, *Legislation of Edward I*, 57.
31 Plucknett, *Legislation of Edward I*, 57, 68.

aftermath of a period of civil war, when many lords were able to acquire seisin of services through the use of force. It was this, then, he suggested, that had brought distraint to the top of the legislators' agenda in 1267.[32] But the application of this standard was also problematic at other times, though perhaps less acutely so.[33] It was all too easy for lords to use distraint to gain seisin of services to which they were not entitled, and then subsequently to rely on this seisin as their title to the services when this was challenged by the tenant through an action of replevin.

More recently, Professor Milsom has emphasized that replevin was originally intended to provide a remedy not against unjust distraint as such, but against lords who refused to release distresses which they had taken in return for 'gage and pledge' (sureties for appearance in the lord's court) — in other words, against lords who were taking measures appropriate to making a claim against their tenants, but then refusing to allow that claim to be put to their own court. Although Milsom's chronology is not entirely clear, he seems to believe that replevin was still performing this function not just at the time 'Glanvill' was written (at the end of Henry II's reign), but also later, and that the question of whether or not a lord was entitled to the services for which he had distrained was then primarily a matter for the lord's own court.[34] By the time 'Bracton' was written the action of replevin had been transformed. It had now become an action which simply allowed a tenant to challenge the lord's distraint. To justify his distraint, a lord needed only to show a 'possessory' title to the services for which he had distrained (a recent seisin of them).[35]

It was certainly a distinctive characteristic of the action of replevin from at least the reign of Henry II onwards (and the action was probably created during Henry's reign) that in it the plaintiff alleged two separate but connected wrongs: that he had been unjustly distrained, and that the distresses so taken had then been detained 'against gage and pledge'.[36] 'Bracton' provides us with the first detailed account of the working of the action. This describes how the action worked in the county court (perhaps in one particular county court) probably at some date in the 1220s or 1230s.[37] It shows the plaintiff making (and probably having to make) both allegations in his initial count,[38] but being allowed to drop one of them once the defendant had made his avowry justifying the distraint, and had denied refusing to release the distresses after an offer of 'gage and pledge'.[39] Thus, in practice, it was possible

32 Plucknett, *Legislation of Edward I*, 54, 68, 71, 74.
33 Plucknett, *Legislation of Edward I*, 52.
34 Milsom, *Legal Framework*, 34.
35 Milsom, *Legal Framework*, 31.
36 It is impossible to prove this assertion for Henry II's reign in the absence of any general account of the action dating from that reign; but it is certainly consonant with such evidence as does survive and with the later evidence.
37 *Bracton*, ii. 439–49. Little in the account helps us to date it. I assume that its composition belongs to the same period as other, more readily datable parts of the treatise, though it is conceivable that it is older and once had an independent existence before being incorporated in the larger work.
38 One passage seems to envisage the possibility that the plaintiff might choose to sue for only one of these two wrongs (*Bracton*, ii. 441) but this probably refers to a later stage in pleading, after the defendant has made his avowry, making it clear that at this stage the plaintiff can, if he wishes, continue to maintain both allegations.
39 That the plaintiff could choose to counterplead the avowry alone seems clear from some answers to avowries that 'Bracton' mentions, which, in effect, amount to claims that the plaintiff was entitled to the unconditional release of the distresses, and that this was refused but which effectively concede that 'gage and pledge' was never offered since such an offer was inappropri-

for plaintiffs to bring the action of replevin (alleging both unjust distraint and detention against gage and pledge) but then to opt to continue only with the allegation of unjust distraint, and thereby (where the distraint was by a lord and for services) to test through this action whether or not the lord's distraint for services had been justified. This is not likely to have been a recent development, as Milsom suggests, for the author seems to go out of his way to make it clear that a plaintiff can, if he so wishes, maintain his allegation of both wrongs, as though this was already uncommon or becoming so.[40] We can see the same thing in replevin actions in the Bench. By 1201 it was possible for a plaintiff here to take issue simply on the justice of a distraint, without also having to take issue on whether or not distresses had been detained against gage and pledge.[41] It is, indeed, possible that this particular characteristic of the action of replevin is a very old one. An allegation of unjust distraint was something, as 'Bracton' tells us, which could be redressed by 'neighbours', and here he may well be thinking of seignorial and hundred courts as well as more informal procedures;[42] and other evidence from the thirteenth century shows us the lords of seignorial and hundred courts claiming to exercise a jurisdiction in such cases without any special authorization and, apparently, merely by virtue of their possession of such courts.[43] If a tenant or other distrainee made a complaint of this kind in the county court, his lord could probably claim the case for hearing in his own court. It was the allegation of detention against gage and pledge which made the plea one which only the sheriff and the county court (and earlier the king and his justices) were competent to hear.[44] Thus, if a tenant or other distrainee wanted to ensure that his complaint of unjust distraint was heard and determined in the county court, it was essential for him to make both allegations. If the king and his advisers had wanted to encourage such cases to come to the county court (or earlier, to the king's courts) they may well have been willing, from a fairly early stage, to allow litigants to give colour to their jurisdiction by making both allegations initially, but then to allow them to continue with one allegation alone. The suggestion is not provable, but the main point remains. There are good reasons for supposing that allowing a tenant or other distrainee to use the action of replevin simply to contest the justice of a distraint was not something new when 'Bracton' wrote, and the practice may well be much older.

'Bracton''s account must also be the starting-point for a discussion of how the question of whether or not a distraint for services was justified was decided during the second quarter of the thirteenth century. As we have already seen, Plucknett's view appears to have been that then, as earlier and later, this was done by reference to whether or not the lord could show a 'short, recent seisin' of the services for

---

ate, e.g. where the lord has distrained for services by judgment of court and the tenant has refused to answer without the king's writ: *Bracton*, ii. 444; where the defendant claims distresses were taken in his several: ibid. ii. 445. That the plaintiff could choose to counterplead the detention against gage and pledge alone is clear from the discussion of damage feasant: ibid. ii. 445; as also elsewhere, when the author takes care to refute the view that the defendant could only be made to answer for detention against gage and pledge when the taking was found to be unjust: ibid. ii. 447.
[40] Above, n. 38. 'Bracton' also explains in a cautionary passage why it might be unwise to do so: *Bracton*, ii. 441.
[41] *CRR* i. 408. For another early example (1206), see *CRR* iv. 266–7.
[42] *Bracton*, ii. 446.
[43] KB 26/143, m. 9; JUST 1/912A, m. 40; CP 40/23, m. 13; CP 40/55, m. 52; *Placita de Quo Warranto*, ed. W. Illingworth and J. Caley (London, 1818), 739, 751.
[44] Above, n. 42.

which he had distrained; and Milsom, too, cites 'Bracton''s account to support his contention that by 'Bracton''s time the question of entitlement was being decided in replevin on a possessory basis. But 'Bracton''s account shows something rather different. The author discusses two different kinds of situation: where there had been no prior litigation between the parties in the lord's own court, and where such litigation had taken place. He considers the first type of situation in two separate passages, and lays down somewhat different rules in each. In the first, he suggests that all a tenant has to do in the county court is to produce 'suit' (witnesses) that distresses had been taken for a service which he does not acknowledge owing. The lord's distraint will then be adjudged wrongful, whether or not he has been in seisin of the services for which he has distrained. A tenant cannot be made to answer for the services without the appropriate royal writ, the writ of 'customs and services'.[45] In the second passage, he suggests that the lord will be allowed to make his avowry for the services for which he has distrained, but that the tenant can make the distraint wrongful simply by responding that he does not owe the services and has never done them. Since this assertion cannot be tested by the county court because it is outside its jurisdiction, it must give judgment for the tenant.[46] His discussion of the second type of situation reveals that a similar rule applies in the lord's court. If the lord has distrained his tenant for a service which he does not acknowledge owing, and the tenant secures the release of his distresses for sureties to appear in the lord's court, he can appear there and simply deny owing the service and refuse to answer for it without a royal writ. If he does this, the litigation should be at an end. The lord's court is only entitled to adjudge the service to the lord if the tenant admits owing it. If it acts without this acknowledgement, then it has exceeded its jurisdiction.[47] It is clear that for 'Bracton' a possessory title to services was not in itself enough. A tenant had also to acknowledge that he owed the service, or be willing to answer for it without the king's writ. 'Bracton''s account suggests that, in his day, the action of replevin was heavily weighted in favour not of lords, as Plucknett suggested, but of their tenants. A similar conclusion is suggested by a passage in 'Bracton' which deals with the situation where a tenant acknowledges a service for which the lord has avowed a distraint, but denies that it is in arrears. Here, the author suggests that if the tenant simply produces sufficient 'suit' (enough witnesses) that the service is not in arrears, the lord will not be allowed to deny this by waging his law, and thus the distraint will be adjudged wrongful.[48]

'Bracton''s account does not stand alone. There is other evidence for the rule that distraint is wrongful if the tenant does not acknowledge owing the service concerned. Although, as we have seen, 'Glanvill' (in book IX) specifically says that the lord may distrain his tenant to answer in his court for the withholding of all or part of his services, elsewhere (in book XII) we find a special form of replevin writ, where the plaintiff's complaint is said to be that: 'R. has taken and detained [his animals] unjustly for customs which he demands from him which he does not acknowledge that he owes.'[49] It is possible that this envisages litigation about these customs, though if so, the use of the phrase 'does not acknowledge that he owes', rather than just 'does not owe', seems strange. It is possible that the 'customs'

---

45 *Bracton*, ii. 439–41.
46 *Bracton*, ii. 444–5.
47 *Bracton*, ii. 443–4.
48 *Bracton*, ii. 446 (in an *addicio* wrongly inserted into a passage on distraint damage feasant).
49 *Glanvill*, 142.

being demanded are non-tenurial dues of some kind, but it is at least equally possible that this writ was intended to enforce the principle found in 'Bracton'. The two parts of 'Glanvill' could have been compiled at different dates, and thus embody different principles. Perhaps, at this stage, the tenant could only claim the protection of the rule by specifically purchasing the king's writ. We can also see the principle being invoked in litigation in the court *coram rege* in 1201 between the earls of Clare and Chester. The earl of Clare sued the earl of Chester for taking animals from his fee 'for customs and services which he demands from that fee which he does not acknowledge owing'.[50] In 1232 we find Hugh of Clive bringing litigation against William le Normaunt for distraining him to do suit of court and attend view of frankpledge. In answer, William claimed that Hugh did owe him suit and that he was in seisin of it. The jury was asked to give its verdict as to which animals he had taken, and as to whether he had detained them for 'suit and services which the same Hugh does not acknowledge'.[51] In fact, in this case, Hugh did not merely deny owing the services; he also denied holding of William. But the principle applied seems to be simply that distraint is wrongful if made for services which the distrainee does not acknowledge owing.

In a fairly small number of replevin cases heard in the Bench during the period prior to 1249 we can see parties to replevin cases taking issue on whether or not the lord was entitled to the services for which he had distrained.[52] In these cases the tenant seems, in effect, to have waived his right to have the issue of entitlement to services determined through a different form of action, and agreed to have it settled in replevin instead: they do not show that a lord could force his tenant to do this. The rule seems to have changed *c.*1250. The Bench plea rolls from 1250 onwards contain significantly larger numbers of replevin cases in which lords avow distraints as made for arrears of service and, in a number of these, issue is taken on whether or not the tenants owe the service concerned.[53] But even when the action of replevin came to function in this way, decisions as to whether or not a lord was entitled to the services for which he had distrained were not, initially at least, always reached simply on the basis of whether or not the lord could show a 'short, recent seisin' of the services for which he had distrained. Thus, in a case of 1260, in which the prior of Harmondsworth avowed a distraint against Robert de Perers for refusing to perform the service of accompanying him throughout England on horseback at the prior's cost, Robert did not deny owing the services but asserted that he and his ancestors had customarily appointed substitutes to perform this service for them, and that he had acted for his father in just this way. But the court would not allow this even to be submitted to a jury. The form of the feoffment was decisive and subsequent seisin, even recent seisin, was judged of no relevance.[54] In a case of 1254 the prioress of Grace Dieu avowed a distraint as made for homage, suit of court and rent, but the tenant, John d'Oyly, claimed that his wife's lord, Rose de

---

[50] *Pleas before the King or his Justices, 1198–1202, I*, ed. D.M. Stenton (Selden Soc. lxvii, 1953), no. 3296; *CRR* i. 383, 425; *CRR* ii. 44.

[51] *Bracton's Note Book*, pl. 677.

[52] E.g. *CRR* vii. 104; *CRR* x. 297 (but the parties do not join issue on the services); *CRR* xv. no. 697.

[53] For such cases from the period prior to 1267, see e.g. KB 26/138. m. 14 (and for related litigation, see KB 26/135, m. 11d); KB 26/148, m. 8; KB 26/154, m. 16; KB 26/165, mm. 8d, 11; KB 26/169, mm. 36d, 56; KB 26/171, m. 62; KB 26/172, m. 5; KB 26/173, m. 1d; KB 26/210, m. 17.

[54] KB 26/165, m. 8d.

Verdun, had only assigned rent from the tenement to the prioress and not granted her the seignory. When the prioress claimed to have been granted the whole of the seignory and to have been seised of the suit till two years previously, she was instructed to bring the charter of grant to court, and not simply allowed to join issue on this seisin.[55] But other cases did concentrate on recent seisin. Thus, in a case of 1260, the prior of Monk's Horton avowed a distraint against Simon of Holt because he had refused to come to his court to make a judgment there (as one of its suitors). Simon denied that he ought to come to the court for this purpose or was accustomed to doing so. The issue actually put to the jury was whether Simon had customarily performed the suit until one year previously.[56] Most replevin cases about services, of the period 1260–7, do, however, seem to be concerned only with fairly recent seisin.[57] The action of replevin seems only just to have been becoming an action in which entitlement to services was decided on a possessory basis on the eve of the enactment of the Statute of Marlborough (1267): it was not, as Plucknett suggested, a long-established characteristic of the action.

III

Extra-judicial distraint was one of three mechanisms that lords employed during the first half of the thirteenth century to secure the performance of services. As Plucknett noted, the oldest of these in origin was proceedings brought in the lord's own court.[58] He believed that such proceedings were still being brought as late as the middle of the thirteenth century, but that they had largely, if not entirely, fallen into disuse by the reign of Edward I.[59] The second was litigation initiated by the lord through the royal writ of 'customs and services'. Plucknett thought that this action was comparatively little used. His characterization of the action suggested good reasons. It was a 'solemn' action, and in it trial was by battle or the grand assize. Thus it was both slow and inconvenient.[60] He also thought that it set a fairly difficult standard of proof for the lord. In order to succeed in this action, it was necessary for him to be able to prove a long-continued seisin of the services claimed.[61] It was extra-judicial distraint that Plucknett seems to have considered as being the most common way for lords to enforce what they considered to be their rights.[62] There is an ambiguity about what Plucknett has to say here: in some passages he seems to assume that distraint was already the most common way of enforcing services at the beginning of the thirteenth century;[63] but in others he

55 KB 26/154, m. 16.
56 KB 26/169, m. 36d.
57 E.g. KB 26/169, m. 56; KB 26/171, m. 62; KB 26/210, m. 17. But for exceptions, see KB 26/173, m. 1d and KB 26/172, m. 5.
58 Plucknett, *Legislation of Edward I*, 56.
59 Plucknett, *Legislation of Edward I*, 55.
60 Plucknett, *Legislation of Edward I*, 56, 68.
61 Plucknett, *Legislation of Edward I*, 52.
62 Plucknett, *Legislation of Edward I*, 55, 56–7.
63 Thus a passage which describes the action of replevin as 'by far the most frequent method of litigating these questions' (and implies the frequent use of distraint) follows straight on from the passage describing the actions of 'customs and services' and *ne vexes*, and appears, like them, to

seems to imply that this only came to be true during the period now under consideration, perhaps as a result of the decline of the jurisdiction of seignorial courts.[64]

For Professor Milsom, as we have seen, extra-judicial distraint was the direct successor, rather than the successful competitor, of proceedings in the lord's court, though his account does perhaps allow for a period of overlap when both existed side by side. He also suggests that there were significant developments in the action of customs and services in the early thirteenth century. In 'Glanvill''s day, it was the remedy of the exceptional lord who was unable to compel his tenant to attend his court and answer for the withholding of services; by 'Bracton''s day, it had become the 'proprietary' remedy for all lords, something like the remedy Plucknett describes.[65]

The decline in the enforcement of services through the lord's own court certainly took place, but rather earlier than Plucknett suggested. His only reason for placing this as late as he did was his belief that 'in the middle of the century Bracton had frequently considered the case of the lord who distrained his tenant by judgment of his court'.[66] We now know, however, that much of the treatise ascribed to Bracton (almost certainly the part including the section on replevin) belongs not to the middle of the thirteenth century but to the late 1220s or early 1230s;[67] and if we can deduce anything at all about the frequency of proceedings about services in lords' courts from what is said in 'Bracton', the treatise suggests that the jurisdiction was already in decline by the time this part of 'Bracton' was written. Other evidence supports an earlier date for the decline of this jurisdiction. The latest in the series of early thirteenth-century cases which refer to distraint by the fee as part of the process intended to secure the tenant's appearance to answer in his lord's court for arrears of service belongs to 1228.[68] Rare are subsequent references to distraint by chattels for arrears of service as having been made by the judgment of a court, and therefore, perhaps, as forming part of the process for securing the appearance of a tenant to answer for services in the court.[69] The explanation for the decline of this jurisdiction is clear. Even in 'Glanvill''s day, it was beginning to look anomalous that the lord might make a tenant answer for services in his court without needing a royal writ, especially since, at this time at least, such proceedings might lead to the tenant losing his tenement.[70] By 1230 at the latest, to judge from the gloss we find on the same passage of 'Glanvill' in the text of the so-called 'Glanvill Revised', it had apparently become the rule that a tenant could refuse to answer in such litigation by claiming the protection of the 'free tenement' rule. He could say that he was not obliged to answer for his free tenement, or anything which 'touched' his free tenement, without the king's writ. The effect of this, as the

be talking about the position from the late 12th c. onwards: Plucknett, *Legislation of Edward I*, 56–7.

64 Plucknett, *Legislation of Edward I*, 52, 55.
65 Milsom, *Legal Framework*, 31–4.
66 Plucknett, *Legislation of Edward I*, 55.
67 S.E. Thorne, 'Translator's Introduction', in id. *Bracton*, iii. pp. xiii–xxxiii.
68 *Bracton's Note Book*, pl. 270.
69 The only Bench replevin cases of Henry III's reign in which the lord specifically avows a distraint as made by the judgment of his court both involve suit of court. In one, the distraint was for an amercement adjudged for defaults at the lord's court: KB 26/169, m. 7d; in the other, simply for defaults at the court (though this possibly means the same): KB 26/200A, m. 14. Neither implies the existence of litigation about the suit.
70 *Glanvill*, 105.

author of the gloss himself suggests, is to prevent lords actually bringing such litigation in their own courts.[71] 'Bracton', too, tells us of the extension of the 'free tenement' rule to cover services owed by the tenant for his tenement. As we have seen, when a tenant was summoned to his lord's court to answer for services or customs, he could deny that he owed the service specified, and he could claim the protection of the rule since the demand was one which 'touched' his free tenement. This would then bring proceedings to a halt.[72] This does not mean that lords' courts ceased to be competent to hear litigation about services initiated by lords. They were still able to do this if the tenant did not invoke the protection of the rule (and not all tenants may have done so); and if all that was in dispute was whether or not particular services were in arrears, then the rule could not be invoked. It was appropriate only where the dispute was about the quantum of services owed. But the overall effect, particularly as the lord could not necessarily know in advance whether or not his tenant would deny liability and invoke the rule, was probably to discourage litigation over service in lords' courts; and this explains the virtual disappearance of references to such litigation after 1230.

The action of customs and services was much easier for a lord to use than Plucknett's account of the action would suggest. One important factor here was the kind of title which the lord needed to make, if he were to succeed in the action. The earliest actions of customs and services enrolled on the Bench plea-rolls do not specify any kind of seisin as the plaintiff's title to the services he claimed; and while this may be the result of drastic abbreviation on the part of the enrolling clerks, this seems unlikely.[73] Once it does become the norm for lords to make a title to the services they are claiming, we do indeed find a few cases in which lords seem to be alleging a long-established seisin of the services they claim, though even in these it often turns out to be a specific, and sometimes quite recent, seisin that they actually rely on subsequently to establish their right.[74] There are also a few cases where lords seem to be relying on a comparatively ancient, though not necessarily long-continued, seisin.[75] But at least as common, indeed probably more common, is reliance on what was clearly a recent, and sometimes a very recent, seisin of the services claimed.[76] It was not, in practice, very difficult to establish or prove a title to services which was adequate for the purposes of bringing this action.

Also important were the methods of proof thought appropriate in this action.

---

71 F.W. Maitland, 'Glanvill revised', in *The Collected Papers of Frederic William Maitland*, ed. H.L. Fisher (Cambridge, 1911), ii. 282. On the date of 'Glanvill Revised', see G.D.G. Hall's note in *Glanvill*, 195–8.

72 *Bracton*, ii. 444.

73 There are only three cases prior to 1220 in which the seisin of the plaintiff or his ancestors is mentioned: *CRR* iv. 292; *CRR* vi. 135; *CRR* vii. 314. Thereafter it becomes much more common and the last case enrolled without such a title (where the case is not settled by agreement or in some way which makes an enrolled title irrelevant) seems to be one of 1242: KB 26/124, m. 30d.

74 See e.g. *CRR* iv. 292; *CRR* vi. 135; *CRR* xii. no. 1453; *CRR* xii. no. 2043; *CRR* xiv. no. 2386; *CRR* xviii. no. 345; KB 26/145, m. 12.

75 See e.g. *CRR* ix. 228; *CRR* x. 30; KB 26/129, m. 13 (1243 case in which, for some of the services claimed, Gilbert de Gaunt relies on the seisin of his ancestor Gilbert, earl of Lincoln (d. 1156). See also *CRR* xiii, no. 1425.

76 For cases where the plaintiff not only claims on his own seisin but also asserts that the defendant has only ceased to perform the services owed at some date in the recent past, see e.g. *CRR* xii. no. 524; KB 26/162, m. 36 (cesser one year ago); *CRR* xv. no. 1570 (cesser one and a half years ago). Seisin by the ward's ancestor at the time of his death (and possibly by the guardian since then) was the only title which a guardian could make and this was necessarily a recent seisin: see e.g. *CRR* ix. no. 25; *CRR* xvi. no. 2347; KB 26/166, m. 20d.

Although battle was sometimes formally offered by plaintiffs at the end of their counts,[77] this does not seem to have been a technical requirement of the action; and there is not a single case in which battle was actually fought.[78] Thus, although battle was probably a theoretical possibility, it was not something that a lord would need to take into account when deciding whether or not to use this action. The grand assize was commonly used to decide the outcome of such cases. It is not at all clear that lords would have seen the finality of the grand assize as any kind of drawback. In fact, if anything, it may have been seen by some as an advantage. Its disadvantage was probably the slowness with which it worked: it required the summoning of electors to elect the grand assize jury prior to the summoning of the grand assize jurors themselves, and with the knights often proving reluctant to appear. But by no means all cases of customs and services were so determined. Trial by an ordinary jury (and perhaps, in theory, at a less decisive level) was also used in many such cases, in all cases involving guardians,[79] in most cases where the plaintiff was claiming villein services,[80] where the seignory had only recently passed to the plaintiff, or there was some other recent transaction relevant to his title to the services,[81] and simply where the plaintiff alleged a recent seisin of the services.[82] In this latter case it seems that the plaintiff could actually insist on jury trial and prevent the defendant getting to a grand assize, though on what seem to be similar facts, plaintiffs did sometimes agree to trial by the grand assize.[83] In other words, lords themselves did at least to some extent determine how their litigation would be determined, and could choose the form of trial that they themselves wanted.

By the end of the reign of Edward I, as we will see, the action of customs and services had become comparatively rare, certainly in the Bench; and most litigation about services took place through the action of replevin. This was certainly not the case in the period that we are now considering. During the whole of the period 1200–67 there is a total of just under fifty replevin cases in the Bench in which we find the defendant avowing as a lord for arrears of service, or in which it is known from other information that this was the purpose of the distraint; and of these, no

[77] For cases where battle was offered, see *CRR* ii. 242 (and *CRR* iii. 36); *CRR* iv. 292; *CRR* vi. 135; *CRR* vii. 314; *CRR* x. 30; *CRR* xi. nos. 308, 1706, 2045, 2441; *CRR* xii. nos. 584, 1453; *CRR* xiv. no. 1898; *CRR* xv. no. 1818; *CRR* xviii. no. 350; KB 26/142, m. 29d; KB 26/162, mm. 26d, 36; KB 26/164, mm. 1d, 14d; KB 26/169, mm. 56, 59d; KB 26/171, m. 18.
[78] For cases in which one or both of the parties showed signs of wanting to go ahead with battle but in which the court successfully deflected this, see *CRR* xi. nos. 1532, 1706, 2045; *CRR* xii. no. 1453.
[79] See cases cited above, n. 76.
[80] *CRR* xi. no. 2045 (though not apparently for this reason); *CRR* xii. no. 2043 (but also because of the plaintiff's recent seisin); KB 26/124, m. 30d; *CRR* xviii. nos. 1382, 1547. But for a grand assize on such a claim, see KB 26/143, m. 15d.
[81] *CRR* xii. no. 1466 (sale to predecessor); *CRR* xiv. no. 1101 (d); *CRR* xv. no. 1959; *CRR* xvi. no. 991; KB 26/129, m. 19; *CRR* xviii. no. 1466.
[82] *CRR* xii. nos. 2043 (but also because villein services are claimed), 2420; *CRR* xiv. no. 2386; *CRR* xviii. no. 350; KB 26/143, m. 24; KB 26/169, m. 2; cf. *CRR* xi. no. 2045 (where one of the arguments advanced by the plaintiff for seeking jury trial rather than joining battle with the defendant is that the defendant ought not to deny his right when he had such recent seisin, up to three years previously).
[83] For cases where the plaintiff may have insisted on jury trial when the defendant wanted trial by the grand assize, see *CRR* xii. nos. 2043, 2420 (despite the defendant producing a charter of the plaintiff's grandfather specifying lesser services); KB 26/169, m. 2 (grand assize rejected because seeks on such recent seisin and is own seisin at hands of defendant). For an apparently similar case where trial was by the grand assize, see KB 26/162, m. 36 (own seisin at defendant's hands till one year previously).

fewer than thirty fall during the period after 1250. By contrast, during the same period there are around 175 cases brought by the writ of customs and services in the Bench. This does not, of course, prove anything about the relative frequency of the two actions in the county court, where most such litigation clearly took place. Still less does it establish that the action of customs and services was more commonly used as a method of enforcing the performance of services during this period than distraint, for not every distraint will have been challenged through an action of replevin. But the relative frequency with which the action of customs and services was brought is, at least, suggestive; and it seems to indicate that in this period distraint may have been less common as a method of enforcing the performance of services than it was later to become. The explanation for this seems to be a two-fold one. As we have already seen, prior to *c*.1250 lords may have been under a considerable disadvantage in using the weapon of distraint;[84] and during the first half of the thirteenth century lords possessed a comparatively simple and handy remedy in the action of customs and services when their tenants failed to perform the services owed.

IV

During the second half of the thirteenth century the action of replevin continued to function as the main legal mechanism for controlling the lord's use of extra-judicial distraint, but the way in which the action worked was affected by a series of changes, some statutory and some non-statutory.

Clause 17 of the Provisions of Westminster (1259), re-enacted in 1267 as Statute of Marlborough, c.21, provided that:

> if anyone's animals are taken and unjustly detained the sheriff can release them without the obstruction or contradiction of the person who took them, once a plaint is made to him about this, if they were taken outside franchises; and if such animals are taken within franchises and the bailiffs of the franchises refuse to release them then the sheriff is to have them released by reason of the default of the said bailiffs.[85]

This clause provided statutory authority for the initiation of actions of replevin through the convenient local mechanism of a verbal complaint to the sheriff of the appropriate county, but there is good evidence that this mechanism had, in fact, long existed without such authority side by side with the procedure for initiating such pleas through a royal writ purchased in chancery. Despite first appearances, then, the legislation did not mark the introduction of a new and more convenient procedure for the initiation of such pleas.[86] It is, indeed, far from clear why this legislation was thought to be necessary at all. Possibly, some doubt had arisen as to

---

[84] Above, 310-12.
[85] *CR 1259–61*, 149; *Statutes of the Realm*, ed. A. Luders *et al.* (London, 1810–28), i. 24.
[86] P.A. Brand, 'The Contribution of the Period of Baronial Reform (1258–67) to the Development of the Common Law in England' (Oxford Univ. D. Phil. thesis, 1974), 165–9.

whether it was proper to initiate replevin litigation by plaint. In at least two eyres of the 1250s juries had made presentments against local sheriffs for holding pleas of replevin 'without warrant', although the article of the eyre under which these presentments were made had simply sought information about sheriffs and others who allowed trial by jury to be used to determine replevin and other litigation initiated without writ. (The rule apparently was that jury trial could only be used in litigation initiated by writ.)[87] Possibly, some actual change had been intended but dropped during drafting, leaving us with a clause which did no more than reaffirm the *status quo*.

Real changes were, however, made by the Statute of Westminster II (1285), c.2. Three sub-sections of this chapter each purport to be directed against different kinds of abuse of the action of replevin by tenants (and other plaintiffs): in other words, they were concerned with tilting the balance of advantage in this action away from the tenant and in favour of his lord. One sub-section dealt with a loophole which had allowed a tenant (or other plaintiff), once he had secured the release of his animals as a preliminary to bringing the action, to sell them or take them outside the jurisdiction before the case was determined and thus, if judgment was given in favour of the lord, prevent the return to him of the distresses that he had originally taken. The remedy provided was to require the plaintiff at the outset of the litigation to find sureties not just to prosecute his case, but also for the return of the distresses if return was adjudged, and to make the bailiff, who had made the release, himself responsible for the value of the distresses if he had failed to secure adequate sureties before making the release.[88] It is unlikely that this had been a major problem prior to 1285. Even if they succeeded in taking the original distresses outside the county, or in selling them once they were replevied, few plaintiffs will have removed or sold all their animals or chattels at the same time, and any that remained were vulnerable to further distraints by their lords. County courts under such circumstances were, moreover, also probably willing and competent to authorize the use of 'withernam' or counter-distraint to force plaintiffs to return the distresses originally taken. The legislators may have overreacted to a comparatively infrequent problem, perhaps in response to a single recent case.

A second sub-section dealt with another such loophole. When a tenant or other plaintiff failed to prosecute his plea, and the lord (or other defendant) obtained a judgment for the return of the distresses by reason of this want of prosecution, it was open to the tenant to replevy the same distresses a second time and bring a second action of replevin (and in theory to continue being non-suited and then replevying in this way indefinitely). The remedy provided was to ensure that when judgment was awarded in the lord's favour in such circumstances, the lord was to get a writ to the sheriff directing him to return the distresses to the lord, a writ which specifically instructed him not to release the distresses a second time without a special judicial writ authorized by the court to this effect. The plaintiff was still to be allowed a second suit initiated by the special judicial writ, but if he again failed to prosecute, or otherwise had judgment given against him, the court was now to adjudge their return to the lord who had made the distraint without possibility of release ('irreplevisable').[89] Again, it is not clear that this was a major problem prior

---

[87] PRO, JUST 1/564, m. 8; JUST 1/233, m. 50; *Statutes of the Realm*, i. 23.
[88] *Statutes of the Realm*, i. 73.
[89] *Statutes of the Realm*, i. 73.

to 1285, though we certainly can see the legislation in action after 1285. A number of replevin pleas are specifically enrolled on the Bench plea rolls as having been initiated by 'judicial writ', and there are also a number of judgments for 'return irreplevisable' recorded there.[90] What is ironic, however, is that although the problem, insofar as it existed, was a problem as much for the county court as for the Bench and other royal courts, the legislation did not apply to these courts, and in a case of 1298 we find one of the justices of the Bench disallowing a plea based on a purported judgment for 'return irreplevisable' made by the Yorkshire county court.[91] This case indicates, however, that at least one county court did attempt to adopt the provisions of the legislation, and there is evidence of a similar move in 1307 on the part of the mayor and aldermen of London.[92]

A third sub-section purported to be concerned with a problem which arose only when tenants brought their action of replevin in the county court or other lower court. In such courts, it was said, when lords avowed a distraint for arrears of service, the tenant was able to disavow holding of the lord and thus have his lord amerced for an unjust distraint (for such a disavowal brought the litigation to an end without more ado). But because the disavowal had been made in a court which did not bear record, the tenant escaped the consequences which such a disavowal would have had in a court which bore record (one of the king's courts), since the lord could not bring an action of right to recover the tenement held by the tenant on the basis of this disclaimer. The remedy given by the statute was to allow all lords intending to avow for arrears of service in lower courts to have the replevin litigation removed into the Bench or Eyre, where any disclaimer would be of record. As I have argued elsewhere, however, there are good reasons for doubting whether it was the practice in all, or even most, local courts prior to 1285 to accept such disavowals as terminating replevin litigation; and there are even better reasons for supposing that the possibility of disavowals not of record occurring in local courts was no more than an excuse proffered by the legislators for allowing lords, as of right, to have replevin litigation removed out of local courts into the Bench, and the Eyre.[93] It is more difficult to discover precisely why lords wished to have the right to secure the removal of replevin litigation of this kind into the Bench. Access to trial by jury for those lords whose opponents had initiated the litigation by plaint rather than writ is one possible explanation, for jury trial was available once the litigation reached the Bench whatever the procedure used for initiating the plea. And with access to jury trial, lords probably also gained access to the possibility of joining issue with their tenants on the quantum of services which those tenants owed, for the position on the eve of the statute seems to have been that, since the county court was not competent to decide litigation about the quantum of services owed in litigation initiated by plaint, the county would give judgment for the tenant if he denied owing the services for which the lord had avowed.[94] Lords

---

90 Not all such actions were, however, recorded as such. The maximum number of recorded cases in any one year is the 11 cases of 1293.
91 BL, MS Add. 5925, f. 42r; and Lincoln's Inn, MS Hale 188, f. 38r (reports of case enrolled as *Stelingflet v. Coygners et al.* on CP 40/122, m. 114d).
92 City of London Record Office, Common Pleas Roll 32, m. 15.
93 P.A. Brand, 'Legal Change in the Later Thirteenth Century: Statutory and Judicial Remodelling of the Action of Replevin', above, 288-91.
94 That the county court was not competent to determine such litigation is clear from the *causa* clause given for a *recordari* writ in a case of Easter term 1285, enrolled on CP 40/58, m. 20d.

may also have wanted to have the plea and its outcome a matter of record in the king's court. A third possibility is that some lords may have wished to raise the stakes in litigation by transferring the case to a court where litigation was perhaps more expensive in the hope of deterring their tenants from pursuing their cases against them.

A fourth sub-section of c.2 is phrased in much more neutral language, citing as its purpose nothing more than a wish that the justices should be 'certain' as to what kind of recent seisin would support an avowry in the action of replevin. It established that a distraint by a lord against his tenant for services could be avowed as reasonable (or just) if it was supported by seisin on the part of the lord's ancestors or predecessors after the limitation date for the assize of novel disseisin (currently 1242).[95] Elsewhere, I have shown that this sub-section was, in fact, much more significant than it appears, for the rule normally observed in replevin cases during the fifteen years or so prior to the statute, and spelled out in a case of 1282, was that a lord could only justify his distraint in the action of replevin if he could show that he himself had been seised of the service he claimed, or that his immediate precedessor in title (normally his immediate ancestor) had died in seisin of it. Thus the statute legitimized the use of distraint in a significantly wider range of situations than had been the case prior to 1285. In a majority of replevin cases of the period 1285–1307 where avowries for services are recorded, lords avowed on their own seisin. This was true in around 57% of the just under 700 cases. But in the remainder they generally relied on the seisin of a predecessor in title. While some of these might have qualified under the old rules, many would not.[96]

The major non-statutory change in the action of replevin during the second half of the thirteenth century was in the form and substance of the lord's avowry. By the 1290s, as we have seen, the lord's avowry was a complex and detailed entity, comprising a number of separate elements: an assertion that the plaintiff or some third party held a specified tenement in a particular village or villages of the defendant by certain specified services (given in full); a statement of the defendant's title to those services (usually, but not invariably, that he or a predecessor in title had been seised of them at the hands of the tenant named, or of his predecessor in title); an assertion that the distraint had been made because certain of the services mentioned were in arrears; and, though this is not found in all enrolments, an assertion that the distraint was made within the lord's fee. This 'standard' avowry was, however, a recent creation and some of its elements were only just then becoming standard. The older practice had been to specify only those services which were in arrears. A full list of all services owed for the tenement, whether or not the services concerned were in arrears, is found occasionally in Bench replevin avowries as early as 1260, but it did not become common until the later 1280s, and did not become the norm until the mid-1290s.[97] This change is probably to be associated with the growth of a belief among the serjeants of the Bench that a lord who failed to list all the services owed to him in an avowry would find himself excluded on a future occasion from claiming or distraining for any of the services omitted. Such a doctrine is found in at least two separate Year Book notes, which

---

95 *Statutes of the Realm*, i. 72–3.
96 See above, 292-94.
97 For one clear example from as early as 1260, see KB 26/165, m. 11.
98 *Year Book 21 & 22 Edward I*, ed. A.J. Horwood (RS, 1873), 361; Lincoln's Inn, MS Misc. 738, f. 99v.

may well be derived from lessons given by law teachers to Bench apprentices. There seem to be no traces of it in decided cases, or even in reports of pleading in such cases.[98] It was an important change, for it allowed plaintiffs (though only if they were the tenants named in the avowry) to take issue with the lord, not just on his right to the services for which he had distrained, but also on any other services which the lord claimed and the tenant denied owing. In this way, replevin became a much more flexible instrument for resolving disputes, and potential disputes, between lords and tenants about services. A second element in the full standard avowry, which likewise is to be found on occasion as early as 1260,[99] but which is only to be found sporadically until the late 1280s and only became standard after 1293, is the statement of title to the services mentioned in the avowry.[100] This was, however, a less significant development, since even prior to this a lord could apparently be forced through pleading to make out a title to the services that he claimed, even if he had not done so in his original avowry.

V

Although proceedings in the lord's court remained a theoretical possibility — and in a small number of replevin cases of Edward I's reign, we do indeed read that a distraint has been made by judgment of the lord's court — the limitations on the jurisdiction of such courts (already discussed) seem to have meant that by Edward I's reign, for almost all practical purposes, the only real alternatives for a lord wanting to enforce his right to services were distraint or the action of customs and services.[101] In the early years of Edward I's reign the action of customs and services was still in common use. Thus, in 1279, we find pleadings in no less than fourteen such cases in the Bench,[102] as compared with just five replevin cases where the distraint is avowed as made for arrears of service.[103] This is, of course, not a reliable

99 The earliest case in which it is to be found is on KB 26/165, m. 8d.
100 But note that it was being asserted as early as 1270 that such a statement was a necessary part of every avowry for services: Cambridge Univ. Library, MS Dd. 7. 14, fos. 387r–v (report of *Wateley v. St. Martin*: KB 26/200C, m. 40d). The court did not agree, though this may have been because the plaintiff was not the tenant named in the avowry (and could therefore not counter-plead the lord's title to the services he claimed).
101 The theoretical possibility of proceedings in the lord's court may be reflected in a Year Book note of the late 13th or early 14th c. (probably giving the doctrine of an anonymous teacher): 'Nota quod dominus non potest advocare justam districcionem super tenentem nisi in duabus causis. Ou par agarde de sa court ou pur services qe sount dues des tenemens . . .': Lincoln's Inn, MS Misc. 738, f. 99v (but he may be thinking of litigation in the court which is not concerned with services). There are many replevin avowries which state that the distraint was made by the judgment of the lord's court, but in all except two cases (CP 40/9, m. 42; CP 40/29, m. 13d) the distraint was for suit of court and awarded by the court after a default there, and the avowry does not seem to presuppose any kind of litigation between lord and tenant over the suit. But for evidence that as late as 1326 such a distraint for suit might lead to litigation about suit in the lord's court determining whether or not the suit was owed, see *Luffield Priory Charters, I*, ed. G.R. Elvey (Bucks. and Northants. Rec. Socs. 1968), 159–60.
102 CP 40/28, mm. 7, 10d; CP 40/29, mm. 49, 54d, 46d, 22d; CP 40/30, mm. 45, 83, 74d, 10d, 3d; CP 40/31, mm. 85d, 63d, 2d. Of these cases, no less than 5 ended with the defendant disavowing tenure of the plaintiff (CP 40/29, mm. 49, 46d; CP 40/30, mm. 45, 10d; CP 40/31, m. 85d) and a 6th case with the defendant simply agreeing to perform the services demanded: CP 40/31, m. 2d.
103 CP 40/29, mm. 13d, 75; CP 40/30, mm. 84d, 24d; CP 40/31, m. 43d.

guide to the relative frequency of distraint and litigation by the writ of customs and services, for much distraint may simply have succeeded in its object of compelling the tenant to perform the services he owed without litigation. Nor, as I have previously acknowledged, is it even necessarily a reliable guide to the relative frequency of contested distraints and litigation by customs and services, for much of this went on in county courts and may not have been in the same proportions there as it was in the Bench. But what does seem to be clear is that there was a steep decline during Edward I's reign in the use of the action of customs and services, both in relative and in absolute terms. Again, our only information is from the Bench, but here it is very noticeable that by 1299 there is only a single such case during the whole year,[104] as compared with some forty-one replevin cases where the avowries are for service arrears.[105] Nor is this relative decline difficult to explain. As we have already seen, two of the changes made by the Statute of Westminster II (1285), c.2 — that allowing lords to remove replevin litigation where they were intending to avow for services into the Bench, and that which allowed them to avow distraints, if they could show any seisin subsequent to 1242 — had the consequence of allowing lords to use distraint in a wider range of circumstances than had hitherto been the case, and with less risk that the distraint would subsequently be challenged and found wrongful; and non-statutory changes in the action of replevin had turned it into a flexible instrument for resolving potential, as well as actual, disputes between lords and tenants over services.[106] We also know, moreover, that lords or their future legal advisers were now being counselled, or taught, to use distraint in preference to litigation. Thus, in the *Modus Componendi Brevia* (c. 1278–85, but revised soon after 1285) the lord is told to bring the action of customs and services only if he were unable to distrain his tenant; and in the *Natura Brevium* (c. 1290) the advice given is that, 'if the lord is wise he will try to recover withdrawn services by distraint . . . before he brings this writ [of customs and services] which is of such a high nature and so perilous in itself' (because of the possibility of the case going to battle or the grand assize).[107] By the later years of Edward I's reign this advice was being followed, and distraint had become the normal remedy for lords whose tenants were withholding their services.

However, there is also some evidence to suggest that, by the latter part of the reign of Edward I, the ready availability of the action of replevin may have been beginning to have the effect of transforming distraint from a weapon for the enforcement of services into a mere preliminary to litigation about title to services, with the consequent growth of legal fictions relating to the distraints mentioned in replevin counts. Thus, we learn from an early fourteenth-century action of mesne that one possible action open to a mesne lord, when his sub-tenant was distrained for services that he himself owed, was to substitute his animals for those taken from

---

[104] CP 40/127, m. 148d: this litigation may well have been collusive, for the parties came to an agreement without any recorded pleading.

[105] CP 40/126, mm. 13, 75, 105, 137, 139, 146, 105d; CP 40/127, mm. 48, 67, 110, 164d, 55d; CP 40/129, mm. 1, 27, 31, 56, 138, 149d, 129d, 118d, 97d, 27d, 20d (*bis*); CP 40/130, mm. 17 (*bis*), 61, 73, 163, 181, 204, 241, 314, 293d, 268d, 259d, 258d, 249d, 125d, 119d, 46d.

[106] Above, 319–21. The elimination of loopholes in replevin procedure which favoured tenants were probably less important here: above318–19.

[107] *Four Thirteenth Century Law Tracts*, ed. G.E. Woodbine (New Haven, 1910), 156–7; Harvard Law Library, MS Dunn 162, f. 163v.

the sub-tenant.[108] The mesne lord would then presumably bring his own action of replevin to challenge the distraint. But if this did happen, it is not reflected in recorded replevin counts. Without exception, these talk only of the plaintiff himself being distrained, never of a sub-tenant being initially distrained, and the tenant then substituting his animals for those of the sub-tenant.[109] Other evidence suggests that we should even be cautious about supposing that every distraint was really quite the forcible seizure which it appears to be. In a case heard in 1302, Richard of Marton alleged among other things that the prior of Guisborough and his men had taken a horse from his stable at Marton. The prior said that he had not taken the horse, but that he had demanded certain services from John and they had agreed to a love-day. They had failed to reach agreement at the love-day, and the prior had said he would now distrain him. Richard had then himself delivered the horse up to the prior without waiting to be distrained. Richard denied this, but the truth of the prior's story was confirmed by a jury.[110] By choosing to deny Richard's claim that he had been distrained, the prior had lost the chance to have the underlying matter in dispute between them discussed, which may indeed have been a dispute about entitlement to services since there is a further replevin plea between them in 1309 which did raise precisely this issue.[111] Other lords in similar circumstances may well have chosen differently, and thus passed over the chance to object that they had in reality not distrained the tenant at all. What one of the Bench serjeants says in this case also suggests that Richard's behaviour was not simple eccentricity on his part, but an accepted part of social norms, for some tenants at least. Serjeant Tothby, apparently acting for the prior, says that 'we are alleging "curtesy" [i.e. on Richard's behalf] and you "villainy" '.[112] Replevin had become a means of litigating about title to services, the preliminary distraint merely the trigger to set off this litigation. The 'courteous' tenant might even save his lord the bother of having to make a distraint by doing this himself. But just how common this practice was it is impossible to estimate; most lords would probably have chosen to ignore the fictitious nature of the distraint and to raise the real issue instead, the dispute between the parties over services.

Extra-judicial distraint was already well established as a mechanism for the enforcement of services by 1200, but its use was effectively restricted by rules enforced through the action of replevin. The great increase in its use during the second half of the thirteenth century — and there probably was such an increase, even if not every 'distraint' of which we read in the plea-rolls was quite what it seems — resulted both from changes in the rules enforced by the courts and practices followed there, and from statutory modifications of the action of replevin. There is no reason to think that its increased use either reflects, or contributed to, any significant increase in seignorial power: for the changes took place, and are understandable only, in the context of the continuing effective control and monitor-

---

108 *Malm'*: 'Coment voet il dire qe nous avoms gre fet: qe quant ses bestes furent prises qe nous feimes la deliverance ou meimes les noz pur les voz ou qe nous avom fet la suite pur H?': BL, MS Add. 35116, f. 189v.
109 But for a case in which the defendant claimed that the plaintiff had forced his way into a pound to substitute a horse for the sheep which the defendant had originally taken in distraint (though both horse and sheep were the property of the plaintiff), see *Neweman v. Pannecak*: CP 40/95, m. 6 (1292).
110 CP 40/144, m. 244d: reported in BL, MS Add. 31826, f. 175r.
111 *Year Books 2 & 3 Edward II*, ed. F.W. Maitland (Selden Soc. xix, 1904), 21–30.
112 'Nus allegoms cortesie e vus vileynie . . .': BL, MS Add. 31826, f. 175r.

ing of the use of distraint through the action of replevin. Extra-judicial distraint remained acceptable and became much more common during the course of the thirteenth century only because it was not what it seemed. It was not a crude form of self-help, wide open to seignorial exploitation at the hands of lords able to use it to accroach additional services from their tenants. It was a convenient procedure for enforcing the payment of arrears where lord and tenant had no disagreement about what was owed, and a satisfactory mechanism for initiating litigation about services in the county court, or in the king's court, where lord and tenant disagreed about what was owed.

16

The Drafting of Legislation in Mid Thirteenth-Century England

A tradition of central royal legislative activity had existed in England since the Anglo-Saxon period, and the continuity of that tradition was never wholly broken even during the period of the first Norman kings, when comparatively little legislation seems to have been enacted. The thirteenth century (and, more particularly, the second half of that century) did, however, witness important developments in that tradition. There was a significant upsurge in the pace of royal legislative activity and a marked change in the care with which both the royal administration and the King's subjects preserved the texts of legislative enactments.[1] What they now took care to keep was normally only the final published text of legislation. This is hardly surprising. There was little practical purpose to be served by preserving documents belonging to the preliminary process of drafting and amendment which lay behind the polished forms of the final text. Consequently any documents which may have been compiled in the course of the drafting process have generally not survived, and for the most part it is only the presence of some obvious inconsistency in the final text of legislation which gives us any kind of clue as to the drafting process which lies behind it.[2]

But there are exceptions; and the major exceptions all relate to those legislative enactments of the thirteenth century which were the products of periods of political upheaval and turmoil. From the process of negotiation and drafting which lies behind the 1215 issue of Magna Carta survive both the so-called 'Unknown Charter' and the 'Articles of the Barons'. Their dating and significance have been discussed recently by Professor J.C. Holt and there is little to be added to his discussion.[3] The present paper is concerned with the various documents belonging to the process of drafting which lies behind the enactment of the Provisions of Westminster in 1259. Historians of the period have long known of the existence of two documents belonging to this drafting process: the 'Petition of the Barons' and the Latin text of the *Providencia Baronum*. In this paper I will show that in fact there survive not two but four distinct documents reflecting the progress of legislative drafting in 1258–9: the

---

[1] H. G. Richardson and G.O. Sayles, 'The Early Statutes', *Law Quarterly Review*, L (1954), 201–23, 540–71.

[2] Cf. T. F. T. Plucknett, *Legislation of Edward I* (Oxford, 1962), pp. 121–2, 159.

[3] J. C. Holt, *Magna Carta* (Cambridge, 1965), pp. 195–6, 296–312; *idem*, 'The Making of Magna Carta', in his *Magna Carta and Medieval Government* (1985), at 217–38; *idem*, 'Magna Carta and the Origins of Statute Law' in his *Magna Carta and Medieval Government*, 289–307 at 292–307.

'Petition of the Barons', a French draft text of the *Providencia Baronum*, the Latin text of the *Providencia Baronum*, and a French draft text of the Provisions of Westminster.[4] The discovery of these new documents allows us to reconstruct much more of the process of drafting that lies behind the Provisions of Westminster than has hitherto been possible. I will also take this opportunity to reassess the nature and significance of the two documents which were already known to historians, the 'Petition of the Barons' and the Latin text of the *Providencia Baronum*.

THE 'PETITION OF THE BARONS'

On 2 May 1258 King Henry III promised on oath to accept the decisions of a committee of 24 as to reforms in the 'state' of the kingdom of England.[5] The committee was to be composed of 12 members of the King's Council and 12 individuals chosen by the magnates and was to hold its first meeting in the second week of June at Oxford.[6] The Parliament which had met in London in April and early May had also apparently adjourned its session to Oxford to the same week of June.[7]

The 'Petition of the Barons', the first of the documents which lies behind the Provisions of Westminster, was apparently drawn up in connexion with this joint meeting of the committee of 24 and of Parliament at Oxford. The introduction to the text of the 'Petition' provided by the Burton annals tells us that the articles contained in the 'Petition' were 'produced' (*prolati*)[8] or (in a second text of the annals) 'published' (*publicati*)[9] under oath (*sub fidei sacramento*) while the King was at Woodstock and the magnates and greater and lesser men and clergy had met at Oxford to make provision and ordination for the reform of the kingdom. Elsewhere, the Burton annalist reproduces a letter from one present at the Oxford Parliament which also talks of the *articuli* being 'expounded' at Parliament.[10]

---

[4] Historians have been aware of the existence of this last text but have misunderstood its nature and significance. See further below, p. 351.

[5] *Documents of the Baronial Movement of Reform and Rebellion, 1258–1267*, selected by R. F. (misprinted as R. E.) Treharne and edited by I. J. Sanders (Oxford, 1973) [hereafter cited as Treharne and Sanders, *Documents*)], pp. 72–6. For recent accounts of the events leading up to this promise see D. A. Carpenter, 'What Happened in 1258', *War and Government in the Middle Ages: Essays in Honour of J. O. Prestwich*, eds. J. Gillingham and J. C. Holt (Woodbridge, 1984), pp. 106–19; idem, 'King, Magnates and Society: the Personal Rule of King Henry III, 1234–1258', *Speculum*, LX (1985), 39–70; H. Ridgeway, 'The Lord Edward and the Provisions of Oxford (1258): A Study in Faction', *Thirteenth Century England I: Proceedings of the Newcastle-upon-Tyne Conference, 1985*, eds. P. R. Coss and S. D. Lloyd (Woodbridge, 1986), pp. 89–99; J. R. Maddicott, 'Magna Carta and the Local Community, 1215–1259', *Past and Present*, No. 102 ((1984), pp. 25–65.

[6] The date fixed for the meeting was one month after Whitsunday (9 June), but this date should perhaps not be taken too literally. It was envisaged that its work would be completed by Christmas.

[7] *Matthaei Parisiensis Chronica Majora*, ed. H. R. Luard (7 vols., Rolls Series, 1872–84), V, 676, 688, 695–6. The adjournment was to the feast of St Barnabas (11 June).

[8] *Annales Monastici*, ed. H. R. Luard (5 vols., Rolls Series, 1864–9), I, 438.

[9] Lichfield MS. 28, f. 70v.

[10] *Annales Monastici*, I, 444.

The 'Petition of the Barons' survives in manuscript in three different versions:

(i) One is incorporated in a copy of the annals of Burton Abbey now in the British Library (Cotton MS. Vespasian E. III, ff. 81r–82v). This text was first printed by William Fulman in 1684 as part of his edition of the Burton annals.[11] The same text was re-edited when a more accurate edition of the same manuscript was produced by H. R. Luard for the Rolls Series in 1864.[12] Luard's text of the 'Petition' was subsequently reproduced by Bishop William Stubbs in his textbook collection of *Select Charters*.[13] Later generations of students and historians have commonly used and cited Luard's edition of the 'Petition' in the form in which it was presented by Stubbs. This divided the 'Petition' up into a series of numbered clauses which may not always correspond to the individual clauses of the original document.[14] It was also Stubbs who gave it the name of the 'Petition of the Barons', a name for which there is no contemporary warrant.[15] Luard's text (and Stubbs's enumeration of the individual clauses) have also been reproduced more recently and with an English translation by R. F. Treharne and I. J. Sanders in their volume of *Documents of the Baronial Movement of Reform and Rebellion*, published in 1973.[16]

(ii) A second text of the 'Petition' is to be found in another manuscript copy of the Burton annals, apparently of the second half of the thirteenth century, which is included in the *Magnum Registrum Album* of Lichfield Cathedral (Lichfield MS. 28, ff. 70v–72r). The existence of a second copy of the Burton annals at Lichfield, which breaks off part of the way through the entry for 1258, appears to have been unknown to historians prior to 1894. In that year R. L. Poole stumbled across the text while examining the manuscripts of the Dean and Chapter of Lichfield for the Historical Manuscripts Commission and he mentioned his find in his report on those manuscripts published in 1895.[17] The existence of this second manuscript copy of the Burton annals was also mentioned in 1924 by H. E. Savage in the introduction to his calendar of that portion of the *Magnum Registrum Album* which is a register of the Dean and

---

[11] Fulman's edition of the Burton annals is to be found in the volume of *Rerum Anglicarum Scriptores* (Oxford, 1684) which he edited, at pp. 246–448. The 'Petition' is printed at pp. 407–10 of this volume.

[12] *Annales Monastici*, I, 183–500. Luard's edition of the text of the 'Petition' is at pp. 439–43. His sidenote at the beginning of the text describes the 'Petition' as the 'Petitions of the barons at Oxford'.

[13] Its full title is *Select Charters and Other Illustrations of English Constitutional History from the Earliest Times to the Reign of Edward the First*. The first edition appeared in 1870 and the final edition (revised by H. W. C. Davis) in 1921 [hereafter cited as *Stubbs' Charters*]. In both editions it appears on pp. 373–8.

[14] The final sentence of clause 1 should probably have been a separate clause (though it may just represent a late and clumsy addition to clause 1). Clauses 17, 18 and 19 should probably not have been separated from clause 16.

[15] The 'Petition of the Barons' is the name given to the text in the running heads of the pages. The title which precedes introduction and text in the main body of the text is the more cumbersome 'Petition of the Barons at the Parliament of Oxford'.

[16] Treharne and Sanders, *Documents*, no. 3 (pp. 76–91).

[17] H.M.C., *MSS. of Lincoln, Bury St Edmund's and Great Grimsby Corporations and of the Deans and Chapters of Worcester and Lichfield*, p. 211.

Chapter of Lichfield;[18] but was apparently unknown to Treharne when he wrote the *Baronial Plan of Reform*[19] and to both Treharne and Sanders when they compiled their volume of *Documents of the Baronial Movement of Reform and Rebellion.*[20] Although the text closely resembles that of the printed manuscript there are a number of passages where the reading of the Lichfield MS. is clearly superior and to be preferred.[21] The Lichfield MS. also differs from the printed version in the omission of clauses 4 and 25. Clause 4 reads like a later, amended (and more generalized) version of clause 5 and it is difficult to believe that the two clauses were intended to appear side by side in the same document. It may well be that the Lichfield MS. preserves a slightly earlier recension of the 'Petition' than that which was known to the scribe of the British Library MS., and that it was only through confusion that the latter reproduced a text which contained both a text of the clause as originally drafted and a text of the amended version of the same clause. If this is so then the omission of clause 24 in the Lichfield MS. may mean that it too was a late addition to the 'Petition'.

(iii) A third text of the 'Petition of the Barons' exists in a volume of transcripts made by the seventeenth-century antiquary and historian Sir William Dugdale, which is now in the Bodleian Library (MS. Dugdale 20, ff. 138v–140r). The first modern historian to draw attention to the existence of this text, though only in passing, was Noel Denholm-Young in an article of 1933.[22] Denholm-Young noted that Dugdale had transcribed the text and other mid-thirteenth-century material from a manuscript associated with the abbey of Darley and suggested that this was possibly to be identified with a manuscript now in the British Library (Cotton MS. Titus C. IX) and that it came from a part of that manuscript now missing. The existence of this third text was also known to Treharne and Sanders and in *Documents of the Baronial Movement of Reform and Rebellion* they purport to print variants between this text of the 'Petition' and the text found in the British Library MS. of the Burton annals in footnotes to the latter.[23] Those footnotes, however, hardly do justice to the extent of the differences between this version and the other two versions. In Appendix 1 I summarize the main significant differences between this version and the other versions of the 'Petition'.

The individual clauses of the 'Petition of the Barons' take a variety of forms. Most ask for the remedying of some particular grievance, stating the matter requiring remedy without going on to suggest what form that remedy should

---

[18] *Magnum Registrum Album*, ed. H. E. Savage (William Salt Archaeological Soc., Collections for a History of Staffordshire, 1924), pp. xxii–xxiii. Its existence was also noted by E. F. Jacob, in an article of 1926: 'The Complaints of Henry III against the Baronial Council in 1261', *E.H.R.*, XLI (1926), 559, n. 3.

[19] R. F. Treharne, *The Baronial Plan of Reform, 1258–1263* (Manchester, 1932), p. 70.

[20] Treharne and Sanders, *Documents*, p. 76, and n.

[21] In clause 7 it reads 'deafforestati' for the 'deafforestari' of the printed text, and in clause 9 'finem' for 'fidem'. In clause 13 it adds 'et' after the first occurrence of 'comitatibus'.

[22] N. Denholm-Young, 'Documents of the Barons' Wars', *E.H.R.*, XLVIII (1933), 558–75 (at 571–2); also reprinted in his *Collected Papers* (Cardiff, 1969), pp. 155–72 (at 168–9).

[23] Treharne and Sanders, *Documents*, pp. 76–90.

take.[24] In two clauses all we find is a complaint about a particular state of affairs without any specific request for a remedy (although this is clearly the implication of the complaint);[25] and a similar implication is also to be read into the three clauses which state matters requiring remedy but neither specifically complain about them nor ask for a remedy for them.[26] A single clause states the matter requiring remedy and also specifies the remedy required or suggested.[27] Six clauses take the form of requests for specific changes or specific legislation.[28]

Meeting specific demands for changes in royal policy did not require legislation, merely a change in policy, or perhaps better still the acquisition of control over the machinery of government by persons committed to making these (and other) changes.[29] The same is also true of a number of other clauses which do not specifically ask for changes in royal policy but to which this was the only appropriate response.[30] Nor was legislation an appropriate response to those clauses in which 'the petitioners were looking for no more than the enforcement of the existing law or rules on the matter in question.[31] But certain clauses of the 'Petition' certainly were asking for changes in the law which could only be achieved through legislation. Clause 1, for example, asked that the law be amended to prevent lords from taking actual seisin after the deaths of their tenants, when they managed to enter the land concerned before the heirs, and more especially to stop such lords committing waste during the period between their taking seisin and their admission of the tenant's heir. It proposed that lords be made liable for damages if they did commit waste in these circumstances, as well as being made liable to an amercement by the King. Clause 3 was also asking for a change in the law, one which would give the other lords from whom tenants-in-chief held their lands the wardship of those lands, leaving the King with the wardship only of the lands held of him in chief, plus the wardship of the minor tenant-in-chief himself.[32] A change in the law was also what was requested and suggested in

[24] Clauses with the formula 'petunt remedium quod' are clauses 2, 7, 9, 10, 13; clauses with the formula 'petunt remedium de' are clauses 11, 12, 16 (though only in the Dugdale MS. – this clause probably continues over the clauses Stubbs numbered 17, 18 and 19), 20, 24, 25, 26, 27, 28.

[25] These clauses are 22 and 23. In clause 22 the phrase only occurs half-way through the clause.

[26] Clauses 14, 21, 29. The final portion of clause 1 (dealing with the exaction of queen's gold on reliefs), which ought to have been a separate clause, follows the same pattern. Clause 8 should also probably have taken the same form. As it stands it is phrased as a request, but it is never made clear what is being requested.

[27] Clause 27.

[28] Clauses 1, 3, 4 and 5, 6, 15. For clause 8, which appears to be of this form but is not, see above, n. 26.

[29] Clauses of this type are clauses 4 and 5, 6, and perhaps clause 15.

[30] E.g. clauses 2, 9 (though legislation would be needed if the change was to be made retrospective), 11, 16 (though only the part concerning the farms of shires and other bailiwicks), 23.

[31] E.g. that part of clause 1 relating to the exaction of queen's gold on the reliefs paid by tenants-in-chief, and clauses 7, 12, 16, 20, 24, 25 and 29.

[32] This is one of the clauses where the reading of the Dugdale text of the 'Petition' makes better sense than the text of either of the Burton annals versions: see below, Appendix I. The clause makes clear that the demand is not for the King to grant them such wardships as a matter of grace, but for a change in the law ('et hoc petunt de jure communi').

clause 27. Here the grievance was that under current law when land was granted in *maritagium* to a husband and wife and the heirs of their bodies the woman concerned, after the death of her husband, could validly grant away the land, despite the fact that no such issue had been born (and despite the fact that the husband's death meant that there was no longer any possibility of such issue being born). The suggestion was to provide the grantor or his heir with a remedy, either through a new form of writ of entry or some other kind of writ, to secure the reversion of the land thus granted after her death. Where only the grievance was described but no specific remedy was suggested, it is sometimes more difficult to be certain as to the kind of remedy the petitioners had in mind. We can be fairly sure that it was some kind of legislative remedy that the framers of clauses 10, 17 and 18 had in mind when they complained of the religious acquiring lands without the consent of the lords of whom those lands were held, or of sheriffs demanding the personal attendance of earls and barons and of the tenants of small parcels of land, which did not include a dwelling, at the sheriff's tourn. It is less clear, but still quite possible, that this was the case with another six clauses of the 'Petition'.[33] Clause 13, for example, complained of the amercement of earls and barons' for default of the common summons at general eyres and forest eyres, when several such eyres were taking place simultaneously. It could presumably have been answered either by a standing royal instruction to the justices concerned to excuse the absence of those attending eyres elsewhere, or by more formal legislation to the same effect. It is difficult, then, to estimate with any real accuracy the number of clauses of the 'Petition of the Barons' which either directly or indirectly sought legislation: at least six and perhaps as many as 12, but in any case less than half the total number of clauses.

Who was responsible for drawing up the 'Petition' and what was their purpose in doing so? For Stubbs the *Petition* was the work of an undefined group of 'the barons' during the period between the adjournment of the London Parliament and its resumption at Oxford; and it constituted a 'list of grievances' for redress by the committee of 24.[34] Treharne originally thought that it was the work of the 12 baronial members of the committee of 24 (or rather of those of the 12 who were in England during the interval between the King's agreement to the committee of 24 and the beginning of the committee's work at Oxford in June), and that it constituted 'a memorandum of definite grievances in administrative and legal matters and in judicial procedure, noted for correction when the barons should have set up the necessary machinery of governmental control';[35] but by 1973 he had come to believe that it was simply 'a statement of grievances' presented by the nobles, though one that was probably drawn up by the baronial 12 in advance of the meeting at Oxford.[36]

There is in fact no evidence to support the suggestion that the 'Petition' was the work of the 12 baronial members of the committee of 24, and it seems

---

[33] Clauses 13, 14, 19, 21, 22 and 28.
[34] W. Stubbs, *The Constitutional History of England* (3 vols., Oxford, 1874–8), II, 74–5.
[35] Treharne, *Baronial Plan*, pp. 69–70.   [36] Treharne and Sanders, *Documents*, pp. 4–5.

improbable that this was the case. We know that the baronial 12 had not yet been chosen when the King issued his letters patent agreeing to abide by the decisions of the committee of 24 on 2 May,[37] and it is by no means impossible that they were in fact only chosen after Parliament had met in Oxford in the second week of June.[38] If so, they can hardly have drawn up the 'Petition' in advance of the meeting at Oxford. Even if they were chosen before the Oxford Parliament assembled, there is still no evidence that they held meetings in advance of the session at Oxford and that they drew up the 'Petition' at such a meeting. If the 'Petition' had been the work of the baronial 12 one might have expected the otherwise well informed Burton annalist to have noticed this fact and to have remarked upon it, but he does not do so. In fact, if anything, his introduction to the document counts against any possibility that the 'Petition' could have been the work of members of the committee of 24. It would hardly have been necessary for members of this committee to have made a public presentation of grievances on oath to a committee of which they themselves were members. It might also have been expected that members of the committee, when drawing up such a list of grievances, would have been rather more willing to suggest remedies for them, since the function of the committee was to reform the state of the realm and not merely to note matters where the state of the realm needed reforming. A final argument against the involvement of the 12 baronial members of the committee in the drawing up of the 'Petition' lies in the sequel, in what was actually done at Oxford by the committee of 24, presumably at the prompting of its 12 baronial members. This bears little or no relationship to the demands and grievances contained in the 'Petition'.[39]

Once we reject the hypothesis that the 'baronial' 12 were the authors of the 'Petition' as both unproven and unlikely, we are driven back to the 'Petition' itself for clues. Some of its clauses seem to suggest that it was the work of (unspecified) 'earls and barons' or just 'barons'. Thus, clause 1 takes the form of a demand by the 'earls and barons';[40] clause 10 seeks a remedy against the religious entering the 'fees' of 'earls and barons' as well as 'others'; clause 11 seeks a remedy against the King usurping the custody of religious houses founded on the fees of 'earls and barons'; clause 13 complains of the amercement of 'earls and barons' for default of common summons when several eyres are taking place simultaneously; clause 17 complains of demands for the personal attendance of 'earls and barons' at the sheriff's tourn; clause 20 complains of sheriffs refusing to accept prisoners taken by 'any earl or baron'

[37] Treharne and Sanders, *Documents*, p. 75.

[38] It is one possible reading of the King's letters patent that they specifically envisage election of the baronial 12 only at that meeting.

[39] Treharne acknowledged this fact but attempted to preserve his hypothesis as to the authorship of the 'Petition' by positing that the 'Petition' was merely part of the 'plan of reform': 'that the Petition was merely a part of the plan of reform is clear from its nature and from a comparison with the Provisions of Oxford, for the only article common to both is that relating to the custody of royal castles': *Baronial Plan*, p. 70. He does not explain how the two parts of the 'plan' came to be separated, or why one part was preserved and the other (and more important) part lost.   [40] Or, in the Dugdale version just 'barons': below, Appendix I.

or (their) bailiff or 'anyone else who has a franchise'; while clause 3 takes the form of a demand in the name of the 'barons' alone. These clauses (with the exception of clause 1) do seem to represent specifically magnate grievances, and suggest that the 'Petition' may have been the work of the magnates present at the Oxford Parliament, perhaps much the same group as that which chose the 12 'baronial' members of the committee of 24.[41] But most of the clauses are not put forward specifically in the name of the 'earls and barons', and a number of them seem most unlikely to have been the work of members of this group. Thus, clause 18 (about demands for attendance at the sheriff's tourn on those holding small parcels of land without a dwelling-place attached), was hardly relevant to the 'earls and barons' who in clause 17 had complained in general terms about demands for their attendance at the sheriff's tourn; clause 19 specifically stated a grievance of 'knights and free tenants' about amercements for non-attendance at sessions of assize justices; clause 25 complained about the misconduct of certain 'magnates et potentiores regni' who had acquired Jewish debts and refused to accept payment from creditors described as 'minores'; and clause 26 appears in part to have expressed the grievances of the merchants of the city of London against certain foreign merchants. These clauses suggest that the so-called 'Petition of the Barons' is probably no more than a collection of petitions from a variety of sources, expressing the interests and grievances of a number of different groups including the 'earls and barons'. It seems possible that they were deliberately solicited by the group of magnates opposed to the King, perhaps as a means of strengthening their hands against him; though they may simply have taken up unsolicited complaints made by these various groups. In any case, it looks as though the 'earls and barons' may in some way have added their imprimatur to the petitions. This may explain why the demand for an end to the commission of waste during primer seisin, the main demand of clause 1, is presented as being made in the name of the 'earls and barons', despite the fact that as drafted it was of no significance to them (other than as a threat to their existing rights).[42]

The 'Petition of the Barons' was very much a first stage in the long process which led eventually to the enactment of the Provisions of Westminster: a first stage at which a number of grievances were aired and remedies proffered for only some of them. In at least two instances clauses (or parts of clauses) in the 'Petition' were to be answered fairly directly and without significant amendment by clauses in the Provisions of Westminster,[43] but more

---

[41] The Burton annals text of the Provisions of Oxford records the names of 11 of the 12 men so chosen under the heading 'Electi ex parte comitum et baronum': Treharne and Sanders, *Documents*, p. 100.

[42] The suggested punishment of such waste by amercement and the awarding of damages was clearly irrelevant to the commission of such waste by the King (the 'chief lord' of all 'earls and barons') and his officials, for neither would be a deterrent in their case.

[43] Clause 10 (on mortmain alienations) was answered by clause 14 of the Provisions of Westminster: *Stubbs' Charters*, p. 393; part of clause 14 (on the amercement of vills not attending coroners' inquests in full numbers) was answered by clause 21: *ibid.*, p. 394.

commonly clauses in the Provisions of Westminster represent a development
and extension of ideas suggested by the 'Petition'.[44] In at least one case (clause
13 of the 'Petition') the Provisions did not contain a clause remedying the
grievance but they did contain a clause (clause 23) which remedied a closely
related grievance.[45] It is also worth noting that at least two of the clauses of the
'Petition' which were seeking specific legislative changes did not succeed in
obtaining them: clause 3 (seeking an end to the prerogative wardship by the
King of the lands of tenants-in-chief held of other lords), and clause 22
(seeking a remedy for the alienation by widows of their *maritagia*). It is to the
documents which shed light on the drafting process which followed the initial
collection of grievances in the 'Petition of the Barons' that we now turn.

THE *PROVIDENCIA BARONUM*

Only one of the clauses of the 'Petition of the Barons' which were asking
either directly or indirectly for legislation is known to have been discussed at
the Parliament of Oxford. John Selden's abstract of a roll then in the
possession of Sir Edward Coke records a decision 'that Relligious persons
purchase not so much'.[46] It appears to attribute this decision to the Oxford
Parliament; and if this is the case we can be fairly certain that at least clause 10
of the 'Petition' was discussed there.[47] Discussion of other such clauses in the
'Petition' was apparently left for a subsequent occasion. Some work may have
been done on them later the same summer. The London chronicle probably
written by Arnulf fitz Thedmar mentions the Earl Marshal, Simon de
Montfort, John fitz Geoffrey and others having daily discussions, sometimes
at the New Temple and sometimes elsewhere, 'on the reform of the usages and

[44] Thus clause 4 of the Provisions (about attendance at the sheriff's tourn), represents a
development of the ideas put forward in clauses 17 and 18 of the 'Petition'; clause 5 of the
Provisions (prohibiting beaupleder fines) represents a development of the idea put forward in part
of clause 14 of the 'Petition'; clause 8 of the Provisions (allowing the overriding of charters of
exemption from jury service), represents a development of the idea put forward in clause 28 of the
'Petition'; clauses 9 and 10 of the Provisions (allowing the awarding of damages against lords who
keep heirs out of their inheritances), represents a development of the main part of clause 1 of the
'Petition'; clause 13 of the Provisions (restricting the power to amerce for default of attendance at
common summonses), represents a development of the idea put forward in clause 19 of the
'Petition'; and clause 22 of the Provisions (restricting the kinds of death for which the *murdrum* fine
was payable), represents a development of the idea put forward in clause 21 of the Provisions. For
the text of these clauses of the Provisions see *Stubbs' Charters*, pp. 391–4.

[45] *Ibid.*, p. 394. Similarly, although there is no clause in the Provisions directly related to clause
29 of the 'Petition' (about superior lords claiming cases removed to the county court for default of
justice), the Provisions do contain a clause (clause 16) which restates the royal monopoly over the
closely related jurisdiction over false judgments: *ibid.*, p. 393. It is also possible that clauses 1–3 of
the Provisions (about suit of court to lord's courts), are related to clause 10 of the 'Petition',
though the latter was only concerned with the undue exaction of suit to county, hundred and
franchisal courts. But for another possible source for this legislation see below, p. 346.

[46] H. G. Richardson and G. O. Sayles, 'The Provisions of Oxford: A Forgotten Document and
Some Comments', *Bulletin of the John Rylands Library*, XVII (1933), 3–33 (at 29).

[47] It should be noted, however, that the 'Petition' appears to be asking for seignorial control
over mortmain alienations, and that this was what lords eventually obtained through clause 14 of
the Provisions of Westminster. Although the quantity of ecclesiastical acquisitions may have been
a factor in the complaint, and in securing the passage of the legislation, it is not reflected in the
details of the enactment.

customs of the realm' and places this sometime after their visit to the Guildhall on 22 July.[48] All three men were members of the council of 15 appointed at the Oxford Parliament to advise the King and to amend and redress all things in need of amendment and redress, and they may have been discussing legal reforms.[49]

Selden's abstract of the contents of Coke's roll also mentions a decision to the effect that 'The Justices et autres sages homes are summoned that between that and the next Parlement they should consider of what ill Lawes and need of reformation there were, and that they meet eight days before the Parlement beginne againe, at the place where it shall be appointed to treat etc.'.[50] Unfortunately this item comes from a portion of the roll which contains material of various dates between 10 July 1258 and February 1259 in no particular order, and is itself undated.[51] The Parliament referred to could be the Parliament scheduled under the regulations laid down in the Provisions of Oxford for 6 October 1258. This would mean that this was a decision taken at the Parliament of Oxford or at its continuation at Winchester.[52] Or it might be a reference to the following Parliament, which was scheduled to meet on 3 February 1259. This would make it a decision of the October Parliament.[53] Treharne and Sanders prefer the former possibility;[54] Powicke the latter.[55] The former is perhaps marginally preferable, if only because it was easier for the justices to find time for such discussions before the opening of Michaelmas term than in the middle of Hilary term.[56] In either case what we seem to have here is evidence of legal experts meeting separately to consider legal reforms, apparently to see if there were any matters other than those already mentioned in the 'Petition of the Barons' which needed reform.

[48] *De Antiquis Legibus Liber: Cronica Maiorum et Vicecomitum Londoniarum*, ed. T. Stapleton (Camden Soc., orig. ser., XXXIV, 1846), pp. 38–9. It is worth noting that the chronicler uses similar terms when describing the Provisions of Westminster themselves: they were, he says, 'composicionem factam per barones . . . super usibus et legibus regni emendandis': *ibid.*, p. 42.

[49] Treharne and Sanders, *Documents*, pp. 104–5, 110–11.

[50] Richardson and Sayles, 'Provisions of Oxford', p. 33.

[51] For the dating of items 23–33 on the roll, see *ibid.*, pp. 6–12 (and note that item 24 belongs to 22 Feb. 1259; item 25 to 28 July 1258 (and succeeding days); item 28 to 4 Aug. 1258).

[52] For the clause of the Provisions of Oxford providing for regular Parliaments meeting on 6 Oct., 3 Feb. and 1 June each year, see Treharne and Sanders, *Documents*, pp. 110–11. The mandate of 4 Aug. to the four knights of each county for inquiries to be made into wrongs, trespasses and excesses committed within their counties envisaged the knights bringing the results of these inquiries to Westminster to the King's Council on 6 Oct. : *ibid.*, pp. 112–5.

[53] Treharne and Sanders, *Documents*, pp. 110–11. Matthew Paris says that it actually met at the octaves of the Purification (9 Feb.): *Matthaei Parisiensis Chronica Majora*, V, 737.

[54] Treharne and Sanders, *Documents*, p. 12. They attempt to link this with the fact that the Parliament actually opened (according to the Winchester annalist) only at the feast of the Translation of St Edward (13 Oct.), suggesting that the opening of Parliament was delayed so that the information on abuses brought by the knights to Westminster on 6 Oct. could 'be analysed by "the judges and wise men" to prepare the way for reforms to be enacted in the coming Parliament': *ibid.*, p. 14. But this would suggest that it should have been arranged that they appear at Westminster on 30 Sept. instead. Richardson and Sayles also seem to hint at a similar date for this clause: 'Provisions of Oxford', pp. 7–8, and n. 1 on p. 8.

[55] F. M. Powicke, *King Henry III and the Lord Edward* (Oxford, 1966), p. 397.

[56] It may also be relevant that it was during this week prior to 6 Oct. that the appointment of Thurkleby, Preston and Hadlow as justices of the Bench was made: *C.P.R.*, 1247–58, p. 652.

Our next real evidence about the progress of the process of legislative drafting comes from the document known as the *Providencia Baronum*. Five different manuscripts contain texts of part or all of this document:

(i) *Cambridge University Library, MS. Mm. I. 27, f. 73v.* This copy of a full text of the *Providencia Baronum* in Latin has been known to historians since it was printed by E. F. Jacob in 1925 in his volume of *Studies in the Period of Baronial Reform.*[57] Jacob's text was subsequently reprinted and translated by Treharne and Sanders in their volume of *Documents of the Baronial Movement;*[58] unfortunately they also thereby reproduced a number of errors in Jacob's text.[59] Jacob believed that this manuscript was the work of one Robert Carpenter of Hareslade, who was 'a contemporary who was interested in and took careful note of the events and enactments of his period',[60] but Denholm-Young showed that the manuscript was in fact written by the Robert Carpenter III who was born in 1258, and that this and other portions of the volume were copied from another manuscript written by his father (Robert Carpenter II) which still survives and is now in Gonville and Caius College Cambridge.[61]

(ii) *Gonville and Caius College, Cambridge, MS. 205/111, pp. 451–6.* This is the manuscript written by Robert Carpenter II from which Robert Carpenter III copied part of the contents of what is now Cambridge University Library, MS. Mm. I. 27. Although Denholm-Young drew attention to this manuscript, and to the text of the *Providencia Baronum* which it contains, in an article of 1935, Treharne and Sanders overlooked its existence when compiling their volume of *Documents of the Baronial Movement* in 1973,[62] and the text of the *Providencia Baronum* which it contains has never been printed. Appendix II to this article notes significant variants between the text of the *Providencia Baronum* in this manuscript and the printed text of the version found in Robert

---

[57] E. F. Jacob, *Studies in the Period of Baronial Reform and Rebellion, 1258–1267* (Oxford Studies in Social and Legal History, VIII, 1925), pp. 366–8. Jacob had previously mentioned the existence of this text in his 1924 article, 'What Were the "Provisions of Oxford"?', *History*, IX (1924), 188–200, at 196.

[58] Treharne and Sanders, *Documents*, pp. 122–31. They also numbered the clauses in accordance with marks which look like paragraph marks in the manuscript, but which seem in fact to function as full stops. This numbering cuts across the sense of the text and will for the most part be ignored here.

[59] The main errors in these texts are: the reading 'constituciones' for the 'consuetudines' of the manuscript at p. 368, line 4 of Jacob's text and clause 13, line 3 of the text in Treharne and Sanders; the reading 'illis' for the 'villis' of the manuscript at p. 368, line 20 of Jacob's text (this error is not reproduced by Treharne and Sanders); the reading 'contradictum' for the 'condictum' of the manuscript at p. 368, lines 22, 24–5, 31 and p. 369, lines 19–20 of Jacob's text and clauses 17, 18, 20 and 25 of the text in Treharne and Sanders (but note that 'contradictum' is the reading of the manuscript at p. 368, line 11 of Jacob's text and clause 15 of the text in Treharne and Sanders); the omission of the word 'causa' between 'attornatum' and 'possit' in line 14 of p. 369 of Jacob's text and line 6 of clause 24 in the text in Treharne and Sanders; the reading 'attornatus' for the 'attornatis' of the manuscript in line 16 of p. 369 of Jacob's text and line 8 of clause 24 in the text of Treharne and Sanders.

[60] Jacob, 'What Were the "Provisions of Oxford"?', pp. 195–6; *idem, Studies*, pp. 78–9.

[61] N. Denholm-Young, 'Robert Carpenter and the Provisions of Oxford', *E.H.R.*, L (1935), 22–35 (reprinted in *Collected Papers of N. Denholm-Young* [Cardiff 1969], pp. 173–86).

[62] Above, n. 61: Treharne and Sanders, *Documents*, p. 122.

Carpenter III's manuscript. Denholm-Young believed that Robert Carpenter II passed in 1259 from the service of William de Lisle, the lord of various manors on the Isle of Wight, into the service of the senior royal justice, Roger of Thurkelby,[63] but C. A. F. Meekings has shown that the evidence adduced in support of this hypothesis does not do so, and that it is in fact most unlikely that Carpenter did become Thurkleby's clerk.[64] Robert Carpenter may, none the less, have had exceptional opportunities in 1258-9 for gaining access to documents connected with the programme of baronial reform. His master, William de Lisle, is known to have been summoned by Aymer de Valence, bishop-elect of Winchester, to attend the Parliament at Oxford with him in June 1258, and is also known to have been a knight in the service of Philip Basset between 1246 and 1262.[65] Philip Basset was chosen at the Oxford Parliament as one of the 12 who were to attend Parliament on behalf of the 'community of the realm';[66] and later (though possibly not until after April 1259) was co-opted as one of the 15 members of the King's sworn council in place of John fitz Geoffrey, who had died in November 1258.[67] Thus Robert Carpenter II, if only at one remove, was close to the political decision-making process in 1258-9.

(iii) *British Library, Cotton MS. Nero D. I, f. 82r.* This partial Latin text of the *Providencia Baronum* is found in the *Liber Additamentorum* of Matthew Paris in a sequence of documents belonging to the period 1253-9.[68] Matthew Paris died in June 1259 and Richard Vaughan notes that this text of the *Providencia Baronum* is the last document to be written in the *Liber Additamentorum* in Matthew Paris's own hand, and that it is followed in the manuscript by copies of two documents of 1258 not in his hand.[69] The abrupt ending of this text part of the way through the clause on attendance at the sheriff's tourn and about half-way through the full text, at the bottom of the recto of a folio of which the verso is ruled but otherwise left blank, is probably to be explained by illness or even death overcoming Matthew Paris while he was copying this document. Luard noted the existence of this text and printed its first three sentences in a footnote to an appendix to his partial edition of the *Liber Additamentorum*.[70] Jacob printed only variants between this text and the text of the *Providencia Baronum* in the Cambridge University Library manuscript, and the same practice was adopted by Treharne and Sanders.[71] Again, however, Jacob's transcription is not wholly to be relied upon and his notes (which were

---

[63] Denholm-Young, 'Robert Carpenter', pp. 27-8 (or *Collected Papers*, pp. 178-9). Here he was following a suggestion made by Jacob: *Studies*, p. 79.

[64] C. A. F. Meekings, 'More about Robert Carpenter of Hareslade', *E.H.R.*, LXXII (1957), 260-9.

[65] Denholm-Young, 'Robert Carpenter', p. 25 (also in his *Collected Papers* at p. 176); *C.P.R.*, 1232-47, p. 463 (I owe this reference to the kindness of Dr David Carpenter).

[66] Treharne and Sanders, *Documents*, p. 104.

[67] Richardson and Sayles, 'Provisions of Oxford', pp. 15-16.

[68] *Matthaei Parisiensis Chronica Majora*, VI, 492-7. On the compilation of the *Liber Additamentorum* see R. Vaughan, *Matthew Paris* (Cambridge, 1958), Chapter 5.

[69] Vaughan, *Matthew Paris*, pp. 10-11, 82-3.

[70] *Matthaei Parisiensis Chronica Majora*, VI, 496, n. 2.

[71] Jacob, *Studies*, pp. 366-8, footnotes; Treharne and Sanders, *Documents*, pp. 122-6, footnotes.

followed in most respects by Treharne and Sanders, who do not themselves seem to have re-examined the manuscript), provide a misleading account of the version of the *Providencia Baronum* contained in this manuscript. A full transcript of it will be found below, at Appendix III.

(iv) *British Library, Additional MS. 15,668, f. 32.* This manuscript is a later thirteenth-century register of the alien Gloucestershire priory of Newent. It contains a hitherto unnoticed Latin text of part of the initial section of the *Providencia Baronum* concerning suit of court.[72] It is preceded in this manuscript by a copy of the sheriff's oath as laid down in 1258, and also of the King's letter of August 1258 to the men of each county notifying them of the appointment of four knights in their county to enquire into grievances.

(v) *Philadelphia Free Library, Hampton L. Carson Collection, MS. LC 14.3, f. 202.* This is a mainly legal manuscript originally compiled in the late thirteenth or early fourteenth centuries and containing treatises relating to estate management, minor legal treatises, a copy of *Britton* and copies of statutes. In the 1320s and early 1330s was added (at ff. 41r–47v) a section of material mainly relating to the Oxfordshire town of Burford.[73] It contains a hitherto unknown text of the *Providencia Baronum* which, unlike all other known texts, is in French. This is reproduced below, in Appendix IV. It also contains another item from the 1258–67 period that is only rarely found in Edwardian manuscripts: a text of the 1264 reissue of the Provisions of Westminster.[74] There is nothing in the manuscript to identify this as a text of the *Providencia Baronum*. It is simply headed *Statutum de sectis curiarum*, with no indication of date, and at the end it simply says *explicit*. None the less a comparison of its text with that of the various Latin versions of the *Providencia Baronum* makes it plain that we are dealing with essentially the same document. It contains 11 sections whose subject matter corresponds exactly with that of the 11 sections of the *Providencia Baronum* in the two fullest Latin manuscripts. These sections also occur in exactly the same order as in those manuscripts, and there is a fairly close resemblance in the content of those sections. It is, however, also clear that this is not simply a straight translation into French of the Latin text of the *Providencia Baronum*, nor vice versa. This emerges clearly if we compare the connecting and introductory passages in this text and in the Latin texts. For the rather tentative 'sic justum et conveniens

---

[72] It reads as follows: 'De sectis curie sic justum et conveniens esse videtur ut scilicet tenens quando ex forma sui feofamenti tenetur ad sectam per verba in sua carta contenta eum faciat in forma feofamenti sui. Illi autem qui feofati sunt per cartas continentes servicium certum pro omni servicio et consuetudine et specialia verba in cartis contenta non tenentur ad sectam nec tenentur decetero de cetero ad ipsam sectam faciendam. Illi autem qui a tempore [32v] conquestus vel a tempore ultra quod accio non conceditur sectam continue fecerunt pro tenementis suis eam faciant sicut antiquitus eam facere consueverunt'.

[73] For a description of the manuscript, see J. H. Baker, *English Legal MSS. in the United States of America, part I: Medieval and Renaissance* (Selden Soc., 1985), no. 162, pp. 57–8 (but Baker wrongly identifies 'Bereford' as Barford, Northants.).

[74] At ff. 173v–175r. This reissue is discussed with reference to the two MSS. then known to contain texts of it in my 1974 Oxford D. Phil. thesis 'The Contribution of the Period of Baronial Reform (1258–1267) to the Development of the Common Law in England', pp. 38–9.

esse videtur' or 'justum et conveniens esse videtur' that introduces the first part of the initial section on suit of court in the Latin text, the French text has the much more definitive words of legislative intent ' . . . est purveu par le Rey e par le Barnage communement'; and the section on adjournments in dower and possessory advowson cases is introduced in the Latin text by the words 'provisum est insuper a domino rege necnon a proceribus condictum' where in the French text we find the much plainer 'derechef est il purveu'. A similar contrast is found in the following section on the overriding of charters of exemption between the 'sic a proceribus condictum est' of the Latin text and the 'issi est il purveu' of the French. We will return later in this paper to the precise nature of the relationship between the French and Latin texts.

When we read the Latin text of the *Providencia Baronum* it becomes clear almost at once that what we are reading is a draft of future legislation rather than an actual legislative text. The 'justum et conveniens esse videtur' of the first clause, the 'videtur autem conveniens' of the third clause and the 'conveniens est' of the tenth clause are all phrases of persuasion rather than authoritative enactment. The phrase that introduces the specimen example of a writ of entry outside the degrees ('forma autem brevis talis in hujusmodi causis competenter esse potest'), is also a tentative one, quite unlike anything we find in actual legislation. There are two opposing and unreconciled views on the attendance of substantial tenants at the sheriff's tourn in the second subsection of clause 5, something possible in a legislative draft though not in a final and authoritative legislative text. Also characteristic of a draft rather than a final text is the material in the final two clauses of the text justifying the legal changes proposed.

Jacob thought indeed that the Latin text gave us a rare glimpse of the actual process of drafting, that it showed 'the royalist side making a proposal and the baronial party on their side . . . confirming, adding to or qualifying it'.[75] In one subsection of clause 5 of the *Providencia Baronum*, that concerned with the attendance at the sheriff's tourn of those possessing substantial holdings, the Latin text of the *Providencia Baronum* does indeed give us a glimpse of a debate, though one in which the second view reported is actually 'contradicting' the first rather than just confirming, adding to or qualifying it. Here the initial proposal was that such landowners should be exempt from attendance at the tourn unless their attendance was specially needed. The opposing viewpoint then given (which is introduced by the phrase 'unde eciam contradictum est . . . ') is that such landowners should only be exempt from attendance if outside the jurisdiction of the tourn at the time its session took place, or prevented from attendance by illness or other good reason. This would, of course, mean that such landholders would normally be required to attend the tourn in the hundred where they resided.[76] Neither viewpoint is ascribed to a particular

[75] Jacob, *Studies*, p. 80. Jacob's view is also taken by Treharne and Sanders (*Documents*, p. 123, n.), despite the fact that Treharne had originally been sceptical of this viewpoint (*Baronial Plan*, p. 133, n. 8).

[76] Jacob's view that the second voice in the debate merely adds a proviso to the initial proposal is clearly wrong: Jacob, *Studies*, p. 81.

group, but if we are to ascribe one view to a 'baronial' side and the other to a 'royalist' side it seems much more probable that the initial proposal came from the 'baronial' side and the second from the King's side rather than vice versa.[77] Elsewhere in the Latin text of the *Providencia Baronum* Jacob thought he had found evidence for the existence of such a dialogue in the use of the term *contradictum*, which he glossed as indicating the reaction of a second group to a proposal rather than as literally revealing a clash of views between the two sides.[78] However, at each of the four places in question what the text actually reads is *condictum*, which means much the same as *provisum* and has no implications of any second voice or viewpoint being involved.[79] Other internal evidence for the existence of any kind of dialogue is very thin. It is possible that the 'provisum est insuper a domino rege necnon a proceribus condictum' of clause 7 and the 'illud autem communiter concessum est et condictum' of clause 6 as well as the 'provisum est eciam de consilio et consensu magnatum et procerum' of clause 9 all imply the existence of a dialogue between King and magnates. It seems more probable, however, that they are simply the common form of legislative drafting and are to be given no greater weight than the 'sic a proceribus condictum est' of clause 8 which, if taken literally, appears to imply that the magnates are competent to legislate without the King's consent. In none of these clauses, in any case, can we see any trace of two separate viewpoints. We must content ourselves, then, with just one clause of the Latin text revealing something of the arguments which went on during the process of drafting; by itself, the Latin text tells us nothing more of that process.

We have the contemporary testimony of Matthew Paris, in the heading to his partial copy of the Latin text of the *Providencia Baronum* in his *Liber Additamentorum*, that this text was 'published' at the New Temple in London with the King's consent in March 1259. It is not wholly clear what sense we should give to the word 'published' in this context.[80] There can be little doubt that it does not mean that these 11 clauses were now promulgated as law in force. There is no evidence of any of them being enforced and, as we have seen, their very language shows them as intended to be a draft rather than actual legislation. It may simply mean, as Treharne suggested, that they were 'read out for discussion'.[81] It seems more likely, however, that at the very least

---

[77] Contrast Jacob, *Studies*, p. 81: 'The next clause exempts prominent landholders from the sheriff's tourn, and the baronial party (if our hypothesis is right) add the proviso that all who have holdings sufficient to guarantee their being peaceful and law-abiding persons shall not be punished for non-attendance if they can show good cause.'

[78] Jacob, *Studies*, p. 80.

[79] Above, n. 59. Denholm-Young also noted Jacob's misreading here: 'Robert Carpenter', p. 32, n. 3 (*Collected Papers*, p. 183, n. 3). It should perhaps be added that in none of these clauses is there any hint of an addition to, or qualification of, a prior proposal: indeed in clause 11 the initial words of the clause are 'condictum est', while in clause 8 the phrase 'sic a proceribus condictum est' is preceded not by any 'royalist' proposal but simply by a phrase explaining what the clause was about.

[80] For previous discussions of this point see Jacob, *Studies*, p.80; Treharne, *Baronial Plan*, pp. 133, 135; Treharne and Sanders, *Documents*, p. 17.

[81] Treharne, *Baronial Plan*, p. 135.

it means also that the text was made publicly available at the New Temple to anyone who wished to have copies of what was being proposed: hence, perhaps, the existence of three independent copies of part or all of the text. It may even mean that the text was in some way circulated to the counties, perhaps as well as being read out at the New Temple. The wording of Matthew Paris's heading certainly sounds as if it may be repeating in part the wording of such a writ.

The date to be ascribed to the Latin text of the *Providencia Baronum* has caused problems for historians. Both the Cambridge Carpenter manuscripts state in their headings to the text that it is the 'Providencia Baronum Anglie anno regni regis Henrici xl secundo'. If taken literally these would mean that it cannot be of a date later than 27 October 1258. Such a date is difficult to reconcile with that of March 1259 given by Matthew Paris. Four different solutions have been canvassed. Treharne and Denholm-Young have both suggested that the main burden of drafting was accomplished prior to late October 1258, but that the draft was not published till March 1259.[82] Richardson and Sayles have suggested that the truncated St Albans version represents a later recension of the *Providencia Baronum*, 'the opening paragraphs of which were practically identical with the first draft . . . '.[83] Powicke has suggested that the Carpenter date was simply the result of scribal error.[84] Jacob, after much thought, plumped for belief in the 'more authoritative and circumstancial' evidence of the *Liber Additamentorum*, and gave as a subsidiary reason the internal character of the text, which was 'the result of more observation and discussion than can have been practicable within two or even three months' time from the beginning of the reform'.[85] It is indeed the circumstantial detail of the *Liber Additamentorum* heading which is convincing, though to that can now be added our knowledge that it must have been written within a few months of the date to which it refers.[86] We also now know that Robert Carpenter was not in 1258–9 right at the heart of things as Thurkelby's clerk (though still fairly close to them at second hand through his service to William de Lisle);[87] and more significantly that he was not very accurate about regnal years, since he was also one regnal year out (though in the opposite direction) when giving a text of the Provisions of Westminster of October 1259, which he ascribes to the regnal year 'xl quarto', though in fact they belong to the regnal year 'xl tercio'.[88] This renders unnecessary any attempt to explain away the regnal year given in the two Cambridge

[82] Treharne, *Baronial Plan*, p. 133; Denholm-Young, 'Robert Carpenter', pp. 32–3 (*Collected Papers*, pp. 183–4); Treharne and Sanders, *Documents*, p. 16.
[83] Richardson and Sayles, 'Provisions of Oxford', p. 8, n. 1.
[84] F. M. Powicke, 'Some Observations on the Baronial Council (1258–1260) and the Provisions of Westminster', *Essays in Medieval History Presented to Thomas Frederick Tout*, eds. A. G. Little and F. M. Powicke (Manchester, 1925), pp. 119–34, at p. 126, n. 4. However, this view seems to have rested on the mistaken assumption that the year was given in the form 'xlij', which is much more easily emended than 'xl secundo'.
[85] Jacob, *Studies*, p. 82. Jacob had previously subscribed to the first of these theories.
[86] Above, p. 336.   [87] Above, p. 336.
[88] This was first noticed by Denholm-Young: 'Robert Carpenter', p. 32 (*Collected Papers*, p. 183).

manuscripts through ingenious theories about Carpenter knowing when the text was actually drafted (though not published), or about there having been two recensions of the text which happen largely to coincide up to the point that one of them breaks off. The two Carpenter texts are simply in error on this point.

What then is the probable context of 'publication' of the Latin text in March 1259? We know that Parliament had met on 9 February 1259 and that it was on 22 February, during this session of Parliament, that the King's Council and the 12 elected by the community sealed a document promising to allow the wrongs done by their bailiffs to be corrected by the justiciar, promising to observe both Magna Carta and the legislation which had already been enacted and future legislation to be enacted before All Saints Day on a number of subjects, and promising also to make their officials take oaths in terms similar to those already enacted for the King's sheriffs.[89] It is conceivable that this same session of Parliament simply continued into March, and that the *Providencia Baronum* was 'published' at this session but towards or at its conclusion. The evidence of the King's movements during February and March 1259, however, suggests that the February meeting of Parliament was over by 26 February, for the King then left Westminster for Windsor, travelling on to Wallingford and Reading before returning to Westminster by way of Windsor, Chertsey and Merton on 20 March.[90] If, as seems probable, the Latin text of the *Providencia Baronum* was published in March at the New Temple in the King's presence, it seems likely that this was between 20 March and the end of the month, and thus almost a month after the parliamentary session had ended. It was also during this same period at the end of March that the King sent out letters patent in French to every county communicating the full text of the document sealed by the members of the King's Council and the 12 on 22 February.[91] The delay of one month in the publication of these letters patent, which are known to have been a product of the February parliamentary session, provides additional reason for thinking that the Latin text of the *Providencia Baronum*, although published only in March, was also in some sense a product of the same parliamentary session. But why the delay? This may simply have been the result of bureaucratic inefficiency. But there is an alternative possibility. It may be that originally there had been no intention to publish either the letters patent of 22 February or the legislation so far drafted, but that there was some pressure placed on the 'reformers' in March to show that they were indeed making some progress in drafting the legislation, and that they were willing to accept as applicable to themselves the reforms they were now enforcing on the King, and that publication only took place as a result of this pressure.[92]

[89] This document survives only in the form it was subsequently published by the King in letters patent of 28 Mar. 1259: see Treharne and Sanders, *Documents*, pp. 130–7.

[90] The information about Henry's movements is derived from the published calendars of Chancery enrolments. [91] Above, n. 89.

[92] It is just conceivable that the protest of the *communitas bachelerie Anglie* is wrongly assigned by the Burton annalist to the Michaelmas Parliament of 1259 and that it really took place in March 1259. It certainly fits better then. For the protest see *Annales Monastici*, I, 471.

We have already seen that the French text of the *Providencia Baronum* is neither simply a translation of the Latin text nor the French original of which the Latin text was itself a translation. We have also seen that it has clauses corresponding to each of the 11 clauses of the Latin text and that they occur in exactly the same order.[93] Two alternative hypotheses seem possible about the relationship between the French and Latin texts: that the French text represents a later recension of the Latin text, or that the French text represents an earlier draft of the Latin text. One feature of the French text which at first sight appears to favour the former hypothesis has already been mentioned: the fact that where the Latin text has merely tentative introductory phrases at the beginning of at least three of its sections the French text uses much more definitive words of legislative intent.[94] Similarly, where the specimen example of a writ of entry outside the degrees is introduced in the Latin text with the very tentative words 'forma autem brevis talis in hujusmodi causis competenter esse potest', in the French text we find at the same point the much more authoritative 'La fourme del bref est ceste . . . '. It looks as though what has once been tentative and uncertain has now been firmed up into the form of definitive legislation. Other evidence apparently pointing in the same direction is the fact that in the French version of clause 5 on attendance at the sheriff's tourn we find only a single consistent viewpoint, and not as in the Latin text two mutually inconsistent opposing viewpoints about the rules which are to apply as to the attendance of the holders of substantial holdings at the tourn.

However, the argument in favour of the second hypothesis is in the end a more convincing one. The strongest evidence in its favour is to be found in the two clauses where there are major differences of substance between French and Latin texts. The second section of the *Providencia Baronum* deals with the division of a tenement which owes suit of court, and in the Latin text appears to deal with two different kinds of situation in which this may occur: where this is the result of inheritance by coheirs, and where this is the result of a tenant granting his lands away to several feoffees. In neither case is more than one suit to be owed for the tenement after division; in both cases those among whom the tenement is divided are to contribute to the cost of the performance of the suit. The French text in the corresponding section, however, is clearly only concerned with the consequences of one kind of division, that between coheirs, and with a variant on this, the situation which arises when some of the coheirs have alienated their shares in an inheritance to third parties. It does not even mention the possibility of a tenement being granted away to several feoffees. If we look at the corresponding section of the eventual Provisions of Westminster (clause 2) we find it purporting to deal with the same two kinds of situation as the Latin text, though it adds to the rules laid down in the draft the additional requirement that in the case of a division between coheirs the eldest coheir is to be responsible for performance of the suit.[95] It is plain then that the Provisions of Westminster represent a further development of the

---

[93] Above, p. 337.   [94] Above, pp. 337–8.
[95] *C.R.*, 1259–61, pp. 146–7.

Latin text; and that the most likely explanation of the relationship between the three texts is that the initial idea contained in the French text was elaborated (and perhaps misunderstood) in the Latin text, and then further elaborated for the eventual legislation. It is not at all likely that the Latin text was simplified for the French version and then once more elaborated (and in exactly the same way) for the eventual legislation. The second such section is that dealing with attendance at the sheriff's tourn. In the Latin text we find an initial subsection agreeing that neither bishops, abbots, priors nor earls or barons are to be required to attend such sessions in future; a second subsection apparently recording two unreconciled views about the attendance at the tourn of those possessing substantial landholdings; a third subsection emphasizing that those who defaulted in attendance at the sheriff's tourn were only to be amerced in accordance with the provisions of Magna Carta; and a final subsection which stipulates that only enough men to 'make inquest' are to be compelled to come to the tourn from individual villages.[96] The French version has nothing corresponding to the final two subsections and has a radically different version of the first two. The first subsection (like that in the Latin text) envisages that abbots, priors, earls and barons will be exempt from attendance at the tourn,[97] but also accepts that those who have large holdings should be exempt in exactly the same manner (and does not record any dissent from this view). Unlike the Latin text, however, it also clearly envisages that members of all these exempt groups will be liable to attend if their presence is specially required for some particular reason. A second subsection then goes on to envisage the conferring of temporary exemptions from attendance on others (not included in these groups) as well: those who are outside the jurisdiction when the tourn is held or prevented from attendance by illness or other good reason . Here too it looks as though the eventual legislation (clause 4 of the Provisions of Westminster) represents a further development of the scheme laid down in the Latin text: for it too does not confer an absolute exemption on those with major landholdings who do not belong to one of the exempt groups (though it does add archbishops, the religious and women to the exempt groups), and it effectively follows the more restricted of the two views given in the Latin text by allowing their absence only when they are not resident in the jurisdiction of the tourn in question. It also follows the Latin

---

[96] This final section may be referring to the attendance of the unfree at the sheriff's tourn to make presentments there. However, in view of the concern of clause 14 of the 'Petition of the Barons' with the attendance of the unfree at coroners' inquests (and their amercement if not all the unfree of the four neighbouring villages appeared), and the fact that the Provisions of Westminster said nothing about the attendance of the unfree at the tourn, but did provide (in clause 21) that the justices in eyre were not to amerce villages for failing to attend fully coroners' inquests (and other inquisitions into crown pleas), provided enough attended for the inquisition to proceed, it seems not improbable that the 'eum' of the Gonville and Caius MS. of the *Providencia Baronum* (with an interlined 's[cilicet] turnum' above it – which Cambridge Univ. Lib., MS. Mm. I. 27 has turned into 'eum turnum'), should read 'inquisicionem'. The only reason for doubt is the reference in the same section to Magna Carta. In the 1217 and 1225 versions this contains a reference to the sheriff's tourn (here called view of frankpledge); but no version refers to the coroner's inquest.

[97] The omission of bishops from the list is presumably an error or an oversight.

rather than the French text in omitting any mention of the exemption from attendance at the tourn of those prevented from attendance by illness or other good reason, and by including a reference to Magna Carta in connexion with the tourn.[98] This again suggests that the French text of this section represents the earliest surviving stage in the textual development; the Latin text a subsequent stage after the text had undergone some revision.

The French text may well represent an initial draft presented by a drafting committee to the February Parliament of 1259. If this is so then the watering-down of the draft as to exemptions from attendance at the sheriff's tourn, and the inclusion in the Latin text of a still more restrictive second view as to the attendance of major landholders not members of one of the exempt groups at the tourn (perhaps the most important of the drafting changes), may well represent the outcome of comments and objections made at that Parliament and may also indicate a significant 'royalist' input into the drafting process at this stage. However, it seems probable that the transformation of the language of statutory enactment into the language of persuasion (a second important element in the drafting changes)[99] belongs to a still later process: that which turned the outcome of the discussions in Parliament in February 1259 into a document made public in March 1259. Such modifications were probably intended simply to make clear that this was only the draft of legislation and not actual legislation. It was perhaps also as part of the process of transforming the outcome of the parliamentary discussions into a document suitable for publication that the *Providencia Baronum* was translated from French (the language in which the drafters appear to have been working), into the Latin of a formal and published document.

The *Providencia Baronum* indicates that as late as February 1259, that is some eight months after the beginning of the 'reform of the realm' initiated at Oxford, the process of law reform had proceeded no further than the preliminary drafting of some 11 clauses of legislation, of which four were devoted to a single topic, suit of court.[100] The 'Petition of the Barons' was plainly one source of inspiration for the legislation which had been drafted. Clause 5 (on exemptions from attendance at the sheriff's tourn) is clearly related to clauses 17 and 18 of the 'Petition of the Barons'. But it is more than simply a translation of those complaints into draft legislation. Both versions of

---

[98] *C.R.* 1259–61, p. 147.

[99] In fact this was not done thoroughly, and elsewhere in the document similar phrases were simply transformed into one of a number of different formulas which appear to suggest actual enactment.

[100] It is just conceivable that other legislation had already been drafted, and that it was only the most recently drafted section of the legislation that was published in March 1259. Against this, however, is the position in the eventual legislation (the Provisions of Westminster of October 1259) of the clauses corresponding to the clauses contained in the *Providencia Baronum* (though, as will be seen, not all the clauses contained in the draft found their place in the eventual legislation): they form clauses 1, 2, 3, 4, 5, 6, 7, 8 and 15 of this legislation. This strongly suggests that they were also the first clauses to be drafted. Also relevant here are the motives behind the publication of the draft legislation. If these were to prove that something was being done, then it is difficult to see why all the draft legislation would not have been published together.

the *Providencia Baronum* go beyond the complaints contained in the 'Petition' to suggest exemption from attendance at the tourn for abbots and priors, and the Latin version also adds bishops. In fact we know that in the case of abbots and priors no change in the law was being proposed, for there had been a judgment in the Exchequer shortly before Easter term 1258 to the effect that the religious were exempt from attendance at the tourn.[101] Thus, in effect, all that was being proposed was a legislative confirmation of an existing rule whose effect would simply have been to ensure that the existing rule was more widely known and enforced. The drafting process had also brought up the question of those who had sizeable holdings but who did not belong to any of the exempt groups, and we can still see in both draft texts the argument advanced for exempting them from attendance: that their holdings alone were sufficient to ensure that they kept the peace and observed the law. The French text also seems to have taken up the issue raised by clause 17 (the demand for exemption from attendance of those with small holdings without a dwelling attached), but proposed rather broader legislation which would effectively have exempted from attendance any not resident in the hundred when the sheriff's tourn was held (whether or not their holdings had houses attached), or who were prevented by sickness or other good cause from attendance. As we have seen, however, this proposal seems to have met with resistance and had been dropped by the time the Latin version of the text was compiled.[102] Similarly, clause 6 of the *Providencia Baronum*, about the exaction of beaupleder fines, is plainly derived from clause 14 of the 'Petition of the Barons'. But again the drafting process has turned a complaint against the exaction of such fines by the justices of the general eyre into a more general prohibition against the exaction of such fines in any court.[103] Clause 8, on the overriding of royal charters of exemption from jury service, is likewise clearly related to clause 28 of the 'Petition of the Barons', which is also concerned with the same problem. Here the French text of the *Providencia Baronum* is closest to the 'Petition', since it too is concerned only with the overriding of such charters in the case of grand assizes where it was necessary to make up the numbers of knights from those with such exemptions. The Latin text also considers the possibility that it may be necessary to override the exemption in other cases as well, and proposes authorizing this too.[104]

It is just possible that clauses 1–4 developed from clause 24 of the 'Petition of the Barons', which sought a remedy for suits newly claimed to county, hundred and liberty courts. However, this seems unlikely, since these clauses

---

[101] The judgment is quoted in writs enrolled on the Memoranda Roll in Hilary term 1259: P.R.O., E.159/32, m. 7d; as also (it seems) in writs enrolled in Easter term 1258: E. 159/31, m. 11.

[102] Above, pp. 343–4.

[103] By the time this clause had been further recast for the Provisions of Westminster (clause 5), it had become a prohibition of the exaction of such fines, not just before the justices in eyre, but also specifically in county courts and in courts baron: *C.R.*, 1259–61, p. 148.

[104] Here, too, the final version of the same clause in the Provisions of Westminster (clause 8) develops the point raised by the Latin text, specifying that the exemption may be overridden, not just for grand assizes, but also for perambulations or where the grantee is the witness to charters or other deeds or for attaints (and adds a general saving for like cases): *C.R.*, 1259–61, p. 148.

are specifically concerned only with suit to seignorial courts, and not with suits owed to the courts specified in the 'Petition'.[105] A much more likely source is one of the complaints made by the clergy at their council held in the summer of 1258, just prior to the Parliament of Oxford. This alleged that ecclesiastics who had been granted land to hold in free alms were being made to do suit of court to the courts of the King, magnates and other lords for the lands they had been given contrary to the form of such gifts, unless they produced evidence of the original gifts and the charters concerned, which had perhaps been lost or destroyed. It established that if distraint was in future made for such suits by the donors or founders concerned or their heirs or successors, they were to be prevented from continuing with them by ecclesiastical censures; similar measures were also to be taken if such suits were demanded by superior lords and such suits had not customarily been done.[106] Here, indeed, we find a concern with the exaction of suit of court to seignorial courts and specifically with the use of distraint to secure its performance. We also find a concern with the rules governing the obligation, and the relationship between the obligation and what is contained in the tenant's charter of feoffment. The *Providencia Baronum* is certainly not a direct borrowing from the ecclesiastical complaint, but it makes an intelligible starting-point for the development of the clauses in the *Providencia Baronum* that are concerned with suit of court.

No such sources have, however, been traced for the remaining four clauses of the *Providencia Baronum*. Two of them (clause 7, on the shortening of the length of adjournments in cases of dower *unde nichil habet*, darrein presentment and *quare impedit*, and clause 9, on the extension of the writ of entry outside the degrees) are both technical legal improvements of the kind that we might expect to have been suggested by the judges and other legal experts consulted on matters in need of reform, and the same is also perhaps true of clause 11, on the extension of the availability of the assize of mort d'ancestor. This does not, however, seem to be the case with clause 10, on the warranting of essoins, since (to judge from the wording of the eventual legislation on this point), the problem was only one which arose in local courts.[107] Here we seem to find a response to a grievance similar to some of the grievances expressed in the 'Petition of the Barons', an indication that there may well have been a continuing lay input into the legislative process as well.

---

[105] Even though franchise courts and the seignorial courts mentioned in the *Providencia Baronum* were both private courts owned by lords, they were conceptually quite distinct. Suit of court was owed to seignorial courts or courts baron by virtue of tenure of land from the owner of the court; suit of court was owed to franchisal courts by virtue of residence within the area of jurisdiction of the court concerned.

[106] *Councils and Synods with Other Documents Relating to the English Church, II (1205–1313)*, eds. F. M. Powicke and C.R. Cheney (2 vols., Oxford, 1964), I, 584. A similar complaint had been made in the previous year: *ibid.*, I, 546.

[107] Clause 15 of the Provisions of Westminster specifies county courts, hundred courts and seignorial courts as those where the warranting of essoins on oath was no longer to be necessary.

THE PROVISIONS OF WESTMINSTER

It was at the Michaelmas Parliament of 1259 that the text of the Provisions of Westminster was finally approved.[108] On 24 October, at or towards the end of the session of Parliament, the Provisions were read out in public in Westminster Hall in the presence of the King and of many earls and barons and of a large number of others.[109]

There survive two official texts of the Provisions, both in manuscripts now in the Public Record Office:[110]

(i) One is on the dorse of the Close Roll for 44 Henry III (C.54/75, m. 17d) where it occurs between entries dated 19 and 22 December 1259. This was taken as the basis of the text printed by the editors of *Statutes of the Realm*,[111] and was again printed *in extenso* by the editors of the Close Rolls of the reign of Henry III.[112] It is certainly not the archetype from which other official texts of the Provisions were derived, for there is clear internal evidence that it was copied rather carelessly from another text, though subsequently emended presumably by reference to that text.[113]

(ii) The second is found on ff. 181r–182v of the Red Book of the Exchequer (E.164/2). This text has never been printed nor even collated with the Close Roll text. It seems probable that it is a contemporary copy of the official text of the Provisions as sent to the Barons of the Exchequer. It appears to have been copied with more care than the text on the Close Roll and should probably be preferred to that text where the two texts differ.[114]

The Provisions as enacted in October 1259 contain a total of some 24

---

[108] A memorandum of decisions taken at this Parliament also survives in two different manuscript versions (in the B.L. manuscript of the Burton annals and in the *Liber Additamentorum* of Matthew Paris): see *Annales Monastici*, I, 476–9; Jacob, *Studies*, 372–4. Treharne and Sanders reprint the Burton annals text and some of the variants from the *Liber Additamentorum* text, but give a misleading account of the relationship between the two: *Documents*, pp. 148–56. This memorandum has also sometimes confusingly been described as the 'Provisions of Westminster'. It is, however, quite clear that it is an internal memorandum not intended for publication, and thus quite different in nature from the statutory Provisions of Westminster, which were formally enacted and published and intended to be enforced as law thereafter.

[109] *De Antiquis Legibus Liber*, p. 42.

[110] There also survive one complete and three incomplete 'unofficial' copies of the Provisions in other manuscripts. These are described and discussed in Brand, 'Contribution of the Period of Baronial Reform', pp. 24, 28–9.

[111] *Stats. Realm*, I, 8–11. This was then reprinted by Bishop Stubbs in *Stubbs' Charters*, pp. 390–4.

[112] *C.R.*, 1259–61, pp. 146–50. This was then reprinted and translated by Treharne and Sanders in *Documents*, pp. 136–49.

[113] Clauses 10, 11 and 16 (as the editors of the printed edition of *C.R.* note in their text) were all omitted by the copyist and had to be inserted in the margin or out of place in the text with marks to show their correct place. There are also two examples of homoeoteleuton (neither noted in the *C.R.* text) where a missing passage has been copied into the margin and noted for insertion at the correct point: between the two occurrences of 'subtractionibus' in clause 3 and the two occurrences of 'mittat' in clause 3.

[114] Its reading 'ante tempus supradictum' in the final sentence of clause 3 is certainly to be preferred to the 'ante tempus supradicte transfretacionis' of the *C.R.* text on grounds of sense alone. Its insertion of 'hundredis' in the list of courts where the beaupleder fine is forbidden in clause 5 also clearly repairs an accidental omission in the *C.R.* text.

clauses.[115] Nine of these are, in essence, further recensions of draft clauses contained in the *Providencia Baronum* of February/March 1259. Clauses 1–3 of the Provisions (on suit of court) represent a major revision of clauses 1–4 of the *Providencia Baronum*[116] and clause 4 (on attendance at the tourn) is also a major revision of clause 5 of the *Providencia Baronum*.[117] Clause 5 (on the beaupleder fine) is merely a more explicit version of clause 6 of the *Providencia Baronum*;[118] but in clauses 6 and 7 we find a substantial amendment of the rules proposed in clause 7 of the *Providencia Baronum*, on giving briefer adjournments in certain types of action, as also an entirely new provision allowing judgment to be given by default in pleas of *quare impedit*. Clause 8 takes up the proposal in clause 8 of the *Providencia Baronum* for allowing the overriding of exemptions from jury-service, but extends considerably the list of situations in which this is to be allowed.[119] Least changed in substance is clause 15, which takes up the proposal in clause 10 of the *Providencia Baronum* and merely adds a list of courts where the warranting of essoins is no longer to be required, and omits the justification given for the reform. Three of these nine clauses can be traced back further to clauses in the Petition of the Barons which seem to have been their inspiration.[120]

A further six clauses of the Provisions of Westminster do not occur in draft form in either version of the *Providencia Baronum* but do clearly represent a response to complaints voiced in the 'Petition of the Barons'. In most cases they go some way beyond merely remedying the grievance voiced in the 'Petition'.[121] The origin of the remaining nine clauses is, however, more problematic.[122] Two of the clauses (both of which had the effect of reducing the possibilities for amercements imposed by the justices in eyre), were

---

[115] In the numbering of these clauses I follow the enumeration of *Stubbs' Charters* (which is also the enumeration followed by Treharne and Sanders). The numbers beside the clauses in the *Stats. Realm* edition of the text refer to the corresponding chapters of the statute of Marlborough.

[116] The first clause has been entirely recast for the Provisions, and now allows lords to distrain for suit of court if they can show that their tenant is obliged to perform suit of court by the wording of his charter, or that he or his ancestors had customarily performed suit of court prior to 1230. The second clause has been amended to make the coheir who holds the share of the eldest coheir responsible for performing suit (with contributions from his fellow coheirs). The third clause has been amended to insert an additional stage of mesne process before a tenant can get judgment against his lord by default, while the fourth clause (also part of clause 3 of the Provisions) has been amended to ensure that lords can only recover damages for withdrawals of suit when this has begun during the period they held their lordship, and to stop them recovering suit by default.

[117] Above, pp. 343–4.   [118] Above, n. 103.   [119] Above, n. 104.

[120] Clauses 4, 5 and 8: above, n. 44.

[121] Thus clauses 9–10 of the Provisions are clearly a response to clause 1 of the 'Petition' (but also cover the case of the tenant who has been in wardship and whose lord refuses to surrender his lands to him when he comes of age); clause 13 of the Provisions is clearly a response to clause 19 of the 'Petition' (but also covers sessions held by escheators and other holders of inquisitions); clause 14 of the Provisions is clearly a direct response to clause 10 of the 'Petition'; clause 21 of the Provisions is clearly a response to part of clause 14 of the 'Petition' (but also covers crown inquests other than coroners' inquests); and clause 22 is clearly a response to clause 21 of the 'Petition' (but establishes the more general principle that the *murdrum* fine is not payable in the case of accidental deaths).

[122] These are clauses 11, 12, 16, 17, 18, 19, 20, 23 and 24.

perhaps suggested by that phrase in clause 14 of the 'Petition' which talked of the 'many other grievances of the pleas of the Crown'.[123] We know that legislation was being contemplated in at least one, and possibly two, of the areas covered by two others of these clauses as early as February 1259, since there is a reference to this in the letters patent of the King's Council and the 12 of 22 February.[124] Four of the clauses seem to be concerned with asserting the rights of the King and of royal justice against seignorial usurpation, or to be directed against seignorial wrongdoing; and are perhaps to be associated with attempts by the King and his followers to rally support from the gentry against their magnate and baronial opponents, a phenomenon also perhaps to be seen in the promises made by the King's Council and the 12 on 22 February.[125]

There also survive a total of five texts of a rather different version of the Provisions of Westminster:

(i) *British Library, Cotton MS. Vespasian E. III, ff. 91r–92v (and 93r).* This is a French text of the Provisions of Westminster with a number of significant differences from the 'official' Latin text.[126] It is found in one of the manuscripts of the annals of Burton, and is immediately followed in that manuscript (without any kind of break) by a text of the memoranda recording other decisions taken at the Westminster Parliament.[127] A single clause (corresponding to clause 24 of the Latin text) occurs in the middle of these administrative memoranda. This text was printed *in extenso* in the late seventeenth century by William Fulman and again by H. R. Luard in 1864.[128]

(ii) *British Library, Cotton MS. Vespasian E. III., ff. 94r–95v.* This is an unskilled and clumsy Latin translation of the French text found in the same manuscript (or rather of an earlier and more accurate version of the French text from which the text in this manuscript was derived),[129] of interest principally

---

[123] Clauses 23 and 24 (though note that the former was not in fact a crown pleas amercement). Clause 23 could also have arisen from consideration of clause 13 of the 'Petition' (about amercement for default of the common summons at the eyre). Amercement for default of the common summons (whatever the extenuating circumstances) was not abolished; but a closely related grievance was.

[124] Their promise is to observe whatever the council ordains between then and the feast of All Saints on the subjects of 'suite de curz', 'amerciemenz', 'gardes socages' and 'ses fermes': Treharne and Sanders, *Documents*, p. 132. The first is clearly a reference to clauses 1–3 of the Provisions, the third a reference to clause 12 of the Provisions and the fourth perhaps a reference to clause 20 of the Provisions. For the possible source of the legislation on socage wardship see Brand, 'Contribution of the Period of Baronial Reform', p. 184.

[125] These clauses are clause 11 (against distraints made outside the fee or in the highway other than by the King); clause 16 (reserving pleas of false judgment to the King); clause 17 (asserting the sheriff's right to release animals taken in distraint, even if taken within franchises); clause 18 (asserting that a royal writ was required to make a tenant answer for his free tenement and to force free tenants to serve as jurors).

[126] These are discussed below.

[127] For those memoranda see above, n. 108. For this manuscript see above, p. 327. The Lichfield MS. of the Burton annals breaks off before the corresponding point has been reached.

[128] *Rerum Anglicarum Scriptores*, pp. 428–31; *Annales Monastici*, I, 471–6 (and 478).

[129] Powicke thought that it was 'an earlier and incorrect, though official translation', 'a rather careless draft by a clerk who did not follow the original intelligently or who wrote it from dictation' (Powicke, 'Some Observations on the Baronial Council', p. 128 and n. 4). Treharne, more perceptively, characterized the text as 'very poor, the language often proving obscure,

because of those passages where it is clear that it is translated from a text that does not contain the errors in the French text in the same manuscript.[130] Again it was printed *in extenso* by both Fulman and Luard.[131]

(iii) *British Library, Cotton MS. Nero D. I, ff. 139r–140v.* This is a second French text of the Provisions of Westminster and closely related to the French text found in the Burton annals. It is found in the *Liber Additamentorum* of Matthew Paris, but was one of the texts added to that volume after Matthew's death. It immediately follows in this manuscript a copy of the memoranda recording decisions taken at the Westminster Parliament. Its chief peculiarity is that it is immediately followed in the manuscript by two clauses in Latin which bear a close resemblance to clauses nine and 11 of the *Providencia Baronum* in the two Cambridge manuscripts, but which also show some signs of subsequent revision.[132] Jacob printed the last six clauses of this version plus the two Latin clauses, but merely noted that the other clauses of this version were (with the exception of one significant variant) much as printed in the Burton annals.[133] Jacob's comment is, however, misleading for there are a number of important differences between the two texts. Appendix V reproduces the whole of this text, noting in the footnotes significant variants between this version and the version found in the Burton annals and the other French versions about to be discussed.

(iv) *Gonville and Caius College, Cambridge, MS. 205/111, pp. 438–50.* This third French text of the Provisions of Westminster is likewise closely related to the texts founded in the Burton annals and the *Liber Additamentorum*. It is in the manuscript written by Robert Carpenter II of Hareslade already discussed in connexion with the *Providencia Baronum*.[134] This text has never been printed although its existence was noted by Denholm-Young.[135]

(v) *British Library, Stowe MS. 386, ff. 6v–8r.* Another French text of the Provisions of Westminster is to be found in this legal manuscript, probably originally compiled at the end of the thirteenth and beginning of the fourteenth centuries. It is in a section of the manuscript which contains mainly statutes from the 1225 reissue of Magna Carta onwards, plus a few minor legal

---

sometimes meaningless, and, in one case at least, actually misleading' and suggested that it was 'a very clumsy and unprofessional attempt to translate into Latin the French text already copied into the chronicle': Treharne, *Baronial Plan*, pp. 165–6.

[130] E.g. in the first clause it correctly states that it is 'viginti novem annis transactis et dimidio' since the King's crossing into Brittany, where the French text mentions only 'vint et nof anz'. For other such passages see the footnotes to Appendix V.

[131] *Rerum Anglicarum Scriptores*, pp. 436–436 bis; *Annales Monastici*, I, 480–5.

[132] Thus clause 9 now has an introductory phrase justifying the extension of writs of entry outside the degrees ('propter fraudem que passim fieri consuevit'); the specimen writ no longer uses the names of prominent members of the King's Council (Roger de Mortimer and Peter de Montfort) but substitutes initials and also has one additional phrase ('per formam dicte dimissionis'), and apparently contemplates the addition of another at the end ('addi post hec clausula: Et quod idem talis ei defecit [?read: deforciat] ut dicit'). So too in clause 11 (which appears here only in a much garbled form), the revision appears to have removed one of the justifications for extending the availability of the assize of mort d'ancestor.

[133] Jacob, *Studies*, pp. 375–6.   [134] Above, pp. 335–6.

[135] Denholm-Young, 'Robert Carpenter', pp. 31, 34–5 (*Collected Papers*, pp. 182, 185–6).

treatises.[136] A second part of the same manuscript contains early Year Book reports of the late thirteenth and early fourteenth centuries.[137] This text has some hybrid features. Its incipit describes it as being a text of the 1263 reissue of the Provisions of Westminster, and it is indeed prefaced by a somewhat modified French translation of the royalist preamble to that reissue.[138] However, the text that follows is (with the exception of a single clause), a close relative of the other French texts of the 1259 Provisions, and it does not omit the clause corresponding to clause 14 of the 1259 Latin version (about mortmain alienations), which was omitted in 1263, or include the two new clauses added to the legislation in 1263.[139] This text has never been printed.

Previous scholars knew only of the French texts of the Provisions in the manuscript of the Burton annals and in the *Liber Additamentorum*.[140] They assumed that the French text represented the original version of the Provisions of Westminster, the version in which they were approved by Parliament and read out in Westminster Hall on 24 October, and that it was then subsequently translated into Latin for circulation as the 'official' text of the legislation.[141] Treharne conceded that the process of translation involved 'defining, hardening, and clearing up many of the less precise passages of the informal Anglo-French'.[142] But the differences between the French and 'official' Latin texts are wider even than this, and cannot be explained as being simply the result of translation. As Treharne himself noted (but did not explain) the

---

[136] This section of the manuscript runs from f. 2 to f. 77. The latest statute it contains is the 1307 Statute of Fines and Attorneys at ff. 76v–77r. It is possible that the early fourteenth-century statutes are an early addition to the original manuscript. A later addition (in a different hand) at ff. 88r–89v is a copy of the Statute of Northampton of 2 Edw. III. The legal treatises include Fet Asaver, Casus Placitorum, Hengham Parva and Cadit Assisa.

[137] This section of the manuscript runs from f. 78 to f. 220 (the front and back covers and first and last folios contain music). The dated material includes reports from the Cambridgeshire eyre of 1299 and from the crown pleas side of the 1302 Cornish eyre, as also of various Bench terms between Michaelmas 1300 and Hilary 1305.

[138] 'Lan del Incarnaciun nostre seynur mil ans deus cent et seysaunte deus, Le rengne le rey Henri fiz Jhon le rey quarantime sept, de nostre fraunche volunte et en nostre plene pouste per nous et nostre conseyl de nus feals et leals fetes fut cestes constitucions souz escrit a la convenablete de la terre par nus et par nostre conseyl, en ceste manere pupplez'. For Latin texts of this reissue see Brand, 'Contribution of the Period of Baronial Reform', pp. 34–7.

[139] The one exception is the clause corresponding to clause 17 of the Latin text (on distraint and the action of replevin). This appears out of place (immediately after the clause on succession corresponding to clauses 9 and 10 of the Latin text). It reads: 'Purveu est ke [si] les avers de alcun humme seyint pris et atort detenuz e le visconte apres la pleynte a li fete les avers sanz desturbement e sanz contradiccion de lui ke les avers prit les purra deliverer si de hors franchise furent pris; e si denz franchise cel maneres de avers furent pris e les baylifs de franchise cels ne vodrunt delivrer dunc le viconte pur defalte de baylifs les avers fra delivrez.' This is recognizably a slightly bungled version of a French translation of the Latin text. For the wholly different phrasing of the same clause in the 'French' version of the Provisions see Appendix V.

[140] Jacob, *Studies*, pp. 72–3; Powicke, 'The Baronial Council', pp. 127–30; Treharne, *Baronial Plan*, pp. 165–6; Treharne and Sanders, *Documents*, p. 136, n.

[141] This appears to be the assumption of Jacob (*Studies*, pp. 87–8). It is certainly the assumption of Powick, ('The Baronial Council', pp. 127–8; *King Henry III and the Lord Edward*, p. 400) and of Treharne (*Baronial Plan*, pp. 165–7; Treharne and Sanders, *Documents*, p. 21).

[142] Treharne, *Baronial Plan*, p. 166.

'official' Latin text omits two clauses found in all the French texts.[143] There are also major differences in the substance of certain of the clauses. Two crucial provisos which are found in the 'official' Latin text of that part of clause 3 which deals with the lord's action for the withdrawal of suit of court (one making it plain that lords are not to be allowed to recover damages if a withdrawal of suit has taken place before they had gained possession of the seignory concerned; the other stipulating that there was to be no judgment by default in this new action), are not to be found in the French text. In the French version of clause 7 of the Provisions there is no mention of the possibility of judgment being given by default in the action of *quare impedit*, though there is in the 'official' Latin text.[144] Less important but still of some significance is the difference between the Latin version of clause 4, which exempts those holding lands in several hundreds from attendance at the sheriff's tourn other than in the hundred where they are living ('nisi in ballivis ubi fuerint conversantes'), and the French version of the same clause, which exempts them from attendance only in hundreds where they have no house ('fors la ou il unt mansiun'); and the difference between the French version of clause 13, which allowed only the chief justiciar and the justices of the general eyre to amerce for default of the common summons, and the Latin version which restricted it to the chief justiciar and the itinerant justices (and thus allowed the justices of forest eyres to continue to impose such amercements).

The most likely explanation for these differences between the French text and the 'official' Latin text is that the French text in fact represents not the final French text from which the 'official' Latin text was translated, but a penultimate draft which was subject to a number of revisions before being finally approved. We therefore have in this text yet another piece of evidence about the drafting process which lies behind the final 'official' Latin text of the Provisions of Westminster, and we can see that technical changes were being made in the legislation even at this late stage in its drafting.[145]

Although October 1259 saw the enactment into law of the Provisions of Westminster, it did not mark the end of the evolution and development of the text of those Provisions. In this respect also the Provisions of Westminster resemble the first issue of Magna Carta of 1215. Just as Magna Carta only reached a definitive form with the reissue of 1225 (after earlier revisions carried out for the reissues of 1216 and 1217), so too the Provisions of Westminster only reached their final form in 1267 with the enactment of the statute of

---

[143] *Ibid.*, p. 166: the two clauses are those prohibiting coroners, sheriffs or other bailiffs amercing vills for non-attendance at inquests and prohibiting justices, sheriffs and other bailiffs from amercing vills for failure to follow the hue and cry, where this has not been raised for good cause.

[144] There may also have been a difference in the provisions regarding mesne process in the action of *quare impedit* between the two texts: but it is difficult to be absolutely certain since the French texts all appear to be corrupt at this point.

[145] It may even be that two of our texts of the French version preserve in their separate variant readings evidence that this penultimate version of the Provisions was written down on a separate roll: see Appendix V, end of clause I (and n. 6).

Marlborough, though in this case there was only one intermediate revision, that undertaken for the first reissue of 1263. A detailed examination of this process is, however, beyond the scope of the present paper.[146]

This paper has shown that it is possible, thanks to the fortunate survival of the relevant documentation, to trace the evolution of the legislation enacted in October 1259 as the Provisions of Westminster through a whole series of preliminary stages. The initial stage was when some of the complaints which were ultimately to be answered by the legislation were included in the miscellaneous collection of grievances and demands known to historians as the 'Petition of the Barons', which was compiled in connexion with the Oxford Parliament of June 1258. The next stage in the process is represented by a preliminary French draft of 11 clauses of legislation which survives in a single and hitherto unknown text in a Philadelphia manuscript. This was probably prepared by a committee including legal experts for the Parliament of February 1259. A Latin translation of this French draft, incorporating a number of important changes in its content, dates from March 1259 and represents a third stage in the evolution of the legislation. This probably incorporates amendments made when the draft was considered by Parliament, but takes its current form (and was translated into Latin) because the amended draft was intended for circulation to a wider public. A fourth stage in the development of the legislation is represented by the various French texts of the Provisions of Westminster, which contain two clauses omitted from the final 'official' Latin version and a number of other significant differences from that version. This seems to represent the penultimate stage in the drafting process: a draft of the legislation prepared for discussion at the October Parliament of 1259. There are still some important gaps in our evidence. In particular, no text has so far been discovered (and probably none survives) of the initial drafting stage of the 15 clauses included in the Provisions of Westminster which are not included in the *Providencia Baronum*. It seems likely that a draft of these clauses was prepared for the April Parliament of 1259, a Parliament about which we are very ill-informed, for no record survives of any of its other decisions. It is also difficult to be certain just how typical the drafting process we have been able to trace was. Clearly the political circumstances were quite exceptional in 1258–9, and it is probably this fact that accounts for the survival of so much material from the drafting process. But it may well be that the process of drafting the major Edwardian statutes was not so very different from what these documents tell us lies behind the enactment of the Provisions of Westminster. In any case, the evidence which does survive from 1258–9 provides us with a rare insight into what normally remains a wholly obscure process: the drafting of legislation in thirteenth-century England.

---

[146] This process is discussed in Brand, 'Contribution of the Period of Baronial Reform', pp. 32–43.

APPENDIX I: *Significant variants in the text of the Petition of the Barons in Bodleian Library, MS. Dugdale 20, ff. 138v–140r.*

Clause 1:

(i) begins 'petunt barones' not 'petunt comites et barones'.

(ii) reads 'libere possessionem terre patris sui habere capiat', instead of 'libere ingrediatur possessionem patris'.

(iii) reads 'et ita fiat de fratre vel sorore, et ita seysina avunculi si obierit sine herede ad nepotem suum filium fratris propinquioris primogenitum, et si frater non habeatur ad liberos sororis vel sororum, et sic de ceteris', instead of 'et ita fiat de fratre vel sorore et de avunculo scisito, si obierit sine herede ad nepotem suum filium primogeniti, et si frater non habeatur ad liberos fratris vel sororis, et sic deinceps' (the Dugdale MS. reading makes better sense).

(iv) reads 'per rationabile relevium et homagium et servicium domino feodi facienda', instead of 'per rationabile relevium et homagium et relevia domino feodi facienda' (the Dugdale MS. reading makes better sense).

(v) adds 'graviter' before 'secundum quantitatem delicti puniatur'.

Clause 3: reads 'tenementorum suorum que sunt de feodis suis talium heredum usque ad legitimam etatem ipsorum', instead of 'tenementorum suorum qui sunt de feodis suis, et heredum usque ad legitimam etatem ipsorum' (the Dugdale MS. reading makes better sense).

Clause 4:

(i) reads 'fidelibus hominibus suis', instead of 'ad fideles suos'.

(ii) reads 'contingere vel evenire', instead of 'evenire vel emergere'.

Clause 5: omitted.

Clause 7: reads 'qui perambulacioni omnium hominum Anglie', instead of 'qui per ambulacionem proborum hominum et per quintamdecimam partem omnium bonorum hominum Anglie'. Here both texts are probably defective and the original text probably read 'qui perambulacione proborum hominum et per quintadecimam omnium bonorum hominum Anglie'.

Clause 8:

(i) reads 'de terris suis propriis et tenencium suorum de novo', instead of 'de terris suis propriis et tenementorum suorum de novo arentatis'. Here again both texts are defective and the original text probably read 'de terris suis propriis et tenencium suorum de novo arentatis'.

(ii) reads 'unde dominus rex vendicat sibi maritagium heredum talium qui ita tenent, et nichilominus servicium sibi indebit' integre', instead of 'unde dominus rex vendicat sibi custodiam heredum talium et nichilominus vendicat servicium omne inde debitum'. Both texts are probably defective.

Clause 9: reads 'totius patrie' instead of 'totius regni'.

Clause 10 (placed after clause 12): omits the 'non' in this clause (which perhaps makes better sense).

Clause 11: reads 'desicut ipsi omnia servicia inde debita domino regi sustineant ut medii', instead of 'cum servicia inde debita domino regi sustineant ut medii'.

Clause 14: reads 'non venerint, omnes de etate xij annorum omnis villat' graviter amerciantur', instead of 'non accesserint, omnes de etate xij annorum predictarum iiij villatarum graviter amerciabuntur'.

Clause 15: reads 'possit firmare castrum supra portum maris vel in insulis infra mare inclusis', instead of 'possit firmare castrum supra portum maris vel supra insulam infra inclusam'.

Clause 16: reads 'Item petunt remedium de vicecomitibus, firmariis ac aliis ballivis libertatum qui capiunt comitatus et ballivas ad firmam, qui habent', instead of 'Item de vicecomitum firmis at aliorum ballivorum liberorum qui capiunt comitatus et ballivas ad firmam qui eciam habent' (the Dugdale MS. reading makes better sense).

Clause 17: reads 'quantum ad diem illum', instead of 'quo ad diem'.

Clause 18:
   (i) reads 'aliquam partem terre, vel duas acras vel tres vel plus vel minus sine manso eidem adjacente', instead of 'aliquam partem terre, scilicet duas acras terre vel plus vel minus sine mansione eidem adjacente'.
   (ii) reads 'tunc pro voluntate vicecomitis amerciatur et dicitur cape finem quia non venit et hoc sine judicio', instead of just 'tunc pro voluntate sua amerciabitur'.

Clauses 19 and 20: omitted.

Clause 21:
   (i) omits 'regni'.
   (ii) reads 'coronatorem' for 'coronatores'.
   (iii) after 'visum factum est' adds 'de ipsis mortuis secundum legem terre'.
   (iv) reads 'et cum' for 'et quia'.

Clause 23: reads 'mercandisis suis' instead of 'mercibus suis'.

Clause 25: supplies the necessary 'vendunt' instead of the 'tradunt' supplied by Stubbs.

Clause 27: reads 'inde feodant' for 'infeodant'.

Clauses 28 and 29 omitted.

APPENDIX II: *Significant variants between the text of the* **Providencia Baronum** *in Gonville and Caius MS. 205/111 and that in Cambridge University Library, MS. Mm. I. 27.*

In the following notes 'the Jacob text' refers to the text of the *Providencia Baronum* taken from Camb. Univ. Lib., MS. Mm. I. 27, printed by E. F. Jacob in *Studies in the Period of Baronial Reform and Rebellion, 1258–1267* (Oxford Studies in Social and Legal History, VIII, 1925), pp. 366–9; 'the Treharne and Sanders text' to the text printed from the same manuscript in *Documents of the Baronial Movement of Reform and Rebellion* selected by R. F. Treharne and edited by I. J. Sanders (Oxford, 1973), pp. 122–30.

1. Reads 'a tempore conquestus' and not just 'tempore conquestus' at p. 366, line 7 of the Jacob text; clause 3 of the Treharne and Sanders text.

2. Reads 'quietanciam' for 'quietam clamanciam' at p. 366, lines 9–10 of the Jacob text; clause 3 of the Treharne and Sanders text.

3. Reads 'Illi autem qui nec per formam cartarum suarum ad sectam tenentur, nec ab antiquo sectam facere consueverunt nisi quod noviter' for 'Illi autem qui nec sectam facere consueverunt nisi quidem noviter' at p. 366, lines 10–11 of the Jacob text; clause 4 of the Treharne and Sanders text.

4. Reads 'hujusmodi seysina' for 'huius habere seisinam' at p. 366, line 14 of the Jacob text; clause 4 of the Treharne and Sanders text.

5. Reads 'ut' for 'et' at p. 366, line 17 of the Jacob text; clause 5 of the Treharne and Sanders text.

6. Reads 'convenerint, ostendere' for 'venerint et ostendere' at p. 367, line 18 of the Jacob text; clause 10 of the Treharne and Sanders text.

7. Reads 'celeritate' for 'sceleritate' at p. 367, line 25 of the Jacob text; clause 11 of the Treharne and Sanders text.

8. Reads 'consuetudines' for 'constituciones' at p. 368, line 4 of the Jacob text; clause 13 of the Treharne and Sanders text (Camb. Univ. Lib., MS. Mm. I. 27 also in fact reads 'consuetudines').

9. Reads 'balliam illam' for 'balliam' at p. 368, line 14 of the Jacob text; clause 15 of the Treharne and Sanders text.

10. Reads 'nec compellantur ad eum' with the words 's[cilicet] turnum' interlined above for 'eum turnum' at p. 368, line 19 of the Jacob text; clause 16 of the Treharne and Sanders text.

11. Reads 'villis' for 'illis' at p. 368, line 20 of the Jacob text (Camb. Univ. Lib., MS. Mm. I. 27 also in fact reads 'villis'). Treharne and Sanders, clause 16 reads 'villis'.

12. Reads 'Illuc' for 'Illud' at p. 368, line 20 of the Jacob text; clause 17 of the Treharne and Sanders text.

13. Reads 'condictum' with the words 'simul edictum' interlined above for the 'contradictum' at p. 368, line 21 of the Jacob text; clause 17 of the Treharne and Sanders text (Camb. Univ. Lib., MS. Mm. I. 27 also in fact reads 'condictum').

14. Reads 'tollantur' with the words 'p. capiantur' interlined above for 'capiantur' at p. 368, line 22 of the Jacob text; clause 17 of the Treharne and Sanders text.

15. Reads 'insuper' with the words 'p. eciam' interlined above for 'insuper' at p. 368, line 23 of the Jacob text; clause 18 of the Treharne and Sanders text.

16. Reads 'proceribus condictum' with the words 'i[d est?] baronibus'

interlined above 'proceribus' for 'proceribus contradictum' at p. 368, lines 24–5 of the Jacob text; clause 18 of the Treharne and Sanders text (Camb. Univ. Lib., MS. Mm. I. 27 also in fact reads 'proceribus condictum').

17. Reads 'actione' with the words 'i[d est?] placito' interlined above for 'actione' at p. 368, line 25 of the Jacob text; clause 18 of the Treharne and Sanders text.

18. Reads 'condictum' for 'contradictum' at p. 368, line 31 of the Jacob text; clause 20 of the Treharne and Sanders text (Camb. Univ. Lib., MS. Mm. I. 27 also in fact reads 'condictum').

19. Reads 'accio' with the words 's[cilicet] placitum' interlined above for 'accio' at p. 368, bottom line of the Jacob text; clause 21 of the Treharne and Sanders text.

20. Reads 'hoc casu' for 'huiusmodi causis' at p. 369, line 4 of the Jacob text; clause 23 of the Treharne and Sanders text.

21. Reads 'ut videlicet' for 'videlicet' at p. 369, line 9 of the Jacob text; clause 24 of the Treharne and Sanders text.

22. Reads 'impotencia' for 'impetencia' at p. 369, line 10 of the Jacob text; clause 24 of the Treharne and Sanders text.

23. Reads 'essoniare, cum per attornatum causa possit ventilari' with the letters 'ri' interlined above the last two letters of 'essoniare' for 'essoniari, cum per attornatum possit ventilari' at p. 369, line 13 of the Jacob text; clause 24 of the Treharne and Sanders text (Camb. Univ. Lib., MS. Mm. I. 27 also in fact includes the additional 'causa').

24. Reads 'attornatis' for 'attornatus' at p. 369, line 15 of the Jacob text; clause 24 of the Treharne and Sanders text (Camb. Univ. Lib., MS. Mm. I. 27 also in fact reads 'attornatis').

25. Reads 'condictum' for 'contradictum' at p. 369, lines 18–9 of the Jacob text; clause 25 of the Treharne and Sanders text (Camb. Univ. Lib., MS. Mm. I. 27 also in fact reads 'condictum').

26. Reads 'ipsos' for 'ipsum' at p. 369, line 20 of the Jacob text; clause 25 of the Treharne and Sanders text.

APPENDIX III: *The* **Liber Additamentorum** *version of the* **Providencia Baronum** *in British Library, Cotton MS. Nero D. I, f. 82r.*

The numbering of the clauses and subclauses has been supplied by the editor.

Heading 'Hec est nova provisio magnatum Anglic publicata apud Novum Templum mense marcio anno regni regis Henrici xliij° propter communem utilitatem tocius regni et ipsius regis de cujus consensu et voluntate processit ipsa provisio et publicatio'.

[1] [i] Justum et conveniens esse videtur ut scilicet tenens quando ex forma sui feffamenti tenetur ad sectam per verba in carta sua contenta eam faciat in forma feffamenti sui.

[ii] Illi autem qui feffati sunt per cartas continentes servicium certum pro

omni servicio et consuetudine et per specialia verba in cartis contenta ad ipsam sectam faciendam de cetero non teneantur.

[iii] Illi autem qui 'a' tempore conquestus vel a tempore ultra quod accio non conceditur sectam continuo fecerint pro tenementis suis eam faciant sicut antiquitus facere consueverunt nisi postmodum inde quietanciam habuerint.

[iv] Illi autem qui nec per formam cartarum suarum ad sectam tenentur nec ab antiquo sectam facere consueverunt nisi quidem noviter per districcionem et voluntatem magnatum aut aliorum ad ipsam faciendam sunt coacti de cetero ad ipsam faciendam non teneantur nec ab aliquo tempore valeat dominis hujusmodi seisina ut per eam accionem aliquam contra tenentes instituere possint.

[2] Provisum est insuper

[i] ut si hereditas de qua secta una tantummodo debetur aut 'ad' participes plures ejusdem hereditatis aut forte ad plurium manus hereditas illa per feffamentum perveniat unica inde fiat secta prout si hereditas integra fuerit fieri debuit aut consuevit, et participes hereditatis predicte contribuant ad sustentacionem secte predicte;

[ii] simili eciam modo contribuere teneantur qui ex feffamento tenent hujusmodi hereditatem nisi feffator eorum eos inde debeat et posset adquietare.

[3] Videtur autem conveniens

[i] quod si dominus curie contra hanc provisionem ad sectam faciendam distringat tunc ad querelam tenentis attachietur quod ad diem brevem sibi prefigendum veniat ad curiam domini regis inde responsurus dum tamen unica precedat essonia et si fuerit imfra regnum; et interim deliberentur averia si que capta fuerint occasione predicta et deliberata permaneant quousque placitum inter eos fuerit terminatum;

[ii] et si illi de quibus querela facta fuerit ad diem sibi per essoniatorem suum datum venire contempserint tunc procedatur ad districcionem per terras et catalla sua quod veniant ad alium diem sibi prefigendum;

[iii] et si tunc ad diem illum non venerint tunc ille dominus curie seisinam amittat illius secte et tenens inde quietus recedat donec ipse qui sectam ipsam exigit sibi perquisierit per breve de recto si sectam illam ulterius exigere voluerit.

[iv] Si vero illi qui sectam exigere voluerint cum venerint ostendere non possint quod secta illa ad ipsos pertineat conquerentibus dampna sua restituant que per districcionem hujusmodi a tempore hujus constitucionis substinuerunt et conquerentes de secta illa quieti permaneant ut predictum est.

[4] [i] Similiter autem si tenentes sectam suam subtrahant ad quam per hanc constitucionem tenentur et quam hucusque fecerint, domini curie sub eadem celeritate justiciam suam consequantur ita quod si tenentes post districcionem factam per terras et catella ad curiam regis venire contempserint domini curie per defaltam tenentium seisinam suam recuperent de secta predicta donec tenentes inde sibi perquisierint si forte prius ad hujusmodi sectam de jure non tenebantur.

[ii] Et subtrahentes sectam illa debitam et consuestam ad dampna domini sui refundendum que per hanc subtraccionem a tempore hujus constitucionis sustinuerunt compellantur

[iii] De aliis autem sectis que ante constitucionem istam subtracte fuerant de quibus actio dominis curie competebat currat accio secundum easdem leges secundum quas currere consuevit.

[5] [i] De turno vicecomitis qui pro pace servanda provisus fuit et ubi essonia locum non habet nec admittitur attornatus sic provisum est ut nec episcopi nec abbates nec priores nec comites nec barones ibi necesse habeant convenire.

[ii] Similiter autem nec alii ampla feoda habentes per que ad legis et pacis observanciam satis sunt astricti, nisi specialiter et ob specialem causam ibi fuerint vocati; unde eciam contradictum est ut qui . . .

APPENDIX IV: *The French text of the* **Providencia Baronum** *in Philadelphia Free Library, Hampton L. Carson Collection, MS. LC 14.3, f. 202.*

The numbering of the clauses and subclauses has been supplied by the editor. This transcript appears with the permission of the Rare Book Department of the Free Library of Philadelphia.

[1] [i] De suite des courtz est purveu par le Rey e par le Barnage communement qe si nul tenant par la fourme de chartre de feoffement est tenu de suite fere face le solum la fourme de son feoffement.

[ii] # Ceus qe feffe sont par chartres ou il ieit certeyne rente nome por touz services et custumes tut yeit[1] suite especefie ne sunt pas tenuz a suite fere desoremes.

[iii] # Cil qe tenent de Cunquest ou de plus long temps e unt fet suite communement[2] pur lor tenemens outre le facent com il soleient auncienement fere.

[iv] # Cil qe sont novelement destreint a suite fere par force e par volente de seignurs ou de autres ne sont pas tenuz desoremes fere le ne le seignurage par encheson de cele manere suite ne pount action aver contre lor tenaunz.

[2] [i] # Si le heritage de[3] une soule suite est due descende a plusors heirs ne fra desore qe une soule suite sicom eole sout fere quant eole feust entiere, mes ly parceners del heritage eyderont a la syute fere e sustenir.

[ii] En mesmes la manere eyderont sil qe feoffe sont de mesme le heritage si il ne pount moustrer qe lor feffor aquiter les deive.

[3] [i] # Si li signur destreigne nul de ces tenantz a suite fere encontre la fourme de ceste provision dont a la pleinte le tenant serra le seignur attache a venir a la court le rey pur respondre de ceo a un bref jour qe lor ert assis. Et si ne averont qe une essoygne si il seient dedenz le reaume; e endementers serront delivere les avers al pleyntif si point iad pris par encheson de la suite e remeindrent delivres desqes le ple entre euz seit terminez.

---

[1] The text is clearly corrupt at this point.   [2] ? Read *continuelment*.   [3] ? Read *dunt*.

[ii] E si ly seignur ne vient garantir son essoygne al jour qe ly est asis lem ly destreindra par terres e par tenemens e par chateuz qe il vienge a un autre jour qe ly asis.

[iii] Et si donqe ne vigne si perdra sa seisine de la suite; et li tenant partira quites desqes li seignur vendra⁴ demander ¹la¹ suite par bref de dreit.

[iv] Et si le seignur ne peot moustrer qe la suite li aporteigne il estora a son tenant touz les damages qe il ad eu pens ceste constitucion par lavantdite destresce; et ly tenanz remeindra quites com il est avantdist.

[4] [i] En mesme la manere avera le seignur hastive dreiture de son tenant si ly sustret suite qe fere ly deyt par dreit et par ceste constitucion. En iteu manere qe si li tenanz apres qe il est destreint par terres e par chateuz ne vent a la court le rey le seignur pur la defaute de son tenant recuvera seisine de lavantdite suite deqes ly tenant par ley de terre se veyle purchaser si ¹il¹ quide qe par dreit suite ne ly ¹la¹ deyve.

[ii] Et si dreite suite a son seignur sutret il serra destreynt a rendre a son seignur touz les damages qe il avera eu par cele suite sustrete del temps de ceste constitucion.

[iii] # De autres suite qe furent sustretes devant ceste constitucion dont ly seygnurages aveynt action vers lor tenanz mesmes la action averont solonc les leys et les coustumes qe soleyent coure.

[5] [i] # Des tourns as viesconte pur la pes garder la ou ensoygne ne attorne ne est receu est il communement purveu qe abbe ne priour, conte ne baron ne autre qe ount large feez parount il sont tenuz a garder la pes e la ley nont mester a venir i, si il ne sont especiaument somons par especial encheson, dont il est communement purveu qe il ne seient amerciez tot ne veignent il a tel terme.

[ii] E en mesme la manere ces qe ne sont mye dedenz la baillye ou sont desturbez par maladie ou par autre noun poer et ceo seit testmonie par francs et par leus ne seit mye destreint si il ne seit grant bosoigne pur enqueste fere sicom il est avant dit.

[6] # Les fynz le⁵ soleynt estre donez as baillifs pur beu pleyder e sanz encheson ne seient mes donez.

[7] # Derechef est il purveu qe en play qe est appele 'unde nichil habet' desoremes seit le jor asis de treis symaignes en treis symaynes; en mesme la manere en lassise del dereyn presentement de eglise et en le play qe ensement est appele 'quare impedit' [f.202v]. Et ceo est pur ceo qe hom ne face boydie a patrons des eglises.

[8] # Des chartres de excepcions qe auchune gentz ount de rey purchace qe il ne seient nent jurez ne en enquestes ne en reconisances issi est il purveu qe si il ne seit grant bosoigne aver les a serment de ceux qe ceuz chartres ount, ceo pur grant assise, ne seit pas destreint a jurer mes en autre poynz salf seit a eux le privilege qe ly reys lor ad grante.

[9] [i] # Derichef il est purveu qe la action le bref qe est apele de entree ne

---

⁴ This has been altered in the MS. to *voudra*.
⁵ Read *ke*.

seit desoremes restreint a degres cum estre sout mes mesmes la prescripcion seit en cest accioun qe est en cele mort de auncestre.

[ii] La fourme del bref est ceste # Ly rey salue le visconte. Comandez a cely qe il adreit e sanz delay rende a B ᶦdeᶦ cel lieu le maner de Stok' ove les apurtenances qe celuy B lessa a celuy a terme qe ja est passe e qe a luy deit torner sicom is est dit; e si il ne face etc.

[10] # Des assoignes est il purveu qe nul ne seit destreint a jurer en sa garantye mes lem crerra la leaute celuy qe se assoygna solum la ley de terre. Mesmes cest est grantez a ceux qe sunt attornez en play ou pur defendre e autresi en languor.

[11] # Derechef est il purveu qe sicom la accion qe est de mortdancestre est grante contre les gardeyns issi ert grant⁶ qar lun bref porreit valer ou lautre par tut ne porreit pas. Et la ou en un meymes cas chesont cheent diverses actions la une ne tout pas lautre, mes nepurquant lem ne poet pas en un meymes cas ensemblement et ᶦaᶦ une foithe user ambedeux.

APPENDIX V: *The French draft text of the Provisions of Westminster in the* **Liber Additamentorum**: *British Library, Cotton MS. Nero D. I, ff. 139r–140v.*

The following text of the French draft version of the Provisions of Westminster is based on that in the *Liber Additamentorum*; but where that text is clearly defective I have emended it and relegated the actual reading of the manuscript to a footnote. I have also noted in the footnotes significant variants from the other manuscript versions of the text. In those footnotes Bi signifies the Burton annals French text; Bii the Burton annals Latin text (I have noted variants from this text only where they seem to indicate differences between the French text from which it was translated and the French text of Bi); C the Gonville and Caius text; S the text in British Library, Stowe MS. 386. For a discussion of these different versions see above pp. 267–9. The numbering of the clauses is mine.

*De sutes de curz a seignurs e purveu issi*¹

[1] De sutes de curz a seignurs est issi purveu ke nul ne seit destraint desoremes a suthe fere a la curt sun seignur si especiaument ne seit contenu en sa chartre ke il deive sa tere tenir par certein servise e fesant siwte a la curt sun seignur, si il u ces ancestres ne le eient fet devant le primer passage le rey ke ore est en² Bretayne, ceo est [f. 139v] asaver xxix anz ad passe e dimi.³ E si nul destraint sun tenant cuntre ceste purveance hastive dreiture en⁴ seit tenue en la curt le rei sicum il est purveu avant⁵ en est roule.⁶

---

⁶ Followed by a blank in the MS. above which is written ? *geners*.

¹ C's introductory heading is *E primes de sewytes de curs cument devent estre fetes*.

² MS. *hors de*. Bi and S read *en*; C *in*.

³ *e dimi* omitted in Bi, though Bii reads *viginti novem annis transactis et dimidio*. S omits *ceo . . . dimi*.

⁴ This word omitted in MS. but supplied from Bi, C.   ⁵ MS. *aval*.

⁶ *sicome il est purveu puis en apres* Bi; *si cum il est purveu apres en cest livre* C; *cum il est purvu apres* S; *sicut provisum est in rotulis de bancho* Bii.

[2] E si il avent ke heritage seit partie entre plusurs parceners de une[7] heritage ke seient cum un heir,[8] li einsne des parceners face la swte pur tuz les autres.[9] E les autres[10] aident al cust de la swte renablement.[11] E si plusurs tenans seient feffe[12] de mesmes cel heritage,[13] jaleplus ne pusse le seignur demander for une swte si cum devant est dit.

[3][14] [i] E si nuls seignurages lur tenans encuntre ceste purveance destreinent dunkes a la plainte le tenanz seient atachez ke il veinent a un bref jur a la curt le rei a respondre ent.[15] A quel jor il averunt un assoigne si il sunt en le reume.[16] E meintenant[17] les avers al plaintif seient deliverez ke par cele acheisun sunt pris e deliveres remainent dekes le play entre eus seit chevi.

[ii] E si ceus ki averunt la destresce fet al jur ke dune lur est par lassoignur u al primer jor si il ne seient assoignez facent defaute, dunkes seit mande al vescunte del pais ke il le face venir a un autre jor. E si dunkes ne veinnent sait mande[18] al vescunte ke il le destreine par kanke il unt en sa bailie, issi ke il respoine al rei des issues e ke il ait lur cors a un autre jur. E pus a cel jur si il ne veignent voit le plaintif sanz jur e les avers remainent delivers, issi ke les seignurages mes ne puissent destreindre par cel acheisun dekes atant ke il eient dereine par play en la curt le rey, sauf as seignurages lur draiture des servises quel ure ke il volent en[19] parler. E si les seignurages veinent en la curt le rey a respondre e les plaintifs poissent lur querele e lur plaintes[20] averer dunkes par jugement de la curt deit recuverer[21] ces damages[22] ke il averat eu par la destresce.[23]

[4] [i] De autre part si les tenanz sustreient a lur seignurages swtes[24] ke il deivent e ke il unt fet pus le devant dit terme par memes la hastive draiture dereinent[25] lur siwtes e recoverent lur damages[26] ensement cume les tenantz de eus.

[ii] Des swtes ke sustretes furent devant le devant dit terme curge la commune ley cum avant.[27]

---

[7] (For the last two words): *come* Bi.

[8] *ke surd cume de un heir* Bi.

[9] *parceners* C. [10] *autres parcenirs* C, S.

[11] Bi makes a mess of the middle of this clause. For the end of the preceding sentence and the whole of this sentence it reads: *al eine des parceners les autres parceners eident al cust a la syute fere resnablement.* Bii does not share this confusion.

[12] This word omitted in MS. but supplied from Bi, C and S. Luard misread the word as *fesse.*

[13] *de un heritage* C.

[14] C gives the heading *De la peyne de ceus ke vunt encontre les dereytes siutes fere* to this clause.

[15] C, S omit this word. Bi reads *a eus.*

[16] C omits the last five words. [17] MS. *meitenant.*

[18] C omits all the text between the two occurrences of *sait mande.*

[19] *ke il en osent* Bi. [20] *lur quereles* Bi, C, S.

[21] MS. *recuvere.* Bi, C, S (for last two words) have *recoverent.*

[22] S omits all the text between *ces damages* in this clause and *lur damages* in the following clause.

[23] *par achesun de cele destresce* Bi; *par la encheysun de cele destrece* C.

[24] MS. *cwtes.*

[25] *destreinent* Bi.

[26] S has lost the whole of the text between *lur damages* and *ces damages* in the previous clause (see n. 22).

[27] *curge a la comune lei communalement* Bi, though Bii reads *et currat communis lex sicut ante.*

De Turns de vescuntes

[5] Derichef purveu est ke as turns[28] de vescuntes ne veine erceveske, esweske, abbe, priur, cunte ne barun ne nule gent de religiun ensement ne femmes si il[29] ni eient especialment a fere, mes scient tenu les turns en la manere ke il furent tenuz es tens as auncestres nostre seignur le rey ke or est. E si nuls eient teres en plusurs hundres[30] ne seient pas destrainz ne ne veinent pas[31] as torns for la u il unt mansiuns[32] e scient tenuz solum la chartre de franchises[33] e solum co ke il furent tenuz en tens le roy Johan e le roy Richard.[34]

[6][35] Purveu est ensement ke en eire de justices ne en cunte ne en curt de barun ne en curt de franchome ne en franchise ne ailurs ne prenge lem mes fin pur bel pleider ne par issi ke la gent ne seient achesune.

[7][36] [i] Purveu est[37] ke en play de duarye ke est al banc doint hem[38] quater jurs par an al mains,[39] co est asaver a checun terme un jur. E si plus poet hem[38] doner plus doint hem.[38]

[ii] Ensement en assises[40] de derain present' e de bref quare impedit des eglises[41] ke sunt vodes doint hom jur[42] de quinzaine en quinzaine u de treis semaines en tres semaines solum co ke le pais est loienz u pres. E si celi ki est enplaide par le bref quare impedit ne veine al primer jur u ne face assoiner[43] sait atache ke il sait a un autre jor. E si a cel jor ne veine ne ne soit assoigne seit destraint par la grant destresce.[44] E pus al jor[45] si il ne veinge seit destraint par tutes sez teres e par tuz ses chateus la grant destresce sicum desus est dit.[46]

[8][47] Des chartres[48] ke lem ad purchace de estre quite des assises e des jurees

28 MS. *turs*; *turns* in Bi. 29 MS. *eles*; *il* in Bi, C, S. 30 *pais* in C.

31 *destreint ke il vyengent* in C.

32 *meysuns e mansiuns* in C; *mansiun* in Bi, S; *domicilia* in Bii.

33 MS. *franchise*; *franchises* in Bi; *les chartres de franchises* in C.

34 *le rei Richard et le rei Johan* in Bi; S reads (for all from *mansiun* onwards): *mes seyunt tenuz les turz sulum la manere quil furunt tenuz el tens le rey Richard et le rey Jhon*.

35 C supplies the heading: *Des fins ke sunt donez avant jugement*.

36 C supplies the heading *De jur aseer au Banc en play de Duere e de dereyn present e pur quey len desturbe presentement*.

37 *Derichef purveu est* Bi, C. 38 *lem* in Bi; *um* in C; *hom* in S.

39 S omits the last two words. 40 *essoines* in Bi, but *assisis* in Bii.

41 *e pur quey um desturb 'le' present 'de' convenable persone as eglises* in C.

42 this word is supplied from Bi, C; S reads *jurs*.

43 MS. *assoines*; *essonier* in Bi; *essonyer* in C; *essoyner* in S.

44 *destreynt par grant destrece cum de sus est dit* C; *seyt la distresse sicum desus est dit* S.

45 *e al autre jur* S.

46 *destreynt par teres e par chatels par la grant destresce sicum desus est dit* S. C omits the whole of the last sentence. Bi has a clearly corrupt version of the latter part of this clause (from n. 43): it reads *al autre jur si il ne vent i seit destreint par totes ses teres et ses chateus par la grant destresce sicome desus est dit*. Bii has a version of the last three sentences which makes better sense than any of the French versions and may be closer to the original. It reads: *Et si ille qui implacitatur per le quare impedit et non veniat ad primum diem nec se faciat essoniare, attachietur quod sit ad alium diem; et si ad diem illum non venerit nec essonietur distringatur per magnam districcionem sicut supradictum est. Et si ille ad primum diem faciat se essoniare si non ad secundum diem venerit per terras et catalla distringatur primo et postea si non venerit per omnes terras suas et omnia catalla distringatur per magnam districcionem sicut supradictum est.*

47 C supplies the heading: *De aquitance de serment par chartres le rey coment sera tenuz*.

48 *chartres le rey* C.

est issi purveu ke si justices veient ke dreiture ne pusse estre tenue sanz le serment de iceus ke la chartre averunt come[49] en grant assise u en poralee[50] u[51] la u il[52] sunt testomonie[53] en escriz u en chartres[54] u en attaintes u en autre cas ke ne poit estre termine saunz serment des chevalers, en cel[55] cas les face lem jurer, sauve a eus lur franchise ailurs.

[9][56] Nul desormes face destresce hors de[57] sun fe ne eins hel real chemin[58] u tote gent pount[59] aler saunz[60] le rey.

[10][61] [i] De autre part si il avent ke le seignur apres la mort sun tenant seisist en sa main ces teres par la reisun ke sun heir seit de denz age e pus kant leir vendrad a son age ne luy voile ces teres rendre sanz play[62] ke li eir recuvere par mort de auncestre[63] sa tere ensemblement ove les damages ke il averad eu par lachesun de la seisine[64] pus son age.

[ii] Ensement si li eir seit de age kant sun ancestre mort e le eir aparant sait[65] ke conu[66] seit e certein[67] en seit[68] le chef seignur ne le bote mie hors ne rens ne prenge ne rens ne ost forsulement face simple[69] seisine. E si le chief seignur le tenge hors par quei li covenge purchacer[70] bref de mort de ancestre u de cosinage[71] recuvere ses damages[72] ausi cum par bref de novel deseisine.

De gardes de socage[73]

[11] De garde de socage[74] est issi purveu ke si tere tenue seit[75] en socage seit tenu[76] en garde par ces parens par la reisun del air ke seit dedenz age ke le gardain ne pust wast fere[77] ne vente ne nul manere de destruction de la tere ke seit en sa garde mes saufment la gard al os lenfant[78] issi ke[79] kaunt il vendrad a sun age le gardein luy respoine leument de ces issues e de pruz de la chose sauve a luy ces renabeles mises. Ne il ne puisse le mariage vendre ne doner si al pru nun del enfant.

---

[49] MS. *ke; come* in Bi; *cum* in C, S.   [50] S omits the last three words.
[51] *un en autre liu* C.   [52] MS. *is; il* in Bi, C, S.
[53] *testmonie nome* C; *sunt summunes* S.   [54] *nomement en chartres ou en escrit* Bi.
[55] *tel* Bi, C.   [56] C adds the heading: *De destresces fere renables.*
[57] *fors en* Bi, but Bii reads *extra.*
[58] *ne en real chemin* Bi; *ne enz al real chemin* C; *ne en le real chemin* S.
[59] *passent et poent* Bi; Bii reads *ire possunt.*
[60] *saunz* is the reading of all the French manuscripts but must be an error for *sauf.* Bii reads *salvo rege* which looks like a translation of *sauf le rey.*
[61] C supplies this clause with the heading: *De eyrs ke recovrent lur eritage par bref de mort de ancestre.*
[62] C supplies *purveu est* at this point.   [63] *par bref de mort de ancestre* Bi.
[64] *detenue* Bi; *disseysine* S.   [65] Bi, C and S omit this word.
[66] *tenu* Bi (but *notus* in Bii); *e tenu pur eyr* C.
[67] C omits the last two words; S reads *et leir aparent et certeyn e conu seyt.*
[68] *enz* Bi; *seyt enz le eritage* C.   [69] *une simple* Bi, C, S.
[70] *par quei il eit cunge ke il pusse purchaser* Bi (but *unde oportet eum perquirere* in Bii); *par que li convynge ke il purchace* C; *par que il purchace* S.
[71] *novele desseysine* C.
[72] MS. *recurne;* Bi has *recovere,* C and S *recovere; sa tere e ses damages* Bi (but just *sua damna* in Bii).
[73] *De gardes de escuage* in MS. (but clearly wrong). This is the heading found in C.
[74] MS. *escuage.*   [75] *ke seit tenue* Bi, C, S.
[76] the last four words are omitted in C.   [77] S adds *ne exil;* Bii also adds *nec exilium.*
[78] *le heir* Bi, C.   [79] Bi omits *issi* (though Bii reads *ita quod*); S reads *et.*

[12]⁸⁰ De autre part purveu est ke escheitur, enquerur, justices assignez as assises prendre ne justices assignez as trespas⁸¹ oir e determiner ne nule autre manere de⁸² bailif eient poer de⁸³ gent⁸⁴ amercier pur defaute de commune sumunse forpris la chef justice e les justices erranz⁸⁵ de tuz plays.

[13]⁸⁶ Purveu est ensement ke nul hom⁸⁷ de religiun ne puise nule tere achater sanz le gre le seignur, co est asaver celi seignur ke est plus prochein saunz mahen.

[14]⁸⁸ Purveu est⁸⁹ des assoines ke nul desoremes ne seit destraint de serement fere al garantie del essoine ne en cunte ne aylurs.

[15]⁹⁰ Nul desoremes forpris le rey ne tenge plai en sa curt de fause jugement fet en la curt de sun tenant kar cel manere de pley apent⁹¹ al rey e a sa corone.

[16]⁹² Purveu est ke si nul⁹³ seit destraint e ces avers tenuz⁹⁴ cuntre wage e cuntre plegge li vescunte quant la plainte li serra fete fraunchement pusse les avers deliverer solum ley de la terre si il seient pris hors de franchise sanz cuntredire e sanz desturber celuy ki les avera pris.⁹⁵ E si il seient pris dedenz franchises e le bailif de la franchise ne les voile deliverer le vescunte les delivere par defaute⁹⁶ le bailif de⁹⁷ la franchise.⁹⁸

[17]⁹⁹ Purveu est ke¹⁰⁰ nul bailif ke acunte deit rendre si¹⁰¹ se sustreit de sun seignur ne¹⁰² ne voile sun acunte rendre e ne eit terre ne tenement dunt il pusse estre destraint sait athache par sun cors issi ke le vescunte en ki bailie il seit trove le face venir a rendre ses acuntes si il seit en arerages.

[18]¹⁰³ Purveu est ke nul haut hom desoremes pusse destraindre ces tenans a respondre de lur franc tenement ne de chose ke a lur franc tenement apent sanz bref le rey; ne ne face ces franc tenans jurer sanz lur gre desicum nul ne les put fere sanz especial comandement le rey.¹⁰⁴

---

⁸⁰ C adds the heading *De amercier pur defaute de commune summunce.*
⁸¹ *a plai de trespas* Bi; *a plaintes e trespas* C; *ne justices asingnez a pleynte de trespas u assises prendre* S.
⁸² Bi, C and S omit the last two words.   ⁸³ *ne puse* S.
⁸⁴ Bi omits this word.
⁸⁵ MS. *la chef justice errant* (also the reading of C); *e les justices erranz* is the reading of Bi and *u justices erranz* the reading of S.
⁸⁶ C adds the heading: *De terres doner a gent de religiun.*   ⁸⁷ *gent* S.
⁸⁸ C adds the heading: *De garentie des essoynes.*
⁸⁹ Bi, C add *ensement.*
⁹⁰ C adds the heading: *De play de faus judement.*
⁹¹ *partent* Bi; *apendent* C.
⁹² C adds the heading: *De avers pris en franchyse e hor de franchyses.*
⁹³ C adds *desoremes.*
⁹⁴ *retenuz* Bi (but Bii has *teneantur*).
⁹⁵ Followed in MS. by *les delivere* (which is redundant).
⁹⁶ MS. *devant*; *defaute* is the reading of Bi and C.
⁹⁷ MS. *ke*; *de* is the reading of Bi and C.
⁹⁸ The version of this clause in S is quite different and evidently a French translation of the Latin text. See n. 139 on p. 351 above.
⁹⁹ In the other manuscripts this clause follows clause [18]. C adds the heading: *De destrece pur acunte rendre.*
¹⁰⁰ S adds *si.*   ¹⁰¹ Bi, C, S omit this word.
¹⁰² *e si il* Bi, C; *e* S.
¹⁰³ C adds the heading: *De respondre de franc tenement e de serment fere.*
¹⁰⁴ *sanz especiaument ke si le rei le eit comande* Bi (Bii has *sine speciali mandato domini regis*).

[19]¹⁰⁵ Purveu est ke nuls fermers en tens de lur fermes ne facent vente, waste¹⁰⁶ ne exil de bois ne de meysuns ne de humages¹⁰⁷ ne de nul autre chose ke al tenemens ke il unt a ferme apent si il ne aient especial escrist ke menciun en face ke il pussent tele vente fere. E si il le facent e scient de co ateint rendent les damages.

Des amercimenz¹⁰⁸

[20] Justices desoremes errans ne amercierunt les vilees en lur eire porce ke chescun home de dusz aunz ne veinent as enquestes fetes devant coroner de mort de homme u de autre chose ke apent a la corone pur quei ke de memes les vilees veinent suffisantment¹⁰⁹ gent par quei lem pusse¹¹⁰ les enquestes fere.

[21] Nul coroner ne vescunte ne autre bailif desoremes ne amercie les vilees pur co ke il ne veignent as enquestes. Mes la u il trovent la defaute seit mis en roule le coroner e presente devant justices erranz ke unt poer¹¹¹ amercier les vilees e nul autre homme.

[22] En eire de justices desormes ne sait murdre esgarde de ceus ke sunt morz par mesaventure fors sulement de ceus ke sunt occis par felunnye.¹¹²

[23] Nul justice ne vescunte ne autre bailif desormes ne amercient les vilees pur uthas levi¹¹³ nient siwy¹¹⁴ si il ne seit leve pur renable achesun cum pur mort de humme de roberye [f. 140v] u de play u de autre cas semblable ke apent especialment a la corone.

[24] Derichef¹¹⁵ si un home¹¹⁶ seit vouche¹¹⁷ a garant de play de terre en eire de justices ne seit my amercie [pur ceo ke il ne est present, de si cum nul franc home ne deit estre amercie]¹¹⁸ pur defaute si del primer jur nun de venue de justices. Mes si le garant seit adunkes en memes le cuntes dunkes seit comande¹¹⁹ al vescunte ke il face venir al terz jur u al quart solum co ke il est loinz u pres si cum custume¹²⁰ est en eire de justices. E si il seit manant en un autre cunte dunkes eit renable somonse de quinzain solum la commune ley.¹²¹

---

¹⁰⁵ C adds the heading: *De ferme tenir a terme.*
¹⁰⁶ Bi and S omit this word (but Bii reads *wastum vendicionem nec exilium*).
¹⁰⁷ *homes* Bi, C; S omits the last two words.
¹⁰⁸ The heading supplied by C for this and the following three clauses is *De amerciemens de viles et de murdre devant justices.*
¹⁰⁹ *forsolement* C.
¹¹⁰ Bi, C and S add *covenablement.*
¹¹¹ Bi adds *a*; C and S add *de.*
¹¹² *par felonie morz* C.
¹¹³ MS. *lem*, followed by some letters partly erased; *huthes leve et* Bi; *hutheyses levez e* C; *huthes leve et* S.
¹¹⁴ *ansywy* C.
¹¹⁵ MS. *Deriches*; *Derichef* in Bi; *Derechif* in C; *Derechef* in S.
¹¹⁶ *si nul* Bi; *se nul home* S.
¹¹⁷ MS. *veuche*; *voche* in Bi, C and S.
¹¹⁸ *pur ceo . . . amercie* supplied from Bi. C also includes a similar passage: *pur ceo ke il le yeyt mye en present, desicum nul franc home ne deyt estre amercie.* The eye of the scribe of the main text (and the scribe of S) evidently jumped in copying from the first to the second occurrence of *amercie.*
¹¹⁹ *ceo* Bi (but *precipiatur* in Bii).
¹²⁰ *contenu* Bi.
¹²¹ *la commune usage de la terre* C.

[25]¹²² Si clerc seit rette de mort de humme u de roberye u de larcin u de autre¹²³ crime ke apent¹²⁴ a la corone e pus seit livere en bayl par le comandement le rey a dusze prudes homes ke il le eient par devant justices a un tel jur¹²⁵ u ke il seit lesse par plegges sanz le comandement le rey,¹²⁶ si les devant dit dusze u les avant dit plegges eient sun cors al primer jur avant par devant justices ne seient pas desoremez amerciez tut ne voile pas le clerc respondre ne a dreiture ester en la curt le rey de sicum il ne furent de autre¹²⁷ plegges ne meinparnurs¹²⁸ for de aver le clerc¹²⁹ avant a cel jor.¹³⁰

¹²² C adds the heading: *De clerk baylle par bayl.*
¹²³ *autre manere de* S.
¹²⁴ S adds *especialment.*
¹²⁵ Bi and C omit the last four words; S omits the last 11 words.
¹²⁶ *ou lesse par pleges par comandement le rei* Bi; *u lesse par plegges (followed by blank) le comandement le Rey*; S omits all from n. 125 onwards.
¹²⁷ *autre chose* Bi, C.
¹²⁸ MS. *mein par iurs*; *main pernant* Bi; *maynparnurs* C. S omits this and the preceding word.
¹²⁹ *le cors le clerc* Bi, C, S.
¹³⁰ Bi, C and S omit the last three words.

17

Hengham Magna: *A Thirteenth-Century English Common Law Treatise and its Composition*

Hengham Magna is a comparatively short English common-law treatise of the second half of the thirteenth century, generally believed to have been composed by Ralph de Hengham, perhaps the most distinguished, and certainly the best known, royal justice of that period. It is for the most part concerned with the technical—but, to contemporary litigants and their advisers, highly important—subject of the procedures appropriate in land litigation initiated by the writ of right; but it also deals, in passing, with topics of more general interest, such as the extent to which the county court could be considered to be a court of record, and the rules about warranty of land. Over fifty manuscript copies of the treatise still survive, almost all of them dating from the late thirteenth or early fourteenth centuries: their number suggests that it was, if only for a brief period, a popular work.

The noted antiquary John Selden was responsible for the appearance, in 1616, of the first printed edition of this treatise. It formed part of a composite volume which also included editions of Sir John Fortescue's *De Laudibus Legum Angliae* and of the other, and even shorter, treatise attributed to Ralph de Hengham, *Hengham Parva*. We owe a modern, critical edition of both this treatise and *Hengham Parva* to the labours of Professor William Huse Dunham junior, who based that edition (which appeared in 1932) on a thorough examination and evaluation of all the surviving manuscripts of the treatise he was able to discover (1).

My purposes in this article are four-fold: to show that the date of the composition of the treatise must be between 1260 and 1272 (and not between 1272 and 1275, as Dunham argued) (2); to demonstrate that the two names used in the treatise as the names of the two opposing litigants

---

(1) *Radulphi de Hengham Summae* (Cambridge Studies in English Legal History: Cambridge, 1932). A list of manuscripts containing the treatise known to Dunham appears on pp. lxxiii-lxxvii (nos. 1-58): to these should be added Oriel College Oxford MS. 46 (ff. 169-179), and the Corporation of London Records Office, *Liber Ordinationum* (ff. 106-115v). In the preparation of this article I have examined all these manuscripts other than the four at Harvard (nos. 37-40), and the manuscripts in the Bodleian Library and the Middleton MSS which contain only small fragments of the treatise (nos. 53, 55 and 56).

(2) A date of between 1256 and 1267 for the composition of the treatise was suggested by T. F. T. Plucknett in his review of Dunham's edition of the two treatises in (1933) 49 *L.Q.R.*, 445-447. As will be clear, I agree with some of Plucknett's criticisms of Dunham's dating criteria, but am not convinced by his alternative dating: and my criticisms were, in fact, formulated before I was aware of Plucknett's work on the subject.

are the names of real people, both of whom were connected with a single village in the county of Sussex, and that there is other evidence in the treatise connecting it with that village (and that the two names are not, therefore, simply fictitious ones, as Dunham thought) (3); to state my reasons for questioning the hitherto generally accepted attribution of the treatise's authorship to Ralph de Hengham; and to suggest an alternative candidate for the authorship of the treatise (4).

I

Dunham's opinion as to the date of *Hengham Magna* was that it "was composed by Hengham sometime after 20 November 1272, and before 15 April 1275" (5), and he was inclined to believe that it was "probably composed quite close to 1275" (6). It was absolutely certain, he asserted, that the treatise was written after 1267 because, as Woodbine had demonstrated, the mesne process described in the treatise for ensuring the attendance in court of the four knights sent to view a man who had essoined himself *de malo lecti* was "that which would obtain subsequent to the statute of Marlborough, 1267" (7). It was, furthermore, only slightly less certain that the treatise was written after 20 November 1272 (the date on which Edward I was proclaimed King of England): for none of the manuscripts which he had collated in detail (which included the two manuscripts that he considered to be the earliest in date of all the surviving manuscripts of the treatise) contained writs running in the name of Henry III in that section of the treatise which contained specimen examples of the different types of writ of right, while all these manuscripts contained at least one reference to Edward I as king, either there or elsewhere in the treatise (8). The treatise must, however, have been written prior to 15 April 1275, the date of the enactment of the statute of Westminster I, because in the earliest manuscripts the limitation date for the action of right given in the final paragraph of the treatise was that which obtained prior to the enactment of that statute and because early manuscripts refer to the possibility of parceners "fourching" in essoins, a practice forbidden by the statute, and also refer to the second attachment as forming part of the mesne process against the four knights sent to view a man who has

---

(3) *The Casus Placitorum, and Reports of Cases in the King's Courts, 1272-1278*, ed. W. H. Dunham (Selden Soc., lxix (1950)) p. xix.

(4) Throughout his edition of the treatise, Dunham refers to it as the *Summa Magna*: I have preferred the title used by Selden. The manuscripts employ a variety of different names for it.

(5) Dunham, *Radulphi de Hengham Summae*, p. lxi.

(6) Dunham, *op. cit.,* p. lxi, note 2.

(7) *Ibid.,* (and p. 33). Woodbine's argument (in *Four Thirteenth Century Law Tracts,* ed. G. E. Woodbine (New Haven, 1910), p. 20 note 1) was that the mesne process described in the treatise consisted of two attachments, *habeas corpus* and the grand distress: but that, had the treatise been composed before the Statute of Malborough, this mesne process would have included at least two writs of distress after the *habeas corpus* stage.

(8) Dunham, *op. cit.,* p. lxi, note 2. It is only fair to add that Dunham conceded the possibility that the "mention of Edward in the MSS . . . [was] a later insertion".

essoined himself *de malo lecti,* a stage of process abolished by the same statute (9). Additional evidence for a date close to 1275 for the composition of the treatise was, Dunham argued, provided by the wording of a passage referring to the statute of Westminster I found in later manuscripts of the treatise, a passage which he was inclined to believe the work of the author of the treatise (*10*).

There is no reason to quarrel with Dunham's arguments for a date prior to 15 April 1275 for the composition of the treatise. The true *terminus ante quem* for its composition, however, is the rather earlier one, of 16 November 1272 (the date of Henry III's death). Evidence that the treatise was composed during Henry III's lifetime is provided by two passages of the treatise. The first passage is one referring to a writ of Henry III's council to the justices of the Bench concerning the computation in leap years of the year and day allowed to a man who has essoined himself *de malo lecti* and who was subsequently pronounced sick by the knights sent to view him. In most manuscripts, Henry III's council is referred to as the "*consilio domini regis*", a phrase appropriate only to the council of a king who, at the time of writing, was still alive; and the year in which the writ was sent by them is referred to as "*anno regni sui xliiii*" where the *sui* must refer back to Henry III and necessarily again presupposes that at the time of composition Henry III was still alive (*11*). The second passage is the one at the very end of the treatise referring to the limitation date for the action of right. In two early manuscripts, the reference is to seisin of the land demanded "*die nec anno quibus Henricus rex avus Henrici regis qui nunc est fuit vivus et mortuus*", which clearly implies that at the time of writing Henry III was still alive (*12*). Now, while it is common enough for copyists to modernize passages in the manuscripts that they are copying—and it is this that explains the fact that all the surviving manuscripts, of which even the best are ". . . quite remote from any hypothetical original—at least three or four generations" (*13*), refer somewhere to Edward I as reigning monarch (*14*)—it is difficult, if not

---

(9) Dunham, *op. cit.,* pp. lxi-lxii (and pp. 25, 33, 50 and note 1).

(*10*) Dunham, *op. cit.,* pp. lxi, note 2, lxxx (and p. 25, note 5).

(*11*) Dunham, *op. cit.,* p. 11: "Et ideo iaci debet tertio die ante diem litis propter computationem dierum in anno bissextili, ut cum detur langido dies a die visus in unum annum et unum diem propter ipsum diem integrum infra tertium diem ante diem litis et eumdem diem litis possit salvari dies excrescens in anno bissextili et computari in integritate anni quo dictum essonium proiectum fuerit. Teste consilio domini regis, ac suo brevi inde directo iustitiariis suis in banco anno regni sui xliii". MSS in which *consilio domini regis* has been emended to *consilio domini H. regis* are Dunham's nos. 11, 13, 57, 58 and the *Liber Ordinationum.*

(*12*) This reading occurs both in Dunham's MS. B (=his MS. no. 24), from whence Dunham prints it as a textual variant in footnote 1 to p. 50 of his edition: and also in Dunham's MS. no. 23, where it has been marked for deletion and the same hand substituted a passage incorporating the post-1275 limitation date.

(*13*) Dunham, *op. cit.,* p. lxxx.

(*14*) Cf. the remarks of Derek Hall a propos of *Hengham Magna* in *Early Registers of Writs,* ed. E. de Haas and G. D. G. Hall (Selden Soc., lxxxvii (1970)), p. xlviii, note 2: "king's names and relationships . . . (are) easily changed by the most ignorant scribe".

impossible, in the case of a treatise of this sort, to conceive of any convincing reason for a scribe or scribes to deliberately alter the text in front of them in order to make it less up-to-date and modern, by making it appear that Henry III rather than Edward I was the reigning monarch. The inescapable conclusion would seem, therefore, to be that the treatise was originally composed during the reign of Henry III. An additional argument for 1272 as a *terminus ante quem* for the treatise is provided by one of the names used in certain manuscripts of the treatise in that section which contains examples of the different types of writ of right. One of these types is that used when the lord of whom the land which is being demanded is held is abroad and the writ is therefore addressed to his bailiffs. In four manuscripts of the treatise, three different named lords' bailiffs are given as alternative addressees of this writ and these include the bailiffs of John fitzAlan of Arundel (*15*). If, as seems probable, these four manuscripts preserve the original text at this point better than the other manuscripts and if the author was using current examples and the names of living persons in his treatise, then the treatise must date from before 1272, since it was in that year that the last John fitzAlan who was lord of Arundel died (*16*).

That 1272 has to be rejected as a *terminus a quo* for the composition of the treatise follows from the arguments already advanced in support of the proposition that the treatise was composed at some time in the reign of Henry III. 1267 must also be discarded as a *terminus a quo* because Woodbine was mistaken in his belief that the mesne process for enforcing the attendance in court of the four knights sent to view a man who had essoined himself *de malo lecti* that is described in the treatise was that which obtained after the passage of the statute of Marlborough in 1267. Whether the third stage of mesne process mentioned in the treatise really is *habeas corpus* or not (*17*), what is clear is that it is a stage of process intervening between the second attachment and the grand distress. What is also clear is that what was enacted by the relevant clause of the statute of Marlborough was that the second attachment should be followed immediately by the grand distress. It follows, therefore, that the

---

(*15*) Dunham's MSS. nos. 1 (=A) (printed by Dunham as his main text: *op. cit.*, p. 3), 33, 44 and 54. In other manuscripts, only two alternative sets of bailiffs are mentioned and those of John fitz Alan omitted.

(*16*) I. J. Sanders, *English Baronies* (Oxford, 1960), pp. 2, 71. As Plucknett notices (*op. cit.*), an even earlier *terminus ante quem* (of 1270) is suggested by another writ in the same section of the treatise, which is addressed to B. archbishop of Canterbury, an initial which only fits Archbishop Boniface of Savoy, who died in July 1270. A single initial, so easily miscopied by a careless scribe, is, however, clearly a less reliable dating criterion than a full name.

(*17*) It is possible that here, as elsewhere, the text of the treatise is corrupt, and that what the author originally referred to was a writ of simple distraint (which incorporated an order to the sheriff to produce the defendant's body, as well as to distrain him).

mesne process described by the treatise was not that which was prescribed by the statute (*18*).

An alternative *terminus a quo* is provided by the passage already quoted (*19*) mentioning a writ from the council of Henry III to the justices of the Bench about the computation of the year and day allowed a man essoined *de malo lecti* in leap years, a writ which is said to have been issued some time in Henry III's forty-fourth regnal year, that is, between 28 October 1259 and 27 October 1260. Plucknett suggested (*20*) that the 44 Henry III of the manuscripts was an obvious error for 40 Henry III; and what was being referred to was clearly the so-called Leap Year ordinance of 1256 (which was "provisum . . . et formatum . . . in presencia regis, Ricardi comitis Corn', Ricardi comitis Glouc', Henrici de Bathon', Henrici de Mar', Henrici de Bratton', Walter de Merton' et aliorum de consilio regis") (*21*): he therefore proposed 1256 as a new *terminus a quo* for the treatise. There is, however, independent evidence for the 1256 ordinance having been reissued, in an almost identical form, in 1260 (*22*), which, like 1256, was a leap year: such a phenomenon can be paralleled by the history of the revised version of the Provisions of Westminster, first issued in January 1263, reissued in identical form only six months

---

(*18*) Plucknett, *op. cit.*, makes the same point. In fact, this particular clause was first enacted in 1263 as one of the additions to the revised version of the Provisions of Westminster then being issued and was only re-enacted in 1267 as part of the stature of Marlborough (*Stat. Realm*, i. 9, note 13). It would not, however, I think be safe to use 1263 as a *terminus ante quem* for the composition of the treatise (as Plucknett's work would suggest) since it would have been quite possible for an author writing after the enactment of the legislation to have made a mistake on such a comparatively minor point: and because it is possible to argue, anyway, that the clause in question was intended to apply only to the mesne process used against defendants, and not to that used against third parties only incidentally involved in proceedings.

(*19*) Above, note 11.

(*20*) *Op. cit.*

(*21*) *Close Rolls, 1254-1256*, p. 414.

(*22*) In B.L. Cotton Claudius D. ii, one of the books of statutes used by the editors of the standard Record Commission edition of *Statutes of Realm*, is to be found an ordinance whose content is almost identical to that of the official, Close Roll version of the 1256 ordinance (above, note 21), and whose form similarly resembles it in being a writ from Henry III to the justices of the Bench: but which differs from the Close Roll version in that the writ is attested by the King at Westminster on an unspecified day and month in his 44th regnal year, instead of at Windsor on 9 May in his 40th regnal year. (*Stat. Realm*, i. 7). In another book of statutes used by the same editors, Liber X of the Exchequer (now P.R.O. E.164/9) an ordinance of similar content and form, but with a royal attestation at Westminster on 5 June in the King's 54th regnal year, is to be found (*ibid.*). While 54 (liv) is easily explained as the result of a scribal error of a common type for 44 (xliv), it is difficult to understand how 44 (xliv), can have come by scribal error to be substituted for 40 (xl), and Westminster to be substituted for Windsor, and the 5 June (quinto die Junii) for 9 May (nono die Maii), particularly when all three changes were in the same short section of the ordinance: and the fact that the King can be shown, from other evidence, to have been at Westminster on 5 June 1260 provides additional support to the hypothesis that the ordinance was in fact reissued on that day. Cf. H. G. Richardson 'Studies in Bracton", *Traditio*, vi (1948), 103.

later (June 1263) and reissued yet again, with no more than a change in the accompanying covering letter, in December 1264 *(23)*.

A similar *terminus a quo* is suggested by the first writ of right in that section of the treatise which contains specimens of the various different possible forms which the writ of right could take. In almost all the manuscripts which contain this section *(24)* the lord to whom the writ is addressed is given the name of Henry Huse *(25)* while the village in which the land demanded is said to be situated is also (in what seems to be the better manuscript tradition) given a name, that of Harting *(26)*, and the county whose sheriff is to act if Henry Huse fails to do so is (again in what seems to be the better manuscript tradition) named as being Sussex *(27)*. Once it is realised that the Huse family were, throughout the thirteenth century, lords of the manor of Harting in Sussex it becomes clear that the name of the lord to whom the writ is addressed is not a fictitious one chosen at random, but, like the names of the other addressees in this section of the treatise, that of a real person: and it seems beyond reasonable doubt that the person whose name is being used is the Henry Huse, who became lord of the manor of Harting on the death of his

(23) Full details will be found in my Oxford D.Phil. thesis "The Contribution of the Period of Baronial Reform (1258-1267) to the Development of the Common Law in England", at pp. 34-39.

(24) Several manuscripts omit this section altogether and refer the reader instead to a register of writs: others contain only this first writ and then omit the remainder of the section.

(25) He is so named in Dunham's MSS. nos. 3, 4, 5, 8, 9, 10, 11, 12, 13, 15, 16, 17, 18, 20, 21, 26, 28, 31, 32, 34, 41, 42, 43, 45, 46, 48, 49, 52, 54 and in the City of London Records Office, *Liber Ordinationum,* and Oriel College Oxford MS. 46. This includes manuscripts from each single one of the various *stemmae* and groups into which Dunham classified the manuscripts *(op. cit.,* p. lxxix). The "Henry Hugon" and "Henry Bous" of Dunham's nos. 27 and 29 are clearly also scribal errors for the same name. The only manuscripts that do include this section, but in which he is not so named, are Dunham's MS. no. 1 (the manuscript he used for his main text), where he is just J. de B, his MS. no. 24 (and B) where he is named Henry de O, his MS. no. 35 where he is named Roger de C, his MS. no. 44 where he is named A. de V, his MS. no. 36 where he has become just "tali domino", his MSS. nos. 30 and 33, where the name has been lost by abbreviation, and his MS. no. 2 where he has become an (unspecified) sheriff.

(26) The land demanded is said to be in Harting ("Herting") in Dunham's MSS. nos. 6, 13, 48 and 54: and the "Hertindon" of his MS. no. 24, "Hertingham" of his MS. no. 4, "Horton" of his MS. no. 52 and "Norton" of his MSS. nos. 26, 28 can all be seen as resulting from scribal errors for "Herting". No other names are found as alternatives to "Herting" at this point: and it is probably significant that the initial "H" is found in place of a name more frequently in the MSS. (Dunham's nos. 1, 2, 3, 5, 9, 11, 12, 16, 20, 25, 32, 35, 45, 49, 57, 58) than is the normal medieval substitute for a name, the initial "N" (found in Dunham's nos. 8, 15, 17, 21, 27, 29, 31, 34, 36, 42, 43, 44 and in the *Liber Ordinationum* and Oriel College MS.). The only other initial found in any manuscript at this point is "D" (in Dunham's no. 30).

(27) Sussex is the county whose sheriff is named in Dunham's MSS. nos. 5, 8, 13, 17, 18, 20, 21, 24, 25, 28, 29, 31, 32, 43, 45 and 58. He is the sheriff of Derbyshire in no. 57, of Huntingdonshire in no. 10, of Lincolnshire in nos. 1, 9, 36 and 44, of Nottinghamshire in no. 7, of Shropshire in no. 4, of Suffolk in nos. 16, 26 and 52, of Surrey in no. 42 and of Yorkshire in nos. 11, and 27 and in the City of London Records Office *Liber Ordinationum.*

father, Matthew Huse, in 1253 (*28*). Henry was still a minor in 1253, and the wardship both of his body and of his lands was granted by the King to John Mansel: he finally came of age in the summer of 1260 and only then obtained livery of his lands (*29*). The correct form of any writ of right brought for lands allegedly held of Henry Huse between 1253 and the summer of 1260 would have been for it to be addressed to John Mansel, as guardian of Henry Huse, and not to Henry Huse himself (*30*): this suggests that if the writ given in the treatise is a copy of one actually issued (as it may be) then the treatise cannot have been composed earlier than 1260, and much the same conclusion seems likely even if the writ is a fictitious concoction, using genuine names, since one might have expected the author of the treatise, if writing before 1260, to have used both Mansel and Huse's names to illustrate the form appropriate where the lord was a minor in wardship instead.

A slightly later *terminus a quo* than either of these may be indicated by some other names and initials used in several manuscripts of the treatise later in the same section, for the form of writ of right used where the lord of whom the demandant claims to hold is out of the realm. The examples given are of writs addressed to the bailiffs of S. bishop of Chichester, an initial which will only fit Stephen Bersted, bishop from 1262 to 1278 (*31*); and to the bailiffs of G. de Clare, earl of Gloucester and Hertford, which must be the Gilbert de Clare, who succeeded his father Richard as earl of Gloucester in 1263/4 (*32*). However, a single initial could easily have been changed by later scribes, as could the name of the current earl of Gloucester, which would be well-known to most people with any interest in the treatise: so, it is perhaps safer to rely upon Henry Huse's name as an indicator of date (the Huse family were not, like the earl of Gloucester, of national significance), together with the reference to the leap-year writ of Henry III's 44th regnal year.

Re-examination of the evidence suggests, therefore, that the treatise was written not, as Dunham argued, between 1272 and 1275, but, at the widest, between 1260 and 1272, and, just conceivably between 1263/4 and 1272: it is possible, therefore, that it was written a whole decade earlier than Dunham's dating would suggest. The significance of this re-dating for the question of authorship of the treatise will be apparent later.

II

The major part of *Hengham Magna* is devoted to a detailed elucida-

---

(*28*) *Cal. Inq. P.M.*, i, no. 285. The only other possible Henry Huse is Matthew Huse's father, whom he had succeeded in 1235 (*Exc. e Rot. Fin*, i, 278), but this seems unlikely.

(*29*) *Exc. e Rot. Fin*, ii 152, 154; P.R.O. K.B. 26/167m. 24d.

(*30*) This is the rule stated in *Early Registers of Writs*, CC5 (rule) and also in *Hengham Magna* itself (Dunham, *op. cit.*, p. 5).

(*31*) The initial S is found with the title bishop of Chichester in Dunham's MSS. nos. 3, 8, 16, 20, 21, 25, 26, 28, 29, 33, 34, 42, 43, 44, 45, 48, 49, 52, 54 and 58.

(*32*) G. de Clare, earl of Gloucester and Hertford, is mentioned in all the MSS. cited in the preceding note, plus Dunham's MS. no. 1.

tion of the procedure applicable to litigation initiated by the writ of right, once such litigation has been transferred to the Bench. Throughout this section of the treatise two names are constantly used by the author as the names of the demandant and tenant: Richard le Jay is normally the name given to the demandant, and William Huse that given to the tenant (33). Nor is this the only part of the treatise where the two names are used: for in those manuscripts which contain a section of specimen writs of right, Richard le Jay is the name normally given to the demandant in the very first of these specimen writs, that which is addressed to Henry Huse and concerns land at Harting in Sussex (34), and William Huse is the name given in several manuscripts not to the tenant in that writ, but to one of the tenants in the variant immediately following that writ (and intended to be read in conjunction with it) (35).

Are these the names of real people? When editing *Hengham Magna*, Dunham expressed no views on this subject: but when, twenty years later, he came to consider the names found in the thirteenth century legal notes he was editing for the Selden Society under the title *Casus Placitorum*, he was as certain that these names were fictitious, a jeu d'esprit on the part of Ralph de Hengham, as he was that some, if not all, of the names found in the notes were genuine:

> "A few notes in the Casus contain the names of litigants, presumably real and not imaginary persons, and others include indirect quotations of pleaders and judges. Surnames of plaintiffs and defenders, Roger de Draitone, Hugh de Chelmewyk, H. Talemasche, and 'the heirs of M. de Brus' have a much more authentic ring than have 'one John' and 'one William' who also appear: and even these Christian names seem less hypothetical than the fictitious litigants, Richard le Jay and William Huse, whom Ralph de Hengham, in his Summa Magna, used recurrently" (36).

This view is, however a mistaken one. Richard le Jay and William Huse are the names of real people living at the time of the composition of the treatise and connected with the village of Harting in Sussex, and, as I

---

(33) But for passages in which their roles seem to have been reversed *see* Dunham, *op. cit.*, pp. 16, 28, 35.

(34) Richard le Jay is the name given to the demandant in this first writ in Dunham's MSS. nos. 2, 3, 4, 5, 6, 7, 8, 9, 11, 12, 13, 15, 16, 17, 18, 20, 21, 24, 25, 26, 28, 29, 31, 32, 34, 41, 42, 43, 45, 46, 48, 49, 50, 52, 54, 57 and 58, and in Oriel Coll. MS. 46 and in City of London R.O. *Liber Ordinationum*. The only alternatives found at this point are I Bek. (in Dunham's MS. no. 1, the manuscript which he used as the basis of his printed text), T (in no. 27), J. de B. (in no. 30), R. de H. (in no. 33), H. de M. (in no. 35), A (in no. 36), and J. de O. (in no. 36).

(35) His name is found at this point in Dunham's MSS. nos. 16, 20, 25, 28, 43, 45, 49. In no. 52 he is named William Huse of Westing' (? for Westherting') and in no. 54 as William Huse of Westring, while in no. 48 he has become William de Westingg'. The William House of nos. 21 and 58, William Heuse of no. 26, the William Louse of no. 8 and William Bous of no. 29 are all clearly scribal variants of the same name, as are the W. de Hus and W. Hus of nos. 31 and 34.

(36) *Casus Placitorum*, p. xix.

hope to demonstrate, there is also other evidence in the treatise to connect it with this village and its neighbourhood.

The Jay family are to be found in the Harting area from the late twelfth century onwards. One Roger Jayus is mentioned at this time as tenant of a mill at Habin in the parish of Harting, a mill the annual rent of twenty-five shillings for which was granted by an earlier Henry Huse to the local abbey of Durford (*37*): and, in a charter which must be dated between 1174 and 1213, a Roger Gaius, probably the same man, can be found granting a croft to the same abbey with the consent of his lord, Henry Huse, and of his own wife and children (*38*). Richard le Jay is first mentioned (as Richard Gay) as one of the jurors of the inquisition *post mortem* held in 1253 into the lands in the county of Sussex held at his death by Matthew Huse (most of which were in Harting) (*39*): and in the Sussex eyre of 1262 the same man is to be found acting as an attorney for Matthew's son, Henry Huse of Harting, in litigation with Isabel, countess of Arundel (*40*). That Richard continued to be connected with Henry Huse is shown by the fact that in 1275 and again in 1279 he is to be found acting as bailiff of the Sussex hundred of Dumpford, which was held in fee by the Huse family and included Harting (*41*), and by the fact that in 1282 he acted as one of Henry Huse's attorneys in a plea in the Bench (*42*): and that he was not just an agent for Henry Huse but also a minor land-owner in the Harting area in his own right is shown by the fact that in the Sussex eyre of 1262 he was named as tenant of three acres of land in East Harting (*43*), and by the fact that in the following Sussex eyre, that of 1279, he is to be found settling land in Harting on his daughter Agnes (*44*), and acquiring land in the next parish of Rogate (*45*). What of the other litigant in the treatise, William Huse? William Huse, presumably some kind of relation to the Huse family of Harting, is a much more obscure person than Richard le Jay: but he is named as the other attorney in the litigation with Isabel, countess of Arundel, in the 1262 Sussex eyre (*46*), and there is other evidence to show him as a minor land-owner in Harting (*47*).

So both Richard le Jay and William Huse can be shown to be the names of real people, alive in the 1260s (the probable date of the composition of the treatise) and both with connections with the village of Harting in Sussex—the village not only named (in several manuscripts) as that in

(*37*) B. L. Cotton Vespasian E. xxiii (Durford Cartulary) f. 12d.
(*38*) *Ibid.*, f. 55d.
(*39*) P.R.O. C132/14 no. 20.
(*40*) P.R.O. JUST/1/912A m. 28.
(*41*) P.R.O. K.B. 27/16m 10d; JUST/1/915m 25d.
(*42*) P.R.O. C.P. 52/Edward I writ-file for the quindene of Trinity, 10 Edward I (inquisition on waste, by the sheriff of Kent).
(*43*) JUST/1/912A m. 6.
(*44*) *Sussex Fines 1248-1307* (Sussex Record Soc., vii (1907)), no. 926.
(*45*) *Ibid.*, no. 915.
(*46*) JUST/1/912A m. 28.
(*47*) *V.C.H. Sussex*, iv. 17.

which was situated the land sought by the first of the specimen writs of right (*48*), but also (in at least two manuscripts, which may well here be preserving the tradition of the original manuscript) (*49*) as that in which was situated the land at stake between the two litigants, Richard le Jay and William Huse, in the litigation in the Bench. Other evidence linking the treatise with Harting and its neighbourhood is provided by the writ given in the treatise ordering four knights to be sent to view the tenant in litigation who was essoining himself *de malo lecti* (*50*). In most manuscripts, he is said to be the tenant in a plea of land in the county of Sussex, and in many manuscripts he is said to be on his sick-bed at a place simply represented by the initial "R". In the two manuscripts, however, which name Harting as the village in which was situated the land at stake between the two litigants in the Bench, that initial R is expanded to read "Reygate" in one manuscript (*51*), and "Regate" in the other (*52*): both best explained as scribal amendments of the little known Rogate, which was the next parish to Harting, and also in the county of Sussex, to change it into the better-known Reigate, which was in the county of Surrey. A final link is provided by the name given to the tenant in the very first specimen writ of right in most manuscripts of the treatise: which is not the plain initial "R" of the manuscript which Dunham chose as the basis of his edition of the treatise (*53*) but either J. de B (*54*), or John de B (*55*), or, more commonly, J. or John Blundel or Blondel (*56*), or J. or John Blundel or Blondel or Blandel of H. (or N. or B.) (*57*), and even once in full, John Blundel of Harting (*58*). Again here, we are dealing with a real person. One Nicholas Blundel had, in the late twelfth century, been granted what seems to have been the same mill at Habin, as that previously held by Roger le Jay (*59*), by the same Henry Huse as that of whom Roger had

---

(*48*) Above, p. 374 and note 26.

(*49*) Dunham's MSS. nos 23 and 54. In both, the place in which the land to be taken into the king's hands by the *grand cape sicut alias* (Dunham, *op. cit.*, p. 27) is situated is said not to be Harting but Welton' (in no. 23) or Delton' (in no. 54): and in no. 23 the tenant is generally called not William but Henry Huse.

(*50*) Dunham, *op. cit.*, pp. 9-10.

(*51*) Dunham's MS. no. 23.

(*52*) In Dunham's MS. no. 54: a superscript "y" has been added to this.

(*53*) Dunham, *op. cit.*, p. 2 (his MS. no. 1): nor the "N" to be found in his MS. no. 36, or "talis" of his no. 46.

(*54*) In Dunham's MSS. nos. 2, 7, 13, 15, 17, 30, 32 and 42. The J. de H. of nos. 24 and 41, the J. de O. of no. 44 and the J. de W. of no. 33 are all presumably the result of scribal errors or emendations.

(*55*) In Dunham's MS. no. 16.

(*56*) J. Blundel in MSS. nos. 20 and 26 (J. Blount in no. 35): John Blondel/Blundell in MSS. nos. 11, 27, 28, 50, 52, 57 and Oriel College MS. no. 46 and City of London R.O. *Liber Ordinationum.*

(*57*) John Blundel or Blandel or Blondel of H. in MSS. nos. 3, 5, 8, 9, 21, 25, 29, 43, 45 and 58; John Blundel or Blandel in N in MSS. nos. 34 and 49; John Blundel or Blandel of B. in MSS. nos. 12 and 54.

(*58*) In MS. no. 48: cf. the John Blundel of Hertinghamham of MS. no. 4. The only other names found here are John Bot in MS. no. 18 and J. de Draytone in no. 31.

(*59*) Above, p. 377.

held it (*60*). John Blundel, clearly a descendant, was holding the mill in 1242, when the abbey of Durford (to whom the earlier Henry Huse had granted the annual rent of twenty-five shillings owed for the mill by Nicholas and his descendants) quitclaimed the rent to Matthew Huse (*61*): he was also its tenant two years later when Matthew granted the rent back again to the abbey (*62*). In 1253 a John Blundel was among the jurors of the inquisition *post mortem* into the lands held at his death in the county of Sussex by Matthew Huse (most of which were in Harting) (*63*), subsequently his son, another Nicholas Blundel (*64*), granted land and the mill at Habin, once held by his father, to Richard le Jay of Rogate, clearly the same Richard le Jay whom we have already seen acquiring land at Rogate (*65*).

It is impossible now to find any trace on the Bench plea-rolls of the 1250s, 1260s, or early 1270s of litigation between Richard le Jay and William Huse or John Blundel (*66*): but the loss of so many of the Bench plea-rolls for this period means that genuine litigation between them cannot be ruled out. Moreover, the fact that the mill at Habin (and probably lands appurtenant to it) once in the hands of a probable ancestor of Richard le Jay, are subsequently, and in unexplained circumstances, to be found in the hands of a man probably the ancestor of John Blundel, and that after John's death, Richard acquired mill and lands from John's son, may perhaps lend at least a degree of plausibility to the hypothesis that there really had, at some stage, been litigation between Richard and John at least, if not between Richard and both John and William. Either way, however,—whether or not there ever had been genuine litigation between them in the Bench—it is clear that the author of *Hengham Magna*, whoever he was, was someone who somehow came to know of Harting and of some of the land-owners of that neighbourhood: that he was using real names of people and of places in his treatise, however much the subsequent manuscript tradition may have tended to disguise the fact. The

(*60*) B. L. Cotton Vespasian E. xxiii, ff. 8-8d.

(*61*) *Ibid.*, ff. 15d-16.

(*62*) *Sussex Fines, 1190-1249* (Sussex Record Soc., ii (1902)), no. 419.

(*63*) C132/14 no. 20.

(*64*) A Nicholas Blundel, possibly the same man, was pardoned 28½ marks which he owed to various Jews of Winchester by the King in November 1265 at the instance of one Robert of Rogate (*Cal. Pat. Rolls, 1258-66*, p. 506): and what may be the same man is found in 1279 and 1288 as the husband of one Margery, who had inherited lands at Elsted, near Harting (JUST/1/914 m. 43; JUST/1/929 mm. 18d, 34, 39).

(*65*) Above, p. 377 and note 45. We know of Nicholas' grant only through the subsequent agreement entered in the Durford cartulary (B.L. Cotton Vespasian E. xxiii ff. 56-56d) between John, abbot of Durford (who occurs as abbot between 1258 and 1297: H. M. Colvin, *The White Canons in England*, Oxford, 1951, p. 403), and Richard. Under this agreement, the abbot remitted five shillings of the twenty-five shillings owed for land and mill, in return for an acknowledgement by Richard that he held the lands which John and Nicholas had once held, of the abbot for 1 lb. of cumin and twenty shillings a year, and Richard's agreement that if the rent got into arrears, the abbot could distrain for it anywhere within the tenements once held by Nicholas and John.

(*66*) I have searched all the surviving rolls for traces of such litigation but in vain.

litigation may or may not have been fictitious: but the litigants certainly
were not.

III

Ralph de Hengham first became a royal justice in 1270, was chief
justice of the court of King's Bench from 1274 to 1289, and served as
chief justice of the Bench from 1301 to 1307 (*67*). Hitherto, it has been
generally accepted that *Hengham Magna* was his work; and there is
contemporary warrant for this belief not only in the title given to the
treatise in most manuscripts (*68*), but also in the *incipit* of one early
manuscript (*69*), which states that "Hic incipit quedam summa quam
dominus Radulphus de Hengham fecit conpendiose de brevibus et placitis
in curia domini regis" (*70*), and in the addition of his name after the
authorial "ego" in the first paragraph of the treatise in another early
manuscript (*71*). So what valid reasons can there be for doubting whether
Hengham really was the author of the treatise?

The first, and most serious, objection to Hengham's authorship
derives from the unfinished and confused state of the text of the treatise
in every surviving manuscript. That it is unfinished is abundantly clear
from the opening paragraph of the work, which makes a number of
promises about what is to follow which are only partly borne out, if at all,
in what really does follow (*72*). In lieu of a section containing all the
various forms of writ of right, writ of entry, writ of dower, writ of escheat,
and writs of assize which we have been led to expect by a promise of
"*brevia . . . de placitis terre*", all that we are given is a section containing
a number of variants of the writ of right and a single example of the writ
of right of dower (*73*). When what we have been promised is an exposition
of the various "delays" which a tenant can enjoy in land actions generally,

(*67*) For brief accounts of Hengham's somewhat eventful career see *Select Cases in the
Court of King's Bench,* Vol. I, ed. G. O. Sayles, (Selden Soc., lv (1936)), pp. liii-liv,
and Dunham, *op. cit.,* pp. xlv-lx.
(*68*) It is normally called *Hengham Magna* or *Summa Hengham* or the like, which imply
authorship by a man named Hengham, if not necessarily this particular Hengham.
(*69*) The manuscript printed by Dunham as his text: it does not occur in other manuscripts of the treatise.
(*70*) Dunham, *op. cit.,* p. 1.
(*71*) At a point corresponding to line 10 of page 1 of Dunham's text. The manuscript
in question is Dunham's MS. no. 47 (and C) which is not, as Dunham thought, a
manuscript of the fifteenth century, but belongs to the thirteenth century (see
M. R. James, *A Descriptive Catalogue of the Manuscripts in the Library of Lambeth
Palace: the Medieval Manuscripts* (Cambridge, 1932) p. 691).
(*72*) Dunham, *op. cit.,* p. 1: "Brevia siquidem domini regis de placitis terre; et qualiter
et quibus dilationibus potest tenens litem differre ante communem apparitionem
in curia, et quomodo petens opponere, et tenens respondere debet; et quibus
casibus potest denegari visus terre et in quibus non; et natura exceptionum tam
peremptoriarum quam dilatoriarum, videlicet, ante visum terre factum et post; ac
modus cirograffandi si per finem factum lis decidatur necnon et exceptiones contra
ipsum finem; ac quedam exemplaria discussionem huiusmodi placitorum iuvantia,
et de iurisdictione curie comitatus et baronis dum lis a tali curia translata fuerit;
inferius suis locis continentur."
(*73*) *Ibid.,* pp. 2-5.

all that we are given is an exposition of the various "delays" which the tenant can enjoy in actions brought by the writ of right (*74*). All that we have to fulfil the promise of a discussion of both dilatory and peremptory exceptions is a very brief discussion of dilatory exceptions (*75*) and the beginnings only of a discussion of peremptory exceptions at the very end of the treatise (*76*). Notwithstanding an initial promise of an exposition of how a demandant makes his count and the tenant his defence, all that we are given in the treatise are heavily abbreviated counts (*77*) and defences (*78*), which seem to presuppose that the subject will be treated at greater length later in the treatise; and the treatise as we now have it contains nothing to correspond to the initial promise of a section devoted to the making of cyrographs and to the possible exceptions that can be made against them (*79*). In the end, the only parts of that initial programme which can be said to have been fulfilled in an adequate manner, are those promising a discussion of the circumstances in which a "view" of land can be claimed (*80*) and a discussion of the jurisdiction of the county court and of the court baron (*81*): and the awkward placing of this latter item in the introductory listing of the intended contents of the treatise suggests that it may in fact have been added subsequently as an afterthought, the author's original purpose having been to deal solely with the *ordo placitandi* in the King's Court. One other piece of evidence also seems to point to the unfinished nature of the treatise as we now have it. In one manuscript—the same manuscript as that which contains at the very end of the treatise one more sentence than the other manuscripts, and a sentence which shows every appearance of being genuine (*82*)—

(*74*) It is this exposition which comprises the major part of the treatise as we now have it from the point at which the author first takes up a description of the *ordo placitandi* in the Bench (at p. 14 of Dunham's text) down to the beginning of the passage on warranty (at p. 45). That the author did originally intend to deal with the procedure in other types of action as well is shown by two cross-references to later sections dealing with those other types of action in that part of the treatise in which the author is dealing with the view: "Et justitiario opus est a modo exprimere in quibus denegatur visus terre et in quibus non, videlicet quantum ad hoc breve hic; alibi quoque simile fiat in aliis brevibus suis locis" (*ibid.*, p. 35), and 'de visu siquidem habendi in placitis intrusionum, dotis et huiusmodi suis locis tractatur" (*ibid.*, p. 36).

(*75*) *Ibid.*, pp. 34-35.

(*76*) *Ibid.*, pp. 49-50: the only type of peremptory exception mentioned is that based on the limitation period of writs of right. It is, perhaps, worth noting that there is one manuscript of the treatise (Dunham's MS. no. 47 and C, for which see note 71), which contains an additional sentence at this point, mentioning a second kind of peremptory exception: "Et qui omittit in narracione descensus nomen unius persone interposite". Although this manuscript was one of those collated in detail by Dunham, he does not mention this additional sentence: it does not, apparently, occur in any of the other manuscripts of the treatise.

(*77*) *Ibid.*, p. 34.

(*78*) *Ibid.*, pp. 34, 35.

(*79*) A further unfulfilled promise is that made later in the treatise (*ibid.*, p. 36) to give the oath of the champion in trial by battle.

(*80*) *Ibid.*, pp. 35-37.

(*81*) *Ibid.*, pp. 5-14.

(*82*) Dunham's MS. no. 47 (C): see above, note 76.

almost at the end of the treatise, and at the end of the discussion on warranty, and immediately preceding the passage about peremptory exceptions (*83*), there appears the rubric "secunda pars summe". What follows hardly deserves the name of a "second part" (*84*), something that the scribe himself seems to have noticed (*85*): it seems certain that the rubric must, therefore, have come from the manuscript from which he was copying, and that this manuscript either had once contained more of the treatise than any surviving manuscript (*86*) or preserved in this rubric the author's unfulfilled intention to continue with the second part of the treatise beyond the point at which the treatise now breaks off (*87*).

That the treatise as we now have it is not only unfinished but also in a state of considerable textual confusion will be clear to anybody who has tried to make sense of the treatise as it is printed by Dunham and as it appears in the manuscripts: all the surviving manuscripts contain a number of clearly misplaced passages, best explained on a hypothesis similar to that which has been advanced to explain a similar feature of Bracton's treatise, that is, that they were in origin supplementary passages, written by the author in the margin of his original manuscript or on loose slips, with no clear indication of where they were to be inserted in the main text and that a subsequent "redactor" of the original manuscript, not the author, then misplaced them when adding them to the text (*88*). One obvious example is provided by the author's discussion of the summoning of the tenant to appear in the Bench. A first sentence on this subject appears, quite out of place, at the end of the section concerning the procedure followed in the county court and prior to a bridging passage which explains that the next section deals with the procedure followed in the Bench (*89*). In at least one manuscript (*90*), the same sentence is then used again a little later on to introduce the first substantive section of what the author has to say on the subject, but at a point in the text where this clearly interrupts what the author is saying on the subject of essoins (*91*). A further section on summoning, clearly following on from this first substantive section, subsequently once more interrupts the author's dis-

(*83*) *Ibid.*, p. 49, line 24.

(*84*) It amounts to little more than nine lines.

(*85*) At the end he wrote: "Hic deest quid de summa que dicitur le Hengham que describit totum ordinem inrotulandi et placitandi in curia domini regis, unde querenda sunt que hic desunt ad tale signum". That he was unable to find any more of the treatise is shown by a subsequent memorandum by the same scribe: 'Memorandum nichil querenda sunt que hic desunt".

(*86*) And the additional material have been lost or misplaced before the scribe began copying it.

(*87*) Either way, it seems clear that this other manuscript was either the author's original manuscript or a close copy of it.

(*88*) Most recently by Professor S. E. Thorne in his "Translator's Introduction" to the reissued Volume I of Woodbine's edition of *Bracton: On the Laws and Customs of England* (Cambridge, Mass., 1968), p. xxxix.

(*89*) Dunham, *op. cit.*, p. 14 (the sentence immediately preceding the heading: "Capitulum V").

(*90*) That which Dunham used for his text.

(*91*) Dunham, *op. cit.*, pp. 14-15.

cussion of essoins (92). Another obviously misplaced section is that concerned with dilatory exceptions (93). As it now appears, it is placed rather awkwardly between two sections both of which are concerned with the procedure for demanding a "view": the passage introducing the discussion of peremptory exceptions suggests that its correct place is immediately before or after the section on voucher to warranty (94). Smaller, but no less obvious, mistakes in arrangement occur also in the placing of the passage relating to the enrolment of a voucher to warranty (95), and in the placing of a passage giving the words a tenant uses when seeking a "view" of land (96).

If, then, we are to accept that Ralph de Hengham really was the author of *Hengham Magna,* we need to believe not only that at some date, probably in the 1260s, with an active legal career of almost forty years still ahead of him, he precipitately abandoned, at a comparatively early stage, a treatise for which not long before he had been conceiving quite ambitious plans; but also that, once he had abandoned it, he then allowed his incomplete treatise to fall into the hands of a scribe whose competence did not even extend to the correct integration into the main body of the text of those additional passages which had been written in the margins or on loose scraps of parchment, and from whose version of the treatise all the existing manuscripts of the treatise descend. And if we accept the alternative hypothesis, suggested by that unique rubric referring close to the end of the treatise to the beginning of a "second part" of the treatise (97), that what we now have is only a fragment of the treatise as actually written, we have to believe that even though Hengham had written a much longer treatise, this never saw the light of day, and that Hengham happily allowed the circulation of only a truncated and mangled version of his great *summa.* Neither hypothesis seems very plausible.

The second argument against Hengham's presumed authorship relates to its style. Contemporary manuscript authority points to Hengham as author not just of *Hengham Magna,* but also of another, and even shorter, treatise, *Hengham Parva* (98). A comparison of the style of the two works reveals major differences between them. To begin with, the author of *Hengham Magna* provided his work with an elaborate, rhetorical

(92) *Ibid.,* pp. 15-16.

(93) *Ibid.,* pp. 34-35.

(94) *Ibid.,* p. 49: "Excursis que in presenti recoluntur quo ad vocacionem waranti et quo ad excepciones dilatorias, de peremptoriis isto loco loqui congruit".

(95) *Ibid.,* p. 42, and note 4. It separates the two parts of a passage relating to the availability of essoins to warrantors, and is itself separated by one of those parts and by a passage giving the form of the writ for the summoning of a warrantor from the other passage to which it belongs, that which gives the words used in court by a tenant vouching to warranty (*ibid.,* p. 41).

(96) *Ibid.,* p. 35. This passage should clearly have been placed with the section giving the *ordo* of procedure in connection with the view. It should probably have been inserted at this point in the text where now are to be found the words by which a tenant seeks a hearing of the writ (*ibid.,* p. 34).

(97) Above, p. 382.

(98) Referred to by Dunham as the *Summa Parva* (*op. cit.,* pp. 51-71).

introduction, that seems to have been written before almost anything else in the treatise (99); whereas *Hengham Parva,* although apparently complete (100), contains no form of introduction but plunges directly into a discussion of the first topic. More generally, it is obvious that the rhetorical question is a favourite literary device of the author of *Hengham Magna* (101), but is almost entirely missing from *Hengham Parva* (102); and, while in *Hengham Magna* one is continually encountering virtually meaningless connective adverbs added solely for rhetorical purposes (103), *Hengham Parva* is almost entirely free of them (104). When wishing to convey the meaning "as for example", the author of *Hengham Magna,* in keeping with his generally florid style, normally uses the word "utpote" (105), whereas the author of *Hengham Parva* uses the plainer "ut" (106) or "veluti" (107) for this purpose; and when the author of *Hengham Magna* wishes to give emphasis to his opinion on a particular subject, he characteristically lapses into the first person singular, most commonly with the word *dico,* to do so (108), a usage which is rare, though not entirely non-existent, in *Hengham Parva* (109). *Vice versa,* among the most characteristic features of the style of the author of *Hengham Parva,* is the recurrent use of *item* as a connective at the beginning of sen-rences (110), and the use of *aliud . . . aliud, alia . . . alia* or *aliquando . . . aliquando* (111) to introduce two or more alternatives: all these devices are absent from *Hengham Magna.*

Even making due allowance for the fact that there must have been a period of anything between thirteen and thirty years (112) between the dates of the composition of the two treatises, it is difficult, in view of the great stylistic dissimilarities between them, to believe that the two treatises really can be the work of a single author: that the same author could or would have changed his style so drastically during the intervening period.

---

(99) This would explain why the list of intended contents of the work promises so much more than it fulfils; and would also explain why the promise of a discussion of the jurisdiction of the county court and of the court baron appears to have been added as an afterthought.

(100) The only hint of any sort that *Hengham Parva* may be unfinished is that provided by the rubric "de brevibus assisarum: et primo de brevi nove disseisine" (Dunham, *op. cit.,* p. 59), which suggests an unfulfilled intention to discuss the other petty assizes as well as novel disseisin.

(101) I have noted some 39 examples in the 50 printed pages of Dunham's edition.

(102) I have noted only 4 examples in the 19 printed pages of Dunham's edition.

(103) The most common of these is "*siquidem*" which occurs no less than fourteen times, others include "*nequaquam*", "*quemadmodum*", "*aliquantislibet*" and "*equidem*".

(104) Even "*quidem*" is only used once.

(105) Dunham, *op. cit.,* pp. 9, 10, 33, 41, 43.

(106) *Ibid.,* pp. 52, 54, 55, 58, 60, 69.

(107) *Ibid.,* p. 60 (twice).

(108) I have noted some 21 different examples of this usage.

(109) I have noted just two examples.

(110) *Ibid.,* pp. 53, 54, 57, 58, 62, 63, 64, 67.

(111) *Ibid.,* pp. 55, 56, 57, 60, 66.

(112) There seems no reason for dissenting from Dunham's view (*ibid.,* p. lxii) that *Hengham Parva* was written between 1285 and 1290.

If this view is accepted, then it is necessary to reject the manuscript authority for attributing both treatises to Hengham, and to attribute one (or perhaps even both) of the treatises to someone else. Fortunately, there does exist some other work which can be attributed to Hengham (*113*): and it is clear from this that it is in the crisp Latin style of *Hengham Parva* and not in the rather florid style of *Hengham Magna,* that we can detect the work of Ralph de Hengham.

There are, therefore, two main arguments against Ralph de Hengham's authorship of *Hengham Magna*. One rests on the unfinished and confused state of the text in all surviving manuscripts of the treatise, and argues that this is difficult, if not impossible, to reconcile with the known chronology of Hengham's life and career. The other rests on a comparison of the style of this treatise and the other treatise attributed to Hengham, *Hengham Parva,* and argues that they are so dissimilar that they are unlikely to have been the work of the same man; that other evidence suggests that it is *Hengham Parva* which is Hengham's work, and that, therefore, the manuscript ascription of *Hengham Magna* to Ralph de Hengham should be rejected. A third argument, though only an argument *e silentio,* against Hengham's authorship is that there is no evidence at all to link him with Richard le Jay, William Huse, John Blundel or the villages of Harting or Rogate: all of whom and all of which must have been known to the author of the treatise.

IV

If Ralph de Hengham was not the author of *Hengham Magna,* then who did write the treatise? The obvious starting-point in a search for the real author is to re-examine the treatise for internal evidence. The first thing to be noticed about the treatise is that its author must have been someone with an extensive knowledge and experience of the Bench: able confidently to state that it rarely happened "in maiori curia domini regis" (by which is meant the Bench) that lords claimed cases for their courts (*114*), able, too, to state it "often" happened that a *responsalis* was disavowed (*115*), also able to state that it was "generally" true that a man who vouched to warranty had previously sought a "view" of the land for which he was being impleaded (*116*), and capable of explaining the exceptional circumstances under which an essoin could be entered on the second rather than the first day of a return-day (*117*) or under which a tenant could safely withdraw from court on the first day of a return-day

---

(*113*) In a Bodleian manuscript (MS. Douce 139) are to be found some anonymous replies, which can be shown to be Hengham's, to a series of questions concerning the law relating to *quo waranto* proceedings, submitted to him by the justices in eyre in Northamptonshire in 1285. See below, pp. 393-443.

(*114*) Dunham, *op. cit.,* p. 7.
(*115*) *Ibid.,* p. 34.
(*116*) *Ibid.,* p. 34.
(*117*) *Ibid.,* p. 16.

without awaiting being called (*118*). It was this same knowledge and experience, too, which enabled him in the treatise to give litigants or their legal advisers practical advice on the procedural hazards to be avoided in litigation (*119*), and to give tenants or their advisers the best possible advice on how to delay making an appearance in court and giving a substantive answer to the demandant's claim for as long as possible (*120*), at the same time reminding them of the possible advantages in doing this (*121*).

Further internal evidence points, more specifically, to someone connected in an official capacity with the Bench as author of the treatise. At each stage in the proceedings, the author gives, in full, not only what litigants, attorneys or essoiners say (in French) in court, but also what is entered subsequently on the plea-roll in Latin recording that stage (*122*): and the relevant judicial writs then issued are not just mentioned but given in full in the treatise (*123*). When the author is explaining what happens in court when an essoin *de malo veniendi* is cast, he mentions not only the words and actions of the demandant (or his attorney) and of the tenant's essoiner, but also those of the crier ("*clamator*") of the Bench and of the *prenotarius,* the chief clerk of the Bench who was the keeper of its rolls and writs (*124*); and the role of the *prenotarius* in checking the date endorsed by the sheriff on a *cape* as that on which land was taken into the king's hands, against the date when the land was replevied is also singled out for special mention in the treatise (*125*). It seems also to be the words

(*118*) *Ibid.,* p. 32.
(*119*) Most of which are, as it were, "signposted" in the treatise by the words "caveat" or "caveat rursus": *ibid.,* pp. 8, 9, 16, 21, 25, 32, 44.
(*120*) Most of the treatise (*ibid.,* pp. 14-45) is devoted to this matter.
(*121*) See in particular the passage (*ibid.,* pp. 15-16) in which the author advises the tenant, even if he has been properly summoned, to deny the fact by waging his law to that effect, and then to default, simply "ad salvandum autumpanlia", that is, in order to secure a sufficient delay to allow the harvesting of the year's crop: and the other passage (*ibid.,* p. 39) where the author speaks of the advantages of the royal writ de *warrantia diei* in securing delay for the tenant as such a delay may enable him to get in the harvest, collect the rents due on a particular day, or outlive his opponent.
(*122*) *Ibid.,* pp. 16, 20, 25-26, 28, 34-25, 38, 39, 41-42.
(*123*) *Ibid.,* pp. 20 (grand *cape*), 26-27 (*scias*), 27 (petty *cape*), 27-28 (grand *cape sicut alias*), 28-29 (*mitte milites*), 33 (attachment of knights sent to view man essoined *de malo lecti*), 35 (view), 41 (summons of warrantor), 43 (*cape ad valenciam*).
(*124*) *Ibid.,* p. 16. The style *prenotarius,* more correctly *protonotarius,* means no more than chief clerk. At this date, the chief clerk was clearly the clerk who was keeper of the rolls and writs of the Bench who, like the justices of the court, but unlike its other clerks, was appointed by, and received a fee from, the Crown. At the time Bracton was writing his treatise, the *protonotarius* of the Bench still kept the "first" plea-roll of the court ". . . cuius irrotulacionem sequi debent omnes alii rotuli subsequentes, et inde trahere originem et auctoritatem (*De legibus,* f. 274 (IV, 113)): subsequently, in 1253, he was ordered to hand over the "first" roll to the chief justice but keep a second roll himself, and to retain custody of the king's writs returned to the court (*Close Rolls, 1251-1253,* p. 374). The keeper of the rolls and writs of Chancery was also on occasion styled *protonotarius* (P. Chaplais, *English Royal Documents, 1199-1461* (Oxford, 1971), pp. 20-21).
(*125*) Dunham, *op. cit.,* p. 25.

of the *prenotarius,* and his words alone, that the author gives us in a short account of what happens when an essoin *de malo lecti* is cast (*126*).

While it is just conceivable that the author of the treatise was a man who had been or was a justice in the Bench, the interest in the minutiae of procedural detail and the close acquaintance with, and interest in, the making of plea-roll enrolments of cases and the formulae of judicial writs, all point strongly to the author being one of the clerks of the court: and his close acquaintance with the functions of the *prenotarius* tend to suggest that among the various clerks, the most likely candidates for authorship of the treatise will be found among the *prenotarii,* the keepers of the rolls and writs. It is, I think, just possible to go further and suggest one particular *prenotarius* as the most likely candidate: his name is John Blundel.

John son of Ralph Blundel is first mentioned in 1241 when, with his brothers William, Tristram and Richard, he made a final concord with one John son of Thomas Blundel (evidently a relation) concerning land at Challock in the county of Kent (*127*). About the same time he is to be found acting as bailiff of the neighbouring royal manor of Ospringe (*128*), possibly during the period that the manor was leased by Robert of Shottenden and others (*129*): and it was probably through Robert, who seems to have been in the royal service from the 1230s onwards (*130*), and to have come from the Shottenden in Kent which is close to

---

(*126*) *Ibid.,* p. 28.

(*127*) *Calendar of Kent Feet of Fines,* ed. I. Churchill, R. Griffin, F. W. Hardman (Kent Archaeological Soc., Records Branch, xv (1956)), pp. viii, 163.

(*128*) Ospringe is about ten miles due north of Challock. John is termed bailiff of Ospringe in a charter of William de Puttewode and his wife Ysoude, confirming a grant by William Esperun to the hospital of Ospinge, to which he is a witness: St. John's College Cambridge, Deeds no. 7/164. In Hilary term 1242, what seems to have been the same land was assured to the hospital by a final concord between its warden and William and Ysoude: *ibid.,* no. 7/165.

(*129*) E371/85m 18d (Pipe Roll, 25 Henry III): Robert of Shottenden, John son of Henry, and Ernulf Cad' owe £55 for a 4-year lease of Ospringe. Robert owes £41 10s. for the corn of Ospringe.

(*130*) He was custodian of the vacant see of Norwich, a position of the sort normally held by royal clerks, in 1236-7 (*Cal. Pat. Rolls, 1232-47,* pp. 157, 159, 173. *Cal. Liberate Rolls,* i. 262, 274, 278, 290). In 1242 he was presented by the King, during a vacancy in the see of Canterbury, to the living of Mersham in Kent and in 1245 to the deanery of Chester, during a vacancy in the see of Lichfield, while in 1247 he was also presented by the king to the prebend of Peasmarsh in the royal chapel of Hastings (*Cal. Pat. Rolls. 1232-47,* pp. 289-447, 509): all preferments of a kind normally associated with royal service. Further evidence that by 1247 he had been for some time in the king's service is provided by a grant to him of ten oaks in the royal forest of Gillingham "ad se hospitandum" (*Close Rolls, 1242-1247,* p. 520) and by a royal mandate copied onto the Close Rolls in that year requiring a certain Italian to be provided with a robe "cum penula de bissis et furrura competenti" of the same kind as that of "R de Sotindon" (=Robert of Shottenden) (*Close Rolls, 1247-1251,* p. 18). By 1251 he was of sufficient importance to be named as one of the three men present in the *curia domini regis* at Guildford for the acknowledgment of a quitclaim by Nicholas de Wauncy (*ibid.,* p. 557), and to be named among the witnesses to royal charters enrolled on the Charter Rolls (C53/43 mm. 5, 2; C53/44 m. 27).

Challock (*131*), that he entered the royal service. By 1252 he seems to have been a fairly senior clerk in Chancery, for in October of that year, he joined with Robert of Shottenden, Henry of Wingham (*132*) and Adam "de Aston" (*133*), all (including John) described in the bond as *clerici domini regis Anglie,* in standing surety by bond to two merchants of Sienna for 60 marks lent to their fellow clerk ("dilecto clerico et socio nostro"), Henry de Maulay for business at the papal *curia* (*134*). The next year, he was involved in organising the preparation of ships from the Cinque Ports for Henry III's expedition to Gascony (*135*), and in buying wine for the Queen at Winchelsea (*136*), and in the following year he was sent to Newcastle-on-Tyne to requisition ships there for the King's service (*137*). It is very probable that John Blundel held the office of keeper of rolls and writs in the Shropshire eyre of January-February 1256 (*138*): and possible that he had held the same office in earlier eyres of the same circuit in the counties of Buckinghamshire, Bedfordshire, Gloucestershire, Worcestershire and Herefordshire from October 1254 onwards. In December 1256 he received robes from the King as a clerk of chancery (*139*); and in March 1257 a hunting licence was granted at the instance of John Blundel, King's clerk (*140*). It was in keeping with his position as a senior Chancery clerk that in April 1257 he was appointed joint-warden of the St. Ives' fair (*141*), and that from 20 May to 9 August 1257 he was joint custodian of the temporalities of the vacant see of Norwich (*142*).

It was probably in October 1257 and therefore after the death of Robert of Shottenden, who had been a justice of the Bench for just over

(*131*) There is a Shottenden in Kent about 1¾ miles WNW of Chilham: Challock is about three miles SW of Chilham. That Robert came from Kent is suggested not only by his lease of Ospringe and his earliest preferment by the Crown being to the church of Mersham (see preceding note), but also by the fact that he was acquiring land at Pickinden in Goudhurst in Kent in 1236 (*Kent Feet of Fines,* p. 133), and by the fact that at his death it was goods which he had possessed at Stockbury and Woodnesborough in Eastry, both in Kent, which were ordered to be seised until his debts were paid (*Close Rolls, 1256-1259,* p. 163). There is, however, no evidence other than his surname to link him with Shottenden.

(*132*) Subsequently (in 1255) Chancellor: and like Shottenden and Blundel of Kent origin.

(*133*) Adam is first mentioned as a royal clerk in 1243 (*Close Rolls, 1242-1247,* p. 95) and is specifically described as a Chancery clerk in 1248, 1250 and 1253 (*Close Rolls, 1247-1251,* pp. 51, 262; *Close Rolls, 1253-1254,* p. 200).

(*134*) P.R.O. C146/9513. John may well have been a royal clerk already in 1245 when, as John Blundel of the diocese of Canterbury, he received a papal indult to hold an additional benefice with cure of souls: such privileges often went to royal clerks (*Cal. Papal Registers,* i, 214).

(*135*) *Cal. Pat. Rolls, 1247-1258,* p. 230: cf. *Close Rolls, 1251-1253,* p. 402.

(*136*) *Cal. Liberate Rolls,* iv, 153.

(*137*) *Cal. Pat. Rolls, 1247-1258,* p. 363.

(*138*) JUST/1/734 m. 38 (note at foot): in the thirteenth century, the keepers of rolls and writs both in eyres and in the Bench were usually by origin Chancery clerks.

(*139*) *Close Rolls, 1256-1259,* p. 17.

(*140*) *Cal. Pat. Rolls, 1247-1258,* p. 544.

(*141*) *Ibid.,* p. 549; *Cal. Lib. Rolls,* iv, 367, 374, 375.

(*142*) *Cal. Lib. Rolls,* vi, no. 900.

a year prior to his death in July 1257 (*142a*) that John Blundel was appointed keeper of the rolls and writs of the Bench (*143*): and he retained that office until dismissed early in 1262 (*144*). His term of office would, therefore, have been such as to have given him first-hand experience of cases heard before Henry of Bath (*145*) and before Roger of Thurkleby (*146*), the only two royal justices whose opinions are cited in the treatise (*147*). Even more significantly, he would have been keeper of the rolls and writs of the Bench when, in 1260, the justices of the Bench received the second writ from the king's council about the computation in leap-years of the year and day allowed a man pronounced sick, which is mentioned in the treatise (*148*), and would, by virtue of his office, have taken official custody of that writ (*149*). Although still alive in 1263, when he is found with his brother Richard, acting as one of the witnesses to a dower settlement between Robert de Crevequer, lord of the Kent barony of Chatham, and Alice, Robert's grandfather's widow (*150*), and, again with Richard, as one of the executors of the will of Alice's late husband, Hamo de Crevequer (*151*), John Blundel was dead by Michaelmas 1265 (*152*). As I have shown, there is nothing in the treatise incompatible

---

(*142a*) *Matthaei Parisiensis Chronica Majora,* ed. H. R. Luard (Rolls Series, 1874-1884), v, 642.

(*143*) His immediate predecessor, Richard de Middleton, received five marks of his annual fee of ten marks at Michaelmas 1257, but by virtue of a writ which suggests that he had already then left office (*Cal. Lib. Rolls,* iv, 402). Blundel received the five marks due to the keeper of rolls and writs at Easter 1258 (*Cal. Lib. Rolls,* vi, no. 2299Y).

(*144*) Payment of his fee as keeper of rolls and writs between Michaelmas 1258 and Michaelmas 1260 was ordered by writs whose enrolment is calendared in *Cal. Lib. Rolls,* iv, 441, 465, 480, 511, 532; and that he still held that office in Michaelmas term 1261 is indicated by the way his name is to be found at the top of mm. 31, 81, 81d, 82, 82d, 83, 83d, 84, 85, 85d, and 86 and at the tail of m. 78 of the surviving Bench plea-roll for that term (K.B.26/171). That he had been removed from office some time before 1 August 1262 is shown by the enrolment of a writ of that date ordering payment to Roger de Leicester of 3½ marks for the expenses of himself and his colleagues in keeping the rolls and writs of the Bench since John Blundel's removal from office: *Cal. Lib. Rolls,* v, 107.

(*145*) Henry of Bath's last period as senior justice of the Bench was from Trinity term 1256 to Easter term 1258.

(*146*) Roger of Thurkleby's last period as senior justice of the Bench was from Michaelmas tern 1258 to Trinity term 1260.

(*147*) Dunham, *op. cit.,* pp. 23, 24, 37 (Bath) and 46 (Thurkleby).

(*148*) Above, p. 149.

(*149*) He was not, of course, keeper of rolls and writs when the first writ was sent to them in 1256, which may explain why he mentions only the second writ.

(*150*) *Close Rolls, 1261-1264,* p. 229.

(*151*) P.R.O. E159/37m. 14d: Richard Blundel had at one time been the steward of Hamo de Crevequer: *Cal. Charter Rolls,* ii, 301.

(*152*) E 159/40m. 3: mandate to the sheriff to levy a debt owed to Peter de Gisors, citizen of London, by the late John Blundel from his executors Hubert la Veyle and Richard Blundel. Hubert and Richard had earlier acted together as the executors of Robert of Shottenden, whose London house(s) they has been intending in 1259 to sell to John Blundel: *Select Cases in the Exchequer of Pleas,* ed. H. Jenkinson and B. E. R. Fermoy (Selden Soc., xlviii (1931)), p. 23, no. 61. They subsequently, still acting as Robert's executors, sold them to Hervey of Boreham, in February 1265: E368/39m. 13d.

with composition prior to 1265, since it could have been written at any date between 1260 and 1272 (*153*); and the sudden, and perhaps premature, death of its author in 1265 would provide a plausible explanation of how a treatise that is so clearly both incomplete and unedited and unrevised could have got into general circulation by, perhaps, the 1270s.

One last feature of the treatise which might also find an explanation in the hypothesis of John Blundel's authorship is the use in the treatise of the real names and places connected with the neighbourhood of Harting. It is, I think, clear beyond reasonable doubt that the John Blundel of Harting mentioned in the treatise (*154*), and the John Blundel who was Chancery clerk and subsequently the keeper of the rolls and writs of the Bench, the suggested author of the treatise, were two different men, though contemporaries. It is hardly likely that a busy and senior Chancery clerk would have had the time to have been one of the jurors for the 1253 inquisition *post mortem* into the Sussex lands held at his death by Matthew Huse (*155*): and none of the quite considerable volume of evidence relating to John Blundel, the Chancery clerk, says anything about a son named Nicholas (*156*), indeed, such evidence as there is suggests that, as befitted a clerk in holy orders, he probably died without issue (*157*). Most of the evidence links John Blundel, the Chancery clerk, with the county of Kent (*158*), though he does seem also to have had interests in Bedfordshire (*159*), Suffolk (*160*), Devon (*161*), and in Sussex, too, though at some

(*153*) Above, p. 375.

(*154*) Above, p. 378.

(*155*) Above, p. 379 and note 63.

(*156*) As we've seen, it was his son Nicholas who succeeded the John Blundel of Harting in the family lands: above, p. 379.

(*157*) In 1259 he settled land which he had probably acquired prior to 1249 (when he was being sued for dower land in Bedfordshire by Maud de Carun: K.B. 26/135m. 6d) at Tempsford in Bedfordshire on himself for life with reversion to his brother, Richard, and Richard's heirs: *Bedfordshire Feet of Fines*, p. 169. This probably means that he had no issue.

(*158*) Above, p. 387: and note that in 1259 he was bringing an action of account against one Richard le Prestre for the time during which Richard had acted as the bailiff of his lands at Challock and "Dene", both apparently in Kent (K.B. 26/162m 32d), that in 1261 and 1262 he joined with his brother Richard and his nephews Roger and Robert in bringing litigation against the prior of Canberbury cathedral priory concerning common of pasture in Challock (K.B. 26/171m. 20, K.B. 26/166m. 2), and that in 1261 he obtained a promise from the King of being presented to the church of Headcorn in Kent (*Close Rolls, 1259-1261*, p. 488).

(*159*) Above, note 157: but note that the Crevequer family of the barony of Chatham in Kent, with whom John Blundel and his brother Richard had connections (above, p. 167), held land in Little Barford, close to Tempsford (*Close Rolls, 1261-1264*, p. 206).

(*160*) Where he was parson of the church of Layham: W. Rye, *A Calendar of the Feet of Fines for Suffolk*, p. 62. K.B. 26/169m. 70. In September 1261 he was entrusted with the mission of explaining on the king's behalf to the men of Norfolk and Suffolk the king's affection and benevolence for them, and that he had no intention to subvert their rights and liberties: *Cal. Pat. Rolls, 1258-1266*, p. 174. It may be no coincidence that the Layham family, who had interests at Layham also held land at Little Barford, close to Tempsford (W. Farrer, *Honors and Knights' Fees*, iii, 177-179).

(*161*) In July 1259 a John Blundel, probably this one, was presented to the church of

considerable distance from Harting (*162*); while John Blundel "of Harting" seems firmly tied to Harting and its immediate neighbourhood. If there really was some litigation in the Bench in the late 1250s or early 1260s involving John Blundel of Harting, might it not have seemed tempting to John Blundel, the Chancery clerk, to make use of this litigation involving his name-sake (who might even have been a distant relative of his) for illustrative purposes in his treatise, thereby allowing him to smuggle his own name into the work? Such a hypothesis could well explain the presence in the treatise of John Blundel of Harting, Richard le Jay and William Huse.

If John Blundel really was the author of the treatise, how did Hengham's name come to be attached to it? There are at least two possible explanations for this. One would be that after John Blundel's death, the manuscript of the incomplete treatise came to the thirteenth century equivalent of a commercial publisher—someone who hired out manuscripts for copying, that he saw no commercial prospect in a *Summa Johannis Blundel,* and for purely commercial reasons attached the name of Hengham, perhaps already by then chief justice of King's Bench, to the work. The other, which reflects rather less credit on Hengham, would be that somehow after Blundel's death the manuscript came to Hengham's hands, that he then put his name to it or perhaps simply lent it to somebody without making it clear that it was not his work but Blundel's, and that therefore when it was copied it was his name which was attached to the treatise. However it happened, we can, I think, be fairly sure that the treatise was not the work of Hengham: and even if we cannot be equally sure that the treatise was the work of John Blundel, there is at least a strong possibility that he is the true author of the treatise.†

Postscript

Further texts of the treatise which have come to light since include Huntington Library, MS. HM 923, ff. 84r-104r; British Library, MS. Additional 22708, ff. 15r-25r; Philadelphia Free Library, MS. LC 14.3, ff. 142r-147v; Philadelphia Free Library, MS. LC 14.6, ff. 31v-45r; Philadelphia Free Library, MS. LC 14.7, ff. 1r-33r; Philadelphia Free Library, MS. LC 14.16, ff. 108v-125v; Philadelphia Free Library, MS. LC 14.19, ff. 148v-166v; Bridgenorth Parish Church, Stackhouse Library MS. 2, ff. 102v-117v; Liverpool Athenaeum, MS. Gladstone 27, ff. 75v-92r.

Poltimore in Devon, and in 1260 he had some sort of claim to the Tidcombe portion of Tiverton: *The Registers of Bishops Bronescombe and Quivil,* ed. F. C. Hingeston-Randolph (London, 1889), pp. 163, 186.

(*162*) He seems to have held a house at Telscombe in Sussex, roughly 30 miles ESE from Harting: in 1260 he was bringing litigation against persons accused of attacking his house there and seizing lambs in the house to the value of thirty shillings (K.B. 26/225 m. 4, K.B. 26/169m. 7, K.B. 26/166m. 22).

†I wish to record my thanks to the late G. D. G. Hall, the late C. A. F. Meekings and Robert Palmer for help and criticism given to me in the preparation of this article.

18

'Quo Waranto' Law in the Reign of Edward I:
A Hitherto Undiscovered Opinion of
Chief Justice Hengham

At the end of this article will be found the text of a set of questions and answers concerning the procedural and substantive law applicable in "quo waranto" cases. These questions and answers survive in at least three different manuscripts: MS. Douce 139 in the Bodleian Library at Oxford, MS. Additional 5761 in the British Library and MS. HM 19920 in the Huntington Library, San Marino, California (*1*).

The first section of this article deals with the question of their authorship and original context. It shows that the questions were drawn up by one of the justices of the Northamptonshire eyre of 1285 (perhaps by the senior justice, John des Vaux) and that, in their original form, they were contained in a schedule attached to a letter to Ralph de Hengham, chief justice of the court of King's Bench. Hengham himself was responsible for the answers and these must date from late 1285 or early 1286. The next section places this consultation in the broader context of the variety of procedures known to have been utilized in later thirteenth century England by the judiciary when faced with difficult points of law which required expert assistance. The third section discusses, in general terms, the development of "quo waranto" law during the years immediately prior to 1285 and the fourth provides a more detailed commentary on the various legal points raised in the individual questions and answers. In this section, the questions and Hengham's answers are paraphrased in English, and the significance of the different views on points of "quo waranto" law thus revealed is explained. These views are also placed in the wider context of the actual practice of the courts in "quo waranto" cases during this period. The final section of the article evaluates Hengham's stance on matters of "quo waranto" law in the context of contemporary disagreements between legal experts on this matter; and speculates on the possible significance of that stance for Hengham's career as a royal justice.

I

Our only real clues as to the format of the original manuscript of this set of questions and answers, the manuscript from which the present text

---

(*1*) It is possible that other copies of it survive in manuscript. The author would be grateful to anyone knowing of the existence of such a copy for drawing his attention to it.

was derived, are those provided by the penultimate paragraph of our text (2). In this paragraph (which seemingly was only copied by mistake) (3) the writer mentions both an opening section of the letter (*littera*), of which the paragraph with its concluding valediction was the final section, and a schedule (*cedula*). The writer asks his correspondent to give his answers to the writer's questions (*premissi articuli*) in the windows (*fenestre*) of the schedule. The obvious inference is that the questions were written on a separate sheet and that the writer left certain parts of this sheet (the so-called 'windows') blank, so that the correspondent could write his answers to the questions in these blank spaces (4). The blank spaces were probably opposite rather than under the individual questions. This would explain why the copyist(s) managed to split what was clearly originally a single question into two separate questions (here numbered 2 and 3) (5) which are separated by part of the answer to that question.

These questions and answers are given no title or *incipit* in two of three texts, and the *incipit* of the Huntington MS. (*Incipiunt notabilia de quo waranto*) is not very helpful. Nor do any of our manuscripts provide any other direct evidence as to the identity of the original writer and his correspondent. It is, however, clear from the content of the individual questions that the person who composed them must have been a royal justice, required in the course of his professional duties to resolve a number of difficulties that had arisen in his court as to the substantive and procedural law that was applicable in "quo waranto" proceedings (6). A further, and more specific, clue as to the writer's identity is provided by question 5, which asks about the

---

(2) Appendix I, below, p. 440.

(3) It is omitted from the version in the Huntington Library MS.

(4) *Fenestra* is not used in this sense in classical latin nor is such a usage recorded in the *Revised Medieval Latin Word-list*. John Baker has drawn my attention to the use of the English word 'windowe' in this sense in the later fifteenth century in *YB Pasch.* 5 4 Edward IV, f. 14, pl. 23.

(5) The actual numbering of the questions is my own work but corresponds to what seems to have been the intentions of the scribes of these texts. On questions 2 and 3 see also below, p. 411.

(6) Each question starts with a brief summary of the point in dispute, followed either by a succinct statement of two different views held on that point (questions 1, 5 and 6) or a statement of a single view from which others are said to dissent (questions 2/3 and 4). Each question conveys an implied request, only made explicit in question 5 (*quid sit agendum*: what is to be done?). It is clear from this that the questioner was someone who needed to be able to resolve these problems. He was thus not a serjeant, merely concerned with advancing a plausible line of argument on behalf of the Crown or of a private client, but must have been a royal justice who needed to adjudicate on such disputes. For evidence that suggests that the differing viewpoints may have been those of the justices themselves and not simply those of the serjeants see below, p. 430.

correct procedure to be adopted in the case of those possessing royal franchises in the county of Northampton, who have not "claimed" those franchises in "the present eyre". This indicates that the writer acted as a justice at one of the two judicial visitations of Northamptonshire, those of 1285 and 1330, at which the possessors of franchises were required to put in a formal "claim" to their franchises, a statement of what franchises they claimed within the county and by what warrant (7). By itself, the handwriting of this section of MS Douce 139 would provide a strong argument against assigning the composition of the questions to as late a date as 1330. This is confirmed by the reference in the answer to question 1 to the king's refusal to be bound by prescription, since after 1293 the Crown accepted that it was bound by the same prescription date as other litigants (8). It is clear, therefore, that the man who drew up the questions was one of the justices of the 1285 eyre.

That gives a choice of some five men: John des Vaux, the senior or chief justice of the eyre, or one of the puisne justices, John of Mettingham (Metingham), William of Saham, Roger Loveday or Nicholas Gras (9). The balance of probability would seem to favour John des Vaux as the writer. If "quo waranto" proceedings in this eyre were heard separately by one of the puisne justices as occurred elsewhere on the same circuit (10), it would seem probable that he would turn first to his judicial colleagues, and in particular to his senior colleague, for advice before approaching an outsider: and that if they were unable to resolve his problems, it would have been thought most fitting for the senior justice to approach an outsider for advice and assistance. *A fortiori,* if "quo waranto" proceedings in this eyre were heard by the justices collectively, it would surely have been thought most proper for it to be the chief justice, des Vaux, who approached the outsider for assistance.

It is plain from his answer to question 2 that the correspondent to whom these questions were sent and who provided authoritative replies to each of them was someone able to speak with authority of the recent practice of the court of King's Bench (11); and his answer to question 1 indicates that he was someone able to speak on behalf not only of himself but also of certain, unnamed colleagues (12). Taken together these references seem to point to Ralph de Hengham, chief justice of the court of

---

(7) A proclamation requiring the submission of such claims only became part of the preliminaries to the eyre in 1278: D. W. Sutherland, *Quo Warranto Proceedings in the Reign of Edward I, 1278-1294* (Oxford, 1963), pp. 25-27, 190-193.

(8) Sutherland, *op. cit.,* pp. 108, 212.

(9) The names of the justices who acted in this eyre are known from the final concords made during it: below, n. 15.

(10) John of Mettingham is known to have held separate sessions for the hearing of "quo waranto" and related pleas with an associate who was not a full justice in the 1281-4 Lincolnshire eyre, the 1286 Huntingdonshire eyre, and the 1287 Bedfordshire eyre: Sutherland, *op. cit.,* p. 35.

(11) Appendix I, below, p. 438.

(12) Appendix I, below, p. 437.

King's Bench since 1274, as having been the recipient of the letter. Evidence that confirms this identification is provided by the reference in the answer to question 1 to litigation between Henry III and H. de la Wade concerning land in a place called "Staunton", a "member" of "Wodestoke" (*13*). Two separate procedural stages in a case in which Henry III was claiming land in an unspecified locality in the county of Oxfordshire which can be shown to be Stanton Harcourt against one Henry de la Wade are recorded on the plea-rolls of the court of King's Bench for Trinity term 1258. There is no reason to suppose that this particular case was of any very great legal significance, that it was the kind of case that any well-informed legal expert would still have remembered a quarter of a century later. Hengham, however, would have had good reason to remember it, since, as a young man, he had acted as de la Wade's attorney in the case (*14*).

The 1285 eyre of Northamptonshire opened on about 30 September and finished on about 8 December (*15*). The reference to the "present" eyre in question 5 indicates that at the time when the questions were written, the eyre itself was still in progress; they can therefore be confidently dated within this fairly short period. When the answers were written is less certain. The questions (and in particular question 5) clearly required a fairly rapid answer: and the writer obviously went to some trouble to ensure that he received Hengham's reply as soon as possible— instructing the messenger who brought the questions to await the reply (*16*), and constructing what amounted to a questionnaire so that

(*13*) Appendix I, below, p. 437.

(*14*) The essoin cast by Hengham as the attorney of de la Wade is recorded on a separate essoin roll of this term: KB 26/157 m. 7. An adjournment of the case, later in the same term, for lack of jurors is recorded on KB 26/158 m. 18. The plea-rolls containing pleading and verdict do not survive. The land in demand, can, however, almost certainly be identified as land in Stanton Harcourt, Oxfordshire ("Staunton"), where both Henry de la Wade and his father held land by hunting serjeanty as of the royal demesne of Woodstock ("Wodestoke"): *Book of Fees*, pp. 103, 235, 589, 830, 1375: *Cal. Inq. P.M.*, ii, no. 620. Hengham probably became involved in the case through his early patron, the royal justice, Giles of Erdington. A long-standing connection can be traced between the Erdington family and Henry de la Wade. At the time of his death, Thomas of Erdington, Giles' father, was in possession of the wardship of Henry and of his land: *Rot. Litt. Claus.*, i. 356b; *Cal. Inq. Misc.*, i. no. 827. In 1225 Rose of Cockfield, Thomas' widow, paid one hundred shillings on behalf of Henry, that he might be allowed to take seisin of his father's land: *Exc. e Rot. Fin.*, i, 125. One of Giles' property transactions was witnessed by Henry (E210/227) and Henry was, like Hengham, one of Giles' executors (CP 40/24m. 27d).

(*15*) These dates, being drawn from the evidence of the feet of fines, are only approximate. The earliest fines are from the morrow of Michaelmas return-day, the week beginning 30 September (CP 25 (1)/174/53 nos. 137-139), and the plea-rolls also give the morrow of Michaelmas as the date of the beginning of the eyre. The latest fines are from the return-day of three weeks after Martinmas, the week beginning 2 December (CP25 (1)/175/55 nos. 201-203). The Peterborough chronicler noted that the eyre lasted for ten weeks, which would confirm these dates: *Chronicon Petroburgense*, ed. T. Stapleton (Camden Soc., original series, xlvii (1849)), pp. 124-126.

(*16*) Appendix I, below, p. 440.

Hengham merely had to write in the answers without needing to rehearse the matter on which he was giving the reply thereby saving him time and effort. It is probable, therefore, that Hengham answered almost immediately, but there is nothing in the surviving evidence to prove this, and it is possible, but unlikely, that he delayed some weeks before replying. The replies are very unlikely to date from any later than early in 1286.

II

From the treatise known as "Glanvill", which was written during the 1180s, we learn of a procedural device apparently of customary origin, which allowed any seignorial court to adjourn a case in which a difficult point of law had arisen into the king's court, in order that it might receive "the advice and the assent . . . of the court of the lord king as to what ought by right to be done in the case". Once the point was settled, the case would be adjourned back into the seignorial court from which it had come, so that the final judgment in the case could be given there (*17*). "Glanvill" also mentions a similar procedure for resolving problems of law that had arisen in cases being heard in county courts: here, however, because the county courts belonged to the king, once a case had been adjourned into the king's court, it would remain there and final judgment be given there also (*18*). Although neither of these procedures seems to have survived into the thirteenth century, this method of dealing with difficult problems—that of formally adjourning a case in which the problem had arisen into a higher and more expert court did survive. In 1217 in the second reissue of Magna Carta local assize justices were authorised to adjourn assizes of novel disseisin and mort d'ancestor in which legal problems had arisen into the Bench (*19*). There is also, as will be seen, evidence from the reign of Edward I of justices in eyre adjourning cases which raised legal problems with which they were unable to cope, to a session of the king's parliament (*20*).

A different method of dealing with such problems was for the court in question to seek the advice of the king's council on the point of law involved, without any formal removal of the case before the council or into any other court. Under this mode of proceeding, judgment in the case on the disputed points would be given by the justices before whom those points had first been argued: but this judgment would be in accordance with the advice which they had received. It is difficult to know how far back this method of resolving legal difficulties goes. There is, however, clear evidence that it was in use by the late thirteenth or early fourteenth

(*17*) *Glanvill*, VIII, 11 (ed. Hall, pp. 102-103).
(*18*) *Glanvill*, VI, 8 (ed. Hall, p. 62).
(*19*) J. C. Holt, *Magna Carta* (Cambridge, 1965), pp. 352-353: this clause was repeated *verbatim* in the 1225 reissue.
(*20*) Below, p. 400. But note that the initiative for removal in these cases came from above rather than below.

centuries in each of the main superior royal courts (21).

This set of questions and answers point to another, and less formal, method of dealing with the same kind of problem: that of taking the advice of an outside expert on the problems (22). Just how common such informal consultations were is not something that can now be stated with certainty. What can be said is that this set of questions and answers does not stand entirely alone as evidence for the existence in the later thirteenth century of such a practice. The so-called *Tractatus de Antiquo Dominico* (23), is a document of the same general type: an expert's opinion. It was evidently delivered in response to a specific request, concerning a difficult point of law relating to ancient demesne tenure that had arisen in an assize of novel disseisin. It may be that such informal consultations were as rare as the surviving evidence for their existence. Many such consultations would, however, presumably have been oral and have therefore gone unrecorded. Even written consultations would normally have been regarded as being of merely ephemeral interest, and as being, in any case, of a confidential nature. The odds would therefore be against the survival of such consultations.

It may be that such informal consultations were a normal part of the practice of the royal courts in late thirteenth century England. During the interval between the adjournments of cases for judgment so often recorded on the plea-rolls and the judgments eventually recorded on those rolls, there may have taken place not only lengthy discussions between the justices of the court, and formal consultations between the justices and the king's council, but also the informal consultation of outside experts.

III

Although certain isolated individual eyres were held in 1275-6, it was only late in 1278 that the first full-scale countrywide eyre visitations of the reign of Edward I began. Two eyre circuits were then established. One started work in the counties of Southern England and was led by John of Reigate. The other started work in the counties of Northern England and was led by John des Vaux. The justices of these circuits had, of course, the normal tasks and jurisdiction of the justices in eyre, as these had

(21) For the eyre see e.g. *Rex* v. *Earl of Gloucester* (Sutherland, *op. cit.,* pp. 195-197); for the court of King's Bench see e.g. *Rex and Boteler* v. *Hopton* (KB 27/128 m. 8d and *Rotuli Parliamentorum,* i. 79); for the Bench see e.g. *Lymesy* v. *Abbot of Westminster* (*Y.B. 6 and 7 Edward II,* ed. W. C. Bolland (Selden Soc., Y.B. series, xv (1918) pp. 43-44).

(22) At about the time the letter was sent, the king's council was in session at Winchester and the court of King's Bench was, as usual, holding its sessions near by: *Select Cases in the Court of King's Bench,* vol. IV, ed. G. O. Sayles (Selden Soc., lxxiv (1955)), p. xcviii. Nonetheless, it seems clear from that part of the letter which was copied as part of the text, and from the tenor of Hengham's answers, that he had been approached informally, and was not answering the questions as a result of having them referred to him for expert advice by the king's council.

(23) Printed by A. J. Horwood in the preface to his edition of *Year-Book 20 and 21 Edward I* (Rolls Series, 1866), pp. xviii-xix.

developed over the previous century. To these were added in 1278 the duty not only of receiving and determining presentments under a large number of additional chapters (the "new" as opposed to the "old" chapters) of the eyre, and hearing and determining plaints made to them, but also of enquiring into what franchises were exercised by franchise-holders within the counties which they visited and by what warrant they claimed to exercise those franchises (24). In practice, too, they had to hear a volume of cases brought in the king's name for the recovery of both land and advowsons that was much larger than had been customary in any of the eyre visitations of the reign of Henry III.

The justices of the "Northern" eyre circuit seem to have been somewhat tardy in commencing the enquiries into franchises (25). However, by the time they reached Northamptonshire in 1285, they had received claims to franchises in at least four counties (26) and had heard pleadings in "quo waranto" and similar actions brought in the king's name in some five counties in all. It could not, therefore, be said that in 1285 the justices of the "Northern" circuit lacked experience of hearing franchise claims and "quo waranto" and related litigation. This makes it, at first sight at least, rather strange that most of the questions sent to Hengham are on what seem to be basic and simple points of "quo waranto" law.

If we are to understand the reasons for this, then the first thing which needs to be borne in mind is the fact that there seems to have been no general consensus among the judiciary as to the main principles of "quo waranto" law. As Sutherland notes, the regulations made in 1278 at Gloucester, while giving detailed instructions as to the procedure to be followed in bringing the question of entitlement to franchises before the justices of future general eyres, had "given no guidance as to what principles of law were to govern [their] judgments" (27). The lack of any authoritative guidance on these matters had led the justices of the "Northern" circuit during the course of the very first eyre in which they heard "quo waranto" business, the Yorkshire eyre of 1279-81, to draw up a memorandum of points relating to "quo waranto" proceedings on which they required guidance (28); and it may well have been because of the large number of unresolved problems raised by "quo waranto" actions in that eyre that all such actions were adjourned into the parliament of

---

(24) A reasonably comprehensive picture of the extent of their jurisdiction is given by the writ of summons. That of the 1285 Northamptonshire eyre is printed in *Chronicon Petroburgense*, pp. 103-104.

(25) There is no evidence that such claims were received in either the 1278-9 Westmorland eyre or the 1279 Northumberland eyre, and it is doubtful whether they were received in the 1278-9 Cumberland eyre.

(26) Sutherland, *op. cit.*, pp. 222-223.

(27) Sutherland, *op. cit.*, p. 29.

(28) The memorandum is printed by Sutherland (*op. cit.*, p. 198). Unlike the document now under discussion, the memorandum simply states the point on which guidance is required, and does not attempt to explain what the different viewpoints on it are.

Michaelmas 1280 (*29*). By 1285 there had, it is true, been what seem to have been authoritative decisions by the king, by the king's council or the court of King's Bench on a number of points of "quo waranto" law: for example, as to the form to be taken by "quo waranto" writs brought for the recovery of franchises (*30*); as to the mesne process to be followed to secure the attendance of defendants in "quo waranto" actions (*31*); as to whether, in actions brought in the king's name for the recovery of land in which the king's attorney counted for the king of the seisin of the king's ancestors, the king was limited by the same statutory prescription as other demandants (which would not allow him to go further back than to the seisin of King Richard) (*32*). But a series of *ad hoc* decisions was no real substitute for a detailed and authoritative exposition of the law relating to "quo waranto" proceedings and related matters (*33*), and any value that it might have possessed was considerably lessened in practice both by the fact that justices were often ignorant of these "authoritative" decisions (*34*) and by the fact that in the absence of any binding doctrine of *stare decisis* they did not consider themselves necessarily bound to follow them (*35*). Moreover, the area in which doubt existed was con-

(*29*) Sutherland, *loc. cit.* The writ ordering this adjournment, which is dated 28 September 1280, is enrolled on m. 33d of JUST/1/1067.

(*30*) Sutherland, *op. cit.,* pp. 196-197 (king's council, 1279). Decisions were made allowing the use of "quo waranto" writs for the recovery of hundreds (king's council, 1279), disallowing their use for the recovery of advowsons (King's Bench, 1280) and disallowing their use for franchises, when the writ failed to specify separately all the places where the franchise was exercised (the king himself, at some date prior to Michaelmas 1280): Sutherland, *op. cit.,* pp. 196-98.

(*31*) "Postea coram rege apud Westm' a die sancti Johannis Baptiste in xv dies hoc anno, quia visum est domino regi et ejus consilio quod predicti justiciarii in placito Quo Waranto procedere debuissent per attachiamentum et postea per districcionem ad conveniendum ipsum abbatem domino regi de predicto placito respondere et non per capcionem alicujus libertatis in manum domini regis, consideratum est quod predicta libertas eidem abbati replegiatur. Et dictum est eidem abbati quod ulterius respondeat . . ." (KB 27/62m. 29d). The rather less revealing enrolment of the same decision made the following term is printed by Sutherland (*op. cit.,* p. 199).

(*32*) Below, p. 138 (the king himself, at some date prior to late 1285). Decisions were also made disallowing the averment that a defendant's ancestor had died seised of the franchise in question as a sufficient plea in answer to a writ of "quo waranto" (king's council, 1279), declaring that a royal confirmation of a private feoffment, in general terms, was no bar to the king's action to recover what had been so granted (King's Bench, Trinity 1285), and declaring that a royal grant of a manor "with its appurtenances" would not suffice as warrant for a franchise as high as return of writs, if made as recently as the reign of Henry III (king's council between 1281 and 1284): Sutherland, *op. cit.,* pp. 119, 125-126, 197.

(*33*) It is not, of course, certain whether such an authoritative exposition would ever have been politically possible in the reign of Edward I.

(*34*) Simple ignorance of what the king had decided about the inapplicability of the statutory prescription to actions brought in his name, is clearly revealed by question 1: below, pp. 402-8.

(*35*) Optimism that the court might be persuaded not to follow an earlier "authoritative" decision rather than ignorance of that decision on the part of pleaders and court seems to lie behind the continued use, even after 1285, of the argument that a general royal confirmation was a bar to the king's suit (Sutherland, *op. cit.,* pp. 125-126) and a renewed attempt in 1287 to use a "quo waranto" writ for the recovery of an advowson (*P.Q.W.,* p. 250).

tinually being expanded under the pressure of the ever more ingenious arguments advanced for the king by his attorneys (*36*): a pressure sufficient not only to reopen matters apparently authoritatively decided in earlier litigation but also to cast doubt even on matters apparently settled by legislative ordinance (*37*). The justices' difficulties were further compounded by a manifest reluctance on their part, a reluctance which if anything increased rather than diminished as time went by, to give judgment on any fundamental point of "quo waranto" law, particularly if that judgment seemed at all likely to go against the king. There were, then, relatively few of their own previous decisions to follow, even had they been so inclined.

Bearing all these considerations in mind, therefore, it is much less surprising than at first seems the case that the justices of the Northampton-shire eyre of 1285 should have been seeking Hengham's guidance on such simple, basic questions of "quo waranto" law. Just how little real progress had been made since 1279 in establishing the main outlines of "quo waranto" law is tellingly demonstrated by a comparison of these questions with the points on which guidance had been sought in the memorandum drawn up by justices of the same circuit half a decade before (*38*). Of the five points contained in that memorandum, only one, as to the mesne process to be followed in "quo waranto" actions, had been settled finally and does not appear among these questions: each of the four remaining points appears, in some form or other, among the questions put to Hengham.

IV

The separate plea-roll on which were recorded almost all the "quo waranto" pleas, and probably other related items of business, heard in the Northamptonshire eyre of 1285, is now lost and very probably no longer in existence (*39*). Some sort of record does, however, survive of five "quo waranto" cases heard in this eyre. It is unfortunate that no definite connection can be established between any of these cases and the points raised in the correspondence with Ralph de Hengham (*40*), since

---

(*36*) The clearest example of this is provided by the process by which it came to be doubted whether seisin since time out of mind was an adequate title to franchises: Sutherland, *op. cit.*, pp. 71-91.

(*37*) For attempts by the king's attorneys to circumvent the 1290 Statute of "Quo Waranto" see Sutherland, *op. cit.*, pp. 99-110. See also, below, pp. 423-34.

(*38*) Above, p. 399.

(*39*) For evidence proving that such a roll did once exist see Sutherland, *op. cit.*, pp. 229-236.

(*40*) Two cases were recorded, by error, on m. 45 of a civil pleas roll of the eyre, JUST/1/619. On the facts stated, one of these cases (*Rex* v. *Wydvill*) could have been the case which give rise to question 4, but the record is too laconic for this to be certain. The other case (*Rex* v. *Cancellis*) raises a problem as difficult as any discussed here: whether a royal grant in general terms could be sufficient warrant for tenure of a hundred. There is a note on the roll of the adjournment of this case into parliament, and presumably the mandate for this had arrived before the letter was sent to Hengham, rendering a reference to him unnecessary. A third

this means that it is now no longer possible to demonstrate the probable connection between each of those points and particular cases heard in the eyre.

What is, however, still possible, is to place the questions and answers in a somewhat broader contemporary context, with the aid of plea-roll material from elsewhere on both eyre circuits and from the two main central courts. It is to this exercise that most of the remainder of the article will be devoted.

Question 1

The first of the questions that were put to Hengham concerned the use by the king of writs of the "quo waranto" form (*41*) in seeking the recovery of "free tenement" (*42*) which he claimed to be part of the "demesne of his Crown" (*43*). Some, it was said, argued that the king was entitled to use writs of this type only when he was seeking the recovery of a franchise of some kind. When what he was attempting to recover was "free tenement", then, whatever the title he was asserting to it, he should use a writ of common form to do so, a writ of a type generally available to his subjects. Others, however, held this view to be incorrect. It was certainly true, they argued, that when the king's title went back to an acquisition (*44*) or an escheat (*45*) of the "free tenement" in question, he was bound to use a writ of common form to assert that title; and in his

---

case (*Rex* v. *Hastings*) survives in an official copy of the late fourteenth century (C260/93 no. 15). The argument of the king's attorney in this case against allowing parceners aid-prayer is strongly reminiscent of one of the views reported in question 2/3: ". . . regiam decet majestatem hujusmodi libertates revocare etate vel parcenaria alicujus non exspectata . . .". It cannot however be the case which gave rise to the question, because it concerns a franchise rather than a "free tenement". A fourth and fifth case, both brought by the king against the abbot of Peterborough, are recorded in full in the abbey's chronicle (*Chronicon Petroburgense* pp. 124-126). The latter raises a problem that is related to that mentioned in question 6: but again the franchise in question is the right to possess a private prison, not one of those mentioned in that question.

(*41*) "Quo waranto" writs summoned a defendant to appear on a certain day in a particular royal court to show "by what warrant" or title he claimed to exercise certain rights.

(*42*) "Free tenement" is used here to denote land or some other form of real property e.g. a seignory, for recovery of which one of the king's subjects would have had to bring a real action e.g. the writ of right, writ of entry, the assize of novel disseisin.

(*43*) The "demesne of the Crown" referred to here is probably to be identified with the lands that had belonged to the Crown when Domesday Book was compiled. The more common term for these lands, which were regarded as the permanent landed endowments of the Crown, was that used elsewhere, "ancient demesne".

(*44*) Apparently any acquisition (whether by gift, purchase or exchange) that had taken place since 1086.

(*45*) In the king's case, this term covered not just a right, analogous to that enjoyed by other feudal lords, to lands which his tenants forfeited for felony, or of which they had died in seisin, without leaving any heir, but also a prerogative right to all lands to which tenants who were subjects of the king of France would otherwise have been entitled, (the so-called lands or escheats of the Normans, Bretons and Flemings).

action he would have to prove the seisin either of himself or of an ancestor (46) within the statutory period of prescription (47). However, when the title alleged was that the "free tenement" was part of the ancient demesne of the Crown, the king was entitled to use a writ of "quo waranto" form to seek to recover it; and, when he did use this writ, he would not have to show that either he or any specific ancestor had ever been in seisin of the "free tenement" sought (since such "free tenement", like all franchises, by "common right" (48) belonged to the Crown), and the tenant of the "free tenement" would be obliged to show a sufficient title to it, even if it did not really belong to the ancient demesne (49). It was further asserted that in this second case the king was not bound by the statutory prescription period.

This is clearly not just an abstract, academic argument concerned solely with the form of words considered most appropriate to the making of the king's claim to "free tenement", in the various different types of circumstances in which such a claim could be made. The form of words used also had wider implications for the way in which the litigation initiated by such writs was to be conducted: and it was some of these, which led the king's attorneys to favour the use, wherever possible, of writs in the "quo waranto" form. But what were these implications?

The first obvious difference between litigation initiated by the two different types of writ lay in the mesne process associated with them: but with regard to this feature at least, the balance of advantage for the king would probably have lain in the use of the common, "precipe" type of writ (50).

A second difference lay in the different modes of pleading considered appropriate to the two types of writ. Here, the balance of advantage for the king clearly did lie in the use of the "quo waranto" writ. In actions brought by the "common" writs, the king, as demandant, would have to make out and prove a title to the "free tenement" he was seeking. In "quo waranto" litigation, where the king was seeking a hundred or

---

(46) In the case of acquisitions, seisin of the "free tenement" in demesne, in the case of feudal escheats, seisin of lordship over the free tenement; in the case of prerogative escheats (apparently overlooked here) seisin by the last person entitled to the "free tenement" before the breach between England and France, or before it descended to a Frenchman.

(47) By Westminster I c. 39 (1275), this was fixed as the period since 1189, the date of Richard I's coronation: *S.R.* i, 36.

(48) This means that there existed a rebuttable legal presumption to that effect.

(49) In other words, it would not be an adequate answer to such a writ to simply deny that the "free tenement" in question had ever formed part of the royal demesne.

(50) A decision of the king's council in the summer of 1281 (above n. 31) had settled that the mesne process to secure the defendant's appearance in "quo waranto" actions was to be the same as that generally used in personal actions: initial summons, attachment and grand distress (repeated indefinitely) with no possibility of judgment for the plaintiff by default. In common actions brought by "precipe", by contrast, mesne process was by "*cape*" (temporary seizure of the "free tenement" in dispute) followed by judgment in favour of the plaintiff by default.

franchise, all he had to do was to fully and correctly name in his writ the hundred or the places where the franchise was exercised (*51*)—without making out any kind of title to them (*52*); and this alone was sufficient to make the defendant show and prove his title to the hundred or franchise, either from a royal grant or from seisin uninterruptedly since time out of mind (*53*). In "quo waranto" litigation brought for the recovery of "free tenement" the king would have at least to specify in his writ whether his claim was that "the free tenement" was ancient demesne wrongfully alienated, a Norman escheat, or the like (*54*): but the burden of proof would still be shifted on to the tenant, who would have to make out and prove his title to the "free tenement" in question (*55*).

A third difference between the two different types of writ, was that only in actions brought by the "common" writs did the statutory prescription date apply, to bar older claims made by the king (*56*). In "quo waranto" actions, possibly because of the mode of pleading considered appropriate to such actions, no prescription barred an action by the king. Again, this might often, if not always, make the "quo waranto" writ preferable for the king's attorneys.

(*51*) Sutherland, *op. cit.*, p. 197 (decision by the king, given prior to Michaelmas 1280).

(*52*) The king's "title" was that all hundreds and franchises in England "naturally" belonged to the Crown, and should "revert" to it unless their present holder could show a sufficient warrant for doing so. The king's council had argued strongly, in 1279, against the inclusion of even the brief phrase ". . . which franchise belongs to our crown" in such writs, on the grounds that this might imply that some types of franchise did not: Sutherland, *op. cit.*, p. 197.

(*53*) But see below, pp. 427-28.

(*54*) The king's council, in making a decision to this effect, suggested that it was necessary simply because there was a considerable amount of land in England which did not fall into any of the categories of types of land to which the king was entitled: ". . . in brevibus 'quo waranto tenet tale manerium' necesse est mencionem facere 'quod est de corona nostra' vel 'quod debet esse in manum nostram tanquam escaeta nostra de terris Normannorum'—multa enim sunt maneria que nec sunt de corona nec de terris Normannorum, propter quod in petitione tenementi conveniens est quod exprimat causam petitionis sue . . ." (Sutherland, *op. cit.*, p. 196). It might also have been argued, however, that specifying, in general terms, what kind of title the king had or claimed to "free tenement" was necessary simply because in such a case there were a number of different kinds of title on which he could be relying: which was not true in the case of franchises.

(*55*) This is clearly assumed in question 1, and in most of the cases brought by "quo waranto" writs for "free tenement" in the decades before and after 1285. It was, however, a matter on which the justices of the Yorkshire eyre of 1279 had been in doubt (Sutherland, *op. cit.*, 198) and there is a "quo waranto" case in the court of King's Bench in Easter 1281 in which the king's attorney seems to have made an initial count alleging that Richard I had been seised of the "free tenement" in question (*Rex* v. *Hervile:* KB 27/60m 17d). In another case in King's Bench in Michaelmas 1280, a vouchee of the tenant seems to have been successful in driving the king's attorney to disclose the seisin on which he was relying and then in taking issue on that seisin (*Rex* v. *St. Elena:* KB 27/57m 31d): while in two cases in the Somerset eyre of 1280 (*Rex* v. *Urtiaco: P.Q.W.*, p. 688; *Rex* v. *Mussegros: P.Q.W.* p. 699), the king's attorney seems to have stated in an initial count when the land sought had been alienated from the royal demesne (which is almost, but not quite, the same thing as stating which king had last been rightfully seised of it).

(*56*) Above, n. 47.

There does exist evidence to show that successful objection had been made prior to 1285 to the use of "quo waranto" writs in seeking one particular type of "free tenement", the advowson (57). Advowsons did, however, constitute a rather special type of "free tenement" (58): and there is no positive evidence to prove that any similar objection had been made to the use of writs of this type when used to claim other types of "free tenement" in either of the eyre circuits or in the court of King's Bench during the preceding decade. Evidence for such a use of "quo waranto" writs is, however, largely confined to the years 1279-1281 (59): and it is possible that some earlier objection had led to their disuse for this purpose, though not to a definitive judgment against such a use.

In his answer to question 1, Hengham dealt first with the specific point on which his advice had been requested: whether or not the king could use "quo waranto" writs for the recovery of ancient demesne "free tenement". His answer seems not to have been based on any weighing up of the intrinsic merits and demerits of allowing the king to do so. He did not balance the desirability of allowing the Crown to recover as expeditiously as possible lands which had been intended to form part of its permanent endowment, resources which it required for administering the realm, against the desirability of ensuring to every tenant of land due process when he was impleaded for it. Instead his answer relied allegedly on what had been the past practice of the courts on this matter. Both "quo waranto" writs and common writs had, he said, been used in the past for this purpose. Writs of the common type had been used when the "free tenement" in question had been in the possession of the king or of one of his ancestors "within time of memory" (60): an instance of this

---

(57) In the case in the court of King's Bench in which judgment was given in Michaelmas term, 1280: *Rex* v. *Prior of Castle Acre* (printed in Sutherland, *op. cit.*, p. 198). The advowson in question was not claimed as "ancient demesne", simply as having belonged to the king's ancestors: but the grounds on which judgment was given, namely that "... tantum tria brevia data sunt placitabilia de advocacionibus etc., scilicet breve de recto, quare impedit, et ultime presentacionis", clearly excludes the use of "quo waranto" writs for the recovery of advowsons, whatever the king's title to them might be.

(58) Special rules applied to them and special legal actions were generally used for litigation about them.

(59) On the "Northern" circuit, such actions are common in the Yorkshire eyre (1279-81) (*P.Q.W.*, pp. 188, 190, 191, 192, 193, 194, 197, 198, 200): but subsequently there is only one example to be found in the Nottinghamshire eyre (1280-1) (JUST/1/670m 4d), and one in the Lincolnshire eyre (1281-4) (*P.Q.W.*, p. 440). On the "Southern" circuit 4 such actions were brought in the Somerset eyre (1280) (*P.Q.W.*, pp. 688, 690, 698, 699), and two in the Dorset eyre (1280) (*P.Q.W.*, p. 180 *bis*), and in the Oxfordshire eyre (1285), there are four cases which look as though they may have been brought by writs in such a form (*P.Q.W.*, pp. 666, 667, 668, 669). In the court of King's Bench, 4 cases brought by such writs were pleaded in Easter term 1280 (KB 27/53mm. 3, 4, 21 and 20d), one in the following Trinity term (KB 27/55m 17d), three in Michaelmas term 1280 (KB 27/57mm 23, 31d, 27d), and two in Easter term 1281 (KB 27/60mm 13, 17d).

(60) That is, within the period of time of which a jury might have cognizance: not necessarily the same thing as the statutory prescription period.

was the case brought by Henry III against Henry de la Wade for his land in Stanton Harcourt (*61*). Writs of the "quo waranto" form had been used to recover land which had been in possession of the king's ancestors only before time of memory; but it was necessary in such a case, if the writ was to be good, that the land be described as royal demesne in Domesday Book (*62*). The recollection of both Hengham and his colleagues was, he said, that of old the writ used by the king for the recovery of Norman escheats was a writ "precipe" (*63*), but that for serjeanties (*64*) the "quo waranto" was used. For land sought by other types of title, the "precipe" was the correct writ: and in such cases the king had to count on the seisin of some ancestor.

The distinction which Hengham draws in his answer between the circumstances where "quo waranto" writs were appropriate for the recovery of ancient demesne "free tenement" and those where a "precipe" was appropriate, though clear and logical, does not in fact reflect the invariable practice of the immediate past either in his own court (*65*) or in the eyre (*66*); nor do the general guide-lines which he laid down on the use of "precipe" and "quo waranto" writs in other situations seem to have been the ones invariably followed in the past, even in his own court (*67*). What his answer provides then, is a rationalisation of what past practice had been: not, as it claims, a faithful representation of that practice.

Hengham went on to comment on the assumptions made in the original question concerning the applicability of statutory prescription

---

(*61*) Above, p. 396, and n. 14.

(*62*) This is probably intended to be a rebuttal of the view expressed by those who argued in favour of the use of the writ that those impleaded by it could not take issue on whether or not the land had ever been part of the royal demesne: above, p. 403, and n. 49 .A similar view to Hengham's seems to have been held by Thornton: ". . . par le precipe si serreyt la dame a respounce par averement du pays, et des aunciene demenes le roy ne deyt nentee avere par pays, eyns deyt par le domesday": below, Appendix II.

(*63*) Of a special form, given in Hengham's answer.

(*64*) That is, for land alienated without licence from (inalienable) royal serjeanties.

(*65*) For "quo waranto" writs brought for ancient demesne of which Henry III had been in seisin see *Rex* v. *d'Aubeny*, *Rex* v. *Gacelyn* and *Rex* v. *St. Elena* (KB 27/53m. 20d; KB 27/55m. 17d.; KB 27/57m. 31d).

(*66*) For another "quo waranto" brought in the Somerset eyre of 1280 for land alienated as recently as the reign of Henry III see *Rex* v. *Urtiaco* (*P.Q.W.*, p. 688).

(*67*) For a "quo waranto" used to seek a Norman escheat in the King's Bench see *Rex* v. *Boteler* (KB 27/57m. 26d): though note that an earlier writ for the same land, quashed because the tenant's wife had not been named as joint-tenant of the land, had been in the form of a "precipe" (KB 27/47m. 1), and that "precipe" writs were used in the cases of *Rex* v. *Mortimer* (KB 27/17m. 12), *Rex* v. *FitzJohn* (KB 27/24m. 7), *Rex* v. *Stirklande* (KB 27/26m. 1d) and *Rex* v. *Leukenore* (KB 27/31m. 11d). Another "quo waranto" was brought for a Norman escheat in the Nottinghamshire eyre of 1280-1: *Rex* v. *Bingham* (JUST/1/670m. 4d). There are also single examples of "quo waranto" writs brought in King's Bench for a Breton escheat (*Rex* v. *Rochechouart*: KB 27/53m. 12d, /55m. 10d) and for an escheat for felony (*Rex* v. *Bonet*: KB 27/49m. 19d).

in actions brought by the king. It was incorrect, he said, to suppose that the king was ever, in law, barred from his action by such prescription; this doctrine had been enunciated by the king himself. In certain cases, the king is reported to have said, he would, as of grace, act as though his right of action was so barred: but he would not accept any such limitation as legally binding in all cases.

In enunciating this doctrine, the king was departing from the earlier doctrine found in "Bracton" which held that the statutory prescription did bind the king in all cases where he was seeking to recover "free tenement", but did not bind him in cases where he was attempting to resume a franchise (*68*). The newer doctrine, excepting the king in some (or all) cases from the statutory prescription, is, however, to be seen at work in practice in at least four cases in the court of King's Bench in the decade prior to 1285. In one the king based his claim on the seisin of King Stephen (*69*); in three others it was based on the seisin of Henry II (*70*). In none of these cases is any challenge recorded to the king's right to bring a case on such an ancient seisin. The same is also true of three cases heard in the eyre during this period (*71*). The only recorded challenge to the practice in this period is found in the case of *Rex* v. *Dean and Chapter of Lincoln* (*72*). This case was initiated in the 1281 Derbyshire eyre, and was adjourned into the 1281-4 Lincolnshire eyre, and thence into the court of King's Bench. It concerned the advowson of the church of Darley, which was claimed on the king's behalf with a count relying on the seisin of Henry II. A challenge was made to this count on the grounds that this was too ancient seisin to be used in such a case (*73*), but eventually (probably in Easter term 1285, when the plea was enrolled) the defendants were told to answer over—that is advised, that their answer was insufficient in law. They then simply denied the seisin alleged, and put themselves on the verdict of a jury. It is by no means improbable that it was this very case which led to the royal pronouncement of which we are informed by Hengham. There is, it is true, no positive evidence, from the plea-roll enrolment itself, to prove that a royal pronouncement lay behind the judgment in this case: but it seems unlikely that on a matter so closely affecting the royal dignity, and leading to so many adjournments, the justices of the King's Bench would have dared to pass judgment without consulting the king and his

---

(*68*) On the date and authorship of Bracton, *see* below, n. 126.

(*69*) *Rex* v. *Archbishop of Rouen:* KB 27/49m. 25d.

(*70*) *Rex* v. *Abbot of St. Augustine's Bristol* (KB 27/37m. 9); *Rex* v. *Abbot of Jumieges* (KB 27/47m. 3): *Rex* v. *Prior of Castle Acre* (KB 27/62m. 5).

(*71*) *P.Q.W.*, pp. 173, 394, 669.

(*72*) JUST/1/152m. 12d; KB 27/90m. 25d.

(*73*) ". . . et dicunt quod non videtur eis quod debeant in hoc casu domino regi respondere ad seisinam antecessoris sui de tam longinquo tempore . . ." This leaves open a possibility that statutory prescription may be inapplicable in certain other circumstances e.g. where "free tenement" is claimed as ancient demesne.

council (74), and without getting a pronouncement very close in content to that reported by Hengham.

"Quo waranto" writs continued to be used in eyres of the Northern circuit for the recovery of "free tenement" apparently without challenge up to the time of its suspension in 1287 (75). Challenges were, however, made in three "quo waranto" cases which were heard in the Bench in 1287, and which were probably adjourned there from eyres on that circuit. In the first of these, heard in Hilary term (*Rex* v. *Prioress of Marlow*) (76), a vouchee of the defendant argued that a "quo waranto" writ ought not to be used by the king since it could not be quashed by the exception of non-tenure, or other exceptions usual in land actions (77). The king's attorney, Gilbert of Thornton, in answer claimed that the "quo waranto" was quite proper when used to seek ancient demesne, and that the king was only obliged to use the "precipe" for acquisitions and escheats, one of the two views reported in question 1 (78). In the other two cases, heard in Michaelmas term (*Rex* v. *Pylet; Rex* v. *Seman*) (79), the defendants simply claimed that "quo waranto" writs only existed for the recovery of franchises, and were not intended to be used for "free tenement" (80); and no reply to their argument is recorded. The eventual outcome of all three cases has not been traced (81). Argument on this point was resumed in the Lancashire eyre of 1292, the first eyre held in the Northern circuit, when that circuit itself was resumed, in the case of *Rex* v. *Holand et al.* (82). Once more the defendants claimed that the "quo waranto" should only be used for franchises. The king's attorney Inge countered

---

(74) As they are known to have done in two other cases enrolled in this term: *Rex* v. *Abbot of Pyn* and *Rex* v. *Bishop of Carlisle* (KB 27/90mm. 33d, 29).

(75) *P.Q.W.*, pp. 84, 94, 241, 243, 253, 257, 260, 261, 296, 673.

(76) CP 40/66m. 2. The case was probably adjourned into the Bench under a general mandate to the justices of the Buckinghamshire eyre of 8 May 1286 (*P.Q.W.*, p. 84).

(77) ". . . et petunt judicium si ad istud breve quod non est breve de recto nec precipe quod reddat etc., quod quidem breve cassari potest per nontenuram et per alias excepciones in regno in placito terre usuales, debeat de libero tenemento suo respondere". On these alleged characteristics see further below, pp. 142-146.

(78) ". . . hujusmodi brevia de recto, sicut precipe quod reddat, locum habent in perquisitis et escaetis et hiis similibus, et non in hiis que sic annexa sint corone domini regis ex prima ejus fundacione et creacione, unde petit judicium." Compare also the related assertion by William Inge in 1287 that the "quo waranto" could be used to seek an advowson, in the same way as it could be used to seek other "free tenement" if it belonged to the ancient demesne, and that the three "normal" writs of advowson had only to be used for "perquisitis et eschatis domini regis .. ." (*P.Q.W.*, p. 250).

(79) CP 40/69m. 75. Both are Cambridgeshire cases, and may have been adjourned into the Bench from the 1286 Cambridgeshire eyre, whose "quo waranto" roll does not survive.

(80) ". . . dicit quod non debet ei ad hoc breve respondere. Quia dicit quod hujusmodi breve provisum fuit et ordinatum pro libertatibus declarandis et non pro petendis tenementa in dominico; unde petit judicium." An identical objection was made in both cases.

(81) All were adjourned, undecided, into the Exchequer.

(82) *P.Q.W.*, pp. 370, 378-9 (the second entry only is printed in Sutherland, *op. cit.*, pp. 210-211).

with two separate arguments. The first was that the difference between the two types of writ lay in the method of proof appropriate to each. The "precipe" was the appropriate writ for lands "at common law" (*83*), where proof of the king's title would be by a jury in the form of a grand assize (*84*). The "quo waranto" was appropriate for lands "not at common law", e.g. ancient demesne lands, as in the present case, where some other form of proof was appropriate (*85*). The second was that, as Henry III had brought a similar writ for part of the lands now in demand in a previous eyre, the king was in seisin of the privilege of using such writs to litigate about these lands. At first, the justices attempted to browbeat the defendants into waiving their objections (*86*), but this was unsuccessful. Eventually, in the next county on the circuit, judgment was given in their favour, accepting their argument in full: and the "quo waranto" ceased to be used on this circuit for "free tenement" (*87*). The use of "quo waranto" writs for free tenement had ceased on the Southern circuit even earlier (*88*).

No further cases in which the king tried to make a claim that would have been barred by the statutory prescription occurred during the Northern circuit eyres prior to their suspension in 1288. Two such cases were, however, brought, apparently without challenge, on the Southern circuit during the same period (*89*). In a case heard in the Bench shortly afterwards (*Rex* v. *Prior of Butley*) (*90*), the practice was once again challenged: and once more defended, on the grounds that it had never been the king's intention, when making the statute, to impose any such

(*83*) i.e. purchases, escheats.
(*84*) The grand assize, the most solemn form of jury trial used in deciding "right" to land, was never used in cases in which the king was demandant. The highest form of jury trial available in such a case was by "jury in place of the grand assize". In both cases, a verdict as to the "greater right" to the land would be given by twelve knights: but, at least in theory, the jury's verdict would be less final than that of the grand assize, if given against the king.
(*85*) Inge was not referring just to the proof by Domesday Book, for in this very case he was offering to prove that King John had been seised of the tenements by means of the records of Chancery or the Exchequer. His argument in this case closely resembles one advanced by Thornton in the report printed in Appendix II. Curiously, royal attorneys had, in the past, not infrequently, been successful in requesting proof by enrolment and, only if no relevant enrolment could be found, by jury, in cases brought by "precipe" writs: see e.g. *P.Q.W.*, pp. 169, 173, 177, 671, 731, 764.
(*86*) *P.Q.W.*, p. 370: the justices are recorded as telling the defendants ". . . quod dicant aliud si sibi viderint expedire."
(*87*) For the sequel to the case, a "precipe" brought for the same lands see *P.Q.W.*, p. 228. The only other "quo waranto" for free tenement on the resumed Northern circuit was another case brought in the Lancashire eyre: *Rex* v. *Waleton* (*P.Q.W.*, p. 382).
(*88*) The last two cases—and it is not even certain that these were brought by "quo waranto"—were in the Suffolk eyre of 1286-7: *P.Q.W.*, p. 734 (*bis*).
(*89*) In the 1286 Norfolk eyre, *Rex* v. *Abbot of Creake* (*P.Q.W.*, p. 488); in the 1287 Hertfordshire eyre, *Rex* v. *Abbot of Faversham* (*P.Q.W.*, p. 287).
(*90*) CP 40/82m. 89d (Trinity term, 1290): the claim which concerned an advowson, was based on the seisin of Henry II.

limitation on himself, more especially when he was attempting to recover those things that belonged to the Crown, as was clear from the words of the statute (*91*). After an adjournment for consultation with the king, the defendant was forced to answer over.

It is a curious fact that actions based on seisins that would have been barred by the statutory prescription are much more common in the resumed eyre circuits of the 1290s than they had been previously: and it is tempting to associate this with the publicity that may have attended the re-affirmation of the legality of this practice in 1290 in *Rex* v. *Prior of Butley*. No less than 35 such cases were brought on the Northern circuit (*92*), and 23 on the Southern circuit (*93*). There continued to be objections to such counts. They were recorded in two cases in the 1292 Herefordshire eyre (*Rex* v. *Grey* (*94*) and *Rex* v. *Mortimer* (*95*)), and in a third case (*Rex* v. *Abbot of St. Alban's*) (*96*) from the 1293 Northumberland eyre. In each of these cases, the defendants were driven by the justices to answer over, but the abbot of St. Alban's was more successful than the other defendants, in securing the adjournment of his case into the Easter parliament of 1293 and the subsequent *ex gratia* confirmation of his possession of what was at stake there by the king (*97*).

It seems probable that this whole rash of cases in 1292-3 created considerable hostility towards the king's use of his immunity, but that the immediate catalyst for the king's surrender on this point was parliamentary discussion arising out of *Rex* v. *Abbot of St. Alban's*. That surrender was announced to the justices of both eyre circuits in writs dated 12 July 1293 (*98*). The new rule was applied by them in cases still pending, even cases in which the pleadings were concluded (*99*). In form, all that the king had conceded was that in future counts made in his name would

(*91*) ". . . intencio ipsius domini regis nunquam fuit ad excludendum seipsum quin petere possit tenementa de seisina quorumcumque progenitorum suorum, et maxin de illis que sunt de pertinenciis corone Anglie etc., et hoc liquet expresse per idc statutum". This is clearly a reference to c. 50 of the statute, which was a general clause saving the king's rights in matters which might tend to the prejudice of himself or of his Crown.

(*92*) There were none in the 1292 Lancashire eyre, but for cases in the 1292 Westmorland eyre (6) see: *P.Q.W.*, pp. 787-790, cases in the 1292-3 Cumberland eyre (15) see *P.Q.W.*, pp. 113, 115-120, 130, 131; and in the 1293 Northumberland eyre (14), see *P.Q.W.*, pp. 585, 587-589, 592, 594-597, 601, 602. All were brought on the seisin of Henry II.

(*93*) There were two cases in the 1292 Herefordshire eyre (*P.Q.W.*, pp. 267, 271), eleven in the 1292 Shropshire eyre (*P.Q.W.*, pp. 674, 678, 679, 682, 683) and ten in the 1293 Staffordshire eyre (*P.Q.W.*, pp. 705, 711, 713, 715, 717). All were brought on the seisin of Henry II.

(*94*) *P.Q.W.*, p. 267: but the king's attorney's answer seems to represent a conflation of two separate arguments, and makes no sense as it stands.

(*95*) *Y.B. 20 and 21 Edward I* (R.S.), p. 68: the case does not seem to have been recorded on the plea-roll.

(*96*) *P.Q.W.*, p. 585: the case concerned the advowson of the priory of Tynemouth.

(*97*) *Select Cases in the Court of King's Bench*, vol. II, ed. G. O. Sayles (Selden Soc., lvii (1937)), pp. 137-141.

(*98*) *P.Q.W.*, pp. 203-352 (printed also in Sutherland, *op. cit.*, pp. 212-213).

(*99*) *P.Q.W.*, pp. 352, 353.

have to observe the statutory prescription: but since, at about the same time the decision was finally made that "quo waranto" writs could not be brought for the recovery of "free tenement" (*100*), their combined effect was to ensure that any tenant of "free tenement", who could show that he and his predecessors in title had held such free tenement continuously since 1189, was safe in that possession from any suit brought against him by the king (*101*).

Questions 2 and 3

There can be little doubt that what the copyist of these questions and answers treated as two separate questions (and answers)—which have been numbered, in accordance with the copyist's intentions, as questions 2 and 3 in the text here printed—formed, originally, but a single question and answer (*102*). This question followed on directly from that put in question 1, and asked what was the proper procedure to follow in actions of "quo waranto" for the recovery of "free tenement", if it was legitimate to use "quo waranto" writs for this purpose. Was it appropriate that in such cases the defendant should be allowed a "view" of the "free tenement" which the king was seeking; and should he be allowed to except to the king's writ on the grounds of non-tenure of what was being sought? Should such a defendant be allowed to pray the aid of his fellow parceners (particularly when one of them was a minor); and should he be allowed to vouch to warranty (particularly when the warrantor was a minor)? Some argued, it was said, that none of these procedures was appropriate when it was a franchise that was being sought by the "quo waranto" writ—and this irrespective of whether the franchise was "jurisdictional" in nature e.g. the franchise of "return of writs", or merely "profitable" e.g. the franchises of "wreck of the sea", and "waif", because franchises were,

---

(*100*) Above, p. 409.

(*101*) It was at least arguable that the king's concession did not apply to "quo waranto" actions, since no count was made in them of the king's seisin: above, p. 135. The author of *Fleta*, who was probably writing soon after 1296 (see H. G. Richardson in *L.Q.R.*, lviii (1947), 377), apparently still held that time did not run against the king for ancient demesne land: "De terris et tenementis regis . . . refert utrum ille terre fuerint dominice terre regis ex antiquo corone annexe vel de escheata vel perquisito, quia de antiquis maneriis per predecessores regis alienatis non currit tempus contra regem sicut contra alium". (*Fleta*, lib. 3. cap. 6, ed. H. G. Richardson and G. O. Sayles, Selden Soc., vol. lxxxix (1972), iii ,12). This opinion would fit well with some of the known facts of the life and career of the main candidate proposed for authorship of the treatise, Matthew of the Exchequer. Matthew was a royal attorney in the 1287 Hertfordshire eyre, and therefore a likely holder of 'royalist' views; and his failure to reflect, in the work, the changes made in the law by the royal mandate of 1293 and the concurrent decision against the use of "quo waranto" writs, might reflect ignorance of an order issued at a time when he was firmly lodged in prison in the Tower of London: Sayles, *Sel. Cases in the Court of King's Bench*, vol. II, pp. cliv-clv.

(*102*) Each of the other questions conforms to the same basic format. An initial statement of the point at issue is followed either by a summary of two opposing viewpoints on the matter, or by a summary of just one.

by their nature, impartible (*103*). They were, however, appropriate when what was being sought was "free tenement" since that, by its nature, was partible etc. Others held the contrary opinion, that none of these procedures was appropriate to any kind of "quo waranto" action, whether for franchises or for "free tenement".

The notion that the king was under a duty not only to preserve intact the royal patrimony of rights and lands, but also to act to recover rights and lands of the Crown lost by his predecessors seems to find its earliest expression in England in the late twelfth or early thirteenth century memorandum "De jure et appendiciis corone regni Britannie et quod sit officium regis" interpolated into a London text of the so-called *Leges Edwardi Confessoris* (*104*). During the Edwardian "quo waranto" proceedings, it was most clearly expounded by the royal attorney, Gilbert of Thornton, in the case of *Rex* v. *Earl Warenne* in the Lincolnshire eyre of 1281-4 (*105*). The earl claimed to exercise the franchise of return of writs in the town of Stamford, on the basis of a grant made to the earl by King Edward I, before he had become king. The king, Thornton argued, was under a duty to reclaim for the Crown all things belonging to that Crown which had been wrongfully usurped or alienated from it, even those things which he had himself, before he became king, usurped from it. This is close to the position of the author of *Fleta* that the king was obliged to revoke all alienations of franchises and "ancient demesne" (including, presumably, even those grants made by himself and by other kings *after* becoming king) (*106*). The idea that the king was under the duty to act in this matter with as much expedition as possible, seems to make its first appearance in 1285. It appears not only in this question, but also, implicitly, in Thornton's argument for the king in the case of *Rex* v. *Hastinges* in the very eyre from which these questions come, that "it is fitting for the king's majesty to revoke such franchises, without awaiting either a minor's coming of age or the presence of parceners" (*107*). It is probably best seen as the logical development of an idea already found in Bracton, that the greater the length of time a franchise was wrongfully usurped from the Crown, the greater was the wrong thereby committed (*108*).

(*103*) And, it must be understood, inalienable and incapable of being viewed.
(*104*) "Debet vero de iure rex omnes terras et honores, omnes dignitates et iura et libertates corone regni huius in integrum cum omni integritate et sine diminucione observare et defendere, dispersa et dilapidata et amissa regni iura in pristinum statum et debitum viribus omnibus revocare". (F. Liebermann, *Die Gesetze der Angelsachen,* i (Halle, 1903) 635: E. Cf. 11, 1A2). But note that this idea had found practical (and perhaps also theoretical) expression rather earlier, in what seems to have been a general resumption of ancient demesne at the beginning of the reign of Henry II: W. L. Warren, *Henry II,* pp. 61, 263 (and authorities there cited).
(*105*) *P.Q.W.,* pp. 429-430.
(*106*) *Fleta,* lib. 3. cap. 6 (III, 12).
(*107*) C 260/93 no. 15.
(*108*) "Diurnitas enim temporis in hoc casu iniuriam non minuit set auget . . ."; Bracton, *De Legibus,* f. 14 (II, 58).

It was, however, also one of the basic principles of the common law that every defendant be allowed an adequate opportunity to defend himself and his rights, even if this was at the cost of causing an additional delay before a full hearing of the case in question. There were convincing reasons for holding that in cases involving title to "free tenement", at any rate (*109*), every defendant ought, in the interests of justice, to be allowed to demand the "view": that is, to seek an adjournment of the case, so that in the interim the plaintiff could indicate to him, on the spot, the precise location of the "free tenement" he was seeking. All that the writ and the count of the plaintiff will have told him is the amount of land demanded, and the village in which it is situated. Quite possibly, the defendant will be in possession of lands in that village in excess of the quantity now demanded, and by virtue of a number of different titles. He cannot know which to plead unless he knows precisely which are being demanded. He may not even hold the land in question, and his failure to secure a view and subsequently plead non-tenure may have the undesirable consequence of allowing the plaintiff to "recover" land in the possession of a third party who has been given no opportunity to appear in court and defend himself. There were, likewise, cogent reasons for allowing a defendant, when he was one of a number of coheirs or parceners between whom an inheritance has been divided, and when he is being impleaded for "free tenement" that had formed part of that common inheritance, to seek an adjournment of the case, while he has his coheirs summoned to join themselves with him in defence of the "free tenement", the procedure known as aid-prayer (*110*). If such aid-prayer was not allowed, this might lead to a defendant losing part or even the whole of his share of the inheritance, without any immediate redistribution of the inheritance being made to compensate him for his loss, even though the loss was caused by no fault of his own (*111*). Moreover, the denial of such aid-prayer might have the effect of depriving the defendant of the assistance of a coheir who possessed the deeds relating to the "free tenement" in question, which might be essential to the defence of it (*112*). Similarly compelling reasons could also be advanced for allowing all defendants, at least in cases where "free tenement" was at stake (*113*), to vouch to warranty and have the case adjourned pending the appearance of the

---

(*109*) A franchise, by contrast, was an incorporeal entity of which it was not possible to be given a view.

(*110*) It was much less clear that such "aid" was appropriate or necessary if the case concerned franchises, if, as was suggested, franchises were impartible. (But see also below, p. 415).

(*111*) This seems to be Hengham's argument in the answer to this question.

(*112*) The parcener in possession of the share of the eldest co-heir might well be in possession of all deeds relating to the whole of the inheritance, or relating to lands in the possession of more than one co-heir.

(*113*) Again these reasons do not apply in the case of franchises, if the argument is accepted that all franchises are, of their nature, inalienable. But on this point, see below, pp. 416-24.

The Making of the Common Law

warrantor. It was clearly unreasonable to deprive the *bona fide* grantee of "free tenement" of the use of a procedure which ensured not only that the grantor assumed the main burden of making a defence of the title of the "free tenement" that had been granted, but also that if the grantor lost, he was at once liable to provide an equivalent in value of what had been lost. It was also possible that the grantor would possess deeds required for a satisfactory defence of the title to the land. Allowing any of these procedures would cause additional delay: and the delay might be considerable in the case of an aid-prayer or voucher to warranty, if one of the coheirs or the warrantor was a minor, since this would mean an adjournment of the case until he came of age. If, however, the arguments in favour of allowing defendants to make use of these procedures, were, in themselves, convincing, the additional delay involved in allowing their use, had simply to be accepted as an unfortunate, but necessary consequence of this. The fact that these procedures were often utilized by defendants simply as a delaying tactic had to be accepted as a necessary evil.

Just where the balance should be struck between these two conflicting principles in reaching a decision on these matters of procedural law outlined in questions 2 and 3 was, therefore, a difficult problem. In 1276 the king's council had been faced with the need to reconcile substantially the same two conflicting principles, when the question was whether or not the king had to obtain a writ—and thus give advanced notice to the defendant, and an opportunity for him to exploit the opportunities for delay—when seeking to recover franchises. The balance struck on that occasion was that he could act, without a writ, when the claim was of usurpation of the franchise by its present possessor, but that he must use a writ to challenge an inherited franchise (*114*). There is, however, no evidence that the particular problem raised by questions 2 and 3 had been discussed much, if at all, prior to 1285. This was probably because prior to this date, the king's attorneys had not insisted quite so strongly on the extreme urgency of the king's duty to resume alienated royal demesne, and had allowed procedures such as voucher to warranty to pass without challenge in the comparatively few "quo waranto" actions brought for "free tenement" (*115*).

(*114*) *De Bigamis*, c. 4 (which claims to be re-enacting a decision made during the reign of Henry III): *S.R.*, i. 43.

(*115*) In *Rex* v. *Vallibus* (*P.Q.W.*, p. 440) in the 1281-4 Lincolnshire eyre, a "quo waranto" for land alienated from a serjeanty, the view was sought and allowed; and an exception of non-tenure had been allowed in *Rex* v. *Earl of Cornwall* (*P.Q.W.*, p. 690) in the 1280 Somerset eyre. For successful vouchers see *Rex* v *Scalleby* (*P.Q.W.*, p. 190), from the 1279-81 Yorkshire eyre, *Rex* v. *St. Elena* (KB 27/53m. 12d, /57m. 31d), from the court of King's Bench (1280), and *Rex* v. *Prioress of Littlemore* (*P.Q.W.*, p. 666), from the 1285 Oxfordshire eyre (where the vouchee was a minor). Note, however, that among the problems troubling the justices of the Yorkshire eyre 1279-81 were whether or not to allow the view, and whether exceptions of non-tenure were allowable in "quo waranto" actions generally: Sutherland, *op. cit.*, p. 198.

Hengham's answer to the question, approving of the use of each of the procedures that had been challenged, again purported to be based on the past practice of the court of King's Bench. In this answer, however, he is willing to go further, and to say that this practice is, also, clearly justified and correct. As was also the case in his answer to question 1, Hengham then goes on to challenge the correctness of a view on which both sides to the original dispute seem to have been agreed: that none of these procedures were allowable when it was a franchise that the king was seeking to recover. On the contrary, he claimed, when the franchise was of such a kind that it was possible to place on it some estimated value (*116*), then aid-prayer ought to be allowed. This is because it was the common practice when the king (or his ministers) were making a division of an inheritance between coheirs, to assign a franchise of this sort to one of them as one of the appurtenances of a manor, and to take its annual value into account when reckoning up the share allocated to him. It would be clearly unfair if this coheir, as a result of being deprived of the possibility of seeking the aid of his fellow coheirs, should—on losing the franchise— find himself with less than his fair share of the inheritance as a whole (*117*).

The subsequent history of this matter is quickly dealt with. "Quo waranto" writs were, as has already been seen (*118*), little used after 1285 to recover "free tenement". Where they were used, defendants did continue to be allowed the view (*119*), to except on grounds of non-tenure (*120*), and to vouch to warranty (*121*). It is of some interest, also, to note that when the case of *Rex* v. *Hastings* was adjourned into the court of King's Bench from the Northamptonshire eyre, the decision was made to allow aid-prayer, despite the objections of the king's attorney (*122*). The case involved the franchise of "view of frankpledge", a franchise on which it was possible to place an estimated annual value: so the decision was precisely in line with Hengham's known views on this matter (*123*).

(*116*) As examples he instanced wreck (the right to objects cast up on the sea-shore in a particular locality) and waif (the right to unclaimed stray animals).

(*117*) The same view is also expressed in Hengham's *Summa Parva*, written between 1285 and 1290: *Radulfi de Hengham Summae*, ed. Dunham, pp. lxii, 68. This provides additional confirmation of Hengham's authorship of the answers.

(*118*) Above, pp. 408-9.

(*119*) For example see *Rex* v. *Sculthorp* (*P.Q.W.*, p. 673) from the 1286 Rutland eyre, *Rex* v. *Abbot of Hayles* (*P.Q.W.*, p. 242), from the 1287 Gloucestershire eyre and *Rex* v. *Moubray* (KB 27/107m. 31), from the court of King's Bench in Michaelmas term 1287.

(*120*) For examples see *Rex* v. *Sculthorp* and *Rex* v. *Moubray*, above n. 119.

(*121*) For examples see *Rex* v. *Sculthorp* (above n. 119) and *Rex* v. *Crokeslee* (*P.Q.W.*, p. 296) from the 1287 Huntingdonshire eyre.

(*122*) C 260/93m. 15. For other cases in which parceners were allowed aid-prayer see: *Rex* v. *l'Estrange* (*P.Q.W.*, p. 91), adjourned from the 1286 Buckingham eyre into the Exchequer before aid was allowed; *Rex* v. *Hastinges* (*P.Q.W.*, p. 294) adjourned from the 1286 Huntingdonshire eyre into the court of King's Bench before aid allowed; *Rex* v. *Paynel*, *Rex* v. *Montalt*, *Rex* v. *Balliol*, *Rex* v. *Hastings* (*P.Q.W.*, pp. 2, 3, 6, 9) in the 1287 Bedfordshire eyre. All these cases concerned view of frankpledge; the last three also concerned waif and warren.

(*123*) Above, n. 117.

Question 4

One of the major unresolved problems of franchise law in 1285 concerned the alienability of franchises *(124)*. Was it possible for a franchise-holder to grant his franchise to someone else, without the king confirming the grant? More specifically, did such a grant pass a title to exercise the franchise that was a sufficient warrant if the king should challenge the grantee's right to exercise the franchise by a "quo waranto"? The first of these questions to directly concern itself with a point of franchise law, question 4, raises this very problem. The problem is not, however, stated in such general terms as these. The question is only concerned with the alienation of franchises of the type that had been characterised in question 3 as "jurisdictional": the examples cited being a shrievalty held in fee, the officer of "keeper" of a hundred, and "return of writs" *(125)*. It is also concerned only with alienations made by those whose own title came from a royal grant of the franchise in question, and therefore excludes consideration of the case of alienations made by those whose title came solely from seisin since time out of mind. Some, it was said, take the view that a valid title to such a franchise could be passed by a grant of this sort made by a franchise-holder whose own title was of this kind. Others do not agree.

It was significant that the franchises mentioned were all of a "jurisdictional" type. In Bracton's treatise, written, at least in part, over half a century before this, but only now coming into general circulation *(126)*, a sharp distinction is drawn between those regalian rights that are "profitable" and those that are "jurisdictional" in nature *(127)*. The "profitable" rights, such as wreck, treasure trove and waif, belong to the king solely "propter privilegium regis". The judicial rights, such as view of frankpledge, the jurisdiction to hear and determine pleas of replevin or theft, and the assize of bread and ale, belong to the king by virtue of his office: because as king, he is responsible for upholding justice and seeing the peace is kept. There is no reason, he argues, why the king should not be allowed, if he wishes, to grant away the "profitable" regalian rights (as "profitable" franchises) for such a grant damages himself alone and does not harm the "common good". There is, however, good reason for

---

(124) For a general discussion of the problem see Sutherland, *op. cit.*, pp. 15, 130-135.
(125) Since Northamptonshire did not possess a sheriff in fee, the first of these franchises was probably included only to make it clear that the question was concerned with the whole category of franchises of this kind, and to put the strongest example of such a franchise.
(126) Professor S. E. Thorne had amply demonstrated that parts of the treatise must have been written in the 1220s and early 1230s at pp. xiii-xxix in his 'Translator's Introduction" to volume III of his new edition with translation of Woodbine's edition of Bracton. He has also there provided good reasons for thinking that Henry of Bracton was only one of the revisers, and not the "author" of the work: *ibid.*, pp. v, xxx-xxxiii. For the date when the treatise comes first into circulation see Thorne's "Translator's Introduction" to Volume I of Bracton, p. xl.
(127) Bracton, *De Legibus*, ff. 14, 55b (II, 58-59, 166-167).

not allowing grants of "jurisdictional" regalian rights (as "jurisdictional" franchises); for the king cannot be competent to grant to others those things which constitute his very Crown. All that the king is competent to do, with regard to regalian rights of this nature, is to "delegate" them to others to administer as his "justices" or agents (*128*).

Since they are merely agents or "justices", acting in the king's name, it follows that such persons are not competent to grant the regalian rights which they are exercising to any third party, unless they have the king's consent to do so (*129*). Arguably, franchise-holders in possession of "profitable" franchises may alienate them without prior royal consent and confirmation (*130*). "Jurisdictional" franchises, however, clearly cannot be so granted. The factual restriction of the question was, therefore, of considerable significance. If the views of Bracton were accepted, the alienation of "jurisdictional" franchises without royal confirmation was certainly ruled out: but without prejudice to the wider question of whether other types of franchise could or could not be so granted.

It was also of significance that the question presupposed that the grantor had acquired his title to the franchise by royal grant. From the 1280s onwards, the king's attorneys frequently challenged the validity in law of seisin since time out of mind as a title to franchises (*131*). No such challenge was generally made to royal grants when pleaded as title (*132*). It was, therefore, possible for Hengham in his answer to assume that the grantor had himself possessed a valid title to the franchise alienated, and concentrate solely on the validity of the alienation (*133*). Moreover, it was sometimes claimed, by those whose title was seisin since time out of mind, that the root of their title was an independent "conquest" of the franchise in question, and not some royal grant made before time of memory (*134*). A franchise-holder who possessed his franchise by virtue of such a title might well, it could be argued, possess a freedom to alienate

---

(*128*) They may, nonetheless, be "agents" or delegates of a somewhat exceptional type, for Bracton nowhere excludes the possibility that such a grant or delegation may be made to a man *and* his heirs.

(*129*) Bracton explains this by reference not to any common law rules relating to agency, but by reference to the civilian and canonist rules concerning "ordinary" and "delegated" jurisdiction. The franchise-holder is to be seen as exercising only a "delegated" jurisdiction, with the king retaining the "ordinary" jurisdiction. Like any other holder of "delegated" jurisdiction, the franchise-holder may not "sub-delegate" to a third party without the consent of the holder of the "ordinary" jurisdiction.

(*130*) Bracton never clearly states his position on this matter.

(*131*) Below, p. 428.

(*132*) For exceptions to this see Sutherland, *op. cit.*, pp. 111-129.

(*133*) In a majority of cases in which challenges were made to the exercise of franchises by the grantees of those whose title was seisin since time out of mind, it was that original title that was attacked by the king's attorney rather than (or as well as) the alienation. For examples see *Rex* v. *Fitzstephen*, *Rex* v. *Brok*, *Rex* v. *Abbot of Woburn*, *Rex* v. *Pugeis*, *Rex* v. *Montgomery* and *Rex* v. *de la Mare et al.* (*P.Q.W.*, pp. 87, 97, 174, 242).

(*134*) Below, p. 428.

that franchise much greater than that of the franchise-holder whose title derived from a royal grant. In the latter case, it was possible to argue that the words of the royal chater granting the franchise to the franchise-holder and his heirs, were, since this was a royal grant, to be interpreted with a strictness that had ceased to be applied to ordinary grants of land by charter in the later twelfth century. It could not be taken as equivalent to a grant to a man, his heirs and assigns, and any attempt at alienation or assignment, would have the effect of causing the forfeiture of the franchise to the Crown, either as a penalty for "unlicensed" alienation (*135*), or through the working of the doctrine of tacit renunciation (*136*). The only way, then, such a franchise could be alienated, was with a royal con-firmation, that was tantamount to a fresh royal grant to the alienee. It was far from clear that any of this was applicable where a franchise had never belonged to the Crown or been granted by it.

The problem raised by this question had only arisen once before in an eyre in the "Northern" circuit, in the case of *Rex* v. *Daniel* (*137*). Judgment was deferred: and there is a note on the roll to the effect that the king and council are to be consulted on the case (*138*). Two further cases on this circuit involved the franchise of warren but both are incon-clusive and it is not clear whether this should be classified as a "jurisdic-tional" franchise anyway (*139*).

Nor are there any cases on this specific problem on the "Southern" circuit (*140*). There are, however, a number of cases on this circuit which do raise the more general problem of the alienability of "jurisdictional" franchises, though without satisfactorily resolving it. In two cases brought by the king against the earl of Gloucester in the 1279 Kent eyre, the king's attorney counterpleaded the earl's attempts to vouch the arch-

---

(*135*) This would be to treat a "franchise" as analogous to "free tenement" held of the Crown, for whose alienation a licence was required. Unlicensed grants could lead to seizure, though normally not to "forfeiture": see J. M. W. Bean, *The Decline of English Feudalism*, pp. 66-79, 98-101.

(*136*) When the original grantee ceased to exercise the franchise, he was held to have tacitly renounced the franchise in favour of the Crown. See Sutherland, *op. cit.*, pp. 9-11, 211-212.

(*137*) JUST/1/152m. 11 (1281 Derbyshire eyre): the franchise was receiving emends for breach of the assize of bread and ale.

(*138*) The case is complicated by the fact that the franchise in question is not mentioned in the charter, but claimed as appurtenant to the franchises of market and fair (which are mentioned). No sequel has been traced.

(*139*) *Rex* v. *FitzThomas* (*P.Q.W.*, p. 190) in the 1279-81 Yorkshire eyre; *Rex* v. *Gousel et al.* (JUST/1/152m. 12) in the 1281 Derbyshire eyre. It should be noted that such a title to franchises was allowed to go unchallenged in the following cases: *Rex* v. *Evere* (*P.Q.W.*, p. 194), in the 1279-81 Yorkshire eyre (where the franchises included gallows); *Rex* v. *Prior of Thurgarton* (JUST/1/670m. 1d), in the 1280-81 Nottinhamshire eyre; *Rex* v. *Wodehay* (*P.Q.W.*, p. 413) in the 1281-4 Lincolnshire eyre; *Rex* v. *Abbess of Polesworth, Rex* v. *Maydenhack, Rex* v. *Bosco,* in the 1285 Warwickshire eyre (*P.Q.W.*, pp. 781, 784).

(*140*) Unless warren be classified as a "jurisdictional" franchise. If so, *Rex* v. *la Susche* (*P.Q.W.*, p. 164), from the 1281 Devon eyre, is the only case in point. Here again judgment was reserved.

bishop of Canterbury to warranty for two "jurisdictional" franchises, with arguments suggesting that such franchises were never alienable. Other arguments were, however, also advanced at the same time against the voucher: and eventually the earl waived it *(141)*. In the 1280 Dorset eyre, a challenge was made, in the case of *Rex* v. *de la Lynde* to the claim of a son of an alienee to the franchises of wreck, gallows and emends of the assize of bread and ale, on the grounds that such franchises were not appurtenant to lands, and so did not pass with them to an alienee: but no final judgment is recorded on the challenge *(142)*. Judgment was, however, given, in the following Somerset eyre, in the case of *Rex* v. *Curtenay,* in favour of an alienee of a hundred *(143)*: and the alienability of "jurisdictional" franchises was not again called into question until the 1281-2 Devon eyre *(144)*. No judgment is recorded on this renewed challenge, but the question was subsequently again allowed to lie dormant until the 1284 Berkshire eyre, when it was once more raised, and left unsettled in the case of *Rex* v. *FitzWarin (145)*.

Hengham's answer to this question indicates that he did not subscribe to the view that all franchises were inalienable. Nor, it would appear was he willing to accept the Bractonian view that these three franchises belonged to a special category of "jurisdictional" franchises, one of whose characteristics was their peculiar inalienability; or the alternative view, that saw those franchises originally granted by royal charter, as the only group of franchises with this characteristic. His view was that two of the franchises (the shrievalty held in fee, and the keepership of a hundred) were serjeanties, and, as such, inalienable without royal consent. The third, however (return of writs), was a franchise resembling markets and warrens, in that the king's own charters "annexed" it to particular manors.

---

(141) P.Q.W., pp. 337-338 (two hundreds), 340 (a separate coroner for the lowy of Tonbridge).

(142) P.Q.W., p. 184: the grantor's title was seisin since time out of mind. Wreck was a "profitable" franchise, the others "jurisdictional".

(143) P.Q.W., p. 693: again the grantor's title was seisin since time out of mind. With regard to two other franchises, claimed by the same defendant on the same title, however (market and fair), judgment was adjourned into parliament. Judgment was given against another defendant in the same eyre who was claiming the view of frankpledge and emends of the assize of bread and ale, by the same title: but probably simply because he failed to show his feoffor's title or to vouch him: *Rex* v. *Abbot of Torre (P.Q.W.,* p. 693).

(144) In the cases of *Rex* v. *Fitzstephen* and *Rex* v. *Scully: P.Q.W.,* pp. 174, 175 (a hundred; view of frankpledge, and emends of the assize of bread and ale). In both cases the alienor's title was seisin since time out of mind, but in both it is alienability of the franchise that is called into question. But note that in other cases from the same eyre, vouchers were allowed by those claiming such franchises by such a title: see e.g. *Rex* v. *la Suche (P.Q.W.,* p. 164), for fair, market, gallows, view of frankpledge, emends of the assize of bread and ale, warren; *Rex* v. *Abbot of Newnham (P.Q.W.,* p. 165) for a hundred, and the sheriff's tourn.

(145) P.Q.W., p. 81. The question was raised by the counterplea of the king's attorney to a voucher by the tenant of a hundred. But similar vouchers went unchallenged in *Rex* v. *Schauford et al. (P.Q.W.,* p. 81) in the same eyre, and in *Rex* v. *Abbot of Thame (P.Q.W.,* p. 664) in the following Oxfordshire eyre.

It therefore passed, like them, with the manor to which it had been annexed to an alienee without a royal confirmation.

The tenants who held by serjeanty of the Crown constituted a heterogeneous group, whose main characteristics were that they owed some form of personal service other than knight service to the king, and that they were liable to the special incidents of tenure in chief by serjeanty, including a requirement that any alienation of land belonging to the serjeanty receive prior royal approval (*146*). It does not seem to have been the normal practice to treat the shrievalties held in fee as serjeanties (*147*), but the idea that they should be so treated is not an unreasonable one. The sheriff-in-fee's income from the pleas of the county and of the hundreds not in private hands, and his custody of the royal castle within the county which acted as the centre for county administration were analogous to the sources of income and landed possessions enjoyed by other serjeanty tenants; and the fairly onerous tasks incumbent on him as sheriff, and performed by deputy, were not dissimilar to the tasks performed by certain other serjeanty tenants, and often carried out by their deputies.

The expression "keeper" of a hundred is an ambiguous one. The reference may be to the hereditary bailiff of a royal hundred. Such a man, in return for the service of making all summonses, attachments and distresses, and performing certain other administrative or quasi-judicial tasks within a hundred, was allowed to hold certain lands within the hundred, or to receive certain fees for the services he performed. Such bailiffs in fee were, certainly, sometimes referred to as serjeanty tenants (*148*). Alternatively, the reference may be to someone who would more commonly be described as the "tenant" or "lord" of a hundred: someone who received all or some of the profits of the hundred, and appointed his own "bailiff" for the hundred (*149*). Again, although such

---

(*146*) For rules relating to serjeanty tenure, generally, see E. G. Kimball, *Serjeanty Tenure in Medieval England* (New Haven, 1936), pp. 208-241.

(*147*) In 1285, there were four, or possibly five, English counties whose shrievalty was held in fee: Cornwall, Lancashire, Westmorland, Worcestershire and (*de facto* at least, but not perhaps *de jure*) Rutland: W. A. Morris, *The Medieval English Sheriff* (Manchester, 1927), pp. 179-182. In each case, the sheriff in fee was also a major baronial tenant-in-chief.

(*148*) Kimball, *Serjeanty Tenure*, pp. 87-88.

(*149*) For evidence indicating that the "lord" of a hundred could, on occasion, be described as merely "keeping" that hundred see the case of *Lovel* v. *Curtenay*, heard in the Bench in Hilary term 1267, where the guardian of the lord of one moiety of the hundred of Coliton in Devon, sued the lord of the other moiety for refusing to allow her in alternate years, "hundredum de Colinton per ballivum suum ... custodire". (KB 26/180m. 10d). To regard the "lordship" of a hundred as a *custodia* (a "keepership", with the implication that it was being kept for someone else, i.e. the king) rather than as a "free tenement" in itself, a piece of real property, would be in keeping with what seems to be a growing tendency in Edward I's reign to emphasize the "franchisal" nature of the "lordship" of hundreds and the possibility, therefore, of such things as the forfeiture of such a "lordship" for misconduct.

tenants were not normally regarded as serjeanty tenants, this would have been not unreasonable. The profits they received from their hundred could be regarded as analogous to the income which most serjeanty tenants received from their land; and their overall responsibility for the administration of their hundred be seen as the service performed in return for that income (*150*).

The franchise singled out by Hengham as alienable was return of writs. This was the franchise which entitled its holder to receive from the sheriff a full copy of every writ addressed to him relating to the area within which it was exercised, and to execute whatever orders those writs contained. Certainly, it was on occasion granted to a particular man to exercise within a named manor or within all the lands he then held, and when such a grant was made, it did resemble the grant of a market or of a fair at a certain named place, or the grant of a warren in all a grantee's demesne lands at certain named places. But it was also, on occasion, granted to the "lord" of a hundred, with respect to all the places within his hundred (*151*): and where a grant of this kind was made, it is much more difficult (if not impossible), in most cases, to see it as being annexed thereby to any particular manor or place in quite the same way.

In any case, it was far from clear that even the franchises of market, fair and warren could be regarded as annexed to particular manors in the manner envisaged by Hengham. As early as the 1279-81 Yorkshire eyre, the king's attorney, Walkingham, had challenged a claim to warren made on the basis of a charter to the grantor of the present claimant, with the argument that the franchise did not pass on the grant of a manor as part of its appurtenances (*152*), and a similar challenge was made by the king's attorney, Gyselham, in the 1281-2 Devon eyre (*153*). There then followed a period during which no such challenges are recorded which came to an end with renewed challenges on both circuits in 1287 (*154*). Challenges were also made on similar grounds in the 1292 Herefordshire eyre (*155*), and judgment given for the king on this point in a case in the 1292-3

(*150*) The lordship of a hundred is certainly described as an "officium" as well as "quasi quedam justiciaria spectans mere ad coronam regis" by the king's attorney Inge in *Rex* v. *Berkle* in the Gloucestershire eyre of 1287 (*P.Q.W.*, p. 256).

(*151*) E.g. *Cal. Ch. Rolls.* i. pp. 121, 183; *Cal. Ch. Rolls*, ii, p. 306.

(*152*) "Warenna est quoddam regale, nec transire potest per aliquod donum, cum non fuerit de aliquibus pertinenciis ad manerium spectantibus": *Rex* v. *FitzThomas* (*P.Q.W.*, p. 190).

(*153*) *Rex* v. *la Susche* (*P.Q.W.*, p. 164),

(*154*) *Rex* v. *FitzWarin* (*P.Q.W.*, p. 248) in the Gloucestershire eyre. The claimant was the alienee of an alienee of the original grantee and claimed that "ipse et feoffatores sui habuerunt et tenuerunt predictam warennam tamquam de pertinenciis predicti manerii a tempore confeccionis predicte carte"; but the king's attorney, Thornton, replied that "libertas warenne de jure communi non pertinet ad aliquod manerium, immo mere procedit a corona regis; nec continetur in carta regis quod aliquis gaudere possit predicta libertate nisi tantummodo predictus Robertus et heredes sui . . ."; *Rex* v. *Prioress of Flixton* (*P.Q.W.*, p. 730), in the Suffolk eyre.

(*155*) *Rex* v. *Helyoun*, *Rex* v. *Solariis*, *Rex* v. *Clyfford*: *P.Q.W.*, pp. 266, 271, 274.

Cumberland eyre (*156*). The question of whether markets and fairs were annexed to particular manors seems not to have been raised until 1292-3, but then two judgments were actually given for the king against claimants who were assigns (*157*). These judgments were given after discussion as to whether all three franchises could be regarded as "appurtenant" to manors had taken place at the Easter parliament of 1293 (*158*). During this discussion, the king "recorded" that on a previous occasion his council had agreed that warren did pass with a manor on alienation, since it was "annexed" to the soil, and penalties for breach of the franchise belonged to the king. His remembrance was, however, that no definite decision had been reached on that earlier occasion with regard to markets and fairs, and the justices now present were, likewise, unaware of any authoritative decision having been made in the past on this point. A decision on the matter was, therefore, deferred until the justices of King's Bench and Common Pleas had time to search their rolls for relevant precedents. Either that search, or a renewed discussion of the matter must have led to the decision that such franchises were not "annexed", which led to the judgments already noted (*159*).

The issue as to whether or not "return of writs" was or could be "annexed" to a particular manor had arisen only in a single case prior to 1285: *Rex* v. *Earl Warenne,* in the 1281-4 Lincolnshire eyre (*160*). In this case, the earl claimed to exercise the franchise within the town of Stamford by virtue of a grant of Stamford and Grantham "with all their appurtenances" made by the future Edward I and subsequently confirmed by Henry III. His case was that Edward had possessed "return of writs" as appurtenant to the town of Stamford, and therefore granted it with it. A decision was eventually reached, in favour of the king, in this case, after it had been referred to the king's council. There were two reasons for this adverse judgment. The first was that Edward had never lawfully possessed the franchise himself, and was therefore in no position to be able to grant it to the Earl. The second was that such a franchise as return of writs could, in any case, not be conveyed by a grant couched in such general terms as those used in this case (*161*). This second argument could be taken to imply that, had the correct form of words been used, explicitly

---

(*156*) *Rex* v. *Seton: P.Q.W.,* p. 118 (heard in the 1292 Westmoreland eyre but judgment not given till Easter 1293).

(*157*) *Rex* v. *Lanc': P.Q.W.,* p. 792 (heard in the 1293-3Cumberland eyre but judgment not given till Trinity 1293); *Rex* v. *Mulcaster': P.Q.W.,* pp. 125-6 (judgment not given till Michaelmas 1293).

(*158*) *Rot. Parl.,* i, 98 (also printed by Sutherland, *op. cit.,* pp. 211-212).

(*159*) Above, n. 157.

(*160*) *P.Q.W.,* pp. 429-430. Other cases about title to this franchise are discussed by M. T. Clanchy in "The Franchise of Return of Writs", *Trans. Roy. Hist. Soc.,* 5th ser., xvii (1967), 67-79.

(*161*) "idem comes ab initio feoffatus fuit de predicta villa cum pertinenciis tantum, in quo quidem feoffamento nichil quod regale est, et maxime returnus brevium transiit nec debuit transire sub illis generalibus verbis . . .". On the interpretation of "general words" in royal charters see Sutherland, *op. cit.,* pp. 113-122.

granting the franchise with the town, it would have legally passed to the earl with it: but, given the facts of the case, the implication may instead be that the subsequent royal confirmation of the grant would, in that case, have specifically provided authority for the earl's exercise of the franchise. In either case, however, it is clear that franchise is not regarded as very closely "annexed" to the town, in the kind of way that Hengham's words would appear to imply.

There are no cases from the decade after 1285 in which a challenge was made to the title of an alienee to a hereditary shrievalty (*162*), or to the title of an alienee to the franchise of return of writs (*163*). There are, however, a number of cases involving both hundred bailiffs (or equivalent officials) and the lords of hundreds. All three cases concerning hundred (or in these cases, wapentake) bailiffs arose in the 1292 Lancashire eyre, and in none was a definitive judgment recorded. In two of these cases, claimants described their office as a serjeanty: presumably with the implied corollary that it was also inalienable (*164*). A third claimant described his office as "annexed and appurtenant" to a manor, while also agreeing that it was a sergeanty (*165*). This may imply that it would pass with the manor on an alienation. The legislation of 1290, accepting seisin since time out of mind as good title for the possession of franchises, though not "free tenement" (*166*), gave added significance to the classification of the "lordship" of a hundred as a franchise or as "free tenement", a special reason for the king's attorneys to try to have it classified as the latter. This was brought out by a case in the 1293 Staffordshire eyre (*Rex* v. *Gryffin*) (*167*) in which the defendant was summoned to show by what warrant he held the *baillia* of the king's hundred of Pirhull. The defendant claimed that he and his ancestors had held it since time out of mind, claiming by implication, the benefits of the 1290 legislation. The king's attorney, in reply, denied that this was a franchise, to which such would be an adequate title, but was driven to waive the denial, and take issue on the seisin alleged. In the event, the jury then found in favour of the king. In a second case (*Rex* v. *Cobeham*) (*168*) in the 1293 Kent eyre

(*162*) No hereditary shrievalties seem ever to have been alienated in this period. The only recorded case during the "quo waranto" proceedings concerning such a shrievalty was that brought in the 1292 Lancashire eyre against the Earl of Lancaster (*P.Q.W.*, p. 338), who was able to show title by grant of Henry III.

(*163*) But note that in a case in the 1287 Gloucestershire eyre concerning view of frank-pledge (*Rex* v. *Valers*: *P.Q.W.*, p. 268), the king's attorney, Inge, went out of his way to deny that any private person possessed the "potestatem aliquem feoffandi de libertate visus franci plegii, nec de plactio vetiti namii del returno brevium nec de aliquibus aliis regiis libertatibus."

(*164*) *Rex* v. *Waleton*, *Rex* v. *Kellet* (*P.Q.W.*, pp. 382, 384).

(*165*) *Rex* v. *Singalton* (*P.Q.W.*, p. 388). It is not, however, said that the manor itself is held by serjeanty tenure.

(*166*) Below, p. 433 and above, p. 410.

(*167*) *P.Q.W.*, p. 709. Since the defendant paid the king 6½ marks a year for this bailiff-ship, it is presumably what would normally be described as the "lordship" of the hundred that he possesses.

(*168*) *P.Q.W.*, p. 365: this case concerns the hundred of Shamwell.

the lordship of a hundred was again treated as a serjeanty in that the king brought a writ of right for its recovery. However, the defendant was allowed to vouch to warranty, as though the hundred was in fact alienable. None of these cases, however, whether concerning the "bailiff-ship" or the "lordship" of a hundred squarely raised and definitively settled the problem raised by the original question.

Nor did this decade see any decisive move to settle the more general problem of whether there was a distinct category of "jurisdictional" franchises, and whether the distinctive feature of this category was that the holders of such franchises were unable to alienate them. The king's attorneys did, on occasion, speak as though there was such a separate category, and as if unalienability was a special characteristic of it (*169*): but this tended to be drowned by the more general cry that all franchises were inalienable (*170*). In a similar fashion, the question of whether there existed a difference in alienability between franchises enjoyed by virtue of a royal charter and those enjoyed by virtue of seisin since time out of mind, tended to be swallowed up and obscured by more general discussion as to whether the latter was ever in itself an adequate warrant for the tenure of franchises, anyway. The end result was, as Donald Sutherland has written, that when "quo waranto" proceedings were halted in 1294 "nothing at all had been done to resolve the question of whether franchises might be alienated" (*171*).

Question 5

Question 5 concerned the correct procedure to be followed when a franchise-holder had failed to respond correctly to the public proclamation requiring all those exercising franchises within the county in which an eyre was being held to put in their claims to those franchises by a certain date. Some, it was said, held that although, in these circumstances, the franchise in question should be seized into the king's hands, it ought to be replevied to the franchise-holder if he so requested (*172*). Others, however, held that, other than in certain exceptional circumstances, the franchise-holder's failure to make his claim at the appointed time, was to be construed as a tacit renunciation of the franchise, and that seizure of the franchise was to cause its permanent re-annexation to the Crown.

(*169*) E.g. in *Rex* v. *Jarpenville*, in the 1286 Buckinghamshire eyre, the king's attorney argued that no private person "habet potestatem aliquem feoffandi de predicto visu [franciplegii] quia est jurisdiccio regalis mere spectans ad dignitatem". (*P.Q.W.*, p. 87); and in *Rex* v. *Peyvere*, in the 1287 Bedfordshire eyre, the king's attorney claimed judgment for the king ". . . ex quo clamat predictum visum franci plegii, que est quedam jurisdiccio regalis de feoffamento private persone qui de jure alicui concedere non potest sine regia confirmacione . . ." (*P.Q.W.*, p. 7).

(*170*) *Cf.* Sutherland, *op. cit.*, p. 133.

(*171*) Sutherland, *op. cit.*, 134. There was one minor exception to this—the franchise of warren: above p. 422.

(*172*) In other words, possession of it was to be restored to him if he found sureties to appear and answer for the franchise.

Replevin of the franchise was, therefore, appropriate only where the franchise-holder was under some disability—e.g. minority, being in prison, absence from the country—which rebutted the presumption of tacit renunciation.

A clause requiring the sheriff of a county in which an eyre was to be held to make a proclamation of the type mentioned in this question had been added to the standard writ of summons for the eyre in 1278, as a direct result of regulations made at Gloucester in the summer of that year (*173*). Subsequent evidence indicates that it was usual for the claims to be made in writing (*174*) and that they normally had to be made at the very beginning of the eyre (*175*). The justices of the "Northern" circuit had, by late 1285, already received such claims in at least four other counties (*176*), and it seems improbable that they had not already had to deal on at least one occasion with a request for the replevin of a franchise seized into the king's hands because its holder had failed to submit his claim by the date specified (*177*). Their apparent hesitation about dealing with this matter now looks even more curious, if it be remembered that the very regulations by which it was arranged that the receipt of such claims should become a regular part of their business, had in fact specifically laid down the procedure to be followed in just such circumstances. These settled that replevin was to be allowed, when requested, but that this was to be conditional on the franchise-holder making an immediate answer for his franchise (*178*).

It is possible that, in the seven years which had elapsed since the regulations were drawn up, they had altogether slipped from the memory of the justices. Most of the provisions which they contained were of an ephemeral nature (*179*) or such as to have an immediate but permanent effect through the alteration of some routine of judicial administration (*180*). There would, therefore, have been little, if any, need for recourse to the text of the regulations during this period: and this could have meant that the regulations themselves had passed into oblivion. Nor is it certain that the justices would have possessed a copy of the text of these regulations that they could have referred to in 1285. Even if it be assumed that a copy was sent to them—and there is no positive evidence

---

(*173*) These regulations are printed in full and discussed by Sutherland, *op. cit.*, pp. 190-193.

(*174*) Sutherland, *op. cit.*, pp. 221-5.

(*175*) Sutherland, *op. cit.*, pp. 221, 224-5.

(*176*) Sutherland, *op. cit.*, pp. 222-223. The eyres in question were those of 1280-1 in Nottinghamshire, of 1281 in Derbyshire, of 1281-4 in Lincolnshire and 1285 in Warwickshire.

(*177*) There is no positive evidence for this, but the routine replevin of a franchise would, presumably, have often gone unrecorded.

(*178*) Sutherland, *op. cit.*, p. 192.

(*179*) E.g. the provision for suspending all proceedings concerning franchises that were then pending before the king's council.

(*180*) E.g. the alterations in the wording of the writ of summons for the general eyre, and in the procedures followed in the eyre.

for this—the vicissitudes of the custody of the official records of the circuit (*181*) could well have meant that they no longer had access to it. Alternatively, it is just possible, that the justices, though aware of the regulations, did not regard them as binding law, but merely temporary administrative orders, which might be disregarded if this was in the interests of the Crown.

It is less difficult to explain why the king's attorneys should have advanced the argument that in normal circumstances unclaimed franchises should be treated as irrepleviable and forfeit. The doctrine of tacit renunciation had already been advanced by them to justify the confiscation of those franchises to which a claimant had a good title but which he had on some past occasion failed to exercise (*182*). The present argument was a natural development of that doctrine. The franchise-holder had been given an adequate opportunity to put in his claim to the franchise he was exercising. If he failed to do so, this might well be the result of a fear of the consequences of close scrutiny of his title, and could, in any case, be construed as a special kind of failure to exercise the franchise. The only people whose failure to put in a claim was not to be construed as a tacit renunciation were those with an excuse for not having done so in some kind of incapacity (*183*).

Hengham's answer to the question is in accordance with the regulations of 1278, even though it does not specifically mention them; and here, at least, his advice seems to have been followed for there is no evidence that forfeiture was ever enforced in the case of late claims during the later Edwardian "quo warranto" proceedings (*184*).

(*181*) The regulations, if sent, would probably have passed into the custody of the keeper of rolls and writs, as did legislative enactments sent to the justices of the Bench: see the memorandum printed by Sayles, *Select Cases in the Court of King's Bench*, vol. I, pp. clix-clx. When the first keeper of rolls and writs on the circuit, Robert of Ipswich, died, the regulations might have remained in the custody of his executors and not been handed over to his successor, Ellis of Sutton: *Cal. Pat. Rolls, 1272-1281*, pp. 295, 304. Alternatively, Sutton might have handed them into the Exchequer with other material belonging to his office in 1284 (*Cal. Pat. Rolls, 1281-1292*, p. 131), and the Exchequer failed to re-deliver them to his successor, Roger of Hales (*Chronicon Petroburgense*, p. 119).

(*182*) Sutherland, *op. cit.*, pp. 9-11.

(*183*) Private law analogies would suggest the inclusion of various other categories in this group, e.g. married women and those *non compos mentis*. The private law doctrine most closely analogous was that which foreclosed all future claim by those who failed to make a claim to land transferred by final concord within a year and a day of its making: Pollock and Maitland, *Hist. Eng. Law*, ii, 101-102.

(*184*) The order issued in 1286-7 by the justices of this circuit to the sheriffs of Bedfordshire, Huntingdonshire and Gloucestershire, during their eyres in those counties, for the irrepleviable seizure of unclaimed franchises (the text of which is printed in Sutherland, *op. cit.*, pp. 200-201), envisaged such a seizure being made not in the circumstances outlined in this question, but where franchises had gone unclaimed through the whole of the sessions of the eyre in the county. This is clear from the exception made for religious houses whose headship had been vacant both at the time the justices started holding sessions in the county, and at the time of their departure from it, after concluding them.

Question 6

The last question, question 6, was also concerned with a point of franchise law. This was whether continuous and peaceful tenure since time out of mind could be considered an adequate warrant for exercising such franchises as return of writs, extracts of the summonses of the Exchequer, view of frankpledge, and possession of a hundred. Some, it was said, argued that such seisin could be regarded as an adequate title, even in the absence of a "special" warrant (*185*) from the king or from one of his ancestors, because the king's ancestors had, through Magna Carta, confirmed all the franchises held by the archbishops, bishops, earls, knights and free tenants of the kingdom, prior to the making of that charter. Others, however, urged a line less favourable to such franchise-holders. Since the king's ancestors had not intended, when granting Magna Carta, to agree to any diminution of the Crown, the clause in question was to be interpreted as confirming only those *libertates* that were appurtenant to "free tenement", not any royal franchises in the proper sense of the word. Such seisin would, nonetheless, under certain circumstances, provide partial evidence of the existence of a valid title. In the case of a lay tenant whose ancestor had come to England at the time of the Norman Conquest and whose title was derived from "conquest" of the franchise (*186*), the seisin would provide evidence of a valid title, provided it was also shown that the franchise-holder possessed the appropriate instruments of punishment, such as gallows, pillory and tumbril. The like combination of evidence could also be taken to demonstrate a valid title in the case of franchises exercised by archbishops, bishops, abbots and priors who held baronies in chief of the king. Such seisin could not, however, provide a valid title for those who had acquired their lands by a private enfeoffment made since the Conquest, since in that case any franchises which they exercised and for which they possessed no royal charter must have been acquired by the grant of private persons, and such grants were invalid. Such franchise-holders would, moreover, it was stated, not be in possession of the appropriate instruments of punishment, which would clearly indicate their lack of legitimate title to the franchise.

Whether seisin since time out of mind was an adequate warrant for the tenure of franchises had come, by 1285, to be one of the major unresolved problems of franchise law. At the very beginning of the Edwardian "quo waranto" proceedings, as Donald Sutherland has shown, tenure of a franchise since time out of mind was generally accepted as a good title to exercise it (*187*). Such titles began, however, to be challenged

---

(*185*) In other words, a charter granting the franchise.

(*186*) This appears to be the sense of the corrupt passage.

(*187*) Sutherland, *op. cit.*, pp. 14, 71-74. This is shown most clearly by the opinion of the king's council of 1279 that ". . . quelibet libertas regia est et ad coronam pertinet nisi ille qui eam habet sufficiens habeat warantum vel per cartam vel [per seisinam] a tempore cujus non extat memoria . . .": Sutherland, *op. cit.*, pp. 196-197.

in eyres on the "Southern" circuit from that held in Dorset (1280) onwards, and in the eyres on the "Northern" circuit from that held in Yorkshire (1279-81) (*188*) onwards, the king's attorneys claiming that franchises were imprescribable (*189*). It appears, however, that, at first, this argument was not advanced with any consistency, and judgment was usually reserved when such a challenge was made (*190*). Then from the autumn of 1285 and as the result, Sutherland suggests, of formal or informal consultations at parliament at Westminster, objection was made quite consistently to all claims to franchises based on such a title: though still judgment was normally reserved when the challenge had been made (*191*).

The plea-roll evidence shows the use of two separate types of argument in support of the claim that seisin since time out of mind be treated as a valid title for the exercise of franchises (*192*). One type conceded that in principle all franchises did belong to the Crown, but claimed either that tenure since time out of mind was evidence of a royal grant made before time of memory (*193*), or that the long tolerance shown by the king and his predecessors for the exercise of a franchise was in effect the equivalent of a royal grant, evidence of tacit consent to the exercise of the franchise (*194*). The other type of argument did not concede that all franchises belonged to the Crown, but held that those franchise-holders whose ancestors had come to England at the time of the Norman Conquest, possessed a legitimate title to their franchises by conquest, by virtue of an independent acquisition of those franchises by their ancestors. This line of argument was reflected in some (if not all) (*195a*) of the offers made to aver "seisin ever since the Conquest" rather than just "seisin since time out of mind" during the "quo waranto" proceedings (*195b*).

(*188*) But note that this was the first "Northern" circuit eyre to hear such pleas in any case.

(*189*) It is tempting to associate this with wider knowledge of the teaching of Bracton that a "special warrant" in the form of a royal charter was necessary to authorise the exercise of any franchise, and that time did not run against the king for the recovery of franchises. Cf. above, n. 126.

(*190*) Sutherland, *op. cit.*, pp. 72-80.

(*191*) Sutherland, *op. cit.*, pp. 80-81.

(*192*) Sutherland, *op. cit.*, pp. 81-85.

(*193*) More particularly, an oral grant made before time of memory, of which there could be no evidence other than long seisin. Selby's argument, for the king, in the 1285 Warwickshire eyre that ". . . nulla prescriptio potest nec debet eidem episcopo conpetere in hac parte, et maxime de returno brevium quod *numquam* consuevit alicui concedi sine speciali waranto et hoc per cortam". (*Rex* v. *Bishop of Worcester: P.Q.W.*, p. 783), was clearly intended to rebut just such a claim.

(*194*) Such an argument would leave intact the theory that all franchises belonged to the Crown, but would rob it of almost all practical significance.

(*195a*) Some offers of such an averment may, however, indicate that the franchise-holder is claiming to hold the franchise by the grant of the Conqueror: this claim is explicitly made in two cases—*Rex* v. *Nonant* in the 1281-2 Devonshire eyre (*P.Q.W.*, p. 167) and *Rex* v. *Lardener* in the 1279-81 Yorkshire eyre (*P.Q.W.*, p. 207).

(*195b*) For clear evidence of the existence of this view see *Rex* v. *Abbot of St. Mary's York*, a "quo waranto" case heard in the Bench in Michaelmas term 1298:

Question 6 reveals the existence of a further variant of the first type of argument, a variant that does not seem to have been recorded or reported in any of the Edwardian "quo waranto" proceedings elsewhere. This is the argument that *Magna Carta* had ratified the title of all those in possession of franchises at the time of its granting, curing any defects in their titles, including failure to possess a "special warrant" for the franchise from the king (*196*). The clause in question appears to be one that first appears in the second Henrician reissue of *Magna Carta* in 1217, and which appears in a slightly modified form in the definitive 1225 reissue (*197*). It seems clear from the context that the original intention of the framers of this clause was no more than to convey the assurance that the granting of certain liberties to the community of the realm as a whole through *Magna Carta* did not imply a revocation of individual grants of liberties and franchises to particular members of that community made at dates prior to that. There was no idea of conceding a general ratification of all franchises, whatever the title of their holder to them might be. Nonetheless, there may have been an earlier precedent for this interpretation of *Magna Carta*. In 1244, the sheriffs of England had received a royal mandate, ordering them to ensure that franchises belonging to the Crown were exercised only by those who were in possession of a sufficient warrant from the king or from his predecessors, or by those who had held such a franchise of old and had exercised it up to the time of "parliament of Runnymede" between King John and his barons (*198*). The most plausible explanation for this latter stipulation would seem to be that the corollary— that all franchises *not* exercised at the time *Magna Carta* was granted were thereby forfeit—was already being deduced from the settled proposition that *Magna Carta* has indeed confirmed all franchises then being exercised (*199*).

CP 40/125m. 260. In this case ,which concerned the abbot's claim to the return of all writs affecting his fee in Marshland, the abbot pleaded as title seisin ever since the reign of King Richard, and before. The king's attorney counter-pleaded that "hujusmodi responsio de prescriptione longi temporis etc. competit comitibus et baronibus, etc. qui per conquestum a diu hujusmodi libertatibus usi sunt etc. et non abbatibus seu aliis viris religiosis etc. quibus libertates tales etc. prius concesse fuerunt per reges etc." The abbot ought, therefore, he argued, be made to produce a specialty from the king or one of the king's predecessors. The case was eventually adjourned *sine die,* in accordance with a royal mandate which gave the justices a choice of doing this or adjourning the case into the next Yorkshire eyre.

(*196*) Logically, of course, this argument should have led to offers to aver seisin at the making of *Magna Carta* and ever since.

(*197*) "Et salve sint archiepiscopis, episcopis, abbatibus, prioribus, templariis, hospitalariis, comitibus, baronibus et omnibus aliis tam ecclesiasticis personis quam secularibus personis libertates et libere consuetudines quas prius habuerunt": J. C. Holt, *Magna Carta* (Cambridge, 1965), p. 356. For the 1217 version see *ibid.,* p. 357, n. 1.

(*198*) *Close Rolls, 1242-1247,* p. 242.

(*199*) The clause in question was not of course part of the text of the 1215 issue of *Magna Carta,* produced by the negotiations at Runnymede. There is, however, little reason to suppose that in 1244 many men were aware of the differences between the text of the 1215 issue and the text of the reissues of 1217 and 1225.

The argument produced to counter this theory of "general ratification" by *Magna Carta* was not, as one might have expected, the obvious one that the "general" words of *Magna Carta* were not to be construed as confirming any particular individual franchises (200). Instead, as already noted, it was countered by the argument that the clause in question cannot have been referring to franchises at all, since the king's ancestors could not have intended to diminish the rights of the Crown when granting *Magna Carta* (201). The "liberties" referred to, then, must have been "liberties" of the kind that were appurtenant to "free tenement"—apparently easements (202).

By this date, the king's attorneys were regularly advancing the argument that the only warrant for the tenure of franchise was a royal charter. Such a view was not, however, advanced even by those who rejected the idea that *Magna Carta* had ratified the possession of franchises: and this is, perhaps, an indication that the viewpoints reflected in the questions are those not of the pleaders on each side, but of the justices during subsequent discussion of the cases (203). They accepted that seisin since time out of mind was *prima facie* evidence of the possession of a valid title, but suggested that more than this was needed to prove the point in full. The additional criterion which the franchise-holder had to satisfy, if he was to prove his title, was the possession of the requisite *"judicialia"*, the instruments of punishment appropriate to the franchise he was claiming (gallows, tumbril, pillory etc.). Of the franchises mentioned in the question, this criterion seems applicable only to view of frankpledge and tenure of a hundred (204). No explanation is provided of what analo-

(200) The king's attorneys frequently argued that "general words" in individual charters were not to be construed as granting or warranting any particular franchises: Sutherland, *op. cit.*, p. 116.

(201) It is probable that Edward I had taken a specific oath to this effect at his coronation, but that his predecessors had solely a moral duty not to do so: E. H. Kantorowicz, *The King's Two Bodies* (Princeton, 1957), p. 356, n. 147.

(202) For use of the term *libertas* to denote an easement see e.g. Bracton, *De Legibus*, f. 220b (III, 162). It is difficult to believe that the passage could have been intended to refer to those franchises that were 'annexed" to free tenement (above p. 000), since such "libertates" are contrasted with "libertates regis" which can only mean franchises in general.

(203) This may also account for the tentative nature of the succeeding argument. Those justices who put forward this argument may have been unwilling to commit themselves too firmly against the view that franchises could only be exercised where the franchise-holder had warranty for this in a royal charter.

(204) In some cases it is said or implied that the only *judicialia* necessary for view of frankpledge are tumbril and pillory e.g. in *Rex* v. *FitzEustace* in the 1286 Norfolk eyre (*P.Q.W.*, p. 483) in *Rex* v. *Tuchet* in the 1286 Rutland eyre (*P.Q.W.*, p. 673), and in *Rex* v. *Ubeston* in the 1286-7 Suffolk eyre (*P.Q.W.*, p. 727). In others, however, the gallows are also included in the list: e.g. *Rex* v. *Tyringham* and *Rex* v. *Jarpenvill* in the 1286 Buckinghamshire eyre (*P.Q.W.*, pp. 84-85, 88) and *Rex* v. *Drayton* in the 1286 Huntingdonshire eyre (*P.Q.W.*, p. 308). All three *judicialia* are treated as appurtenant to a hundred in *Rex* v. *Curtenay* in the 1280 Somerset eyre (*P.Q.W.*, p. 693). Only gallows are specifically mentioned as such in *Rex* v. *Countess of Aumale* in the 1280-1 Hampshire eyre (*P.Q.W.*, p. 769) and *Rex* v.

gous criterion can be applied in the case of the other franchises mentioned, or other franchises in general. Nor, curiously, is there any kind of justification attempted for the adoption of this criterion. It is not explained why it should be true that it was only those franchise-holders, whose seisin of a franchise had originated in a valid transaction, that were in possession of such *judicialia*.

There seems to be no evidence that the possession of *judicialia* was ever in practice adopted, whether before or after 1285, as a criterion for distinguishing between valid and invalid claims to the tenure of a hundred based on immemorial seisin, nor even of it being argued that such a criterion should be adopted. The same is true prior to 1285 of claims to view of frankpledge. Thereafter, however, arguments are found urging the application of this criterion, particularly during the period from 1286 to 1289 when, as Sutherland had already noted, particular attention was being paid to this franchise (*205*). In some cases, it is clear that all that is being urged is that failure to possess the requisite *judicialia* is analogous to holding the view in the absence of a royal bailiff, an abuse of the franchise that justifies its forfeiture (*206*). In other cases, however, it is quite clear that failure to possess such *judicialia* is being treated as evidence that seisin of the franchise was wrongfully acquired (*207*). Such arguments were normally combined with others, and judgment, as in most other "quo waranto" cases, respited. There is, however, at least one case in which judgment was given for the king wholly or partly on the basis of such an argument (*208*).

Hengham's answer to this question shows him once more in disagreement with both the views expressed in the original question. Provided it was proved to the satisfaction of a "good" inquisition, seisin since time out of mind was, he said, an adequate warrant for the tenure both of frankpledge and of return of writs: the other franchises he ignores. Such seisin is, it seems, a good warrant not because such titles have been ratified

---

Bishop of Salisbury in the 1281 Wiltshire eyre (*P.Q.W.*, p. 804), but tumbril and pillory are probably included by implication.

(*205*) Sutherland, *op. cit.*, p. 80.

(*206*) E.g. in *Rex* v. *Prior of Hospitallers* and *Rex* v. *Tuchet*, in the 1286 Rutland eyre (*P.Q.W.*, pp. 672-673). On the forfeiture of franchises for abuse see Sutherland, *op. cit.*, pp. 141-142.

(*207*) E.g. in *Rex* v. *FitzEustace* in the 1286 Norfolk eyre (*P.Q.W.*, p. 483); *Rex* v. *Ubeston* in the 1287 Suffolk eyre (*P.Q.W.*, p. 727); *Rex* v. *Hussey* in the 1286 Rutland eyre (*P.Q.W.*, p. 671); *Rex* v. *Prior of Christchurch, Canterbury* in the 1286 Buckinghamshire eyre (*P.Q.W.*, pp. 86-87) and *Rex* v. *Riddal* and *Rex* v. *Drayton* in the 1286 Huntingdonshire eyre (*P.Q.W.*, pp. 294-5, 308). Thornton's objection, for the king (in the 1286 Rutland eyre) to a defendant's claim to exercise this franchise on the grounds that long seisin was no valid title *especially* to those whose ancestors did not come at the Conquest, is probably also a reflection of this theory, rather than the product of any special knowledge of the family history. Neither the doweress exercising the franchise nor her warrantor, possessed the requisite judicialia: *Rex* v. *Paunton* (*P.Q.W.* p. 671).

(*208*) *Rex* v. *Drayton*, above, n. 207.

by *Magna Carta* but, simply, because there are many franchise-holders who exercise their franchise with this as their only title. This appears to be an argument based solely on political expediency, but it is just possible that what Hengham is saying is that the combined evidence of long tenure and tenure by a large number of people is, in itself, sufficient to create a general "custom" in favour of such franchise-holders which makes up for their lack of a "special warrant" from the king (*209*). Hengham goes on then to mention a further group of franchise-holders who may be entitled to exercise these particular franchises (*210*), even though they do not possess a royal charter specifically authorising them to do so. These are those franchise-holders who possess a royal charter of an older type that simply grants that the king's official shall not enter the lands of the grantee (*211*). If, during the long period after the Conquest when pleas that are now brought by writ were brought instead by plaint, these franchise-holders or their ancestors or predecessors had always taken "bills" from the sheriff (*212*), and if once writs had been invented, they had refused to allow the king's officials to enter their lands or to execute any royal mandate in them, but insisted that all mandates be "returned" to them for execution (*213*), they were, he argued, fully entitled to exercise the franchise of return of writs, even though their charter did not mention it and could not have done so, as the franchise was not then invented (*214*).

Hengham tacitly rejects the idea that the possession of *judicialia* can be used to distinguish those whose immemorial seisin commenced

(*209*) That "antiqua approbata et usitata consuetudo" is a sufficient title for franchises is asserted by the writ used by the plaintiff in *Prior of Blyth* v. *Cressy*, heard in the King's Bench in Easter 1277 (KB 27/31m. 8) "Antiqua consuetudo unde non est memoria" is mentioned as one valid title to franchises in *Rex* v. *Earl of Gloucester* in the 1279 Kent eyre (Sutherland, *op. cit.*, pp. 196-197).

(*210*) Or perhaps just the single franchise of return of writs.

(*211*) Again, the passage is a little obscure, but this seems the plausible interpretation of it.

(*212*) These "bills" are presumably either written instructions from the sheriff for the summoning of defendants to the county court, or summaries of plaints made by plaintiffs, transmitted to the franchise-holder for trial in his court.

(*213*) For the development of the "return of writs", a process which postdates the invention of the returnable writ, see M. T. Clanchy, "The Franchise of Return of Writs", *Trans Roy. Hist. Soc.*, 5th series, xvii (1967), pp. 59-82.

(*214*) Presumably Hengham would have also held that a similar seisin would have to be demonstrated by those claiming this franchise without charter by seisin since time out of mind. Certainly such a seisin was demonstrated in a *quo waranto* case (*Rex* v. *Countess of Aumale*) heard in King's Bench in Easter 1280 (KB 27/53m. 21): for the knights of the jury found that the countess and her ancestors "postquam returnum brevium provisum fuit semper habuerunt returnum brevium et placitaverunt placita eorundem brevium que vicecomites placitant in comitatu; et antequam returnum aliquod fuit provisum, antecessores ejusdem comitisse placitaverunt eadem placita per billias". It may be that it was this case which had stimulated Hengham's awareness of the historical background to the development of this franchise for he was chief justice of King's Bench at the time.

It is, however, possible that the verdict simply reflected the need to satisfy criteria already established by Hengham and others, as a result of existing knowledge of that development.

with a valid transaction, and who therefore now have a valid title to their franchise. He is more concerned to register a positive dissent from the associated assertion that it was possible to discriminate on this matter between those whose ancestors had come at the Conquest and those who were unable to show this. Unfortunately, it is not clear what reasons he had for doing this. What he says is that those who propose to make such a distinction can be answered by pointing out that those franchise-holders who had acquired a manor with its franchises by virtue of a grant in *maritagium,* a grant for service, a grant by way of alms, or a grant by way of exchange, and who have then exercised the franchises, will be able to use the same plea in their defence as the magnates who had granted them the manors would have done, if the grant had not been made. There are at least three possible interpretations of this:

(1) Hengham may have accepted the view that any restrictions on alienation only applied if the franchise had been acquired by royal grant. If a franchise was acquired by "conquest", then the seisin of the alienees and of the alienors since that conquest will be as good a title as the continuous seisin of the heirs of the conqueror.

(2) Hengham may be saying that if a grant took place before the limit of legal memory, then it will be true that the alienees will be able to show continuous seisin since time out of mind, and that, as a matter of law, such seisin is a sufficient title to exercise a franchise. There will therefore be no difference between such seisin when it is proved by alienees and such seisin when it is shown by the original tenants of the franchise.

(3) Hengham may be starting from the supposition that both view of frankpledge and return of writs are franchises of the type that is appurtenant to land, and that they will pass, therefore, with the land to which they are "annexed". If this is so, then in law a joint seisin since time out of mind by both grantor and grantee will be as good as one by the grantor alone.

There is no evidence that Hengham's views on these matters exercised a significant influence on the justices of the "Northern" circuit between 1285 and 1288. At most, they may have played some part in reinforcing the unwillingness of the justices to give judgment in cases raising such points, despite the pressure of the king's attorneys to give judgment in them for the king. The statute of "Quo Waranto", enacted at the Easter parliament of 1290, established that continuous seisin of any franchise since time out of mind was a valid warrant for the exercise of that franchise *(215)*. It seems probable that the statute was largely the result

---

(215) The procedure originally envisaged by the statute was a complicated one, which had the merit of theoretically preserving intact the "royalist" theory that all franchises could be exercised only by virtue of a "special" warrant from the king. The defendant whose title to this franchise was immemorial seisin was to be allowed to plead such seisin in his defence, and would have to prove it to the satisfaction of a jury. A favourable verdict would not, however, be followed by an immediate judgment confirming the defendant's possession of the franchises.

of political pressure exerted by the magnates on Edward I. However, although Hengham was by then in disgrace (*216*), his past advocacy of the view that such titles were valid may have done something towards the creation of the climate for the statutory confirmation of the validity of such titles. In any case, despite some determined rear-guard actions by the king's attorneys (*217*), the statute did in practice solve the problem: and, therefore, seisin since time out of mind was accepted as a valid title to franchises.

V

In 1285 the Court of King's Bench was still the regular court with the closest links to the king, in some senses the king's own private court, and this was still shown most graphically by the way in which it moved round the country with him. It might have been expected, therefore, that the chief justice of the court, Ralph de Hengham, would adopt a generally "royalist" line, the line most favourable to the king, in the controversies that arose over "quo waranto" law. His answers to these questions indicate, however, that this was not so. In the controversy over the use of "quo waranto" writs for the recovery of "free tenement" (Question 1), Hengham adopted the essentially moderate line that these writs should be used only where this was unavoidable, because it was impossible to prove seisin within time of memory (*218*). In informing his correspondent of the king's decision that statutory prescription was not to apply in his case, Hengham seems not to have been expressing an opinion, whether for or against, that particular decision—with its high "royalist" overtones—but simply to have been telling him about a decision which under current constitutional custom, they were both obliged to accept (*219*). His views on the procedural delays available to defendants in "quo waranto" actions (Question 2) clearly reflected little sympathy for the claims made on the king's behalf by his legal representatives for special treatment (*220*). In holding that the franchises of return of writs, warren and market would pass to an alienee without a royal confirmation (Question 4) and, more

---

When a favourable verdict was given the case would be adjourned to allow the defendant to take a copy of the official record to Chancery and obtain letters patent confirming him in possession of the franchises, and it would then be on the basis of those letters patent that judgment was given. The procedure bears a close resemblance to that followed for the pardoning of those who had committed homicide by accident or in self-defence: see N. D. Hurnard. *The King's Pardon for Homicide* (Oxford, 1969), pp. 44-54. In practice, however, as soon as the eyres resumed in 1292—and possibly due to a deliberate change of policy on this point—those who pleaded and proved such titles were adjourned *sine die* without being required to produce letters patent confirming their title. Sutherland, *op. cit.*, pp. 91-96, 203-205.

(*216*) Dunham, *Radulfi de Hengham Summae*, pp. liii-lvi.
(*217*) Sutherland, *op. cit.*, pp. 99-100.
(*218*) Above, pp. 405-6.
(*219*) Above, p. 407.
(*220*) Above, p. 415.

generally, in his rejection of the view that there existed any general rule against the alienation of the franchise without royal consent, Hengham can be seen to have taken a remarkably "unroyalist" line (*221*). Hengham's rejection of the idea of construing failure to put in claims to franchises at the correct time as tacit renunciation of those franchises (Question 5) may simply indicate that he did remember the earlier regulations on this point. If not, he was again choosing the more "liberal" side as that which he supported (*222*). Lastly, his view that seisin since time out of mind was a sufficient warrant for the tenure of franchises (Question 6) was an opinion, that, in 1285, clearly put him in the "liberal" camp—even if it was a view that was eventually accepted by statute as the correct one (*223*).

The picture that emerges from his answers of a man with "liberal" views on "quo waranto" law is one which fits in well with what little is known of Hengham's views on matters of law that were politically sensitive (*224*). Such information as we have is provided by a well-known story told by Bereford C.J. early in the region of Edward II, shortly before Hengham's death (*225*). Isabel de Forz, countess of Aumale, had been summoned to one of Edward I's parliaments, to answer the king "on any matter that should be alleged against her" (*super sibi obiciendis*). When she appeared, no less than thirty separate charges were laid against her, in the king's name, by one of the justices. She had objected to this, on the grounds that the writ which summoned her ought to have specified the matters with which she was now charged. Two justices present had spoken in favour of upholding the writ. Hengham, however, had spoken forcefully against it. The law of the land was, he said, that no-one ought to be taken by surprise in the king's court, nor deprived of a proper warning of the matters with which they were to be charged. The writ was duly quashed.

No corruption was actually proved against Hengham in 1290. His disgrace followed conviction on a very minor matter of technical negligence in sealing an incorrectly dated judicial writ (*226*). His replacement as chief justice of King's Bench, Gilbert of Thornton, had, as the king's attorney on the "Northern" circuit eyres of the 1280s, frequently advanced high "royalist" views on the king's behalf (*227*); and, soon after his appointment as chief justice, he joined with the other justices of King's

---

(*221*) Above, pp. 419-20.

(*222*) Above, p. 426.

(*223*) Above, pp. 431-2.

(*224*) There were, of course, a considerable number of cases raising legal points that were politically sensitive during Hengham's time as chief justice of King's Bench. The collegiate nature of the court, and the lack of "reports" of cases there, means, however, that we have no means of knowing how far decisions recorded in these cases reflect Hengham's own views.

(*225*) *Y.B. 3 Edward II*, ed. F. W. Maitland (Selden Soc., Y.B. series vol. iii (1905)), p. 196.

(*226*) *Radulfi de Hengham Summae*, ed. Dunham, pp. liv-lv; *Sel. Cases in the Court of King's Bench*, vol. I, ed. Sayles, pp. lxvii-lxviii.

(*227*) Sutherland, *op. cit.*, pp. 83-84, 126, 128.

Bench in giving judgment for the king in a number of cases where the king's attorneys had disputed claims to franchises based on seisin since time out of mind on the grounds that this was no title to franchises, thereby leading to the political crisis which was eventually settled by the enactment of the statute of "Quo Waranto" and the revocation of these judgments (*228*). It is, then, at least a possibility that Hengham's dismissal and disgrace in 1290 were for political reasons, because Edward I wished to secure a more "royalist" chief justice of the King's Bench, and, more specifically, one who could be relied upon to take the correct line in "quo waranto" cases (*229*). Hengham's rehabilitation and appointment as chief justice of Common Pleas in 1301 may also, perhaps be, after all, a result of other political factors: though a discussion of these would be beyond the scope of the present article.

In these questions and answers, we possess the opinions of one of the greatest legal experts of late thirteenth century England on topics that were among those mostly disputed in his day. For this, for the evidence they provide on the practice of informal inter-judicial consultation, and for the light they shed on some of the differing opinions held on the matters in dispute, this set of questions and answers deserves a small but honoured place among the sources for the history of the common law in their period.*

(*228*) Sutherland, *op. cit.*, pp. 94-97.
(*229*) The Chronicler, Pierre de Langtoft, said that Hengham lost his place not for corruption, but for being "difficult". "Sir Rauf de Hengham tant ad despute Ke del bank le rais perdu ad le see". (quoted by Sayles in *Sel. Cases in the Court of King's Bench*, vol. I, p. lxviii).

*I wish to record my thanks to Professor Donald Sutherland, to Dr. Robert Palmer, and to Dr. Paul Hyams for their criticism of earlier drafts of this article. The final version also owes much to the valuable criticism of my wife, Vanessa.

APPENDIX I

The text here printed is taken from ff. 154v-155v of MS. Douce 139 in the Bodleian Library at Oxford. I have also noted significant variants from the other two texts in the footnotes. Variants from British Library MS. Additional 5761, ff. 99r-100r are cited as *A*; those from Huntington Library MS. HM. 19920, ff. 62v-64r are cited as *H*. The individual questions and answers are not numbered in any of these manuscripts, but have been given numbers for ease of reference. The same considera-tion has dictated some alterations in the original paragraphing and in the punctuation of the text.

[1] Ad primum (*1*) utrum domino regis competat accio ad recuper-andum dominicum corone sue a corona sua separatum (*2*) per breve quod vacatur "quo waranto". Sunt aliqui qui dicunt quod hujusmodi breve de "quo waranto" non jacet de libero tenemento set tantum de libertatibus regiis a corona separatis et quod domino regis non (*3*) competunt nisi communia brevia sicut (*4*) quibuslibet privatis personis ad liberum tenementum suum recuperandum. Et sunt aliqui qui dicunt quod de perquisitis et aliis eskatis domini regis injuste alienatis non competunt domino regis nisi communia brevia et ubi oporteat quod (*5*) dominus rex doceat de seisina propria vel antecessorum suorum et ubi currit prescripcio versus ipsum regem sicut contra quemlibet alium, set de antiquis dominicis corone et de libertatibus regiis que faciunt ipsam coronam a corona separatis breve de "quo waranto" tenet locum et ad primum formatum (*6*) fuit nec ttenet ibi locum prescripcio nec oportet quod dominus rex doceat de aliqua seisina, cum de jure communi hujusmodi ad coronam pertineant. Et dicunt quod si rex scire vellet quo waranto aliquis terram suam teneret, licet terra sua non esset de antiquo dominico, oportuit tenentem (*7*) pro se sufficiens warantum ostendere.

Ad que responsum fuit quod visum (*8*) est utrumque breve videlicet "precipe etc." et maxime de dominicis (*9*) que fuerunt in manibus regum tempore cujus haberi potest memoria, ut visum fuit inter regem H[enricum] et H[enricum] de la Wade de toto tenemento suo in Staunton "quod est membrum de Wodestoke"; visum est eciam breve

---

(*1*) *A* and *H* omit these two words.
(*2*) In the main MS., the last four words have been misplaced and are to be found at the end of the sentence after *quo waranto*.
(*3*) In the margin of the text of the main MS. opposite this point (between the third and fourth lines of the text) is to be found the word *proposiciones*, which appears to refer to the whole of the first paragraph.
(*4*) This is the reading of *A* and *H*. Our main MS. reads: *sint*.
(*5*) This word is supplied from *A* and *H*.
(*6*) This is the reading of *A* and *H*. Our main MS. reads *fozratum*.
(*7*) rectius: *tenenti*.
(*8*) *H* reads *usitatum*.
(*9*) *H* reads (for the last five words) *et summone etc., precipe in casu quod rex petit aliquod in dominico et maxime jacet de dominicis.*

"quo waranto tenet tale manerium quod est de antiquo dominico etc.", et hoc de dominicis que fuerunt in manibus regum ante tempus memorie. Et (*10*) ad hoc quod illud breve sit bonum oportet esse securus quod comperiatur antiquum dominicum in libro de Domesday. De eskaetis Normannorum antiquitus non fuit visum aliud breve, ut socii mei et ego recolimus, quam tale "precipe A. etc. quod juste etc. reddat nobis tale manerium quod debet esse in manu nostra (*11*) tanquam eskaeta nostra de terris Normannorum". De serjantiis jacet "quo waranto". De aliis terris que fuerunt in manibus regum et injuste occupatis (*12*) generaliter jacet "precipe etc." (*13*) Et in hiis habet rex necesse narrare de seisina alicujus predecessoris. Et quo ad prescripcionem sciatis quod dominus rex ore suo proprio dixit quod non wlt artari ad aliquam prescripcionem. Dixit tamen quod voluit aliquibus facere graciam, set hoc pro voluntate sua (*14*).

[2] Item super eodem si breve de "quo waranto" locum tenere debeat, si competat (*15*) tenenti visus terre, excepcio non tenure, proparcenaria (maxime ubi particeps fuerit infra etatem), waranti vocacio (ubi warantus fuerit infra etatem). Et sunt aliqui qui dicunt quod hec omnia locum habere debent, cum hujusmodi antiquum dominicum est liberum tenementum et sui natura partibile, licet dominus rex hujusmodi dominica a corona separata sine mora tenetur revocare, etate alicujus minoris non (*16*) expectata.

Ad quod responsum fuit quod tam in "quo waranto" quam in "precipe" (*17*) per que rex proposuit recuperare tenementa in Banco Regis hucusque concessus est visus et videtur quod visus necessarius est. Item excepcio de nontenura hucusque in eodem Banco fuit allocata. Item auxilium proparcenarie concessum est et merito concedendum, quia ipsemet rex post mortem tenencium suorum dividit hujusmodi inter coheredes per extentam, propter quod (*18*) non solum de tenementis, immo de omnibus que ad certum annuum commodum extendi possunt, concessum est auxilium parcenariorum. Item waranti vocacio necessario debet concedi, sive warantus sit plene etatis sive infra etatem, et debet expectari etas.

[3] De libertatibus autem regiis a corona separatis ut ae returno

---

(*10*) *H* reads *Set.*

(*11*) Followed in the main MS. by a redundant *de terris Normannorum.*

(*12*) MS.: *occupati. A* reads *occupate.*

(*13*) *H* reads for the last two sentences *De serjantiis et de aliis terris ut de perquisitis, escaetis et alio modo excepto antiquo dominico in manibus regum dudum existenti non jacet similiter precipe etc. quo waranto tenet tale tenementum etc., ubi hujusmodi tenementum injuste occupatum fuerit super regem.*

(*14*) *H* adds another sentence here *Et breve quod dicitur summone etc. quo waranto tenet visum franciplegii et naturaliter jacet de libertatibus regiis a corona sua separatis recuperandis.*

(*15*) *H* reads *Item si in casu quo breve de quo waranto locum habet competit.*

(*16*) *A* and *H* read for the last two words *minime.*

(*17*) *H* reads *Ad que responsum est: tam in "precipe" quam in "summone" de quo waranto.*

(*18*) *H* reads *dividit hereditatem heredum tenencium suorum inter hujusmodi coheredes per extentam et hoc.*

brevium, officio ministrorum regis et de hujusmodi que spectant ad
jurisdiccionem, et wreyk' et weyf' et hujusmodi que spectant ad
commodum corone et que sui natura non sint partibilia non jacet
paracenaria, waranti vocacio et hujusmodi, set oportet quod deforcians
qui plene etatis fuerit ostendat warantum de domino rege vel amittere
debet. Alii sunt qui in contrarium senciunt (*19*).

Ad quod responsum fuit quod licet libertates regie wreyk' et weyf'
non sint, ut dicitis, de suit natura partibilia potest tamen unum
manerium ad quod spectant hujusmodi libertates assignari uni heredi in
proparte et coheredi potest assignari aliud manerium ad quod hujusmodi
libertates non pertinent, et hujusmodi particio fiy per regem multociens.
Si igitur petantur versus unum heredem libertates sue, necesse est quod
habeat auxilium participis, alioquin unus participum haberet plenam
propartem, alio sine (*20*) culpa exheredato.

[4] Item cum dominus rex concesserit alicui quod sit vicecomes suus
de feodo vel quod habeat returnum brevium vel quod custos sit
hundredi, et ille cui dominus rex sic concesserit predictum officium, isne
regia (*21*) voluntate alteri concesserit, si concessio hujusmodi private
persone deforcianti poterit esse sufficiens warantum. Sunt quidam qui
dicunt quod jure nulla, et quidam qui dicunt quo concessio valida (*22*).

Ad quod (*23*) responsum fuit quod qui habet custodiam hundredi vel
sit vicecomes de feodo, cum sint serjantie, videtur quod sine (*24*) rege
nullo modo possunt alienari. De returno brevium aliud est et warrena,
mercato et hujusmodi que per factum regis sunt annexe maneriis, quia
cum totum manerium alienatur in illa alienacione transeunt cum manerio.

[5] Item quid sit agendum de illis qui libertates habent regias in
comitatu Norht' et qui illas in presenti itinere non clamaverunt licet
publice (*25*) proclamatum fuit quod omnes illi qui libertates regias
clamare voluerunt essent in presenti itinere ad illas clamandas (*26*). Sunt
enim quidam qui dicunt quod predicte libertates non clamate capiende
sunt in manum domini regis et replegiande sunt cum petite fuerunt per
plevinam; sunt alii qui dicunt quod capiende sunt domino regi irreplegi-
abiles et quod corone regis annexe debent esse, cum domini libertatum
hujusmodi (*27*) libertatibus tacite renunciant; set hoc non est intelligendum

---

(*19*) *H* omits this sentence.

(*20*) This word is supplied from *A* and *H*.

(*21*) *A* and *H* read *regis*.

(*22*) *A* reads (for the last nine words) *talis concessio de jure nulla est et sunt qui dicunt quod concessio valida est.*

(*23*) This word is supplied from *A* and *H*.

(*24*) Followed in the main MS. by the word *herede* which is marked for deletion.

(*25*) MS.: *pullice. A* reads *pupplice.*

(*26*) *H* substitutes for this sentence the following *Item quid sit agendum de illis qui postquam proclamatum fuerit publice in itinere quod omnes illi qui aliquas libertates in tali comitatu habere clamant essent tali die tali loco itineris ad ea clamanda et non venerint ad clamanda.*

(*27*) *H* reads (for the last twenty-one words) *sunt quidam qui dicunt quod capiende sunt in manum domini regis per defaltam tanquam forisfacte corone domini regis annexe, maxime cum domini hujusmodi libertatum.*

de illis qui sunt infra etatem vel in prisona vel extra regnum Anglie
vel hujusmodi.

Ad quod responsum fuit: libertates capte in manum domini regis
pro eo quod post proclamacionem non calumpniate fuerunt replegiande
(*28*) sunt cujucumque etatis domini extiterint, et postquam replegiate
fuerint habeant domini suas responsiones.

[6] Item sunt aliqui qui a tempore quo non exstat memoria clamant
habere libertates regias ut returnum brevium, extractas summonicionum
scaccarii, et qui clamant habere hundreda ad coronam regis spectancia et
similiter visum franciplegii, ubi debent inquiri de latronibus et eorum
recetattoribus, de purpresturis super regem (*29*) factis post ultimum
visum, de falsis mensuris et ponderibus, de assisis fractis (*30*) et
hujusmodi que in turno vicecomitis debent inquiri et que omnia mere
sunt regalia. In quo casu diversimode sentitur. Dicunt quidam quod
omnes illi qui hucusque (*31*) libertates pacifice possiderunt illis guadere
debent inperpetuum licet de domino rege vel progenitoribus suis
speciale warantum non habuerint, cum in magna carta libertatum
contineatur quod archiepiscopi, episcopi, comites, barones, milites,
libere tenentes habeant libertates suas quas ante confeccionem predicte
carte habuerunt. Et sunt aliqui qui ita exponunt quod progenitores
domini regis non intellexerunt per magnam cartam (*32*) libertatum
aliquid subtrahere de corona Anglie, et dicunt quod predicta carta
tantum se extendit ad libertates ad liberum tenementum non spectantes
et non ad libertates regis (*33*). Et dicunt quod licet hujusmodi longa
seysina valere debeat aliquibus non tamen omnibus; set dicunt quod
forte valere potest comitibus, baronibus, magnatibus, militibus (*34*), et
libere tenentibus quorum antecessores (*35*) in conquestu Anglie statum
suum tenuerunt, et illis qui statum talium (*36*) modo habent (*37*), et qui
habent furcas, pilloria, tumberella et hujusmodi, per quod liquere possit
(*38*) quod hujusmodi libertas eis adhereat, et eciam de archiepiscopis,
episcopis, abbatibus, prioribus et hujusmodi qui baronias de domino
rege tenent in capite et qui habent furcas, tumberellum, pilloria et
hujusmodi indicia (*39*), set de illis qui per privatas (*40*) personas sunt

---

(*28*) *H* reads *replegiabiles*.
(*29*) This is the reading of *H*. The main MS. reads *sine regi. A* reads *sine rege*.
(*30*) *H* reads *assisa panis et cervisie fracta*.
(*31*) *A* reads *hucusque hujusmodi*; *H* reads *hujusmodi*.
(*32*) Followed in the main MS. by a redundant additional *cartam* which is marked for
    deletion.
(*33*) *A* and *H* read *regias*.
(*34*) *H* reads *baronibus, militibus et aliis magnatibus*.
(*35*) The last two words are written over an erasure in the main MS.
(*36*) *talium* is the reading of *A*. The main MS. reads *suum calm*.
(*37*) *H* reads (for the last seven words) *et iullis eciam valere potest quorum antecessores in
    conquestu Anglie statum suum tenuerunt et illis eciam qaui statum talem modo habent*.
(*38*) The last four words are written over an erasure in the main MS.
(*39*) *H* reads *judicialia*.
(*40*) Followed in the main MS. by the word *sunt* which is marked for deletion.

feofati de terris et tenementis, et ubi feofatores de jure communi hujusmodi libertates regias concedere non potuerunt (*41*), et qui non habent furcas, tumberella, pillorium (*42*) et hujusmodi, videtur quod longa seysina talibus valere non debeat pro waranto.

Quapropter dileccionem vestram suppliciter exoro quatinus diligenciam vestram circa premissa adhibere velitis et me de premissis articulis sicut prius supplicavi in principio hujus littere per latorem presencium reddere cerciorem, et responsionem vestram scriptum (*43*) in fenestris predicte cedule mihi remittere velitis (*44*). Valete (*45*) in eo quem peperit virgo singularis (*46*).

Ad que responsum fuit quod (*47*) cum multi habent visum franciplegii sine carta (*48*) et similiter returnum brevium, si quis ostendere possit per bonam inquisicionem quod ea habuit a tempore cujus non extat memoria sufficiens est eis warantum. Quia bene scitis (*49*) quod nullus per antiquam cartam habet returnum brevium aut visum franciplegii, set habent quidam quod ministri regis non intrent terras suas, et hoc est sufficiens warantum illis qui ante returnum brevium ceperunt bilettas quando brevia non fuerunt et postquam brevia fuerunt illis qui non (*50*) permiserunt ministros regis ingredi nec execucionem alicujus mandati regis in terris suis exequi nisi haberent returnum brevium, quia fere omnia que nunc (*51*) placitantur per brevia per magnum tempus post conquestum placitabantur per querimonias. Illis qui volunt facere differenciam inter comites, barones et alios qui (*52*) venerunt ad conquestum Anglie et alias privatas personas (*53*) bene potest responderi quod magnates illi qui in maneriis suis predictas habuerunt libertates si unum manerium dedissent in maritagium vel alicui pro servicio suo vel in elemosina cum predictis libertatibus vel illud excambiissent et illi ad quos maneria illa devenerunt modo quo predictum est usi extiterint libertatibus illis per eandem responsionem se tueri possint (*54*) per quam se tueruntur hujusmodi magnates vel eorum heredes.

(*41*) *H* adds *aliquibus assignatis*.
(*42*) This word is supplied from *A*.
(*43*) *rectius scriptam*.
'(*44*) *A* omits this word.
(*45*) This word is supplied from *A*.
(*46*) *A* places this paragraph at the very end, after the response to question 6. *H* omits it entirely.
(*47*) This word is supplied from *H*.
(*48*) The last two words are supplied from *H*. *A* reads *sine cartis*.
(*49*) *H* reads (for the last two words) *satis liquet*.
(*50*) The last word is interlined in the main MS.
(*51*) This is the reading of *A* and *H*. The main MS. wrongly reads *nunc*.
(*52*) *H* reads *quorum antecessores*.
(*53*) *H* adds the gloss *id est alios de communi populo*.
(*54*) *H* adds *si calumpniati fuerunt*.

APPENDIX II

This report is taken from f. 392v of MS. Dd.7.14 in the University Library at Cambridge (55). There is a second version of what is clearly the same report in British Library MS. Harley 25, f. 215v, from which it was subsequently copied in a version which differs only in orthography into British Library MS. Additional 35116 (at ff. 227r-v). Significant variants from the first of these two manuscripts are noted in the footnotes where this manuscript is referred to as *YY*. The two British Library MSS. are arranged by form of action. This report is to be found in a section of miscellaneous pleas in both. In the Cambridge University Library MS. it occurs as part of a section of reports of cases both from the Common Bench and from the Eyre of various dates between 1270 and 1290 running from f. 369v to f. 394v. William of Saham's appearance as a justice and Gilbert of Thornton's appearance as king's serjeant in the report suggest that it is a case heard on the "northern" eyre circuit between 1278 and 1287. The heaviest concentration of identifiable eyre cases in this section comes from the 1284 Leicestershire and 1285 Warwickshire and Northamptonshire eyres. Since Thornton was absent in Ireland at the time the 1284 Leicestershire and 1285 Warwickshire eyres were held, the report certainly cannot be from either of those eyres. It is more than possible that it comes from the 1285 Northamptonshire eyre itself, since the two preceding reports and the three succeeding reports are from that eyre. A passage found at the end of this report only in the British Library MSS. also suggests that the case was ultimately decided in the same eyre and may specifically refer to the justices taking advice before giving judgment (56).

Edward Rey de Engleterre porta un bref vers la dame de E. et demaunde par queu garaunt ele clama tener le maner de C. ke apent a sa coroune cum ceo ke en askun tens fut des auncyene demenes (57).

Kall' (pur la dame) respond ke cety bref de "quo warento" est fourme (58) sur franchises et non pas sur terre ne tenement et demaund jugement de cety bref.

Thornton' (59). Si le Rey demaunda (60) cum sun dreyt de la seysine sun auncestre ou de sa seysine demene dunk diseyt ben. Mes nostre seygnur le Rey le demande cum aunciene demeyne ke apent a la

---

(55) On this MS. see *YBB 20 & 21 Edward I* (Rolls Series), pp. xi-xx.
(56) See below, note 70.
(57) *YY* adds *le Roy*. In the margin of the main MS. opposite this first paragraph are the words *Quo Warrento*.
(58) *YY* reads *fundu*.
(59) *YY* wrongly ascribes this speech to Tothby (*Thoud'*).
(60) *YY* reads *demaundast le maner*.

coroune, et le "quo warento" est especialement done a *(61)* ceo ke apent a la coroune; demandum [jugement etc.].

Kall'. Cety bref deveryt estre un "precipe quod reddat" et dusum aver la veuue *(62)*; mes en le "quo warrento" ne gist pas la veuue, dunt cety bref ne gist pas en teu cas *(63)*.

Thorton'. En le "quo warrento" de franchises *(64)* ne gyst pas la veuue, pur ceo ke jurisdiccioun neyt pas veable *(65)*; mes en cety bref de terre git la veuue *(66)*. Et la ou vous dites ke ceo devereyt estre un "precipe" ne dites nent ben, pur ceo ke par le "precipe" si serreyt la dame a respounce par averement du pays, et des auncienes demenes le Roy ne deyt nent estre avere par pays eyns deyt par le Domesday, pur quey cety bref est especial a demander aunciene demene *(67)*.

Kall'. Si cety bref deyt luy tener dunk est ceo *(68)* le premer ke unke fut fet *(69)* en teu cas.

Saham. Cety bref est bon. Dites outre *(70)*.

---

(61) *YY adds* demander.
(62) *YY adds* pur ceo qe nous ne pooms en cesti bref allegger nountenure *(the* ne *is superfluous here).*
(63) *YY reads* et en le "quo warranto" ne deit hom pas aver la vewe, par qei nous demandom jugement.
(64) *YY reads* de fraunchise nent veable.
(65) *YY reads* pur ceo qe ceo nest mie chose veable.
(66) *YY adds* pur ceo qe on bref "precipe quod reddat".
(67) *YY reads (for the whole of this sentence)* Et si serra la dame recu par pais de averrer qe ceo nest mie aunciene demene et le aunciene demene le rey ne deit mie estre averre par pais, par qei cesti bref est especiale a demander aunciene demeine.
(68) This is the reading of *YY*. The main MS. reads *esse*.
(69) *YY reads* vew.
(70) *YY reads* Saham dit qe le bref fut bon, mes nepurquant il furent a jugement sil feut bon ou noun etc. E au drein avoient la vewe e le bref agarde bon par les Justices ov avvis en le counte de Norhampton' *(quod mirum fuit desicom* "precipe quod reddat" *eust etc.).*

19

Ireland and the Literature of the Early Common Law

I

When King John crossed the Irish Sea to visit his lordship of Ireland in the summer of 1210, his main purpose was to hunt down the fugitive William de Braose, his wife and children, and to punish those Anglo-Irish magnates who had given them refuge—William Marshal and Walter and Hugh de Lacy (*1*). John did, however, also find time during the two months he spent in Ireland to issue a charter relating to the observance of the common law of England within the lordship of Ireland (*2*). It is unfortunate that this charter survives neither in the original nor in any contemporary or later copy, official or unofficial (*3*). There are, however, several references to it in later letters patent and close, and from these references it is possible to piece together a general picture of its form and contents (*4*).

The charter was issued on the initiative of King John, whose seal it bore, and it appears to have been drafted by the men of discretion and legal expertise ("viri discreti et legis periti") whom he had brought with him to Ireland (*5*). The King also succeeded in securing some kind of consent to the issuing of the charter from the magnates of Ireland and a promise from them, under oath, that they would abide by its terms; and

---

(*1*) G. H. Orpen, *Ireland under the Normans* (Oxford, 1911-1920), 2. 235-67.

(*2*) For previous discussions of this charter and its context *see* Orpen, 2. 270-7; W. J. Johnston, "The first adventure of the common law", *L.Q.R.* 36 (1920), 9-30 at 13-4; H. G. Richardson and G. O. Sayles, *The Irish Parliament in the Middle Ages* (Philadelphia, 1952), p. 12; G. J. Hand, *English Law in Ireland, 1290-1324* (Cambridge, 1967), p. 2; A. J. Otway-Ruthven, *A History of Medieval Ireland* (1968), pp. 81-2.

(*3*) All the chancery rolls of the relevant regnal year are now lost.

(*4*) The principal references to it are in enrolments of letters patent of 29 June 1226, 10 December 1226, 28 October 1233 and 9 September 1246, and enrolments of letters close of 8 July 1226, 8 May 1228 and 27 January 1257. These have been transcribed or calendared in *Pat R. 1225-32*, pp. 48, 96; *C.P.R., 1232-47*, pp. 31, 488 (these are transcribed in full in *Early Statutes, Ireland*, ed. H. F. Berry (1907), 1. 24-5 and *Rymer's Foedera*, 1.1.266); *R.L.C.*, 2.128; *C.R. 1227-31*, p. 45; *C.R. 1256-9*, p. 120.

(*5*) Knowledge of the contribution of "viri discreti et legis periti" to the making of the charter comes from the letters patent issued in favour of the justiciar, Geoffrey Marsh, in December 1226. It is reasonable to assume that they embody information communicated by Marsh himself. Marsh was in a position to know what had happened in the summer of 1210, for he was then in Ireland and rendered military assistance to King John: Orpen, 2. 248. For these legal experts, see also below, p. 445.

both of these may have been recorded in the charter itself (6). The charter was subsequently kept for safe custody in the Exchequer at Dublin (7). There is a fairly general agreement among the later documents referring to the charter that it contained a general statement of principle that, in future, English laws and customs—in other words, the common law of England—were to be observed in the lordship of Ireland and two of them suggest that the charter went on to give some sort of summary or explanation of the main rules of the English common law which were to apply in Ireland (8). Which rules were thus expounded and how succinctly or clearly they were explained cannot now be known; but it seems clear that it did include some of the rules of the criminal law, and that the resulting charter was sufficiently brief for it to be thought feasible for the justiciar of Ireland to have the whole charter read to the assembled archbishops, bishops, abbots, priors, earls, barons, knights, free tenants and bailiffs of counties of the lordship in 1228 (9).

John's Irish charter of 1210 was not, of course, the first attempt to reduce to writing the main rules of the English common law: the treatise known as *Glanvill* had already performed that task, and probably in a

(6) The charter is said in the letters patent of December 1226 to have been issued at the request of the Irish, and in the letters patent of 1233 King John is said to have decreed that English law be observed in Ireland with the common consent of "all" the men of Ireland. The letters close of 1228 mention the oath of the magnates of Ireland to observe the charter.

(7) This fact is mentioned only in the letters patent of December 1226, but there is every reason to believe that it is true: above, n. 5. The letters close of 1228 clearly assume that the new Justiciar, Richard de Burgh, will have ready access to the charter.

(8) The letters patent of December 1226 state that King John ". . . statuit et precepit leges Anglicanas teneri in Hibernia; ita quod leges easdem in scriptum redactas reliquit sub sigillo suo ad Scaccarium Dublinie", while the letters close of 1228 order the Justiciar to have the charter read and to order the audience for this reading ". . . quod leges illas et consuetudines in carta predicta contentas decetero firmiter teneant et observent".

(9) When the justiciar was ordered in May 1228 to have the charter read out and to secure that its terms were observed in future, the King conceded that on two matters, presumably included in the charter or directly affected by its terms, there should be no immediate enforcement, but a continuance of the *status quo* until a fortnight after Michaelmas. This concession to the magnates of Ireland concerned the death *(mors)* and chattels of murdered Irishmen *(Hibernensium occisorum)*. The reference to the "death" of murdered Irishmen suggests that the charter may specifically or, by apparent implication, have extended to all the native Irish living within the lordship the full protection of the criminal law, so that their murder would be accounted a felony and punished accordingly. The later, and perhaps also the earlier, rule was that such a killing only required the payment of compensation to the lord of the Irishman concerned: Hand, pp. 201-3. The reference to the "chattels" of murdered Irishmen is more obscure. Native Irishmen who were convicted of felony were subject to the rigours of the common law. John's charter may have made it clear that their chattels were forfeit to the King on conviction and did not pass to their lords. This may have changed an earlier rule; *cf.* the charter of Geoffrey de Joinville, lord of the liberty of Meath, allowing his tenants to have the chattels of "their" Irishmen on conviction: *Calendar of the Gormanston register*, ed. J. Mills and M. J. McEnery (Royal Society of Antiquaries of Ireland, extra volume, 1916), pp. 176-7.

much more satisfactory manner, over twenty years earlier. But *Glanvill,* whatever the author's connections with the King's court may have been, appears to have been the product of private enterprise; and the lost charter of 1210 represents the first attempt to produce anything resembling an official *summa* of the English common law. In this, it was, of course, a precursor not just of many of the clauses of *Magna Carta,* which represent a codification and reaffirmation of existing rules and principles, but also of many clauses in English statutes of the later thirteenth century, which perform a similar function; it should also be seen perhaps as a precursor of the statute of Wales of 1284, which was an attempt to summarize some of the main rules of the later thirteenth century common law for application in the conquered Welsh territories. It is, furthermore, just possible that there is some connection, if only a distant one, between the charter and the second great treatise of the common law, which has long been known as *Bracton.* Professor Thorne's work has made it plain that Henry of Bratton's connection with *Bracton* is merely that of a reviser, and shown that the bulk of the treatise was composed in the late 1220s and early 1230s by William Ralegh and his circle (*10*). It is not implausible to hypothesize that one starting-point for the work might have been the outline of the common law produced for the charter of 1210. The great royal justice of John's reign, Simon of Pattishall, was among the "viri discreti et legis periti" who accompanied King John to Ireland; and the King is likely to have utilized his services and those of his clerks in the making of the charter (*11*). Among those clerks is likely to have been Martin of Pattishall, who was in Simon's service for the whole of King John's reign and perhaps longer (*12*). William Ralegh in turn served his apprenticeship as Martin of Pattishall's clerk, and might have come across a copy of, or drafts connected with, the charter of 1210 among Martin's papers (*13*). William Ralegh may even have gone to Ireland himself, as clerk to Martin or Simon of Pattishall: he was certainly in a clerical position in the courts by 1214, and could possibly have been in a similar position as early as 1210. In that case, he might himself have worked on the drafting of the charter. The great treatise could have started life as an extended commentary on the charter of 1210 or as an attempt to produce a more adequate account of the whole of the common law than that contained in the charter.

What remains to be seen is just how important the charter of 1210 really was in the process of the transmission of the English common law

(*10*) *Bracton: On the laws and customs of England,* ed. G. E. Woodbine, translated and revised by S. E. Thorne (Cambridge, Mass., 1968, 1977), 3. xiii-lii.

(*11*) *Rot. de Lib.,* p. 188.

(*12*) *Rolls of the Justices in Eyre for Lincolnshire (1218-9) and Worcestershire (1221),* ed. D. M. Stenton, SS 53 (1934), xvi-xviii.

(*13*) C. A. F. Meekings, "Martin Pateshull and William Raleigh", *B.I.H.R.* 26 (1953), 157-80; idem, "Martin de Pateshull of good memory, my sometime lord", *B.I.H.R.* 48 (1974), 224-9.

to Ireland. An incautious reading of the later documents referring to the charter might well suggest that the charter was responsible for the introduction of the common law into Ireland: that overnight, and at one single stroke, the whole of the common law was, through the agency of the charter, introduced into Ireland. Yet it is clear that many of the procedures associated with the nascent common law were in operation in Ireland prior to 1210. There is good evidence for the use not only of trial by a jury of twelve men but also, more specifically, of the availability in Ireland of the assizes of novel disseisin and mort d'ancestor, and of the utilisation by Irish litigants of the writ of right, the writ *de rationabilibus divisis* and the writ of naifty (*14*). There is also evidence of the use in

(*14*) As early as 1192, the city of Dublin was promised that no *recognicio* would be held in the city: *Historic and Municipal Documents, Ireland*, ed. J. T. Gilbert (RS, 1870), pp. 51-5; at some date between 1192 and 1199, a *recognicio* of twelve men was heard in the so-called "county court" of Dublin: *Chartularies of St. Mary's Abbey, Dublin*, ed. J. T. Gilbert (RS, 1884-1886), 1. 145-6; and in 1200 King John insisted that no *recognicio* be taken in Ireland save in his court: *Rot. Chart.*, p. 99. Almost certainly *recognicio* means trial by a jury of twelve men in each of these contexts. In 1199 payment was promised in England for an assize of novel disseisin for land in Ireland: *Rot. de Obl.*, p. 27; in February 1204, the justiciar of Ireland was told to make it known that the limitation date for such assizes for land in Ireland was in future to be the King's first coronation: *Rot. de Lib.*, pp. 105-6; and in November 1204 the justiciar was given authority to issue such writs for use in Ireland himself: *R.L.P.*, p. 47. The assize of novel disseisin was a procedure for remedying the unjust dispossession of freehold tenants of land; to use the procedure, a litigant had to be able to show that he had been dispossessed in the recent past, since the limitation date specified in the writ necessary to initiate his plea. Payment was promised in England for assizes of mort d'ancestor for land in Ireland on several occasions from 1199 onwards: *Rot. de Obl.*, pp. 26, 40, 200-1, 214, 297, 382; and in November 1204 the justiciar was authorised to issue such writs himself provided the land in demand was half a knight's fee or less: *R.L.P.*, p. 47. The assize of mort d'ancestor was a procedure that allowed a litigant to assert a right to land which was based on the fact that a close relative had died in possession of it: to use the procedure, a litigant had to be able to show that the relative had died in the fairly recent past, since the limitation date specified in the writ necessary to initiate his plea. At the same time, the justiciar was also authorised to issue writs of right, with a similar limitation: *R.L.P.*, p. 47; and in 1205 half a mark was promised in England for a writ of right for half a knight's fee in Ireland: *Rot. de Obl.*, p. 330. The writ of right was the comparatively slow procedure for the assertion of title to land which had to be used by those litigants unable to make use of the assizes of novel disseisin and mort d'ancestor. In 1199 Walter de Ridelesford, in an entry subsequently cancelled, is recorded as promising payment for, among other things, a writ "de rationabilibus divisis inter ipsum et vicinos suos": *Rot. de Obl.*, p. 76; in 1201 the Irish head of the order of Hospitallers, at Kilmainham, offered money "pro litteris domini regis habendis de rationabilibus divisis suis inter terras suas et terras vicinorum suorum": *Rot. de Obl.*, p. 175; and in November 1204 the justiciar was given power to issue "breve de divisis faciendis inter duas villas exceptis baroniis" in Ireland: *R.L.P.*, p. 47. The writ *de rationabilibus divisis* was a procedure for settling boundary disputes between neighbouring land-owners in neighbouring villages. A writ of naifty issued in May 1204 survives in a later transcript: *Chart. St. Mary's Dublin*, 1.90; and in November 1204 the justiciar was authorised to issue the "breve de fugitivis et nativis" himself: *R.L.P.*, p. 47. The writ of naifty was a procedure by which lords asserted their right of ownership over unfree tenants: by this date, the procedure seems normally to have been used to initiate litigation between lord and tenant as to whether or not the tenant was unfree.

Ireland, as modes of proof, of trial by battle and of the ordeals of cold water and hot iron; and of the practice of outlawing fugitive felons (*15*). The use of these procedures clearly also implies that many of the concepts and rules of the early common law were thought to be applicable in Ire'and; and there is other evidence to suggest that the concept of "reasonable dower" was considered applicable there, and that there was already seignorial wardship of minors holding land by knight service, and even a royal claim to the prerogative wardship of all lands held by tenants-in-chief (*16*). It is, nonetheless, probable that the charter of 1210 was the first authoritative statement that the law followed in the courts of the lordship of Ireland was to be identical with the common law of England in all respects and in all details: that the courts of the lordship were not to be free to reject certain rules and practices of the common law as developed by the King's courts in England while accepting others, and the rules specifically mentioned in the charter may have been intended to displace other, contrary rules hitherto observed in Ireland (*17*). In practice,

(*15*) In 1185 William FitzMaurice was granted the right to the franchises of holding trial by battle, and the ordeals of hot iron and cold water (and the associated right of possessing an ordeal pit): *Chartae, Privilegia et Immunitates* (Irish RC, 1829-30), p. 5; and in 1192 the citizens of Dublin were exempted from trial by battle: *Hist. and Munic. Documents*, pp. 51-5. In 1200 King John enunciated the principle that only his court in Ireland was competent to pronounce outlawry: *Rot. Chart.*, p. 99. For possible evidence of the use of indictment in Ireland in 1207 *see R.L.P.*, p. 77, and for the use of the criminal appeal in 1208 *see Rot. Chart.*, pp. 176, 178.

(*16*) Evidence for the applicability to Ireland of the concept of "reasonable" dower—that is, the right of the widow of a deceased tenant to a life tenancy of one-third of his lands—is in an order of 1205 to the bailiffs of the earl Marshal in Leinster to ensure that a named widow received her "reasonable" dower: *Rot. de Obl.*, p. 321. Evidence for seignorial wardship in general and prerogative wardship in particular is provided by the charters of 1208 re-granting Leinster to William Marshal and Meath to Walter de Lacy which specifically allow the grantees wardship of the lands of tenants-in-chief who hold of them within their liberties: *Rot. Chart.*, pp. 176, 178. His right of prerogative wardship generally allowed the king to enjoy the wardship of all the lands which belonged to a tenant-in-chief who was under age: not only the lands which were held of the king, but also those held of other lords.

(*17*) F. H. Newark in his *Notes on Irish Legal History* (Belfast, 1960), p. 6 vouched the evidence of Matthew Paris for a story "told in later years that King Henry [II] held a council at Lismore 'where the laws of England were by all freely received and confirmed with due solemnity' ", and accepted that this story was "not improbable" if it was "taken to mean that there was some sort of a declaration that the Norman barons and such Irish Kings as had done homage to Henry would have their relations *inter se* governed by English Law". However, as Orpen showed long ago, the chronicle passage concerned is a distorted reference to a council held at Cashel, though called by the bishop of Lismore, at which were received and accepted not the English common law but ecclesiastical regulations followed in England: Orpen, 1. 274-7. The only evidence relating to the earliest period of the Anglo-Norman lordship which might be taken to imply some general decision as to the use of English law in Ireland by the English settlers is the much later reference (in 1283) to a charter said to have been issued by King Henry II in favour of the Ostmen of the city and county of Waterford, allowing them the use of "English" law: C 66/102 m. 9, calendared in *C.P.R. 1281-92*, p. 78. This would, of course, only make sense if there had already also been a decision that the English settlers themselves were to use "English" law. However, although the 1283 Patent Roll

the attempt to impose uniformity was not completely successful, but it is conceivable that the charter of 1210 did lead to a much greater degree of uniformity between the common law of England and that of Ireland than would otherwise have been the case (*18*). The charter may also have been important in helping to reinforce the principle first, albeit only indirectly, enunciated in the charters of 1208 re-granting the liberty of Leinster to William Marshal and the liberty of Meath to Walter de Lacy: that there was to be no room for the development of a separate law or custom, differing from the common law, within the great liberties of Ireland (*19*). The charter may have spelt out this principle in direct terms; if not, it was, nonetheless, soon being taken as authority for this position (*20*). Given the wide extent of these two liberties, the principle thus stated was of enormous importance for the future development of the law of the lordship of Ireland.

II

Registers of writs survive in manuscript in some quantity from the mid-thirteenth century onwards (*21*). They contain the formulae of those original writs which could be obtained by or for potential litigants from the English royal chancery for the initiation of litigation, and of some other writs potentially of interest to litigants or to their legal advisers: they do not reflect those sides of the routine activities of chancery which did not possess any great interest for litigants or lawyers (*22*). The earliest

entry speaks as though the king (or his officials) had seen a charter in such terms ("Quia per inspeccionem carte domini H. regis filii Imperatricis quondam domini Hibernie proavi nostri nobis constat quod Custumanni (sic) nostri Waterford' legem Anglicorum in Hibernia habere et secundum ipsam legem judicari et deduci debent . . ."), it seems not improbable that all that they had seen was the charter of Henry II to the Ostmen of Waterford, of which there is a transcript in the Carew Mss. (for which *see* Appendix, below, p. 113), and which merely grants the king's protection to them as his liegemen. The Patent Roll entry may simply reflect a much later and, in its terms, anachronistic understanding of what Henry II's charter had granted the Ostmen of Waterford.

(*18*) For a discussion of the question of how far, and in what ways, Irish common law varied in the later thirteenth and early fourteenth centuries from that of England *see* Hand, ch. 9. For the related question of the treatment of the native Irish at common law *see* Hand, ch. 10.

(*19*) *Rot. Chart.*, pp. 176, 178. Both charters allowed the King to hear allegations of delay or failure to do justice and false judgment against the liberty courts, indirectly a means of enforcing legal uniformity.

(*20*) The letters patent of December 1226 referring to the charter of 1210 are addressed to the barons, knights and free tenants of Leinster and clearly imply that the charter, and the principles which it enunciates, are applicable within that liberty: *Pat. R., 1215-25*, p. 96.

(*21*) For a survey of the manuscript registers which survive *see Early Registers of Writs*, ed. E. de Haas and G. D. G. Hall, SS 87 (1970), xxiii-xxvi.

(*22*) It is to be noted that none of the early registers contains the formulae of the writ *diem clausit extremum* for holding an inquisition *post mortem*, of any of the various types of writ of *liberate, computate* etc., nor even of many of the types of royal charter or grant. This must be a matter of some importance for our view of the extent to which the registers were of official Chancery provenance.

surviving registers are the seven which appear, in substance, to predate the enactment of the statute of Merton in 1236 (*23*).

Of these seven pre-Mertonian registers, one stands somewhat apart from all the others. It is the register contained in the Cottonian manuscript Julius D. ii (*24*). It alone is preceded by what purports to be a copy of letters patent of Henry III, addressed generally to all his subjects in Ireland, and dated at Canterbury on 10 November in that king's twelfth regnal year (1227). These letters patent explain to the addressees that the King is sending them, enclosed within the letters patent themselves, a formulary of writs of course ("formam brevium de cursu"), in order that justice may be done in Ireland in the circumstances explained in the formulary by means of writs of the appropriate form running in the name of, and under the seal of, the justiciar. The King further explains that his reason for doing this is his wish that justice be provided for all complainants in the kingdom of Ireland in accordance with the custom of the kingdom of England (*25*). The register appears, then, to represent a formulary of writs of course sent by Henry III to Ireland in November 1227.

This "Irish" register of writs has been known to legal historians since it was re-discovered by Maitland in 1889 (*26*). Until 1970, there was general acceptance of the view that the Cottonian manuscript preserved a copy of a register that was actually sent from England to Ireland in 1227 (*27*). In that year, however, the late Derek Hall subjected the register (and covering writ) to a detailed re-examination and reached the conclusion that ". . . the weight of evidence is against the view that the Register was sent to Ireland" in 1227 (*28*). His reasons for doing this related both to the covering letters patent and to the contents of the actual register.

There are two quite separate difficulties about accepting the genuineness of the letters patent as they stand. The first is that Henry III was not at Canterbury on 10 November 1227 but at Westminster (*29*). The second is that there is no trace of any such letters patent on the patent rolls for

---

(*23*) *Early Registers*, pp. cxix-cxxi.
(*24*) BL Cott., Julius D. ii, ff. 143b-147b and 150a.
(*25*) *Early Registers*, p. 1.
(*26*) F. W. Maitland, "The introduction of English law into Ireland", *E.H.R.* 4 (1889), 516-7; reprinted in his *Collected Papers,* ed. H. A. L. Fisher (Cambridge, 1911), 2.81-3.
(*27*) W. J. Johnston, "The First Adventure of the Common Law", *L.Q.R.* 36 (1920) at 22; E. Curtis, *A History of Medieval Ireland* (1938), p. 121; A. G. Donaldson, *Some Comparative Aspects of Irish Law* (Durham, N.C., 1957), p. 6; A. J. Otway-Ruthven, "The Medieval Irish Chancery" in *Album Helen Maud Cam* (Studies presented to the international commission for the history of parliamentary institutions, 24 (1961)), 2.117-138 at 121; Hand, pp. 2-3.
(*28*) *Early Registers*, pp. xxxiii-xl. Hall's argument was accepted by Geoffrey Hand in his article "English Law in Ireland, 1172-1351", *N.I.L.Q.* 23 (1972), 393-422 at 399.
(*29*) He had, however, been at Canterbury as recently as 2 November: *Early Registers,* p. xxxvii, and n. 5.

that year, or any related document on any other surviving chancery roll (*30*). The difficulties relating to the register are more complex. Let us start with the limitation dates given in the register for the assizes of novel disseisin and mort d'ancestor and the writ of naifty. These are incorrect for the year 1227, whether they be regarded as English limitation dates, left in the register out of ignorance of those applicable in Ireland, or as Irish limitation dates (*31*). The limitation date given in the register for novel disseisin is "after our last crossing from Ireland into England" ("post ultimam transfretacionem nostram de Hibernia in Angliam"). In England, in 1227, the correct limitation date for the assize was "after the last return of our father, John, from Ireland into England" ("post ultimum redditum domini J. patris nostri de Hibernia in Angliam"); in Ireland, the correct limitation date was the same (perhaps somewhat differently expressed) or "after the first coronation of our father John at Canterbury". The limitation date given in the register for mort d'ancestor is "after the coronation of our father, Henry" ("post coronacionem H. patris nostri"). In both England and Ireland in 1227 this should have been "after the first coronation of King Richard, our uncle" ("post primam coronacionem R. regis avunculi nostri"). The limitation date given in the register for the writ of naifty is "after our first coronation" ("post primam coronacionem nostram"). In England it should probably have been the same as for mort d'ancestor; in Ireland, the same or "after the capture of Dublin" ("post capcionem Dublin"). Derek Hall also made a detailed comparison of the formulae of the individual writs in the "Irish" register with those of another register of the 1220s (CA) and those found in later registers and was driven to the conclusion that those in the "Irish" register "represent an earlier stage of development . . . than CA", and were so different that it was "difficult to regard [the register] as an official chancery production of November 1227" (*32*). A final difficulty relates to the tangled history of the writ *de rationabilibus divisis* in Ireland (*33*). Letters close of November 1237 suggest that the writ had been withdrawn from use—or, but this is less likely, simply had its status altered, making it no longer a writ of course—by Richard Duket and Simon of Hale, when they had been

---

(*30*) *Early Registers*, pp. xxxix-xl. Hall argues—and, in my view, quite correctly—against Maitland that one would expect to find the letters patent enrolled, even though there would have been little point in enrolling the register of writs itself. *Cf.* the enrolled version of the letters close of 1234 sending a copy of the writ *de rationabilibus divisis* to Ireland, which records the covering letter but not the formulae of the writ: *C.R. 1234-7*, p. 157.

(*31*) *Early Registers*, pp. xxxv-xxxvii.

(*32*) *Early Registers*, p. xxxiv.

(*33*) *Early Registers*, p. xxxix. I am unable to follow Hall (ibid., pp. xxxviii-xxxix) in finding major difficulties in reconciling the form of the writ *de excommunicato capiendo* found in the register with the practice with regard to contumacious excommunicates enjoined on the justiciar in January 1227. It is difficult to believe that the justiciar was intended to issue and seal a writ for the arrest of a contumacious excommunicate that was directed to himself, rather than to the appropriate local sheriff.

sent to Ireland by the King to itinerate there (*34*). Duket and Hale appear
to have travelled to Ireland in the spring of 1228 (*35*). Hale was back in
England by the summer of 1229 and does not appear to have returned to
Ireland subsequently (*36*). It is, as Hall noted, difficult to believe that
Duket and Hale would have dared to abrogate the writ or caused it to
cease being a writ of course, if it was included in a formulary of writs of
course that had been sent so recently to Ireland for use there by the King.

Most, though not all, of the arguments advanced by Derek Hall
against the acceptance of the letters patent and the register as copies of
documents actually sent from England to Ireland would be met and
answered if we were to adopt the hypothesis that the scribe who copied
these two items into the manuscript made two small alterations in the
text of the letters patent when he copied them. The suggestion, which is
tentatively advanced here, is that the scribe, who is known to have been
working in Canterbury during the first half of the reign of Henry III,
altered whatever place there was in his exemplar in the dating clause of
the letters patent into the more familiar Canterbury, and that he changed
an initial "J" (standing for "Johannes") at the very beginning of the
letters patent into the initial "H" (standing for "Henricus") (*37*). Such
alterations—however annoying or misleading they may be to historians—
are not out of keeping with the known habits and practices of other
medieval copyists. With both letters patent and register re-dated to
November 1210, the difficulty in explaining why they were not recorded
on the chancery rolls disappears. The loss of all the chancery rolls of
John's twelfth regnal year leaves us free to assume that the letters patent
were enrolled on the rolls which are now missing. The limitation date
given in the register for novel disseisin ("after our last crossing from
Ireland into England") is not one that is known to have been in use in
either England or Ireland in 1210, but too little is known of the law of the
lordship in this period for us to be certain that it was not so used. It
would certainly make grammatical sense as a limitation date fixed for
Ireland in November 1210, since by then John had visited Ireland twice—
in 1185 and again in the summer of 1210. If it was, then the alteration of
the English limitation date in 1218 to "after the last return of our father,
John, from Ireland into England" would simply have brought England
into line with the existing Irish rule (*38*). The limitation date given in the

(*34*) *C.R. 1234-7*, p. 501.

(*35*) *Pat. R., 1225-32*, pp. 180, 183.

(*36*) *Pat. R., 1225-32*, p. 299. Duket returned to Ireland in the summer of 1229 (*Pat. R.,
     1225-32*, p. 258; *C.R. 1227-31*, pp. 193, 194, 197; *C.L.R. 1226-40*, pp. 134, 139)
     and again in 1233 (*C.R. 1231-4*, p. 186; *C.P.R. 1232-47*, pp. 10-1).

(*37*) For evidence as to the provenance of the manuscript and where and when it was
     copied *see Early Registers*, p. xxxiii (and references there cited).

(*38*) For the limitation dates applicable in England and Ireland in 1210 and later *see
     Early Registers*, pp. xxxv-xxxvii. Such a limitation date would have been more
     recent than those normally set in this period, but not excessively so. In June 1199,
     a limitation date only 8 months earlier was used in England; in spring 1202, one of

register for mort d'ancestor ("after the coronation of our father, Henry"), also makes good grammatical sense in a register of 1210 during the reign of a king whose father's name was Henry (II). It was moreover the limitation date in use in England for this assize in 1210. In Ireland, it is believed that the limitation date in use in 1210 was that fixed in 1204— "after the crossing of King Henry our father from Ireland into England", and it was from this limitation date that a change was requested in 1219. Yet when the change was actually made in 1222, it was said to be a replacement for the equivalent of the limitation date found in the register ("after the first coronation of King Henry our grandfather") as though it were believed in England that this was the proper term. The limitation date given for naifty is also grammatically possible ("after our first coronation") but remains an implausible limitation date for the action in 1210 in either country (*39*). Redating the register to 1210 would also explain the archaisms in some of the writ formulae noticed by Hall, and would make much more plausible the action of Duket and Hale with regard to the writ *de rationabilibus divisis* (*40*).

The suggested re-dating of the writ and register to 1210 would have two further advantages. Hall was driven to ascribe to the copyist responsibility for what he described as the "wholly inappropriate *Incipit*"— "Here begins the formulary of writs of course for the justices to be appointed" ("Incipit forma brevium cursalium ad justiciarios constituendos") (*41*). Yet this *incipit,* though clearly inappropriate in 1227, could very well have made good sense in an Irish context in 1210. Prior to John's visit in 1210, there is no evidence of royal justices engaged in judicial work in Ireland (*42*). There was only the justiciar of Ireland, working through the king's court in Ireland or the so-called county court of Dublin—the only "county court" mentioned in Ireland at this date and possibly in reality the same institution as the king's court in

---

about 12 months earlier: D. W. Sutherland, *The Assize of Novel Disseisin* (Oxford, 1973), p. 55. It may be significant also that when a change was requested in the limitation date used for the assize of mort d'ancestor in Ireland in 1219 (below, n. 39), there was no request made for a change in the limitation date for the assize of novel disseisin.

(*39*) In Ireland, the limitation date in use in 1204 was "after the capture of Dublin". At some date not ascertained prior to 1237 it had been moved forward only as far as "after the first coronation of King Richard". In England the correct limitation date would probably have been "after the first coronation of our father, King Henry".

(*40*) It might also explain the omission of any writ of prohibition to court christian for lay chattels and debts. Such writs may only have become writs of course after 1220: G. B. Flahiff, "The writ of prohibition to courts christian in the thirteenth century", *Medieval Studies,* 6 (1944), 261-313 at 277.

(*41*) *Early Registers*, pp. xxxiv, n. 2, and 1.

(*42*) The only reference to royal "justices" refers to them as being engaged, probably in 1207, with the levying of royal taxation: H. G. Richardson and G. O. Sayles, *The Administration of Ireland, 1172-1377* (Irish manuscripts commission, 1963), pp. 29-30; Richardson and Sayles, *Irish Parliament*, p. 47. It cannot be assumed that they were necessarily engaged also in judicial work.

Ireland (*43*). By 1218, there were "justices itinerant" in Ireland, other royal justices as well as the justiciar, and it is not implausible to suppose that this change was connected with John's visit of 1210: that the decision was then taken that there should be justices itinerant in Ireland, but their appointment perhaps deferred till other arrangements, such as the sending of the register of writs, completed (*44*). The *incipit* would then mean— "the formulary of writs of course for use in connection with the justices who are to be appointed"—a not unreasonable description of a register many of whose writs are returnable before "justiciis nostris ad primam assisam cum in partes illas venerunt".

The sending of a register of writs to Ireland in November 1210 also makes much better sense. It can be seen as a direct follow-up, after John's return to England, of the decision, announced in the charter, that the English common law should be applicable as a whole in Ireland. The full range of English writs of course was now to be made available in Ireland through the justiciar. The delay can be explained by the need to make certain adaptations of the English writs for use in Ireland and perhaps by the lack of ready access to a copyable text of the register of writs while the King was in Ireland. The sending of a register to Ireland in November 1227 makes much less sense. It is difficult to believe that once the decision had been taken in 1210 that the English common law should be applicable as a whole in Ireland, the justiciar would have remained unable to issue more than the limited range of writs which he was authorised to issue in 1204, and that litigants wishing to initiate other types of action, which could readily be initiated in England by writs of course, would have had for the next seventeen years to go or send to the English chancery to acquire the appropriate writ (*45*). Yet if the justiciar was in 1227 issuing a full range of writs of course, this fact is unlikely to have been unknown to the King and his advisers in England, and would suggest that any covering letters patent sent with the register should not have implied—as these letters patent so clearly do—that the writs of course were now being made available in Ireland for the first time.

The suggested emendation of the covering letters patent accompanying the "Irish" register of writs must, in the absence of conclusive evidence, remain tentative, but there are strong arguments in favour of these emendations and the consequent redating of letters patent and register to 1210. If these arguments are accepted, then we possess in the "Irish"

(*43*) For references to the king's court in Ireland *see Rot. de Obl.,* pp. 36, 79; *Rot. Chart.,* p. 99; *R.L.C.,* 1.7; *R.L.P.,* pp. 45, 46, 76. For references to the county court of Dublin *see Pleas before the King or his justices, 1198-1202,* ed. D. M. Stenton, SS 67, 68 (1948, 1949), 1. no. 3169; *Rot. de Obl.,* pp. 180-1; *R.L.P.,* p. 77; *Chart. St. Mary's Dublin,* 1. 29-30, 145-6.

(*44*) *Exc. e Rot. Fin.,* 1.11 and *see R.L.C.,* 1.451. In 1226 it was believed or remembered that arrangements as to the taking of the assizes for the lands and fees of the bishops of Ferns, Ossory, Kildare and Leighlin—crosslands within the liberty of Leinster—dated from John's visit in 1210: *R.L.C.,* 2.128.

(*45*) The 1204 authorisation is enrolled on *R.L.P.,* p. 47.

register the only register of writs belonging to the reign of King John: and the register can resume its place, indeed take its rightful place for the first time, in the history of the transmission to Ireland of the English common law.

III

A series of letters patent and letters close, containing statements as to the English practice or rules on particular matters of law or legal procedure, were sent from England to Ireland during the 1220s and 1230s. At first sight, these would appear to indicate that the charter of 1210 was not a success in transplanting the corpus of the English common law to Ireland, and that knowledge of even quite elementary rules was sti'i lacking in Ireland. Closer examination of them will, however, lead to a somewhat different conclusion, and suggest that the charter of 1210 may in reality have been rather more successful.

Let us examine them in chronological order:

(1) The earliest such statement appears in letters close of 1223 (*46*). These explain that, in England, it is the practice to allow the defendant in an action *de rationabilibus divisis* to choose battle or "other means", *i.e.* the grand assize, as modes of proof in his defence, as in the writ of right. In Ireland, as the King is informed, the practice is to decide such disputes by the verdict of an ordinary jury. The King orders that the Irish procedure be brought into conformity with that of England.

The action *de rationabilibus divisis* was well-established in Ireland, pre-dating John's visit of 1210 (*47*). It seems probable that the explanation for this mandate is that the procedural rules to be followed in the action—more rational, as it happened, than those followed in England— had become established at that time, and that this variation between English and Irish rules had not been noticed or specifically dealt with in 1210. This mandate was now required to secure the enforcement of t. main principle behind the 1210 charter—the identity of English and Irish law—in this one matter (*48*).

(2) The next such statement comes in letters patent of 1226 (*49*). These explain that it is the English rule that a widower should enjoy the right of curtesy—possession of all of the lands which his late wife held in her own right—for life, whenever the couple have had born to them at least one child who was not still-born, and that this right was not adversely affected even if the wife's heir was the child of a previous marriage and that child had come of age. The letters patent are addressed to the barons,

---

(*46*) *R.L.C.*, 1.497.
(*47*) Above, p. 446 and n. 14.
(*48*) Some modification of the English procedure to meet Irish conditions was authorised in the following year: *R.L.C.*, 1.532. For the subsequent history of the action *see* above, p. 450, and below, p. 456.
(*49*) *Pat. R., 1225-32*, p. 96. It is the same letters patent which have so much to say on the subject of King John's charter of 1210: above, p. 450, and below, p. 456.

knights and free tenants of Leinster and ordered them to see that the rule is applied in a case in the court of the earl marshal (of Leinster) between Maurice fitzGerald and the justiciar, Geoffrey Marsh, and in any similar case that might arise there (*50*).

Although a right of curtesy as ample as that here described was the settled rule of the later medieval common law, it is far from clear that it was anything near as well settled a rule in this period. *Bracton* indicates that one leading English royal justice of the period, Stephen of Segrave, held the opinion that an heir of an earlier marriage who was of age should exclude his step-father from enjoyment of curtesy (*51*). If the suitors of the court of Leinster—for such they must be—were minded to give judgment for Maurice fitzGerald or were in doubt on the matter, their error or doubt was a reasonable one, supported by good authority, and not a mark of ignorance.

(3) Letters close were sent to the justiciar, Geoffrey Marsh, in 1227, containing a rehearsal of the English practice with regard to contumacious excommunicates, denounced by the ordinary. Again, these do not neces-sarily imply a previous ignorance in Ireland of the appropriate pro-cedure (*52*). The same letters close more particularly enjoin on the justiciar action with regard to certain canons of Louth, excommunicated by the archbishop of Armagh: and it would not be straining the wording of the mandate to see it as primarily intended to secure action in this one case and, secondarily, as being intended not so much to inform the justiciar of a procedure of which he was ignorant but, more probably, to deprive him of a discretion which he may hitherto have exercised in deciding whether or not to act on receiving a "signification" from an ordinary.

(4) In 1229 letters patent were sent to Richard de Burgh, the new justiciar of Ireland, reminding him of the English rule that the daughters of an elder son who had died in his father's lifetime were not allowed to implead their uncle (a younger son of the same father) for the father's inheritance—a particular application of the general *casus regis* rule (*53*). He was ordered to ensure that the rule was enforced by forbidding the continuation of litigation brought in the earl marshal's court (of Leinster) by the two daughters of Raymond de Roche against their uncle Gerald (*54*).

There is no reason to infer from this mandate that the rules associated with the *casus regis* were not known in Ireland in 1229. All that it is legitimate to conclude is that the suitors of the court of Leinster may not

(*50*) Geoffrey Marsh had been the third husband of Eva, daughter and coheiress of Robert de Bermingeham, who had inherited the "barony" of Offaly, an "honorial barony" of the liberty of Leinster. Maurice fitzGerald was Eva's son and heir by her first husband, Gerald fitzMaurice: Orpen, 3.65, n. 1 and 4.128.

(*51*) *Bracton*, ff. 437b-438 (4.360).

(*52*) *R.L.C.*, 2.166.

(*53*) *C.R. 1227-31*, p. 236.

(*54*) For the background to this litigation *see* E. St. J. Brooks, *Knight's Fees in Counties Wexford, Carlow and Kilkenny* (Irish manuscripts commission, 1950), pp. 146-8.

have been aware of these rules or, perhaps more probably, did not consider the liberty of Leinster to be bound by them. If the latter be the case, then perhaps these letters patent should be seen in the context of the earlier letters patent concerning the right of curtesy, also relating to a case in the court of the liberty of Leinster, as spelling out clearly that the liberty of Leinster was not to be allowed to develop its own separate legal customs, differing from those of the royal courts in England and Ireland.

(5) Letters patent were sent to the people of Ireland in 1233, forbidding them to bring suits in court christian about the advowsons of churches or chapels, about lay fees or concerning chattels, unless the latter were connected with a marriage or a will. Accompanying letters patent, addressed to the ecclesiastics of Ireland, warned them against entertaining such litigation in their courts. These jurisdictional rules were again justified by reference to the rules followed in England on such matters (55).

The reason for the issuing of these letters patent is not clear. It seems extremely unlikely that they constituted the first attempt to define legally the limits on ecclesiastical jurisdiction in Ireland. It is possible, though, that the jurisdictional limits which they contain are more restrictive than any contained in John's charter of 1210 or enforced in Ireland prior to 1233 (56). Alternatively, the jurisdictional limits on the church courts, though well known, may have been in practice widely ignored, and the letters patent have been intended solely as a reminder of these existing rules.

(6) In the following year—1234—letters close were sent to the justiciar of Ireland, instructing him to allow the use of the writ *de rationabilibus divisis* in Ireland, and enclosing a copy of the relevant writ formula, as used in England (57).

The immediate context of this mandate appears to have been a dispute about boundaries between Peter de Bermingeham and Maurice Comyn (58). As has already been seen, the writ was not previously unknown in Ireland—indeed, its use there went back to the beginning of the thirteenth century—but it had apparently been abrogated in 1228 or 1229 by the English justices, Richard Duket and Simon of Hale (59). The

---

(55) *C.P.R. 1232-47*, p. 31. A full text is printed in *Statutes and ordinances and acts of the parliament of Ireland, King John to Henry V*, ed. H. F. Berry (Dublin, 1907), pp. 24-25.
(56) The prohibition of pleas relating to lay chattels being heard in court christian may well have been new. As has been seen (above, n. 40), there is no writ of prohibition for the prevention of the hearing of such pleas in the "Irish" register.
(57) *C.R. 1234-7*, p. 157.
(58) *Ibid*. The following writ orders the justiciar to see that either of them is issued the writ if he asks for it. Peter de Bermingeham had been in England with the justiciar earlier in the same year, and had been granted an annuity receivable at the Dublin Exchequer while in the King's service in Ireland: *C.P.R. 1232-47*, pp. 70-2. In 1236 he acted as one of the itinerant justices in Ireland: Richardson and Sayles, *Admin. Ire.*, p. 132.
(59) Above, pp. 451, 454.

letters close of 1234 were not introducing the writ and action into Ireland for the first time, merely attempting to secure the revival of their use (60).

(7) The year 1236—the year of the enactment, in England, of the statute of Merton—witnessed the sending of two certifications of English law and custom to Ireland. The first, transmitted to Ireland in May 1236 along with a text of the statute of Merton itself, concerned the trial of the issue of special bastardy (61). This certification was sent in answer to a series of questions as to the correct procedures to follow in such cases, the details of which suggest that the problem had arisen in connection with a case then before the courts in Ireland (62).

The puzzlement of the justiciar and of the archbishop of Dublin as to the correct procedure for the trial of the issue of special bastardy was not a matter of Irish ignorance of a settled English common-law procedure. The correct procedure to be followed in such cases was still a matter under discussion in England at the time the letters close were sent, and the Irish request for information seems clearly to indicate an awareness in Ireland that the matter was a contentious one on which royal instructions were required (63).

(8) The second certification of English law and custom to Ireland in 1236 was sent to the justiciar, Maurice fitzGerald, in August of that year. It explained the rules as to tenurial arrangements which were applicable when an inheritance was divided between parceners, and is the mandate subsequently found in English collections of statutes as the *Statutum Hibernie de Coheredibus* (64).

The immediate context for this certification, as the letters close themselves reveal, was information reaching the King that the justices itinerant in Ireland—at this date, probably the only royal justices in the lordship—were uncertain as to what the correct rules were (65). Although the letters close speak as though the rules concerned were old and well-established, it seems clear that this is not in fact the case, and that the

(60) The attempt does not appear to have been a success, to judge from subsequent letters close of 1237: *C.R. 1234-7*, p. 501.
(61) *C.R. 1234-7*, p. 354.
(62) The case is not, however, identified and can, perhaps, now not be identified.
(63) The course of the dispute about special bastardy is most succinctly discussed in *Council and Synods, with other documents relating to the English church, volume II*, ed. F. M. Powicke and C. R. Cheney (Oxford, 1964), 1. 198-9.
(64) *C.R. 1234-7*, pp. 375-6; *S.R.*, 1. 5.
(65) The knights mentioned in the letters close as the oral source of this information may well have been acting as messengers for the justices itinerant. Certainly, two of the men who, in Easter term 1236, were acting as justices itinerant in the king's court at Dublin, were on this same day given safe conducts to come to England for consultation with the King: *Chart. St. Mary's Dublin*, 1. 164; *C.P.R. 1232-47*, p. 157. It is possible that the difficulties had arisen in litigation connected with the division of the inheritance of Thomas fitzAnthony, who had died in 1229: Orpen, 2. 136, n. 5; Brooks, pp. 46-7. One of the daughters was married to Gerald de Roche, who was probably responsible for securing the issue of the letters patent of 1229 concerning the *casus regis:* above, p. 455.

matter is one on which it is not unreasonable to find Irish justices doubtful and hesitant (*66*).

(9) The last of this series of certifications of English law to Ireland was one sent in 1238. This informed the justiciar that it was the English rule that when a bastard died without issue his land escheated to the lord of whom it was held. He was also sent a copy of the writ of escheat appropriate to these circumstances as used in England (*67*).

It seems clear that the main purpose of this mandate was the one disclosed, almost incidentally, in its last sentence: that of ensuring that the writ (and action) were available to Robert de Hyda and his wife for litigation they wished to initiate. The writ, then, was probably not in use in Ireland prior to 1238: it is not one included in the "Irish" register, and had probably only quite recently come into use in England (*68*). It does not, however, necessarily follow that the associated legal rule—that the land of a bastard dying without issue escheated—was not already known in Ireland and observed there, though it probably seemed as well to repeat the rule when sending the writ.

The general conclusion to be drawn from a detailed study of these letters patent and close, then, is that they are not necessarily evidence of a general ignorance of the rules of the common law in Ireland, but are explicable in terms which would allow for a considerable degree of knowledge of those rules in Ireland. The appeal in these mandates to the law and custom of England can be seen, perhaps, as an attempt to foreclose any argument on the Irish side as to the validity of the rules communicated, an authority against which they were unable to appeal, as bound by the general principle enunciated in the charter of 1210 of the identity of Irish and English law.

IV

It was the late G. J. Turner, the editor of the early pleading manual known as *Brevia Placitata,* who was the first to suggest that the manual might have Irish connections. He thought it possible that when John fitzGeoffrey went to Ireland as justiciar in 1245 ". . . the King sent him a formulary of writs, encoupements and defenses for the use of himself and his fellow justices", a first version of *Brevia Placitata,* though the earliest surviving version of the text was, he suggested, a subsequent revision of that formulary, made and issued in 1259-60 in England (*69*). More recently, Professor Hand has expressed an inclination to accept ". . . the suggestion . . . that when John fitzGeoffrey became justiciar a formulary of writs

---

(*66*) F. Pollock and F. W. Maitland, *History of English Law before the reign of Edward I* (Cambridge, 1898), 2. 276-8.
(*67*) *C.R. 1237-42,* p. 123.
(*68*) The earliest example I have so far noticed of an action apparently initiated by such a writ is in Easter term 1229: *C.R.R.,* 13. no. 1880.
(*69*) *Brevia Placitata,* ed. G. J. Turner, SS 66 (1947), p. xxvii.

and pleadings was provided for his use" and that this subsequently ". . . may have become the basis of the collection known as *Brevia Placitata*". He also suggested a possible connection between the formulary and a royal mandate of 1246 stating that "the King 'vult quod omnia brevia de communi jure que currunt in Anglia similiter currant in Hibernia' " (70).

The hypothesis is, however, one for which there is almost no evidence. Two, or perhaps three, out of the twelve manuscripts of the treatise collated by Turner give the name of John fitzGeoffrey as that of the lord to whom the first writ in the treatise—the writ of right patent—is addressed, and John fitzGeoffrey was justiciar of Ireland from 1245 to 1256 (71). But John fitzGeoffrey was a major land-owner in England as well, his name is not used elsewhere in the treatise, and the other names and places used in it—with one exception—do not appear to have any connections with Ireland (72). In one manuscript only—out of the three manuscripts which give a precedent for the writ of right of advowson—the advowson claimed is that of the church of St. Mary, Kilkenny, in Ireland, but the very fact that it is described as being "in Ireland" makes it improbable that the exemplar from which it was drawn was composed in or for Ireland (73). Even if this exiguous evidence be thought enough to connect the treatise with Ireland, it still does not demonstrate the truth or probability of the even less credible proposition that *Brevia Placitata* was an official pro- duction sent to John fitzGeoffrey in Ireland. Such a production, even after subsequent revision, would surely have gone out of its way to proclaim its origins and the status these could be taken to confer on it. As for the royal mandate of 1246 quoted by Professor Hand, it would seem that this marks not an extension, or an intended extension, of the availability of writs and forms of action in Ireland to match their avail- ability in England—a context into which the official production of *Brevia Placitata* might just fit—but something quite different. The passage is not quoted by Professor Hand in full but goes on in the original to explain that it is the King's wish that such writs should run in Ireland "sub novo sigillo regis" (74). The mandate probably marks the point at which the change was made from the earlier practice of writs being issued in the name and under the seal of the justiciar to writs running in the name and under the seal of the King (75). It may also reflect the King's expressed intention, now that the liberty of Leinster had come into his hands pend-

(70) Hand, p. 3.
(71) *Brevia Placitata*, pp. 1, 41, 73, 96, 114, 126, 153.
(72) *The Complete Peerage*, ed. V. Gibbs and H. A. Doubleday, 5 (1926), 433-4.
(73) *Brevia Placitata*, p. 46; cf. pp. 6, 158. In the same manuscript, the demandant is given as prior David of Kilkenny.
(74) *Rymer's Foedera*, 1.1.266.
(75) During the justiciarship of Maurice fitzGerald, justiciar from 1232 to 1245, writs were still issued in the justiciar's name: *Chart. St. Mary's Dublin*, 1. 57-8. This was in accordance with the letters patent that accompanied the "Irish" register: above, p. 101. By 1254, writs were certainly running in the King's name: *Chart. St. Mary's Dublin*, 1. 194.

ing the division of the Marshal inheritance, of ensuring the permanent suppression of the separate chancery of Leinster, which had issued writs in the name and under the seal of the lords of the liberty, but whose activities had already been suspended when this mandate was issued (76).

In fact it is the later and more sophisticated pleading manual, *Novae Narrationes*—or at least, its numerically strongest tradition, that of the "C" texts—which has a much stronger claim to some connection with Ireland. Although, so far as they can be identified, the precedents contained in the text all seem to be drawn from cases heard in the English courts, almost all the manuscripts contain Irish place-names and some contain personal names connected with Ireland which appear to have been substituted for the original English place and personal names (77). Most manuscripts of the "C" text give a variant count of the writ of right of wardship for a lord claiming wardship of land held by socage tenure under the custom of the lordship of Ireland; and in two specimen counts, suit of court is mentioned as being performed every fortnight, a frequency apparently legal in Ireland but illegal in England under legislation of 1234 (78). It seems clear that the archetype of the "C" texts—or, at least, a manuscript from which all were descended, was copied in Ireland or altered with Irish requirements in mind: so that *Novae Narrationes* may be regarded as evidence of the continuing influence of the lordship of Ireland on the literature of the common law.

For many purposes it is possible to treat the Common Law, in the earlier phrases of its history, as though it were a purely English phenomenon, and such a treatment will not lead to any serious distortion of the legal historian's perspective. The literature discussed in this article does, however, provide a convincing demonstration of the fact that for other purposes such a treatment is seriously defective; and that the legal historian must remember that from very early in its history the Common Law developed as an Anglo-Irish legal system—the legal system not just of England but also of the lordship of Ireland. This article has suggested that the initial impulse for the writing of *Bracton* may have come from the work done in preparing a statement of English law for promulgation in Ireland by King John in his charter of 1210; and that the

---

(76) The King's intentions had been explained in letters close sent to the seneschal he had appointed to administer Leinster earlier that year: *C.R. 1242-7*, p. 432. The parceners of the liberty did, however, later enjoy the right of issuing their own writs.

(77) *Novae Narrationes*, ed. S. F. C. Milsom and E. Shanks, SS 80 (1963). The most commonly occurring placenames are Colp (Co. Meath) and Lusk (Co. Dublin), but there are also references to Trim, Navan and Slane (all in Co. Meath). The personal names with Irish connections include John or J. Plunkett (found in some MS. versions of C41, C46, C53, C96) and possibly the Richard le Blund of C53.

(78) The variant count for the writ of right of wardship is C212. For the history of this Irish custom *see* Hand, pp. 178-186. The counts mentioning suit performed fortnightly are C40 and C45. For other evidence of suit being performed this frequently *see Red book of Ormond*, ed. N. B. White (Irish manuscripts commission, 1932), p. 2. The English legislation of 1234 is recorded in *C.R. 1231-4*, pp. 588-9.

earliest surviving register of writs was copied from an official register prepared and sent to Ireland shortly after John's return from Ireland in 1210. The statements of English law sent to Ireland in the 1220s and 1230s may well have played a part in the development of the common law not only in Ireland but also in England. The need to state clearly what the English rule was may, paradoxically, have helped to create a single, fixed rule in England: and, as has been seen, at least one of these statements— the 1236 mandate on parcenry—found its way into English collections of statutes as the *Statutum Hibernie de Coheredibus*. That the Irish connection continued to be of some importance for the literature of the early common law—and, therefore, for the Common Law as a whole—is shown by the main manuscript tradition of the early fourteenth century pleading manual, *Novae Narrationes,* which clearly descends from an archetype produced in the lordship of Ireland. Discussion of the literature of the early common law must, it seems, therefore, bear in mind that the Common Law was the legal system not just of England but also of the lordship of Ireland, since the process of transmission of English law to Ireland was a significant factor in the creation of the literature of the early common law.

APPENDIX: HENRY II'S CHARTER TO THE OSTMEN OF WATERFORD

Henry II's charter to the Ostmen of Waterford appears to survive only in a transcript contained in the Carew manuscripts in Lambeth Palace Library (in MS. 632 on f. 234a *recto*). It is to be found in a volume which contains transcripts of other material relating to the city of Waterford and was presumably transcribed from an original charter or copy in the city archives.

"Henricus dei gratia Rex Anglie dux Normanie et Aquitanie et Comes Andegavie archiepiscopis episcopis comitibus baronibus justiciariis vicecomitibus et omnibus ballivis et fidelibus suis omnium terrarum suarum salutem. Sciatis quod Hostmanni de Waterford homines mei legii sunt et ipsi et omnia sua sunt in manu et custodia mea et proteccione mea et ideo (*1*) precipio quod ipsi et omnes res sue firmam pacem et securitatem habeant per totam terram meam in eundo redeundo et moram faciendo ubicunque fuerint in terra mea faciendo rectas consuetudines (*2*) suas. Et precipio quod vos possessiones suas custodiatis et manuteneatis et protegatis sicut meas proprias ita quod eis nullam molestiam vel injuriam vel violentiam faciatis aut fieri permittatis et si quis super hoc in aliquo forisfecerit plenariam eis inde sine dilatione justiciam fieri faciatis. Teste magistro Johanne Cumin, Hugone Mordag, Radulpho filio Stephani camerario, Michell Billet, Willelmo de Bending. Apud Taytinton" (*3*).

(*1*) MS. *idio.*
(*2*) MS. *rectis custuetudinis.*
(*3*) ? *recte* Gaytinton.

20

Ralph de Hengham and the Irish Common Law

When the Anglo-Norman settlers came to Ireland from 1169 onwards they brought with them Anglo-Norman customary law. In the early thirteenth century the decision was taken in principle that the nascent common law of England should be the law followed in all the courts of the lordship. That decision was followed up soon afterwards by the transmission to Ireland of a register of writs based on that used in the English chancery to be used by the justiciar's clerical staff when writing writs for litigants who wanted to initiate litigation in the courts of the lordship; and (during the 1220s and 1230s) by a series of certifications of English law sent to the lordship *(1)*. Thereafter such certifications cease, but we do know of a number of different mechanisms through which the common law of the courts of the lordship of Ireland was kept in reasonably close correspondence with the common law of the English royal courts: the sending of English legislation to Ireland for its publication and application within the lordship *(2)*; the exercise by the English court of King's Bench of a jurisdiction in review over judgments made in the courts of the lordship *(3)*; the appointment of men with experience in the English courts as judges in Ireland *(4)*; the training in England of lawyers who were going to practise in Ireland *(5)* and the use in Ireland of English common law manuals *(6)*. This article provides evidence for the operation of yet another such mechanism and one whose existence has not hitherto been suspected: the informal consultation of a leading English judge by one or more of his colleagues serving in the courts of the lordship.

That evidence is provided by the text transcribed in the appendix at

---

(1)| P. Brand, "Ireland and the Literature of the Early Common Law", above, pp. 247-51.

(2) G. J. Hand, *English Law in Ireland, 1290-1324* (Cambridge, 1967), 4-5 and chapter 8; P. A. Brand, "King, Church and Property", above, pp. 247-51.

(3) Hand, *op. cit.*, 14-19 and chapter 7.

(4) Hand, *op. cit.*, 21-25, 46-7, 94-5; F.E. Ball, *The Judges in Ireland, 1221-1921* (London, 1926), I, book I, *passim*; R. Frame, *English Lordship in Ireland, 1318-1361*, 94.

(5) By far the earliest reference to this practice is that to be found in *Cal. Pat. Rolls, 1281-1292*, 269. I owe this reference to Mr. David Higgins. The next reference known to me comes from over a century later: *Cal. Chancery Rolls, Ire.* 149b, no. 99.

(6) The most likely explanation for the Irish place and personal names found in the "C" texts of *Novae Narrationes* is that the treatise had early on been brought to Ireland and been used here before it found its way back to England: Brand, "Ireland and the Literature of the Early Common Law", 460. There is also evidence that the early treatise known as *Natura Brevium* found in Harvard Law Library Ms. 162, British Library Mss. Additional 22708 and Harley 673, Bodleian Library Ms. Rawlinson C 897 and Cambridge University Library Ms. Hh. 3.11 was written or altered with a specifically Irish audience in mind.

the end of this article. It comes from a manuscript now in Lincoln's Inn, Miscellaneous 738. The manuscript consists mainly of Year Book reports of the reign of Edward I, arranged in the first fifty-one folios roughly in term and regnal year sections, and thereafter very roughly in sections corresponding to the various forms of action. Our text comes from the middle of an undated section of reports of assizes of novel disseisin (which runs with some interruptions from f.57r to f.80v) and occurs with two other reports of cases concerning advowsons, one an assize of darrein presentment and the other an action of *quare non admisit*. The first, and longest, part of our text appears to be a full transcript of an entry from a plea roll made for one of the courts of the lordship of Ireland, recording pleadings on an assize of darrein presentment concerning the right to present a rector to the church of 'Moygorban' (apparently the modern Magorban in co. Tipperary in the barony of Middlethird and some five miles east of Cashel). The reference in this enrolment to the last presentment having been made in the reign of king Henry, the father of the present king, and to the rector having then been instituted by 'Martin' archbishop of Cashel indicates, as we might have expected, that this enrolment also belongs to the reign of Edward I (Martin is presumably a copyist's error for the Marianus who was archbishop of Cashel from 1223 to 1237). A second indication of date is provided by the references in the text to the statute of Westminster – or, more precisely, on one occasion to the statute of Westminster II – which indicate that the case must have been heard after 1285, the year of the enactment of that statute.

It is, however, the final part of the text with which we are here principally concerned. This section starts with the name *Hengham* and then goes on, initially in the first person, to comment on the main point of legal difficulty raised in the course of pleadings on the Magorban assize of darrein presentment. This concerned the use of the exception of plenarty. The assize of darrein presentment had originally been created in the reign of Henry II to give a swift legal remedy to those patrons of ecclesiastical livings who faced opposition when trying to have their candidates admitted and instituted to those livings when they became vacant on the death or resignation of the previous incumbent; and the writ which initiated proceedings on the assize ordered the summoning of twelve jurors to give their verdict as to "which patron in time of peace presented the last parson who is dead to the church of X, *which is vacant* as it is said" *(7)*. The assize was not an appropriate form of action for the patron if the church already had an incumbent and so was not vacant. It was a legitimate answer for a defendant in such proceedings to make an exception of *plenarty* alleging that the church concerned was not vacant but he would generally have to produce *prima facie* evidence

(7) Glanvill, ed. G.D.G. Hall (London, 1965), XIII, 18-19 (pp. 160-1); *Bracton,* transl. S.E. Thorne and ed. G.E. Woodbine (Cambridge, Mass., 1968-1977), f.238 (III, 206).

that this was so in the form of letters of institution and admission from the appropriate authorities. The justices who were hearing the assize would then normally write to the local bishop for a certificate on the matter, since whether or not a church was vacant was a matter admitted to lie properly within his cognisance. That certificate would then be taken as final and binding. It had, however, long been recognised that there were circumstances in which a substantial injustice might be done if the defendant was allowed to make his exception of plenarty in this way and the bishop's certificate was then accepted as final *(8)*. Part of chapter 5 of the statute of Westminster II had been concerned with one of these: where the bishop had admitted the defendant's candidate to the living despite the plaintiff having contested his right to present and initiated proceedings through the assize within six months of the beginning of the vacancy *(9)*. The bishop had done wrong by so doing and would be tempted to make a false certificate to protect himself against legal proceedings by the plaintiff. Another such situation – it was sometimes argued – was that which arose when a religious house had wrongfully gained possession of an advowson and had then presented itself to the church and been admitted by the bishop. Once this had happened there would never again be a vacancy in the living, and so no chance for the rightful patron of the advowson to regain possession of that advowson through an assize of darrein presentment brought during a vacancy. If he wished to recover his advowson he would need instead to bring the much slower and more hazardous writ of right of advowson. Why should a religious house be allowed to take advantage of its own wrongdoing in this way? Should it not be made to answer the true patron's claim to the advowson in the possessory assize of darrein presentment, notwithstanding the fact that the church was not in fact vacant? *(10)*. In the Magorban assize the defendants, the prior and convent of Athassel, had made an exception of plenarty, saying that they held the church to their own use (that is, as rectors as well as patrons) and claiming that they had so held the church for at least forty years. They also argued that the only circumstances in which the plaintiff would be entitled to bring the assize, notwithstanding the fact that the church concerned was not in fact vacant, were those mentioned in chapter 5 of the statute of Westminster II and that this could not be the case here since much more than six months had elapsed since the last vacancy. The plaintiff, Walter of Stanton, had, however, argued that the church was properly speaking merely "incumbered" rather than "full" because the prior and convent were wrongfully in possession of it through a grant made by his father's guardian, who had no power to make such grants. He argued that in these

---

(8) J.W. Gray, "The Ius Praesentandi in England from the Constitutions of Clarendon to Bracton", *Eng. Hist. Rev.*, lxvii (1952), 481-509 at 496-8.

(9) *Statutes of the Realm*, i. 76.

(10) For an English *quare impedit* case where this view seems to have been followed see *Eye* v. *Abbot of Reading:* CP 40/49, m.32 (Easter term 1283).

circumstances they should not be allowed to benefit from the exception of plenarty and that the assize should give its verdict on his claim instead.

The author of the opinion remembered having seen divergent judgments on this very point. Martin of "Lytebirii" had held that when a religious house in these circumstances made the exception of plenarty all it needed to do was to claim that it had been in possession of the church for a long period of time and the exception was then to be allowed and the bishop asked for his certificate. Richard of "Midd", however, had held that in such circumstances the religious house ought to make at least a *prima facie* case that they had been duly admitted to the church at the presentation of the true patron of the advowson before the exception was to be allowed; and this would mean that they would need to show who the incumbent of the church was, since when that incumbent had held the church, at whose presentation he had been admitted and by which ordinary he had been instituted. The writer seems to think that the latter is the better view.

Who are these two men whose judgments are recalled by the author of the opinion? Martin of "Lytebirii" must be the Martin of Littlebury who was a senior justice of one of the English eyre circuits in 1262-3 *(11)*, chief justice of the Bench at Westminster from 1268 to 1272 and then chief justice of the court of King's Bench from 1273 to 1274 *(12)*. Richard of "Midd" seems to be the Richard of Middleton who was a puisne justice under Martin of Littlebury in his eyre circuit of 1262-3, and then senior justice of an eyre circuit of his own in 1268-9 *(13)* before becoming chancellor of England from 1269 to 1272.

The appearance of the name "Hengham" at the start of the opinion suggests some connection between the opinion and the best-known English royal justice of the reign of Edward I, Ralph de Hengham. Hengham's career as a judge commenced at the very end of the reign of Henry III with his appointment as a puisne justice in eyre in 1271-2 and as the senior justice of an eyre circuit in 1272 *(14)*. It continued with his appointment as a puisne justice of the Bench in 1273-4 and as chief justice of King's Bench (in succession to Martin of Littlebury) from 1274 until his disgrace in 1290 *(15)* and concluded with a final period as chief justice of the Bench from 1301 to 1309 *(16)*. That the opinion is in fact the work of Hengham is suggested by the close similarities that exist between its style and general form and the style and form of the only other such opinion of his that is known to survive *(17)*. The author's cita-

---

(11) D. Crook, *Records of the General Eyre* (Public Record Office Handbooks, 20), 131-3.
(12) *Select Cases in the Court of King's Bench under Edward I*, vol. I, ed. G.O. Sayles (Selden Soc. lv (1936)), xlix, cxxix-cxxx.
(13) Crook, *op. cit.*, 131-3, 135-7.
(14) Crook, *op. cit.*, 139-42.
(15) *Select Cases . . . King's Bench*, vol. I, liii, cxxx-cxxxi, cxxxv.
(16) *Select Cases . . . King's Bench*, vol. I, cxxxviii-cxxxix.
(17) P. Brand, "Quo Warranto Law in the reign of Edward I: a hitherto undiscovered opinion of Chief Justice Hengham", above, pp. 393-441.

tion of judgments by Littlebury and Middleton would certainly also fit Hengham for he is known to have reminisced on other occasions about judgments made by both these men (18). Hengham's career before his appointment as a royal justice is obscure. Sayles and Meekings both noted evidence showing him as a clerk in the service of Giles of Erdington, who had been a justice of the Bench between 1251 and 1255 and who thereafter acted as a commissioner for the hearing of possessory assizes (19). Hengham's knowledge of judgments given by Littlebury and Middleton suggests that during the 1260s he may also have been a clerk in the service of these two justices (20).

There is no evidence that the Magorban assize was ever removed to England for hearing and it seems clear that Hengham's opinion is not a formal judgment on the point of law involved. What it does read like is Hengham's other known unofficial opinion, one on *quo warranto* law given in response to questions submitted to him by the judges of the Northamptonshire eyre of 1285, though without the clues which that contained as to the means by which his opinion had been sought (21). In this instance we can only conjecture that the formal record of the Magorban assize was sent to him in England with some sort of covering note asking for his advice on the point of law involved, and that the opinion represents his answer to that request. As to the precise date of the opinion and of the hearing of the assize it is impossible to be certain; but it seems most likely to have been after his appointment as chief justice of the Bench in England in 1301 or just possibly to have been between the enactment of the statute of Westminster II in 1285 and Hengham's disgrace and dismissal in 1290. Nor can we say for certain who it was that asked for his advice. It might have been one of the justices of the Dublin Bench. The obvious candidates in the early fourteenth century are the English-born judges: Simon of Ludgate (chief justice of the Dublin Bench from 1298 to 1302), Robert of Littlebury (puisne justice of the Dublin Bench from 1300 to 1303) or Thomas of Snitterby (puisne justice of the Dublin Bench from 1295 to 1307) (22). An alternative possibility is one of the justices of the co. Tipperary eyre of 1305-7. The one obvious candidate here is John of Fressingfield though he only sat as a justice for

---

(18) For his reminiscence of a case heard by Martin of Littlebury *see* British Library Ms. Additional 31826, f.373v. For his reminiscence of a case heard by Richard of Middleton, probably in the 1268 Oxfordshire eyre *see* British Library Ms. Egerton 2811, ff. 157r-v.

(19) *Select Cases . . . King's Bench*, vol. I, liii, n.3; C.A.F. Meekings, "More about Robert Carpenter of Hareslade", *Eng. Hist. Rev.*, lxxii (1957), 260-9 at 262.

(20) Hengham may also have served as a clerk in the court of King's Bench in the late 1250s and early 1260s. For another reminiscence by him of the practice of Hugh Bigod, the justiciar, see British Library Ms. Additional 31826, f.127v.

(21) Above, n. 17.

(22) H.G. Richardson and G.O. Sayles, *The Administration of Ireland, 1172-1377* (Irish Manuscripts Commission, 1963), 150-2. On their English origins see Ball, *Judges in Ireland*, I, 57-9.

part of the eyre *(23)*. Whatever the precise circumstances, however, the real importance of this opinion is that it provides us for the first time with evidence for yet another way in which the development of the common law in the lordship of Ireland was influenced from England during the reign of Edward I.

Postscript

In Cambridge University Library MS. L1.4.18, ff. 142v-143r, towards the end of a register of writs of c. 1281 there occurs a *regula de advocacione ecclesiarum* which reads as though it may be the answer of a second justice to the same Irish query about the appropriate procedure to be followed in the assize of darrein presentment:

Consultacio super ambiguis in brevibus super assisis ultime presentacionis et qualiter in Anglia proceditur, videlicet si in predictis brevibus responsum fuerit quod ecclesia plena fuerit et non vacans: tunc interrogandum est a respondente de quo sit plena et ad cujus presentacionem et a quo patrono. Quod si respondens velit proponere et afferre, demandandum est episcopo loci quod super hoc justiciariis ad certum diem certificet. Et si forte respondens premissa nolit proponere responsio ejus pro nullo debet haberi. Contingente autem quod viri religiosi quicumque se apposuerunt et fuerunt defendentes fiantque eciam de se ipsis fuere *(1)* plenam, debent ostendere quid habeant de patronatu et de collacione ordinarii. Quod si nec possint nec velint ostendere pro nulla eorum habeatur responsio. Et si forte querens dicat quod ecclesia de talibus religiosis non est plena nisi per intrusionem quam in eam ipsam fecerint et alii quod *(2)* assensu et voluntate *(3)* veri patroni et collacione ordinarii tunc ex responsione querentis emergit inquisicio per patriam capienda etc.

(1) *MS.*: fere.
(2) *MS.*: aliis que.
(3) *MS.*: volunte.

---

(23) Richardson and Sayles, *Administration of Ireland,* 144. On his English origins see Ball, *Judges in Ireland,* I, 59.

APPENDIX*
Lincoln's Inn Ms. Miscellaneous 738 ff. 70r-70v.

Assisa venit recognitura quis advocatus tempore pacis presentavit ultimam personam que mortua est ad ecclesiam de Moygorban que vacat ut dicitur et cujus advocacionem Walterus de Stanton' dicit ad se pertinere et quam advocacionem prior de Athessel et Galfridus le Bryt predicto Waltero deforciant ut dicit. Et unde predictus Walterus dicit quod quidam Rogerus de Stanton' proavus suus cujus heres ipse est ultimo presentaviit ad predictam ecclesiam quemdam clericum suum nomine Robertum de Ros ad quam presentacionem suam fuit admissus ad eandem ecclesiam et in eadem institutus per Martinum archiepiscopum Casselensem tempore pacis tempore Henrici regis patris regis nunc.

Et predictus Galfridus venit per attornatum suum et pro se dicit quod in nullo deforciat predicto Waltero de Stanton' advocacionem predicte ecclesie nec aliquid in eadem advocacione clamat.

Et predictus prior venit et dicit quod predicta ecclesia non vacat sed est plena de se et conventu suo in proprios usus, unde petit judicium si ad istud breve debeat respondere desicut non fuit impetratum infra tempus semestre prout per statutum domini regis ordinatum est in brevibus advocacionum de advocacione possessoribus *(1)*. Et quod predicta sunt vera paratus est verificare ubi et quando debet etc.

Et petitum fuit a predicto priore per quem patronum *(2)* fuit ipsa plena taliter. Et predictus prior dicit quod ubi clamat eam in proprios usus habeat ibi duos status, videlicit patroni et persone; nec tenetur ad hoc breve respondere per cujus feoffamentum aut per quem titulum habet hujusmodi ecclesie patroniam postquam predicta ecclesia est plena. Et pone quod aliquis jus non habens presentandi presentaverat ad aliquam ecclesiam et ejus presentatus fuerit admissus et in eadem institutus ille qui verus est patronus vivente presentato *(3)* et instituto non habet aliquod recuperare per breve de advocacione possessorium nisi breve suum infra tempus semestre fuerit impetratum et hoc statutum Westm' testatur, unde petit judicium desicut paratus est verificare plenitudinem ut supradictum est et plenitudo per predecessores ipsius prioris et per se ipsum continuata per quadraginta annos et amplius postquam Walterus qui queritur fuit plene etatis xxj annis elapsis si ultra

---

* I wish to acknowledge the kind permission of the Masters of the Bench of Lincoln's Inn in allowing me to see manuscripts belonging to the Inn and to publish the following text. I am also grateful to the librarian of Lincoln's Inn, Mr. G. Holborn, for his assistance to me while consulting the manuscripts.

(1) Ms. *possessorium.*
(2) Ms. *patronem.*
(3) This has been altered in the Ms. from *presentatu.*

premissa ad *(4)* aliquod tangens accionem suam tenetur respondere. Et predictus prior requisitus si aliquid aliud velit dicere vel ponere se inde in assisam predictam dicit quod non.

Et predictus Walterus *(5)* venit per attornatum suum et dicit quod predicta ecclesia vacua est et non plena immo pocius incumbrata, quia dicit quod predictus Rogerus die ultime presentacionis ad eandem ecclesiam predictum Robertum de Ros sicut etc.; et postea mortuo predicto Rogero et Henrico filio et herede predicti Rogeri quidam Thomas filius et heres ipsius Henrici pater predicti Walteri qui nunc petit cujus heres ipse est fuit infra etatem et in custodia Walteri Bryt et ille Walterus Bryt tempore custodie sue contulit ecclesiam predictam et ejus advocacionem priori et conventui de Athessel ad tenendum in proprios usus qui semper hactenus nostram *(6)* ecclesiam sic incumbratam tenuerunt nec unquam ad eam presentaverunt. Et dicit quod exceptio de semestri tempore non competit alicui in hoc casu nisi episcopo nec debet retardari assisa quia nulli alio *(7)* accrescit jus vacante ecclesia vel incumbrata nisi episcopo per lapsum temporis. Et dicit quod secundum Westm' de ecclesia que plena est habet intelligi de aliqua mortali persona ad presentacionem alicujus quia tunc lapsum temporis semestris adquisitum est illo patrono seisina *(8)* juris patronatus; sed predictus prior non est in illo casu. Et predictus Walterus de Stanton' petit quod premissa inquirantur per assisam; et predictus prior noluit se ponere inde in assisam sed petit judicium ut supra.

Hengham. In consimili casu vidi diversa judicia. Quia dominus Martinus de Lytebirii statim cum viri religiosi allegassent plenitudinem ecclesie a longinquo tempore statim sine ostensione quod aliquid haberent de patrono vel episcopo adjudicavit mandari episcopo quod super hoc inquiretur. Et Ricardus de Midd' statum suum reputans insufficiens sentivit et dixit quod nisi ostenderent quod ecclesia illa esset plena ad presentacionem veri patroni vel quasi per admissionem alicujus ordinarii vel quasi quod ecclesia fuit vacans et *(9)* oporteret ulterius respondere quia hec sunt [f.70v] interroganda – a quo plena, a quo tempore, ad cujus presentacionem et ad cujus ordinarii admissionem. Et si hec sunt interroganda tunc erit ad ea respondenda quod dixi superius quamvis propter magnam vim quia in isto brevi de possessione non est distinguendum de vero patrono vel vero ordinario. Sed ostensis supradictis mandandum erit episcopo.

---

(4) Marked for insertion in place of *ob* which is marked for deletion.
(5) Name left blank in Ms.
(6) Sic in Ms.
(7) Ms. *alii.*
(8) Ms. *patroni seisitus.*
(9) Altered in Ms. from *ut.*

Index

Abingdon, Berkshire, abbey of 2, 3, 305
abjuration 113, 132
adjournment of litigation into higher court
  in cases of difficulty 397, 399-400
advocatus 10
advowson, use of *quo waranto* writs to claim 405
aid-prayer, availability in *quo waranto* cases 415; reasons for allowing 413
aids, reasonable 305-6
Aldborough, William of 130
Aldbrough, Richard of 69
Alneto, Herbert de 81
Ambrose, master 1
ancient demesne, royal duty to recover 412; use of *quo waranto* to claim 402-3, 405-6
Anstey, Richard of 1
Anstey case, the 1
apprentices of the Bench 60-1
Ardern, John de 260-1
Arderne, Adam de 11
Argentan, Reginald de 5
Armagh, co. Armagh, archbishop of 29, 45, 259, 262, 277, 457
Arnesby, Richard of 11
Arnold, M.S. 71
articles of the eyre, charges for copies of 183; revised to include question on mortmain alienations 253-4
Arundel, Robert 81
Ashbourne, Ellis of 42; Roger of, serjeant of the Dublin Bench 29, 36, 42, 54; Roger of, mayor of Dublin 36
  Reginald of 188
assizes, ad hoc commissions to hear prior to 1241 138-9; adjournment of difficult cases into Bench 397; establishment of

territorial circuits to hear 139; changes in system of hearing in 1285 139-40; personnel appointed to hear 139, 140, 141;
  See also gaol delivery
Aston, Adam of 388
Athassel, co. Tipperary, priory of 467
Athy, John of 38, 50; William of 30, 38, 41, 54
attorney, inability to disavow what had said 8-9; inability to speak the language of the Bench 18; possibility of appointing stranger as 15-16; stewards and bailiffs acting as 15, 16;
  See also professional attorneys
Atwater, Geoffrey, of Ditchingham 131
auditores querelarum, activities of 104; appointment of 104, 105, 126; different groups of 106-7; reasons for appointment of 105-6
avowries for services in replevin cases, changes in 320-1; seisin required in 292-5, 308-9, 310-11, 312-3, 320-1

Babwell, Suffolk, priory of 132
Bacun, John 173, 176-7, 195-6, 197
Bagod, Thomas 54
Bainard, Fulk 5
Baker, J.H. 57, 71
Balliol, Gilbert de 3
Ballyboggan, co. Meath, priory of 276
'Balycur' alias 'Dissertale', co. Meath 260-1
'Balyhokyn', co. Dublin 45
Bampton *see* Kirkbampton
Bardfield, Great and Little, Essex 35
—, Ralph of 7; William of 26-7, 29, 35-6, 41, 48, 54; Katherine his wife 35
Bardulf, Hugh 92

Bardwell, William of 126
Barford, Edmund of 54;
   See also Bereford
'barrators' 14
Barre, Hamon de la 11
Barry, John 31; Richard 124
Basoche, William de la 234
Basset, Ralph 81; Richard 52; William 92
Bassingfield, Nottinghamshire 124
Bath, Somerset, bishop of *see* Burnel;
   prior of 263
—, Henry of 103, 142, 152, 389
battle, offered in actions of customs and
   services 316
Battle, Sussex, abbey, abbot of 3;
   chronicle of 2-3; court of 2
Bayfield, John of 35
Bean, J.M.W. 242-3
Beaubec, Normandy, abbey of 259, 277;
   See also Beybeg
Beaulieu, co. Louth 39
Beckingham, Ellis of 107, 109, 118, 122,
   130, 143, 187-8, 197
Belet, Michael 92, 93, 141
Bench (Common Bench), adjournment of
   assizes into 397; increase in business in
   19; knowledge of by author of *Hengham
   Magna* 385-7; origins of 86-9; use by
   wealthier litigants 18;
   See also apprentices; chief clerk;
   chirographer; clerks of the Bench;
   professional attorneys of the Bench;
   professional serjeants of the Bench
Bench in the reign of Edward I,
   complement of justices in 120-1;
   divisions of 122-3; effects of increase
   in normal length of judicial careers in
   143-4; participation of outside justice in
   hearing in 127; period of office of chief
   justices of 120; predominance of longer-
   serving justices in 144; recruitment of
   keepers of writs and rolls as justices of
   196-7;
   See also professional attorneys of the
   Bench of the reign of Edward I;
   professional serjeants of the Bench of
   the reign of Edward I
Benhall, Robert of 131
Beningbrough, Yorkshire 36
—, Henry of 25, 36, 47, 54
Bereford (Barford), William of 11, 73,

117, 142-3, 155, 162-3;
   See also Barford
Berkeley, Nicholas of 21
Bermingeham, Peter de 458
Bernard, the king's scribe 81
Berstead, Walter of 146
Berwick, John of 183
Beybeg (Beaubec), co. Meath 259-60
Biggin, Northamptonshire 9
Bigstrup, Matthew of 6, 7
bill of exceptions, refusal of 127, 155-6
bills and presentments at General Eyre
   sessions, responsibility of chief clerk of
   the Crown for 181
Binham, master Stephen of 1
Bladis, Hugh de 8
Blaxhall, Suffolk 118
Blewbury, Robert son of William of 4-5
Blound, John le, of Gowran 44, 45-6
Blund, master David le 40, 41, 55;
   Richard le, of Arklow 32, 37-8, 41, 55
Blundel, John, of Harting 378-9, 390-1;
   John son of Ralph 387-91; his family
   387, 389; Nicholas 378
Bocking, John of 11
Bodleian Library, Oxford, MS. Douce
   139 393-4, 436-42
Boncretien, Stephen 5
Bonquer, William 72
Boyland, Richard of 8, 108, 109, 111,
   117, 154-5, 157-8, 195
Brabazon, Roger 119, 143, 160
Bracton 17-18, 73, 78, 149, 227, 236, 309-
   11, 314-15, 407, 412, 416-17, 447, 457
Bracton, Henry of 237, 447
Bradbrig *see* Broad Bridge
Bradfield, Robert of 11
Bradford, John of 174, 188, 189
Braham, William son of Roger of 130
Braose (Brewosa), Richard de 231;
   Alice his wife 231; William his son 231;
   William de 445
Brandeston, Suffolk 118
Brattleby, Lincolnshire, barony of 3
Bray, master Henry de 103
Brevia Placitata 8, 63, 460
Brewosa *see* Braose
bribe, 109;
   See also judicial ethics
Bridgetown, co. Cork, prior of 259
Bridgwater ('Ponte'), John of 34-5, 41,

47, 55
Bristol, Robert of 36-7, 41, 48, 55;
  William of 37
British Library
  MS. Additional 35116 69;
  MS. Harley 25 69, 70;
  MS. Lansdowne 467 61
Britton 228
Broad Bridge [in Bosham], Sussex 229
Broad Bridge ('Bradbrig'), John of 229;
  Alice his daughter 229
Brok, Laurence del 157
Brompton, William of 105, 108, 110-111,
  118, 122, 124-5, 127, 130, 153-4, 170,
  179, 186, 191-2, 194, 197
Brough under Stainmore, Westmorland,
  church of 127
Brown, Hugh 40
Brundon, Essex 126, 133
Buckingham, William of 5
Bucuinte, John 6
Buildwas, Shropshire, abbey of 261
Burford, Oxfordshire 338
Burgh, Hubert de 61; Richard de 457
Burnel, Robert, bishop of Bath and Wells,
  chancellor 248
Burnham, Norfolk 296
Burton, Staffordshire, abbey, annals of
  149-50, 327-9, 349-50
Bury St Edmund's, Suffolk, abbot of
  125, 126;
  See also Babwell
Butley, Suffolk, prior of 129

Camarthen, John of 38, 55
Campbell, J. 114
canon lawyers 1
Canterbury, Kent, abbey of St Augustine's
  3; archbishop of *see* Pecham; court of
  archbishop of 1
Cantok *see* Quantock
Cardiff, John of 32, 40, 55; Nicholas of
  55; Richard of 31
caricature of justice's face 125
Carlisle, bishop of 127
Carpenter, Robert, of Hareslade 335,
  336, 340-1
Carrick, Philip of 37, 55
Carwel, William, of Ireland alias Carewel
  le Forester 131
Cashel, co. Tipperary, archbishop of

46, 257, 466
Casus Placitorum 63-4, 228
casus regis 457-8
causidicus 2, 10
Cave, John of 179, 189, 193, 194
Cernes, Nicholas of 179, 194
cessavit per biennium, limitations on use
  123
Challock, Kent 387
champerty, prohibition of, by London
  legislation of 1259 10; forbidden to
  royal officials 151
champion, allegation that man is hired 6
chancery, responsible for granting all
  Irish mortmain licences prior to 1316 267
chancery clerks, possible early
  involvement in legal education 64-7;
  See also inns of chancery
chantry college, intended foundation of
  268; advantages from 272
Chaumflour, Nicholas de 55
Chertsey, John of 186, 191; Richard of 191
Chester, earl of 312
—, John of 179-80, 193
chief clerk, of the chief justice of the
  Bench 175-6
—, of the chief justice of the General Eyre
  181
—, of the chief justice of King's Bench
  179-80
—, of the Crown in the General Eyre 181
Chignall Zoyn, Essex 128
Childwick, Geoffrey of 7; Clarice his
  wife 231
Chillesford, Suffolk 118
Chilton, Robert of 2
chirographer of the Bench, fees charged
  by 184; functions of 174; oath taken by
  189; value of office 184;
  See also final concords
chirographs *see* final concords
Church Stanton, Devon, church of 188
Cirencester, Gloucestershire, abbey,
  abbot of 4; cartulary of 4-5; court of 4-5
Cirographer, Simon son of William le 174
Clare, earl of 312
Claver, John le 69
clerks of the court, clerical status of most
  200-1; do not become serjeants 200;
  fees charged by 183-4; laymen among
  188; nature of duties 200; oaths taken

by 189; promotion to judicial office
196-9; solidarity among 169; sources of
income of 182-9; statutory regulation
of conduct of 189-90;
See also misconduct
clerks of the Bench, acting as attorneys
184; as writers of plea rolls 169-71;
as writers of judicial writs 171-2;
misconduct *see* misconduct; numbers
in the reign of Edward I 170-2; senior
clerks and functions 172-8;
See also chief clerk of the chief justice of
the Bench; chirographer; keeper of
rolls and writs in the Bench
clerks of the General Eyre 180-2; oath
taken by 189;
See also chief clerk of the Chief Justice
of the General Eyre; chief clerk of the
Crown in the General Eyre
clerks of King's Bench 179-80; act as
attorneys 184;
See also chief clerk of the chief justice of
King's Bench
Clive, Hugh of 312
Clonard, co. Meath 279
Clonturk, co. Dublin 35
Cobham, John of 116; William of 146
Coke, Sir Edward 135
Colchester, Richer of 10
Coleville, Robert de 7
Collon, co. Louth 262
Colswain 3; Picot son of 3
Common Bench *see* Bench
Comyn, Maurice 458
consultation, informal written, of outside
experts 398; of the chief justice of
King's Bench by an Eyre justice
through
letter 393-7; of an English judge by
Irish judges 465-72; of the king's council
by royal justices in cases of difficulty
397-8, 399; of the king's court by county
courts 101, 397; of the king's court by
seignorial courts 99-100, 397
Cork, co. Cork, nunnery to be established
at 268
Cornwall, Edmund earl of 119, 161, 166;
Richard earl of 9, 119
Cornwall, Richard of 181
counts, education in making 57;
emergence of standard counts 17;

need to correspond with writ 97; shift
from first person to third 17
county courts, integration into national
system 100-1; not allowed to award
return irreplevisable 319
court, inns of *see* inns of court
courts, attendance at, as part of legal
education 58, 60-1
Coutances, bishop of 80
Coventry, Alexander of 11
Cressingham, Hugh of 182
Crevequer, Hamo de 389; Alice widow of
389; Robert de 389
'crib', the 61
Crich, Derbyshire 301
Criol, Peter de 3
Crowland, Lincolnshire, abbot of 6
Culworth, William of 145
'curtesy' 323
curtesy, right of 456-7
custom of county 82, 86
custom of the king's court 79, 93
custom of England, development prior to
Henry II's reign 206; development
under Henry II 100, 101; prohibits
mortmain alienation without lord's
consent 234
custom of lordship of Ireland, giving
wardship to lords of socage tenants 462
custom and legal rules 206, 221
customs and services, action of, methods
of proof used in 315-6; title needed in
315; use made of 316-7, 321-2

Dallinghoo, Robert of 28, 55
damages, assignment in Dublin Bench to
clerks, officials and serjeants 24;
assignment to clerks in England 184
Darley, Derbyshire, abbot of 301
Deanham, John of 69; William of 69
'de', addition of, by Weyland family 116
defamation, of court clerk 169; of royal
justice 155
Denholm-Young, N. 335-6
Dent, Yorkshire 36
—, Thomas of 36, 42, 55
Dialogus de Scaccario 95
disavowal of lords in action of replevin
prior to 1285 288-90, 319-20
disavowal of what said in court by attorney
8-9; of serjeants 7, 8, 17; of serjeants in

Ireland 24

disseisin, customary restraints on 209, 210; method of preventing mortmain alienations 236-7; punishment for actions to lord's disinheritance 234; punishment for breach of feudal obligations 208-9

distraint by chattels, advice to lords to use 322; early use against sub-tenants 307-8; fictions in relation to 322-3; lord must be able to show seisin of services to use 124; origins of extra-judicial 218-19, 221, 303-8; primary remedy for lords 123; specifically authorised by court 306-7, 314, 321; wrongful where tenant not acknowledge owing service 311-12

distraint by the fee, end of use in service cases in seignorial courts 314; requires judicial authorisation 307

Divisiones Brevium 73-4

Dover, Kent, port of 113

Downpatrick, co. Down, hospital of St John 250; priory of St Patrick 250

Drogheda, co. Meath, community of 259-60

Dublin, city of, custumal of 24, 49; mayor and bailiffs of 249; as place of origin of Irish serjeants 36-7

—, Holy Trinity (Christ Church) cathedral priory 263; St Mary's abbey 251, 260; St Michael's church 263; St Thomas's abbey 257, 279

Dublin Bench, clerks of *see* Berkeley and Morton;
See also professional serjeants of the Dublin Bench

Dublin Exchequer 446

Ducket or Duket, Richard 5, 50, 452-3, 458

Duleek, co. Meath, priory of 249, 250

Dunham, W.H., jr. 369-91 *passim*

Dunmow, Gilbert of 109

Dunstable, Bedfordshire, annalist of priory of 105

Durford, Sussex, abbey of 377, 379

Durham, co. Durham, bishop of 129

East Dereham, Norfolk, church of 188

Easton, John of 10

ecclesiastical jurisdiction, limitations on 458

Edgfield, Nicholas of 42, 55

Edward I 34-5, 103; accepts statutory prescription period 410-11; claims in his name for land and advowsons during Eyre circuits 399; declares self not bound by statutory prescription period 407-8; the 'English Justinian' 135; grant made by while lord Edward 412, 422; significance of reign as period of major legal change 287; supposed change in attitude to punishment of those convicted of judicial misconduct 105, 108

Eldkinge, Roger 229

Eleanor, wife of Edward I 35, 129

Englefield, William of 146

Englishmen, acting for Abingdon abbey after the Norman Conquest 2

English proverb quoted by justice 125

Erdington, Giles of 469

escheators, articles of enquiry of 252; certificates on reasons for seizure of property 257; responsibility for seizure of land alienated into mortmain without royal licence 252-3

Essex, earl of 82

—, Swein of 80

estoppal, limitations on 123

ethics *see* judicial ethics; misconduct; professional misconduct

Eu, count of, court of 3

Exchequer, beginnings of regular judicial business in 86-9; estimate of revenue by 138; identical with king's court at Westminster 88-9; justiciar's presence in 89, 92; origins of the Bench in 86-9; *See also* Dublin Exchequer; justiciar

—, Matthew of the 73, 411

Exeter, Richard of 48

Eyre *see* General Eyre

Eyville, Roger d' 240

fair, franchise of holding 421-2

false judgment, allegations of 99

falsiloquium 7

Farlington (Ferlington), Henry of 231; John his son 231; Sara his wife 231

Farningham, master Ralph of 72, 182

fenestra 394

Ferlington *see* Farlington

Fifhide, William de 71

final concords, charges for making 184;

creation of remainders under 227;
drawn up by chirographer in the Bench
174; drawn up by keeper of writs and
rolls in General Eyre 181; evidence of
dominant role of royal justices in
sessions of the General Eyre 83-4, 84-5;
procedure when litigant challenges
genuineness of 85; volume in the
Common Bench by early fourteenth
century 184; wrongly levied 191-2
Fishburn, Thomas of 11
FitzGeoffrey, John 460-1
FitzGerald, Maurice 457, 459
FitzHervey, Osbert 142
FitzJohn, John 119
FitzMaurice, Thomas 52
FitzNeal, Richard 88, 92, 141
FitzPeter, Geoffrey 141
FitzReinfrey, Roger 92, 93
FitzRichard, Simon 29, 39, 41, 55
FitzThedmar, Arnulf, London chronicler
10-11
FitzWilliam, Adam 145
—, John 51, 52
Fleta 73, 228, 411, 412
Flinton, Thomas of 289-90
Fokeram, William 33
Forester, Henry 55
formedon *see* writ of formedon
Fortescue, sir John 57
Foss, Edward 114
Francheville, Mabel de 1
franchises, alienability of 416-24;
   annexation to manors 419-20, 433;
   conquest as title to 417-18, 427, 428;
   decisions on law relating to 400, 422;
   jurisdictional and profitable 411-12,
   416-17, 424; reasons for absence of
   settled law relating to 399-401; tacit
   renunciation 418, 424, 426; title by
   royal grant 417-18; title by seisin time
   out of mind 417-18, 427-34
Frechenvill, Ralph de 301
free tenement, rule requiring royal writ
   for litigation concerning *see* original writ
Fressingfield, John of 182, 469
'friends', agreements to ensure presence
   at lawsuits 3-4; role in providing advice
   and speaking for litigants 16-17
Fulham, Robert of 7
Furness, Lancashire, abbot of 249,

259-60, 277
Fyncheden, William de 71

Galeye, Adam de la 27, 55
gaol delivery, assize circuit justices made
   responsible for 140; creation of circuit
   panels for 140; special commissions for
   140
Gedding, Rannulf of 92
General Eyre, core justices drawn from
   the Bench 137-8; creation in the reign
   of Henry II 82-4; jurisdiction extended
   in 1278 399; mortmain seizures by
   justices of 253-4; permanent groups of
   justices appointed to hold in 1278 138,
   150, 398-9; supposed creation in the
   reign of Henry I 79-80; suspension
   during Edward I's reign 138; visitations
   of reign of Henry II 84, 137; visitations
   planned individually prior to reign of
   Edward I 137;
   See also articles of the eyre; bills and
   presentments; chief clerk; clerks of the
   General Eyre; itinerant justices
Gerard, Henry, of Guildford 109, 192-3
Gernegan, Hugh 9
Gernoun, John 39-40, 41-2, 55
Gerveys, John 55
Giffard, Alexander 45
Giffard alias Gifford, John 8, 11
Gisleham, William of 116, 117, 158-9,
   421
Glanvill 17, 78, 79, 85, 86, 97-101, 208,
   212, 217, 222, 225, 234, 305-6, 307,
   311-12, 314, 397, 446-7
Glanvill Revised 314-15
Glanvill, Ranulf de 2, 79, 92, 210
Glen, Richard of 10; Roger of 55
Gloucester, earl of 9
Gosbeck, Hugh of 108, 129-30
Gosfield, Richard of 11
Gothemund, John 46
Grace Dieu, Leicestershire, prioress of
   312-13
grand assize, causing removal of litigation
   98-9, 100; use in action of customs and
   services 316
Grantchester, John of 28, 37, 41, 55;
   Alice his wife 37
grants to secure representation at
   particular courts 4; to secure support at

courts 3-4
Gras, Nicholas 395
Grey, William de 128
Gruys, Richard 10
Guestling, John of 142
Guisborough, Yorkshire, prior of 323

Hagbourne, Berkshire 4-5
Hadlow, John son of Richard of 186, 195;
  Nicholas of 147
Hale, Sir Matthew 78
—, Simon of 453, 458
Hales, Henry of 175, 176, 188
Hall, G.D.G. 65, 451-5
Halleton, Peter de 46
Hambury, Henry of 42
Hamo *dapifer* 3
Hand, Geoffrey 133, 460-1
Hanwood, Matthew of 55
Hareng, Ralph 5
Harmondsworth, Middlesex, prior of 312
Harpley, John of 10
Harrowden, Adam of 196; Simon of 170
Hartforth (Hertford), Robert of 117,
  159-60
Harting, Sussex 374, 376-9
Hautayn, Hamon 104
Havering, Richard (de Ulmis) of 8
Heliun, Walter de 119
Hemmington, Richard of 146
Hengham Magna 8, 369-91; authorship
  380-91; date 370-5; manuscripts 369,
  391; style of writing 383-5; textual
  confusion of surviving manuscripts
  382-3; unfinished state 380-2
Hengham Parva 383-5; difference in
  style from *Hengham Magna* 383-5
Hengham, Ralph de 61, 105, 107, 108,
  110, 118, 126, 127, 143, 152-3, 155-6,
  162, 175, 177, 179, 180, 193, 194, 292,
  380-5, 393-442 *passim*
Henry II, anti-feudal policy of 214-15,
  224-5; contribution to making of
  English law forgotten 78; deliberate
  changes initiated by 101-2; Irish grants
  by 261, 449-50, 463; peace with king
  Stephen 211; rediscovery of
  importance 78
Henry III, claim to land by 396, 406;
  obtains services of all the serjeants of
  the Bench for case against Hubert de

Burgh 6
heritability, beginnings of in England
  207-8, 210
Herriard, Richard of 142
Hertford *see* Hartforth
Heydon, Thomas of 174
Heym, Stephen 119
hibernicus, status of land held by 258-9
Higham, Roger of 11, 302
Holm, James of 124
Holt, Simon of 313
Honne or Houne, Maurice 45
Hook Norton, Oxfordshire, barony of 3
Hopton, Walter of 109-110, 111, 116,
  154-5
Horton, John of 41, 55
Hotot, Richard de 7
Houghton, John of 11
Howard, William 117, 163
Humphreys, W.H. 228
hundred, office of 'keeper' of 416, 420-1,
  423
Huntingdon, Huntingdonshire, prior of
  186, 192
Hurstbourne, master Thomas of 142
Huscarl, Roger 50, 156-7
Huse, Henry 374-5; 377; Matthew 375,
  377, 379; William 376-7
Hyda, Robert de 460

Ibstone, Ellis of 52
Ilchester, Richard of, archdeacon of
  Poitou and bishop of Winchester 92
Inge, William 73, 408
Ingham, John of 69
Inkbarrow (Inteberge), Nicholas son of
  John 26-7, 46
inns of chancery 57; creation 58; teaching
  in 57
inns of court 56; beginnings of education
  at 59-60; creation 58-9; education
  in 57-8
inquest of sheriffs (1170) 82, 103
inquisitions *ad quod damnum* into
  mortmain alienations 241-2, 262, 263,
  270-3, 278-9
Inteberge *see* Inkbarrow
Ireland, English law in prior to 1210
  448-9; extension of English legislation
  to 247-8, 250-1, 465; king John's visit
  to (1210) 445; the king's courts in

454-5; mechanisms through which Irish and English common law kept in step 465; register of writs sent to 451-6; royal justices in 454-5; royal mandates sent to relating to observance of English legal rules 456-60; writs to run in king's name in 461

Irish judiciary, appointment of men with English court experience to 465; *See also* Dublin Bench

Iseny, Adam d' 234

itinerant justices, of reign of Henry I, as presiding officers, not judges 81-2; of early part of reign of Henry II also perhaps presiding officers 82; *See also* General Eyre

Ives, E.W. 59-60

Jacob, E.F. 335, 338-9, 340

Jay, Richard le 376-9; his family 377

John, king, charter of on observance of English law in Ireland 445-50; Irish grant by 261; Irish visit in 1210 445; mandate in favour of bishop of London 235; register of writs sent to Ireland by 453-6

Johnstone, H. 104

judicial ethics, enforcement of 152-6; enunciation of standards of 149-52; *See also* misconduct; oaths of office

judicial writs, clerical signatures added to 171-2; function of 171; payments for writing of 183; required for second release of distresses 318-9; supervision of chief justice's chief clerk over writing of 175, 179; use to initiate pleas of replevin 319; when and where written 171, 180

judicialia, possession of 430, 431

jury trial not available in county court for actions by plaint 318, 319; by serjeants and attorneys of Dublin Bench, asked for by clerk accused of misconduct 21

justices, effects of increase in length of service 143-4; emergence of full-time 141-2; emergence of professional 167-8; employment of trained canonists and civilians 72; employment of university graduates 72; end of clerical recruitment 167; information needed about 113-14; laymen employed 156;

long-serving 141-4; payment of regular salaries 144; preference for serjeants previously employed by king 165-6; serjeants gain monopoly of appointment 165-7; significance of magnate sponsorship for appointment 166; *See also* judicial ethics; oaths of office

—, of the Anglo-Norman period, role of 80

—, of the reign of Henry II, building up of 'core' group of long-serving experts 91-3, 141; role of 89

—, of the reigns of Richard I and John, long-serving 142

—, of the reign of Henry III, beginnings of regular payment of 145-6; long-serving 142

—, of the reign of Edward I, geographical origins 116; length of service 142-3; links with magnates 129; long-serving 142-3; payment 147-8; previous experience 157-66; recruitment of serjeants 117; recruitment of court clerks 117-18; recruitment of magnate administrators 118-19; role of senior court clerks in supplementing 176-8, 181-2, 196; social origins 116

justiciar, chief, and hearing of ordinary litigation by the Exchequer 89; presence not necessary for Exchequer to hear such litigation 89; revival of office in period of baronial reform 137, 147

—, local, role of 80-1

keeper of rolls and writs in the Bench, clerical staff of 174; functions 173-4, 176-7, 386-7, 389; payment 182-3; promotion 196-8; *See also* Bacun, Blundel, Leicester, Littlebury, Lovel

—, in the General Eyre 180-1, 183, 388, 426; *See also* final concords

—, in King's Bench 179

Kelloe, William of 11

Kells in Ossory, co. Kilkenny, prior of 250

Kemp, Brian W. 95

Kenilworth, Warwickshire, prior of 234

Kenley, Walter of 28

Kent, county court 3

Keppok, John 32

Keu, Henry le 179
Kilkenny, co. Kilkenny, church of St Mary 461
king's attorney *see* Brok;
    See also king's serjeants
King's Bench, complement of justices 137;
    forerunners 136; increase in business in second half of thirteenth century 20; jurisdiction 136-7; jurisdiction in error over Irish cases 465; origins 136; role of stewards of the household in 137;
    See also chief clerk; clerks of King's Bench; keeper of rolls and writs in King's Bench
king's council, consultation in cases of difficulty by royal justices 397-8; decision on matter of *quo waranto* law 422; reference of case to for punishment 169-70; role in mortmain licensing system 241, 262, 270, 273; role in trial of royal justices in 1290 107, 127-8
king's court, sessions of General Eyre regarded as sessions of 86; sessions of Exchequer hearing ordinary cases described as sessions of 88
king's courts of the reign of Henry II, distinctive characteristics of 89-97
—, of the reign of Edward I, increase in number of manned by own staffs of full-time justices 135-41
king's serjeants, in England 8, 11; ingenuity in argument on king's behalf 401
    see also Brok, Gisleham, Thornton and Walkingham
—, in Ireland *see* Bardfield, Barford, Bridgwater, FitzRichard, FitzWilliam, Gernoun, Hanwood, Neville, Oweyn, Petit, Preston, St Edmund's, Staines
Kinsham, Adam of 11
Kinton, John of 55
Kirkbampton, Bampton, Cumberland 230
Kirton, Suffolk 130
Knighthood, receipt of 118
Knockgraffon, co. Tipperary 46
Knyvet, John 71

Lacy, Hugh de 443; Walter de 260, 450
Laffan *see* Lessayn
Lancaster, Edmund earl of 119, 160

—, John of 69
language of the court, serjeants' ability to speak 18; inability of some attorneys and litigants to speak 18
Launeye, William de 27
Laver (Laufare), Nicholas of 200
learned laws, influence on common law educational methods 72
lectures giving basic introduction to common law 61-2; other possible lectures 62-7; possible effect on form of avowry in replevin cases 320-1
legal education in England 30-1; beginnings of 57-75 *passim*; for Irish lawyers 31, 465
legal education in Ireland 31-2
legal experts, brought to Ireland by king John 445
legal fictions, distraint as involuntary seizure of chattels 323; distraint of chattels of mesne lord 322-3; offer of gage and pledges alleged in replevin 301, 309-10
legal memory, limit of 77-8
legal profession, criteria for existence of 5; in existence by reign of Edward I 11-14; reasons for emergence 20
    See also professional attorneys; professional serjeants
Leges Edwardi Confessoris, London text of 412
Leges Henrici Primi, 15, 16, 91, 94, 219, 305
Leghe, Henry de la 179, 194
legislation, origins in discussion sparked off by single case 244, 290, 318; publication of 240, 347; publication in Ireland 247-8;
    See also Ireland; legislative drafting; London; *Questiones Compilate de Magna Carta et aliis Statutis*; 'readings'
legislation of the reign of Henry II, references to in *Glanvill* 78
—, Assize of Essoiners (1170) 96
—, Assize of Northampton (1176) 214, 216, 217
—, Assize of Windsor (1179) 99
—, Lost Assize relating to attorneys 15-16
—, Lost Assize restricting area of application of mort d'ancestor 225
legislation of John's reign: Magna Carta (1215) 325, 447

legislation of the reign of Henry III:
—, 1217 reissue of Magna Carta 427, 429-30; c.12 397; c.39 235; c.43 235-6
—, 1225 reissue of Magna Carta 427, 429-30; c.29 296
—, 1228 ordinance against mortmain alienations by tenants in chief 236
—, 1234 legislation on appointment of attorneys in local courts 16
—, 1234 legislation on frequency of court sessions 462
—, 1236 Statute of Merton 459
—, 1236 *Statutum Hibernie de Coheredibus* 459-60
—, 1256 Leap Year ordinance 371, 373; possible 1260 reissue 373-4, 389
—, 1259 Provisions of Westminster, draft texts of 349-52, 361-7; official texts of 347; publication of 347; relationship to the Petition of the Barons 348-9; relationship to *Providencia Baronum* 348; sources for 348-9; c.14 238-40; c.17 317-18
—, 1263 reissue of the Provisions of Westminster 239
—, 1264 reissue of the Provisions of Westminster 239, 337
—, 1267 statute of Marlborough 239, 352-3; c.9 294; c.21 317-18
legislation of the reign of Edward I, general importance 135
—, 1275 Statute of Westminster I, cc. 25-30, 190; c.25 151; c.27 183; c.28 189-90, 191, 192, 193; c.29 13; c.33 14; c.39 77
—, 1278 Statute of Gloucester 62
—, 1279 Statute of Mortmain 240-4, 245-6, 248-51, 269
—, 1284 Statute of Wales 447
—, 1285 Statute of Westminster II 71; c.1 (de Donis) 70, 72, 74, 227-8; c.2 288-95, 318-21; c.5 466-7; c.21 123-4; c.30 139-40; c.31 127; c.32 247, 251, 258, 263; c.35 177; c.44 183, 184; c.49 151, 190, 193
—, 1290 Statute of Quo Waranto 401, 423, 433-4, 436
—, 1292 Ordinance on Attorneys in the Bench 12, 61
—, 1293 Ordinance on Assize Courts 140
—, 1299 Statute of Fines, c.3 140

legislation of the reign of Richard II: 15 Richard II, c.5 247, 251, 257-8
legislative drafting, associated with Magna Carta 325; associated with the Provisions of Westminster (1259) 325-67 *passim*; clues to in inconsistencies in final texts 325
Leicester, Robert earl of 92
—, Peter of 107; Roger of 109, 111, 118, 122, 130, 153-4, 182-3, 197
Leinster, Ireland, court of earl marshal of 456-8; liberty of 461-2; writs issued by chancery of 462
Lenfaunt, Robert 56
Lessayn alias Laffan, William 56
Levynthorpe, Adam de 239
Lewes, Sussex, honour court of 237
Lewknor, Geoffrey of 146; Thomas of 128
Lexington, Robert of 142
Lichfield, Henry of 170
Limerick, co. Limerick, hospital of St Cross 258
limitation dates for writs 452-4; *See also* prescription period
Lincoln, Lincolnshire, Robert de Chesney, bishop of 81; prior of hospital at 234
Lincoln, Henry de Lacy, earl of 119, 159, 161, 162, 166
Lincoln's Inn, MS. Miscellaneous 738, 466
Lisle, John de 11
Littlebury, Martin of 118, 185, 468-9; Robert of 130, 173, 185-6, 191, 197, 198, 469
Llanthony Secunda, Gloucestershire, prior of 249, 250
Locard, Richard 40, 56
London, city of, adopts provisions of 1285 statute 319
—, ordinances of 1244 6, 10; ordinances of 1259 10-11; ordinances of 1264 11; ordinances of 1280 12
—, professional lawyers in courts of 10-12, 18
London, bishop of 235; church of St Swithin, Candlewick Street 180; *See also* Tower of London
Lonlay, France, abbey of 277
Louth, co. Louth, canons of 457
—, earl of 276

loveday 323
Loveday, Roger 395
Lovel, John 127; master John 72, 163-4, 174, 197
Lovetot, John de 105, 108, 111, 116, 121, 122, 129, 130, 153, 192-3
Lowther, Hugh of 11
Lucy, Godfrey de 92; Richard de 3, 82, 92, 95
Ludgate, Simon of 35, 42, 469
Ludham, Robert of 104
Luffield, Buckinghamshire, prior of 237
Lushill, John of 181
Lusignan, Aymer de 119
Lynn, Nicholas of 8

Macotyr (McCotyr), Reginald 40-1, 56
Magorban, co. Tipperary, church of 466
Maitland, F.W. 227, 236, 303-4, 451
Malet, Robert 116, 119, 132, 161
Mallore, Peter 119, 162, 196
Manning, Richard 46-7
Mansel, John 7, 231, 375; Robert 26
Margery, Reginald son of 229
market, franchise of 421-2
Marsh, Geoffrey 457
Marshal, Henry, of Guildford 118, 161-2, 182, 198-9
—, William 445, 450
marshalsea court 137
Marton, Richard of 323
Mashbury, Essex 126
Maulay, Henry de 388
Meath, Ireland, bishop of 279
Meleti, master Peter of 1
Mellifont, co. Louth, abbey of 262-3
Mells, Nicholas of 196
Mettingham, John of 73, 106, 116, 119, 120, 127, 143, 160-1, 162, 171, 395
Middleton, Richard of 146, 468-9; William of 183, 197
Midgley, William of 69
Milsom, S.F.C. 101, 203-25 *passim*, 228, 304-5, 309, 314
misconduct, allegation of, against clerk of Dublin Bench 21; allegations of, against court clerks 169-70, 179-80, 181, 190-6; allegations of, against chief justice Weyland 126-31; allegations of, against justices 186; fines paid by justices for 110; investigation of, by local officials 106; modification of judicial oath after allegations of, in 1289-90 151; punishment of local officials for, in 1289-93 103; punishment of non-judicial royal officials for, in 1289-93 103; punishment of justices for, prior to 1289 103-4; punishment of royal justices for, in 1289-93 108; statutory rules to prevent, by court clerks 189-90; *See also* judicial ethics; professional misconduct
Modus Componendi Brevia 64, 293, 322
Moion, Durand de 81
Monasteranenagh, co. Limerick, abbot of 44
Monewden, Suffolk 131, 132
Monk's Horton, Kent, prior of 313
Montpellier, Thomas of 42
More, William de la 230; his wife Agnes 230
mort d'ancestor, assize of 213-4; effects of 219; original purpose of 214, 216, 224
mortmain alienations, challenges to royal seizures of unlicensed 256-61; definition of 233, 245; requests to pardon unlicensed 261-3; royal assistance to lords in controlling 235, 237-8, 249; royal licences for 241-2, 246; seignorial control over 234-8, 242, 246, 249; seizure into king's hands of unlicensed 250, 252-6; seizure by lords of unlicensed 251-2; statutory restrictions on 235-6, 238-40, 242-4, 245-6, 247, 249, 267-86
mortmain licences for Irish property, fines paid for 273, 280, 283-4; geographical spread of 268, 276, 282; nature of transactions licensed 268-9, 276-7, 282-3; quantity and value of property 269-70, 277-8, 283; process for obtaining 270-4, 278-80, 283; role of English chancery in granting 267, 274, 280; role of Irish chancery in granting 274-5, 280-1; types of licence granted 267-8, 275-6, 281-2; types of recipient 268, 276, 282
Morton, Geoffrey of 37; William of 21
Moulton, Thomas of 25
Moze, John of 126

'Moyglas', co. Limerick 25
Munteny, John de 127
Musters, Peter de 228; Christine his wife 228

Naas, co. Kildare, hospital at 279
Narracio de Passione Justiciariorum 104
Natura Brevium 31-2, 64-5, 322, 465
neighbours, accompany litigant to court 2
Neville, John de 35, 48, 56
Newent, Gloucestershire, register of priory of 337
Norfolk, Roger Bigod earl of 51-2, 53, 119, 129, 131, 232
non-professional serjeant, permission of justices sought for use of 9
non-royal courts, making of judgments in 90-1; measures taken in Henry II's reign to integrate into national legal system 97-101; periodic sessions held by 93-4, 462; use of action of replevin to challenge judgments of 295-8
Normaunt, William le 312
Northamptonshire eyre of 1285, consultation by one of justices of 395-7; loss of *quo waranto* roll from 401; record of five *quo waranto* cases from 401
Norwich, Norfolk, burgesses of 181 prior of 195
Nottingham, Simon of 174; William of 174
Novae Narrationes 32, 462, 465
novel disseisin, assize of, development of regular civil remedy 212-13, 215-16; effects of 218; original purpose 212-13, 215-16, 222-4
Nugent, Gilbert de 261
nunnery, expected benefits from establishment of 272

oath of office, of court clerks 189; of judges 149-51
Odiham, Walter of 248-9
'office' of serjeant, in England 10; in Ireland 27, 28, 30;
    See also suspension
Old Ross, co. Wexford 52
original writs, authorisation of novel by leading justices 127; required for litigation concerning free tenement 97-8; required for litigation in royal

courts 96, 97-8, 217, 218, 219, 225;
    required for service litigation 314-15;
    restrictions on types available 96;
    study of 57; use of helps foster growth of legal argument 96-7;
    See also register of writs
Ormond, earl of 276
Ormsby, William of 117, 164
Osney abbey, Oxfordshire, abbot of 193;
    annalist of 105-6
Ospringe, Kent 387
Oweyn, Roger 51
Oxburgh, Norfolk 116
Oxford, parliament of (1258) 326, 330-2, 333
—, Oxfordshire, hospital of St John the Baptist 237
—, John of, bishop of Norwich 92
Oxnead, John of, chronicler 105
Oylly, John d' 312-3; Nigel d' 3

Pakeman, William de 10
Pakenham, John of 8, 10
Palmer, Robert C. 203, 209-10, 215-16, 219
Panxworth, Norfolk 228
parceners, tenurial arrangements between 459-60
Paris, Matthew, St Alban's chronicler 6-7; his *Liber Additamentorum* 336-7, 339-40, 350
Parles, Eustace de 155; John de 155
Pashley, Edmund of 69, 73
Pattishall, Martin of 447; Simon of 141-2, 447
Pecham, John, archbishop of Canterbury 243-4
Pembroke, David of 52
pensions *see* retainers
Perers, Robert de 312
Peterborough, Northamptonshire, abbey of, Anglo-Saxon chronicle from 81;
    chronicle of 9, 10; *Descriptio Militum* of 3
—, abbot of 9, 10, 188; sacristan of 9
Petit, William 42, 56
Petition of the Barons (1258) 326-33;
    authors of 330-2; legislative changes sought by 329-30, 332-3; origins 326;
    recensions of 328; as source for the Provisions of Westminster (1259) 348-9;
    subsequent discussion of 333-4; texts of

326-8, 354-5; c.10 238, 333

Philadelphia Free Library MS. LC 14.3 74

Picot, William 48

Pierrepoint, Henry de 124; Annora his wife 124

Pitte, Gilbert de la 191

placitator 1-3, 10

Planaz (Planez), John de 5, 7

plea roll enrolment, allegation of deliberate change in 108-9, 129-31, 179, 191, 194; allegation of deliberate fraud in making 21, 181, 193, 195; allegation of falsification by entering backdated attorney appointment 169; charge by clerks for making 184; charge for copy for nisi prius proceedings 183; crossed through by clerk 196; inability of clerks to produce competent 194; playing on title of litigant 9; recording sighs and tears of defendant 9; role of chief clerk of chief justice in supervising making of 175, 179; role of chief clerk in dictating 181, 195

plea rolls, beginning of 95-6

—, of Bench, access to 175; clerical signatures on 170, 196; clerks engaged in writing 169-71; copying of roll of chief justice by junior justices 109; responsiblity of keeper of rolls and writs for producing Rex roll 173, 191; safe custody matter for chief justice's chief clerk 175

—, of the General Eyre, responsibility of keepers of rolls and writs for compiling Rex rolls 180

—, of King's Bench, signatures on 179

pleading, oral, education in 57-8

plenarty, exception of 466-8

Plucknett, T.F.T. 242, 287, 292-3, 304, 308-9, 313-14

Plunket, John 32, 38-9, 48, 56

Poer, William le 49; John his son 49

pone 100-1; availability for defendants in replevin actions prior to 1285 290-1

Ponte *see* Bridgwater

Pontoise, John de, bishop of Winchester 104, 107

Postwick, Norfolk 228

Powicke, F.M. 340

Prat, Alan 12-13

precedents, search of rolls of King's Bench and Bench for 422

prenotarius see keeper of rolls and writs

prescription period, application to *quo waranto* actions 404; application to royal claims of free tenement 403, 406-8, 409-11; king accepts application to own claims 410-11

Preston, Gilbert of 116, 142, 199; Robert of, Irish serjeant and justice 42, 56; Robert of, clerk in the General Eyre 181, 188, 194-5; Roger of 42

professional attorneys of the Bench, reasons for eventual emergence 19-20; reasons for late emergence 19

—, of the Bench in the reign of Henry III: account for only small proportion of recorded appointments in 1260 9; evidence for existence 9; small numbers in 1260 9

—, of the Bench in the reign of Edward I: allegations of misconduct against 12; expansion in numbers during reign of Edward I 14; functions performed by 22; measures to limit numbers and restrict admissions to ranks 12; punishment for deception 13; punishment for failure to exercise proper skills 13; recognised as having special professional skills 12-13; special term used for 12

—, of the Dublin Bench: agreements to act for clients 44; difficulties in identifying 44-5; functions 43; identified 45-7; record of appointments 43-4; smallness of numbers 53

—, in the Exchequer 14

—, in the General Eyre 12

—, in King's Bench 12, 14

—, in London city courts 12

professional lawyers, absence in 1150s 2; absence in Anglo-Norman period 2-5; arrangements mistakenly seen as proving existence in Anglo-Norman period 2-5; beginnings of appointment as royal justices 156-66; differences of appointment as royal justices 156-66; differences between court clerks and 200-1; proto-professional of early thirteenth century 5-6; reasons not needed before later twelfth century 17; shortness of professional memory of 294;

See also professional attorneys; professional serjeants

professional misconduct, allegations of made against attorneys 12; legislation relating to 13; punishment of 13-14; *See also* misconduct

professional negligence, punishment for 45

professional serjeants, in city, fair and county courts 12, 19; in city, county and liberty courts in Ireland 48-9

—, of the Bench, activity of individuals in early thirteenth century 6; intermediaries between court and litigants 18; reasons for early emergence 18; reasons for predominance in eyre 18; reasons for predominance in King's Bench 18-19

—, of the Bench of the reign of Henry III 6-7; individuals identified 7-8; mediation by 7; use by litigants 8-9

—, of the Bench of the reign of Edward I, ability to speak language of court 18; functions performed 23; individual practitioners listed 11; numbers of serjeants employed by individual litigants 23; overlap with serjeants of the General Eyre 11; overlap with serjeants of King's Bench 14; possessing knowledge of the learned laws 72-3

—, of the Dublin Bench, ability to bring litigation by bill 30; absence of direct evidence on functions 23; closed group with monopoly by early fourteenth century 30; earliest evidence for 50-2; family ties with the Irish judiciary 42; geographical origins 34-41; liable to be assigned to litigants by the court 25, 30; longer term agreements with clients 25-8, 29; multiple employment by litigants 24; promotion to judiciary 41-2; salaries of 28-9; taxation of salary by the court when assigned to litigants 25

—, of the General Eyre, evidence of existence in the reign of Henry III 10; individuals active in the 'northern' eyre circuit of 1280s 11

—, in Ireland, list of known serjeants of period 1290-1350 54-6

—, in the Irish General Eyre 47-8

—, in the Irish justiciar's court, liability to be assigned to individual litigants 47; overlap with serjeants of the Dublin Bench 47

—, in London city courts, evidence for existence by 1259 10; legislation intended to make their use superfluous in certain kinds of litigation 10-11; legislation to prevent acting as essoiners 11; reasons for early emergence 18

protonotary of the Bench 175

Providencia Baronum (1259), context of its publication 341; date of 339, 340-1; different texts of 335-8, 355-61; French version of 337-8, 342-4; nature of its publication 339-40; nature of text 338-9; sources of inspiration for 344-6; stage in drafting process 344-6

Pulteney, John de 71

Quantock (Cantok), master Thomas of 49, 174, 187, 248

questio disputata 70-1

Questiones Compilate de Magna Carta et aliis Statutis 71

quo waranto proceedings, arrangements for hearing 395; claims to franchises made at 395, 399, 424-6; decisions on points of law relating to 400; failure to make claim in 424-6; justices of General Eyre given responsibility for hearing 399; regulations of 1278 on 399, 425-6; *See also* franchises; writ of *quo waranto*

Quy, John of 11

Rabayne, Ellis de 119, 162; his wife Maud 162

Raleigh, William of 447

Ralph, Alice widow of Reginald son of 229

Ramsey, Huntingdonshire, abbey 11

—, John of 11, 192

Ranworth, Norfolk 228

Rathcon, co. Tipperary 33

'Rathdrum', co. Tipperary 26

Reading, John of 56

'readings' on the statutes, earliest evidence of 71-2; as element in legal education 58

Reed, Suffolk 191

—, John son of Roger of 191-2

Reedy, William T., jr. 79

register of writs 450; contents of 450; as element in legal education 65-7; 'Irish' 451-6; pre-Mertonian 451

Reigate, John of 398

relief, liability of religious houses to pay 302

religious houses in Ireland, intended foundation of new 268

remainders, creation of prior to 1285 227; protection of prior to 1285 227-32

replevin, action of, initiation by judicial writ after 1285 319; initiation by plaint 317-18; origins 308-10; return irreplevisable awarded in 318-19; significance of two wrongs alleged in 309-10; sureties for return required in 318; use to challenge distraints for services 302-3, 306, 316-17; use to challenge judgments of non-royal courts 295-8; as way of determining questions of title to services 312 *See also* avowries; disavowal of lords

reports of cases, early 10, 11, 121-5; as source of information on justices 114; use in education 68-70

epresentation in legal proceedings, availability prerequisite to development of legal profession 15; limitations on use under Anglo-Norman custom 15, 16-17

retainers, paid to senior court clerks 185-7; paid to serjeants of the Dublin Bench 26-9

return of writs, franchise of 416, 421, 422-3, 432

Retford, Robert of 176, 198

Reve, Martin le 47

Richardson, H.G. 156, 305, 340

Richild, Ralph de 228; his wife Idonea 228

Ridel, Geoffrey, archdeacon of Canterbury and bishop of Ely 92

Ripley, Derbyshire 301

Ripon, Anger of 175-6

Riseholme, Lincolnshire 3

Roche, Gerald de 457; Raymond de 457

Rochester, Solomon of 107, 154-5, 182, 186, 195

Rockingham, Robert of 5

Rogate, Sussex 377, 378

Rome, papal court of audience at 1

Rose, Robert of 181

Rothbury, Gilbert of 143, 164, 199

Sackville, William de 1

Saham, William of 107, 111, 152-3, 179, 194, 395, 442

Sale, Robert de la 181

St Alban's, Hertfordshire, abbot of 7; cellarer of 7; monk of *see* Paris

St Alban's, master Lawrence of 6; Reginald of 10

St Andrew in the Ards, co. Down, priory of 276

St Benet Hulme, Norfolk, abbot of 195

St Edmund's, Robert of 51; Walter of 169

St Evroult, France, abbot of 126

St Katherine's by Leixlip, co. Dublin, priory of 279

St Martin, Abel de 8

St Michael, Robert de 31

Sancta Brigida, Roger de 46

salary, of royal justices 145-8; of serjeants of the Dublin Bench 25, 28-9; of senior court clerks 182-3

Savan, Roger, of Bridgwater 191

Sayles, G.O. 156, 183, 184, 187, 305, 340

Scarborough, Robert of 42

Scarning, master Thomas of 107

Scotter, Roger of 11

Scrope, Henry le 73

Searle, Eleanor 2

Seaton, master Roger of 72, 120, 185

Segrave, Stephen of 457

seignorial courts, challenge to constitution of 296; challenge to judgments of 295-8; challenge to jurisdiction of 296-8; decisions on succession 207-8, 217-18; disciplinary jurisdiction 208-9, 218-9; integration into national court system 97-9; nature and functioning prior to reign of Henry II 203-10, 219-20; role in controlling mortmain alienations 237; use in enforcement of services 303-4, 307-8, 314-15, 321

Sempringham, Lincolnshire, prior of 127, 171, 188

serjeants, difference from attorneys 16; early thirteenth century references to activity of 6; extension of availability of 17; participation in making of judgments 6, 10; twelfth century

forerunner of 16-17;
  See also non-professional serjeant;
  professional serjeants
serjeanty, tenure by 420-1, 423
services, mechanisms to secure *see*
  customs and services, distraint,
  seignorial courts
sessions, continuous within terms or
  within visitations of new royal courts
  93-4; periodic of older courts 93-4
Shardlow, John of 69
Shenholt, Henry of 181, 195
Shottenden, Kent 387-8
Shottenden, Robert of 387-8
sheriffs, commissioned to hear litigation
  100; holding office in fee 416, 420, 423;
  See also inquest of sheriffs
Siddington, master Thomas of 72, 110,
  111, 154-5
Skutterskelfe, William of 10
Slebech, Pembrokeshire, preceptor of 193
Smithfield, East, Middlesex 126
Snitterby, Nicholas of 30, 34, 42, 56;
  Thomas of 34, 42, 469
Sotton *see* Sutton
special bastardy, trial of 459
Spigurnel, Henry 164-5
Spitzer, Anne 115
Staines, John of 48, 56; Nicholas of 56
Stamford, Lincolnshire 412, 422
Stanford, Norfolk, church of 188
Stanton, Hervey of 116, 118, 162, 177-8,
  188; Walter of 467
Stanton Harcourt, Oxfordshire 396, 406
Stapenhill, William of 56
Stapleton, Nicholas of, royal justice 108,
  109, 110, 111, 155
'State Trials' of 1289-93 103-112, 126-31,
  138, 152-5, 190-5, 435-6
statutes *see* legislation
Stenton, Doris M. 5, 156
—, F.M. 220
Stephen, Gilbert son of 186
stewards of the royal household 137
Stoneleigh, Warwickshire, prior of 234
Stowe, William of 11
Strand, Stephen of the 7
Stratton, Adam of 103, 111
Stubbs, William 135, 327, 330
Sturmyn, John 170
stultiloquium 7

subinfeudation, control of 234
Sudbury, Robert of 7
substitution, control of 233
suit of court 5
suitors 17, 89-91
Sully, William of 38, 47, 56
Summerson, Henry 133
suspension from office, as punishment for
  champerty under London legislation of
  1259 10; as punishment for misconduct
  of professional lawyers under 1275
  legislation 13-14
Surdeval, Walter de 127
Sutherland, Donald W. 215, 393-436
  passim
Sutton, Ellis of 116, 118, 181, 183, 199
Sutton ('Sotton'), Michael of 33-4, 56

teachers of law, senior apprentices as
  68-70; senior chancery clerks as 64-7;
  student interruption of 62;
  See also lectures; legal education
Templars, master of the 240
testate succession to land 208, 217-8, 225
Thirkleby, Roger of 142, 389
Thorne, S.E. 59-60
Thorney, William of 8
Thornton, abbot of 289-90
—, Gilbert of 10, 11, 52, 73, 117, 158,
  408, 412, 435-6, 442
Thorp, master Robert de 161
Threekingham, Hugh of 56; Lambert of
  118, 129, 161-2, 197-8
Thurston, Suffolk, church of 188
tolt 98
Thrussington, Leicestershire, church of
  188
Tothby, Gilbert of 323
Tout, T.F. 104, 114, 125
Tower of London, imprisonment in 155;
  special gaol delivery session at 113
Tractatus de Antiquo Dominico 398
Tractatus super statutum Westmonasterii
  secundi 71
Treharne, R.F. 330, 334, 339, 340, 351-2
Trimley, Suffolk 130
Turner, G.J. 460
—, R.V. 72, 91, 156-7
'Turvylauneyston', co. Dublin 27

Ufford, Robert of 128

Ulster, earl of 268
universities, English, and study of common law 57, 73-4; influence on common law educational methods 72
university graduates, employment as royal justices 72-3
Uppingham, Rutland, church of 187
Upton, Robert of 169
uses, feoffments to, to use of ecclesiastics 247, 257, 273-4

Van Caenegem, R.C. 212
Vaux, John des 395, 398
Verdun, Rose de 312-13; Thomas de 128
Vescy, William de 254
view, reasons for allowing in actions to recover free tenement 413
view of frankpledge, challenges to proceedings at 297-8; title to 427, 430, 431
'villainy' 323
Vincent, Walter 56
visual aids, use of, in law teaching 62
voucher to warranty, reasons for allowing in cases involving title to free tenement 413-14

Wade, Henry de la 396, 406
Walerand, Robert 119
Walkingham, Alan of 11, 117, 158, 421
Wallingford, Peter of 69
Walsingham, Norfolk, prior of 296
Walter, Hubert 92, 95
Walton, master Simon of 72
Wandsworth, John of 10
Warkton, Northamptonshire, church of 188
Warmington, Northamptonshire, church of 188
warren, franchise of 419, 421-2
Warwick, Nicholas of 11, 302
Waterford, co. Waterford 263; Ostmen of, grant by Henry II to 449-50, 463
—, hospital of St Leonard 263
Watford, master William of 104
Waxham, Alan of 7
Werry, John 230; Margaret daughter of Avice 230; Theophania daughter of Avice 230; William 230
Westmill, Hertfordshire 128
Westminster, Middlesex, abbey of 188, 237
Westminster hall 7, 187
Weston, William of 52
Weyland, Herbert 115; his wife Beatrice 115-16
—, Herbert (another), 130; his wife Margaret 130
—, John 118
—, Thomas 105, 106, 107, 108, 110, 111, 113-133, 153-4, 185; family origins 115-16; his first wife Anne 118; his second wife Margery 126, 133; his son John 133
—, William 116, 119-20, 126
Wheatfield, Robert of 92
Whitby, Yorkshire, abbot of 239
Whitchester, Roger of 146
Wichio, master Robert of 187
William, John son of 10
Willoughby, Richard of 42
Wilton [in Ellerburne], Wilton in Pickeringlithe, Yorkshire 231
Wimborne, Walter of 118, 152, 180
Wingham, Henry of 388
Winterbourne (Wyntreburne), Edeline of 229
'withernam' 318
Witnesham, Suffolk 116, 132
—, Stephen of 115
Wogan, John 182, 254
Wolmerston, Robert of 10
Woodbridge, Suffolk, priory of 133
Woodworth, William of 47
writ files of writs returned into court, charges for searching in 183; responsibility of keepers of writs and rolls for custody 173-4, 180-1
writ *de excommunicato capiendo* 457
—, *de rationabilibus divisis* 448, 452-4, 456, 458-9
—, of customs and services *see* customs and services
—, of escheat for bastardy 460
—, of formedon in the descender, use by remainderman 228, 230
—, of formedon in the remainder 227-8, 231-2
—, of formedon in the reverter, use by remaindermen 228-30
—, of purpresture 98
—, of *quo waranto*, application of

prescription period to 404; mesne
process on 403; mode of pleading
appropriate to 403-4; mode of proof
appropriate to 409; procedures
appropriate to 411-15; successful
objection to use to claim advowsons 405;
use to claim ancient demesne 405-6, 408;
use to seek free tenement 402-11
—, of right 98, 210-2; effects of
introduction 216-17; original context
210-12, 215, 221-2; procedures
applicable in 411-15
—, of right of dower 98
writs of course, abrogation of 453; made

available in Ireland 455, 460
writs *see also* judicial writs; limitation
dates; original writs; register of writs
Wye, Kent 2
Wyntreburne *see* Winterbourne

Year Books *see* reports
York, archbishop of 129; church of St
Andrew within Sempringhamite priory
at 171
—, John of 69

Zoyn, John de 128; Margaret and Violetta,
his sisters and heirs 128